Selected Works of
RICHARD SIBBES

Including
Memoir of Richard Sibbes, D.D.
Description of Christ
The Bruised Reed and Smoking Flax
The Sword of the Wicked
The Soul's Conflict with Itself and Victory
over Itself by Faith
The Saint's Safety in Evil Times
Christ is Best; Or St. Paul's Strait
Christ's Suffering for Man's Sin
The Church's Visitation
The Ungodly's Misery
The Difficulty of Salvation
The Saint's Hiding-Place in the Evil Day

Edited by
Alexander B. Grosart

Printed on acid free ANSI archival quality paper.
ISBN: 978-1-78139-862-3.
© 2017 Benediction Classics, Oxford

"God knows we have nothing of ourselves,
therefore in the covenant of grace,
He requires no more than He gives,
but gives what He requires,
and accepts what He gives."

"See a flame in a spark, a tree in a seed.
See great things in little beginnings."

CONTENTS

	PAGE
PREFACE,	xiii
MEMOIR OF RICHARD SIBBES, D.D.,	xix
APPENDIX TO MEMOIR,	cxxxi

DESCRIPTION OF CHRIST............MATT. XII. 18,	1
Notes,	31
THE BRUISED REED AND SMOKING FLAX............MATT. XII. 20,	33
Epistle Dedicatory,	35–37
To the Christian Reader,	38–41

PART I. CHRIST WILL NOT BREAK THE BRUISED REED.

The text opened and divided. What the reed is, and what the bruising,	43, 44
Those that Christ hath to deal withal are bruised,	44
Bruising is necessary, 1. before conversion; 2. after conversion,	44
Use. Not to be rash in judging such,	44
Christ will not break the Bruised Reed,	45
Confirmed from his borrowed titles, relations, offices,	45
Use 1. Go boldly to the throne of grace,	46
Use 2. Despair not in thy bruisings,	46
Use 3. See the contrary to this in Satan,	46
(1.) Signs, (2.) Means, (3.) Measure, (4.) Comfort to the bruised,	46–48

PART II. NOR QUENCH THE SMOKING FLAX.

Grace is little at the first,	49
Use. Not to be discouraged at small beginnings,	49
Grace is mingled with corruption,	50
Use. Hence we judge so variously of ourselves,	50
Christ will not quench small and weak beginnings—	

	PAGE
Because it is from him, ...	51
Because it is for him, ...	51
Use 1. No more should we: therefore—	
1. Let all men in general carry themselves with moderation; yet with wisdom to discern those that are not such, and tenderness towards beginners, . .	51, 52
2. In particular to admonish of this, (1.) ministers, (2.) the church, (3.) magistrates, (4.) private Christians: that they quench not good things in others by their —example, slanderings, censuring and judging them —[1.] for matters indifferent, [2.] for weaknesses, .	53–57
Use 2. Examine whether we be such as Christ will not quench:	
1. Rules how to examine ourselves, . . .	58
2. Signs whereby to examine ourselves, . .	59
Some scruples of heart answered, that keep us from the comfort of our examination, ...	62
Use 3. We are encouraged to set upon duties, notwithstanding our weaknesses and disabilities, . . .	65
A case about indisposition to duty resolved, . . .	66
Two doubts of acceptance, either, 1. From scruples about duties; 2. Ignorance of our condition in Christ, . .	67
Weaknesses what, ...	68
How to recover lost peace, ...	69
Use 4. Let us frame our conceits accordingly, and not believe Satan's representations of Christ to us, . . .	71
Or of us unto ourselves, ...	71
Use 5. Reproof of such as sin against this merciful disposition in Christ, as those do,—	
1. That go on in ill courses, either from despair, or presumption, or a wilful purpose to quench the light that is in them, ...	73
2. That neglect good courses from hopes to have comfort, because Christ is thus merciful, . . .	74
3. That ill requite so gracious a Saviour as Christ is, (1.) by neglecting his Mediatorship, (2.) or by being cruel to him in his [1.] members, [2.] name, [3.] by divisions in opinion, ...	75, 76
4. That walk contrary to Christ in their dealing with the tender, for their own gain, . . .	77
5. That despise and stumble at this low stooping of Christ,	77

PART III. UNTIL HE SEND FORTH JUDGMENT UNTO VICTORY.

	PAGE
Explanation of the words, ...	77, 78
The matter whereof is drawn out into six conclusions— .	78
Conclusion 1. Christ is so mild that yet he will rule those that enjoy the comfort of his light mildness, . . .	79
Use. For trial to discern who may lay just claim to Christ's mercy, ...	79
Conclusion 2. The spiritual government of Christ is joined with judgment and wisdom, ...	80
Use 1. Spiritual wisdom and judgment is excellent, and in what respects, ...	81

	PAGE
Why Satan envies and spiteth it,	81
It is most necessary for the managing of a Christian's course,	81
Where true wisdom and judgment is, there Christ sets up his government,	82
The best method for practice,	83
Use 2. There is no true judgment where the life is ill governed,	83
Conclusion 3. Christ's government is victorious,	84
1. In every private Christian,	84
2. In the church in general,	85
Why the victory seems sometimes to go on the contrary side,	85
Use 1. Comfort to weak Christians: the least spark in them, if it be right, will prevail,	86
(1.) Signs whether there be any such grace in us as will be victorious,	87
(2.) Means to be used that it may be so,	88
Use 2. To admonish—1. nations and states, 2. families, 3. every one in particular, (1.) for himself, (2.) his friends, to side with Christ, and to embrace his government,	91
Use 3. To inform us that then Popery must come down,	91
Conclusion 4. As Christ's government shall be victorious, so it shall openly appear, it shall be brought forth to the view of all to victory,	91
Use. Deceit and error shall be laid open to shame,	92
Conclusion 5. This government is advanced and set up by Christ alone,	93
In all spiritual essays look for strength from Christ, and not from thyself,	94
Conclusion 6. This prevailing and victory shall not be without fighting,	95
Because it is—1. government, 2. spiritual government, 3. government with judgment,	95
Use. It is no sign of a good condition to find all quiet,	96
Wheresoever Christ cometh, there will be divisions,	97
Miserable are those men that stand out against him, and are still under Satan's government,	97
Conclusion and general application of this third part,—to encourage Christians to go on comfortably and cheerfully, with confidence of prevailing, both in respect, 1. of ourselves, although beset with corruption; and, 2. the church, although compassed with enemies,	97
Notes,	100, 101
THE SWORD OF THE WICKED............Ps. XLII. 10,	103
Notes,	117, 118
THE SOUL'S CONFLICT WITH ITSELF, AND VICTORY OVER ITSELF BY FAITH............Ps. XLII. 11.	119
Dedication,	121

CONTENTS.

	PAGE
To the Christian Reader,	122–127
Verses by Benlowes and Quarles,	128, 129

CHAP. 1. General observations upon the text, . . 131
    2. Of discouragements from without, . . . 133
    3. Of discouragements from within, . . . 136
    4. Of casting down ourselves, and specially by sorrow. The Evils thereof, ... 142
    5. Remedies of casting down: to cite the soul, and press it to give an account, ... 144
    6. Other observations of the same nature, . . 148
    7. Difference between good men and others in conflicts with sin, ... 153
    8. Of unfitting dejection: and when it is excessive. And what is the right temper of the soul herein, . 155
    9. Of the soul's disquiets, God's dealings, and power to contain ourselves in order, . . . 160
    10. Means not to be overcharged with sorrow, . . 162
    11. Signs of victory over ourselves, and of a subdued spirit, 169
    12. Of original righteousness, natural corruption, Satan's joining with it, and our duty thereupon, . 172
    13. Of imagination: sin of it, and remedies for it, . 178
    14. Of help by others: of true comforters, and their graces. Method. Ill success, ... 191
    15. Of flying to God in disquiets of souls. Eight observations out of the text, ... 197
    16. Of trust in God: grounds of it: especially his providence, ... 202
    17. Of graces to be exercised in respect of divine providence, ... 207
    18. Other grounds of trusting in God: namely, the promises. And twelve directions about the same, . 212
    19. Faith to be prized, and other things undervalued, at least not to be trusted to as the chief, . . 218
    20. Of the method of trusting in God, and the trial of that trust, ... 221
    21. Of quieting the spirit in troubles for sin: and objections answered, ... 226
    22. Of sorrow for sin, and hatred of sin, when right and sufficient. Helps thereto, . . . 232
    23. Other spiritual causes of the soul's trouble discovered and removed: and objections answered, . 237
    24. Of outward troubles disquieting the spirit; and comforts in them, ... 239
    25. Of the defects of gifts, disquieting the soul. As also the afflictions of the church, . . . 242
    26. Of divine reasons in a believer, of his minding to praise God more than to be delivered, . . 244
    27. In our worst condition we have cause to praise God. Still ample cause in these days, . . . 248
    28. Divers qualities of the praise due to God. With helps therein. And notes of God's hearing our prayers, 252

		PAGE
CHAP. 29. Of God's manifold salvation for his people; and why open, or expressed in the countenance,		258
30. Of God, our God, and of particular application,		262
31. Means of improving and evidencing to our souls that God is our God,		267
32. Of improving our evidences for comfort in several passages of our lives,		271
33. Of experience and faith, and how to wait on God comfortably. Helps thereto,		277
34. Of confirming this trust in God. Seek it of God himself. Sins hinder not: nor Satan. Conclusion and soliloquy,		282
Notes,		289–294

THE SAINT'S SAFETY IN EVIL TIMES..................Ps. VII. 14, . . 295

Notes, ... 313

THE SAINT'S SAFETY IN EVIL TIMES, MANIFESTED BY ST PAUL, FROM HIS EXPERIENCE OF GOD'S GOODNESS IN GREATEST DISTRESS.................2 TIM. IV. 17, 18, 314

Notes, ... 334

CHRIST IS BEST; OR, ST PAUL'S STRAIT...............PHIL. I. 23, 24, 335

Notes, ... 350

CHRIST'S SUFFERINGS FOR MAN'S SIN.............................MATT. XXVII. 46, 351

Notes, ... 369

THE CHURCH'S VISITATION ....1 PET. IV. 17–19, 371

Notes, ... 384

THE UNGODLY'S MISERY................................1 PET. IV. 17, . 385

THE DIFFICULTY OF SALVATION ....1 PET, IV. 18, . 395

THE SAINT'S HIDING-PLACE IN THE EVIL DAY.........1 PET. IV. 19, . 401

Notes, ... 410

THE SAINT'S HIDING-PLACE IN THE EVIL DAY.........1 PET. IV. 19, . 411

PUBLISHER'S PREFACE

The last decade has presented a problem to Christian publishers which has not had to be faced since the 1850's and 60's, namely, in what order to reprint the best writings of the Puritan period. Only twenty years ago no publisher in the English-speaking world anticipated that this question would ever again be relevant, yet today, with young people in many parts of the world reading seventeenth-century books, the same healthy problem has returned.

While the present publisher has given independent thought to the subject of Puritan reprints our decisions on priorities bear a resemblance to those of nineteenth-century publishers. About the year 1860 James Nichol, an Edinburgh publisher, projected a series of 'Standard Divines of the Puritan Period' and a parallel series of 'Puritan Commentaries'. Six Edinburgh ministers formed a 'Council of Publication' to guide and support the endeavour. Before that date, however, along with some other leading Puritans, John Owen and John Flavel had already been reprinted at various times in the nineteenth century and the same two have had pride of place today.[1] James Nichol's reprints began with four authors—Thomas Goodwin, Thomas Adams, Samuel Ward and Richard Sibbes. Of these four the most important, with the possible exception of Goodwin, was Richard Sibbes whose several works were for the first time collected and issued in seven volumes, 1862–64.

This book is a reprint of Volume one of the Nichol edition. For two principal reasons it has been decided to publish it separately from the rest. First, there is here contained not only Sibbes' most famous works, *The Bruised Reed* and *The Soul's Conflict*, but in fact all the material which Sibbes himself issued in his own lifetime. Second, it has appeared to the present publisher, that with so many Puritans to choose from, there is a strong case for re-issuing some of the foremost works of a number of authors rather than the whole works of a comparative few. The re-issue of the remaining six volumes of Nichol's edition of Sibbes is not therefore currently contemplated.

[1] *The Works of John Owen*, reprinted in 16 volumes, 1965-68, and *The Works of John Flavel*, 6 volumes, 1968.

As already stated, other sets of Puritan authors were reprinted before Sibbes but the latter's Works came to have one not inconsiderable advantage over them. James Nichol gave to a young Scottish minister by the name of Alexander Balloch Grosart (1827–99) the opportunity to edit the text of Sibbes' various works. The task was a much-needed one, for hitherto, though a number of the Cambridge Puritan's works had been reprinted, they were mutilated and disfigured with blunders which no earlier editor or proof-reader had attempted to eliminate. Grosart's execution of his task was masterly; it set a standard for editorial work on the Puritans which has not been bettered to this day and it laid the foundation for Grosart's subsequent reputation as an authority on the seventeenth century.

The reader will see that Grosart's editorial work has been extensive. He has compared with care the text of earlier editions of Sibbes and indicated by footnotes the variant readings that occur. There are also notes supplied at the end of each treatise, referred to in the text by the letters *a*, *b*, *c*, etc. As for the material itself, Grosart assures us, 'in nothing save the modernising of the orthography and punctuation are Sibbes' words touched'. Some readers may not wish at the outset to be detained by Grosart's lengthy Memoir of Sibbes but, as interest grows, this part of the book, despite its antiquarian lore, will be found to have its own fascination. The fact that no writer on Sibbes prior to Grosart had gone beyond a five-page biography indicates the extent of the editor's research in preparing this volume!

Something of Grosart's own career deserves to be recorded in a reprint which owes so much to him. Born in 1827, he concluded his education in arts at Edinburgh University though, for reasons which are not made clear in the brief records available, he left without taking a degree. Certainly his later years proved that his scholarship was far above the common order, a fact duly recognized when the University of Edinburgh gave him the honorary degree of Doctor of Laws and St. Andrews that of Doctor of Divinity.

In 1851 he began a course of study in the theological hall of the United Presbyterian Church, and a little more than four years later he was licensed by the presbytery of Edinburgh. His first charge was at Kinross, and it was in the Manse of Kinross, on the Western shore of Loch Leven, that his toil on the Puritans commenced. On the completion of his new edition of Sibbes he turned to the hardly less arduous work of editing the writings of Thomas Brooks whose Collected Works Nichol duly published in six volumes in 1866 and

1867. At the same period Grosart supplied for Nichol's Puritan Commentary Series biographical accounts of John King, John Rainolds, Henry Airay, Thomas Cartwright, Richard Stock, Richard Bernard and Edward Marbury. In the year that Marbury on *Obadiah and Habakkuk* was issued, 1865, Grosart moved south to a Liverpool church. In 1868 he accepted a call to another Presbyterian Church in Lancashire, at Blackburn, and there sustained a ministry lasting almost a quarter of a century. His closing years were spent in retirement in Dublin—to which city his wife belonged—and there he died in March, 1899. His extensive private library was largely shared between the British Museum and Princeton University.

Grosart wrote several religious works of his own, and even some hymns, though all these have now been lost to view. Probably his most useful work was his volume, *Representative Nonconformists*, published in 1879, in which he wrote on Howe, Baxter, Rutherford and Matthew Henry. His principal literary energies, however, continued to go to editing and it is hard to suppose that any other worker excelled him or exceeded his output in this his chosen field. At least 170 volumes were edited by his pen. They included a considerable measure of secular literature from the sixteenth and seventeenth centuries. *The Dictionary of National Biography* gives Grosart high praise and tells us that his 'editions of old authors were privately issued in very limited editions to subscribers at high prices, and the business arrangements were conducted by himself. His handwriting was peculiarly small and often illegible. He spared neither time nor trouble in searching for rare volumes and recondite information, and in the course of his career travelled widely, ransacking the chief libraries of France, Germany, Italy and Russia, as well as those of England, Scotland and Ireland. . . . By means of his elaborate series of reprints of Tudor and Jacobean writers, whose works were rare and almost inaccessible, he conspicuously advanced the thorough study of English literature.'

In all the fields of literature which Grosart covered after his early days in Kinross he never found a richer mine than the works of Richard Sibbes, and many have shared the view that James Nichol never did a better thing than produce this reprint. C. H. Spurgeon did not think that all the Edinburgh publisher's choices were the right ones but in the early selection of Sibbes he heartily concurred: 'Sibbes,' he wrote, 'never wastes the student's time; he scatters pearls and diamonds with both hands.' In recent days another, who like Sibbes and Spurgeon gave long years to preaching in the heart of London, has called for a renewed reading of this Puritan. 'The Puritans,' writes Dr. Lloyd-Jones in his *Preaching and Preachers*, 'are almost invariably helpful but there are Puritans and Puritans! . . . I shall never cease to be grateful to one of them called Richard Sibbes who was balm to my soul at a period in my life when I was overworked and badly overtired, and therefore subject in an unusual manner to the onslaughts of the devil. In that state and condition . . . what you need is some gentle tender treatment for your soul. I found at that time that Richard Sibbes, who was known in London in the early seventeenth century as "The Heavenly Doctor Sibbes" was an unfailing remedy. His books *The Bruised Reed* and *The Soul's Conflict* quietened, soothed, comforted, encouraged and healed me.'

With this reprint Sibbes once again ceases to be a rare item to be sought only on the secondhand market. The present publisher re-issues it in the full confidence that it will contribute to the deepening of the Holy Spirit's work in the people of God of this and future generations.

January 15, 1973.

MEMOIR OF
RICHARD SIBBES

MEMOIR OF RICHARD SIBBES, D.D.

CHAPTER I.

'MEMORIALS' THAT MIGHT HAVE BEEN.

Izaak Walton—Dr William Gouge—Richard Baxter—John Davenport, B.D.—
Leading 'Puritans'—Sibbes's own indifference.

THERE are more than common reasons to cause regret that hitherto there has not been, and in this later time can scarcely be, a worthy life of the '*heavenly*' RICHARD SIBBES (the adjective, like the 'venerable' Bede, the 'judicious' Hooker, the 'holy' Baxter, being the almost invariable epithet associated with every mention of his name, through many generations after his departure).* I look upon my own gatherings, after no small expenditure of time and endeavour, all the more sorrowfully because of these reasons. I would fain have placed upon the honoured forehead of the author of the 'Bruised Reed' and 'Soul's Conflict' a wreath of 'amaranthine flowers;' but alas! have instead with difficulty gleaned a few crushed and withered leaves, some poor spires of faded grass and braids of grave-stone moss, with perchance a sprig of not altogether scentless thyme; whereas in the course of my researches, I have come upon various notices and scintillations of revelation, which shew how different it might have been had contemporaries discharged their duty. These tantalizing indications

* 'Heavenly.' The famous Dr Manton thus speaks of him : 'This is mentioned .... because of that excellent and peculiar gift which the worthy and reverend author had in unfolding and applying the great mysteries of the gospel in a sweet and mellifluous way ; and, therefore, was by his hearers usually termed the "sweet dropper"—sweet and heavenly distillations usually dropping from him with such a native elegancy, as is not easily to be imitated.'—(To the Reader .... Commentary .... on 2 Cor. i.). 'That "heavenly" man,' says Zachary Catlin ; and Neal, 'His works discover him to have been of a "heavenly," evangelical spirit.'—(Hist. of the Puritans, vol. i. 582, edition, 3 vols. 8vo, 1837.)

of personal knowledge, and of reserved and now lost information, may perhaps most fitly introduce our narrative.

First of all, in that 'Last Will and Testament,' over which so many eyes have brimmed with unsorrowing tears—drawn out ' in a full age,' very shortly before the venerable writer went up to lay his silver crown of gray hairs at His feet—good, gentle, blithely garrulous Izaak Walton bequeaths, among numerous other tokens and legacies, his copies of the 'Bruised Reed' and 'Soul's Conflict,' and there gleams upon the antique deed, like a ray of sunlight, these noteworthy words about them :—'To my son Izaak, I give Doctor Sibbes his Soul's Conflict, and to my daughter his Bruised Reed, DESIRING THEM TO READ THEM SO AS TO BE WELL ACQUAINTED WITH THEM.'* Nor was this the only expression of esteem for Sibbes by the 'old man eloquent.' In a copy of 'The Returning Backslider,' now preserved in Salisbury Cathedral library, he has written this inscription :—

'Of this blest man, let this just praise be given, .
Heaven was in him, before he was in heaven.—IZAAK WALTON.'

Pity that either Wotton was not assigned to another, or that Richard Sibbes made not a sixth to the golden five 'Lives' of this most quaintly-wise and wisely-quaint of all our early English biographers. How lovingly, how tenderly, with salt of wit and warbling of poetic prose, would he have made 'sacrifice to the memory' (his own phrase) of Master Richard Sibbes, the more than equal of Donne or Herbert, Sanderson or Wotton, and only in degree, not in kind, beneath Hooker himself.

Again, in Sibbes's own will, the usual sum was left to Dr William Gouge of 'Blackfryer's, London,' to preach a funeral sermon. The wording runs, 'To my reverend frende Dr Gouge, I doe give as a testimony of my love, twenty shillings, desiring him to take the paynes to preach my funeral sermon.' Pity once more that this noble preacher, whose great 'Exposition of Hebrews' is worthy of a place beside the kindredly-massive folios of John Owen, having preached it, as he doubtless did, gave not his 'sermon' to the press. Spoken by one who was his fellow-student at the university, and who knew and greatly loved him, while men's eyes were yet wet for him, while the tones of his 'sweet-dropping' voice (Manton's word) still lingered in the groined roof of the chapel of Gray's Inn, it must have contained not a little that we of the nineteenth century would have prized. It is vexatious that importunity should have got printed this large-thoughted man's

* 'Will of Walton.' Introductory Essay to 'The Angler' by Major, 4th edition, 1844, pp. xlii.-vi.

funeral sermons, for a 'Mrs Margaret Ducke!' and numerous others equally unknown, and secured not this.

Further, Richard Baxter, his survivor for upwards of half a century, might have been the biographer of Sibbes. In the story of his earlier days, in that marvellous 'Reliquiæ Baxterianæ,' which won the heart of Coleridge, he speaks gratefully of him :—'About that time [his fifteenth year] it pleased God that a poor pedlar came to the door that had ballads and some good books, and my father bought of him Dr Sibbes's Bruised Reed. This also I read, and found it suited my state and seasonably sent me, which opened more the love of God to me, and gave me a livelier apprehension of the mystery of redemption, and how much I was beholden to Jesus Christ.'* This circumstance alone, observes Granger, in his meagre and chary fashion missing the right word 'immortal,' would have rendered his (Sibbes's) name memorable.'† How priceless would have been a life of Sibbes from this like-minded man, as a companion to his Alleine! How thankfully should we have spared half a dozen of his 'painful' controversial books for half a dozen pages of such a memoir!

Nor is my roll of casualties—shall I say?—done. In the address 'to the Christian Reader,' prefixed to 'The knowledge of Christ indispensably required of all men who would be saved' (4to, 1653), of JOHN DAVENPORT, who, like Gouge, was Sibbes's contemporary, coadjutor, and bosom friend, he informs us of a grievous loss to himself and to us :—'My far distance from the press,' he says, dating from his sequestered 'study in Newhaven,' New England, 'and the hazards of so long a voyage by sea, had almost discouraged me from transmitting this copy; foreseeing that whatsoever $\sigma\phi\alpha\lambda\mu\alpha\tau\alpha$‡ are committed by the printer, men disaffected will impute it to the author; and being sensible of my great loss of some manuscripts by a wreck at sea, together WITH THE LIVES OF SUNDRY PRECIOUS ONES, about six years since.' From the peculiarly close and endeared friendship between the two, there can be little doubt that among those precious ones would be Richard Sibbes.

Then again, we have Thomas Goodwin, Thomas Manton, and Philip Nye, Simeon Ash, and Jeremiah Burroughs, John Sedgwick, Arthur Jackson, James Nalton, and John Dod, John Hill, John Goodwin, Robert Towne, Joseph Church, Lazarus Seaman, William Taylor, Ezekiel Culverwell, in truth, all the foremost puritan names of the period, as the writers of 'Prefaces,' 'Epistles,' 'Dedications.'

* 'Baxter,' R. B., pp. 3, 4, lib. i., pt. 1, 1696, folio.
† 'Granger,' Biog. Hist. of England, 2d edition, 1776.
‡ That is, 'slips, blunders.'

addresses 'To the Reader,' in the original quartos and duodecimos as they were issued in quick succession. In these there are provoking hints, so to speak, of withheld information. Thus say Ash, Nalton, and Church : ' The scope and business of this epistle is not so much to commend the workman (whose name is a sweet savour to the church), as to give a short and summary view of the generals handled in this treatise. THOUGH MUCH MIGHT BE SAID of this eminent saint, if either detraction had fastened her venomous nails in his precious name, or the testimony of the subscribers of this epistle might give the book a freer admission into thy hands.'* Again, John Goodwin thus pleads : ' Good reader, to discourse the worth or commendations of the author, especially the pens of others having done sacrifice unto him in that kind, *I judge it but an unpertinency*, and make no question but that if I should exchange thoughts or judgments with thee herein, *I should have but mine own again*.'† A sketch of our saintly Calvinist by the great Arminian would have been worth having.

Once more, Arthur Jackson, William Taylor, and James Nalton, deem any enlargement supererogatory : ' WE NEED SAY NOTHING OF THE AUTHOR, his former labours sufficiently ' speak for him in the gates,' his memory is HIGHLY HONOURED AMONGST THE GODLY LEARNED. He that enjoys the glory of heaven needs not the praises of men upon earth.'‡

Further, how many pleasant memories lay behind, when Jeremiah Burroughs thus poured out his reverence and love : ' Bless God for . . . . : this work, AND THE MAN THAT INDITED IT, a man, for matter always full, for notions sublime, for expression clear, for style concise—a man spiritually rational and rationally spiritual— one that seemed to see the insides of nature and grace and the world and heaven, by those perfect anatomies he hath made of them all.'§

Finally (for it were endless to cite all), in the ' Marrow of Ecclesiastical History' (folio, 1675), in the address 'to the Christian Reader,' signed 'Simeon Ash, John Wall,' we read : 'Here, *we might have given in a true though short character* of some precious servants and ministers of Christ, whose graces were admired whilst they lived, and whose memory their surviving friends do much honour, viz., Dr Preston, SIBBES, Taylor, Stoughton,' &c.

There are again and again such things, in every variety of loving

---

* 'To the Reader,' Heavenly Conference betwixt Christ and Mary, 12mo, 1654. 4to, 1656.

† 'To the Reader,' Exposition of 3d chapter of Philippians, &c., 4to, 1639.

‡ 'To the Reader,' Glorious Feast of the Gospel, 4to, 1650.

§ 'To the Reader,' The Christian's Portion, 12mo. 1638.

epithet, but we look in vain for any adequate memorial of the tender and tenderly treasured friendships; for even the welcome gossip that abounds, of far inferior men.

The 'evil days and evil tongues,' the crowding and trampling of events, England's 'Ιλιὰς κακῶν, that made men hold their breath and ask, 'What next?' explains, if it does not mitigate, the neglect of Sibbes's friends to place on record their knowledge and wealth of regard for him. He departed when the shadows of great calamities were falling, huge and dark, over the nation—calamities that were to recall, as with a clarion-blast, John Milton from Italy; and it is easily to be understood, how, under such circumstances, there was delay issuing in forgetfulness. To all this must be added Sibbes's own splendid indifference to any blazoning of his name or fame, other than what might come spontaneously. His three small volumes—all that were published during his own life, under his own sanction—were literally compelled from him. Of the first, the 'Bruised Reed,' he tells us, with a touch of complaint, almost of anger, *'To prevent further inconvenience,* I was drawn to let these notes pass with some review, considering there was an *intendment of publishing them by some who had not perfectly taken them.* And these first as being next at hand.' Of the 'Soul's Conflict,' he says also, ' I began to preach on the text about twelve years since in the city, and afterwards finished the same in Gray's Inn. After which, *some having gotten imperfect notes, endeavoured to publish them without my privity.* Therefore, to do *myself right, I thought fit to reduce them to this form.*'

All this was the expression, not of passing irritation, much less of petulancy wearing the vizard of modesty, but of principle. For, in his 'Description of Christ,' the introductory sermons to the 'Bruised Reed' (which are now restored to their proper place), he had deprecated all eagerness after human applause. ' Let us commit the fame and credit,' says he, ' of what we are or do to God. *He will take care of that,* let us take care to be and to do as we should, and then *for noise and report,* let it be good or ill as God will send it. . . . . *If we seek to be in the mouths of men, to dwell in the talk and speech of men,* God will abhor us. . . . . Therefore let us labour to be good *in secret.* Christians should be as minerals, rich in the depth of the earth. That which is least seen is his (the Christian's) riches. We should have our treasure deep; for the discovery of it, we should be ready when we are called to it; and for all other accidental things, let it fall out as God in his wisdom sees good. . . . . God will be careful enough to get us applause. . . . . As much reputation as is fit for a man will follow him in being and doing what he should. *God will look to that.* Therefore we should not set up sails to our own meditations, that unless we be carried with the wind of applause, to be becalmed, and not go a whit forward, but we should be carried with the Spirit of God, and with a holy desire to serve God and our brethren, and to do all the good we can, and never care for the speeches of the world, ... We should, from the example of Christ, labour to subdue this infirmity, which we are sick of naturally....' Then, in words that have the ring of Bacon in them, 'We shall have glory enough, and be known enough to devils, to angels, and men, *ere long.* Therefore, as Christ lived a hidden life—that is, he was not known what he was, that so he might work our salvation, so let us be content to be hidden ones.' More grandly, and even more like a stray sentence from 'The Essayes,' he elsewhere gives the secret of his unconcern as to what men might say or leave unsaid of him. 'THERE WILL BE A RESURRECTION OF CREDITS, as well as of bodies. We'll have glory enough BY AND BY.' The very ease, nay, negligence of that 'by and by' (recalling Henry Vaughan's 'other night,' in his superb vision of the great ring of eternity), sets before us one who 'looked not at the things that are *seen and temporal,* but at the things unseen and eternal,' one who would shine not in the lower firmament of human fame, but up higher, in the 'new heavens,' as a star for ever and ever.

With all explanations, and all the modesty of Sibbes himself, we cannot help lamenting that his contemporaries so readily acquiesced in his choice of being a 'hidden one.'

But I must now try to put together such particulars as have been found, and in proceeding to do so it can only be needful to remind those who have attempted similar service, of the Greek proverb— Τοῖς σίτου 'ἀποροῦσι σπουδάζονται οἱ ὄροβοι—which may be freely rendered, ' Chick-peas are eagerly sought after when we lack corn.'

CHAPTER II.

PARENTAGE AND BIRTH—BIRTH-PLACE AND SCHOOLS.

Suffolk—Martyrs and 'Puritans'—Name, its various orthography—Bishop Mountagu—'*Blue blood*'—Tennyson—Birth-place, Tostock, not Sudbury—Zachary Catlin—The old English Village—Removal to Thurston—The 'Wheel-wright'—School at Pakenham—Richard Brigs—The 'boy father of the man'—John Milton—Contemporary 'boys'—Grammar-school at Bury St Edmunds—Father begrudges 'expense'—Master Sibbes put in the 'wheel-wright's' shop—Friends step in.

RICHARD SIBBES was a native of Suffolk, one of the great martyr and puritan counties of England, that furnished many of the early fugitives to Holland, a very unusual proportion of the emigrants to New England (whose lustrous names are still talismans over the Atlantic), and nearly a hundred of the 'ejected' two-thousand of 1662. The name 'Sibbes' is variously spelled. The spelling now given, and adopted in our title-page, is his own signature to his own dedications and 'epistles to the reader.' But he is frequently called Sibbs, and such is the orthography of his Will, as well as of his heirs and their descendants. There is a third variation, Sybbes or Sybesius. But it is the Latinized form, as it occurs in Richterus Redivivus.* A fourth, Sibs, is common to many of the original editions, and furnishes a side-thrust in a play upon the word to Bishop Mountagu, in his 'Appello ad Cæsarem' (1625), that over-clever 'Defence.' Even thus early Sibbes was speaking bravely out in his post at 'Gray's Inn' against the semi-popish practices of the prelates; and the venal bishop, afraid to strike openly, must needs hint dislike in this taunt, 'So .... with our Puritans, very *Sibs* unto those fathers of the society, every moderate man is bedaubed with these goodly habiliments of Arminianism, popery, and what not, unless he will be frantic with them for their holy cause.'† This may, perchance, be a mere jesting use of the word 'sib,' but the capital S and plural, and the man, seem to indicate an intended hit at our author, ever outspoken against such as the unquestionably astute but also unquestionably unscrupulous Richard Mountagu. The earliest occurrence of the name that I have met with is in a Robert Sibbes or Sybbs of Cony-Weston, Norfolk, who, in 1524, purchased Ladie's Manor, Rockland-Tofts, which again was sold by his son and heir, also a Robert, in 1594.‡ Perhaps, by further inquiries, it might be possible to connect the neighbouring Norfolk with the Suffolk Sibbeses; and, though I have searched in vain in Burke's 'Armoury,' and all through the Davy 'Suffolk MSS.,'§ for genealogical record, it is possible that further research might even shew 'blue blood' in the descent of the author of the 'Bruised Reed.' But it would serve

---

* 'Richterus Redivivus.' In a curious letter of Christopher Arnold, containing new and apparently unused information about Milton. Writing to Geo. Richter (from Lond., A.D. 7 Aug. (*sic*) 1651, printed in Richterus Redivivus, p. 485), he says, 'In Academia Cantabrigiensi vir peramans mei, Abrah. Whelocus, Arab. atque Anglosaxonicæ Linguarum Professor et Bibliothecarius publicus codices manuscriptos cum primis Græcos, &c. .... Obstupui in Johannitica (bibliotheca), cum mihi magnum sacrorum librorum Græcobarbarorum copiam ostenderent, a benefactore quodam anonymo, suasione Richardi Sybbes, S. Th. Prof. et hujus Coll. quondam socii senioris, A.D. 1628, dono oblatorum.'

† 'Appello ad Cæsarem, a Just Appeale from Two Unjust Informers.' By Richard Mountagu. 4to, 1625, p. 139.

‡ Blomefield's Norfolk, vol. i., pp. 481–82.   § In British Museum. Addl. MSS.

little purpose to do so, or to prove him '*sib*' to this, that, or the other great family. The far-fountained 'red' ichor that has come down from

'The grand old gardener and his wife'*

suffices, the more especially as, at the time of his birth at least, our author's family was assuredly lowly, and of the people :

'Kind hearts are more than coronets,
And simple faith than Norman blood.'†

In all preceding notices, Sudbury, the old town, so far back as Edward III.'s times inhabited by the Flemings, is given as Sibbes's birth-place. 'At Sudbury,' says Neal ('History of the Puritans'), and Brook ('Lives of the Puritans'), and so all the 'Biographical Dictionaries.' '*Nigh* Sudbury,' says Fuller; '*At the edges* of Suffolk, *near* Sudbury,' says Clarke. This is a mistake. The town, 'as great as most, and ancient as any,' according to Thomas Fuller, that can boast of Thomas Gainsborough and Thomas Constable later, as natives, and of Faithful Teate, William Jenkyn, and Samuel Peyto earlier, as ministers, can afford to give up an honour to which it has no claim. Tostock, not Sudbury, was his birth-place. The 'registers' of the period, of Sudbury and Tostock alike, have perished; but a contemporary manuscript 'Memoir' of Sibbes, from the pen of Zachary Catlin (of whom more anon), which the stream of time, while engulphing so much else of what was precious and what was worthless, has floated down and placed by lucky accident in my possession, states the fact. As this contemporary manuscript must be frequently laid under contribution in the sequel, it may be as well to give here its proem, which is sufficient, apart from what will subsequently appear, to attest its authority and trustworthiness. 'At the request of a noble friend, Sir William Spring, I have here willingly contributed to the happy memory of that worthy man of God, Dr Sibbes, a few such flowers as I could collect, either from the *certain relation of those that knew his first education, or from mine own observation of him* at that distance whereat we lived. And if anything here recorded may seem convenient for his purpose, who is (as I am informed)

---

* and † Tennyson. 'Lady Clara Vere de Vere'. Even were it possible to trace the name of Sibbes up to 'Norman blood,' we must remember our Scottish proverbs :—

A' Stuarts are no *sib* to the king, } = Though of the same name,
A' Campbells are no *sib* to the duke, } not of the same family.

Moreover, as he says himself of another (Sherland), 'What should I speak of these things, when he has personal worth enough? I need not go abroad to commend this man, for there were those graces and gifts in him that made him so esteemed, that verily I think no man of his place and years lived more desired, and died more lamented.' ('Christ is Best,' page 347 of this volume of the works.)

about to publish the lives of some worthies deceased, I shall think my labour well bestowed. For I am not of that philosopher's mind, who lighting upon a book newly put forth, entitled, "The Encomium of Hercules," cast it away, saying, *Et quis Lacedæmoniorum eum vituperavit?* accounting it a needless work to praise him whom no man did or could find fault withal. I rather judge it a commendable thing to perpetuate and keep fresh the memory of such worthy men whose examples may be of use for imitation in this declining and degenerate age.'* I give his *ipsissima verba* of the birth-place, as above, and embrace in the quotation the birth-date as well. 'But I come to the matter. This Richard, the eldest son of Paul Sibs and Johan [= Joanna ?] was born at Tostock, in Suffolk, four miles from Bury, anno domini 1577.'† The source of the blunder of making Sudbury the birth-place is evidently confounding '*Bury*' St Edmunds with Sud*bury*. Tostock is 'nigh' the former, but not 'nigh' the latter, and cannot at all be described as 'on the edges' of Suffolk, being fifteen or twenty miles in the interior. Tostock, to which I thus restore, if not in the popular sense a great, at least a revered, name, and one of which any place might be proud, remains to-day very much as we may suppose it to have been two hundred years ago, except perhaps that 'its tide of work has ebbed away,' and it is now wholly rural. It is a small sequestered village in Thedwestry hundred, about, as we have seen, four miles from Bury St Edmunds, and about thirteen miles from Sudbury.

> 'A quaint, old, gabled place
> With Church stamped on its face.'

Exactly such a 'village' as 'Our Village' has made dear to us all. Its few picturesquely scattered houses cluster around an unenclosed 'common' (once abundant in 'merry England,' but now sparse), and present fine specimens of what every year is seeing disappear—the peaked-roofed, mossy-thatched, or saffron-tiled 'homes' of our forefathers of the 16th and 17th centuries, with every 'coign of vantage' of the over-hanging upper storeys and lozenge-paned windows,

> 'Held by old swallows on a lease of love
> Unbroken, immemorial;'

and little gardens a-front flinging out into the air the breath of

---

* Above and throughout I modernise the orthography; but in Appendix A to this Memoir I reprint from my MS. the whole very interesting document. Thither I refer for further information concerning its author.

† Neal gives 1579, and is followed by others; but the misprint is corrected by the statement that his death took place in 1635, in his 57th year, which, however, ought to be 58th. The 'Registers' of Tostock that remain commence long subsequent to 1577, and hence the date of his birth-*day* is lost.

old-fashioned flowers. It is pleasant in our day to come upon such a virgin spot.

> 'For it is well, amid the whirr
> Of restless wheels and busy stir,
> To find a quiet spot where live
> Fond, pious thoughts conservative,
>   That ring to an old chime,
>   And bear the moss of time.
>
>   .   .   .   .   .   .
>
> 'And sweeter far and grander too
> The ancient civilisation grew,
> With holy war and busy work
> Beneath the spire and round the kirk
>   Than miles of brick and stone
>   In godless monotone.'

The 'church,' lichened and lady-ferned, but in excellent preservation, is approached by a fragrant lane that strikes off from 'the rectory,'

> '   .   .   .   where the budding purple rose,
>   Prolific of its gifts, the long year through
>   Breaks into beauty.

It is dedicated to St Andrew.

> 'Nor gargoyle lacks, grotesque and quaint,
> Nor saintly niche without its saint,
> Nor buttress lightsome, nor the tower,
> Where the bell marks the passing hour,
>   And peals out with our mirth,
>   And tolls our earth to earth.'

The 'font'—from which no doubt little Richard Sibbes was baptized—is noticeable. The 'benches' are of dark oak, grotesquely carved. The graves around are ozier-woven, and on some of the stones, the once great Suffolk name of Bacon, is still to be read; also in the wrecks of the 'Registers' that remain, the mighty name of Wolsey occurs, as elsewhere in the neighbourhood (by a strange link with Germany and the Reformation), is to be found that of Luther. We visited the primitive hamlet on one of the finest of English September days, and our Scottish eye and heart were touched with the quiet English scenery, long familiar by the 'landscapes' of Suffolk's Gainsborough and Constable, and her poets, Bloomfield and Crabbe. There were the 'Cart on a Road,' 'Cows crossing a Ford,' 'Boys a-straddle on a Gate,' the 'Stile,' ringed with honey-suckle, and now the glowing, and now the bleak originals of 'The Farmer's Boy' and of 'The Borough.' Tostock was a cheery, sunny, many-memoried birth-place; to this hour, with its sister-villages, possessing traditions of martyrs and reformers, Rowland Taylor and Yeoman, and, farther off,

Hooper and Coverdale and John Rogers, and legends of the Tudors and the Commonwealth. For a 'Puritan' none could have been more fitting, for all around were the family seats of grand old Puritan worthies, Barton-Mere, Talmach Hall, Pakenham, Nether Hall, where 'godly ministers' were ever welcome to the Barnardistons and Brights, Veres and Brooks, Winthrops and Riches, Springs and Cavendishes, and the Bacon stock.

But Sibbes was very soon removed thence to Thurston, a similar hamlet only about three miles distant. Here, our old worthy the Vicar of Thurston informs us, Mr and Mrs Sibbes 'lived in honest repute, brought up and married divers children, purchased some houses and lands, and there both deceased.'

There will be something to say afterward of these 'divers children' who were 'married;' but it is to be regretted that, the 'registers having perished, no positive light can be cast on the dates of the decease of the elder folks, except that the father was dead before 1608. Concerning him this is Catlin's testimony : ' His father was by his trade a wheel-wright, a skilful and painful workman, and a good, sound-hearted Christian.' 'Skilful and painful'* were very weighty words then, particularly 'painful,' which was the highest praise that could be given to a laborious, faithful, evangelical minister of the gospel. It is found in many an olden title-page, and underneath many a grave, worn face. A 'mill-wright,' or 'wheel-wright,' for they are interchangeable, was by no means an unimportant 'craftsman' in those days. In country places, such as Thurston and Tostock, where division of labour could not be carried so far as in the large towns, the 'wheel-wright' was compelled to draw largely upon his own resources, and to devise expedients to meet pressing emergencies as they arose. Necessarily this made him dexterous, expert, and 'skilful' in mechanical arrangements. If thus early, the whole of Smiles's description, on whose authority I am writing this,† does not hold (for he speaks of him devising steam-engines, pumps, cranes, and the like) ; yet in those primitive days, perhaps more than some generations later, such tradesmen were, in all cases of difficulty, resorted to, and looked upon as a very important class of workmen ; while the nature of their business tended to make them thoughtful, decided, self-reliant. The cradle of little Richard, therefore, would seem to have been rocked at a fireside not altogether unprosperous. And yet there must have been in the outset somewhat of poverty and struggle, or, the elder Sibbes will need the full benefit of Catlin's character of him. For our guileless

* Painful = full of pains, *i.e.*, painstaking, laborious.
† Smiles's Life of Brindley, in Lives of the Engineers, vol. i. p. 312.

chronicler, carrying us swiftly onward, adds immediately thereafter, 'This Richard he brought up in learning at the grammar school, *though very unwillingly in regard of the charge.*' We will in charity give Master Paul Sibs, wheel-wright, the benefit of the vicar's testimony, and ascribe the 'unwillingness' to the *res angustæ domi.* Whether or not the 'charge,' I fear, had prematurely removed the little fellow from the school to the wheel-wright's bench, but for his own bookish tastes, and the watchful interest of friends. This is explicitly affirmed in what follows. The sentence above, that tells us of the unwilling school-learning, through the 'charge,' thus continues—'had not the youth's strong inclination to his books, and well profiting therein, with some importunities of friends, prevailed so far as to continue him at school till he was fit for Cambridge.' Most truly the 'boy was father of the man.' I turn again to the Izaak Walton-like words of the Vicar of Thurston. He says—'Concerning his love to his book, and his industry in study, I cannot omit the testimony of Mr Thomas Clark, high constable, who was much of the same age, and went to school together with him at the same time, with one Mr Richard Brigs (afterward head master of the Free School at Norwich), then teaching at Pakenham church. He hath often told me that, when the boys were dismissed from school at the usual hours of eleven and five or six, and the rest would fall to their pastime, and sometimes to playing the wags with him, as being harmless and meanly apparelled (for the most part in leather), it was this youth's constant course, as soon as he could rid himself of their unpleasing company, to take out of his pocket or satchel one book or other, and so to go reading and meditating till he came to his father's house, which was near a mile off, and so he went to school again. This was his order, also, when his father sent him to the Free School at Bury, three or four miles off, every day. Whereby the said Mr Clark did then conceive, that he would in time prove an excellent and able man, who of a child was of such a manly staidness, and indefatigable industry in his study.'* Milton's immortal portraiture of '*The* Child' may be taken to describe Master Richard :—

> 'When I was yet a child, no childish play
> To me was pleasing; all my mind was set,
> Serious to learn and know, and thence to do,
> What might be public good.'—*Paradise Regained.* [B. i. 201-204.]

The 'school near Pakenham church' has long since disappeared,

* '*Staidness*' is the very word Lord Brooke uses to describe the youthhood of Sir Philip Sidney: and indeed his whole description is reflected in the above. Cf. the Life of the renowned Sir Philip Sidney (ed. 1652), pp. 6, 7.

and no memorial whatever has been transmitted of it. The mansion of Pakenham was the seat of the Gages, whence the mother of Sir Nicholas Bacon, father of *the* Bacon, came ; and later was the residence of Sir William Spring, at whose request Catlin drew up his notice of Sibbes. Probably, we err not in tracing back the after-friendship with Sibbes to those school-boy days. One likes to picture little Master Richard in his leathern suit (not at all uncommon at the period), studiously walking day by day from Pakenham to Thurston, and home again. Nor can we avoid thinking of other 'boys,' who were then likewise 'at school,' and destined to cross one another's paths. Not a few of them will be found united in intimate friendship with the little leathern-suited pupil of Master Brigs. With others he came into conflict. They are relegated to a footnote.*

Having obtained all that he could, apparently, at the school of Master Brigs (of whom nothing has come down), little Richard, as our last citation from the vicar's manuscript has anticipated us in stating, was sent to Bury St Edmunds, to the 'Free School' there, by which must be intended the still famous 'School' founded by Edward VI. ; and we can very well understand the zest with which one so thoughtful and eager would avail himself of the advantages of such an institution. Dr Donaldson has failed to enrol Sibbes among the celebrities of the school, an omission which, it is to be hoped, will

---

* Contemporary 'boys.' The greatest of all, Master Willie Shakespeare, rising into his teens, has only very lately been tossing his auburn curls at Stratford 'school;' and, still a 'boy,' is now wooing his fair Anne Hathaway. Master Joseph Hall is playing about Bristow Park, Ashby-de la-Zouch, under the eye of Mistress Winifred, of whom he was to write so tenderly as his more than Monica. Away in the downs of Berks, diminutive Willie Laud is playing at marbles under the acacia-walk of Reading. Master George Herbert is ruffling the humour of his stately brother, afterwards Lord Herbert of Cherbury, the '*doubter*,' by overturning a glass of malmsey on his slashed hose and 'roses of his shoon.' In not distant Tarring, Master John Selden is already storing up in the wizard cave of memory those treasures of learning the world is one day to marvel at. Masters Phineas and Giles Fletcher are truanting in the linden glades of their father's vicarage. Masters George Wither and Francis Quarles are agog (in strange contrast with their grim scorn of such 'gaudery,' by-and-bye) over their new lace-frill. Master William Browne is chasing the butterflies in Tavistock. Masters Ussher and Hobbes are perchance busy over their A B C. Francis Beaumont and John Fletcher are still asunder. Master Massinger, tossing ha'pence under the minster of Salisbury, no vision yet of the 'Virgin Martyr,' and no shadow of the '*stranger's* grave' he is to fill. Moreover, as Master Sibbes was thus footing it between Thurston and Bury, men were alive who had seen martyr-faces, 'pale i' the fire.' In the words of Bourne, of a few years earlier, 'The English air was thick with sighs and curses. Great men [were] heavy-hearted at the misery which had fallen upon the land . . . . and he [may] have listened to their earnest, mournful talk. (Memoirs of Philip **Sidney**, by H. R. Fox Bourne, 8vo, 1862, pp. 9, 10.)

henceforward be supplied, for any school may boast of a name so venerable as the author of the 'Bruised Reed.' In the 'registers of the school the name of Sibbes has not been recorded. One would have been glad to know some of his schoolmates. I am not aware that history or biography has named any of them, none at any rate more distinguished than himself. The statutes and other documentary manuscripts of the school have been lost, and nothing is known of its celebrated scholars till 1610—long subsequent to Sibbes—when the list is headed by that twin-brother to Pepys, Sir Symonds D'Ewes. Only one Master is given before 1583, a Philip Mandevill. In 1583, the office was filled by a John Wright, M.A., and in 1596, by Edmund Coote, M.A., who seems to have published his 'English Schoolmaster' (hardly to be placed beside 'The Schoolmaster' of Roger Ascham, though not without merit), during his short term of office.

The earliest extant list of 'boys' is dated 1656. It is a fine glimpse of the student-boy old Catlin gives, leisurely footing from Pakenham to Thurston, and it is to be remembered he did the same to the more distant Bury. We can avouch that, in this good year Eighteen hundred and sixty-two, twenty-fourth of Queen Victoria I., few more pleasant rural roads can be found than that which now winds from Thurston to Bury. On either side are picturesque hurdle-fences tangled with purple cornel, or hedge-rows odorous with hawthorn spray. But it must have been very different in Master Richard's time. Macadam was still unborn; and even a century and half later, Arthur Young[*] has anything but praise for this turnpike. 'I was forced,' he tells us in reference to it, 'to move as slow in it as in any unmended lane in Wales. For ponds of liquid dirt, and a scattering of loose flints, just sufficient to lame every horse that moves near them, with the addition of cutting vile grips across the road, under the pretence of letting the water off, but without effect, altogether render at least twelve out of these sixteen miles (between Bury and Sudbury) as infamous a turnpike as ever was beheld.' Alas! for bookish, studious Master Richard, if he found his school-walk such a Slough-of-Despond.

Sent to Bury 'Free School' (visiting which I looked up at the time-stained bust of its youthful royal founder with interest for Sibbes's sake, who, perchance, practised his first Latin in spelling out the not over-elegant or accurate inscription beneath), there would, no doubt, be rapid advancement. But the 'child' had become a 'lad,' and again there was threatened interruption to his school-learning. I

[*] 'Six Weeks' Tour through the Southern Counties of England and Wales.' 2d ed. 1769. Pp. 88, 89.

find an objurgation rising to my lips against this so 'unwilling' father; but it is silenced by the recollection of the vicar's testimony: 'He was a skilful and painful workman, and a good, sound-hearted Christian.' Master Catlin, I suspect thy sweet-nurtured charity was blind to Master Paul Sibs's penuriousness! It may have been, again let us say, pressure of circumstances, many mouths to be fed, multiplied 'work' demanding another pair of hands. Still it is not altogether what we should like, to find Master Richard again hindered. 'His father,' continues our vicar, 'at length *grew weary of his expenses for books and learning*, took him from school, bought him an axe and some other tools, and set him to his own trade, to the great discontent of the youth, wnose genius wholly carried him another way.' So Master Paul Sibs proposed, but Another disposed. The lad was destined to work for his generation—and many generations—with other tools than these.

CHAPTER III.

STUDENT AND PREACHER AT CAMBRIDGE.

Leaves Bury St Edmunds for 'St John's College,' Cambridge—Greaves—Knewstub—Rushbrook—Enters as 'sub-sizar'—Jeremy Taylor '*pauper scholaris*'—Progress—Degrees—B.A.— 'Fellow' — M.A.—'Taxer' — B.D.—Paul Bayne — '*Conversion*'—A 'Preacher'—Lectureship of 'Trinity,' Cambridge—Memorial—'Hobson'—Accepts—Results—Samuel Clarke—Thomas Cawton—John Cotton—'Word in season' to Thomas Goodwin—Prevalent 'preaching.'

Once more vigilant friends stepped in. They saw the 'youth' set utterly against the grain, at the wheel-wright's bench. 'Whereupon,' approvingly, with the faintest touch of rebuke, chronicles good Zachary Catlin: 'Mr Greaves, then minister of Thurston, and Mr Rushbrook, an attorney there, knowing the disposition and fitness of the lad, sent him, *without his father's consent*, to some of the Fellows of St John's College of their acquaintance, with their letters of recommendation; where, upon examination, he was so well approved of, that he was presently entertained as a sub-sizar, shortly after chosen scholar of the house, and at length came to be Fellow of the College, and one of the taskers of the university; his father being hardly brought to allow him twenty nobles a year towards his maintenance in Cambridge, to which some good friends in the country, Mr Greaves, Mr Knewstub, and some others, made some addition, for a time, as need required.' I am sure all my readers will wish that we knew more of those 'good friends.' All honour to the memory of 'Mr Greaves and Mr Rushbrook.' Of 'Mr Knewstub,' the scholarly, the pious, the brave-hearted, no admirer of the Puritans needs to be informed. His is truly a historic *clarum et venerabile nomen.* His letter of recommendation to St John's College would have the greater weight, in that he was one of its greatest lights, and, subsequently, its benefactor. One is pleased, nevertheless, to learn that it was 'upon examination,' not mere 'recommendation,' the youth was received. He was then in his eighteenth year. Entered as a sub-sizar, which is even beneath a sizar, young Sibbes must have been placed at a disadvantage. Jeremy Taylor, however, was entered as '*pauper scholaris*,' lower still. That has transfigured, if not ennobled, the lowly 'sizar.' Certainly the more honour is due to those who, starting with the meanest, have won for themselves the highest places. How many who entered among the highest are forgotten, while the lapse of time only brightens the lustre of our 'sub-sizar' and the '*pauper scholaris.*'

The career of Sibbes at the university was singularly successful, and indicates in the son of the wheel-wright of Tostock and Thurston, no common energy and devotion to study. It is probable that his 'school-learning' at Pakenham and Bury St Edmunds, alike, was frequently interrupted and hindered. Nevertheless, he seems to have at once placed himself abreast of the most favoured students. The records and registers of St John's College, shew that he passed B.A. in 1598-9; was admitted 'Fellow' 3d April 1601, commenced M.A. in 1602, taxer (the 'tasker' of Catlin) in 1608, was elected 'College Preacher' feast of 1st March 1609, and graduated B.D. in 1610.

We must return upon these dates. When Sibbes, in 1595, proceeded to Cambridge, '*without the consent of his father*,' but with kind words of cheer and something more from Mr Greaves, Mr Knewstub, and Mr Rushbrook, it does not appear that he had any specific intentions in regard to the future. An academic life was evidently his ambition; but to what profession, whether divinity, law, or medicine, he was ultimately to devote himself, was probably left undetermined. An event, or more accurately, *the* one great event and 'change' in every man—his *conversion* (I like and therefore use the good old puritan, because Biblical, word), in all likelihood led him to decide to serve God in the ministry of the gospel of his Son. Paul Bayne, sometimes Baine and Baines, one of the most remarkable of the earlier '*Doctrinal* Puritans' (that name of stigma imposed by Laud), whose 'Letters,' second only to those of Samuel Rutherford, and other minor books, were long the chosen fireside reading of every puritan household, and whose 'Exposition of Ephesians' is worthy to take its place beside Rogers and Byfield on Peter, Jenkyn on Jude, Petter on Mark, Elton on Colossians and Romans, Newton on John, and their kindred folios, that lie now-a-days like so many unworked mines of gold—had succeeded Perkins as preacher at St Andrew's, Cambridge, 'and it pleased God,' says Clarke, 'to make him an instrument of the conversion of that holy and eminent servant of Christ, Dr Sibbes.' Sibbes himself is reverently reticent on the momentous matter, even in his preface to Bayne's 'Exposition of the first chapter of Ephesians' (published separately in 1618), making no allusion to it; but it probably took place somewhere about 1602–3.* In 1602, having passed M.A., he shortly thereafter became a 'preacher.' By 1608 'he was a preacher of good note.' Where he did preach we are not informed. In his address to the reader prefixed to the 'Soul's Conflict,' he states that the 'Sermons' which compose it had been preached first of all 'about twelve years' before 'in the city,' *i.e.*, London, and afterwards at 'Gray's Inn.' I have utterly failed to come upon any memorial of this 'city' ministry; but it is probable that it was commenced between 1602 and 1607. Elected 'College Preacher' in 1609, he must have been then well known and distinguished.

In 1610, when he had graduated B.D., another very important event happened. In that year a 'Memorial' was addressed to him, which, in so far as I can learn, appears to have been the origin of the subsequently celebrated 'Trinity Lectureship,' held since by some of the greatest names of the church. The memorial gives us

* 'Conversion .... reticent.' This is quite in accord with Sibbes's declared sentiments. I would refer the reader to 'The Description of Christ,' pp. 30, 31. There he will find not more sound than admirably expressed counsels and warnings as to the 'vainglory' of publishing abroad things too solemn to be so dealt with. I assume the responsibility of affirming, that at no period have those warnings been more demanded than the present. Every one who 'loves the Lord,' who prays and longs for the coming of 'the kingdom,' who mourns the wordliness and coldness of all sections of Christ's divided church, must rejoice in the past two years' awakening and 'revival.' I would gladly recognise the work of the Spirit of God in much that has taken place. I verily believe very many have been 'born again,' and more who were half asleep have been stirred and quickened. At the same time, it were to be unfaithful and untruthful to blink the 'evil' that has mingled with the 'good.' It becomes every reverent soul to protest against those premature declarations of 'conversions,' and publication of 'experiences' that have got so common. It is perilous to forget the Master's words, Luke xvii. 20. Paul was fourteen years a 'servant' of Christ before he made known his ineffable rapture and vision. Modern 'converts,' do not allow as many hours to expire ere their whole story is blazoned in the public prints. Surely a thing so awful and so sacred, unless in very exceptional instances, is for the ear of God alone. The Tract Societies would act wisely if they circulated by thousands as a 'Tract for the Times,' Sibbes's priceless words of 'Vainglory.'

insight into the popularity of Sibbes as a preacher.* The orthography and wording of the original are retained :—

'A Coppye of the general request of the inhabitants of o^r p'ishe deliv'ed to Mr Sibs, publique p'acher of the house of Cambridge.

'We whose names ar heerunderwritten, the Churchewardens and P'ishioners of Trinity p'ishe in Cambridge, with the ful and fre consent of Mr Jhon Wildbore o^r minister, duely considering the extream straytnes & div'se other discomodities concerning the accustomed place of y^r exercise & desireing as much as in vs lyeth y^e more publique benefit of yor ministery, doe earnestlye entreat you wold be pleesed to accept of o^r p'ishe Churche, which al of vs doe willinglye offer you for & concerning the exercising of yo$_r$ ministery & awditorye at the awntient and usual daye & houre. In witnes hereof wee have heervnto set to o^r hands this 22th (*sic*) of Novebe$_r$ 1610. 'JOHN WILBORE, Minister.
'EDWARD ALMOND,
'THOMAS BANKES, } Churchewardens.
(Signed also by 29 Parishioners.)

The churchwardens of the parish having kindly permitted access to their 'Records,' I find amongst them a list of the names of the subscribers to the lectureship in the several parishes of the town, with the amount of each person's subscription, which runs generally 13s. 4d., 10s., and 6s. 8d. per annum. Three gave £1 per annum each, of whom one was Mr Hobson, the carrier, immortalised by Milton, and later by Steele in the 'Spectator,' and to this day a 'household word' in Cambridge, in kindly eccentric association with the proverb, 'Hobson's choice, that or none,' which no one book-read will need explained. One thing is noticeable, that a goodly number of the signatures to the memorial are with marks +. This is of the last interest and not a little touching. The 'common people' heard Sibbes, like his Master, 'gladly,' and the 'straytnes of the place' hindered others. This is a sign of change for the better in Cambridge very worthy of observation. The old longing after that full preaching of the gospel which had characterised the period of Perkins's seraphic yet pungent ministry, was revived. Sibbes responded to the memorial, and immediately it was felt that 'Trinity' had a man of mark as its 'Lecturer,' the coequal of Bayne of St Andrew's. How those saintly servants of the same Lord would rejoice to be fellow-helpers of each other, the younger 'serving' with the elder, as a son with a father. The lectureship of 'Trinity' was a complete success. Besides the townsmen, many scholars resorted to him, whereby he became, in the words of Clarke, a 'worthy instrument of begetting many sons

* 'Trinity Lectureship.' The 'Memorial' is given by Mr Cooper in his Annals of Cambridge, iii. 168.

and daughters unto God, besides the edifying and building up of others.'*

We have incidental confirmations of the weighty testimony of the 'Pastor of St Bennet Fink, London.' More generally, in that curious little rarity of Puritan biography, 'The Life and Death of that Holy and Reverend man of God, Mr Thomas Cawton'† (1662), we read 'He conscientiously and constantly laboured to counter-work those factors of hell, and drove a trade for God in bestirring himself to insinuate into any lad that was ingenious, and was very successful therein, to the astonishment and confusion of his opposers. Many had great cause to bless God for him, and their first acquaintance with him, for his bringing them to Dr Preston's and *Dr Sibbes, his Lectures* in those times.' More specially, Cotton Mather, the Thomas Fuller of New England, tells us of one memorable conversion through his instrumentality—John Cotton, who was in turn the 'leader to Christ' of a greater than himself, Dr Preston, and whom Oliver Cromwell himself addressed as 'my esteemed friend.'‡

It were like to rubbing off with coarse fingers the powder from a moth's wing, in any wise to change the loving and grave narrative. It is as follows :—'Hitherto we have seen the life of Mr Cotton while he was not yet alive! Though the restraining and preventing grace of God had kept him from such outbreakings of sin as defile the lives of most in the world, yet like the old man who for such a cause ordered this epitaph to be written on his grave, "Here lies an old man who lived but seven years," he reckoned himself to have been but a dead man as being "alienated from the life of God," until he had experienced that regeneration in his own soul, which was thus accomplished. The Holy Spirit of God had been at work upon his young heart, by the ministering of that reverend and renowned preacher of righteousness, Mr Perkins; but he resisted and smothered those convictions through a vain persuasion, that if he became a godly man 'twould spoil him for being a learned one. Yea, such was the secret enmity and prejudice of an unregenerate soul against real holiness, and such the torment which our Lord's witnesses give

* Clarke, Lives of Thirty-two English Divines, 3d edition, 1677, folio, p. 143.
† 'Cawton,' p. 11.
‡ Cotton and Cromwell. The letter of the great Protector, alluded to, a very striking one, will be found in Brook's Lives of the Puritans, iii. 158–9. It is also given with characteristic annotation in Carlyle's 'Cromwell,' iii. 221–225 (3d ed. 1850). When, may I ask in a foot-note, will America give us worthy editions of the still inedited and uncollected 'Works' of John Cotton, Thomas Hooker, Davenport, and others of their kindred? Surely this were better than much that has been reprinted over the Atlantic.

to the consciences of the earthly-minded, that when he heard the bell toll for the funeral of Mr Perkins, his mind secretly rejoiced in his deliverance from that powerful ministry by which his conscience had been so oft beleaguered; the remembrance of which things afterwards did break his heart exceedingly! *But he was at length more effectually awakened by a sermon of Dr Sibs,* wherein was discoursed the misery of those who had only a negative righteousness, or a civil, sober, honest blamelessness before men. Mr Cotton became now very sensible of his own miserable condition before God; and the errors of those convictions did stick so fast upon him, that after no less than three years' disconsolate apprehensions under them, the grace of God made him a thoroughly renewed Christian, and filled him with a sacred joy which accompanied him into the fulness of joy for ever. For this cause, as persons truly converted unto God have a mighty and lasting affection for the instruments of their conversion, *thus Mr Cotton's veneration for Dr Sibs* was after this very particular and perpetual, and it caused him to have the picture of that great man in that part of his house where he might oftenest look upon it.'*

Various similar *memorabilia* might be here adduced from the Puritan 'Biographies' and 'Histories.' One additional 'word in season,' spoken to Dr Thomas Goodwin, may suffice. In his earlier days this celebrated divine leant to Arminianism rather than to Calvinism, and it was through Sibbes that his views were cleared, to his life-long satisfaction, on the point of Jesus Christ being the Head and Representative of his people. It is also recorded that, in familiar discourse with Goodwin, Sibbes said, 'Young man, if you ever would do good, you must preach the gospel, and the free grace of God in Christ Jesus.'† The counsel was as a 'nail in a sure place,' and no reader of Goodwin needs to be told how fully and magnificently he sets forth the 'grace' of God in Christ.

Well was it that such men as Paul Bayne and Richard Sibbes were preachers in such a place and at such a time. From contemporary accounts it is apparent, that notwithstanding the profound impression 'on the town' by Perkins, and notwithstanding that there were a few who, Mary-like, 'kept all the things' they had heard from him, 'and pondered them in their hearts,' Cambridge was sunken down, as a whole, to all its former indifferentism and formality. The preaching that was fashionable among the 'wits' of

* Cotton. Magnalia Christi Americana: or the Ecclesiastical History of New England, book iii., c. i., § 5, p. 15. Folio, 1702.

† Robert Trail, A.M., Justification by Faith, Works, vol. i. p. 261 (edition 4 vols. 8vo, 1810).

the university was a very different thing from the stern reproofs, bold invectives, burning remonstrances, prophet-like appeals of William Perkins. What was now cultivated and extolled was a frivolous, florid eloquence, that boasted itself on its deftly-turned tropes, its high-flown paraphrases of the classics, especially Seneca and Cicero, and the Fathers, the multiplied quotations of the 'sermons' published shewing like purple patches on a thread-bare robe. There was trick of manner, mellifluous cadence, simpering refinement, nothing more. The Senhouses *et hoc genus omne* sprinkled *eau-de-cologne* over their hearers (if they durst, it had been '*holy* water'), while parched lips were athirst for the '*living* water'—tickled the ear when the heavily-laden soul sought pardon, the weary rest, the bruised balm. The cross lifted up on Calvary beneath the pallid heavens—the cross as proclaimed by Paul—was 'vulgar,' and to be kept out of sight. The awful blood must first be wiped off—the coarse nails withdrawn. Whoso gainsays, let him turn to their extant 'Sermons.' But amid the faithless some faithful were found. There were some not ashamed of *the* gospel,' some who could stand and withstand 'the loud laugh.' The 'townspeople' would have that which the 'collegians' (so they called them) rejected. In such circumstances we may conceive that the ministry of Sibbes could scarcely fail to be a ministry of power. 'The Day' alone will fully reveal its fruits.

CHAPTER IV.

'PREACHER' AT GRAY'S INN, LONDON.

'Deprived' of Lectureship and 'Outed' from Fellowsnip—Sir Henry Yelverton—'Preacher' at Gray's Inn—Correction of date—The ' Chapel'—The ' Inn'—Segar MS.—The Auditory—Lord Bacon.

From 1610 to 1615, Sibbes held his lectureship and other honours without molestation. But in the latter year he was deprived ('outed,' says Clarke) both of his fellowship and lecture. Even thus early Laud was at work against all Puritanism and 'preaching ;' and this was the manner of his working. However, as in many other instances, while there was unquestionable hardship and hurt done by the double deprivation, it 'fell out for the furtherance of the gospel.' Sir Henry Yelverton, that 'constant patron to godly ministers,' stepped in and secured the 'preachership' of 'Gray's Inn,' London, for him. All preceding authorities give 1618—the 'Synod of Dort' year—or 'about 1618,' as the date of this well-timed appointment. This is incorrect. I found the following entry in the 'Order-Books:'*

'Quinto die, Feb. A.D. 1616.

'At this penton [pension] Mr Richd. Sibbs is chosen preacher of Graies Inne; and it is ordered that he shal be continually resident, and shall not take any other benefice or livinge.' †

This appointment introduced him at a bound to the first society of the metropolis.

Among the treasures of the British Museum is a noble folio, drawn up from the books of 'Gray's Inn,' by Segar, one of the society's former 'butlers.' ‡ In it, with superb blazonry of shield and scutcheon, and all the 'pomp of heraldry,' are registered the names of those who were resident 'readers, benchers, ancients, barristers, students,' from the earliest date. If one had the Greek of Homer, or the 'large utterance' of Milton, or even the rhetoric of Macaulay, it were possible to revivify the auditory of the 'chapel.' A more illustrious can scarcely be imagined. The flower of the old nobility, the greatest names of the state and of history, men who mark epochs, were embraced in it. I have looked through the roll from 1616 to 1635—the period of Sibbes's office—and almost at random I note Abbots and Ashleys, Audleys and Amhersts, Bacons and Barnardistons, Boyles and Brookes, Bradshaws and Barrows, Cromwells and Cholmleys, Cornwallises

* 'Order Books.' These are deposited at 'Gray's Inn,' where I had the privilege of an unrestricted examination of them. The volume from which I make all my excerpts, is a huge folio, marked 'Gray's Inn. Book of Orders. II. of Eliz. to XVIII. of Chs. II.'

† 'Chapel' of 'Gray's Inn.' I cull from the above authority a record of the foundation of the 'preachership' to which Sibbes was elected:—

CHAPELL.

'It appeareth as well by a deed of the Cort of Augmentacons, bearinge date the 10th of November, in ye 33th (*sic*) yeare of ye reigne of King Henry 8. As also by an Exemplificacon thereof, made ye 12th November in ye said yeare. As also by another Exemplificacon thereof, granted by ye late Queen Elizab., dated at Westminster the 12th of ffebruary, in the fourth yeare of her reigne. That ye treasurer of ye Cort of Augmentacons, of ye said revenue of ye crowne, for the time beinge, should yearely pay out of ye said treasurres to ye treasurer of ye house of Graye's Inn, Nigh Holborne, in ye county of Midd. for ye time being, ye sume of vi xiij iiij^d (£6, 13s. 4d.), in recompense of a yearly stipend of vij xiij iiij (£7, 13s. 4d.), wch. was duely proved before ye said Cort of Augmentacons to be issuinge out of ye possessions of ye late monasterie of St Bartholomew in Smithfield, besides London; and of right payable, time out of mind, by ye prior and convent of the said monastrie and their p'decessors, for ye findinge of a chaplaine to celebrate divine service in ye chapell of Graye's Inn aforesaid, for ye students, gent., and fellowes of ye said house,' &c. &c. &c.

‡ 'Segar.' Harleian MSS., 1912. 94, c. 25. Plut. xlvii. E folio.

and Chetwinds, Drakes and Egertons, Fairfaxes and Fitzgeralds, Nevills and Pelhams, Riches and Sidneys, Staffords and Stanleys, Standishes and Talbots, Wallers, and Vaughans, and Veres.* Truly the wheel-wright's son has a worthy audience; ay, and what is better, he is worthy of the audience.

At the date of Sibbes's appointment, the greatest of all the names enumerated, Francis Bacon, had 'chambers' in Gray's Inn; and, after his fall, was a permanent resident.† When it was dark with him, he had Sibbes for his 'preacher.' Am I wrong in thinking that the touching appeal of the stricken Lord Chancellor to his peers, recorded by every biographer, 'I am a *bruised reed*,' may have been a reminiscence of the golden-syllabled words which he had heard from the 'preacher' at Gray's Inn?

I know not that the author of the Bruised Reed is once named

---

* 'Gray's Inn.' I may give in a foot-note, from Segar's folio, the earlier history of the Society with which the name of Sibbes is so indissolubly associated. Having recited certain ancient mediæval-Latin records, which are also supplemented by prior relations to the Dean and Chapter of St Paul's, the chronicler proceeds:—

'By all wch severall offices, it appeares that the said manor of Portepole, now Gray's Inne, or within ye which a part of Graye's Inne is now situate, was anciently the Inheritance of the Grayes. But I do not find in any of ye said former, &c. . . . that any Gray, lord or owner of ye said manor or messuage, did at any time reside there. Reginald de Gray, in ye 44th year of ye reign of Kinge Edw. 3, for ye yearly rent of Q (?), as is mentioned in ye office, then found after his decease. And in ye wch office (the same beinge in form^r inquisitions named mesuagium), is thereby found to be hospitium and in lease whereby it's manifested yt. ye house then and yet knowne by the name of Gray's Inn, was demised to some p'sons of speciall regard and rank, *and not to meane ones, or p'sons of meane or privat behav^r*, but to such as were united into a Society p'fessinge ye lawes, that in those dayes begunn to congregat and setle themselves within ye Court (?) as an associated company entertayning hospitalitie together. And then this house grew to be off an higher title in denominacon and became to be totally termed by ye Intitulacon of Hospitium in Portopole. And it also appeareth that ye said Reginald de Gray devised ye said messuage as aforesaid in ye reigne of King Edw. 3, in his lifetime, and at his death was held for hospitium and by the jury before whom ye said inquisition was taken in ye said 44th yeare of Edw. 3d (a° 1370), was found to bee hospitium, and not mesuagium. Imediatly whereupon ye said hospitium is called Grey's Inne, or Hospitium Graiorum, for that that estate had been soe long and by soe many severall descents in yt name,' &c. &c. &c.

This quaint and curious narrative, which I believe is now for the first time published, explains the origin of the name 'Gray's Inn.' Those interested will find much additional information in Segar,—all the more valuable that many of the originals were destroyed by a fire at Gray's Inn. These missing portions have been transcribed, but not very accurately, for the Hon. Society.

† 'Bacon and Gray's Inn.' See an interesting chapter of an unusually interesting, but not very accurate, book, Meteyard's 'Hallowed Spots of Ancient London' (4to, 1862), entitled 'York House, Strand, and Gray's Inn,' pp. 80–99. An engraving of 'Gray's Inn' is given on page 90. I need hardly say that all the old buildings, and the 'faire gardenne,' with its Bacon-planted elms, have long disappeared.

in all Bacon's writings, but then neither is Shakespeare. Still, I cannot help rejoicing that, in his closing years of humiliation and penitence, while he was building up the Cyclopean masonry of his 'Novum Organum,' he had Richard Sibbes to lift his thoughts higher. I delight to picture to myself the mighty thinker and the heavenly preacher walking in the 'faire gardenne' of the Inn, holding high and sanctified discourse.* I fancy I can trace the influence of Sibbes on Bacon, and of Bacon on Sibbes. There are in Sibbes many aphoristic sayings, pregnant seeds of thought, felicitous 'similies' (so marked on the early margins), that bear the very mintage of the 'Essays;' and again there is in them an insight into Scripture, a working in of its cloth-of-gold with his own meditations, an apposite quotation of its facts and words, that surely came of the sermons and private talk under the elms with Sibbes. It is something to know that two such men knew each other.

The 'Bruised Reed' and 'Soul's Conflict,' and indeed nearly all his works, present specimens of the kind of preaching to which the auditory of 'Gray's Inn' listened from Sunday to Sunday. One is gladdened to think that such men heard such preaching, so wise, so grave, so fervid, so Christful. There grew out of it life-long friendships.

CHAPTER V.

PROVOSTSHIP OF TRINITY COLLEGE, DUBLIN.

Archbishop Ussher—Dr John Preston—Letter of Sibbes—Sir William Temple—Letters of Ussher to Archbishop Abbot and the Hon. Society of Gray's Inn—Sibbes to Ussher—Archbishop Abbot to Ussher—Declines the Provostship.

Installed as 'preacher' at Gray's Inn, Sibbes seems to have acted up to the letter of his appointment; which, it will be remembered, required that he was 'to be continually resident,' and 'to take no other benefice or living.' This he continued apparently to do, with the exception of occasional 'sermons' in the 'city' or in Cambridge, until 1626. In that year new honours came to him. Archbishop Ussher sought to have him made provost of Trinity College, Dublin; and he was elected, on the death of Dr John Hills, 'Master' of St Katherine Hall (now College), Cambridge. A very interesting correspondence remains in relation to

* One asks wistfully if they took any note of one William Shakespeare, who, within three months of the appointment to the 'preachership' at 'Gray's Inn,' was laid beside his little Hamnet by the Avon! (Died, 23d April 1616.)

the former, which I would now introduce. He had long been in intimate friendship with the illustrious primate of Ireland, who, on his visits to London, was wont to invite himself to his 'study.'[*] One early notice of their mutual regard is contained in a portion of a letter from Dr John Preston to Ussher. It is as follows: 'March 16. 1619.—Your papers you shall surely have with you; and if there be no remedy that I cannot see you myself, I shall entreat you *to make plain to Mr Sibbes* (or whom else you will) the last point especially, when the LXX weeks began, though I should speak to you about many other things.'[†] The following brief letter of Sibbes himself a few years onward, 1622, gives us a further glimpse of their relations, as well as of various memorable names and occurrences. Ussher was then Bishop of Meath.

Mr R. Sibbs to the Bishop of Meath.[‡]

I could not, Right Reverend Sir, omit so fit an opportunity of writing unto you as the coming of two of my worthy friends, Sir Nathaniel Rich and Mr Crew; though it were but to signify unto you that I retain a thankful and respectful remembrance of your lordship's former love and kindness. Mr Crew is already known unto you; Sir Nathaniel, I think, a stranger yet unto you; you shall find him for sincerity, wisdom, and right judgment worthy your inward acquaintance. How matters stand here you shall have better information from those worthy gentlemen than from me. For Cambridge matters, I suppose your lordship hath already heard that Dr Ward is chosen professor in Dr Davenant's place; there is hope of Mr Preston's coming to be lecturer at Lincoln's Inn, which place is now void. Mrs More, Mr Drake and his wife, Mr Dod, with others that love you heartily in the Lord, are in good health, the Lord be praised. Sir Henry Savil hath ended his days, secretary Murray succeeding him in Eton, but report will prevent my letter in this and other matters. Sir, I long to see your begun historical discourse of the perpetual continuity of a visible church, lengthened and brought to these latter times. No one point will stop the clamour of our adversaries more, nor furnish the weaker with a better plea. Others not very well affected to the Waldenses, &c., for some tenets . . . have gone about to prove what you do some other ways. But perhaps the present exigence of your Church is such as taketh up your daily endeavours and thoughts. And I know the zeal of your heart for the public good will put you forward for whatsoever is for the best advantage of the common cause. I fear lest the encountering with that daring chal-

---

[*] 'Ussher and Sibbes.' Brook's 'Lives of the Puritans,' vol. ii. p. 416. From Brook's own copy, interleaved and containing additional MS. notes. In the library of Joshua Wilson, Esq., Tunbridge Wells.

[†] 'Preston and Ussher.' This and the succeeding correspondence I take from 'The whole Works of the Most Rev. James Ussher, D.D., Lord Archbishop of Armagh and Primate of all Ireland. With a Life of the Author, and an Account of his Writings. By Charles Richard Elrington, D.D., Regius Professor of Divinity in the University of Dublin. Dublin: Hodges & Smith. 16 vols. 8vo, 1847, *seq*.' See vol. xvi. p. 378. Elrington supersedes Parr (who also gives the most of the letters), and I therefore take the whole from him.

[‡] 'Sibbes to Usher.' Letter ccclxiii. Vol. xvi. p. 395, 396.

lenger breed you a succession of troubles. How far you have proceeded in this matter we know not. The Lord lead you through all conflicts and businesses, with comfortable evidence of his wisdom in guiding you, and goodness in a blessed issue.

Your Lordship's in all Christian affection and service,

R. SIBBS.

Gray's Inn, March 21. 1622.

Advancing to 1626–27, Ussher was now archbishop and primate, and involved in an imbroglio of political and ecclesiastical difficulties. His was only a splendid exile. He writes, half-mournfully half in dread, under date 'Feby. 9th, 1626 :'—'As for the general state of things here, they are so desperate that I am afraid to write anything thereof.'* He was specially 'troubled' in the matter of 'Trinity College,' of which he was the patron. Sir William Temple was provost, and from his great age, utterly inefficient, and even in dotage. There were perpetual disputes between him and the 'fellows,' so much so that the removal of the provost, in some quiet manner, was felt to be the only method of preserving the discipline and good order of the college. To this Ussher addressed himself, and ultimately persuaded the old man—a not unhistoric name—to resign, on condition that Sibbes took his place. This we learn from a letter of the primate to Archbishop Abbot, to whom, on 10th January 1626–27, he writes :—'The time is now come wherein we have at last wrought upon Sir William Temple to give up his place, *if the other may be drawn over.*' That 'other' was Sibbes. But all difficulty about the resignation, with or without conditions, was unexpectedly removed by the death of Sir William, who expired on the 15th of January 1626–27, five days only after the date of Ussher's letter,—upon which he again wrote Abbot in favour of Sibbes. The whole correspondence is of the last interest, and is self-explanatory. It may now be given in order, the more so, that, excepting one of the letters, it has been overlooked or left unused :—

The Archbishop of Armagh to the most Reverend GEORGE ABBOT, *Archbishop of Canterbury.*†

MY MOST GRACIOUS LORD,—When I took my last leave of you at Lambeth, I made bold to move your grace for the settlement of the provostship of our college here upon some worthy man, whensoever the place should become void. I then recommended unto you Mr Sibbes, the preacher of Gray's Inn, with whose learning, soundness of judgment, and uprightness of life I was very well acquainted ; and it pleased your grace to listen unto my motion, and give way to the coming over of the person named, when time required. The time, my lord, is now come, wherein we have at last wrought Sir William Temple to give up his place, if the other may be

* Ussher, xv. 365–6. † Ussher, letter cxxi. xv. 361–2.

drawn over. And therefore I most humbly entreat your grace to give unto Mr Sibbes that encouragement he deserveth; in whose behalf I dare undertake that he shall be as observant of you, and as careful to put in execution all your directions, as any man whosoever. The matter is of so great importance for the good of this poor church, and your fatherly care, as well of the church in general, as our college in particular, so well known, that I shall not need to press you herein with many words. And therefore, leaving it wholly to your grace's grave consideration, and beseeching Almighty God to bless you in the managing of your weighty employments, I humbly take my leave, and rest,

Your grace's in all duty, ready to be commanded,

J. A.

Drogheda, January 10. 1626.

At the same time, the primate addressed a similar letter to the 'Honourable Society of Gray's Inn,' to deprecate their putting any obstacles in the way of Sibbes's acceptance. By a slip of the pen, he inserts—'*Lincoln's*,' instead of 'Gray's' Inn. As himself formerly 'preacher' in 'Lincoln's,' the mistake was natural :—

*The Archbishop of Armagh to the Honourable Society of Gray's-Inn.**

MY MOST WORTHY FRIENDS,—I cannot sufficiently express my thankfulness unto you for the honour which you have done unto me, in vouchsafing to admit me into your society, and to make me a member of your own body. Yet so is it fallen out for the present, that I am enforced to discharge one piece of debt with entering into another. For thus doth the case stand with us. Sir William Temple, who hath governed our college at Dublin these seventeen years, finding age and weakness now to increase upon him, hath resolved to ease himself of that burthen, and resign the same to some other. Now of all others whom we could think of, your worthy preacher Mr Sibbes is the man upon whom all our voices have here settled, as one that hath been well acquainted with an academical life, and singularly well qualified for the undertaking of such a place of government. I am not ignorant what damage you are to sustain by the loss of such an able man, with whose ministry you have been so long acquainted; but I consider withal, that you are at the well-head, where the defect may quickly be supplied; and that it somewhat also tendeth to the honour of your Society, that out of all the king's dominions your house should be singled out for the place unto which the seminary of the whole Church in this kingdom should have recourse for help and succour in this case. And therefore my most earnest suit unto you is, that you would give leave unto Mr Sibbes to repair hither, at leastwise for a time, that he may see how the place will like him. For which great favour our whole Church shall be obliged unto you: and I, for my part, shall evermore profess myself to rest

Your own in all Christian service, Ready to be commanded,

J. A.

Drogheda, January 10. 1626.

Further :—

The Archbishop of Armagh to the most Reverend GEORGE ABBOT, *Archbishop of Canterbury.*†

MY VERY GOOD LORD,—I wrote unto your grace heretofore concerning

---

* Ussher, letter cxx., xv. 363–4.   † Ussher, letter cxxi., xv. 365.

the substitution of Mr Sibbes into the place of Sir William Temple. But having since considered with myself how some occasions may fall out that may hinder him from coming hither, and how many most unfit persons are now putting in for that place, I have further emboldened myself to signify thus much more of my mind unto you, that in case Mr Sibbes do not come unto us, I cannot think of a more worthy man, and more fitted for the government of that college, than Mr Bedel, who hath heretofore remained with Sir Henry Wotton at Venice, and is now beneficed about Berry. If either he, or Dr Featly, or any other worthy man whom you shall think fit, can be induced to accept of the place; and your grace will be pleased to advise the fellows of the college to elect him thereunto ; that poor house shall ever have cause to bless your memory for the settlement of it at such a time as this, where so many labour to make a prey of it.

Of the 'occurrences' that might 'fall out' to hinder Sibbes from coming, the primate had been informed in our next letter :—

MR R. SIBBS *to the Archbishop of Armagh.**

RIGHT REV. AND MY VERY GOOD LORD,—I answered your letters presently upon the receipt of them, but out of a mind diversely affected as divers things presented themselves to me ; it much moved me when I perceived your great care of the place, the cost, the trouble, the more than ordinary inclination towards me, far beyond any deserts of mine. Yet as I signified to your grace, when I consider God's providence in raising me so little before, to another place, and that compatible with my present employment here in London, it moveth me to think it were rash to adventure upon another place. And I have entered into a course of procuring some good to the college, which is like to be frustrate, if I now leave them, and they exposed to some who intend to serve their own turn of them. The scandal whereof would lie upon me. The judgment of my friends here is for my stay, considering I am fixed already, and there must be a call for a place ; as to a place, they allege the good which may be done, and doubtfulness of good succession here ; and that it were better that some other man had that place that were not so fixed here. These and such like considerations move them to think, that when your lordship shall know how it is with me at this time, that you will think of some other successor. Nothing of a great time so much troubled me. I humbly desire you, my lord, to take in good part this my not accepting, considering now there be other difficulties than were when you were in England with us. It is not yet openly known that I refuse it, that so you may have time of pitching upon another. I write now this second time, fearing lest my former letter might miscarry. I could set the comfort by you against many objections, were not that late chief in Cambridge. I count it one part of my happiness in especial manner, that ever I knew your lordship ; the remembrance of you will be fresh in my heart whilst I live, which will move me to desire the multiplying of all happiness upon you and yours.

I have not delivered the letter to my lord of Canterbury, because it hath reference to the business as it concerneth me. The Lord continue to honour you in his service for the good of many, and to keep you in these dangerous times.—Your Grace's to command in the Lord,

R. SIBBS.

Gray's Inn, Feb. 7. A.D. 1626.

I humbly desire you to remember my service and respects to Mrs Ussher.

* Ussher, letter ccclxxxvi., x vi. 440–1.

Upon receipt of this the primate wrote :*—' But now very lately, even by the last packet, I have received a letter from Mr Sibbs, signifying his doubtfulness of accepting the place of provost here (he having beine *at the same time* chosen head of another college in Cambridge), which hath much altered our intentions.' A few days later, Ussher was informed more definitely by Dr Samuel Ward of Sibbes's election to the Mastership of 'Catherine Hall.' I give an extract, with context, as it introduces to us an eminent ornament of Sibbes's circle :—

Dr SAMUEL WARD *to* USSHER—London, ' Feb. 13. 1626.'†

The 25th of January deceased your good friend and mine, Mr Henry Alvey, at Cambridge. I was with him twice when he was sick : the first time I found him sick, but very patient and comfortable. He earnestly prayed that God would give him patience and perseverance. The later time I came he was in a·slumber, and did speak nothing : I prayed for him, and then departed. Shortly after he departed this life. He desired to be buried privately, and in the churchyard, and in a sheet only, without a coffin, for so, said he, was our Saviour. But it was thought fitting he should be put in a coffin, and so he was : I was at his interring the next day at night. Thus God is daily collecting his saints to himself. The Lord prepare us all for the *dies ascensionis*, as St Cyprian styleth it. Since the death of Dr Walsall, Dr Goslin, our vice-chancellor, and Dr Hill, master of St Katherine Hall, are both dead. In their places succeed, in Bennet College, Dr Butts ; in Caius College, Mr Bachcroft, one of the fellows ; *in Katherine Hall, Mr Sibbes of Gray's Inn.*

Notwithstanding Sibbes's intimation, that he had not delivered the primate's letter to Abbot, he must have subsequently changed his mind, and done so. To Ussher's recommendation, Archbishop Abbot lent a cordially willing ear. This appears by his letter in reply, which would also seem to indicate that Sibbes had been persuaded to go over to Ireland, probably to consult personally with his friend :—

The most Reverend GEORGE ABBOT, *Archbishop of Canterbury, to the Archbishop of Armagh.*‡

MY VERY GOOD LORD,—I send unto you Mr Sibbes, who can best report what I have said unto him. I hope that college shall in him have a very good master, which hitherto it hath not had. You shall make my excuse to the fellows that I write not unto them. You shall do well to pray to God that he will bless his church ; but be not too solicitous in that matter, which will fall of itself, God Almighty being able and ready to support his own cause. But of all things take heed that you project no new ways ; for if they fail you shall bear a grievous burden ; if they prosper, there shall be no thanks to you. Be patient, and tarry the Lord's leisure. And so commending me unto you, and to the rest of your brethren, I leave you to the Almighty, and remain,

        Your lordship's loving brother,   G. CANT.

Lambeth, March 19. 1626.

Sibbes no doubt found, on his arrival in Dublin, that the ' place

* Ussher, letter cccxci., xvi. 453.   † Ussher, xv. 369.   ‡ Ussher, xv. 375

was likely to prove harassing, and to lead him into controversy. A sentence from a letter of Joseph Mede, in like circumstances, explains his declinature :—' I would not,' he writes to Ussher, ' be willing to adventure into a strange country upon a litigious title, having seen the bad experience at home of perpetual jars and discontents from such beginnings.' * Similar reasons, combined with the attractions of Gray's Inn and Cambridge, led Sibbes to return, leaving the provostship of Trinity College, Dublin, to be filled by the afterwards revered Bishop Bedell.

CHAPTER VI.

MASTER OF CATHARINE HALL, CAMBRIDGE.

Accepts Mastership—Relaxation of ' order' at Gray's Inn—Founder of Catharine Hall and its celebrities—Its condition—' Troublous times'—Dr John Preston—Trinity Lectureship—Bishopric declined—Friendship between Sibbes and Preston—Fellow-labourers—Conversion of Preston—The effect of the preaching of the two Puritan Masters—Auditory of St Mary's—Memorials of Trinity Lecture—Success of Sibbes as Master—Clarke and Fuller—Fellows.

Having declined the Provostship of Trinity College, Dublin, Sibbes at once accepted the Mastership of Catharine Hall, Cambridge, to which, as has been narrated, he was almost simultaneously elected. No record remains of the influence used to secure this coveted and often contested honour for the ' outed' Fellow and ' deprived' Lecturer. It is not improbable that it was to Dr John Preston, the Puritan Master of the 'nest of Puritans' (so his enemies designated it), Emmanuel, that he was indebted. Preston was then in the height of his favour with the Duke of Buckingham,—the acceptance of whose patronage is one of the stains upon the memory of the Puritans. He had long been in close friendship with the preacher of Gray's Inn.

There must have been some relaxation of the ' order' under which Sibbes accepted the appointment of preacher to Gray's Inn,—to admit of his accepting the mastership of Catharine Hall, without resignation of the other. The statute is very explicit, as will be seen :—' 15 Nov. 40 Eliz. (1598–9).—The divinity-reader to be chosen shall be nominated, having *no ecclesiastical preferment* other than a prebend without cure of souls, nor readership in any other place ; and shall keep the same place as long as he continues thus qualified, and no longer ; and to be charged with reading but twice a week, except when there is a communion.'†

* Ussher, as *ante*, p. 455–56, vol. xvi.
† This ' order' was made in the term previous to the election of the successor of

There were then, as now, the two distinct offices of reader, sometimes called chaplain, and of preacher, sometimes called lecturer, and as in above order, 'divinity-reader.'* So that it was the more easy to arrange for Sibbes's absence during the week. From an entry, under date 19th Jan. 1612, we learn that 'The preacher, ye chaplain, ye steward . . . . . . were to be allowed such commons as *gentlemen*.'† Not as 'gentleman' merely, but as associate and friend, was Sibbes regarded. The anxiety of the 'ancients, barristers, students,' to retain his services, would also smoothe the way to place in practical desuetude the 'order' as to '*no other ecclesiastical preferment*.' Be all this as it may, Sibbes entered on the mastership of Catharine Hall forthwith. ‡

Catharine or Katharine Hall, on whose Mastership Sibbes thus entered, was then, as it continues, one of the minor Colleges of the University. Yet is it not without its own celebrities, even the foremost names of English theology, Church and Puritan, before and since. It proudly tells of John Bradford the martyr, John Maplet, John Overall, William Strong, Ralph Robinson, Ralph Brownrig, John Arrowsmith, William Spurstowe, James Shirley (the dramatist), John Lightfoot, Thomas Goodwin, John Ray, William Wotton, John Strype, Thomas Sherlock, Joseph Milner, and has recently lost Charles Hardwick. It was founded by a Robert Woodlark, D.D., § (whose name has passed away like his namesake's song of a previous summer), in 1475; and took its name in honour of the 'virgin and martyr St Katherine.' Its original endowment, beyond 'the tenements and garden,' was small for even those days.

a certain Dr Crooke, who was preacher from 1583 to 1599. His successor was a Mr Fenton, elected 7th Feb., 41st Eliz., 1598-99. In respect to the preacher being unmarried, the 'order' was rigid, and probably explains why Sibbes remained so to the end. I cull a couple of entries that don't say very much for the chivalry of the Gray's Inn authorities :—1612, 'A fine paid upon change of life.' 1630, 'Noe women to come into any pt. of ye Chapell.' 1647, 'No familie to bee in the house.'—Segar MS.

* 'Chaplain.'—I note certain little memoranda in relation to the 'Chaplain,' as distinguished from the 'preacher:' the later from Segar, being one of the items included in the destroyed originals—the warrrant itself having perished; and the earlier from the 'order book' at Gray's Inn :—1625, Warrant (granted) to pay to the treasurer of Gray's Inn £6 : 13 : 4, June 25. yearly, during pleasure, for a chaplain to read service daily in the chapel there. An earlier entry runs thus :—'5th Feb. 1620. Mr Finch allowed 4/ a week for reading in the Chappell.'

† 'Order-Book' Gray's Inn, p. 16, Segar MS.

‡ In Carter's History of the University of Cambridge (pp. 202-6), and Graduati Cantabrigienses, Dr Brownrig is erroneously stated to have been elected Master of Catharine Hall in 1631. Even so accurate a writer as Mr Russell ('Memorials of Fuller', p. 114) repeats the blunder.

§ 'Dr Woodelark.' The Cambridge Antiquarian Society have published a Catalogue of Books presented by the founder to 'Catharine Hall.'

It had some subsequent 'benefactors,' among whom appear, earlier and later, Barnardistons and Claypoles. At the period of Sibbes's election, the buildings were dilapidated, the revenues limited, the students few in number. But he threw his whole soul into his office, and speedily not only attracted a fair share of young men, but also persuaded his many noble and wealthy friends to become 'benefactors.' So early as 1630, there were no fewer than twenty-eight new entries of students; and, by that time, the hall was renovated and adorned.

Sibbes entered on his mastership in 'troublous times.' When deprived of his 'lectureship' at Trinity—which in all probability, as we said, originated with the memorial addressed to him by the parishioners—he was succeeded by a John Jeffrey, of Pembroke Hall, who resigned in 1624. Upon his resignation a remarkable contest for the situation ensued. The 'townsmen'—who were now leavened with Puritanism through his preaching, and that of his associates—were desirous of electing Dr Preston; and to make it better worth his acceptance, raised the stipend from £40 or £50, to £80 a year. He was opposed by Paul Micklethwaite, fellow of Sidney College, who was supported by the Bishop of Ely, Francis White, a creature of Laud's, and the heads of colleges. It is difficult to understand on what plea there was interference with the 'townsmen.' They had themselves originated the lectureship; had themselves appointed Sibbes, had themselves supported it. But the matter came before the king at Royston, and so intense was the royal wish to root out Puritanism, his primate inciting him to the dastardly work, that Dr Preston was actually offered a bishopric, the see of Gloucester being then void. He refused to withdraw. He accepted and entered upon the lectureship. All honour to the man who spurned a mitre, its honours and revenues alike, when offered at the price of proving false to the earnest desires of 'the people' to have the gospel, the very gospel, preached to them,—wherein, in the high but truthful encomium of Goodwin, he did 'bow his more sublime and raised parts to lowest apprehension.'* When Sibbes returned to Cambridge therefore, he found in Preston one like-minded, while equally did Preston find in him one worthy to stand by his side, and 'display a banner because of the truth.'

Preston and Sibbes, from the date of the mastership of the latter, were the two great centres of influence in Cambridge, in so far as the *preaching* of the gospel was concerned. They loved one another with a love that was something wonderful. They were as

* To the Reader. . . . Sermons before His Majesty, 1680. 4to.

David and Jonathan in earlier, and as Luther and Melanchthon in later, days. They were never found apart when anything was to be done for THEIR MASTER. To the last it was so; and when the prematurely old Master of 'Emmanuel' died, he left all his papers to his beloved friend the Master of Catharine Hall, along with John Davenport, sending words of kindly greeting by Lord Say and Seale to Gray's Inn. As Sibbes's return to Cambridge, and association with Preston, formed a marked era in his life and life-work, it is needful to dwell for a little on the history of his friend.

Dr Preston was a man of extraordinary force of character and splendour of eloquence, and burned with the zeal of a seraph. Very remarkable were his antecedents. For years, like John Cotton, he had been the glory of the 'wits' for his learning and faculty of utterance. But by John Cotton's first sermon after his 'change,' he had been smitten as between joints and marrow, soul and spirit, and thenceforward had known nothing but Christ Jesus crucified. Cotton Mather tells the story of his conversion finely, and we may pause over it for a moment. 'Some time after this change upon the soul of Mr Cotton,' he says, 'it came to his turn again to preach at St Mary's; and because he was to preach, an high expectation was raised through the whole university that they should hear a sermon flourishing indeed with all the learning of the whole university. Many difficulties had Mr Cotton in his own mind, and what course to steer.' And then he proceeds to tell how he decided ' to preach a plain sermon, even such a sermon as in his own conscience he thought would be most pleasing unto the Lord Jesus Christ; and he discoursed practically and powerfully, but very solidly, upon the plain doctrine of repentance.' What then? 'The vain wits of the university, disappointed thus with a more excellent sermon, that shot some troublesome admonitions into their consciences, discovered their vexation at this disappointment by their not humming, as according to their sinful and absurd custom they had formerly done; and the vice-chancellor, for the very same reason also, graced him not as he did others that pleased him. Nevertheless,' adds Mather, 'the satisfaction which he enjoyed in his own faithful soul abundantly compensated unto him the loss of any human favour or honour; nor did he go without many encouragements from some doctors, then having a better sense of religion upon them, who prayed him to persevere in the good way of preaching which he had now taken.' And then he continues, with exultation, 'But perhaps the greatest consolation of all, was a notable effect of the sermon then preached. The famous Dr

Preston, then a fellow of Queen's College in Cambridge, and of great note in the university, came to hear Mr Cotton, with the same "itching ears" as others were then led withal. For some good while after the beginning of the sermon, his frustrated expectation caused him to manifest his uneasiness all the ways that were then possible; but before the sermon was ended, like one of Peter's hearers, he found himself "pierced at the heart." His heart within him was now struck with such resentment of his own interior state before the God of heaven, that he could have no peace in his soul, till, with a "wounded soul," he had repaired unto Mr Cotton, from whom he received those further assistances wherein he became a "spiritual father" unto one of the greatest men in his age.'*

These were men who believed in a 'living,' presiding God, and who were not ashamed to recognise, nor afraid to avouch, 'the finger of God,' the very interference of God, as real as when the Lord met Saul of Tarsus, in the turning of a human soul to Himself. They saw in Sibbes reaching the conscience of John Cotton, and in John Cotton touching the heart of Dr Preston, so many links of the mighty chain of predestination, whose last link is fast to the throne of the Eternal. They are weaker and not wiser men who scorn such faith. It is not to be wondered at, then, that in the correspondence of the Puritans in Cambridge of this period, it was felt to be 'of God,' that quick as one preacher of the word, in its blessed height and depth, breadth and length, was removed thence, another succeeded. William Perkins was taken away, but Paul Bayne was 'sent' in his room. Paul Bayne was removed, and Sibbes was sent; Sibbes was 'outed,' and John Preston took his place; and now while the Master of Emmanuel was longing for one who might be a fellow-helper with him, again came Richard Sibbes. The hearts of the praying few were cheered, and under the awakening, rich, full, grand, proclamations of the 'grace of God that bringeth salvation,' all Cambridge was moved. Preston was from day to day at Emmanuel and Trinity, and Sibbes from day to day at Catharine Hall, preaching as 'dying men to dying men;' knowing nothing among them save Jesus Christ and him crucified, yea, regarding the demand of the 'wits' for 'polite' preaching as but an awful echo of the olden cry, 'Let him come down from the cross and we will believe him.'

From the title-pages of the early editions of their Sermons, we find that they were, again and again, appointed to preach at St Mary's, the church of the whole University. On these occasions

* Magnalia, as *ante* page 16.

there was such a galaxy of men assembled as could not have been seen elsewhere in all the world. The effect was electric, among gentle as among simple. It rejoices one to scan the roll of the names of those who were then Masters, Fellows, and Students, and all of whom were found in attendance on the preaching of Sibbes and Preston. With relation to Sibbes, we read 'The Saint's Safety' and 'Christ is Best,' 'Christ's Sufferings for Man's Sin' and 'The Church's Visitation,' and 'The Saints' Hiding-place,' with deepened interest, as, turning to the original title-pages, we find they were addressed to auditories that included the foremost names of the age. The dates inform us that these sermons, which are almost unrivalled for largeness, I might even say grandeur, of thought, richness of gospel statement, impressiveness and pungency of application, and music of diction, were delivered when the several colleges sent to St Mary's names such as these. Foremost stands John Milton, then at Christ's, and himself writing sonnets on the very themes of Sibbes's discourses. Next comes Jeremy Taylor, just entered '*pauper scholaris,*' as Sibbes assumed the Mastership. Behind him, already renowned as a 'public orator,' mark George Herbert. Side by side with him rises the girlish face, with its strange shadow of sorrow, of Matthew Wren, destined to belie God's handwriting in that face, by becoming a 'persecutor.' Very different is the next that meets our eye, William Gouge, of King's. And beside him is one who will be the preacher's successor at Catharine Hall, Ralph Brownrig, looking wistfully upward with his large, beaming eyes. Snug in some sequestered pew, taking keen note of all in that marvellous memory of his, see Thomas Fuller. Worn and weary, yet moved to listen, picture Edmund Castell and Abraham Whelock. Sitting at the foot of the pulpit stairs are Charles Chauncy and Richard Holdsworth, and dreamy Peter Sterry from Emmanuel. Taking notes, and wishing the hour-glass were turned again, is Joseph Mede. Fronting the preacher, and intent as any, lo! the young Lord Wriothesly, son of Shakespeare's Earl of Southampton, and young Sir Dudley North, son of Lord North of Kirkling, both of Sibbes's own college, St John's. Linking himself arm-in-arm with the preacher as he descends, mark stormy John Williams, afterwards Bishop and 'Lord Keeper.' And thus might be recounted, almost by the hundred, names that still shine like a winter's night of stars. St Mary's pews and lobbies, crowded, above and below, with such hearers, to such preachers, is a noticeable mark of progress.*

Perhaps I cannot better illustrate the advance of Puritanism

* I have gathered these names, after Masson (Life of Milton, i. 92-99), from numerous sources, but mainly from Cooper's 'Annals of Cambridge,' Wood's 'Athenæ'

in Cambridge than by here submitting a hitherto unpublished document of this period, 1626–27, recovered from the 'Churchwardens' books of the parish.* It very strikingly reveals the interest pervading the community in the Trinity lectureship.

The document explains itself. I adhere to its orthography—

'Whereas, such p'sons as are interessed in the seates of the gallerie of this church ("Trinity") to sit there dureinge the time of the lecture, haveinge paid for the same to the p'ish, and yet, notwithstanding, are displaced by others haveinge not interest there, to their greivance and wronge; and, unles redresse herein be speedely had, such p'sons soe greived will withdraw their cotribucons from the said lecture. For remedie whereof, it is ordered and agreed unto, by a joynt consent of all the p'shioners, that from henceforth noe p'son nor p'sons of what condyc'on soever, except such who have interest in the seats, shal be permytted to goe up into the galleries untyl the bell have done tollinge; and then, yf any place be voyd, or may be spared to p'mytt, in the first place, grave divines, and after them such others as shall be lyked of by such as shall keep the dore; and yf any who have interest in the seates shall bringe any stranger to be placed there, and will have him to have his place in the gallerie, then such p'son bringing such stranger, to keepe belowe, and take his place els where for such tyme; and yf any person interessed in the seats doe not repair to the church before the bell have done tollinge, then he to lose his place for that tyme.

'It is likewise ordered, by ye like consent, that such p'sons as have interest in any of ye seates in ye church, shall not have it particularly to themselves to place and displace whom they will, but only to have ye use of the seats, duringe the tyme of the lecture, for theire owne p'sons, and to receave into them such other of the parish, yf any such come, as shall belonge to such seate, and such others likewise as are people of qualitye who doe contribute to ye lecture; and not to receave any children into their seats.

'It is further ordered that noe seats eyther in ye galleries or in ye church shall hereafter be disposed of to any wthout the consent of the parishiners at a publiq meetinge in the church.†

Thus moving the 'whole city,' Sibbes and Preston went hand-in-hand; and long after they were gone, when a very different spirit

(by Bliss), Fuller's 'Worthies' (by Nichols), and the 'Lives of Nicholas Ferrar, and of Matthew Robinson,' two of, I trust, a series of like 'Biographies,' under the scholarly editorial care of Mr Mayor of St John's. Consult also the 'Memoirs' of each name given. All, however, wishing to get real insight into Cambridge-life of the period, I must again and again refer to Mr Masson's 'Milton.' Sibbes's popularity and success is testified by all who write about him, and I can trace none who was so frequently called to preach in St Mary's.

* From 'Between the Churchwarden's Accounts for 1626 and 1627, Trinity Parish, Cambridge.' Kindly pointed out to me by Mr Wallis, and obligingly transcribed, with his usual exactness, by Mr Cooper.

† It may be as well to round off, in a foot-note, such additional memoranda as are in my possession about the lectureship. On 11th May 1630, there was again interference and controversy, Dr Thomas Goodwin being the lecturer. A letter respecting it was addressed to the vice-chancellor by Dudley Carleton, Viscount Dorchester, one of the principal secretaries of state. This 'letter' may be here given from

reigned in Cambridge, born of the wild licence of the Restoration, white-headed men would recall their honoured names with a sigh.

But, while thus faithful as a 'servant of Jesus Christ' in preaching, Richard Sibbes had the faculty of government. Catharine Hall soon found itself on an equality with its sister colleges. He returned from Sunday to Sunday, while the 'Courts' sat, to Gray's Inn, and was ever forward to plead the claims of his 'little house,' with his noble friends there.

We have many testimonies to his influence and usefulness in both. Of the former, Samuel Clarke observes: 'About the year 1618 (1616), he was chosen Preacher to Gray's Inn, one of the learnedest societies in England, where his ministry found such general approbation and acceptance that, besides the learned lawyers of the house, many noble personages, and many of the gentry and citizens, resorted to hear him, and many, till this day

the Baker MSS. (xxvii. 137), as inserted in Cooper's Annals of Cambridge (iii. 229-30).

To my Reverend Friend Mr Dr BUTS, *Vice-chan, &c.*

SIR,—By reason of his Majesties late directions concerning lecturers, that they should read divine service according to the Liturgy, before their lectures, and the afternoone sermons to be turned into catechising, some doubt hath beene made of the continuance of the lecture at Trinity Church, in Cambr. which for many yeares past hath beene held at one of the clocke in the afternoone, without divine service read before yt, and cannot be continued at that hower, if the whole service should be reade before the sermon begin. Whereupon his Majestie hath been informed that the same is a publick lecture, serving for all the parishes in that town (being fourteen in number), and that the university sermon is held at the same tyme, which would be troubled with a greater resort than can be well permitted, yf the towne sermon should be discontinued: and that the same being held at the accustomed hower, there will be tyme enough left after that sermon ended, and the auditory departed thence to their own parish churches, as well for divine service as for catechising in that and all other churches in the towne, which could not well be, yf divine service should be read in that church before the lecture; besides the catechising in that church, would hereby be lost. Upon these motives his Majesty, being graciously pleased that the said lecture may be continued at the accustomed hower, and in manner as yt hath been heretofore used, hath given me in charge to make knowne to you his royall pleasure accordingly, but under this caution, that not only divine service, but catechising be duely read and used after that sermon ended, both in that and the rest of the churches of the towne; and that the sermon doe end in convenient tyme for that purpose, soe as no pretext be made, either for the present or in future tyme, by color of the foresaid sermon, to hinder either divine service or catechising, which his Majestie is resolved to have maintained. And so I bidd you heartily farewell, and rest, Yours to doe you service, DORCHESTER.

From Whitehall, the 11th of May 1630.

Mr Cooper annotates: 'Randolph in a poem "On Importunate Dunnes," after a curious malediction on the Cambridge tradesmen, adds—

"And if this vex 'um not, I'le grive the town,
With this curse, State, put *Trinity-lecture* down."'

Randolph's Poems, ed. 1643, p. 119.

(1674–77), bless God for the benefit which they received of him.'*
Besides this, various regulations and 'orders' as to seats and right
of entrance in the order-books, inform us of over-crowded attendance.
Thus, under 1623, 'All strangers to be kept out of the Chapell at
Sermon, but such as are brought in by some of yᵉ society.' Perhaps even more significant of a crowd is what follows : 'And all yᵉ
gentlemen to goe out of yᵉ Chappell bare-headed in decent manner.'

Of the latter, again, Clarke says, 'About the year 1625, or '26, he
was chosen Master of Katharine Hall in Cambridge, the government
whereof he continued till his dying day ; and, indeed, like a faithful
governor, he was always very solicitous and careful to procure and
advance the good of that little house. For he procured good means
and maintenance, by his interest in many worthy persons, for the
enlargement of the College, and was a means and instrument to
establish learned and religious Fellows there; inasmuch as, in his
time, it proved a very famous society for piety and learning, both in
Fellows and Scholars.'† To the same effect, though with characteristic quaintness, Fuller testifies, 'He found the House in a mean
condition, the wheel of St. Katharine having stood still (not to say
gone backwards) for some years together ; he left it replenished with
scholars, beautified with buildings, better endowed with revenues.'‡
Somewhat boastfully, perhaps, Daniel Milles, in his list of Masters,
thus describes Sibbes :—

'Ricardus Sibbs, Sacræ Theologiæ Professor,§ omnium quos præsens
ætas viderit vir pientissimus, concionator mellitissimus, qui haud paucorum
corda suavitate dicendi emolliit, et vivendi sanctitate ad bonam frugem
plane rapuit. Hic erat qui collegium istud partim temporum injuria,
partim Præfectorum socordia et avaritia bonis suis spoliatum, et omni
honore exutum, ad pristinam famam et dignitatem restituit, quiaque erat
apud omnes pios autoritate maximâ, largam benefactorum messem, in hoc
vacuum gymnasium feliciter diduxit. Adeo ut non nudo Præfecti nomine
dignus videatur, sed alter fundator censeri debeat.'

Other testimonies, as of Eachard,‖ might be given, were it needful ;
and, indeed, the tribute of Sir Philip Sidney to Hubert Languet
must have been his, from many,

" . . . . hating what is naught,
   For faithful heart, clean hands, and mouth as true.
   With his sweet skill my skill-less youth he drew
   To have a feeling taste of Him that sits
   Beyond the heaven, *far more beyond our wits.*'
              (*Arcadia*, Book iii. pp. 397–8, ed. 1755.)

Of the Fellows, during Sibbes's Mastership, may be named Anthony

* 'Clarke,' as *ante*, p. 144.   † 'Clarke,' as *ante*, p. 144.
‡ Fuller, 'Worthies,' edited by Nichols. 2 vols. 4to. 1811. Vol. ii. p. 848.
§ *i.e.*, D.D.   ‖ 'Eachard,' History of England, p. 451.

Pym (1628), probably a relative of *the* John Pym, who was a personal friend, and mentioned in his will; William Spurstowe (1630);*
John Sibbes (1631), his nephew; Charles Pym (1631), brother of Anthony; Roger Fleetwood (1632); Joseph Spurstowe (1634).

CHAPTER VII.

SIBBES AND LAUD—' THE PALATINATE.'

The Puritans watched—The Elector Palatine—Disasters—Shame of England—Battle of Prague—Frederick and Elizabeth fugitives—Persecution—Circular Letter by Sibbes, Gouge, Taylor, and Davenport—Citation before the Star-Chamber—Pronounced 'Notorious Delinquents.'

All the emotion and interest to hear such preaching as was that of Sibbes and Preston, while it gives a measure of the progress of Puritanism (using the word in its recognised historic and lustrous sense), is also to the student of the period a measure of the hate with which the king (in so far as he had stamina enough to hate) and Bishop Laud, now rising into notice, regarded it. So early as 1611, the latter was a '*whisperer*,' a '*busy-body*,' ever going about with sly, stealthy-paced, panther-like foot-fall, and keen, cold eye, if by any means, he might possess himself of *secrets*. Between Gray's Inn, and Catharine Hall, and St Mary's, with not unfrequent 'sermons' elsewhere, Sibbes had noble vantage-ground for noble service, and he was occupying it to the full; and Laud was ready to pounce upon him. I have now to narrate the occasion. Sibbes was not a man to narrow his activities to his own immediate sphere, or to his own country. He watched with profoundest interest the progress of the great Protestant sister-countries, rejoicing in their joy and mourning with their mourning. In 1620, he had spoken burning words 'of the Palatinate;' words that reveal the common shame of England for her king's pusillanimous desertion of the Elector Frederick, a man true and good in himself, and knit by the tenderest ties to the king of England. From shore to shore the nation had rung with acclaim over revolting Bohemia—the land of John Huss and many martyr-names. They had said 'Amen' to the rejection of Ferdinand II., and their hearts beat high for the Elector Palatine chosen in his stead, when he fearlessly said 'Yes' to the call. History tells the tragic sequel.

* Spurstowe. The date, 1630, of Spurstowe's 'fellowship' (he was afterwards Master), shews that Mr Masson has made a slip in enumerating his name among the distinguished 'fellows' under Dr Hill's Mastership. Life of Milton, i. 97. I cannot make even this small reference to Mr Masson without, in common with every literary man since the issue of his book, acknowledging my indebtedness to his industry, and almost prodigal elucidation and illustration of contemporary events and names.

Then opened what proved the 'Thirty Years' War,' in which the emperor, and pope, and the king of Spain were leagued against Frederick, and against the Protestant Union in him. All Europe looked on. Our own England was humiliated, all but treasonous, as James talked his foolish talk and lived his unclean life, and forgot daughter, son-in-law, Protestantism—all. Driven to do something, he did his little when too late. In November 1620, the Protestants were smitten in one decisive battle—Prague; and Frederick and his queen, losing Bohemia, losing the Palatinate, losing all, fled as refugees to Holland. What followed, only the great sealed 'book' above will declare. The triumphant enemy 'played havoc;' and, through many dark and terrible years, the sufferings of the Protestants of Bohemia and the 'palatinate,' were something unimaginable. The cry reached England, and public help was sought and denied. But it went not everywhere unheard, unheeded. The Puritans, Sibbes among the first, recognised their brotherhood, and out of their own private resources sought to do a little, if it were only to shew their sympathy. I have been fortunate enough to recover a touching memorial of their efforts. Preserved among very different papers in Her Majesty's Record Office is a 'circular' letter, which, in the pathos of its simple words, goes right to the heart. Here it is:—

Whereas, a late information is given to his Matie of the lamentable distresses of two hundred and forty godly preachers, with their wifes and families, and sundrie thousands of godly private persons with them, cast out of their house and homes, out of their callings and countreys, by the furie of the mercilesse papists in the Upper Palatinate, whose heavie condicion is such as they are forced to steale their servises of religion in woods and solitarie places, not without continual feare and damage of their lives; and whose present want is such as they would be very thankfull for coarse bread (and) drinke if they could gett it. As tenderinge the miserie and want of deare brethren and sisters, desire all godly persons to whom these presents may come, as fellowe feeling members of the same body of Jesus Christ, to comiserate their present want and enlarge their hearts and hands for some present and private supply for them till some publique means (which hereafter may be hoped) may be raised for their reliefe, assuring themselves that whatsoever is cast into heaven, and falleth into the lappe of Christ in his members, shall return with abundant increase in the harvest; neither lett any be discouraged least their bounty should miscarrie, for we knowe a sure and safe way whereby whatsoever is given shall undoubtedly come to their hands to (whom) it is intended.

2 Martii 1627. (Signed) THO. TAYLOR.
RICHARD SIBBS.
JOHN DAVENPORT.
WILLIAM GOUGE.*

* 'Circular.' Described in 'Calendar of State Papers, Domestic Series of the Reign of Charles I., 1627-28.' By John Bruce, 1858 (Longman).

One of two copies of this affecting 'circular' is endorsed by Laud, and the names noted so carefully, that the Sibbs within is corrected to Sibbes without. One marvels what ground even a Laud could find for opposition, much less persecution, in so piteous an appeal. But when there is a will to hurt or hinder, an occasion is not ill to devise. Perchance the vehement words, '*merciless papists*,' stung. At any rate, the four honoured men, Richard Sibbes, William Gouge, Thomas Taylor, John Davenport, were summoned before the Star Chamber, and reprimanded. It is not at all wonderful that William Prynne, in his 'Canterburie's Doom,' should ask, '*By what law of the land*'—a question, by the way, that rings all through the charges of this extraordinary book, like a Gerizzim curse—' did they convert Doctor Gouge, Doctor Sibbes, Doctor Taylor, and Master Davenport, as notorious delinquents, only for setting their hands to a certificate upon entreaty, testifying the distressed condition of some poor ministers of the Palatinate, and furthering a private contribution among charitable Christians for their relief, when public collections failed ?'

It does not appear what further steps, if any, were taken ; but one thing is certain, the miserable persecution did not 'silence' Sibbes. For he not only preached, but published passionately rebuking words against the national lukewarmness. 'What,' asks he, 'shall the members of Christ suffer in other countries, and we profess ourselves to be living members, and *yet not sympathize with them?* We must be conformable to our Head, before we can come to heaven.'* What a pass things had reached, when those in authority would have shut even the hand of private charity against such sufferers ! It is impossible to restrain indignation when reading of James's more than poltroonly, more than mean, desertion of his own 'flesh and blood,' not to speak of Protestantism ; but doubly base was Laud's interference to stamp out as a pestilent thing, this little effort to relieve 'godly preachers and private persons.' It only added to that thunder-cloud, which in a few years was to launch its lightnings on his own head, and whose preluding shadows were even now darkening the sky: such retribution as comes

'When the quick darting lightning's flash
Is the clear glitter of His golden spear.'†

---

* 'Soul's Conflict.' † Cecil and Mary, by Jackson, p. 19 (1858.)

CHAPTER VIII.

SIBBES AND LAUD AGAIN—'THE IMPROPRIATION FEOFEES.'

The Preacher of Gray's Inn under surveillance—Controversy not sought by Sibbes—Loyal to Church and State—The Puritans no 'Schismatics'—Witness-bearing—Wonder and yet no Wonder—Laud's 'Beauty of Holiness'—'Solemnity'—Persecution—'Silencing'—William Prynne—Puritan Literature—Laudian-Bishop's Literature—Sibbes against Popery—Lord Keeper Finch—The 'Impropriation' Scheme—Sibbes a 'Feoffee'—Checks upon Laud—'Overthrow' of 'Feoffees'—Confiscation—Banishment—Verdict upon Laud.

The Star Chamber citation, because of The Palatinate, with its result—a severe reprimand, and treatment as of 'notorious delinquents,'—was only a slighter issue of that unsleeping and vengeful resolution to suppress all Puritanism, which through upwards of a quarter of a century, Laud had planned. Accordingly, though defeated in the matter of the Palatinate, in so far as '*silencing*' Sibbes and his compeers was concerned, they, in common with all the 'good men and true' of the period—for really it appears that every man of note in his day, who was not his creature, was the object of his annoyance—were *watched*.* Nor is it at all difficult to understand, that such preaching as was being heard from Sunday to Sunday at 'Gray's Inn,' and down in Cambridge, and by crowds in St Mary's, when reported to him, as everything was reported—must have been superlatively offensive. We do not find Sibbes mixed up with the controversies of the day. There is in his works a noteworthy absence of those fires of intolerant passion that burn so fiercely in many of the writings and actings of his contemporaries. Never once do we meet with him in the ante-chamber of 'the Court,' or mingling with the venal crowds that in unholy rivalry bade high and higher, or more properly low and lower, for place, seeking to cover their 'multitude of sins,' not with charity, but lawn sleeves. He lived serenely apart from the miserable squabbling and personal resentments, and exacerbations of the semi-political, semi-theological polemics that agitated state and church. He was loyal, even tenderly charitable to those in authority; and true to the church, if only the church would be true to him, by being true to its Head. Let us hear what he was saying about both in those days. Of the State he thus speaks:—'Sometimes it falleth out that those that are under the government of others are most

---

* 'Watched.' Scattered up and down Sibbes's writings are various indications of his knowledge of this espionage, *e. g.*, 'So in coming to hear the word of God, some come to observe the elegancy of words and phrases, *some to catch advantage, perhaps, against the speaker, men of a devilish temper.*'—('Bowels Opened,' pp. 130–31.)

injurious, by waywardness and harsh censures, herein disparaging and discouraging the endeavours of superiors for public good. In so great weakness of man's nature, and especially in this crazy age of the world, *we ought to take in good part any moderate happiness we enjoy by government;* and not be altogether as a nail in the wound, exasperating things by misconstruction. *Here love should have a mantle to cast upon the lesser errors of those above us. Oftentimes the poor man is the oppressor by unjust clamours. We should labour to give the best interpretation to the actions of governors that the nature of the actions will possibly bear.*'* Similar sentiments abound. Of the Church we have many wise and considerate words. He had no wish for separation: none of the Puritans had, until they were driven to it. So far from seeking to divide 'the church' and injure it—the refrain of many an accusation—Sibbes has sarcasms that perhaps might have been spared, against those who even then felt they could not remain within her pale. 'Fractions,' he says, with an approach to unkindness very unusual with him, 'always breed factions.' He could not mean it; but this was capable of being turned by Laud to his own account. He was quick as a sleuth-hound to discern taint of treason. But we have more full and explicit statements. Thus with more than ordinary vehemence he expostulates, accuses :—' What a joyful spectacle is this to Satan and his faction, to see those that are separated from the world fall in pieces among themselves! Our discord is our enemy's melody. *The more to blame those that for private aims affect differences from others, and will not suffer the wounds of the church to close and meet together.*'†

Was this man, so truly a man of peace, one to track and keep under surveillance, as though he had been at once traitor and fanatic? Whence came it? The answer is too easy. Though 'slow to speak,' and sweet-natured to a fault, he was fearless when the occasion demanded it.‡ Even immediately on saying the above,

---

* Bruised Reed, e. ix. † Bruised Reed, c. xvii.

‡ 'Sweet-natured to a fault.' Brook ('Lives of the Puritans,' ii. 419) remarks: 'This reverend divine was eminently distinguished for a meek and quiet spirit, being *always unwilling to offend those in power.*' This is too general, for however gentle, Sibbes, when roused, spoke out with no thought of who might be, or might not be, offended. For, says he, 'It argues a base disposition, either for frown or favour, to desert a good cause in evil times' ('Bowels Opened,' 1st edition, 1639, 4to, p. 45). Brook continues, from Calamy (Calamy's Account, vol. ii. pp. 605, 606): 'This trait in his character will appear from the following anecdote: —A fellowship being vacant in Magdalen College, for which Archbishop Laud recommended his bell-ringer at Lambeth, with an evident design of quarrelling with

he takes care to guard himself from misconstruction, by adding :—
'Which must not be understood, as if men should dissemble their
judgment in any truth where there is just cause of expressing themselves; for the least truth is Christ's, and not ours : and therefore
we are not to take liberty to affirm or deny at our pleasure. There
is a due in a penny, as well as in a pound ; *therefore we must be
faithful in the least truth, when season calleth for it.*' But
again, so gentle and unpolemic was he, he continues finely :—' But
in some cases peace, by keeping our faith to ourselves, Rom. xiv.
22, is of more consequence than the open discovery of some things
we take to be true : *considering the weakness of man's nature is
such, that there can hardly be a discovery of any difference in
opinion, without some estrangement of affection.* So far as men
are not of one mind, they will hardly be of one heart, except where
grace and the peace of God, Col. iii. 15, bear great rule in the heart.
*Therefore, open show of difference is never good but when it is
necessary;* however some, from a desire to be somebody, turn into
by-ways, and yield to a spirit of contradiction in themselves.'*
And then, Leighton-like, he turns away from the distractions
around him, and thinks of the 'rest that remains.' 'Our blessed
Saviour, when he was to leave the world, what doth he press upon
his disciples more than peace and love ? And in his last prayer,
with what earnestness did he beg of his Father that they might be
one, as he and the Father were one ! John xvii. 21. But what he
prayed for on earth, we shall only enjoy perfectly in heaven. *Let
this make the meditation of that time the more sweet to us.*'†
Even so—

> 'Search well another world; who studies this,
> Travels in clouds; seeks manna where none is.'‡

One wonders, and yet does not wonder, how such a peaceable
and loveable man came to be thus harassed. But what has the
dove done to make the serpent strike its fang into it ? Simply

them if they refused, or of putting a spy upon them if they accepted, Dr Sibbes, who
was ever unwilling to provoke his superiors, told the fellows that Lambeth-house
would be obeyed; and that the person was young, and might in time prove hopeful.
The fellows therefore consented, and the man was admitted.' This 'anecdote'
carries improbability in the face of it, and neither Calamy nor Brook adduce any
authority. Sibbes could have no voice in 'Magdalen,' in the election or rejection of
a 'fellow.' Nor is there the slightest memorial of such an appointment as is stated.
Surely if it had been made, name and date would have been notorious. Amid the
many charges against Laud, this has no place either in Prynne or elsewhere.
Calamy is not guilty, ordinarily, of introducing mere idle gossip, but it would seem
that in the present instance he has.

* and † Bruised Reed, c. xvii.

‡ Henry Vaughan, Silex Scintillans. Edition by Lyte, 1847, page 17.

crossed its path. What the lamb, to cause the wolf to take it by the throat? Again, simply *crossed its path.* Sibbes had done that with Laud. While the king, under his mitred councillor's tuition, was straining every nerve to un-Sabbath Sunday, Sibbes and his co-Puritans held fast its inviolable authority. While proclamations, unsanctioned by Parliament, were issued to substitute the May-pole for the Cross, the Book of Sports for the Book of God, and the village green for the sanctuary, Sibbes held up the cross and summoned the people to the sanctuary. While all doctrinal preaching, all declarations of the *grace* of God in Jesus Christ, was sought to be put down (precursor of the infamous 'Directions'), Sibbes avouched his Calvinism, and spoke with no bated breath of Arminianism. While *churchmen* of the school of Laud would have men regard transubstantiation as a '*school nicety,*' bowing to the table of the 'Lord, as '*becoming reverence,*' images in churches worthy 'commemoration,' sacerdotal absolution and confession to a priest as '*proper things,*' the Lord's Supper not as a sacrament, but as a sacrifice,—Sibbes protested, and gave them their proper designation, with no periphrasis or courtly phrase, of papistical innovation and delusions of the devil. I am not sure that I would make all his and the Puritans' side-thrusts against 'the papist' my own. I fear I cannot acquit either them or him of 'upbraiding,' and even blameable uncharity for the men, in the honesty of his indignation against their doctrines and measures. But we must not forget the circumstances of 'the time.' He was old enough to remember the Armada, sent to his own Suffolk shore under a pope's blessing, and a 'bull' being nailed to the palace-door with a pope's ban. He was cognizant of innumerable plots, not merely against our religious, but also our civil, liberties. He heard claims asserted, not for equality, but supremacy. And then there were those high in authority, coquetting with that popery that had incarnadined England with her best blood, and had been got rid of at a cost inestimable. He could not but speak, and, speaking as a patriot and Protestant, it was not easy to '*prophesy smooth things.*' Perhaps Laud would have endured Sibbes's bold and passionate rebuke of the prevailing sins of the age, and even, however galled, have winked at his full and fervid assertions of the principles of the reformation from popery, and clear and articulate condemnation of Arminianism, had he gone no further. But words were not only to be answered with words, be it granted unadvised words, with occasional kindredly unadvised words. Action was to be met with action, if 'the church' were not to be only a masked re-establishment of popery, and if the Calvinism of its fathers were not to degenerate into *ultra*-Arminianism ; and it was done, as we shall see. Peter Heylin was now at the ear of Laud ; and Hacket observes, that 'they that watched the increase of Arminianism, said, confidently, that it was from the year 1628 that the tide of it began to come in, and this because it was from that year that 'all the preferments were cast on one side.'* Similar is the testimony concerning the favour shewn to popery. Thus opposing Laud in his two darling objects, it is easy to foresee that one like Sibbes, resident in London, could not fail to come into conflict with the vigilant and suspicious head of the church. Nor are we to suppose that, if *he* was watched by Lambeth's police, Lambeth went unwatched. How far the primate was going in his 'papistical tendencies,' may be gathered from one notorious exhibition. Besides its bearing on the persecution springing out of the impropriation scheme, it gives point to a suggestive hit by Sibbes, which was probably the thing that stung Laud to further action against him and his coadjutors in another blessed work. I therefore give the record of it from the admittedly authoritative pages of Rushworth and Wharton, *in extenso* :—On Sunday the 16th of January 1630-1, a new church—St Catherine Creed—in Leadenhall Street, was consecrated. It had been re-built, and had been suspended by the primate from all divine service, sermons or sacraments, until it should be re-consecrated. Laud and a number of his clergy came in the morning to perform the ceremony. Then as strange and sad a 'performance' as ever men beheld was enacted, regard being had to the fact that the performer was the Protestant Primate of England :—

'At the bishop's approach to the west door,' says Rushworth, 'some that were prepared for it cried, with a loud voice, "Open, open, ye everlasting doors, that the king of glory may enter in!" and presently the doors were opened, and the bishop, with some doctors, and many other principal men, went in, and immediately, falling down upon his knees, with his eyes lifted up, and his arms spread abroad, uttered these words : "This place is holy ; the ground is holy: in the name of the Father, Son, and Holy Ghost, I pronounce it holy." Then he took up some of the dust, and threw it up into the air, several times, in his going up towards the chancel. † When they approached near to the rail and communion-table, the bishop bowed towards it several times ; and, returning, they went round the church in procession, saying the 100th Psalm, and after that the 19th Psalm, and then said a form of prayer, commencing, "Lord Jesus

* Hacket . . . Life of Williams, Lord Keeper. Pt. ii. p. 42 and p. 82.

† Masson, 'Life of Milton,' i. 350, adds here this foot-note :—This was sworn to on Laud's trial by two witnesses; but Laud denies it, and moreover, says that, if it had been true, it would not have been a popish ceremony, as the Romish pontifical prescribes, not 'dust,' but 'ashes' to be thrown up on such occasions.

Christ," &c., and concluding, " We consecrate this church, and separate it unto thee, as holy ground, not to be profaned any more to common use." After this, the bishop being near the communion-table, and taking a written book in his hand (a copy, as was afterwards alleged, of a form in the Romish pontifical, but according to Laud, furnished him by the deceased Bishop Andrewes), pronounced curses upon those that should afterwards profane that holy place by musters of soldiers, or keeping profane law-courts, or carrying burdens through it; and at the end of every curse, bowed towards the east, and said, "Let all the people say, Amen." When the curses were ended, he pronounced a number of blessings upon all those that had any hand in framing and building of that sacred and beautiful church, and those that had given, or should hereafter give, any chalices, plate, ornaments, or utensils; and at the end of every blessing, he bowed towards the east, and said, " Let all the people say, Amen." After this followed the sermon, which being ended, the bishop consecrated and administered the sacrament in manner following :—As he approached the communion-table, he made several lowly bowings; and coming up to the side of the table, where the bread and wine were covered, he bowed seven times; and then, after the reading of many prayers, he came near the bread, and gently lifted up a corner of the napkin wherein the bread was laid; and when he beheld the bread, he laid it down again, flew back a step or two, bowed three several times towards it, then he drew near again, and opened the napkin, and bowed as before. Then he laid his hand on the cup, which was full of wine, with a cover upon it, which he let go again, went back, and bowed thrice towards it; then he came near again, and lifting up the cover of the cup, looked into it, and seeing the wine, let fall the cover again, retired back, and bowed as before. Then he received the sacrament, and gave it to some principal men; after which, many prayers being said, the solemnity of the consecration ended.'

That was the sort of thing that the primate and his like-minded bishops, sought to impose on men as 'SOLEMNITY!' That '*mountebank* holiness' (it is Sir Philip Sidney's word of scorn) was to be its translation of the grand old ' Beauty of Holiness,' (1 Chron. xvi. 29; Ps. xxix. 2, and xcvi. 9).* It is no light occasion that

* ' Beauty of holiness.' The vehement words of John Milton, stern as Jeremiah. a few year later, are memorable, and may not be passed by :—' Now for their demeanour within the church, how have they disfigur'd and defac't that more than angelick brightnes, the unclouded serenity of Christian religion, *with the dark overcasting of superstitious coaps and flaminical vestures.* . . . Tell me. ye priests, wherefore this gold, wherefore these roabs and surplices, over the gospel? Is our religion guilty of the first trespasse, and hath need of cloathing to cover her nakednesse? What does this else but cast an ignominey upon the perfection of Christ's ministery by seeking to adorn it with that which was the poor remedy of our shame? Believe it, wondrous doctors, *all corporeal resemblances of inward holinesse and beauty are now past.*' (The Reason of Church Government, B. II. ch. ii. p. 154. Mitford's Milton. Prose Works, vol. i. Pickering.) Elsewhere, denouncing the 'chaff of over-dated ceremonies,' he thus describes the Laudian ' prelaty :'—' They began to draw down all the divine intercourse betwixt God and the soul, yea, the very shape of God himself, into an exterior and bodily form, urgently pretending a necessity and obligement of joining the body in a formal reverence and worship circumscribed: they hallowed it, they fumed it, they sprinkled it, they bedecked it, not in robes of calls for one's judgment of another in so awful and sacred a thing as his religion, however it may be darkened by superstition, or lightened by the fires of the wildest fanaticism. Deplorable, therefore, as this mummery may be to us, we may not pronounce that it was an unreal, much less that it was a farcical thing to its chief actor. Such a soul as his, so small, so narrow, may have found channel deep enough for its reverence in such return upon an effete ritualism. We may agree with Macaulay's epithet of 'imbecile,' but not with the Puritan's angry charge of 'hypocrite.' But when one realises that prison, fine, the knife, the shears, persecution to the death, were the award of every honest soul that refused to regard as the 'Beauty of Holiness' such exaggerations of even popery, it is hard to withhold an anathema, ringing as Paul's, on the memory of him who devised, and of the craven bishops who cravenly enforced them. There the spider-soul sat, in its craft, spreading out its net-work over broad England, and by its Harsnets and Curles, Mountagus and Buckridges, Bancrofts and Wrens, and Mainwarings, united in a brotherhood of evil, sought to entrap all who held to the divine simplicity of the New Testament. The secret threads, revealed by the tears of the persecuted, as by the morning dew is revealed the drop-spangled and else concealed web of the open-air spider, thrilled news up to the hand that grasped all, and forth the fiat went. 'Within a single year, at this period,' says Neal, 'many lecturers were put down, and such as preached against Arminianism or the new ceremonies were suspended and silenced, among whom were the Rev. Mr John Rogers of Dedham, Mr Daniel Rogers of Wethersfield, Mr Hooker of Chelmsford, Mr White of Knightsbridge, Mr Archer, Mr William Martin, Mr Edwards, Mr Jones, Mr Dod, Mr Hildersam, Mr Ward, Mr Saunders, Mr James Gardiner, Mr Foxley, and many others.' *

We have the burning words of Prynne, that at a 'later day,' in the day of his humiliation, the primate had to meet. Thus forcibly is the charge put—nor was it ever touched :—

'As he thus preferred Popish and Arminian clergymen to the chief eccle-

pure innocency, but of pure linen, with other deformed and fantastic dresses, in palls and mitres, gold and gewgaws, fetched from Aaron's old wardrobe or the flamen's vestry; then was the priest sent to con his motions and his postures, his liturgies and lurries, till the soul, by this means of overbodying herself, given up to fleshly delights, bated her wing apace downwards.' In our own day, one has characterised the same phenomenon, as presented by Tractarianism, which, indeed, was the harvest of the baleful seed sown by Laud, as 'a thing of flexions and genuflexions, postures and impostures, with a dash of man-millinery.'

* Hist. of Puritans, Vol. i. p. 589, &c. (ed., 3 vols. 8vo, 1837.)

siastical preferments in our church, so, on the contrary, (following the counsel of Cautzen, the Mogonutive Jesuit, in his politics, see 'Look about you'), he discountenanced, suspended, silenced, suppressed, censured, imprisoned, persecuted most of the prime, orthodox, diligent preaching ministers of the realm, and forced many of them to fly into America, Holland, and other foreign places, to avoid his fury, only for opposing his popish innovations, and expressing their fears of the change of our religion. Not to trouble you with any forementioned instances of Mr Peter Smart, Mr Henry Burton, Mr Snelling, and others, we shall instance in some fresh examples. . . . .' Mr Samuel Ward's case, and Mr Chauncy's case, are then narrated. 'To these we could add,' he proceeds, 'Mr Cotton, Mr Hooker, Mr Davenport, Mr Wells, Mr Peters, Mr Glover, and sundry other ministers, driven into New England and other plantations.' And then 'Dr Stoughton, *Dr Sibbes*, Dr Taylor, Dr Gouge, Mr White of Dorchester, Mr Rogers of Dedham, with sundry more of our most eminent preaching, orthodox divines, were brought into the High Commission, and troubled or silenced for a time by his procurement upon frivolous pretences, but in truth because they were principal props of our Protestant religion against his Popish and Arminian innovations.'*

Now, we have the actual books containing the actual preaching of these men, and the numerous others who shared their persecution. They are in our libraries; and he must be either a bold or a very foolish man, not only rash, but reckless, who gainsays that, *remove these books from the Christian literature of the period and you remove the very life-blood of that literature.*

The most recent, truthful, and catholic of 'the church' historians, Mr Perry,† admits that all the practical writers of the age were of the Puritans and sufferers for nonconformity; and he names a few, Willet and Dyke, Preston and Byfield, Bolton and Hildersam, and Sibbes. 'This fact,' he candidly observes, 'must needs have told with extreme force against the interests of the church. It was doubtless alleged that the church divines could only speak when their position or their order was menaced, but in the face of the great and crying sins and scandals of the age they were dumb and tongue-tied;' and he might have added, in view also of the gross ignorance and darkness in which whole districts of the country were shrouded.

I should make larger reservation or exceptions in favour of 'church' writers than Mr Perry does; for I find in Thomas Adams and Anthony Farindon, and others, whom I love equally with the foremost of the Puritans, the same preaching with theirs. Still it remains that the men whom Laud delighted to honour were the men who were vehement enough to bring men to 'the church,' but not at all concerned about bringing them to Christ; ready to dispense

* 'Canterburie's Doom,' pp. 362, *seq.* 1646, folio.

† The History of the Church of England from the death of Elizabeth to the present time. By the Rev. G. G. Perry, M.A., Rector of Waddington. Vol. I. 1861. (Saunders. Otley, & Co.) See C. ix. p. 326.

the sacraments, but oblivious of their antitype; swift to jangle in hot controversies on 'super-elementation,' but cold about the one transcendent change; reverers of the altar, but despisers of the cross. We have defences of the church, its tithes and dignities, its upholstery and repairs, *ad nauseam*. We have the primate himself fervid about his genu-flexions and reverence to the *name* of Christ, and the name only; and a Mountagu, ribald as Billingsgate against holy Samuel Ward. They were, as was jested of a modern Lord Chancellor, buttresses rather than pillars of 'the church.' We look in vain all through the extant writings of the bishops named, from Laud downward, for anything approaching one earnest, heartfelt utterance as from a servant of Jesus Christ to perishing sinners, one living word to men as 'under wrath,' nay, for one flash of genius, one gush of human feeling. They had no answer for the 'Anxious Inquirer' as he cried—

'I am a sinner, full of doubts and fears,
Make me a humble thing of love and tears.' *

There exists not a more meagre, inane, contemptible literature, taken as a whole, than that composed of the Laudian books *proper*; for it were a historic blunder, as well as a slander, to include Hall or Ussher or Bedell or Davenant among them, from the mere accident of their first appointment, more or less, coming from Laud. Yet we must believe that what they printed and gave to the world was their best, and at least was the preaching their auditories heard. On the other hand, it equally remains unchallengeable that the men whom Laud delighted to persecute were the only men then in England who were really discharging, in the fear of God, their office of preachers of the gospel, men, at the same time, of generous loyalty, and lovers, with the deepest affection, of that reformed church from which they were driven in 1662.

Such having been the state of things, it is only what we should expect, to find even the unpolemic and gentle Sibbes speaking out against the doings and tendencies of the men in authority. There is a time to be silent, *and* a time to speak. Fealty to truth demanded plain words, and translating of words into acts. Nor was either awanting. For words take these, over which we can conceive even the rheumy eyes of the primate flashing fire. They are taken from sermons preached during this period, and afterwards fearlessly published. I venture to italicise some few lines:—

'What spirit shall we think them to be of that take advantages of the bruised-ness and infirmities of men's spirits to relieve them with false peace for

* Hartley Coleridge, Poems, ii. p. 387 (edition 1851).

their own worldly ends? A wounded spirit will part with anything. Most of the gainful points of popery, as confession, satisfaction, merit, purgatory, &c., spring from hence, but they are physicians of no value, or rather tormentors than physicians at all. *It is a greater blessing to be delivered from "the sting of these scorpions" than we are thankful for.* Spiritual tyranny is the greatest tyranny, and then especially when it is where most mercy should be shewed; yet even there some, like cruel surgeons, delight in making long cures, to serve themselves upon the misery of others. It bringeth men under a terrible curse, "when they will not remember to shew mercy, but persecute the poor and needy man, that they might even slay the broken in heart," Ps. cix. 16.

'Likewise, to such as raise temporal advantage to themselves out of the spiritual misery of others, join such as raise estates by betraying the church, *and are unfaithful in the trust committed unto them*, when the CHILDREN SHALL CRY FOR THE BREAD OF LIFE, AND THERE IS NONE TO GIVE THEM, *bringing thus upon the people of God that heavy judgment* of a spiritual famine, starving Christ in his members. Shall we so requite so good a Saviour, who counteth the love and mercy shewed in "feeding his lambs," John xxi. 15, as shewed to himself?

'Last of all, they carry themselves very unkindly towards Christ, who stumble at this his low stooping unto us in his GOVERNMENT and ORDINANCES, that are *ashamed of the simplicity of the gospel*, that count preaching foolishness.

'They, out of the pride of their heart, think they may do well enough without the help of the WORD and SACRAMENTS, and think CHRIST TOOK NOT STATE ENOUGH UPON HIM, AND THEREFORE THEY WILL MEND THE MATTER WITH THEIR OWN DEVICES, whereby they may give the better content to flesh and blood, *as in popery.*'*

Elsewhere, in his most eloquent sermon entitled 'The Saint's Safety in Evil Times,' he thus fearlessly speaks:—

'I beseech you consider, what hurt have we ever had by the "Reformation" of religion? Hath it come naked unto us? Hath it not been attended with peace and prosperity? Hath God been "a barren wilderness to us?" Jer. ii. 31. Hath not God been a wall of fire about us? which if he had not been, it is not the water that compasseth our island could have kept us.†

Once more, in the 'Ungodly's Misery,' also 'preached' at this period, we have these plain-spoken words:—

'What is the gospel but salvation and redemption by Christ *alone?* Therefore, Rome's church is an apostate church, and may well be styled an adulteress and a whore, because she is fallen from her husband Christ Jesus. And what may we think of those that would bring light and darkness, Christ and Antichrist, the ark and Dagon, together, that would reconcile us, as if it were no great matter?'‡

Still again, in his exceeding precious sermons on Canticles, he strikes high, even right at the prelates, on their neglect of abounding error:—

'Thus,' says he, 'popery grew up *by degrees*, till it overspread the

* 'Bruised Reed,' page 77. ‡ 'Ungodly's Misery,' p. 388.
† 'Saint's Safety,' page 312.

church, *whilst the watchmen that should have kept others awake* FELL ASLEEP THEMSELVES. And thus we answer the papists when they quarrel with us about the beginning of their errors. They ask of us when such and such an heresy began; we answer, THAT THOSE THAT SHOULD HAVE OBSERVED THEM WERE ASLEEP. Popery is a " mystery," that *crept into the church by degrees* UNDER GLORIOUS PRETENCES. *Their errors had modest beginnings.*

These two words, 'glorious pretences,' must have been treasured up by Laud. They reappear in his 'Answers' to the 'Charges' against him, as I shall notice anon.

These were fiery words, and given to the world in print, the former in 'The Bruised Reed,' in 1629-30, the latter in 'The Saint's Safety,' in 1632-3, they could not fail to rouse the primate. Almost immediately upon his appointment to the preachership of Gray's Inn, Laud had sought to have him deprived and silenced; for tidings had reached him of the Trinity lectureship and the evangelical 'soul-fatting' (good old Bolton's word) preaching there. But Lord Keeper Finch had interfered to defeat his machinations, a right good service by not the best of men I fear, which he did not forget to plead when he stood at the bar of the House. Thus did he bring it up, the little quarto containing the full 'speech' being now before me :—' I hope for my affection in religion no man doubteth me. What my education was, and under whom I lived for many yeares, is well knowne. I lived neere thirty years in the society of Gray's Inne; and if one (that was a reverend preacher there in my time, Doctor Sibs) were now living, he were able to give testimony to this House that when a party ill-affected in religion sought to tyre and weary him out, he had his chiefest encouragement and help from me.' Let the erring Lord Keeper have the benefit of this redeeming trait.

Defeated in this earlier effort, Laud postponed, but did not abandon, his purpose. He soon found a pretext. As was observed before, Sibbes was a man of beneficent action as well as of beneficent words; and holding as he did that the church was for the nation, and not the nation for the church,—that the ministry was for the preaching of the gospel,—he joined hand and heart in counterworking those schemes, that, by quenching every 'golden candlestick' within which burned the oil of the sanctuary, sought to bring back the darkness and superstitions of the worst of popish times. Things had come to the crisis of endurance. If Laud and his myrmidons would 'deprive,' 'out,' 'silence,' 'persecute' the humble, faithful, godly preachers of salvation by grace, who were bearing the 'heat and burden' of work, and would intrude men, from the bishop to his humblest curate, who enforced a thinly-veiled popery in practice, and *un*scriptural, *anti*scriptural teaching in doctrine, something was demanded that should neutralise such doings. What was devised is matter of history. 'Feoffees' were appointed—the sacred 'twelve' in number—to raise funds, and buy in from time to time such 'impropriations' as were in the hands of laymen, when they could be purchased, and then to appoint therein as lecturers those who would really do the work of preaching. Superadded was the appointment of similar lecturers in the more neglected regions where lay-impropriations were not purchasable. Years before Sibbes had expressed his earnest wish that a 'lecturer' were in every dark corner of England.* It was a noble enterprise, and was nobly responded to. The best and wisest, the purest and holiest men of the age, took their part in the undertaking. I hesitate not to avouch, that there was scarcely a man whose name is now remembered for good, but was found subscribing amply and co-operating zealously for its accomplishment. The national heart was stirred, and it was found to beat in the right place. Sibbes, along with his old friends and coadjutors, Davenport and Gouge, was appointed one of the 'Feoffees.' It needs not to be told how this drew down the vengeance of Laud. The scheme had been more or less hindered from its inauguration in 1626, but not till 1632-3 (coincident with Sibbes's defences of 'The Reformation from Popery') was open action taken. The delay was caused by no relenting, much less forgetfulness. But events in the interval had transpired to 'give pause.' James had died, and his son reigned in his stead. The plague had passed over the metropolis in 1625, and there was 'lamentation and woe' in tens of thousands of households, again returning dolefully in 1630. There were political movements, also, that whitened to pallor the proudest cheek. One 'Mr Cromwell' had come up to Parliament in 1627-8. Besides 'the Petition of Right,' and the extorted and memorable *Soit fait comme il est desiré*, and the 'Declaration,' most uncourtly words fell from Masters Pym and Hampden and Eliot, and many others. But very especially was there plain-speaking, in his own stammering but forcible and resolute fashion, by 'Mr Cromwell' about increase of 'popery.' The House of Commons resolved itself into a Committee of Religion. Let Thomas Carlyle, tell the issue. 'It was,' says he, 'on the 11th day of February 1628-9, that Mr Cromwell, member for

* His words are memorable: 'If it were possible, it were to be wished that there were set up some lights in all the dark corners of this kingdom, that might shine to those people that sit in darkness and in the shadow of death.'—(Saint's Safety, p. 331 of the present volume.)

Huntingdon (then in his thirtieth year), stood up and made his first speech, a fragment of which has found its way into history, and is now known to all mankind. He said: "He had heard by relation from one Dr Beard (his old schoolmaster at Huntingdon) that Dr Alabaster (prebendary of St Paul's and rector of a parish in Herts) had preached flat popery at Paul's Cross; and that the Bishop of Winchester (Dr Neile) had commanded him, as his diocesan, he should preach nothing to the contrary. Mainwaring, so justly censured in this House for his sermons, was, by the same bishop's means, preferred to a rich living. If these are the steps to church-preferment, what are we to expect?"* We shall probably not greatly err if we conclude that even the 'red face' of Laud blanched under that question of 'Mr Cromwell,' knowing as he well did that the facts named were only two out of many, and knowing also the 'stuff' of which the men were made who were upon the inquisition. Then came 'remonstrances' and 'declarations' stronger still, and they who drew them up meant to have what they demanded. True, the chief speakers were 'indicted' in the Star-Chamber, and ultimately sent to the Tower, 'Mr Cromwell,' and 'Mr Pym,' and 'Mr Hampden' alone excepted (marvellous and suggestive exceptions). There lay Denzil Holles and Sir John Eliot, John Selden, Benjamin Valentine, and William Couton, Sir Miles Hobart and William Longe, William Strode and Sir Peter Hayman. For eleven years it was decreed to be penal so much as to speak of assembling another Parliament. There were 'wars and rumours of wars,' too. Every one who at all knows the time can see that a constraint which could not be disregarded was put upon Laud in the matter of his persecuting for religion. He durst not go in the teeth of the unmistakeable menaces of the last memorable Parliament. He noted down everything, and certainly would not fail to note down what Rous and Pym, Eliot and Selden, had said. Let us hear a little of what was said. Francis Rous, trembling like an old Hebrew prophet with his 'burden,' had denounced that 'error of Arminianism which makes the grace of God lackey it after the will of man,' and called on the House to postpone questions of goods and liberties to this question, which concerned 'eternal life, men's souls, yea, God himself.' Sir John Eliot repudiated the claim that 'the bishops and clergy alone should interpret church doctrine; and, professing his respect for some bishops, declared that there were others, *and two especially*, from whom nothing orthodox could come, and to empower whom to interpret *would be the ruin of national religion*.' John Selden, grave and calm, referred to individual cases in which

* Cromwell's Letters and Speeches, 3d edition, i. 29.

Popish and Arminian books were allowed, while Calvinistic books were restrained, notwithstanding that there was no law in England to prevent the printing of any books, but only a decree in Star-Chamber.' And then on one occasion the whole House stood up together, and vowed a vow against '*innovations in the faith.*' The issue of that, passed with closed doors, and with clenching of teeth and gripping of sword-hilts, none will soon forget. We have to do with only one of the three 'Resolutions :—' Whoever shall bring in innovation of religion, or by favour or countenance seem to extend Popery or Arminianism, or other opinion disagreeing from the true and orthodox church, shall be reputed a capital enemy to this kingdom and commonwealth.'*

After these things it is remarkable that the king, a man without mind, and Laud, a man without either mind or heart, should at all have adventured to go against the mind and heart of England. But so it was. There was of necessity greater secrecy, very much of covert plotting against the liberties, civil and religious, of England. The 'feoffees' at last, borne with involuntarily from 1626, were summoned before the Star Chamber and High Commission both. And that was but the execution of Laud's cherished purpose from the beginning. For in that strangest of strange 'Diaries,' the oddest combination, that ever has been written, of piety and grovelling superstition, of faith and the most babyish credulity, (for Pepys' is wisdom itself in comparison†), we light upon this entry:—

'Things which I have projected to do, if God bless me in them—
'III. To overthrow the feoffment, dangerous both to Church and State, going under the specious pretence of buying in impropriations.'

Opposite these words, a few out of many equally deplorable, that a little onward came to be to their writer terrible as the mystic 'handwriting' of Babylon's palace-wall, is inscribed 'DONE.' And it was *done*—for the moment; but it was a tremendous success to its doer. If only Nemesis had been touched with ruth to blot out the handwriting! But no! There the entry stood, when perhaps not altogether lawfully or honourably, at least not courteously, the diary was seized :—

* Consult for the facts introduced Masson's Life of Milton, i. 181, 329, *seq.*; Carlyle's 'Cromwell;' John Forster's 'Statesmen of the Commonwealth,' and others of his historical works about this period.

† Pepys. I do not know if his prescient entry in favour of the Puritans has been remarked. Having witnessed Ben Jonson's 'Bartholomew Fair,' he jots down, 'And is an excellent play; the more I see it the more I love the wit of it; *only the business of abusing the Puritans* begins to grow stale, and of no use, *they being the people that at last will be found the wisest.*' See Index of any edition of 'Diary' under 'Bartholomew Fair.'

'Feb. 13. 1632.

'*Wednesday.*—The feoffes that pretended to buy in impropriations were dissolved in the Chequer Chamber. *They were the main instruments for the Puritan faction to undo the Church.* THE CRIMINAL PART RESERVED.'*

Reserved! Ay, and transferred!

Those who had engaged in the impropriation scheme, including Sibbes, having been thus summoned before the Star-Chamber, were dealt with, not as honourable and good men, but as 'criminals and traitors.' The verdict was—CONFISCATION of the funds and BANISHMENT of the men!

Some fled to Holland, some to New England.† Had the nation's

---

* Laud's 'Works,' vol. iii. p. 216, 217.

† Of the 'fugitives' associated with Sibbes in the 'feoffees' scheme, the most eminent was John Davenport. In Anderson's Life of Lady Mary Vere, in 'Memorable Women of Puritan Times,' some very touching letters of his are given from the Brit. Museum MSS. (Birch 4275, No. 69). Two extracts will shew the anxiety in which these godly men were kept, and at the same time shew how far they were from wishing to be 'schismatics,' or in any way to injure the church. First of all, while he and Sibbes and others were under the ban of the 'High Commission' as mentioned above, he writes, ' I have had divers purposes of writing to your honour, only I delayed in hope to write somewhat concerning the event and success of our High Commission troubles; but I have hoped in vain, for to this day we are in the same condition as before, delayed till the finishing of the session in Paliament, which now is unhappily concluded without any satisfying contentment to the king or commonwealth. *Threatenings were speedily revived against us by the new Bishop of London, Dr Laud, even the next day after the conclusion of the session.* We now expect a fierce storm from the enraged spirits of the two bishops; ours, as I am informed, hath a particular aim at me upon a former quarrel, so that I expect ere long to be deprived of my pastoral charge in Coleman Street. But I am in God's hand, not in theirs, to whose good pleasure I do contentedly and cheerfully submit myself.'

A more beautiful charity, or more modest assertion of conscience, than in our next extract, can scarcely be imagined.

'Be not troubled, much less discouraged, good madam, at any rumours you meet with concerning my present way. The persecution of the tongue is more fierce and terrible than that of the hand. At this time I have sense of both...... The truth is, I have not forsaken my ministry, nor resigned up my place, *much less separated from the church*, but am only absent a while to wait upon God, upon the settling and quieting of things, for light to discover my way, being willing to lie and die in prison, if the cause may be advantaged by it, but choosing rather to preserve the liberty of my person and ministry for the service of the church elsewhere, *if all doors are shut against me here*....... The only cause of all my present sufferings is the alteration of my judgment in matters of conformity to the ceremonies established, whereby I cannot practise them as formerly I have done; *wherein I do not censure those that do conform* (nay, *I account many of them faithful and worthy instruments of God's glory*; and I know that I did conform with as much inward peace as now I do forbear; in both my uprightness was the same, but my light different). In this action I walk by that light which shineth into me....... With much advice of many ministers of eminent note and worth, I have done all that I have done hitherto, and with desire of pitching upon that way wherein God might be most glorified. In his due time he will manifest its truth.'

tongue not been cut out—no Parliament sat for years!—there had been stormy debates on that!

So far as Sibbes was concerned, it does not appear that any part of the sentence was ever put into execution. He continued preacher at Gray's Inn, and Master of Catharine Hall. This assures us that powerful friends, the Brooks and Veres, Manchesters and Warwicks, must have stood by him. But there was no compromise on his part. I find that almost like a menace, and most surely a defiance, Sibbes introduced into a sermon, preached immediately after the decision, an explicit eulogy of Sherland, the recorder of Northampton, for what he had done toward the impropriation scheme; and published the sermon.*

Still it was crushed, the 'monies' confiscated,* the 'purchases' reversed, the whole holy enterprise branded, and its agents disgraced. One thing is to be recalled. Among the 'things projected,' Laud enumerates, with imbecile forgetfulness, precisely such a scheme of purchase of 'impropriations'—by HIMSELF.† So that it stands confessed that not the thing itself was dangerous and illegal, but the doers of it. Let only him and his appoint to the places, and all was well and right. But let men such as Sibbes, Gouge, Taylor, Davenport in the Church, and the foremost men for worth in the State, their enemies themselves being witnesses, be the appointers, and instantly it smells of 'treason, stratagem, wiles.' These or those dangerous to Church and State? What is the award of posterity? And yet defenders have been found for the transparently mendacious and infamous act. Such jeer at the paltry minority of Puritanism, oblivious of what a living poet has finely expressed—

'. . . . . You trust in numbers, I
Trust in One only.' ‡

Let us see how Laud himself met it when it came in awful resurrection back upon him. Every one is aware that the suppression of the 'feoffment-impropriation' scheme formed one of the counts in the great roll of accusation, whose issue was the block on Tower Hill. A careful record was kept of charges and answers, and the whole have been republished in the Works of Laud. It is but fitting that what he had to say should appear. Here, then, are 'charge' and 'defence.' The whole case, so vital as between Laud and the Puritan worthies, among whom Richard Sibbes was prominent, can then be judged of :—

* See 'Christ is Best,' in the present volume, p. 349.
† See the whole list in his works, as after-referenced.
‡ Cecil and Mary, as *ante*, p. 10.

That whereas divers gifts and dispositions of divers sums of money were heretofore made by divers charitable and well-disposed persons, for the buying in of divers impropriations, for the maintenance of preaching the word of God in several churches; the said archbp., about eight years last past, wilfully and maliciously caused the said gifts, feoffments, and conveyances, made to the uses aforesaid, to be overthrown in his majesty's Court of Exchequer, contrary to law, as things dangerous to the Church and State, under the specious pretence of buying in appropriations; whereby that pious work was suppressed and trodden down, to the great dishonour of God and scandal of religion.

This article is only about the feoffments. That which I did was this: I was (as then advised upon such information as was given me) clearly of opinion, that this was a cunning way, under a glorious pretence, to overthrow the church government, by getting into their power more dependency of the clergy than the king, and all the peers, and all the bishops in all the kingdom had. And I did conceive the plot the more dangerous for the fairness of the pretence; and that to the State as well as the Church. Hereupon, not "maliciously" (as 'tis charged in the article), but conscientiously, I resolved to suppress it, if by law it might be done. Upon this, I acquainted his majesty with the thing, and the danger which I conceived would in few years spring out of it. The king referred me to his attorney, and the law. Mr Attorney Noye, after some pause upon it, proceeded in the exchequer, and there it was, by judicial proceeding and sentence, overthrown. If this sentence were according to law and justice, then there's no fault at all committed. If it were against law, the fault, whate'er it be, was the judges', not mine; for I solicited none of them. And here I humbly desired, that the Lords would at their leisure read over the sentence given in the exchequer,* which I then delivered in; but by reason of the length, it was not then read. Whether after it were, I cannot tell. I desired likewise that my counsel might be heard in this and all other points of law.

1. The first witness was Mr Kendall.† He says, that speaking with me about Presteen, 'I thanked God that I had overthrown this foeffment.'

2. The second witness, Mr Miller,‡ says he heard me say, 'They would have undone the church, but I have overthrown their feoffment.' These two witnesses prove no more than I confess. For in the manner aforesaid, I deny not but I did my best in a legal way to overthrow it. And if I did thank God for it, it was my duty to do so, the thing being in my judgment so pernicious as it was.

3. The third witness was Mr White, one of the feoffees.§ He says, 'that coming as counsel in a cause before me, when that business was done, I fell bitterly on him as an underminer of the church.' I remember well his coming to me as counsel about a benefice. And 'tis very likely I spake my conscience to him, as freely as he did his to me; but the particulars I remember not; nor do I remember his coming afterwards to me to

---

* Sir Leolin Jenkins hath a copy of it out of the records of the exchequer. W. S. A. C. (See Rushworth's Collections, vol. ii. pp. 151, 152.)

† 'William Kendall.'—Prynne's Cant. Doom, p. 388.

‡ 'Tempest Miller.'—Ibid.

§ John White. He was, in 1640, M.P. for Southwark, and chairman of the Committee for Religion. He was commonly called 'Century' White from the title of his celebrated tractate, 'The First Century of Malignant Priests,' (Wood. Ath. Ox. iii. 144, 145).

Fulham; nor his offer 'to change the men or the course, so the thing might stand.' For to this I should have been as willing as he was; and if I remember right, there was order taken for this in the decree of the Exchequer. And his majesty's pleasure declared, that no penny so given should be turned to other use. And I have been, and shall ever be, as ready to get in impropriations, by any good and legal way, as any man (as may appear by my labours about the impropriations in Ireland). But this way did not stand either with my judgment or conscience.

1. First, because little or nothing was given by them to the present incumbent, to whom the tithes were due, if to any; that the parishioners which payed them, might have the more cheerful instruction, the better hospitality, and more full relief for their poor.

'2. Secondly, because most of the men they put in, were persons disaffected to the discipline, if not the doctrine, too, of the Church of England.

'3. Thirdly, because no small part was given to schoolmasters, to season youth *above*, for their party; and to young students in the universities, to purchase them and their judgments to their side, against their coming abroad into the church.

'4. Fourthly, because all this power to breed and maintain a faction, was in the hands of twelve men, who were they never so honest, and free from thoughts of abusing this power, to fill the church with schism, yet who should be successors, and what use should be made of the power, was out of human reach to know.'

5. Because this power was assumed by, and not to themselves, without any legal authority, as Mr Attorney assured me.

He further said, 'that the impropriations of Presteen, in Radnorshire, was specially given to St Antolin's, in London.* I say the more the pity, considering the poorness of that country, and the little preaching that was among that poor people, and the plenty which is in London. Yet because it was so given, there was care taken after the decree, that they of St Antolin's had consideration, and I think to the full. He says, 'that indeed they did not give anything to the present incumbents, till good men came to be in their places.' Scarce one incumbent was bettered by them. And what then? In so many places not one 'good man' found? 'Not one factious enough against the church, for Mr White to account him good?' Yet he thinks 'I disposed these things afterwards to unworthy men.' 'Truly, had they been at my disposal, I should not wittingly have given them to Mr White's worthies.' But his majesty laid his command upon his attorney, and nothing was done or to be done in these things, but by his direction. For Dr Heylin, if he spake anything amiss concerning this feoffment, in any sermon of his† he is living to answer it; me it concerns not. 'Mr Brown in the sum of the charge omitted not this. And I answered as before. And in his reply he

---

* This impropriation was, after the forfeiture, granted by King Charles I. to the rector of Presteign for ever. This grant was revoked during the Rebellion, but confirmed by King Charles II. at the beginning of his reign.

† The Sermon to which reference is here made, was preached by Heylin, at St Mary's, Oxford, July 11. 1630, at the Act. The passage relating to the feoffees will be found in Prynne (Cant. Doom, p. 386), who transcribed it from a MS. copy of the Sermon in Abp. Laud's study; and in Heylin (Cypr. Ang. p. 199, Lond. 1671). who appears in his turn to have transcribed it from Prynne.

turned again upon it, that it must be a crime in me, because I projected to overthrow it. But, under favour, this follows not. For to project (though the word 'projector' sounds ill in England), is no more than to forecast and forelay any business. Now as 'tis lawful for me, by all good and fit means, to project the settlement of anything that is good; so is it as lawful, by good and legal means, to project the overthrow of anything that is cunningly or apparently evil. And such did this feoffment appear to my understanding, and doth still.' As for reducing of impropriations to their proper use, they may see (if they please) in my Diary (whence they had this) another project to buy them into the church's use. For given they will not be. But Mr Pryn would shew nothing, nor Mr Nicolas see anything, but what they thought would make against me.

Of this Defence, it must be said in the apophthegm of Helps, 'It would often be as well to condemn a man unheard, as to condemn him upon the reasons which he openly avows for any course of action.'* Still, in common with the whole of the 'Answers,' as tragically told in the 'History of the Troubles,'† it exhibits no little astuteness and dexterity, and more than all his resoluteness in assertion of conscience. There is also characteristic strategy shewn in his retreats behind others who acted with him, now Attorney-General Noye, and now the king himself, with an almost humorous contrast in the surrender of Heylin to his fate. While then we cannot altogether deny that an answer (not reply merely, but answer) is returned, nor that his infamy was shared; yet there lies behind all the indisputable fact, that here was an association of the very salt of Church and State, seeking from their own resources to purchase in a legal way,—in the very way their accuser himself had done, and still proposed to do,—'impropriations' in the hands of laymen who were not only willing, but wishful, to part with them, and to place therein, through the recognised authorities, men of kindred character with themselves, in order that the gospel might be fully preached, and the people cared for—and Laud prevents. It is not more strange than sad, that in this nineteenth century, men should be found maintaining that Laud did right —that in entering among ' the things to be done,' the overthrow of the 'Feoffees,' or the frustration of an earnest effort whereby men of God, in the truest sense, would have '*fed* the flock of God, which he hath redeemed with his own blood,' he came to a resolution, and in the execution of it performed a service, to be remembered and praised, not deplored. But, indeed, such defences only mask a deeper hatred. For often, as Lovell Beddoes puts it—

* Thoughts in the Cloister and the Crowd. 1835, 12mo, page 9.
† The History of the Troubles and Trial of Archbishop Laud. Works (edited by Scott and Bliss in 'Anglo-Catholic Library'), vol. iv. pp. 302–306.

'These are the words that grow, like grass and nettles
Out of dead men; and speckled hatreds hide,
Like toads, among them.'*

There is always a certain nimbus of glory around a decollated head, and I am disposed to concede that a truer man, great among the small, fell on Tower Hill than he whose face paled on the awful block of Whitehall window, though it was a king's and has been canonized as a martyr's. There was a stout-heartedness in the face of fearful odds in the stricken and forsaken primate throughout his trial that commands a measure of respect; and, perhaps, such is the inscrutable mystery of poor human nature, he deceived himself into a conscientious suppression of all consciences that differed from his own. Neither would I forget that one or two, or even three or four—Hall and Prideaux, Ussher, Davenant, and William Chillingworth—may be named, who, self-contradictorily, were advanced in the church more or less by him.† I will not conceal this, though historic candour compels me to affirm that, in so far as they fell in with his wishes (taking Bishop Hall as an example), they stained the white of their souls, and that Ussher and the apostolic Bedell and Chillingworth protested against the ultimate development of his views and actings.

I gladly give him all praise for his honest and courageous word to the king, when his irreverent Majesty came in too late and interrupted 'prayers.' It was a brave and worthy request that he made that the king should be present 'at prayers as well as sermon every Sunday.' ‡

I found no common joy also in coming, in the arid pages of the 'Diary,' upon these pitying words about a very venerable Puritan, gleaming like a drop of dew, or even a human tear :—'In Leicester the dean of the Arches suspended one Mr Angell, who had continued a lecturer in that great town for these divers years, without any license at all to preach, yet took liberty enough. I doubt his violence hath cracked his brain, and do therefore use him more tenderly, *because I see the hand of God hath overtaken him.*' §

Brook ('Lives of the Puritans'‖) testily criticises the entry. The conclusion was false, for the 'violence' of the good Angell was the 'fine frenzy' of a man in awful earnest, in a fashion which Laud could not so much as apprehend. Still he is entitled to the full advantage of it, and to have it placed beside the kindred touch-

---

* Poems: Posthumous and Collected, vol. i. p. 109.

† 'Advanced.' The most has been made of this in the following acute and, in certain respects, valuable pamphlet :—' A Letter to the Rev. J. C. Ryle, A.B., in Reply to his Lecture on "Baxter and his Times." By a Clergyman of the Diocese of Exeter. Exeter, 1853. 8vo.'

‡ Diary, Nov. 14. 1626.   § Ap. for 1634, pp. 325–6.   ‖ Brook, iii. 236.

ing notices of his dying servants, his love for whom is remarkable.*
But with every abatement, unless we are to blur the noblest names of
the Christianity of England; to write 'false' against its truest, and
refuse honour to men who, rather than fail in fealty to what they
believed was written in the word of God, hazarded all that was
dear to them; unless we are to overtop the loftiest intellects by one
of the lowest, and sanctified genius and learning by one who was
no scholar, and even could not write tolerable English, we must
denounce every attempt to exalt and extol the morbid craving for
an impossible 'uniformity' of this hard, cruel, unlovingly zealous,
and unlovable man, around whom there hangs but a single gentle
memory of tenderness to frailty or mercy to penitence; from whose
pen there never once flowed one true word for Christ or the salvation of souls; from whom, in his darkened end, there came not so
much as that remorseful touch that wins our sympathy for a Stephen
Gardiner, '*Erravi cum Petro at non flevi cum Petro.*'† Claver-
house, the 'bloody,' and the first Charles, the 'false,' have been
idealised. We look upon their pensive faces, and feel how traitorous
they must have been to their better nature. But Laud it is not possible to idealise. The more, successive biographers have elucidated
his history; they have only the more made him a definite object of
contempt. He was elevated above men who, by head and shoulders
(and we know what the head includes), were taller than himself.‡
The stilts fell from beneath him, and he found his level, as 'imbecile' (it is Lord Macaulay's word), as contemptible, as worthless
a man as ever rose to power—a mitred Robespierre. A certain
party are voluble in pronouncing their judgments upon the victims
of Laud. It were to play false to truth to let them go unanswered;
and the present is undoubtedly an occasion demanding such answer
and out-speaking. But—

> 'I say not that the man I praise
> By that poor tribute stands more high,
> I say not that the man I blame
> Be not of purer worth than I;

* Laud's servants. I give one entry in Diary:—'Sept. 23. 1621.—Thy. Mr
Adam Torless, my ancient, loving, and faithful servant, then my steward, after he
had served me full forty-two years, died, to my great loss and grief.'

† Gardiner. Foss's Judges of England, v. 370.

‡ A few wise words from 'Thoughts in the Cloister and the Crowd' may enforce
our remarks—'Perhaps it is the secret thought of many that an ardent love of power
and wealth, however culpable in itself, is nevertheless a proof of superior sagacity.
But in answer to this it has been well remarked, that even a child can clench its
little hand the moment it is born; and if they imagine that the successful, at any
rate, must be sagacious, let them remember the saying of a philosopher, that the
meanest reptiles are found at the summit of the loftiest pillars.' (Pp. 20–1.)

> But when I move reluctant lips
> For holy justice, human right,
> The sacred cause I strive to plead
> Lends me its favour and its might.'*

CHAPTER IX.

SIBBES'S 'INTRODUCTIONS' TO WORKS OF CONTEMPORARIES.

Whitaker—Duke of York—Paul Bayne—Henry Scudder—Ezekiel Culverwell—Dr John Preston—John Smith—John Ball—Richard Capel.

But I turn the leaf, and pass on in our 'Memoir.' And it is a pleasant change to turn from a Laud, chaffering over the breadth of a phylactery; from a Mountagu, overwhelming holy men, such as Samuel Ward, with the ribaldry of a 'Gagg for the new gospel!—no, a new gagg for an old goose!' from a Wren, tracking every 'two or three' who sought to meet together in the name of the Lord, to Richard Sibbes at his post, discharging his duties as a minister of Christ through 'good and evil report,' and sustaining the kindliest relationship with all the 'good men and true' of his contemporaries. There are pleasant memorials of the latter in various occasional productions, such as 'prefaces' and 'epistles dedicatory,' which Sibbes from time to time prefixed to good books of good men. These I would now bring together. They give us some very precious glimpses of his society, from a pretty early date to near the close. They are, indeed, so many little 'essays' on religious subjects, written in his very best style, and breathing all the sweetness, and informed with all the spirituality, of his larger writings. Where can we turn to more felicitous words about 'faith,' and 'prayer,' and 'holiness,' and the 'Christian life'? while there is a modesty of praise of the author introduced, whether living or dead, in striking contrast with the adulation then prevalent. First of all, I find among the 'Epicedia in Obitum Gul: Whitakeri,'† a copy of Greek verses to the memory of that truly great man, whose mother was Elizabeth Nowell, sister of Dr Alexander Nowell, and who, if he had found such a biographer as Nowell has in Archdeacon Churton, would be better known to the present generation. As a Master of Sibbes's own College of St John's, and as having married a sister first of Samuel and Ezekiel Culverwell, and next the widow of Dudley Fenner, and in every-day association with the Culverwells

---

* 'Passion-Flowers,' by Mrs Howe. Boston, 1854, p. 113.
† Works, Geneva, fol. 1610, vol. i. p. 706; previously published in 1596. 4to.

and Fenners, Cartwright, Fuller, Chadderton, and Dod, Whitaker could not but be known and esteemed by him. He was venerated by all parties. He was, says even the atrabilious Anthony Wood, 'one of the greatest men his college ever produced, the desire and love of the present times and the envy of posterity, that cannot bring forth a parallel.'* 'The learned Whitaker,' observes Leigh, 'the honour of our schools and the angel of our church, than whom our age saw nothing more memorable.'† 'Who,' exclaims Bishop Hall, 'ever saw him without reverence, or heard him without wonder?'‡ Whitaker died in 1596, the second year of Sibbes's studentship. It is significant that the verses of such a mere youth received a place beside the tributes of the greatest men of the age:—

> Τὴν ὀρθὴν πάροδον πολλοῖς, 'ραιστῆρα Παπιστῶν
> Σαυτὸν γνωρίζεις, Οὐϊτάχηρε, σοφοῖς
> Ἔξοχος ἁπάντων, ὁ δ' ἀνεδραμεν ἐρνεῖ ἴσος,
> Καὶ Μουσῶν ὀρθῶς τὰς ἀνέωγε θύρας.
> Εὔθετα τ' ἐκδίδου, 'ρ' ἔμφρων καὶ πλοῖα κυβερνῶν
> Τὴν λύμην κακὴν ζῶν τε θανών τ' ἔφυγε.
> Νῦν γε ἀείμνηστον φήμην, κῦδος τε μέγιστον,
> Λιπών, πηγάζει δόγματα θεσπέσια.
>
> R[ICHARD] S[IBBES].§

It is hardly worth while turning these verses into English, but one remark is suggested by them. Spite of the ''ραιστῆρα Παπιστῶν' (= hammer of the papists), won by his controversies with Campian and Bellarmine and others, Bellarmine thought so highly of Whitaker that he sent for his portrait, and gave it a prominent place in his study; and when his friends were introduced to him he used to point to it and say, 'he was the most learned heretic he ever read.'‖

Though it anticipates the order in date, it may be as well to introduce here the only other verses of Sibbes that are known (this time Latin)—on the birth of the Duke of York:—¶

---

* Fasti Oxon. (ed. by Bliss, vol. i. p. 210, &c.)

† Edward Leigh's Treatise of Religion and Learning, folio, 1656, p. 363.

‡ Quoted in Leigh, *supra*, p. 364. Hall wrote an English 'Elegy' and Latin verses on Whitaker. The former will be found in Caroli Horni Carmen Funebre in Obitum Ornatissimi viri Gul., Whitakeri, &c. Lond. 4to, 1596. The latter prefixed to Whitaker's Prælectiones, 1599, 4to. Both, in Hall's Works by Peter Hall, xii. 323–25 and 330. § Given *verbatim et literatim* from the volume of Whitaker.

‖ Wood's Athenæ, *ante*. For full notice of Whitaker, with, as usual, ample authorities, consult Cooper's Athenæ Cantab., vol. ii., p. 196, *seq*.

¶ From 'Ducis Eboracensis Fasciæ a Musis Cantabrigiensibus,' 1633, p. 6. For pointing out both the Greek and Latin verses I am indebted to Charles H. Cooper, Esq., Cambridge, not more erudite than willing to place his multitudinous collections at the disposal of a fellow-labourer.

IN NATALEM DUCIS EBORACENSIS AUSPICATISSIMUM.

Anglia ter felix, ternâ jam prole beata :
  Pax regno namque est pignore firma novo.
Major si ex populi numero sit gloria regis ;
  Natorum ex numero an non magè surgit honos ?
Candidiora nitent tria Lilia, tresque Leones
  Exultant, sceptra ut nobilitata vident,
Fratribus et binis stipatur utrinque Maria :
  Delicias junctas cum Patre Mater habet.
Regia stirps crescit ; crescunt hinc gaudia regni :
  Crescat et hinc summo gloria summa Deo !

At Tu, Magne puer, Regum de stemmate germen,
  Cura Dei, Patriæ spes nova, vive, vige.
Gloria Te niveis semper circumvolet alis,
  Teque ipso major crescito, parve puer !
Gratia te et virtus semper comitentur euntem !
  In vultu et labris sessitet ipsa *Charis* !
Angelicusque chorus tua stet cunabula circum,
  Sitque *Duci* semper *Dux* DEUS atque *Comes!*
Et nati natorum, et qui nascentur ab illis
  Perpetuent seriem, *Carole* magne, tuam !
Germinet usquè, ferax jam faustè, regia vitis
  Germinet, O fructus edat et usquè novos !

R[ICHARD] S[IBBES], *Aulæ Sanctæ Catharinæ Præfectus.**

It were a waste of pains to translate these lines. Neither their subject nor their merit claims this.†

It is clear that Sibbes wanted the *afflatus* of the poet, of whom the old axiom, one of the world's *memorabilia*, must ever hold, *nascitur non fit.* And alas! for the '*gratia*,' and other prayers! for this Duke of York became the Second Charles of England.

Returning upon our chronology, Paul Bayne, whose 'ministry' along with Sibbes has been described in an earlier part of this Memoir,‡ having died in 1617, there was issued immediately a quarto volume containing an Exposition of the 1st chapter of the Epistle to the Ephesians.§ Its main theme is 'Predestination,' one of the '*doctrinal*' points forbidden by royal proclamation to be discussed. Soberly, wisely, suggestively, and with much beauty of wording does Sibbes introduce his 'father in the gospel.'

'Notwithstanding the world's complaint of the surfeit of books (hasty wits being over forward to vent their unripe and misshapen conceits), yet

---

* This also is given *verbatim* from the volume.

† Perhaps the classical scholar will agree with me, that in the couplet,
  Gratia te et virtus semper comitentur euntem,
  In vultu et labris sessitet ipsa Charis !
= 'May grace itself sit on thy countenance and lips,' we have a reminiscence of a fragment from Diodorus πειθώ τις ἐπικάθισεν ἐπι τοις χείλεσιν = 'Persuasion sat upon his lips.' Quoted in Keightley's History of Greece, p. 160.

‡ See pages xxxvi, xxxviii.

§ Commentary on 1st Chapter of Ephesians, handling the controversy of Predestination, 4to, 1618.

in all ages there hath been, and will be necessary uses of holy treatises, appliable to the variety of occasions of the time; because men of weaker conceits cannot so easily of themselves discern how one truth is inferred from another, and proved by another, especially when truth is controverted by men of more subtile and stronger wits. Whereupon, as God's truth hath in all ages been opposed in some branches of it; so the divine providence that watcheth over the church, raised up some to fence the truth, and make up the breach. Men gifted proportionably to the time, and as well furnished to fight God's battles, as Satan's champions have been to stand for him: neither have any points of Scripture been more exactly discussed, than those that have been most sharply oppugned, opposition whetting both men's wits and industry, and in several ages men have been severally exercised. The ancientest of the fathers had to deal with them without (the Pagans), and especially with proud heretics, that made their own conceits the measure of holy truth, believing no more than they could comprehend in the articles of the Trinity, and natures of Christ, whence they bent their forces that way, and for their matter wrote more securely. Not long after, the enemies of grace, and flatterers of nature, stirred up St Augustine to challenge the doctrine of God's predestination and grace out of their hands, which he did with great success, as fitted with grace, learning, and wit for such a conflict, and no Scriptures are more faithfully handled by him, than those that were wrested by his opposites, and such as made for the strengthening of of his own cause. In other writings he took more liberty, his schdlars Prosper, Fulgentius and others interest themselves in the quarrel.

In process of time, men desirous of quiet, and tired with controversies, began to lay aside the study of Scriptures, and hearken after an easier way of ending strife, by the determination of one man (the Bishop of Rome), whom virtually they made the whole church; so the people were shut up under ignorance and implicit faith, which pleased them well, as easing them of labour of search, as upon the same irksomeness of trouble in the eastern parts, they yielded to the confusion and abomination of Mahometism.

And lest scholars should have nothing to do, they were set to tie and untie school knots, and spin questions out of their own brain, in which brabbles they were so taken up, that they slightly looked to other matters; as for questions of weight they were schooled to resolve all into the decisive sentence of the see apostolic, the authority of which they bent their wits to advance; yet then wisdom found children to justify her: for Scriptures that made for authority of princes and against usurpation of popes, were well cleared by Occam, Marsilius, Patavinus, and others, as those of predestination and grace by Ariminensis, Bradwardine, and their followers, against Pelagianism, then much prevailing. At length the apostasy of popery spread so far, that God in pity to his poor church, raised up men of invincible courage, unwearied pains, and great skill in tongues and arts to free religion, so deeply enthralled; from whence it is that we have so many judicious tractates and commentaries in this latter age. And yet will there be necessary use of farther search into the Scriptures as new heresies arise, or old are revived, and further strengthened. The conviction of which, is then best when their crookedness is brought to the straight rule of Scriptures to be discovered. Besides, new expositions of Scriptures will be useful, in respect of new temptations, corruptions in life and cases of conscience, in which the mind will not receive any satisfying resolution, but from explication and application of Scriptures. Moreover, it is not unprofitable that there should be divers treatises of the same portion of Scriptures, because the same truth may be better conveyed to the conceits of some men, by some men's handling than others', one man relishing one man's gifts more than another. And it is not meet that the glory of God's goodness and wisdom should be obscured, which shineth in the variety of men's gifts, especially seeing the depth of Scripture is such, that though men had large hearts, as the sand of the sea shore, yet could they not empty out all things contained; for though the main principles be not many, yet deductions and conclusions are infinite, and until Christ's second coming to judgment, there will never want new occasion of further search and wading into these deeps.

In all which respects this exposition of this holy man, deserves acceptance of the church, as fitted to the times (as the wise reader will well discern). Some few places are not so full as could be wished, for clearing some few obscurities; yet those that took the care of setting them out, thought it better to let them pass as they are, than be over-bold with another man's work, in making him speak what he did not, and take them as they be. The greatest shall find matter to exercise themselves in; the meaner, matter of sweet comfort and holy instruction, and all confess, that he hath brought some light to this excellent portion of Scripture.

He was a man fit for this task, a man of much communion with God, and acquaintance with his own heart, observing the daily passages of his life, and exercised much with spiritual conflicts. As St Paul in this epistle never seemeth to satisfy himself in advancing the glory of grace, and the vileness of man in himself, so this our Paul had large conceits of these things, a deep insight into the mystery of God's grace, and man's corruption: he could therefore enter further into Paul's meaning, having received a large measure of Paul's spirit. He was one that sought no great matters in the world, being taken up with comforts and griefs, unto which the world is a stranger; one that had not all his learning out of books; of a sharp wit, and clear judgment: though his meditations were of a higher strain than ordinary, yet he had a good dexterity, furthered by his love to do good, in explaining dark points with lightsome similitudes. His manner of handling questions in this epistle is press, and school-like, by arguments on both sides, conclusions, and answers, a course more suitable to this purpose than loose discourses.

In setting down the object of God's predestination, he succeeds him in opinion, whom he succeeded in place;* in which point divines accord not who in all other points do jointly agree against the troubles of the church's peace, in our neighbour countries; for some would have man lie before God in predestinating him, as in lapsed and miserable estate; others would have God in that first decree to consider man abstracted from such respects, and to be considered of, as a creature alterable, and capable either of happiness or misery, and fit to be disposed of by God, who is Lord of his own to any supernatural end; yet both agree in this: First, that there was an eternal separation of men in God's purpose. Secondly, that this first decree of severing man to his ends, is an act of sovereignty over his creature, and altogether independent of anything in the creature, as a cause of it, especially in comparative reprobation, as why he rejected Judas, and not Peter; sin foreseen cannot be the cause, because that was common to both, and therefore could be no cause of severing. Thirdly, all agree in this, that damnation is an act of divine justice, which supposeth demerit; and therefore the execution of God's decree is founded on sin, either of nature, or life, or both. My meaning is not to make the cause

* Perkins.

mine, by unnecessary intermeddling. The worthiness of the men on both side is such, that it should move men to moderation in their censures either way. Neither is this question of like consequence with others in this business, but there is a wide difference between this difference and other differences. And one cause of it, is the difficulty of understanding, how God conceives things, which differs in the whole kind from ours, he conceiving of things altogether and at once without discourse, we one thing after another, and by another. Our comfort is, that what we cannot see in the light of nature and grace, we shall see in the light of glory, in the university of heaven ; before which time, that men should in all matters have the same conceit of things of this nature, is rather to be wished for, than to be hoped. That learned bishop (now with God) that undertook the defence of Mr Perkins, hath left to the church, together with the benefit of his labours, the sorrow for his death, the fame of his worth, an example likewise of moderation, who, though he differed from Mr Perkins in this point, yet shewed that he could both assent in lesser things, and with due respect maintain in greater matters.* If we should discern of differences, the church would be troubled with fewer distempers ; I speak not as if way were to be given to Vorstian, lawless, licentious liberty of prophecy ; that every one, so soon as he is big of some new conceit, should bring forth his abortive monster : for thus the pillars of Christian faith would soon be shaken, and the church of God, which is a house of order, would become a Babel, a house of confusion. The doleful issues of which pretended liberty, we see in Polonia, Transylvania, and in countries nearer hand. We are much to bless God for the king's majesty's firmness this way, unto whose open appearing in these matters, and to the vigilancy of some in place, we owe our freedom from that schism, that troubleth our neighbours.

But for diversity of apprehensions of matters far remote from the foundation ; these may stand with public and personal peace. I will keep the reader no longer from the treatise ; the blessing of heaven go with it, that through the good done by it, much thanksgiving may be to God in the Church ! Amen. R. SIBBS.
Gray's Inn.

Our next name is Henry Scudder, whom Richard Baxter and John Owen united to praise while he was alive. In 1620, he published his inestimable little treatise, worthy companion to his 'Christian's Daily Walk in Holy Security and Peace,' entitled 'Key of Heaven, the Lord's Prayer Opened.'† To it Sibbes prefixed a 'Recom-

---

* The 'learned bishop' is Robert Abbot, Bishop of Salisbury, and the reference is to his 'Defence of the Reformed Catholick of W. Perkins against Dr W. Bishop.' 4to, 1611.

† A Key of Heaven : the Lord's Prayer opened, and so applied, that a Christian may learn how to pray, and to procure all things which may make for the glory of God, and the good of himself, and of his neighbour. Containing likewise such doctrines of faith and goodness, as may be very useful to all that desire to live godly in Christ Jesus. The second edition, enlarged by the author. Mat. vii. 7, Ask, and it shall be given you ; seek, and ye shall find ; knock, and it shall be opened unto you. *Oratio justi clavis cœli.* London : Printed by Thomas Harper, for Benjamin Fisher, and are to be sold at the sign of the Talbot in Aldersgate Street. 1633. This 'Key' has been erroneously included among Sibbes's own writings, *e. g.*, Brook (' Lives of Puritans, ii. 420), and even in Dr Bliss's Sale-Catalogue.

mendation,' which is in itself an Essay on Prayer, of rare value. Scudder was a contemporary of Sibbes in Cambridge, of Christ's Church. Afterwards he became successively minister at Drayton, in Oxfordshire, and at Collingborn-Dukes, in Wiltshire. In the year 1643, he was chosen one of the 'Assembly of Divines,' and was exemplary in his attendance. His books are pre-eminently scriptural and practical, and there are occasional similes and scraps of out-of-the-way incidents of a quaint beauty and appositeness. It is easy to understand that such a man would be dear to Richard Sibbes.* Thus he writes :—

To be much in persuading those that be favourites of some great person, to use that interest for their best advantage, were an endeavour somewhat needless, considering natural self-love inclineth men in such cases to be sensible enough of their own good. Yet so dull is our apprehension of matters that are of an higher nature, that though we have the ear of God always open unto us, and free access to the throne of grace through Christ who appeareth in heaven for us, carrying our names in his breast, yet we need stirring up to improve this blessed liberty, though the whole world be not worth this one prerogative, that we can boldly call God Father. This disproportion of our carriage ariseth in part from Satan's malice, who laboureth to keep us in darkness, that we believe not, or mind not our best privileges, which if we did, how glorious would our lives appear! how comfortably and fruitfully should we walk! what honour should God have by us! what sweet sacrifice from us! how should we overlook all opposite power! But now by reason we are prone to believe Satan, and the lies of our own heart; and ready to call truth itself into question, as if these things were too good to be true, no marvel if we pass our days so deadly. For what use of an hidden and locked up treasure, if we use not this key of prayer to fetch from thence for all our need? What benefit of all the precious promises made in Christ unto us, unless we allege them unto God, and with a reverend boldness bind him with his own word, which he can no more deny, than cease to be God? If we took these things to heart, God should hear oftener from us, we would be more in heaven than we are, seeing we should bring as much grace and comfort from God as we could bring faith to grasp and carry away.

Besides this fore-mentioned mindlessness of our privileges, since the fall the soul naturally loveth to spend and scatter itself about these present sensible things, and cannot without some strife gather itself together, and fix upon heavenly things. Now this talking with God requireth an actual bent of the mind, and carrieth up the whole soul into heaven, and exerciseth, as all the parts, so all the graces of the soul, faith especially, prayer being nothing else but the flame of faith. And Satan knowing that when we send up our desires to God, it is to fetch supply against him, troubleth the soul, weak of itself, with a world of distractions. Where he cannot corrupt the doctrine of prayer (as in popery) with heresies and superstitious follies, there he laboureth to hinder the exercise of it. Wherein we should be so far from being discouraged, that we should reason rather that must needs be an excellent duty which is so irksome to the flesh, and which the devil so eagerly sets against. This should encourage us to this exercise, wherein

* Scudder. Consult Brook's 'Lives of the Puritans,' ii. 504, *seq.*

lieth all our strength, that if in spite of Satan's annoyance and our own indisposition, we will set upon this duty, we shall find ourselves by little and little more raised up to heaven, and our hearts more and more enlarged, God rewarding the use of that little grace we find at the first, with increase of strength and comfort. To him that hath (in the exercise of that he hath) shall be given more. We should labour not to be ignorant of Satan's enterprises, who besides his diverting our minds from prayer, and disturbing us in it, laboureth by all means to draw us to some sin, the conscience whereof will stop our mouths, and stifle our prayers, and shake our confidence, and eclipse our comfort; which he oft aimeth more at than the sin itself unto which he tempteth us. We should labour therefore to preserve ourselves in such a state of soul, wherein we might have boldness with God, and wherein this gainful trading with him might not be hindered.

To pass over many other causes of the neglect of this intercourse, and dealing with God by prayer, we may well judge, as one of the chief, a self-sufficiency whereby men dwell too much in themselves. He that hath nothing at home will seek abroad. The poor man (saith Solomon) speaketh supplications. If we were poor in spirit, and saw our own emptiness, it would force us out of ourselves. Alas! what temptation can we resist, much less overcome, without fresh succour? What cross can we endure without impatience, if we have not new support? What success can we look for, yea, in common affairs, without his blessing? What good can we do, nay, think of, without new strength? When we do any good by his power, do we not need pardon for the blemishes of our best performances? What good blessing can we enjoy, so as we defile not ourselves in it, without a further blessing, giving us with the thing the holy use of it? Yet we see most men content to receive blessings as they come from God's general providence, without regarding any sanctified use by prayer, whereas holy men, knowing that God will be sought unto even for those things of which he hath given a promise, Ezek. xxxvi. 37, in obedience to this his divine order, desire to receive all from him as a fruit of their prayers. And God's manner is to keep many blessings from his children until they have begged them, as delighting to hear his children speak. The consideration whereof moveth those that have nearest communion with God to acknowledge him in all their ways, depending on him for direction, strength, success, whereupon he delighteth in shewing himself more familiarly unto them in the sweetest experiences of his love, guiding them by his counsel whilst they abide here, and after, bringing them to glory, Ps. xxxvii. 24. As other graces grow in those that are in the state of grace, so this spirit of prayer receiveth continual increase upon more inward acquaintance with God, and their own estates. Whence they can never be miserable, having God to pour forth their spirits and ease their hearts unto, who cannot but regard the voice of his own Spirit in them. But of ourselves, such is our case, that God who knoweth us better than we know ourselves, saith, we know not what or how to pray, Rom. viii. 26. This language of Canaan is strange unto us. Which our blessed Saviour in mercy considering, stirred up a desire in his disciples to be taught of him the Son, how to speak to the Father. Where thereupon he teacheth them a form, which for heavenly fulness of matter, and exactness of order, sheweth that it could come from no other Author.

This holy pattern comprising so much in so little, all things to be desired in six short petitions, it is needful for the guides of God's people to lay open the riches of it to the view of those that are less exercised. An endeavour which his excellent majesty thought not unbeseeming the greatness of a king. For the use of a set form of prayer, and this in special, I will make no question; yet in the use of this prayer, we may dwell more in the meditation and enforcing such petitions as shall concern our present occasions. For instance, if ever there were time of praying, 'Let thy kingdom come,' let Christ arise and his enemies be scattered, then certainly now is the time for us to ascend up into heaven by our prayers, and awake Christ, that he would rebuke the winds and waves, and cause a calm; that he would be strong for his church, in maintaining his own cause. It is God's manner, before any great work for his church, to stir up the spirits of his beloved ones to give him no rest. How earnest was Daniel with the Lord immediately before the delivery out of Babylon, Dan. xi. And undoubtedly, if we join the forces of our prayers together, and set upon God with an holy violence, he would set his power, his wisdom, his goodness on work for the exalting of his church, and ruin of the enemies of it. Now is the time for Moses his hands to be upheld, whilst Amalek goeth down.

The prevailing power of prayer with God in times of danger, appeareth not only in the sacred history of the Bible, but hath been recorded in all ages of the church. In the primitive church, A.D. 175, the army of Christians was called the thundering legion, because, upon their prayers, God scattered their enemies with thunder, and refreshed themselves with showers in a great drought.

After, in the good Emperor Theodosius his time, A.D. 394, upon an earnest prayer to Christ, the winds fought from heaven for him against his enemies, as they did for us in 1588. And continually since, God never left the force of faithful prayer without witness. If we would observe how God answereth prayers, we should see a blessed issue of all the holy desires he kindles in our hearts; for he cannot but make good that title whereby he is styled, 'a God hearing prayer,' Ps. lxv. 2, which should move us to sow more prayers into his bosom, the fruit whereof we should reap in our greatest need. It would be a strong evidence in these troublesome times of the future good success of the church, if we were earnest in soliciting Christ with these words which himself hath taught us, 'Let thy kingdom come.' For put him to it, and 'he will never fail those that seek him,' Ps. ix. 10. He loveth importunity.

But to speak something of this treatise of this godly and painful minister of Christ, which is written by him without affection, as desirous to clothe spiritual things with a spiritual manner of writing, the diligent and godly reader shall observe a sound, clear, substantial handling of the greatest points that naturally fall within the discourse, and a more large and useful unfolding of many things, than in former treatises. It appeareth he sought the good of all; so that, besides the labours of other holy men, there will be just cause of blessing God for his assistance in this work. To whose blessing I commend both it and the whole Israel of God.

Gray's Inn. R. SIBBES.

Passing on to 1623–4, we have a delightful 'epistle' prefixed to Ezekiel Culverwell's 'Treatise of Faith . . . . . applied especially unto the use of the weakest Christians.'* This little volume had

---

* A Treatise of Faith. Wherein is declared how a man may live by faith, and find relief in all his necessities. Applied especially unto the use of the weakest Christians. By Ezekiel Culverwell. The just shall live by faith. The seventh

passed through seven editions by 1633; and it were well if its popularity could be revived; for it overflows with profound thought, sagacious counsel, pungent appeal, and true eloquence. But let Dr Gouge characterise it and its author. 'God,' he says, 'sent Ezekiel Culverwell, as of old he sent Ezekiel Buzi, to set forth the promises of God more plentifully and pertinently than ever before; and that to breed faith where it is not, to strengthen it where it is weak, to settle it where it wavereth, to repair it where it decayeth, to apply it aright to every need, to extend it to sanctification as well as to justification, and to point out the singular use of it in matters temporal, spiritual, and eternal.' And he adds—'What I say of him, I know of him;· for from mine infancy have I known him, and under his ministry was I trained up in my younger years, he being at least two-and-twenty years older than myself.'*

Let us now read Sibbes's 'Epistle to the Christian Reader:'—

The leading of a happy life (the attainment whereof this treatise directeth unto) is that which all desire, but God's truth only discovereth, and faith only enjoyeth. In the first Adam, our happiness was in our own keeping; but he, by turning from God to the creature, made proof what and whence he was; a creature raised out of nothing, and without the supporting power of him in whom all things consist, subject to fall into a state worse than nothing again. Hence God, out of his infinite power, and depth of goodness intending the glory of his mercy, in restoring man, would not trust man with his own happiness; but would have it procured and established in the person of a second Adam, in whom we recover a surer estate than we lost in the first. For though Adam's soul was joined to God, yet that knitting was within the contingent and changeable liberty of his own will; but now we are brought to God in an everlasting covenant of mercy, by faith in Christ; who, by taking the nature of man into unity of his person, and not the person of any, became a public person, to be the author of eternal salvation to all that receive him; and so gathering us that were scattered from God, into one head, bringeth us back again to God, by a contrary way to that whereby we fell, that is, by cleaving to God by faith, from whom we fell by distrust. A fit grace for the state of grace, giving the whole glory to God, and emptying the soul of all self-sufficiency, and enlarging it to receive what is freely wrought and offered by another. Thus we come to have the comfort, and God the glory of mercy; which sweet attribute moved him to set all other attributes on work to make us happy. Out of the bowels of which mercy, as he chose us to eternal salvation in Christ, so vouchsafeth he all things necessary to life and godliness. And as the same love in God giveth us heaven, and furnisheth us with all things needful in the way, until we come thither; so the same faith which saveth us, layeth hold likewise on the promises of necessary assistance, comfort, provision, and protection: and

edition, corrected and amended. Ephes. vi. 16, 'Above all, taking the shield of faith.' Rom. xv. 4, 'Whatsoever things were written aforetime, were written for our learning, that we through patience and comfort of the Scriptures might have hope.' London: Printed by J. D. for Hen. Overton, and are to be sold at his shop at the entering in of Pope's-head Alley, out of Lumbard Street, 1633.

* 'To the Christian Reader,' prefixed to Treatise of Faith, *supra*.

this office it performeth in all the several stations of this life, until it hath brought us unto the enjoying of him 'in whose presence is fulness of joy for evermore,' Ps. xvi. 11.

We see that same love in parents, which moveth them to give an inheritance to their sons, moveth them likewise to provide for them, and to train them up in experience of their fatherly care. So it pleaseth our first and best Father, besides the main promise of salvation, to give us many other rich and precious promises, that in taste of his goodness and truth in these, we may at length yield up our souls to him, as to our faithful Creator, 1 Pet. iv. 19, with the more assured comfort; and the longer we live here, be more rooted in faith. 'I know whom I have trusted,' 2 Tim. i. 12, saith aged St Paul. But alas! how little is that we know of his ways, Job xxvi. 14, because we observe him not, making good his word unto us! 'All his ways are mercy and truth,' Ps. xxv. 10, and every 'word is a tried word,' Ps. xii. 6. For the better help of God's people, to know their portion in those good things, which their father not only layeth up for them, Ps. xxxi. 19, for times to come, but layeth out for them here as his wisdom seeth fit; this reverend and holy man of God hath compiled this treatise, wherein he layeth open the veins of promises hidden in the Scriptures, to the view of every Christian, and digesteth them in their orders; and withal, sheweth their several value and use, for the beautifying of a holy life; which wits less exercised, of themselves, would not so well have discerned.

Now that we may the rather benefit ourselves by this treatise, it will not be inconvenient to know these four things.

First, that it supposeth a reader grounded in the knowledge of the nature and properties of God, of Christ and his offices, of the covenant of grace, and such like: because as in an arch, one stone settleth another, so there is such a linking together of points in divinity, that one strengtheneth another. For from whence hath faith that efficacy, but because it is that which is required in the covenant, to lay hold on the free promises? And whence have the promises their strength, but from the constant nature of Jehovah; who giveth a being to his word, and is at peace with us, by the all-sufficient sacrifice of the Mediator of the new covenant? Words have their validity from the authority of the speaker. Were not faith founded on the word of an infinite God, so thoroughly appeased, the soul would sink in great temptations, whereas now even mountains vanish before a believing soul. For what can stand against Christ, who is able to subdue all to himself? Hence it is, that now we are by faith, Phil. iii. 21, safer than Adam in Paradise, because we have a promise, which he wanted. Safer it is to be as low as hell with a promise, than in paradise without it, because faith wrought by the power of God, hath what strength God hath, on whom it resteth, and therefore worketh such wonders: God honouring that grace, which honours him so much.

But howsoever the knowledge of these things serveth the argument in hand; yet it must not be expected, that he should be long in these things, which are but coincident, and should be foreknown: which I speak, because some of weaker judgment, not considering the just bounds of treatises, may expect larger handling of some things. Whereas he hath laboured especially to furnish the argument in hand, and not to load the discourse.

In the second place, it must be known, that the fruit of these things belong to such as are in Christ, in whom all promises are yea and amen, made and performed. He that by the immortal seed of the word and Spirit is born again, may claim a title to that he is born unto. These promises be as well his inheritance, as heaven itself is. For clearing of this, there be three degrees of promises; one of salvation to absolute and personal obedience; but this, by reason of weakness of the flesh, driveth us to a despair of ourselves, and so to the second promise of life by Christ. This requireth nothing but receiving by faith, which is wrought in those that are given to Christ, whilst grace is offered, the Spirit clothing the words with a hidden and strong power, and making them operative; when they are commanded to believe, their hearts are opened to believe. To persons in this estate, are made a third kind of promises, of all that is needful in this world, until all promises end in performance. Of both these promises, and the last especially, this book speaketh.

Thirdly, it must be pressed upon those that mean to profit, that they resolve to come under Christ's government, and be willing to be led by the Spirit into all revealed truth. Wisdom is easy to such as are willing; and the victory is as good as gotten, when the will is brought from thraldom to base affections, to resolve to be guided. For such a heart lieth open to God's gracious working, and the Spirit readily closeth with such a spirit, as putteth not bars of obstinacy.

Notwithstanding, we must know in the fourth place, that when we are at the best, we shall yet be in such a conflicting state, as that we shall long after that glorious liberty of the sons of God, after we have done the work God hath given us to do. For God will have a difference betwixt heaven and earth; and sharpen our desire of the coming of his kingdom, which nothing doth so much, especially in times of outward prosperity, as those tedious combats of the inner man. And yet let this raise up our spirits, that it is so far that this remainder should prejudice our interest in happiness, that thereby we are driven every day to renew our claim to the promise of pardon, and so to live by faith until this unclean issue be dried up. These sour herbs help us to relish Christ the better. Moreover, though in this life our endeavours come short of our desires, and we always allow a greater measure than we can attain unto; yet we may, by stirring up the graces begun in us, and by suing God upon those promises of his Spirit and grace, whereby he hath made himself a debtor unto us, come to that measure, whereby we shall make the profession of religion glorious, and lovely in the eyes of others, and comfortable to ourselves; and so shine far brighter than others do. Why then do we not, in the use of all sanctified means, beg of God, to make good the promises wherein he hath caused us to trust? Do we not, beside life of our bodies, desire health and strength to discharge all the offices of civil life? And why should we not much more (if the life of God be in us) labour after health and vigour of Spirit, and for that anointing of the Holy Ghost, whereby we may do and suffer all things, so as we may draw others to a liking of our ways? The truth is, Satan laboureth to keep us under belief of particular promises, and from renewing our covenant, in confidence, that God will perfect the work that he hath begun, and not repent him of his earnest. So far as thus we cherish distrust, we lie open to Satan. Strengthen faith, and strengthen all. Let us therefore at once set upon all duties required, and be in love with an holy life, above all other lives, and put ourselves upon God's mercy and truth; and we shall be able from experience, so far to justify all God's ways as that we would not be in another state for all the world. What greater encouragement can we wish, than that our corruptions shall fall more and more before the Spirit, and we shall be able to do all things through Christ that strengtheneth us?

To make these ways of God more plain unto us, this pains is taken by this man of God. Not to disparage the labours of other holy men (as far as I can judge), there is nothing in this kind more fully, judiciously, or savourily written, with greater evidence of a spirit persuaded of the goodness and truth of what it sets down. And though (distinct from respect to the author) the treatise deserveth much respect, yet it should gain the more acceptance, especially of those that are babes and young men in Christ, that it is written by a father of long and reverend esteem in the church; who hath begun in all these rules to others. As for our bodies, so for our souls, we may more securely rely on an old experienced physician. He commendeth it unto thee, having felt the kindly working of it upon himself. The Lord by his Spirit convey these truths into thy heart, and upon good felt hereby in thy soul, remember to desire God that he may still bring forth more fruit in his age, until he hath finished his course with credit to the gospel, and an assured hope of a blessed change.

Gray's Inn. RICHARD SIBBES.

We place along with this another 'epistle' by Sibbes, prefixed to another small book by Culverwell. The copy of this in my library, was formerly in the possession of Charles I., and has his royal arms enstamped in gold on each side. Judging from its appearance, it must have been well read. The book is entitled, 'Time Well Spent in Sacred Meditations, Divine Observations, Heavenly Exhortations;' and the 'Epistle Dedicatory' is addressed to an 'excellent Christian woman,' who seems to have been greatly beloved by Sibbes, Mrs More.* It runs as follows :—

To the right worshipful and truly religious Mrs MORE.

RIGHT WORSHIPFUL AND WORTHY MRS MORE.—The church of God hath not only benefit by exact and just treatises knit together in a methodical dependency of one part from another, but likewise of sententious independent speeches, that have a general lustre of themselves, as so many flowers in a garden, or jewels in a casket, whereof every one hath a distinct worth of themselves; and this maketh them the more acceptable, that being short they are fitter for the heart to carry, as having much in a little.

This moved this reverend man of God, to spend what spare hours his sickness would afford him about thoughts in this kind. He was many years God's prisoner under the gout and stone, such diseases as will allow but little liberty to those that are arrested and tortured by them. So fruitful an expense of time in so weak and worn a body is seldom seen, scarce any came to him but went away better than they came; God gave much strength of spirit to uphold his spirit from sinking under the strength of such diseases. It were a happy thing if we that are ministers of Christ, would on all conditions and times think of our calling, that our office is not tied to one day in a week, and one hour or two in that day, but that upon all fit occasions we are to quicken ourselves and others in the way homeward, as guides to heaven. We read not of the opening of heaven but to some great purpose. So it should be with the man of God, he should not open his mouth and let any thing fall (so far as frailty and the necessary occurrences of human life will permit) but what might minister some grace to the hearers.

The reason why I made choice of you to dedicate them unto, is not that

* Mrs More. She is named in his Will

I might discharge mine own debt unto you with another man's coin, but that I could not think of any fitter than yourself, whom this ancient minister of Christ esteemed always very much for eminency of parts and grace, and you him as a man faithful, and one that maintained his ministerial authority with good success in his place; God allotting your habitation in your younger years in that part of the country where he lived, and where you first learned to know God and yourself. In those times those parts were in regard of the air unhealthful, yet that air was so sweetened with the savoury breath of the gospel, that they were termed the holy land. Hereupon I thought meet to commend these sententious speeches by your name to others. Which though (divers of them) may seem plain, yet what they want in show they have in weight, as coming from a man very well experienced in all the ways of God. The Lord follow you with his best blessings, that you may continue still to adorn the gospel of Christ in your place!

Yours in all Christian service, R. SIBBES.

Before passing on to other 'Epistles' of a public kind, I would here introduce a letter to Ussher, of probably 1628–29, which happens to have been preserved. It reveals to us the keen zest and interest with which Sibbes observed what was transpiring, 'Petition of Right,' and the like. It falls in here fittingly as an introduction to the next 'Epistle,' as there is in it a passing notice of the last illness of the 'Master' of 'Emmanuel.'

MR R. SIBBS *to the Archbishop of Armagh.*

RIGHT REVEREND,—My duty and service premised. I am forced of the sudden in midst of straits and distractions to write unto you, your servant being presently to depart here: but I choose rather thus to express my remembrance of your grace, than to let slip so fit an opportunity. I hope I shall always carry you in my heart, and preserve that deserved respect I owe to you, who are oft presented to me as one that God hath shewed himself unto in more than ordinary measure, and set up high in the affections of the best. I know not the man living more beholden to God, in those respects, than yourself. It went for current here a while that you were dead, which caused the hearts of many to be more refreshed upon hearing the contrary. It is very ill losing of men of much meaner service in the church in these almost desperate times. Yesterday there was an agreement between the two houses about a petition of right, whereby the liberty of the subject is like to be established. Here is much joy for it, if it prove not a lightning before death. Our fears are more than our hopes yet. Doctor Preston is inclining to a consumption, and his state is thought doubtful to the physicians. The neighbour schism getteth still more strength with us. . *Boni deficiunt, mali perficiunt.* I cannot now enlarge myself, your servant hastening hence. The Lord still delight to shew himself strong with you, and to shield you in the midst of all dangers, and glorify himself by you, to the great comfort of his church, and the disheartening of his enemies! I desire your grace to remember my respect to your wife, humbly thanking you both for your undeserved love.—Your Grace's in all Christian service, to be commanded, R. SIBBS.*

May 27.

* Ussher, *ante* xvi. letter ccccxxii.

We have a series of prefaces, in union with John Davenport, to various posthumous works of Dr John Preston, of whom I have had occasion to speak repeatedly in this memoir. I trust that the time is not distant when we shall have a worthy edition of his writings to place beside those of Sibbes. No books had such a wide, nay, universal audience through many generations. Edition followed upon edition, and now it is not easy to collect them all. It is mournful to think how Cambridge neglects her most illustrious sons!

The Preston epistles call for no comment beyond an explanatory word. I give them in order:—

I. The 'New Covenant or Saint's Portion.'*

Dedication.

Illustrissimis, et Honoratissimis Viris, Theophilo Comiti Lincolniensi, et Gulielmo Vice-Comiti Say et Sele, Dominis suis submississimè colendis has Johannis Prestoni, S.S. Theol. Doct., et Collegii Immanuelis Magistri Primitias Devotissimi, Tam Authoris, Dum Viveret, Quam Ipsorum, Qui Supersunt, Obsequii Testimonium, L.M.D.D.D.

RICHARDUS SIBS.
JOHANNES DAVENPORT.

To the Reader.

It had been much to have been desired (if it had so pleased the Father of spirits), that this worthy man had survived the publishing of these and other his lectures; for then, no doubt, they would have come forth more refined and digested; for, though there was very little or no mistake in taking them from his mouth, yet preaching and writing have their several graces. Things livened by the expression of the speaker, sometimes take well, which after, upon a mature review, seem either superfluous or flat. And we oft see men very able to render their conceits in writing, yet not the happiest speakers.

Yet we, considering (not so much what might have been, as) what now may be for the service of the church, thought good rather to communicate them thus, than that they should die with the author. He was a man of an exact judgment and quick apprehension, an acute reasoner, active in good, choice in his notions; one who made it his chief aim to promote the cause of Christ and the good of the church, which moved him to single out arguments answerable, on which he spent his best thoughts. He was honoured of God to be an instrument of much good, whereunto he had advantage by those eminent places he was called unto. As he had a short

---

* The New Covenant, or the Saint's Portion: a Treatise unfolding the All-Sufficiency of God, Man's Uprightness, and the Covenant of Grace. Delivered in fourteen sermons upon Gen. xvii. 1, 2; whereunto are adjoined four sermons upon Eccles. ix. 1, 2, 11, 12. By the late faithful and worthy minister of Jesus Christ, John Preston, Dr in Divinity, Chaplain in Ordinary to his Majesty, Master of Emmanuel College in Cambridge, and sometimes preacher of Lincoln's Inn. The fourth edition, corrected. 'He hath given a portion to them that fear him: he will ever be mindful of his covenant,' Ps. cxi. 5. London: Printed by I. D. for Nicholas Bourne, and are to be sold at the south entrance of the Royal Exchange. 1630, 4to.

race to run, so he made speed, and did much in a little time. Though he was of an higher elevation and strain of spirit than ordinary, yet, out of love to do good, he could frame his conceits so as might suit with ordinary understandings. A little before his death (as we were informed by the Right Honourable the Lord Viscount Say and Sele, in whose piety, wisdom, and fidelity he put great repose), he was desirous that we should peruse what of his was fit for public use.

We are not ignorant that it is a thing subject to censure to seem bold and witty in another man's work, and, therefore, as little is altered as may be. And we desire the reader rather to take in good part that which is intended for public good, than to catch at imperfections, considering they were but taken as they fell from him speaking. And we entreat those that have anything of his in their hands, that they would not be hasty, for private respects, to publish them, till we, whom the author put in trust, have perused them. We purpose (by God's help) that what shall be judged fit shall come forth. We send forth these sermons of God's All-Sufficiency, and Man's Uprightness, and the Covenant of Grace first, as being first prepared by him that had the copies, and because the right understanding of these points hath a chief influence into a Christian life. The Lord give a blessing answerable, and continue still to send forth such faithful labourers into his harvest!

RICHARD SIBS.
JOHN DAVENPORT.

II. The 'Breastplate of Faith and Love.'*

Dedication.

Illustrissimo, Nobilissimoque Viro, Roberto Comiti Warwicensi, Johannis Prestoni, S.T.D., et Collegii Immanuelis Q.† Magistri (cujus tutelæ, dum in vivis esset, Primogenitum suum in Disciplinam et Literis expoliendum tradidit), posthumorum tractatuum partem de natura fidei, ejusque efficacia, deque amore et operibus bonis, Devotissimi, tam authoris, dum viveret, quam ipsorum qui supersunt, obsequii testimonium. M.D.D.D.

RICHARDUS SIBS.
JOHANNES DAVENPORT.

To the Christian Reader.

CHRISTIAN READER—Innumerable are the sleights of Satan, to hinder a Christian in his course towards heaven, by exciting the corruption of his own heart to disturb him, when he is about to do any good; or by discouraging him with inward terrors, when he would solace himself with heavenly comforts; or by disheartening him under the fears of sufferings,

---

* The Breastplate of Faith and Love. A treatise, wherein the ground and exercise of faith and love, as they are set upon Christ their object, and as they are expressed in good works, is explained. Delivered in 18 sermons upon three several texts, by the late faithful and worthy minister of Jesus Christ, John Preston, Dr in Divinity, chaplain in ordinary to his Majesty, Master of Emmanuel College in Cambridge, and sometimes Preacher of Lincoln's Inn. The fourth edition. 'But let us who are of the day be sober, putting on the breastplate of faith and love,' 1 Thess. v. 8. 'What will it profit, my brethren, if a man say he have faith, and hath not works? Can faith save him?' James ii. 14. Imprinted at London by R. Y. for Nicholas Bourne and are to be sold at the south entrance of the Royal Exchange. 1634.

† Qu. 'quondam?'—ED.

when he should be resolute in a good cause. A type whereof were the Israelites, whose servitude was redoubled when they turned themselves to forsake Egypt. Wherefore we have much need of Christian fortitude, according to that direction, 'Watch ye, stand fast, quit yourselves like men,' 1 Cor. xvi. 13; especially since Satan, like a serpentine crocodile pursued, is by resistance put to flight.

But as in wars (which the Philistines knew well in putting their hope in Goliath) the chief strength of the soldiers lieth in their captain, so in spiritual conflicts all a Christian's strength is in Christ, and from him. For before our conversion we were of no strength; since our conversion we are not sufficient of ourselves to think a good thought. And to work out from the saints all self-confidence, God, by their falls, teacheth them 'to rejoice in the Lord Jesus, and to have no confidence in the flesh.'

Whatsoever Christ hath for us, is made ours by faith, which is the hand of the soul enriching it by receiving Christ, who is the treasure hid in the field, and with him, those unsearchable riches of grace, which are revealed and offered in the gospel; yea, it is part of our spiritual armour. That which was fabulously spoken of the race of giants is truly said of a Christian, he is born with his armour upon him; as soon as he is regenerate he is armed. It is called a breastplate, $Θώραξ$, 1 Thess. v. 8, because it preserves the heart; a long, large shield, $Θυρεός$ of $θύρα$, Eph. vi. 16 (as the word signifieth), which is useful to defend the whole man from all sorts of assaults. Which part of spiritual armour, and how it is to be managed, is declared in the former part of the ensuing treatise, in ten sermons.

Now, as all rivers return into the sea whence they came, so the believing soul, having received all from Christ, returneth all to Christ. For thus the believer reasoneth, Was God's undeserved, unexpected love such to me that he spared not his only-begotten Son, but gave him to die for me? It is but equal that I should live to him, die for him, bring in my strength, time, gifts, liberty, all that I have, all that I am, in his service, to his glory. That affection, whence these resolutions arise, is called love, which so inclineth the soul that it moveth in a direct line towards that object wherein it expecteth contentment. The soul is miserably deluded in pursuing the wind, and is taking aim at a flying fowl, whilst it seeks happiness in any creature; which appears in the restlessness of those irregular agitations and endless motions of minds of ambitious, voluptuous, and covetous persons, whose frame of spirit is like the lower part of the elementary region, the seat of winds, tempests, and earthquakes, full of unquietness; whilst the believer's soul, like that part towards heaven which is always peaceable and still, enjoyeth true rest and joy. And indeed the perfection of our spirits cannot be but in union with the chief of spirits, which communicateth his goodness to the creature according to its capacity. This affection of love, as it reflecteth upon Christ, being a fruit and effect of his love to us apprehended by faith, is the subject of the second part of the following treatise, in seven sermons.

The judicious author, out of a piercing insight into the methods of the tempter, knowing upon what rocks the faith of many suffers shipwreck; that neither the weak Christian might lose the comfort of his faith through want of evidences, nor the presumptuous rest upon a fancy instead of faith, nor the adversaries be emboldened to cast upon us, by reason of this doctrine of justification by faith only, their wonted nicknames of Solifidians and Nullifidians; throughout the whole treatise, and more especially in the last sermon, he discourseth of good works as they arise from faith and love. This is the sum of the faithful and fruitful labours of this reverend, learned, and godly minister of the gospel, who, whilst he lived, was an example of the life of faith and love, and of good works, to so many as were acquainted with his equal and even walking in the ways of God, in the several turnings and occasions of his life. But it will be too much injury to the godly reader to be detained longer in the porch, We now dismiss thee to the reading of this profitable work, beseeching God to increase faith, and to perfect love in thy heart, that thou mayest be fruitful in good works.

Thine in our Lord Jesus Christ,   RICHARD SIBBS.
JOHN DAVENPORT.

III. The Saint's Daily Exercise. *

To the Reader.

COURTEOUS READER,—To discourse largely of the necessity and use of this piece of spiritual armour, after so many learned and useful treatises upon this subject, may seem superfluous, especially considering that there is much spoken to this purpose, for thy satisfaction, in the ensuing treatise, wherein, besides the unfolding of the nature of this duty (which is the saint's daily exercise), and strong enforcement to it, there is an endeavour to give satisfaction in the most incident cases, want of clearing whereof is usually an hindrance to the cheerful and ready performance thereof. In all which, what hath been done by this reverend and worthy man we had rather should appear in the treatise itself, to thy indifferent judgment, than to be much in setting down our own opinion. This we doubt not of, that, by reason of the spiritual and convincing manner of handling this argument, it will win acceptance with many, especially considering that it is of that nature wherein, though much have been spoken, yet much more may be said with good relish to those that have any spiritual sense; for it is the most spiritual action, wherein we have nearer communion with God, than in any other holy performance, and whereby it pleaseth God to convey all good to us, to the performance whereof Christians find most backwardness and indisposedness, and from thence most dejection of spirit, which also in these times is most necessary, wherein, unless we fetch help from heaven this way, we see the church and cause of God like to be trampled under feet. Only remember, that we let these sermons pass forth as they were delivered by himself in public, without taking that liberty of adding or detracting, which perhaps some would have thought meet; for we thought it best that his own meaning should be expressed in his own words and manner, especially considering there is little which perhaps may seem superfluous to some, but may, by God's blessing, be useful to others. It would be a good prevention of many inconveniences in this kind, if able men would be persuaded to publish their own works in their lifetime; yet we think it a good service to the church when that defect is supplied by giving

* The Saint's Daily Exercise; a Treatise unfolding the whole Duty of Prayer. Delivered in five sermons upon 1 Thes. v. 17. By the late faithful and worthy minister of Jesus Christ, John Preston, Dr in Divinity, Chaplain in Ordinary to his Majesty, Master of Emmanuel College in Cambridge, and sometime Preacher of Lincoln's Inn. The fourth edition, corrected. 'The effectual fervent prayer of a righteous man availeth much,' James v. 16. 'If I regard iniquity in my heart, the Lord will not hear my prayer,' Ps. lxvi. 18. London : Printed by W. I. for Nicholas Bourne, and are to be sold at the south entrance of the Royal Exchange. 1630. 4to.

some life to those things, which otherwise would have died of themselves. The blessing of these labours of his we commend unto God, and the benefit of them unto thee, resting thine in our Lord Jesus Christ,

RICHARD SIBS.
JOHN DAVENPORT.

IV. The Saints' Qualification. *

Dedication.

Illustrissimo, Nobilissimo Viro, Philippo, Pembrochiæ, et Montis Gomerici Comiti, Baroni Herbert de Cardiffe et Sherland, Ordinis Garterii Equiti, Regiæ Domus Camerario, Regiæ Majestati a Secretioribus Consiliis, &c., triplicem hunc Johannis Prestoni, S.S., Theologiæ Doct. Colleg. Immanuelis Nuper Magist. et Regiæ Majest. a Sacris, Tractatum, de Humiliatione, Nova Creatura, Præparatione ad Sacram Synaxin, in Devotissimæ, Tam authoris, quam Ipsorum, Observantiæ Testimonium, L.M.D.D.D.

RICHARDUS SIBS.
JOANNES DAVENPORT.

To the Christian Reader.

The good acceptance the sermons of this worthy man have found amongst well-disposed Christians, hath made us the willinger to give way to the publishing of these, as coming from the same author. The good they may thus do prevails more for the sending of them forth than some imperfections (that usually accompany the taking of other men's speeches) may do to suppress them. Something may well be yielded to public good in things not altogether so as we wish. They are enforced upon none that shall except against them, they may either read or refuse them at their pleasure. The argument of them is such as may draw the more regard, being of matters of necessary and perpetual use.

For 'Humiliation' we never so deeply see into the grounds of it (sinfulness of nature and life); or, so far as we see, look upon it with that eye of detestation we should; and therefore a holy heart desireth still further light to be brought in, to discover whatsoever may hinder communion with God, and is glad when sin is made loathsome unto it, as being its greatest enemy, that doth more hurt than all the world besides, and the only thing that divides between our chief good and us. As this humiliation increaseth, so in the like proportion all other graces increase; for the more we are emptied of ourselves, the more we are filled with the fulness of God. The defects of this appear in the whole frame of a Christian life,

---

* The Saints' Qualification: or, a treatise—1, of humiliation, in ten sermons; 2, of sanctification, in nine sermons; whereunto is added a treatise of communion with Christ in the sacrament, in three sermons. Preached by the late faithful and worthy minister of Jesus Christ, John Preston, Doctor in Divinity, chaplain in ordinary to his majesty, master of Emmanuel College in Cambridge, and sometime preacher of Lincoln's Inn. The third edition, corrected. 'When men are cast down, then thou shalt say, There is lifting up: and he shall save the humble person,' Job xxii. 29. 'Cast away from you all your transgressions, whereby ye have transgressed, and make you a new heart, and a new spirit,' &c., Ezek. xviii. 31. 'He that eats my flesh and drinks my blood, dwelleth in me and I in him,' John vi. 56. London; Printed by R. B. for N. Bourne, and are to be sold by T. Nicholes at the Bible in Pope's-head Alley. 1637. 4to.

which is so far unsound as we retain anything of corrupted self, unhumbled for.

The foundation of Christianity is laid very low; and therefore the treatise of 'Humiliation' is well premised before that of the 'New Creature.' God will build upon nothing in us. We must be nothing in ourselves before we be raised up for a fit temple for God to dwell in, whose course is to pull down before he build. Old things must be out of request before all become new; and without this newness of the whole man from union with Christ, no interest in the new heavens can be hoped for, whereinto no defiled thing shall enter, as altogether unsuitable to that condition and place. Nothing is in request with God but this new creature, all things else are adjudged to the fire; and without this it had been better be no creature at all. By this we may judge of the usefulness of discourses tending this way. One thing more thou art to be advertised of (courteous reader), and that is, of the injurious dealing of such as for private gain have published what they can get, howsoever taken, without any acquainting either of those friends of the author's that resided in Cambridge (to whose care he left the publishing of those things that were delivered there) or of us, to whom he committed the publishing of what should be thought fit for public view of that which was preached in London. Hereby not only wrong is done to others, but to the deceased likewise, by mangling and misshaping the birth of his brain; and therefore once again we desire men to forbear publishing of anything until those that were entrusted have the review. And so we commit the treatise and thee to God's blessing.

RICHARD SIBS.
JOHN DAVENPORT.

In 1632, Sibbes introduced to the world the excellent folio of John Smith on 'The Creed,'* and the well-known and still vital treatise of John Ball on 'Faith.'† John Smith was 'preacher of the word at Clavering in Essex.' He succeeded Bishop Andrewes as lecturer in St Paul's Cathedral. Anthony Wood speaks of him as being skilled in the original languages, and well acquainted with the writings of the ablest divines. He died in November 1616.‡

* An Exposition of the Creed; or, an Explanation of the Articles of our Christian Faith. Delivered in many afternoon sermons, by that reverend and worthy divine, Master John Smith, late preacher of the Word at Clavering in Essex, and sometime Fellow of St John's College, in Oxford. Now published for the benefit and behoof of all good Christians, together with an exact table of all the chiefest doctrines and uses throughout the whole book. 'Uprightness hath boldness.' Heb. xi. 6, 'But without faith it is impossible to please him: for he that cometh unto God must believe that he is, and that he is a rewarder of them that diligently seek him.' At London: Imprinted by Felix Kyngston, for Robert Allot, and are to be sold at his shop, at the sign of the Black Bear, in Paul's Churchyard. 1632.

† A Treatise of Faith. Divided into Two Parts, the first shewing the Nature, the second the Life of Faith, both tending to direct the weak Christian how he may possess the whole word of God as his own, overcome temptations, better his obedience, and live comfortably in all estates. By John Ball. Hab. ii. 4, 'The just shall live by his faith.' The third edition, corrected and enlarged. London: Printed by Robert Young, for Edward Brewster, and are to be sold at his shop, at the sign of the Bible, upon Fleet Bridge. 1637. 4to.

‡ Wood's Athenæ (ed. by Bliss), ii. 188. And see Chalmers's Biog. Dict., *sub. voce*

So far as I have been able to read his folio, I must regard Sibbes's Introduction as its most valuable feature. Pearson, indeed, overshadows all such works. John Ball has been very lovingly written of by very many. Wood and Clarke, Thomas Fuller, and Richard Baxter, and Simeon Ash join in speaking 'well' of him. His books, larger and smaller, are worthy of a place beside those of Sibbes. His 'Power of Godliness' (1657), a thin folio, is marked by extraordinary acquaintance with the workings of the human heart. There are touches of weird subtlety, and one in reading can easily understand the stillness of his auditory. His treatise on 'Faith' is rich and practical.* With these few words, let us turn to the two 'epistles:'—

I. Smith on the Creed.

To the Christian Reader.

It is available, for the better entertainment of this work, to know something concerning the author, concerning the work itself, and concerning the argument; for the author, my acquaintance with him was especially towards the declining part of his years, at what time (as they speak of the sun towards setting) the light and influence which comes from worthy men is most mild and comfortable. The gifts of men then, perhaps, are not so flourishing as in their younger time, but yet more mature, and what cometh from them is better digested. In the prime of his years he was trained up in St John's College, in Oxford, being there Fellow of the House, and for piety and parts esteemed highly in the University of those that excelled in both. Afterwards he grew to that note that he was chosen to read the lecture in Paul's, succeeding therein that great, learned man, Doctor Andrewes, late Lord Bishop of Winchester, which he discharged not only to the satisfaction, but to the applause of the most judicious and learned hearers, witnessed by their frequency and attention. Not long after he was removed to a pastoral charge in Clavering, in Essex, where being fixed till his death, he shined as a star in his proper sphere.

This good man's aim was to convey himself by all manner of ways into the heart, which made him willingly heard of all sorts; for witty things only, as they are spoken to the brain, so they rest in the brain, and sink no deeper; but the heart (which vain and obnoxious men love not to be touched), that is the mark a faithful teacher aims to hit. But because the way to come to the heart is often to pass through the fancy, therefore this godly man studied by lively representations to help men's faith by the fancy. It was our Saviour Christ's manner of teaching to express heavenly things in an earthly manner; and it was the study of the wise man, Solomon, becoming a preacher, to find out pleasant words, or words of delight, Eccles. xii. 10. But when all pains are taken by the man of God, people will relish what is spoken according as their taste is. It falleth out here as it doth in a garden, wherein some walk for present delight, some carry flowers away with them to refresh them for a time; some, as bees, gather honey, which they feed on long afterwards; some, spider-like, come to suck that which may feed that malignant and venomous disposition that they bring with them. There cannot be a better character of a man than

* Consult Brook, 'Lives of the Puritans,' ii. 440, *seq.*

to observe what he relisheth most in hearing; for as men are, so they taste, so they judge, so they speak. Ezekiel, besides prophetical gifts fit for so high a calling, had no doubt a delightful manner of expression of himself, whereupon the wickeder sort of Jews, engaged in sinful courses, came to hear him but as a musician to please their ears, neglecting the authority of his person and the weight of his message, Ezek. xxxiii. 32. It is no wonder, therefore, if in these days people stick in the bark and neglect the pith; though sometimes it falleth out with some, as with Augustine hearing Ambrose, whilst they bite at the bait of some pleasing notions, they are, at the same time, catched with the Spirit's hook.

He was skilful in the original languages, and thereupon an excellent textman, well read in writers that were of note in the several ages of the church, which made him a well furnished and able divine. His judgment was clear and his conscience tender, and, which helped him most, he brought to the great work of the ministry an holy and gracious heart, which raised and carried him to aims above himself and the world. In his conversing he was modest, fruitful, wise, and winning; in his expressions witty and graceful, insomuch that he hath left a fresh and sweet remembrance of them to this day. Towards his end he grew more spiritual, setting light by all things here below, and only waited (as his expression was) for the coming of the Comforter; at length, his work being finished, breathing out his life with that wish of the spouse, 'Yea, come, Lord Jesus,' Rev. xxii. 20. Thus much I thought not unfit to be made known of the man.

Now, for the work itself, it must be considered by the learned reader that these things were spoken, though to a people high-raised in knowledge, and more refined than ordinary by his teaching, yet to the people, not with a purpose that they should come to the view and censure of the learned. But though they were delivered to the people, yet are they not so popular, but (if my love to the man and the work deceive me not) they will leave the best reader either more learned or more holy, or both. It must, therefore, be remembered, for the more favourable acceptation of this work, that these sermons were taken by one of his parish, a man, though pious and of good parts, yet not skilful in the learned languages; and therefore it must needs be that many apt and acute sentences of the fathers, by which this learned man did use to beautify and strengthen the points he delivered, are fallen to the ground and lost, for lack of skill to take up. But howsoever much of the spirits be lost, yet here you have the corpse and bulk of the discourse, and not without some life and vigour, wherein this is peculiar in his manner of handling, that he hath chosen fit texts of Scripture to ground his exposition of every article upon.

Now, for the argument itself, the Creed, I think it fit to premise something, because it hath been omitted by the author, or at least not gathered with the rest. The Creed is of middle authority, between divine and human, and called the Apostles' Creed, not only for consanguinity with the apostles' doctrine, but because it is taken out of the apostles' writings, and therefore of greatest authority next to the Scriptures. It is nothing else but a summary comprehension of the counsel and work of God concerning our supernatural condition here and hereafter. The doctrine of salvation is spread through the Scriptures as spirits in the arteries and blood in the veins, as the soul in the body. And here, for easier carriage, the most necessary points are gathered together, as so many pearls or precious stones, that we might have a ready use of them upon all occasions, being, as it were, a little Bible or Testament that Christians of all ranks, as suited for all conditions, may bear about with them everywhere without any trouble. In every article there is both a shallow and a depth, milk for babes and meat for strong men. Though there be no growth in regard of fundamental principles (which have been alike in all ages of the church), yet there hath and will be a proficiency in regard of conclusions drawn out of those principles. The necessities of every Christian, and the springing up of unsound opinions in the church, will continually enforce diligence and care in the further explication and application of these fundamental truths.

It will not, therefore, be amiss to set down a few directions for the more clear understanding of the Creed, and for the better making use of it. And first, for the understanding of it, it hath the name of Creed or Belief, from the act exercised about it, to shew that it doth not only contain doctrine to be believed, but that that doctrine will do us no good unless, by mingling it with our faith, we make it our belief. Therefore, both the act and the object are implied in one word, Belief. Secondly: From the execution in creation and incarnation we must arise to God's decree; nothing done in time which was not decreed before all times, ' Known unto the Lord are all his works from the beginning of the world,' Acts xv. 18. Thirdly: We must arise from one principal benefit to all that follow and accompany it, as in forgiveness of sins, follow righteousness, peace, and joy, the spirit of sanctification, Christian liberty, &c. Though the articles be nakedly propounded, yet are we to believe all the fruits and privileges. So to God's creating of heaven and earth we must join his providence in upholding and ruling all things in both. Fourthly: In the consequent we are to understand all that went before by way of cause or preparation, as in the crucifying of Christ, his preceding agony and the cause of it, our sins, and the love of God and Christ in those sufferings, &c. Fifthly: Though we are to believe circumstances as well as the thing itself, yet not with the same necessity of faith, as it is more necessary to believe that Christ was crucified than that it was under Pontius Pilate; though when any circumstance is revealed we ought to believe it, and to have a preparation of mind to believe whatsoever shall be revealed. Yet in the main points this preparation of mind is not sufficient, but there must be a present and an expressed faith. We must know that, as in the law, he that breaketh one commandment breaketh all, because all come from the same authority; so, in the grounds of faith, he that denies one in the true sense of it denies all, for both law and faith are copulatives. The singling out of anything is contrary to the obedience of faith. *Fides non eligit objectum.*

For particular and daily use, we must know, first, that every article requires a particular faith, not only in regard of the person believing, but likewise in regard of the application of the article believed; or else the devil might say the creed, for he believes there is a Creator, and that there is a remission of sins, &c.; but because he hath no share in it, it enrageth him the more. Our adversaries are great enemies to particular faith, and think we coin a thirteenth article when we enforce particular assurance, because, say they, particular men are not named in the Scripture, and what is not in Scripture cannot be a matter of faith. But there is a double faith, a faith which is the doctrine we do believe, and faith which is the grace whereby we believe; and this faith is a matter of experience wrought in our hearts by the Spirit of God. It is sufficient that that faith which we do believe is contained in the Scriptures. Now whereas they object that we make it a thirteenth article, their fourteenth apostle adds to these twelve many more articles of faith, which he enforceth to be believed, with the same necessity of faith as these twelve; neither hath he only entered upon Christ's prerogative in minting new articles of faith, but likewise they have usurped over all Christian churches by adding Roman to the catholic church in the creed. A bold imposture!

But for special faith, the main office of the Holy Spirit is in opening general truths, to reveal our particular interest in those truths, and to breed special faith whereby we make them our own, because the Spirit of God reveals the mind of God to every particular Christian, 1 Cor. ii. 11, 12; for as the things believed are truths above nature, so the grace of faith whereby we believe is a grace above nature, created as a supernatural eye in the soul, to see supernatural truths.

Secondly, Where sacred truths are truly apprehended, there the Spirit works an impression in the soul suitable to the things believed; every article hath a power in it which the Spirit doth imprint upon the soul. The belief of God to be the Father Almighty breeds an impression of dependence, reverence, and comfort. The belief and knowledge of Christ crucified is a crucifying knowledge. The true knowledge and faith in Christ rising, is a raising knowledge. The knowledge of the abasement of Christ is an abasing knowledge; because faith sees itself one with Christ in both states. We cannot truly believe what Christ hath wrought for us, but at the same time the Spirit of Christ worketh something in us.

Thirdly, It is convenient for the giving of due honour to every person to consider of the work appropriated to every one: all come from the Father; all are exactly performed by the Son in our nature for the redemption of those that the Father hath given him. The gathering out of the world of that blessed society (which we call the church) into an holy communion, and the sanctifying of it, and sealing unto it all the privileges believed, as forgiveness of sins, resurrection of the body, and life everlasting, &c., proceed from the Holy Ghost.

Fourthly, It has pleased the great God to enter into a treaty and covenant of agreement with us his poor creatures, the articles of which agreement are here comprised. God, for his part, undertakes to convey all that concerns our happiness, upon our receiving of them, by believing on him. Every one in particular that recites these articles from a spirit of faith makes good this condition, and this is that answer of a good conscience, which Peter speaks of, 1 Pet. iii, whereby being demanded what our faith is, every one in particular answers to every article, I believe; I not only understand and conceive it, but assent unto it in my judgment as true, and consent to it in my will as good, and build my comfort upon it as good to me: this act of belief carries the whole soul with it.

Fifthly, Though it is we that answer, yet the power by which we answer is no less than that whereby God created the world and raised Christ from the dead. The answer is ours, but the power and strength is God's, whereby we answer, who performs both his part and ours too in the covenant. It is a higher matter to believe than the common sort think it. For this answer of faith to these truths, as it is caused by the power of God's Spirit, so is it powerful to answer all temptations of Satan, all seducements of the world, all terrors of conscience from the wrath of God and the curse of the law; it setteth the soul as upon a rock above all.

Sixthly, These articles are a touchstone at hand to try all opinions by, for crooked things are discerned by bringing them to the rule. What directly, or by immediate and mere consequence, opposeth these, is to be rejected as contrary to the platform of wholesome doctrine. That one monster of opinions, of the bread into the body of Christ by transubstantiation, overthrows at once four articles of the Creed—the incarnation of Christ, ascension, sitting at the right hand of God, and coming to judgment; for if Christ's body be so often made of a piece of bread, being in so many places at once here upon earth, how can all these articles be true?

Again, seventhly, These grounds of faith have likewise a special influence in direction and encouragement unto all Christian duties. A holy life is but the infusion of holy truths. Augustine saith well, *Non bene vivitur, ubi bene de Deo non creditur:* men of an ill belief, cannot be of a good life; whereupon the apostles' method is, to build their exhortations to Christian duties upon the grounds of Christian faith. But we must remember, that as faith yields a good life and conscience, so a conscience is the vessel to preserve the doctrine of faith, else a shipwreck of faith will follow. If there be a delighting in unrighteousness, there will not be a love of the truth; and if we love not the truth, then there will be a preparedness to believe any lie, and that by God's just judgment, 2 Thes. ii. 12.

Eighthly. As these fundamental truths yield strength to the whole frame of a Christian life, so they are so many springs and wells of consolation for God's people to draw from; whereupon that good Prince George Anhalt (who in Luther's time became a preacher of the gospel), intending to comfort his brother Prince John, raiseth his comfort from the last three articles —remission of sins, resurrection of the body, and life everlasting; which, as they have their strength from the former articles, are able to raise any drooping spirit, and therefore in the greatest agonies it is the readiest way to suck comfort from these benefits. But I omit other things, intending only to say something by way of preface. And thus, good reader, I commend this work unto thee, and both it and thee to God's blessing.

Thine in the Lord, R. SIBBES.

II. Ball on 'Faith.'

The Preface to the Reader.

Glorious things are spoken of the grace of graces (faith) in the Scriptures, God setting himself to honour that grace that yields up all the honour unto him in Christ: who indeed is the life of our life, and the soul of our soul. Faith only as the bond of union bringeth Christ and the soul together, and is as an artery that conveys the spirit from him as the heart, and as the sinews which convey the spirit to move all duty from him as head, whence St Paul maketh Christ's living in us, and our living by faith all one, Gal. ii. 20. Now that which giveth boldness and liberty to faith, is not only God's assignment of this office to it in the covenant of grace to come unto Christ, and unto him in Christ, to receive grace, but likewise the gracious promises whereby the great God hath engaged himself as a debtor to his poor creature, for all things needful to life and godliness, until that blessed time when we shall be put into a full possession of all things we have now only in promise, when faith shall end in fruition, and promises in performances.

Faith first looks to this word of promise, and in the promise to Christ, in whom and for whom they are yea and amen, both made and performed. And in Christ it eyeth God in whom it last resteth, as its proper centre and foundation; otherwise how should we weak sinful creatures dare to have any intercourse with God that dwelleth in that light that none can attain unto, if he had not come forth and discovered his good pleasure in Christ the substantial Word, and in the word inspired by the Holy Ghost for the good of those whom God meant for to make heirs of salvation? Now these promises whereon all our present comfort and future hope dependeth lie hid in the Scriptures, as veins of gold and silver in the bowels of the earth, and had need be laid open, that God's people may know what upon good grounds to lay claim unto. Those, therefore, that search these mines to bring to light these treasures, deserve well of God's church. We commend (and not without cause) the witty industry of those that from springs remote bring rivers to cities, and by pipes from these rivers derive water to every man's house for all domestical services; much more should we esteem of the religious pains of men that brings these waters of life home for every man's particular use, in all the passages and turnings of this life.

In which regard, I do not doubt, but the pains of this godly, painful, and learned man will find good entertainment of all children of the promises that hope to inherit them, who hath with great pains, and with good evidence of spiritual understanding, endeavoured to clear most matters concerning faith, and likewise discovered the variety and use of the promises, with teaching Christians how to improve their riches in Christ here spread before them, how to use the shield of faith and the sword of the Spirit upon all occasions, that so they might not only be believing but skilful Christians, knowing how to manage and make the best advantage of their faith and the word of faith. Which if they could do, there would another manner of power and beauty shine in their lives than doth. He is a man that hath formerly deserved well of the church, but in more special manner fitted for a treatise of this nature, as having been put to it to know by experience what it is to live by faith, having in sight for matters of this life very little whereupon to depend. Those that are driven to exercise their faith cannot but find God faithful, as never failing those that trust in him, they see more of God than others do.

If it be objected that others of late time have digged in the same mine and laboured in the same field, and to good purpose and success, I answer, it is true, the more this age is bound to God that directs the spirits of men to so useful, so necessary, an argument, seeing without faith we have no communion with the fountain of life, nothing in this world that can yield settled comfort to ground the soul upon, seeing without it the fairest carriage is but empty and dead morality, neither finding acceptance with God nor yielding comfort to us in our greatest extremities, and by it God himself and Christ, with all that he hath done, suffered, conquered, becometh ours and for our use. Besides, none that I know have written in our language so largely of this argument; and such is the extent and spiritualness of this heavenly point, that many men and of the greatest graces and parts, may with great benefit to the church dive and dig still into this mystery. Neither let any except against the multitude of quotations of Scriptures; they are brought under their proper head, and set in their proper place, and the matter itself is cut out into variety of parts. Store (as we used to speak) is no sore, we count it a delight to take out of a full heap; the more light the conviction is the stronger; what suits not at one time will suit our spirits and occasions at another, and what taketh not with one may take with another. But the full and well handling of matters in this treatise carries such satisfaction with it, that it frees me from necessity of further discourse, and mine own present weakness of body taketh me off. Only I was willing to yield that testimony to the fruitful pains of a faithful labourer in God's vineyard, and I judge it deserved. Receive it, therefore, Christian reader, with thanks to God that stirreth up such helpers of that faith by which we live, stand, conquer, and in which we must die, if we look to receive the end of our faith, the salvation of our souls.

RICHARD SIBBES.

The last epistle known to me is prefixed to a very striking and suggestive book, to wit, Richard Capel's 'Treatise of Temptations.'* Nearly related to the noble family of Capel, he was yet a staunch Puritan and 'Nonconformist:' his son Daniel having also been one of the 'ejected' of 1662. He was very much esteemed by Sibbes, who left to him a memorial 'ring' in his will.† The book itself is well fitted to comfort the despondent, and may be placed beside Brook's 'Precious Remedies for Satan's Devices,' which it somewhat resembles, though wanting in the wonderful learning and ingenuity of illustration of that most learned and vivid of the later Puritans. The 'epistle' follows :—

To the Christian Reader.

After the angels left their own standing, they envied ours, and out of envy became both by office and practice tempters, that they might draw man from that happy communion with God, unto that cursed condition with themselves. And success in this trade hath made them both skilful and diligent, especially now, their time being but short. And if neither the first or second Adam could be free from their impudent assaults, who then may look for exemption? The best must most of all look to be set upon as having most of Christ in them, whom Satan hates most, and as hoping and disheartening of them, to foil others, as great trees fall not alone; no age or rank of Christians can be free. Beginners he labours to discourage; those that have made some progress, he raiseth storms against; those that more perfect he labours to undermine by spiritual pride; and above all other times, he is most busy when we are weakest, then he doubles and multiplies his forces, when he looks either to have all, or lose all. His course is either to tempt to sin or for sin. To sin, by presenting some seeming good to draw us from the true good, to seek some excellency besides God in the creature, and to this end he labours in the first place to shake our faith in the word; thus he dealt with Adam, and thus he dealeth with all his posterity. And besides immediate suggestions, he cometh unto us, by our dearest friends, as unto Christ by Peter; so many tempters, so many devils in that ill office, though neither they or we are oft aware of it; the

---

* Tentations: their nature, danger, cure. By Richard Capel, sometime Fellow of Magdalen College in Oxford. The sixth edition. The fourth part left enlarged by the author, and now there is added his remains to the work of Tentations. To which thou hast prefixed an abridgment of the author's life, by Valentine Marshall, of Elmore, in Gloucestershire. 1 Cor. x. 13, There hath no tentation taken you, but such as is common to man: but God is faithful, who will not suffer you to be tempted above that you are able; but will with the tentation also make a way to escape, that ye may be able to bear it. London: Printed by Tho. Ratcliffe, for John Bartlet, long since living in the Goldsmith's Row in Cheapside, at the Gilt Cup; since at St Austine's Gate; now in the New buildings on the south side of Paul's near St Austine's Gate, at the sign of the Gilt Cup, and at the Gilt Cup in Westminster Hall, over against the Upper Bench. 1659.

† Consult Brook, *supra*, iii. 259 *seq.*

nearest friend of all our own flesh, is the most dangerous traitor, and therefore most dangerous because most near, more near to us than the devil himself, with which, if he had no intelligence, all his plots would come to nothing; this holding correspondence with him, layeth us open to all danger; it is this inward bosom enemy that doth us most mischief. When Phocas (like another Zimry) had killed his master, Mauricius the emperor, he laboured like Cain, to secure himself with building high walls, after which he heard a voice telling him, that though he built his walls never so high, yet sin within the walls would undermine all. It is true of every particular man, that if there were no tempter without, he would be a tempter to himself; it is this lust within us that hath brought us an ill report upon the creature. This is that which makes blessings to be snares unto us; all the corruption which is in the world is by lust, which lieth in our bosom, 2 Pet. i. 4, and as Ahithophel, or Judas, by familiarity betrayeth us, yea, oftentimes in our best affections, and actions, nature will mingle without* zeal, and privy pride will creep in, and taint our best performances with some corrupt aim. Hence it is, that our life is a continual combat. A Christian, so soon as new born, is born a soldier, and so continueth until his crown be put upon him; in the mean time our comfort is, that ere long, we shall be out of the reach of all tentation; 'the God of peace will tread down Satan under our feet,' Rom. xvi. 20. A carnal man's life is nothing but a strengthening and feeding of his enemy, a fighting for that which fighteth against his soul. Since Satan hath cast this seed of the serpent into our souls, there is no sin so prodigious, but some seed of it lurketh in our nature; it should humble us to hear what sins are forbidden by Moses, which if the Holy Ghost had not mentioned, we might have been ashamed to hear of, they are so dishonourable to our nature; the very hearing of the monstrous outrages committed by men, given up of God, as it yields matter of thanks to God for preservation of us, so of humility, to see our common nature so abused, and so abased by sin and Satan. Nay, so catching is our nature of sin, that the mention of it, instead of stirring hatred of it, often kindles fancy to a liking of it; the discovery of devilish policies and stratagems of wit, though in some respects to good purpose, yet hath no better effect in some, than to fashion their wits to the like false practices; and the innocency of many ariseth not from the love of that which is good, but from not knowing of that which is evil.

And in nothing the sinfulness of sin appears more than in this, that it hindereth all it can, the knowledge of itself, and if it once be known, it studieth extenuation, and translation upon others; sin and shifting came into the world together; in St James his time, it seems that there were some that were not afraid to father their temptations to sin, upon him that hateth it most (God himself), whereas God is only said to try, not to tempt. Our adversaries are not far from imputing this to God, who maintain concupiscence, the mother of all abominations, to be a condition of nature as first created, only kept in by the bridle of original righteousness, that from hence, they might the better maintain those proud opinions of perfect fulfilling the law, and meriting thereby. This moved St James to set down the true descent and pedigree of sin; we ourselves are both the tempters and the tempted; as tempted we might deserve some pity, if as tempters we deserve not blame. In us there is both fire and matter for fire to take hold on. Satan needs but to blow, and oftentimes not that neither; for many, if concupiscence stir not up them, they will stir up concupiscence. So long

* Qu. 'with our?'—Ed.

as the soul keeps close to God and his truth, it is safe; so long as our way lieth above, we are free from the snares below. All the danger first riseth from letting our hearts loose from God by infidelity, for then presently our heart is drawn away by some seeming good, whereby we seek a severed excellency and contentment out of God, in whom it is only to be had. After we have once forsaken God, God forsakes us, leaving us in some degree to ourselves, the worst guides that can be; and thereupon, Satan joins forces with us, setting upon us as a friend, under our own colours; he cannot but miscarry that hath a pirate for his guide. This God suffereth to make us better known to ourselves; for by this means, corruption that lay hid before, is drawn out, and the deceitfulness of sin the better known, and so we are put upon the daily practice of repentance and mortification, and driven to fly under the wings of Jesus Christ. Were it not for temptations, we should be concealed from ourselves; our graces as unexercised, would not be so bright, the power of God should not appear; so in our weakness, we would not be so pitiful and tender towards others, nor so jealous over our own hearts, nor so skilful of Satan's method and enterprises, we should not see such a necessity of standing always upon our guard; but though, by the overruling power of God, they have this good issue, yet that which is ill of itself, is not to be ventured on, for the good that cometh by accident. The chief thing wherein one Christian differs from another is watchfulness, which though it require most labour, yet it bringeth most safety; and the best is no farther safe, than watchful, and not only against sins, but tentations, which are the seeds of sin, and occasions which let in tentations. The best, by rash adventures upon occasion, have been led into temptations, and by temptation into the sin itself; whence sin and temptation come both under the same name, to shew us that we can be no further secure from sin, than we be careful to shun temptations. And in this every one should labour so well to understand themselves, as to know what they find a temptation to them. That may be a temptation to one which is not to another; Abraham might look upon the smoke of Sodom, though Lot might not; because that sight would work more upon Lot's heart than Abraham's. In these cases a wise Christian better knows what to do with himself than any can prescribe him. And because God hath our hearts in his hand, and can either suspend or give way to temptations, it should move us especially to take heed of those sins, whereby, grieving the good Spirit of God, we give him cause to leave us to our own spirits; but that he may rather stir up contrary gracious lustings in us, as a contrary principle. There is nothing of greater force to make us out of godly jealousy 'to fear always.' Thus daily 'working out our salvation,' that God may delight to go along with us, and be our shield, and not to leave us naked in the hands of Satan, but second his first grace with a further degree, as temptations shall increase. It is he that either removeth occasions, or shutteth our hearts against them, and giveth strength to prevail over them; which gracious promise you cannot be too thankful for. It is a great mercy when temptations are not above the supply of strength against them. This care only taketh up the heart of those who, having the life of Christ begun in them, and his nature stamped upon them, have felt how sweet communion and acquaintance with God in Christ, and how comfortable the daily walking with God, is; these are weary of anything that may draw away their hearts from God, and hinder their peace. And therefore they hate temptations to sin as sin itself, and sin as hell itself, and hell most of all, as being a state of eternal separation from all comfortable fellowship with God. A man that is a stranger from the life of God, cannot resist temptation to sin, as it is a sin, because he never knew the beauty of holiness; but from the beauty of a civil life, he may resist temptations to such times * as may weaken respect, and from love of his own quiet, may abstain from those sins that will affright conscience. And the cause why civil men fear the less disturbance from temptations is, because they are wholly under the power of temptation, till God awaken their heart. What danger they see not, they feel not, the strong man holds his possession in them, and is too wise, by rousing them out of their sleep to give them occasion of thoughts of escape. None more under the danger of temptation, than they that discern it not; they are Satan's stales, 'taken by him at his pleasure,' whom Satan useth to draw others into the same snare. Therefore Satan troubleth not them, nor himself about them; but the true Christian fears a temptation in everything. His chief care is, that in what condition soever he be, it prove not a temptation to him. Afflictions, indeed, are more ordinarily called temptations, than prosperity, because Satan by them breedeth an impression of sorrow and fear, which affections have an especial working upon us in the course of our lives, making us often to forsake God, and desert his cause. Yet snares are laid in everything we deal with, which none can avoid but those that see them. None see, but those whose eyes God opens; and God useth the ministry of his servants for this end, to open the eyes of men, to discover the net, and then, as the wise man saith, ' In vain is the net spread before the sight of any bird.' *Domine, quis evadet laqueos istos multos nisi videat istos? Et quis videbit istos, nisi quem illuminaveris lumine tuo? ipse enim pater tenebrarum laqueos suos abscondit.* Soliloq. cap. 16. Which goeth under Augustine's name. Tom. 9

This moved this godly minister, my Christian friend, to take pains in this useful argument, as appeareth in this treatise, which is written by him in a clear, quick, and familiar style; and for the matter and manner of handling, solid, judicious, and scholar-like; and which may commend it the more, it is written by one that, besides faithfulness and fruitfulness in his ministry, hath been a good proficient in the school of temptation himself, and therefore the fitter, as a skilful watchman, to give warning and aim to others; for there be spiritual exercises of ministers more for others than for themselves. If by this he shall attain, in some measure, what he intended, God shall have the glory, thou the benefit, and he the encouragement to make public some other labours.—Farewell in the Lord,

RICHARD SIBBES.

These 'epistles' and 'prefaces' shew the cordial relations sustained by Sibbes towards his fellow-divines and contemporaries; and down to a late period, the booksellers found it a profitable advertisement to say of a book, 'Recommended by Dr Sibbes.' †

---

* Qu. 'sins?'—ED.

† 'Recommended by Dr Sibbes.' The various books of Preston are usually thus advertised; and those of Burroughs, Hooker, and Cotton as 'approved by Dr Sibbes.'

CHAPTER X.

SIBBES VICAR OF TRINITY, CAMBRIDGE—PEACE-MAKER.

Presentation to Vicarage of Trinity by the King—Another relaxation of 'order' of Gray's Inn—Lord Keeper Williams—'Tender Conscience'—'Consolatory Letter' —Thomas Goodwin—' Summer visits'—Earls of Manchester and Warwick— Truro and Say and Seal—Brooks and Veres—Thurston—'Mother and brethren.'

From the manner in which Sibbes escaped the practical effects of the 'High Commission' and 'Star-Chamber' decisions, in striking contrast with Davenport and Hooker, and others of the fugitives to Holland and New England, and from the fearless way in which he continued to preach the same sentiments, it is evident that he must have personally commanded the weightiest regard, and secured influence that could not be disregarded. In 1627, he passed D.D. In 1633 (shortly after the overthrow of the 'Feoffees' scheme, which makes it the more memorable), he was presented by the king, Charles I., on its resignation by Thomas Goodwin, who scarcely held it a year,* to 'the vicarage of the holy and undivided Trinity, in the town of Cambridge.' We have the fact in the 'Fœdera:—

'Ricardus Sibbes, clericus, in Sacra Theologia Professor, habet consimiles Literas Patentes de presentatione ad Vicariam sanctæ et individuæ Trinitatis in Villa Cantabrigiæ, Diocesis Eliensis, per resignationem ultimi Incumbentis ibidem jam vacantem, et ad nostram presentationem pleno jure spectantem; et deriguntur hæ Literæ Reverendo in Christo Patri Domino Francisco Eliensi Episcopo. Teste Rege apud Westmonasterium, vicesimo primo die Novembris 1633.' †

This 'presentation' speaks much for Sibbes; for at this date Laud was filling every place with men of his own kind. We have not the means of determining by what influence this appointment was obtained. One tells us Goodwin resigned 'in favour of Sibbes,' but that could scarcely be, inasmuch as he at the same time resigned all his offices and honours in the University. Besides, the difficulty is only removed back a stage; how did it come about that a Puritan resigned and another stepped into his place? It may be that it was a tacit recompence for the former injustice of 'outing' him from his lectureship of Trinity and his fellowship; but it is more probable that on the 'Feoffees'' decision, the powerful friends of the preacher at Gray's Inn interfered in such a way as to let the primate understand that they, at any rate, were not to be trifled with; and that then he secured, or at least did not hinder, this 'presentation.'

But there is the further difficulty of the 'order' of Gray's Inn, that their preacher was not only to be continually resident, but

* Rymer's Fœdera, xix., 440, No. 81, ed. 1732.   † *Ibid.*, xix., 536.

likewise to have no other ecclesiastical preferment. As Sibbes actually accepted and acted as vicar, the 'order' must once more have been relaxed in his favour. Indeed, I suspect that 'order' was originally passed for a personal object and from a personal reason. The immediate predecessor of Sibbes was a Mr Fenton,—in all likelihood, though no Christian name appears in the 'Order-Books' of Gray's Inn, the same with Roger Fenton, D.D., who was a great pluralist, and who died 16th January 1615-16. He held the prebend, rectory, and vicarage of St Pancras, and the rectory of St Stephen's, Walbrook, and also the vicarage of Chigwell, Essex, till his death. Probably he neglected his duties as preacher at Gray's Inn. Hence the check put upon his successor.* For one so faithful in the discharge of his office, and who was regarded by all as a personal friend, there would be no great difficulty in making arrangements, in order to his accepting the 'presentation,' and still continuing the honoured preacher of Gray's Inn.

It is greatly to be lamented that the most diligent and persistent research has failed to add any memorials to the fact of his entrance on the vicarage of Trinity. Though he must have been non-resident, he would have many opportunities to officiate during 'vacation' time at the Inn.

This is the last public honour recorded as having been conferred upon Sibbes. What remains to be told partakes of the privacy of his daily life.

One little fact, half-casually recorded in that extraordinary folio, 'Scrinia Reserata: a Memorial offer'd to the great deservings of John Williams, D.D., who some time held the place of Lord Keeper of the Great Seal of England, &c., &c., &c., by John Hacket, late Lord Bishop of Litchfield and Coventry,' 1693—a book *sui generis*, and than which none gives profounder insight into the 'form and pressure of the age,'—brings out a very beautiful side of Sibbes's character, and dates to us, if I err not, one of the most interesting, biographically, of his minor writings. Vindicating Williams—a vindication which, the more successful it is, the more it damages the strangely contradictory character of the Lord Keeper—from the rumour of favouring Puritans, Hacket thus introduces Sibbes :—

'Another rank for whose sake the Lord Keeper suffer'd, were scarce an handful, not above three or four in all the wide Bishoprick of Lincoln, who did not oppose, but by an ill education seldom used the appointed ceremonies. Of whom when he was certified by his commissaries and officials.

---

* 'Check put upon his successor.' For these facts and the inference from them I owe thanks to Dr Hessey he sent for them, and confer'd with them with much meekness, sometimes remitted them to argue with his chaplain. If all this stirred them not, *he commended them to his old collegiate Dr Sibbes*, or Dr Gouch (Gouge), *who knew the scruples of these men's hearts*, and how to bring them about, the best of any about the city of London.'*

There is such a fascination, spite of all his errors, or it may be crimes, about the hot-blooded Welshman, so stormy and impulsive, so wise and yet so foolish, that one is glad to find, that even when he was 'Lord Keeper,' and surrounded by very different men, he forgot neither him who was once his humble fellow-student of St John's, nor the staunch puritan of ' Blackfryers,' William Gouge, also a contemporary at Cambridge, but—

'They had been friends, when friendship is
A passion and a blessedness;
And in a tender sacrament
Unto the house of God they went,
And plighted love,—caressing
The same dear cup of blessing.

'They had been friends in youth, most dear;
In studious night, and mirthful cheer,
And high discourse, and large debate,
Unmixed by bitterness or hate—
Their fellowship, I ween,
A pleasant thing had been.'

It is specially pleasing to know what was the occasion of again associating the students of earlier years—to wit, tender dealing with tender consciences. I like to place that over against his after humiliating repudiation of all Puritans, extorted from him while under the shadow of a charge of treason, and in a letter to LAUD.† He was truthful in his favour; untruthful in his disfavour. The fact also dates, as I have intimated, one of the minor writings of Sibbes, which illustrates how he would discharge the office assigned to him. It is entitled:—

A CONSOLATORY LETTER To an afflicted Conscience: full of pious admonitions and Divine Instructions. Written by that famous Divine, Doctor SIBBS: and now published for the common good and edification of the Church. Ecclesiastes vi. 18, *Be not thou just overmuch, neither make thy selfe overwise; wherefore shouldest thou be desolate.*

[Woodcut portrait. Ætat: Suæ 58.] London, Printed for *Francis Coules.* 1641.‡

---

* i. 95. 'Scrinia' seems to have been a favourite title. The historical student will recall also ' Scrinia Ceciliana.'

† Works of Laud. vi. pp. 312–314. Sept. 9. 1633.

‡ For a copy of this excessively rare 'Letter,' published in a thin 4to, pp. 6, I am indebted to the kindness of Joshua Wilson, Esq., Nevill Park, Tunbridge Wells, who has devoted much time to good purpose in investigating the history, and biography, and bibliography of Puritanism. His 'Historical Inquiry concerning the Principles, &c., of English Presbyterians ' (1835) has not gathered all its renown yet.

I introduce this 'Letter' here, retaining its orthography :—
Deare Sir,

I understand by your Letter, that you have many and great tryals; some externall and bodily, some internall and spirituall: as the deprivall of inward comfort, the buffetings (and that in more then ordinary manner), of your soule, with Satans temptations: and (which makes all those inward and outward, the more heavy and insupportable) that you have wanted Christian society with the Saints of God, to whom you might make knowne your griefes, and by whom you might receive comfort from the Lord, and incouragement in your Christian course.

Now that which I earnestly desire in your behalfe, and hope likewise you doe in your owne, is that you may draw nearer to God, and be more conformable to his command by these afflictions; for if our afflictions be not sanctified, that is, if we make not an holy use of them by purging out the old leaven of our ingenerate corruptions, they are but judgments to us, and makes way for greater plagues: Ioh v. 14. And therefore the chiefe end and ayme of God in all the afflictions which he sends to his children in love, is, that they may be partakers of his holinesse, and so their afflictions may conduce to their spirituall advantage and profit, Heb. xii. 10. The Lord aymes not at himselfe in any calamities he layes on us, (for God is so infinitely all-sufficient, that we can adde nothing to him by all our doings or sufferings) but his maine ayme is at our Melioration and Sanctification in and by them. And therefore our duty in every affliction and pressure, is thus to think with our selves: How shall we carry and behave our selves under this crosse, that our soules may reap profit by it? This (in one word) is done by our returning and drawing nearer to the Lord, as his holy Apostle exhorts us, Iames iv. 8. This in all calamities the Lord hath a speciall eye unto, and is exceeding wroth if he finde it not.

The Prophet declares *That his anger was not turned from Israel, because they turned not to him that smote them,* Isa. i. 4, 5. Now it is impossible that a man should draw nigh to God, and turne to him, if he turne not from his evill wayes: for in every conversion there is *Terminus à quo*, something to be turned from, as well as *Terminus ad quod*, something to be turned to.

Now, that we must turn to, is God; and that we must turne from, is sinne; as being diametrally opposite to God, and that which separates betweene God and us.

To this purpose we must search and try our hearts and wayes, and see what sinnes there be that keepe us from God, and separate us from his gracious favour: and chiefly we must weed out our speciall bosom-sins. This the ancient Church of God counsels each other to doe in the time of their anguish and affliction, Lam. iii. 39, 40, *Let us search and try our wayes, and turne againe to the Lord*: for though sinne make not a finall divorce betwixt God and his chosen people, yet it may make a dangerous rupture by taking away sense of comfort, and suspending the sweet influence of his favour, and the effectuall operation of his grace.

And therefore (deare Sir) my earnest suit and desire is, that you would diligently peruse the booke of your conscience, enter into a thorow search and examination of your heart and life; and every day before you goe to bed, take a time of recollection and meditation, (as holy *Isuac* did in his private walkes, Gen. xxiv. 63), holding a privy Session in your soule, and indicting your selfe for all the sins, in thought, word, or act committed, & all the good duties you have omitted. This self-examination, if it be so strict and rigid as it ought to be, will soone shew you the sins whereto you are most inclinable (the chiefe cause of all your sorrowes), and consequently, it will (by God's assistance) effectually instruct you to fly from those venomous and fiery serpents, which have so stung you.

And though you have (as you say) committed many grievous sinnes, as abusing God's gracious ordinances, and neglecting the golden opportunities of grace: the originall, as you conceive of all your troubles; yet I must tell you, there is another *Coloquintida* in the pot, another grand enormity (though you perceive it not) and that is your separation from Gods Saints and Servants in the Acts of his publike Service and worship. This you may clearly discern by the affliction it selfe, for God is methodicall in his corrections, and doth (many times) so suite the crosse to the sinne, that you may reade the sin in the crosse. You confesse that your maine affliction, and that which made the other more bitter, is, that God tooke away those to whom you might make your complaint; and from whom you might receive comfort in your distresse. And is not this just with God, that when you wilfully separate your selfe from others, he should separate others from you? Certainly, when we undervalue mercy, especially so great a one as the communion of Saints is, commonly the Lord takes it away from us, till we learne to prize it to the full value. Consider well therefore the haynousnesse of this sin, which that you may the better conceive, First, consider it is against Gods expresse Precept, charging us not to forsake the assemblies of the Saints, Heb. x. 20, 25. Again, it is against our own greatest good and spirituall solace, for by discommunicating & excommunicating our selves from that blessed society, we deprive our selves of the benefit of their holy conference, their godly instructions, their divine consolations, brotherly admonitions, and charitable reprehensions; and what an inestimable losse is this? Neither can we partake such profit by their prayers as otherwise we might: for as the soule in the naturall body conveyes life and strength to every member, as they are compacted and joyned together, and not as dis-severed; so Christ conveyes spirituall life and vigour to Christians, not as they are disjoyned from, but as they are united to the mysticall body, the Church.

But you will say *England* is not a true Church, and therefore you separate; adhere to the true Church.

I answer, our Church is easily proved to be a true Church of Christ: First, because it hath all the essentialls, necessary to the constitution of a true Church; as sound preaching of the Gospell, right dispensation of the Sacraments, Prayer religiously performed, and evill persons justly punisht (though not in that measure as some criminals and malefactors deserve:) and therefore a true Church.

2. Because it hath begot many spirituall children to the Lord, which for soundnesse of judgement, and holinesse of life, are not inferiour to any in other Reformed Churches. Yea, many of the Separation, if ever they were converted, it was here with us: (which a false and adulterous Church communicated.)

But I heare you reply, our Church is corrupted with Ceremonies, and pestered with prophane persons. What then? must we therefore separate for Ceremonies, which many think may be lawfully used. But admit they be evils, must we make a rent in the Church for Ceremonious Rites, for circumstantiall evils? That were a remedy worse than the disease. Besides, had not all the true Churches of Christ their blemishes and deformities, as you may see in seaven *Asian* Churches? Rev. ii. and iii. And though you may finde some Churches beyond Sea free from Ceremonies, yet notwithstanding they are more corrupt in Preachers, (which is the maine) as in prophanation of the Lord's day, &c.

As for wicked and prophane Persons amongst us, though we are to labour by all good meanes to purge them out, yet are we not to separate because of this residence with us: for, there will bee a miscellany and mixture in the visible Church, as long as the world endures, as our Saviour shewes by many parables: Matth. xiii. If therefore we should be so overjust as to abandon all Churches for the intermixture of wicked Persons, we must saile to the Antipodes, or rather goe out of the world, as the Apostle speaks: it is agreed by all that *Noahs* Arke was a type and embleme of the Church. Now as it had been no lesse then selfe-murder for *Noah*, *Sem*, or *Iaphet*, to have leapt out of the Arke, because of that ungracious *Cains** company; so it is no better then soule-murder for a man to cast himself out of the Church, either for reall or imaginall corruptions. To conclude, as the Angell injoyned *Hagar* to returne, and submit to her Mistris *Sarah*, so let me admonish you to returne your selfe from these extravagant courses, and submissively to render your self to the sacred communion of this truly Evangelicall Church of *England*.

I beseech you therefore, as you respect Gods glory and your owne eternall salvation, as *There is but one body and one spirit, one Lord, one Baptisme, one God and Father of all, who is above all, and through all, and in us all; so endeavour to keep the unity of the spirit in the bond of peace*, Eph. iv., as the Apostle sweetly invites you. So shall the peace of God ever establish you, and the God of peace ever preserve you; which is the prayer of

Your remembrancer at the Throne of Grace   R. Sibs.

The preceding 'Letter,' the more valuable because of the paucity of such memorials of Sibbes, was in all likelihood addressed to Thomas Goodwin, D.D., who has been designated the Atlas and patriarch of Independency. Francis White, Bishop of Ely, within whose jurisdiction the Church of Trinity, Cambridge, lay, being one of the ultra-zealous adherents of Laud, had put every obstacle possible in the way of Goodwin's acceptance, and subsequently of his installation; but he was ultimately installed as vicar, having passed from the curacy of St Andrew's, Cambridge, thereto. On the succession of Laud to the primacy, his special charge to his bishops was to watch over the lecturers, and 'watch over' had a terrible significance. White harassed all within his diocese who sought to preach evangelically. He renewed his attacks upon Goodwin. The result was, that, dissatisfied with the restrictions imposed upon preaching that truth which, from the time of Sibbes's barbed words to him, he had found to be the very life of his own soul, he resigned at once his vicarage, lectureship of Trinity, and fellowship of Catharine Hall, and removed, as it would appear, to London, where he began to propagate his new views and conclusions in regard to church government. He shrank not from the name, then of evil omen, of 'Separatist.' † The

* Qu. 'Cham's?'—Ed.
† Consult Dr Halley's Memoir of Goodwin in this series, II, xxiii–iv.

whole circumstances of the case, their previous friendship, their mutual sentiments, warrant, I apprehend, the supposition that this grave, loving, skilful, and admirable letter was addressed to Thomas Goodwin. If so, it was unsuccessful in winning him back to 'the church.' Methinks Sibbes would have acted more faithfully as well as more consistently, had he followed the example of his friends, Goodwin, John Cotton, John Davenport, Thomas Hooker, Samuel Stone, and their compeers. The spirit that pervades his letter is worthier than his arguments. It seems difficult to see how Goodwin could have remained within the pale of the church, gagged and hindered as he was in what was to him momentous beyond all earthly estimate;. and it was equally impossible to give 'assent and consent' to what those in authority pronounced to be the 'beauty of holiness,' and teaching of the Book of Common Prayer. Sibbes allowed of neither. By the powerful influence of his many friends, while certainly, as we have seen, summoned before Star Chamber and High Commission, he held on in his way of preaching the same gospel everywhere. That explains his remaining within the church. Who doubts for a moment, that, if his mouth had been shut, as was Goodwin's, on the 'one thing,' Sibbes would have placed himself beside his friend? Perhaps there would have been more of lingering effort to get above the difficulties, more pain in sundering of the ties that bound him to the church, more sway given to heart than head. Still the final decision, beyond all debate, would have been that of the 'two thousand' of 1662. The more shame to those who compelled such loyal lovers of 'the church' to leave her. This letter gives us insight into Sibbes's method of procedure in dealing with the scruples of the conscientious. It is to be regretted that we have no more of such letters, and none of his conversations with them. But we have the fact, upon various authority, that he was at all times ready to speak a word in season, and on principle, contrived to *sanctify* all his intercourse with his fellow-men, as well more privately as publicly. He had many opportunities of influencing for good some of the finest minds of the age; and he availed himself of such opportunities. He was wont, Samuel Clarke informs us, 'in the summer time, to go abroad to the houses of some worthy personages, *where he was an instrument of much good*, not only by his private labours, but by his prudent counsel and advice, that upon every occasion he was ready to minister unto them.'* Charles Stanford has well limned to us such visits in Alleine's day. If you wish, he says, 'to see what Puritan life was like in "the high places," go with Mr Alleine and

* Clarke, *ante*, p. 145.

his brother Norman, to spend an evening with Admiral Blake at his country house at Knowle.'* Instead of Alleine let us go with Sibbes, and instead of Admiral Blake at Knowle, let the visit be to John Pym, or to Lady Mary Vere, or to Sir Robert and Lady Brooke, or any of those great and true families, whose heads

'. . . . . bore, without abuse,
The grand old name of gentleman,'

and 'feared God,' and were 'lovers of all good men.' Suppose Colonel Hutchinson and the Puritan Admiral to be also guests. There would be the simple meal,—the Bible would be brought in, —there would be prayer,—there would be conversation such as Christians love, and which they can only have when in 'their own company,'—there would probably be discourse, in logical forms, on some of the mysteries of Christian truth,—of course, there would be reasonings over some 'case of conscience.' Dr Gouge would be apt to get prosy, in discussing the opinions of Fragosa, Talet, Sayrus, and Roderiques, or of Doctors Ursinus or Lobetius; Master Davenport would interpose a 'why' or 'how;' and Richard Sibbes would close with some sweet words from John or the Lord himself, modestly confirming his own elucidations of them from Bernard, or with a quaint saying from Luther, or a wise apophthegm from Augustine. Then there would be a flow of graceful and varied talk, not only on politics ('Petition of Right,' and so on), but on books, pictures, gardening, or the last scientific experiments of the 'Oxford Society;' and the tall-browed statesman, and the great sailor, 'would affect a droll concern to prove before the ministers, by the aptness and abundance of their Latin quotations, that in becoming 'leader in the House' and admiral, they had not forfeited their claim to be considered good classics.' You could not find better types of the winning, yet stately Christian gentleman, than among such Puritan circles ; and where will you match their 'fair ladyes?' We have confirmation of the 'visits' and of their results in the several 'epistles' and 'dedications' of his posthumous writings. Each of these records personal intercourse and kindnesses, and the tenderest cherishing of his memory. He was a frequent guest with the Earls of Manchester and Warwick, and Ladies Anne and Susanna, their Countesses, Lord Say and Seal, Lord Roberts, Baron Truro, and Lady Lucie his consort, but most of all with the Brooks and Veres, with whom he lived on the most familiar terms. The 'dedications' and 'epistles' will be found in their respective

* Joseph Alleine: his Companions and Times, pp. 131–2; and Hepworth Dixon's Life of Blake, p. 267. I accommodate, rather than quote from Stanford's picturesque and masterly work.

places; but, as it reflects interesting light and mutual honour on both, I must introduce in full the 'epistle dedicatory' of the 'Fountain Sealed,' to 'the truly noble and much honoured lady, the Lady Elizabeth Brooke, wife to Sir Robert Brooke,' and also glean a few biographic sentences from others. The 'epistle' to Lady Brooke, one of the most remarkable women of England, at a period when there were many such, is as follows :—

To the truly noble and much honoured lady, the LADY ELIZABETH BROOKE,
wife to Sir Robert Brooke.

'Madam,—Besides that deserved interest your Ladyship held in the affections and esteem of this worthy man more than any friend alive, which might entitle you to all that may call him author, this small piece of his acknowledgeth a more special propriety unto your Ladyship. For though his tongue was as the pen of a ready writer in the hand of Christ, who guided him, yet your Ladyship's hand and pen was in this his scribe and amanuensis, whilst he dictated a first draught of it in private, with intention for the public. In which labour, both of humility and love, your Ladyship did that honour unto him which Baruch, though great and noble, did but receive in the like transcribing the words of Jeremiah from his mouth, wherein yet your Ladyship did indeed but write the story of your own life, which hath been long exactly framed to the rules herein prescribed. We, therefore, that are intrusted in the publishing of it, deem it but an act of justice in us to return it thus to your Ladyship, unto whom it owes even its first birth, that so, wherever this little treatise shall come, there also this that you have done may be told and recorded for a memorial of you. And we could not but esteem it also an addition of honour to the work, that no less than a lady's hand, so pious and so much honoured, brought it forth into the world, although in itself it deserveth as much as any other this blessed womb did bear. The Lord, in way of recompense, write all the holy contents of it yet more fully and abundantly in your ladyship's heart, and all the lineaments of the image of Jesus Christ, and seal up all unto you by his blessed Spirit, with joy and peace, to the day of redemption.—
Madam, we are your Ladyship's devoted, THOS. GOODWIN.
PHILIP NYE.

It was no uncommon thing for ladies moving in the highest circles thus to 'take down' the sermons of their ministers, or discharge the office of amanuenses. Contemporaneously with Lady Brooke we find Lady Elizabeth Rich, another of Sibbes's friends, transcribing and preparing for the press WILLIAM STRONG's great folio 'Of the Covenants.'* Of Lady Brooke, her biographer Parkhurst states, among many other things of note, that—

'She used a mighty industry to preserve what either instructed her mind or affected her heart in the sermons she had heard. To these she gave great attention in the Assembly, and heard them repeated in her family. And thus she would discourse of them in the evening; and in the following week she had them again repeated, and discoursed the matter of them to some of her family in her chamber. And besides all this, *she wrote the substance of them,* and then digested many of them into questions and

* 1678. Dedication by Theophilus Gale to Lady Elizabeth Rich.

answers, or under heads of common-places, and then they became to her matter for repeated meditation. And by these methods she was always increasing her knowledge, or confirming the things that were known.'*

Addressing Lord Roberts, Baron Truro, and Lady Lucie, John Sedgwick thus commences his 'dedication' of the 'Beams of Divine Light :'—

'RIGHT HONOURABLE AND TRULY NOBLE,—It was not so much the nobility of your blood, as that of grace given unto you from the divine hand, *which did so much interest you in the love and esteem of that worthy servant of Christ*, the author of this work, in whom Urim and Thummim met, whose whole course being a real and vital sermon, sweetly consonant to the tenor of his teaching, made him amiable living and honourable dead, in the opinion of as many as well knew him. This was the thing, I suppose, which wrought unto him from you, *as well as from many others of your noble stock and rank*, more than an ordinary esteem.'†

Again, in like manner he addresses Robert, Earl of Warwick, and Lady Susanna, in 'Light from Heaven :'—

'For me to commend the author, were to make the world to judge him either *a stranger unto you, or a man that had not ingratiated himself with you whilst he lived near unto you.* I well knew that he had an honourable opinion of you both, and of yours. . . . . You that knew and loved him so well shall, in vouchsafing to read over these ensuing sermons, find his spirit in them.'‡

These 'testimonies' might be greatly multiplied, and it is very pleasing to know that one who so carried about with him the 'sweet savour' of Christ was thus welcomed at the Kimboltons, and Cockfields, and Hevinghams, and other of the family seats and castles of the nobility and gentry. It is especially honourable to Sibbes that he received such cordial welcome from the nobles and gentry of his own native county of Suffolk. The Tostock 'wheelwright's' son reversed the too often true saying of a prophet not being without honour 'save in his own country and among his own kin.' The Day will declare the good effected by these summer visits and 'conferences in private, done aptly, pithily, and profitably . . . . much in few words.'§

While thus a visitor among the 'great ones,' he did not forget his birth-place or school-boy haunts, his 'mother, and brethren.' I turn here to the manuscript of the Vicar of Thurston :—

'Anno Domini 1608. I came to be minister of Thurston, and he was then a Fellow of the College, and a preacher of good note in Cambridge, and we soon grew well acquainted. For whensoever he came down into the

---

* Quoted in Wilford's 'Memorials and Characters,' folio, 1741, page 210. Consult pp. 209–213, and Appendix xvii.
† Ep. Ded., 4to, 1639. ‡ Ep. Ded., 4to, 1638.
§ 'Epistle Dedicatory' to 'Evangelical Sacrifices,' 4to, 1640.

country to visit his mother and brethren (his father being deceased) he would never fail to preach with us on the Lord's day, and for the most part twice, telling me that it was a work of charity to help a constant and a painful preacher, for so he was pleased to conceive of me. And if there were a communion appointed at any time he would be sure not to withdraw himself after sermon, but receiving the bread and wine at my hands, he would always assist me in the distribution of the cup to the congregation.'

The church of Thurston, in which Sibbes thus ministered, has only within these two years disappeared. Its great tower fell, and it was found necessary to rebuild the whole. This has been done nearly in fac-simile of the original.* The parsonage of the excellent vicar remains. It has degenerated into a kind of farmer's house, but on a recent visit I found many traces of former elegance and comfort. It is two-storied, with lozenge-paned windows, and heavy sculptured doorway. In front is an avenue of noble chesnuts and beeches, and pollard limes. The 'garden' must have been of considerable extent. Imagination was busy calling up Sibbes and Catlin walking arm-in-arm along the mossed avenue. I stepped across the threshold of the ancient house, sat down by the carved mantel-pieced fireside with reverence. It was something to know that there our worthies had many and many a time exchanged loving words, perhaps smoked a pipe.

Finely does the vicar continue his personal reminiscences of the visits to Thurston, and of his friend's kindnesses. We must again listen to him :—

'As for his kindness to his kindred, and neglect of the world, it was very remarkable. For this I can testify of my own knowledge, that, purchasing of Mr Tho. Clark and others in our town a messuage and lands at several times to the value of fifty pounds per annum, he paid the fines to the lords but never took one penny of the rents or profits of them, *but left the benefit wholly to his mother and his two brethren* as long as he lived. So much did this heavenly-minded man of God' ('heavenly' seems instinctively to drop from every one who writes of him) 'slight this present world (which the most men are so loth to part withal when they die) that he freely and undesired parted with it whilst he lived, requiring nothing of them but only to be liberal to the poor. Nay, over and besides, if any faithful, honest man came down from Cambridge or London, where he lived, by whom he might conveniently send, he seldom or never failed to *send his mother* a

---

* An engraving of the church as it was before its fall is given in one of those privately printed family histories, for which we are indebted to the love of the Americans towards their mother country. 'The Brights of Suffolk, England; represented in America by the descendants of Henry Bright jun., who came to New England in 1630, and settled in Watertown, Massachusetts. By J. B. Bright. For private circulation. Boston. 1 vol. royal 8vo. 1858.' See opposite page 109. This book is of the deepest interest, well arranged, and illustrated lavishly with portraits and other illustrations.'

piece of gold, for the most part a ten shilling piece, but five shillings was the least,* and this he continued as long as his mother lived. And would she have been persuaded to exchange her country life for the city, he often told me that he would willingly have maintained her there in good view and fashion, *like his mother*, but she had no mind to alter her accustomed course of life in her old days, contenting herself with her own means, and that addition which her son made thereunto.'

And still farther the good old man continues, with a love and reverence most affecting, and that only a *true* man could have secured :—

'For his special kindness to myself, in particular, I cannot omit that, being trusted by personages of quality with divers sums of money for pious and charitable uses, he was pleased, among many others, not to forget me. At one time he sent me down three twenty-shilling pieces of gold enclosed in a letter, and at two other times he delivered to me with his own hand two twenty-shilling pieces more; and so far was this humble saint from pharisaical ostentation and vainglory, and from taking the honour of these good works to himself, that he plainly told me that these gratuities were not of his own cost, but being put in trust, and left to his own discretion in the distribution, he looked upon me as one that took great pains in my ministry and in teaching scholars, and at that time labouring under the burden of a great charge of children, and so thought me a fit object of their intended charity. And from myself his love descended down to my son for my sake, for whom (before he had ever seen him, being then at the grammar-school at Bury, he then, chosen Master of Katherine Hall, promised me a scholarship there of five pounds a year, and to provide for him a tutor and a chamber. And such was his constancy of spirit and his reality, that whatsoever promise he made me he would be sure both to remember it and to make it good as freely as he first made it, that was unasked and undesired. And for these manifold kindnesses all that he desired at my hands was no more but this, *that I would be careful of the souls of my people, and, in special, of his mother, his brethren, and his sisters*, and would give them good counsel in their disposing themselves in marriage, or upon any other occasion, as I saw they stood in need. And this one thing I may not pass over concerning myself, that in his last will and testament he gave me a legacy of forty shillings, with the title of " his loving friend," which I the rather mention, because I had not the least thought to have been in that sort remembered by him at his death, living at no less distance from him than of threescore miles. In a word, such was the lowliness of this sweet servant of God, such his learning, parts, piety, prudence, humility, sincerity, love, and meekness of spirit (whereof every one was a loadstone to attract, unite, and fasten my spirit close to his), that I profess ingenuously no man that ever I was acquainted withal got so far into my heart or lay closer there, so that many times I could not part from him with dry eyes. But who am I? or what is it to be beloved of me, *especially for him that had so many and great friends as he had?* Yet even to me the great God is pleased to say, " My son, give me thy heart," and this poor and contrite heart I know he will not despise; and this heart of mine, as small as it is, yet is too great to close with a proud, profane, worldly, malicious heart, though it be in a prince. But true virtue and

---

* This may fairly be considered equal to a pound of our present money.

grace are the image of God himself, and where they are discerned by wisdom's children they command the heart and are truly lovely and venerable, whereas carnal notions and unmortified affections (whereof this man of God was as free as any man I know living), they do render a man, whatever he be, if not hateful and contemptible, yet at least less lovely and honourable. But my love to this good man hath transported me beyond my purpose, which was to speak of some things less visible to others, especially concerning his first education. For when he came to the university and the city, there his life and actions were upon a public theatre, and his own words, without a trumpet, would praise him in the gates. As for his kindness to his kindred and to myself, I know none that took more notice of them than I, and therefore I could not hide them from the world upon this occasion without some kind of sacrilege.'

Thanks, chatty Zachary, for thy golden words! Thou wert a meet companion of Richard Sibbes! Would that we might recover thy '*Hidden Treasure*,'* for, of a truth, it must breathe thy very spirit! All the notices of the author of The Bruised Reed and Soul's Conflict harmonise with the tribute of the vicar of Thurston. Whether it be Clark or Thomas Fuller, Prynne or Eachard, or his numerous 'prefacers,' he is invariably spoken of with the most touching kindliness.

CHAPTER XI.

'THE BEGINNING OF THE END.'

Retrospect—Character—Humility—the English Leighton—his 'Cygnea-Cantio' vel Concio.

We have now reached 'the beginning of the end.' A few months later, and Richard Sibbes lay dying. But at this point, I would observe, that up to the latest he continued faithfully to execute his office as a '*preacher of the word.*' Left alone (for Preston was gone: and Cotton, and Davenport, and Hooker, and many others of his circle, were fugitives in New England), he had ever-increasing demands made upon him, and no 'door of entrance' was opened into which he did not enter, still

'Hoping through the darkest day.'†

He continued to preach at Gray's Inn, in the good old way, the simple gospel that Paul preached, and that of all men JOHN CALVIN, following Augustine, in his estimate, had best interpreted.

---

* The following is the title, from Crowe's Catalogue of our English writers on Old and New Testament, &c., 1668:—'Hidden-Treasure, two sermons on Mat. xiii. 44. 4to. 1633.' Can any reader help to this?

† Poems by Currer, Ellis, and Acton Bell, p. 34, 12mo. 1846.

He resided with enlarged acceptability as Master of Catharine Hall, adding to its Fellows, and Students, and Revenues, and from 1632–3, he was, as already recorded, Vicar of Trinity, Cambridge. One incidental sentence informs us, that he was very fully, if not over, occupied, even before his presentation to the Vicarage of Trinity. It occurs at the close of the address 'To the Christian Reader' prefixed to 'The Bruised Reed :' 'What I shall be drawn to do in this kind,' he says, '*must be by degrees, as leisure in the midst of many interruptions will permit.*'

His was a self-sacrificing, self-consuming life. Quaintly does Mather put it of another. 'There,' he says, ''twas that, like a silk-worm, he spent his own bowels or spirits to procure the " garments of righteousness" for his hearers ; there 'twas . . . he might challenge the device and motto of the famous Dr Sibs, a wasting lamp, with this inscription, " *Prælucendo pereo*," or, " My light is my death." '*

Another casual reference indicates earlier personal sickness. He closes one of his 'Epistles' prefixed to Ball† by saying, 'Mine own weakness of body taketh me off.'

His published writings afford the best evidence of what stamp his preaching was. The most cursory reader is struck with the Paul-like kindling of emotion, the Paul-like burning of utterance, as often as the name of Christ occurs ; and it is most interesting to mark the majestic procession of his words as he walks along some great avenue of thought, leading up to the cross, and from the cross, in farther vista, to the house of many mansions, and to the throne of sculptured light. Very beautifully does Clarke put this :—

His learning was mixed with humility, whereby he always esteemed lowly of himself, and was ready to undervalue his own labours, though others judged them to breathe spirit and life, to be strong of heaven, speaking with authority and power to men's consciences. His care in the course of his ministry was to lay a good foundation in the heads and hearts of his hearers. And though he were a wise master-builder, and that in one of the eminentest auditories for learning and piety that was in the land, as was said before, yet according to the grace which was given to him (which was indeed like that of Elisha in regard of the other prophets, 2 Kings i. 9, the elder brother's privilege, a double portion), *he was still taking all occasions to preach of the* FUNDAMENTALS *to them ;* and amongst the rest, of the incarnation of the Son of God, one of the chief fundamentals of our faith, one of the chief of those wonders in the mercy-seat which the cherubim gaze at, which the angels desire to pry into, 1 Pet. i. 12. And preaching at several times, and by occasion of so many several texts of Scripture concerning this subject, there is scarce any one of those incomparable benefits which accrue to us thereby, nor any of those holy impressions which the meditation hereof ought to make on our hearts, which was not by him

* Life of Urian Oakes. Magnalia Am. as *ante*, b. iv. pp. 186, 187.   † *Ante* p. cvi.

sweetly unfolded, as may appear by those sermons now in print. 'And therefore,' saith a reverend divine, ' the *noted humility of the author* I less wonder at, finding how often his thoughts dwelt upon the humiliation of Christ.'*

The 'reverend divine' referred to was Thomas Fuller, who plays with the conceit in his own wisely-witty way. We cannot pass it by :—

He was most eminent for that grace which is most worth, yet costs the least to keep it, viz., *Christian humility.* Of all points of divinity, he most frequently pressed that of Christ's incarnation ; and if the angels desired to pry into that mystery, no wonder if this angelical man had a longing to look therein. A learned divine imputed this good doctor's great humility to his much meditating on that point of Christ's humiliation when he took our flesh upon him. If it be true what some hold in physic, that *omne par nutrit suum par*, that the vitals of our body are most strengthened by feeding on such meats as are likest unto them, I see no absurdity to maintain that men's souls improve most in those graces whereon they have most constant meditation, whereof this worthy doctor was an eminent instance.†

Aye, quaint and loveable Fuller, and there is a higher authority than 'physic' for it, even 2 Cor. iii. 18, ' We all, with open face beholding as in a glass the glory of the Lord, *are changed into the same image* from glory to glory, even of the Lord, the Spirit.'

Thus growing in holiness and humility, Richard Sibbes passed along his ' pilgrimage.' We have found that he lived in troublous times, and that he did not escape his own share of its trials and persecution. It had argued time-serving or a cold neutrality had it been otherwise. We find him also taking a fitting stand for 'the truth,' and speaking brave and noble words, and flinching not from giving them to the world. At the same time, it must be apparent to all who have followed our memoir thus far, that naturally Sibbes was of a ' meek and quiet spirit,' willing to bear and forbear much. I picture him as an English 'Leighton,' as *he* has been pourtrayed in a little volume of ' poems,' entitled ' The Bishop's Walk.'‡ We have to change very little in the scenery, have but to translate ' Dunblane' to the ' fair garden' lined with elms, of Gray's Inn, or to the acacia-bordered 'Walk' of St Catherine Hall, Cambridge, or, perhaps, to the bosky glades of the Veres, or Brooks, or Manchesters, or Warwicks. I invite my readers to judge :—

* Clarke, *ante* p. 144.
† Fuller's ' Worthies,' *ante* p. 343 of vol. ii.
‡ The Bishop's Walk and the Bishop's Times, By Orwell. Cambridge : Macmillan and Co. 1861. The measure will reveal the source of earlier quotations in this memoir ; and certainly the gifted author promises to take a high place among the poets of Scotland. It may be noted here, that among the few Puritan books in the library of Leighton (preserved at Dunblane) are Sibbes's Bruised Reed (6th edition, 1638) and Soul's Conflict (4th edition, 1638).

Two hundred years have come and gone,
Since that fine spirit mused alone
On the dim walk, with faint green shade
By the light-quivering ash-leaves made,
   And saw the sun go down
   Beyond the mountains brown.

Slow pacing with a lowly-look,
Or gazing on the lettered book
Of Tauler, or A Kempis, or
Meek Herbert with his dulcimer,
   In quaintly pious vein
   Rehearsing a deep strain:

Or in the Gold-mouthed Greek he read
High rhetoric, or what was said
Of Augustine's experience,
Or of the Gospel's grand defence
   Before assembled lords,
   In Luther's battle-words.

Slow-pacing, with a downcast eye,
Which yet, in rapt devotion high,
Sometimes its great dark orb would lift,
And pierced the veil, and caught the swift
   Glance of an angel's wing,
   That of the Lamb did sing;

And with the fine pale shadow, wrought
Upon his cheek by years of thought,
And lines of weariness and pain,
And looks that long for home again;
   So went he to and fro
   With step infirm and slow.

A frail, slight form—no temple he,
Grand, for abode of Deity;
Rather a bush, inflamed with grace,
And trembling in a desert place,
   And unconsumed with fire,
   Though burning high and higher.

A frail, slight form, and pale with care,
And paler from the raven hair
That folded from a forehead free
Godlike of breadth and majesty—
   A brow of thought supreme
   And mystic, glorious dream.

And over all that noble face
Lay somewhat of soft pensiveness
In a fine golden haze of thought,
That seemed to waver light, and float
   This way and that way still,
   With no firm bent of will.

God made him beautiful, to be
Drawn to all beauty tenderly,
And conscious of all beauty, whether
In things of earth or heaven or neither;
   So to rude men he seemed
   Often as one that dreamed.

But true it was that, in his soul,
The needle pointed to the pole,
Yet trembled as it pointed, still
Conscious alike of good and ill;
   In his infirmity
   Looking, O Lord, to thee.

Beautiful spirit! fallen, alas,
On times when little beauty was;
Still seeking peace amid the strife,
Still working, weary of thy life,
   Toiling in holy love,
   Panting for heaven above:

I mark thee, in an evil day,
Alone upon a lonely way;
More sad-companionless thy fate,
Thy heart more truly desolate,
   Than even the misty glen
   Of persecuted men.

   For none so lone on earth as he
   Whose way of thought is high and free
   Beyond the mist, beyond the cloud,
   Beyond the clamour of the crowd,
      Moving, where Jesus trod,
      In the lone walk with God.

We have here the very man before us, and the very books he loved, and the very age he 'fell on,' and from which he was 'taken away.' Looking at the portrait, over and over engraved for the early quartos and duodecimos, and his one folio, Richard Sibbes must have been a man of larger mould, of more massive head, ampler brain-chamber, keener vision than Robert Leighton.* As

---

* Russell, in his 'Memorials of Fuller' (1844), and Mr Mayor, in his prefatory remarks to Catlin's MS., from the Baker MSS., have anticipated the comparison of Sibbes with Leighton. The former says—'Dr Richard Sibbes . . . a writer surpassed by none in that purity and depth of true spirituality, which also characterised

one studies the ruff-girted 'Master'-capped face, a more robust soul looks out from the benignant eyes. The seamed and lined forehead tells of deeper thinking, not without storms of doubt and wrestling (that always *so* leave their mark, like the waves on the sea-shore sands, as though the soul's mystic sea beat there). But the 'inner men,' in their spiritual-mindedness, unworldliness, meekness, humility, peacefulness, surely very closely resemble one another.

But now the stage darkens for 'the end,'

> 'Like a cave's shadow enter'd at mid-day.' *

He has to preach but other two 'sermons,' and then go forth on the last great journey. With strange fitness he chooses for his texts, John xiv. 1, 2, 'Let not your heart be troubled; ye believe in God, believe also in me. In my Father's house are many mansions; it it were not so, I would have told you.'

CHAPTER XII.

'THE VALLEY OF THE SHADOW OF DEATH.'

Last Illness—Finishes 'The Soul's Conflict'—Draws up his 'Will'—
'Falls on Sleep.'

Having preached the last of these two 'sermons,' he 'fell sick that very night, June 28,' with some un-named illness. Feeling that he was indeed dying, he, on 'July 1,' put the finishing touches to his 'Address to the Christian Reader,' for the 'Soul's Conflict,' which had been passing through the press during his absence at Cambridge. Glancing over the proof-sheets, he detected certain passages which he found misunderstood, and noticed them; but apparently was too weak to do more. On the 4th, he 'set his house in order,' by revising and altering his 'last will and testament.' He had many friends, gentle and simple, and it is with no common satisfaction that it is in our power to present this closing memorial :—†

Leighton in a succeeding age,' p. 81. The latter—'When we consider the beauty of Sibbes' language, and the gentleness of his temper, in both which respects he almost deserves the name of the Puritan Leighton, we cannot but wonder at the general neglect which has obscured his memory,' p. 253.

* 'Adon:' Poems. By Mrs Clive. 1856. P. 39.

† Extracted from the Principal Registry of Her Majesty's Court of Probate, in the Prerogative Court of Canterbury.

'IN THE NAME OF GOD, AMEN, I, RICHARD SIBBS, Doctor of Divinity, weake in body, but of p'fect memory, doe make and ordaine this my last will and testament, in manner and forme followeing: First, I comend and bequeath my soule into the hands of my gratious Saviour, whoe hath redeemed it wth his most pretious blood, and appeares now in heaven to receave it, with humble thankes that he hath vouchsafed I should be borne and live in the best tymes of the gospell, and have my interest in the comforte of it; as alsoe, that he hath vouchsafed me the honour of being a publisher thereof wth some measure of faythfullnes. My body I would have to be buried at the discretion of my executors. And as for that outward estate that God. in his rich goodnes, hath blessed me wthall, my minde and will is as followeth: First, I give and bequeath unto my brother Thomas Sibbs of Thurston, in the countie of Suffolk,* all my messuages, lands, and tenements, with the appurtenances, lyeing and being in Thurston aforesaid, or elsewhere, for and dureing the terme of his naturall life; and after my said brother's decease, to John Sibbs, sonne of my late brother John Sibbs, and now a student at Katherine Hall, in Cambridge,† and to his heires for ever: Item, I give unto my sister, Margaret Mason, fourtie pounds; and unto the children of my late sister, Susann Lopham, deceased, the some of thirty pounds, to be equally devided amongst them; as likewise, I give unto the children of my late sister, Elizabeth King, deceased, the some of fourtie pounds, to be equally devided amongst them; the said threescore and ten pounds, soe given to the children of my said sisters, I would have payed to the said children, severally and proporconably, at the dayes of their marriage, or when they shall accomplish their severall ages of one-and-twenty yeares, or otherwise sooner, at the discretion of my executors: Item, I give unto my uncle Sibbs, yf he be liveing, fourtie shillings; and unto the children of my late aunte . . . . . who dwelt in or neer Waldingfeild, in Essex,‡ the some of three pounds: Item, I give unto my cosen, Jeremy Huske, unto my cosins, Anne Beckett and Elizabeth Beckett, to every of them fourtie shillings: Item, I give unto the poore of the said towne of Thurston twentie shillings: Item, I give unto such of my poore kindred as are now dwelling at Stowlangton,§ in Suffolke, or elsewhere, whoe are now knowne to my executors, fourtie shillings, to be disposed according to the discretion of my executors: Item, I give unto James Joyner of London, whoe hath beene very faithfull in his service unto me tenn pounds; and to my loveing frends, Mr Dermer, haberdasher, dwelling on Ludgate Hill, twenty shillings, and to his wife twentie shillings, and to Widdow Dermer twentie shillings; and to my good friends Goodman Pinkaur and Goodman Rocke, dwelling in Perpoole Lane, to each of them twenty shillings: Item, I give unto Mr Nicholas Parry, steward of Grayes Inne, three pounds; and to Mr Guy, cheife cooke there, a ring of tenn shillings; and to his under servants, to be disposed at his discretion, the some of twenty shillings in the whole: Item, I give unto the three cheife butlers of Grayes Inne, to every of them, twenty shillings; alsoe, I give unto the inferiour servants of that house twenty shillings, to be disposed of according to the discretion of the steward; and as for that Hono^{ble} Society of Grayes Inne, I have nothing to bequeath unto it but the prayers of a sicke and dyeing man, that it may continue to be still a semenary of worthy men,

---

* See B in Appendix to this Memoir.   † *Ibid.*
‡ This is a slip. It is in Suffolk, near Sudbury, on borders of Essex.
§ Stowlangtoft, three miles from Thurston.

whoe may be alwayes ready to maintaine religion and justice, wth humble thankes for all their kindnesse and loveing respects towardes mee: Item, I give unto my auncient and deare frend, ould Mr Mew, in remembrance of my love, one of Mr Downham's books, called a Direccon to a Christian Life;* and to my deare and very worthy frend, Mr John Pym,† a ring of fourtie shillings: Item, I give unto my very good frend, Mr William Mew, one silver spoone, now in the custody of James Joyner aforenamed: Item, I give unto the poore of the parrish where I shal be buried twenty shillings: Item, I give unto my very worthy, religious, and bountifull frend, Mrs Mary Moore,‡ as a poore remembrance of my harty love unto her, one ryng of fourtie shillings; and to my very worthy frends Sr Robert Brooke of Langly, to his lady,§ and to his brother, Mr John Brooke, to each of them a ring of fourtie shillings; and to my kind frend, Mr Stevens of Gloucestershire, a ring‖ of twentie shillings; and to my worthy friend, Mr Capell, ¶ late preacher in Gloucestershire, twenty shillings: Item, I give five pounds to the poore of the p'ishes of Trinity and St Andrews, in Cambridge: Item, Whereas there is due unto me, from the Colledge of St Katherine, in Cambridge, one hundred pounds, for wch Mr Goodwyn and Mr Arrow Smith** stand bound to mee, haveing the seale of the said colledge for their securetie, I doe hereby give and bequeath unto the said colledge, for ever, the said some of one hundred pounds, for the setling of a scholarship of fower pounds p. ann.; to wch said schollership my will and desire is, that my kinsman, John Sibbs, aforemenconed, shal be first elected and admitted; and that in all future eleccons, when the same shal be void in tyme to come, yf any of my kindred shal be then students in the said colledge, the p'son soe of kynne to me shal be p^rferred before another: Item, I give unto my loveing frend, Mr Catline, preacher of Thurston, fourtie shillings: Item, I give unto my good frend, Mr Almond of Cambridge, fyve pounds, praying him to imploy the same for the benefit of his sonne and my godsonne: Item, I give unto my godsonne, Richard Clerk, fortie shillings; and whereas, by the will of Mrs Gardiner, late of London, widdow, deceased, I was desired to dispose a certain some of money, in such manner as in her said will is specified, all wch money hath beene accordingly disposed, excepting only fyve pounds, payable unto Mr Symons of Katherine Hall, my will therefore is that payment be made of the said fyve pounds unto Mr Symonds aforesaid; and to my reverend frende, Dr Gouge, I doe give, as a testimony of my love, twenty shillings, desiring him to take the paynes to preach my funerall sermon:††. Item, My will is, that my reverend frend, Mr Downeham, shall have two of those bookes of his owne making backe againe wch were by him delivered unto me, and are remayning in my studie at Grayes Inne; all the rest of my goods and chattles, my funerall, debts, and legacies being payed and discharged, I give unto my brother and kinsman before named— that is to saie, to my brother Thomas Sibbs, and my nephew John Sibbs, formerly menconed, whome, together wth John Godbold of Grayes Inne,

---

* Published 1622, and entitled 'A Guide to Godliness; or, a Treatise of a Christian Life.' The author was John Downame or Downham, B.D., brother of George, Bishop of Derry. He died 1644.
† See references *in loc.* at p. cxxxvii, Appendix A
‡ Sibbes dedicates Culverwell's 'Time Well-spent' to her, *ante* p. xciii, *seq.*
§ See reference *in loc.* p. cxxxvii, Appendix A.
‖ *Ibid.* ¶ *Ibid.* ** Drs Goodwin and Arrowsmith.
†† See Mr Mayor's note *in loc.* Appendix A.

Esquire, I doe hereby ordayne, constitute, and appoynt to be the executors of this my last will and testament, giving unto the said Mr Godbould a peece of my owne plate, such as himself shall choose out of that plate of myne, which is now in the custody of the said James Joyner; and I doe entreate my worthy and very loveing frends, Sr Nathaniel Rich, Sir Nathaniell Barnardiston,* and Sr William Spring, Knighte,† to be overseers of this my will, desireing my executors, in all things of difficulty, to be advised by them in the execution of the same; and as a remembrance of my love to every of the said overseers of my will, I give unto each of them a ring of twentie shillings.—In wittnes whereof I have hereunto set my hand and seale, this fourth daye of July, in the eleaventh yeare of the raigne of our sov'aigne Lord Charles, by the grace of God, kinge of England, Scotland, France, and Ireland, defender of the faith, &c., and in the yeare of our Lord God 1635. Signed, sealed, and published to be the last will and testament of the said Richard Sibbs in the presence of us.

PROBATUM fuit testamentum sup^{r}scriptum apud London coram ven^{li} viro magistro Willimo Merricke legum doctore : Surrogato ven^{lis} viri Domini Henrici Marten militis, legum etiam doctoris, curiæ prerogativæ Cantuar. magistri, custodis sive com^{rii} legitime constituti; undecimo die mensis Julii anno Domini millesimo sexcentesimo tricesimo quinto, Juramentis Thomæ Sibbs et Johannis Sibbs duorum executorum in senior ‡ testamento nominatorum : Quibus commissa fuit administracio omnium et singulorum bonorum piriu (?) et creditorum dicti defuncti de bene et fideliter administrando eadem ad sancta dei evangelia juratis : Reservata potestate similem commissionem faciendi Johanni Godbould Ar : alteri executori etiam in senior ‡ testamento nominato cum ven'it eand^m petitum.'

His will was drawn up on Saturday the 4th, and then he quietly waited his 'change.' '*Paulisper O senex, oculos claude, nam statim lumen Dei videbis*' ('Shut thine eyes a little, old man, and immediately thou shalt see the light of God'§).

Thus remembering his kinsmen and friends left behind, even the humblest, and looking UPWARD, he 'WALKED THROUGH the valley of the shadow of death,' and went, from the Sabbath below (*it was a Sabbath morning*) to the Sabbath above, to 'be with the Lord.' 'Blessed are the dead who die in the LORD. . . . Yea, saith THE SPIRIT, for they rest from their labours, *and their works do follow them,*' Rev. xiv. 13. He died 5th July 1635, in the 58th year of his age. An entry in the 'Register' of St Andrew's Church, Holborn (within which parish Gray's Inn is situate), tells us he was buried there on the next day :—

---

* Sir Nathaniel Barnardiston. The 'Rich' and 'Barnardiston' families are historic in their warm support of the Puritans. It were superfluous to annotate names that are found in every Puritan 'History.'

† Sir William Spring, Knt. He was of Pakenham, near Bury St Edmunds, of the ancient family of Lavenham. See Burke's 'Extinct' Baronetcies; also *ante* page xxvi.

‡ Qu. 'superscripts ?'—ED.

§ Sozomen, lib. ii. cap. ii. Stanford's Alleine, p. 21.

'1635. July 6. Richard Sibbes, D.D., sometime preacher in Gray's Inn, died in his chambers at Gray's Inn, 5th.'*

1.

'Servant of God! well done;
Rest from thy loved employ;
The battle fought, the victory won,
Enter thy Master's joy.'
—The voice at midnight came;
He started up to hear:
A mortal arrow pierced his frame.
He fell,—but felt no fear.

2.

Tranquil amid alarms,
It found him in the field,
A veteran slumbering on his arms,
Beneath his red-cross shield:
His sword was in his hand,
Still warm with resent fight,
Ready that moment at command,
Through rock and steel to smite.

3.

The pains of death are past,
Labour and sorrow cease,
And life's long warfare closed at last,
His soul is found in peace.
Soldier of Christ! well done;
Praise be thy new employ;
And while eternal ages run
Rest in thy Saviour's joy. †

I would have my readers turn to the perhaps over-garrulous, yet interesting 'reflections' upon the death of Sibbes,‡ and add only a few words by Ashe, Church, and Nalton:—

'This bright star, who sometimes with his light refreshed the souls of many of God's people while he shone on the horizon of our church, set, as we say, *between the evening of many shadows and the morning of a bright hoped-for reformation,* which, though for the present (1654) overcast, yet being so agreeable to the mind of Jesus Christ, and ushered in with the groans and prayers of so many of his saints, we doubt not but will in God's own time break forth gloriously, to the dissipating of those clouds and fogs which at the present do eclipse and darken it.' § Even so:—

'God's saints are shining lights; . . . .
They are indeed as pillar-fires,
    Seen as we go;
They are that city's shining spires
    We travel to.' ‖

A. B. G.

---

* It has been found impossible to identify his grave; no stone, the simplest, marks it. Is there to be no memorial raised?

† James Montgomery, 'The Christian Soldier.' Poetical Works, p. 305, ed. 1 vol. 8vo. 1851.

‡ Appendix A, p. cxxxviii, *seq.* See also B, pp. cxl–xli, in Appendix, for notices of Sibbes's family and name; and C, p. cxli, for references concerning his successors at Gray's Inn and Catharine Hall

§ 'To the Reader,' Heav. Conf. between Christ and Mary, 12mo. 1654.

‖ Vaughan, as *ante* p. 39.

APPENDIX TO MEMOIR.

A, page xxvi, *et alibi.*—ZACHARY CATLIN.

It has been deemed proper to give in full, in this appendix, the 'Memoir' of Sibbes, drawn up by Zachary Catlin (the manuscript of which, as has been stated, is in my possession). Accordingly it is subjoined, *verbatim et literatim* from the original holograph with signature. Two copies of this 'Memoir' are preserved at Cambridge; one among the Baker MSS. (xxxviii. 441–446); the other, recently presented, in University Library.* That by Baker has been edited with scrupulous fidelity by Rev. J. E. B. Mayor, M.A.; and forms one of the 'Communications' of the Cambridge Antiquarian Society (read December 1. 1856, No. vii. pp. 252–264). It is to be regretted that it abounds with the most singular misreadings; for which Baker, not Mr Mayor, must be held responsible. Mr Mayor's notes, characteristically full of out-of-the-way reading, are appended. They are marked M. That in University Library, Mr Cooper informs me, 'is a transcript written about 1750, and contains some slight verbal variations from the Baker MS.,' but he adds, 'these variations can be of little value, because the scribe read the olden hand so imperfectly, that he throughout calls the subject of the memoir "Gibbs."'

Of Catlin very little is known beyond the incidental notices of himself and father, in his memoir of Sibbes. The 'Diary of John Rous, incumbent of Santon Downham, Suffolk, from 1625 to 1642, edited by Mary A. E. Green, (Camden Society, 4to, 1856,)' introduces him thus :—

'Upon Shrovemoonday, February 13. [A.D. 1632], Mr Catlin preaching at Bury, gave out before his sermon that it was good the ministers of the combination wold meete to consulte of the making of the combination, that those ministers that wold doe good might be put in seasonably for it. I learned since, that a newe-come minister was put in first in the combination, to beginne on Plough Moonday, but as it seemed would not goe before the graver preachers, and, therefore, lefte the day unprovided; but Mr Catlin by entreaty, preached at that time, *ex improviso*, and after wold have beene freed of this his owne time, but could not (thus he said before the sermon), and in his sermon said thus much obiter, which I heard. We are blamed for our churches, but it is certaine, that these courtes extracte more from us than will repayer our churches, adorne them, and keepe them so.' Pp. 68, 69. <small>Thirston.— Mr Catlin's sermon.</small>

* A third is in Harl. MSS., 6087, fol. 17.

Mr Mayor has overlooked the marginal-note, 'Thirston,' when he asks if our Zachary Catlin were 'the Mr Catlin mentioned by John Rous.' 'Thirston,' *i.e.*, Thurston, gives the answer in the affirmative.

Mr Cooper has favoured me with a note of various Catlins of the several colleges, Cambridge. There is a Zachary Catlin of Christ's, B.A. 1598, M.A. 1602. This was probably our Zachary. There is a Jonathan Catlin of Catharine-Hall, B.A. 1631, M.A. 1635, who was most likely the son mentioned as cared for by Sibbes.

The name, spelled 'Catling' and 'Catlyn,' occurs in Mr Bright's volume (*ante* page cxxi), as an 'overseer' in the will of one of the Nether-hall Brights, and elsewhere as a 'witness' (see pp. 108, 128). I have been unable to trace to any library the two sermons published by him (*ante* page cxxiii). Considerable 'Notes' on the family and name of Catelyne or Catlin (unpublished), will be found in 'Davy's Suffolk Collections,' vol. xlvi. (pp. 312–24). . . . Pedigrees C, Caa—Cha; Mus. Brit. Jure Emptionis, 19, 122. Plut. clxxvi. E. With these slight memoranda, I beg now to submit, 'Dr Sibbs, his Life, by Zachary Catlin.'

At the Request of a Noble Friend, S[ir] W. Spring,* I haue here willingly contributed to the happy memory of that worthy man of God Doctour Sibs a few such Flowers, as I could collect, eyther from the certain Relation of those yt knew his first Education, or from mine own observation of him, at that distance, whereat we lived. And if any thing here recorded, may seem convenient for His purpose, who is (as I am informed) about to publish the Lives ‡ of some Worthyes lately deceased, I shall think my labour well bestow'd. For I am not of that Philosopher's mind, who lighting upon a Book newly put forth, entitled, The encomium of Hercules, cast it away, saying, Et quis Lacedæmoniorum eum vituperavit? accounting it a needles § work to prayse him, whom noe man did, or could find fault withal. I rather iudge it a commendable thing, to perpetuate and keep Fresh the Memory of such worthy men, whose examples may be of use, for Imitation, in this declining, and degenerate Age. But I come to the matter.

Mr Clark of London.†

He was born 577. This Richard, the eldest Son of Paul Sibs and Johan, was born at Tostock‖ in Suffolk, 4 miles from Bury, anno domini 1577, from whence his Parents soon removed, to a Town adioining, called, Thurston, where they lived in honest Repute, brought up, and maried divers children, purchased some Houses and Lands, and there they both Deceased. His Father was by his Trade, a Wheelewright, a skilful and painful workman, and a good sound harted Christian. This Richard he brought up to Learning, at the Grammar Schole, though very ¶ unwillingly, in regard of the charge, had not the youth's strong Inclination to his Book, and wel profiting therein, with some Importunity of Freinds prevailed so far, as to continue him at Schole, til he was fit for Cambridge. Concerning his

His industry in his study. loue to his Book, and his Industry in study, I cannot omit the Testimony of Mr. Thomas Clark, High Constable, who was

---

* See Prynne's 'Canterb. Doome,' p. 376.—M.

† Mr Clark of London. Probably 'Samuel Clarke,' who included a Memoir of Sibbes in his 'Thirty-two lives' (*ante* p. xxxvii), without however using Catlin's MS. Perhaps as the volume was published in 1652, and the MS. is dated November 1st of that year, it may not have reached him in time. But neither does any trace of it appear in subsequent editions.—G.   ‡ 'Plan' in Baker, by Mr Mayor.—G.

§ 'Useless' in Baker, by Mr Mayor. I designate the remaining mis-readings by M. B.—G.   ‖ 'Tastock' in M. B.—G.   ¶ 'Yet' in M. B.—G.

much of the same Age, and went to schole, together with him, at the same Time, wth one M^r· Rich. Brigs (afterward, Head Master of the Free Schole at Norwich) then teaching at Pakenham church. He hath often told me, that when the Boies were dismist from Schole, at the usuall Houres of eleuen, and 5, or 6, and the rest would fal to their pastime, and sometimes to plaiing the Waggs with him, being haimlet* and meanly apparel'd, for ye most part in Leather, & was this Youth's constant course, as soon as he could rid himself of their unpleasing company, to take out of his Pocket or Sachel, one Book or other, and so to goe reading† and meditating, til he came to his Father's house, wch was neere a mile of, and so as he went to Schole agen. This was his order also, when his Father sent him to the Free Schole at Bury, 3, or 4 Miles off, every day. Whereby ye said M^r· Clark, did then conceive yt he would in Time prove an excellent and Able man, who of a child was of such a manly staydnes § and indefatigable industry in his study. His Father at length grew weary of his expenses for books and learning, took him from Schole, bought him an Axe and some other tooles, and set him to his own Trade, to the great discontent of the youth, whose Genius wholy caried him another way. Whereupon, M^r· Greaves ‖ then Minister of Thurston, and M^r· Rushbrook an Attorney there, knowing the disposition and fitnes of the lad, sent him, without his Father's consent, to some of the Fellowes of S^t· John's colledge, of their acquaintance, with their Letters of Recommendation, where, upon examination, he was so wel approved off, that he was presently entertained as a Sub-sizar, shortly after chosen Scholer of the House, and at length came to be Fellow of ye Colledge,¶ and one of the Taskers of ye University, His Father being hardly brought to allow him 20 Nobles a yeare toward his maintenance in Cambr., to which some good friends in the country, M^r. Greaves,** M^r. Knew-stub,†† and some others, made some addition, for a Time as need required.

$ἐὰν\ ἦ\ φιλ$-
$ομαθής$, $ἰσῆ$
$πολυμαθής$.
Tis one signe of a scholar to be $φιλόπονος$.
—Ascham.‡

His profiting in Cambr.

Anno domini 1608, I came to be Minister of Thurston, and he was then a Fellow of the Colledge, and a Preacher of good Note in Cambr., and wee‡‡ soon grew §§ wel acquainted, for whensoeuer he came down into ye Country, to visit his Mother and brethren (his Father being deceased) he would never faile to preach with us, ‖‖ on the Lords day, and for the most part, twice, telling me, that it was a work of charity, to help a constant and painful preacher, for so he was pleased to conceiue of me. And If there were a Communion appointed at any Time, he would be sure not to with-draw himselfe after sermon, but receiving the Bread and wine at my hands, he would always assist me in the distribution of ye cup to the congregation.

As for his kindnes to his kindred,¶¶ and neglect of the world, it was very remarkable, for this I can testify of my own know-ledge, that purchasing of M^r· Tho. Clark, and others in our Town, a Mesuage and Lands, at seueral times, to the value of fifty pounds per annum, he paid the Fines to the Lords, but never took one peny of the Rents or profits of them, but left the Benefit wholly to his

His kindnes to his kindred and his singu-lar neglect of ye world.

---

* ' Humble ' in M. B.—G.   † ' Studying ' in M. B.—G.
‡ Not given in M. B.—G;   § ' Stryde ' in M. B.—G.   ‖ ' Gwinn ' in M. B.—G.
¶ ' That house ' in M. B.—G.   ** ' Graves ' in M. B —G.
†† See Brook's ' Puritans,'vol. ii. p. 308, seq.; Clarke's ' Lives of Thirty-two Eng-lish Divines,' ed. 1677, p. 133; Geffrey Whitney's ' Emblems,' p. 223; Bancroft's ' Daungerous Positions,' pp. 5, 57 (Bk. 2, c. 10), 44 (Bk. 3, c. 2), 120, 122, 143; Sutcliffe's ' Answere to Throckmorton,' p. 47; Prynne's ' Canterb. Doome,' p. 376.—M.   ‡‡ ' Was ' in M. B.—G.   §§ ' Grown ' in M. B.—G.
‖‖ ' Me ' in M. B.—G.   ¶¶ ' Friends ' in M. B.—G.

Mother, and his 2 Brethren,* as long as he liued. So much did this Heavenly-minded Man of God slight this present world (which the most men are so loth to part withal, when they Dye) that he freely and undesired, parted with it, whilst he liued, requiring nothing of them, but only to be liberal to the poore. Nay ouer and besides, if any faithful honest man came down from Cambridge or London, where he liued, by whom he might conveniently send, he seldome or never fayled to send his Mother a Peice of Gold, for the most part, a ten shillings Piece, but 5 shillings was the least, and this he continued as long, as his Mother liued. And would she haue been persuaded to exchange her Country Life for the citty, he often told me, yt he would willingly have maintain'd her there, in good view and fashion, like his Mother, but she had no mind to alter her accustomed course of Life, in her old daies, contenting her self with her own Meanes, and that Addition, wch her Son made thereunto.

His special kindness to me. And for his special kindnes to my self, in particular, I cannot omit, that being Trusted by Personages of Quality, with diuers sumes of mony, for pious and charitable uses, he was pleased, among many others, not to forget Me. At one Time he sent me down three Twenty shillings peices of gold inclosed in a Letter: and at 2 other Times, deliver[ed] me, with his own hand, two Twenty shilling pieces *His singular humility.* more: and so far was this Humble Saint from Pharisaical ostentation, and vain glory, and from taking the honour of these good works to himself, that he plainly told me, that these Gratuities were not of his own cost, but being put in Trust, and † left to his own Discretion, in the distribution, he lookt upon Mee as One, that took great Paines in my ministry, and in teaching Scholers, and at that Time Labouring under the Burden of a great charge of children, and so thought me a fit object of their intended charity. And from myselfe His love descended down to my Son, for my sake, for whom ‡ (before he had euer seen him, being then at the Grammar Schole at Bury) he, then chosen M^r of Katherin Hal, promis'd me a Schollership there, of 5 pound a yeare, and to provide for him a Tutour and a chamber. And such was his constancy of *His reality in his promises. Pollicitis dives quilibetis esse potest.§* spirit, and his Reality, that whatsoeuer promise he made me, he would be sure, both to Remember it, and to make it good, as freely as he first made it, that was, unaskt and undesired: and for these manyfold kindnesses, all that he desired at my hands, was no more but this, that I would be careful of the soules of my people, and in special of his Mother, his Brethren, and his sisters, and would give them good counsel, in their disposing themselves in Marriage, or upon any other occasion, as I saw, they stood in need. And this one thing, I may not passe over, concerning myself, that in his last wil and Testament, he gave me a Legacy of 40 sh. with the Title of his Loving Freind, wch I the rather mention, because I had not the least thought, to haue been in yt sort remembered by him, at his Death, liuing∥ at no lesse distance from him, then of three score miles. In a word, such was the Loueliness of this sweet ¶ seruant of God, such his learning, parts, piety, prudence, humility, sincerity, Loue and meeknes of Spirit (whereof euery one was a Lodeston to attract unto, and fasten my spirit, close to his) that (I professe ingenuously) no man yt euer I was acquainted withal, got so far into my hart, or lay**

---

* 'Brothers' in M. B., and so elsewhere. § Not in M. B.
† 'As' in M. B.—G ∥ 'Being' in M. B.—G.
‡ 'For whom' dropped in M. B.—G. ¶ 'Same' in M. B.—G.
** 'Was' in M. B.—G.

so close therein: So that many Times I could not part from him, with dry eyes. But who am I? or what is it to be belov'd of me, especially for Him, that had so many and so great Friends, as he had? yet even to Me, the great God is pleased to say, My son give me thy Heart, and this poor and contrite hart, I know, he wil not despise, And this Hart of mine, as small as it is, yet is too great, to close with a Proud, Profane, worldly, malicious hart, though it be in a Prince. But true* Vertue and Grace, are the Image of God himself, and where they are discerned † by Wisdom's children, they command the Hart, and are truly louely and venerable, whereas Carnal, vitious, and unmortified Affections (whereof this Man of God, was as Free, as any man, I know liuing) they do render a man (whateuer he bee), if not hateful and contemptible, yet at least less louely and honourable. But my Love to this good Man hath transported me beyond my purpose, wch was to speake of some things, lesse visible to others, especially concerning his first Education: for when he came to the University and the Citty, there his Life, and Actions were upon a publick Theatre, and his own works, without a Trumpet, would prayse him in the Gates. As for his kindnes to his kindred, and to my selfe, I know none, yt took more notice of them, then I, and therefore I could not hide them from the world (upon this occasion) without some kind of Sacriledge.

<small>Prov. 23 26. Psal. 51. 17.</small>

<small>Prov. 31. 31 and 23.</small>

<small>His death July 5th 1635 ætat 58.</small>

But from his Life, I passe to his Death, and the disposing of his worldly estate, wherein are some things very Remarkable, and coming to my certain knowledge and observation, I neyther wil, nor dare ‡ conceal them. His Death was some what soden; for having preach't at Graye's Inne, upon the Lords Day, on that sweet Text, Joh. xiv. 1, 2, 'Let not your Harts be troubled, ye belieue in God, Believe also in me. In my Father's House are many Mansions,' as if he had presag'd his own Death, he fel sick that very night, and died on ye Tuesday|| following, being the 5th of July A.D. 1635. Ætatis suæ 58, his Physitian, that knew his Body best ¶ being then out of ye Citty; yet having his senses, and some respite of Time, as he set his Soule, so he set his House in order, revising his former will, and altering, what he thought fitt to be altered. And first, he Bequeathed and commended ** his Soule, into the hands of his gracious Saviour, who Redeemed it, with his most precious Blood, and appeared then in heaven, to receive it. He gave him humble thanks, that he had vouchsafed him, to be born, and to live, in the Best Times of the Gospel, *(mark this)* and to have his Interest in the comfort of it. As also that he had vouchsafed him the Honour of being a Publisher of it, with some measure of Faithfulnes (mark this, you that contemne ye office of the ministry). His Body he ordered to be buried, at the pleasure of his Executors. And for his worldly estate, wherewith God had blessed him, he thus disposed of it. His House and Lands at Thurston, to the value of 50 lib. a year, or more, he gave to his youngest and only Brother then liuing, Thomas Sibs, for ye terme of his natural Life, and the Remainder to John Sibs, the son of John, his second Brother deceased: and between these two, he diuided all his

<small>His Cygnea Cantio vel concio §</small>

<small>His last will.</small>

<small>Note.</small>

<small>How he disposed his lands and personal estate.</small>

---

* 'This' in M. B.—G.   † 'Discovered' in M. B.—G.   ‡ 'Doe' in M. B.—G.
§ This is the title given to Whitaker's last 'sermon,' published 1599, 4to.—G.
|| This is a slip for Sunday. See Memoir, page cxxx., and title-page of 'last sermons,' in this volume.—G.
¶ 'Best' in M. B.—G.   ** 'Committed' in M. B.—G.

personal estate, which clearly amounted to 650 lib. (his large Legacies, and funeral charges being discharged and satisfied) making them, ye exequestors of his Wil and Test^t. To the children of his 3 sisters deceased he gave 110 lib. To other poore kindred 13 lib. To his faithful Servant, James Joynar, 10 lib. To other 5 in London, 5 lib. To the poore of the parishes of Trinity and St Andrew's in Cambridge, 5 lib. To the poore of the Parish of Thurston, and of the parish, where he should be buried, 2 lib. To the Steward of Grayes Inne, 3 lib. To the 3 cheife Butlars, 3 lib. To their Servants, 1 lib. To the chiefe Cook, a Ring of 10 sh. To his under Servants, 1 lib. To his deare and worthy Friend M^r. Jo. Pym,* a Ring of 2 lib. To S^r. Robt Brook † of Langley, his Legacies given out 288 lib. 10 sh. Lady, and Brother, 3 Rings of 6 lib. To Mr. Stephens‡ a Ring of 2 lib. To Mr Capell,§ Preacher, 1 lib. To his loving friend Mr. Catlin, Preacher of Thurston, 2 lib. To Mr. Almond of Cambr. for his Son (ye Doctours Godson), 5 lib. To his Godson Richd Clark, 2 lib. To Mr. Gouge ‖ of London, whom he requested to preach at his Funeral, 1 lib.¶ To Sr Nath. Rich ;** to Sr Nath. Barnardiston ;†† and to Sr Wm Spring, Supervisors of his will, 3 Rings of 3 lib. To Mrs Mary Moore, a Ring of 2 lib. To Mr. Jo. Godbold of Gray's Inn Esq., one of ye exequatours of his Will, the best peice of plate he had, valued at 10 lib. To Katherin-Hal in Cambr, for the setling of a Scholarship of 4 lib. per annum for ever, 100 lib. All wich Legacies amount to the total summe of 288 lib. 10 sh.

His enlarging Katherin Hal. During the Time yt he was M^r. of Kath-Hal, he was the Meane by his great friends, of buying in the Inne, adioininge ye Colledge, called The Bull, and so of enlarging the Buildings of the Colledge, to the value of 500 lib. as I am informed: But I leave this to ‡‡ a *melius Inquirendum*. O what a Pious and charitable disposition do these things discouer, in this precious Saint, to be had in everlasting Remembrance.

* Besides the common sources for Pym's life, consult the 'Charisteria and Epist Eucharist.' of Degory Whear, his tutor and acquaintance of many years' standing. 'Charist.' Dedn. and pp. 101, 102; 'Epist. Eucharist.' Nos. 21—28. Pym was a friend and connection of Brownrigg's. B's 'Life,' pp. 190, 191.—M.

† Sir Robert Brook of Langley, his Lady . . . . See 'Dedication' of 'Fountain Sealed' (*ante* page cxix)—G.

‡ Dr Stephens, editor of 'Statius,' Master of Bury? 'Life of Isaac Milles,' 1721, pp. 8-12, 74.—M.

§ Richard Capel, Wood's 'Athenæ,' ed. Bliss, iii. 421, Clark's 'Lives' (as above), p. 303 *seq*.—M.

‖ Dr Wm. Gouge. See his life in Clark (as above), p. 234 *seq*., Harwood's 'Alumni Etonenses,' p. 202, Wm. Lilly's 'Life,' ed. 1774, p. 29, Prynne's 'Canterb. Doome,' p. 362, Life of Row' in Clark's 'Lives of Eminent Persons,' (1683), pt. ii. p. 106, Brook's 'Lives of the Puritans,' iii. 165, *seq*.—M. Also 'Memoir' prefixed to his Exposition of 'Hebrewes,' folio, 1655, vol. i.—G.

¶ From a tract bound in the volume marked R. 10. 16 in the University Library of Cambridge (p. 525) it appears that 10s. was commonly charged to the poor, and 20s. to the rich, for a funeral sermon. The tract contains the answer of George Finch (a Cambridge man, brother to Lord Finch) to the articles against him A.D. 1641.—M.

** See Birch's James I., vol. ii., p. 55, and Whear's 'Charisteria,' p. 127.—M.

†† See his life in Clarke's 'Lives of Eminent Persons,' (1683), pt. ii., p. 105, *seq*. Cf. *ibid.* pp. 161, 163, 169, 172, 175; Calamy's 'Account,' pp. 636, 637; 'Contin.' p. 786.—M.

‡‡ The Black Bull was given by will to Cath. Hall by Dr Gostlin, for the founding of six scholars, &c.—M.

I shal conclude with an Observation, wch I made of the Time, when this holy man, and some other Godly and precious Divines, were taken out of this world, by the wise Providence of God. Tis that of ye Prophet Is: 57, 1. That Righteous and merciful men are taken away, from the Evill to come. They enter into Peace, and rest in their Graues, as in Beds of Sleep. Thus ye Lord said, concerning good Josia, I wil gather thee to the Fathers, and thou shalt go to thy Grave in Peace, And thine eyes shall not see all ye Evil, wch I wil bring upon this place. In like manner, the Lord took away, about the same Time, with this Reverend man diuers, that their eyes might not see that great Evils, then ready to break out, upon these 3 kingdoms. To instance in some few, D^r. Sibs died July 5, 1635 ; M^r. Sam. Ward,* that Worthy Preacher of Ipswich, was censured in the High commission, and silencet in October follow^g ye same yeare 1635, and died, as I remember 1638. The Irish Rebellion, the slaughter of 100,000 Protestants in a yeare, the long, fatal war, between the King and Parl^t.

M^r. Rogers† also, that Zealous and powerful Preacher of Dedham in Essex, died Octob: 15 : 1636. And I may not forget my own father also, M^r. Robert Catlin,‡ an aged and a faithfull Minister in Rutlandshire, about four score yeares old died July 24 : 1637 : who Being unable any longer to serue his great Pastoral cure, he came over to Barham, neere Ipswich, to dy amongst his children (here) in Suffolk : who lying on his sick Bed, heard M^r. Fenton, a Minister relating the Heavy censure, that was then newly passed upon the Bishop of Lincoln, and Deane of Westminster, Doctour Williams, reputed at that Time a very good Man, whom my Father knew to be a great Freind to the Good ministers in his Diocese, and a great enimy to the setting the Tables Altarwise, and to the Altar worship, wch then began to be much advocated, and one that had done many munificent works of charity, and had given yearely a great summe to the Releife of the Lady Elizabeth. The Bishop, by the malice of Archbishop Laud and others his enemies, was suspended in the High Commission ab officio or beneficio, censured in the Star-Chamber, fined 10,000 lib. and cast into the Towre of London about July 15, 1637 : from whence he was fetchet out the beginning of this Parl^t. Nov. 3d, 1640, with great applause. My Father, I say, hearing of this Bishop's censure (wherein my Brother Wm. Catlin, a minister was deeply concerned, as being a witness for ye Bishop), He brake out into these words, before the 2 Ministers, and others then present in the chamber. Alas poore England, thou hast now seen thy best daies; I that am 4 score yeares old, and I have in al my time seene no alteration in Religion, nor any foreign Enemy setting

---

* See Brook's 'Lives of the Puritans,' vol. ii. p. 452, *seq.*, with the authors there cited; also Heylin's 'Cyprianus Angl.' p. 120, *seq.*; Prynne's 'Canterb. Doome,' pp. 157, 159, 361, 375 ; Birch's 'James I.,' vol. ii, pp 226, 228, 232 ; Clark's 'Lives of Eminent Persons' (1683), pt. ii. pp. 154, 159 ; D'Ewes' 'Autobiography,' vol i. p. 249 ; Calamy's 'Account,' p. 636 —M. Also Mr Ryle's Memoir, prefixed to his 'Sermons' in present series (see Adams's, iii.).—G.

† See his life in Brook's 'Lives of the Puritans,' vol. ii. p. 421 : and Bastwick's 'Utter Routing,' p. 474, Prynne's 'Canterb. Doome,' pp. 363, 373, Calamy's 'Account,' p. 606, Clark's 'Lives of Eminent Persons' (1683), p. 64 (Life of Blackerby), Mather's 'Life of T. Hooker,' p. 8, Mather's 'Life of John Cotton,' pp. 24, 25.—M. Also Chester's 'John Rogers' . . . pages 245, *seq.* (1 vol. 8vo, 1861).— G.

‡ This account has been printed in Brook's 'Lives of the Puritans,' vol. ii. pp. 428, 429.—M.

foot in England, nor any Ciuil wars, amongst ourselves, do now forsee euil
daies a comming. But I shal go to the grave in Peace. Blessed be that
God, whom I have served, who hath accepted my weake service, and wil
be mine exceeding great reward. And within a few houres, he departed
this Life, and lies Buried in the Chauncell of the Parish Church at Barham, Doctour Young of Stow Market,* preaching at his Funeral: and as
he Blessed God (with D^r· Sibs) yt he had lived in the best Times of the
Gospel, so there was no great difference in the Time of their death. And
shortly after the death of these men were those sparkles of discontent
kindled between the Scots and us, wch were the sad Præludia, or beginnings
of this late Universal Conflagration. The King went against
<small>King went against ye Scots. March 1638.</small> the Scots, as far as York, in March 1638: and the Scots were
proclaimed Traitours in the Churches of England, in April
following, and though this Proclamation were revoked, yet who
knows not, what Tragical events have follow'd in al the 3 Kingdoms, to
this very day,† to the astonishment of Heaven and Earth. This is ye
<small>Bezæ Ep. 70.</small> very observation of Reverend Beza in his 70th Epistle: That
as often as God kindleth and setteth vp these Lights (men of
singular graces and special use in ye church) so often he testifies his good
wil to y^{ose} Times and Places in a certen special and peculiar manner. But
when he extinguishes these Lights and puts them out, it must be accounted
as an evident testimony of his sore Displeasure. For (saith he) it is
apparant in al Histories that when greivous Tempests are comming upon a
People, The Lord is wont to withdraw his especial servants into the Haven
beforehand, wch agrees with y^t of ye Prophet Isay 2. 2, 3, 5. Behold ye
Lord wil take away out of Judah and Jerusalem ye Judges and ye Prophets;
the Wise man and ye Councellour and ye Honourable: and the People
shal bee oppressed one of another etc. And no marvel, for such men are
the το κατεχος . . . meanes as a shield to keep off the wrath of God from
<small>Gen. 7. 16. 11. 13.</small> the Places where they live. The Lord with held the Flood
of waters from ye old world, til Noah was safely shut up in the
Ark, and the very selfe same day (saith the Text) were the Fountaines of
the Deep broken up and the windowes of Heaven opened. The
<small>Gen. 13. 22.</small> Angel told Lot he could do nothing against wicked Sodom, till
<small>2 Chron. 34. 28, and 36. 6.</small> he was got out of that place. The Lord held off the king of
Babilon from beseiging Jerusalem til good Josia was at rest.
<small>Josephus.</small> And ere the Roman Army sate down before it, the Lord by a
Miracle warned the Christian Jewes to remove from thence to
<small>Augustine.</small> Pella. Again, no sooner was that worthy Bishop of Hippo
St Augustin deceased, but the Citty was taken and sacked by the Goths
<small>M. Luther.</small> and Vandals. No sooner was Martin Luther translated to a
better Life, but the Smalcaldick warre brake out wch wasted
almost al the Protestants in Germany. No sooner was that
<small>D. Pareus.</small> worthy man, aged Pareus taken from Heydelberg, but presently
Marques Spinola with his Army entered the Town. And no sooner had
the Lord taken away these worthy Divines, but presently the Fire of war
<small>Psal. 11. 3.</small> and confusion (a iust punishment for our great and crying
sins) brake out upon these 3 nations. For if the Foundations
(of Religion and Government) be cast down and destroy'd, what can the
Righteous do. The voice of wise men is not heard in the cry of Fooles:
The counsel of moderate and unbiased men is not regarded in such a

---

* The celebrated Scottish tutor and friend of John Milton.
† From 'very day,' on to 'The Lord in Mercy,' not in M.-B.—G.

Tempest of clamour, violence, and confusion. Such men would have been slighted and lay'd aside in such Times as these. The Lord therefore hath put them into their safe harbour and Haven of Rest, while wee that survive are tossed to and fro upon the turbulent Eurypus of Anabaptistical, Anarchical, Fanatical, and Atheistical barretings and Vittlitigations.*

The Lord in Mercy vouchsafe to stil the Raging of the waters, Ps. 65. 7. and the madnes of (that many headded monster) the People, Isay. 39. 8. that once more his faithful Servants in these 3 Nations, may Matt: 8. 25. enjoy a blessed calm. That there may yet once again, be Peace and Truth in our Daies. Lord save us, or we perish.

Compiled and attested, by Zachary Catlin, Minister of Thurston, Nov. 1. 1652: Anno ætatis 69: currente.

(I have presented Catlin's MS. to 'University Library,' Cambridge).

B, pages xxix and cxxxi.—SIBBES'S FAMILY AND NAME.

The Will of Sibbes (*ante* p. cxxviii, *seq.*), enumerates various relatives deceased and alive. His father had died before 1608, and his mother, Catlin informs us, also predeceased him. Dr Sibbes himself never married, perhaps through the 'order' of Gray's Inn, that forbad its 'preacher' to marry. The name seems to have utterly died out, not in Suffolk merely, but everywhere. While all the other Puritans of this Series are living names, I have failed to trace any Sibbes beyond 1787. No doubt the blood has been transmitted in the issue of the several sisters named in the 'Will.'

The following *memorabilia* from the sources enumerated above each, contain all that I have been able to collect about the family and name.

I. Catharine-Hall 'Registers.'
(1.) John Sibbes, B.A. 1635 (mentioned in 'Will').
(2.) Richard . . . B.A. 1664, M.A. 1668. (See entry in Thurston 'Register,' Mo. 2.)
(3.) Robert . . . B.A. 1675.
(4.) Richard . . . B.A. 1716.

II. Tostock 'Registers.'
The merest fragment of the 'Registers' of Tostock has been preserved; and the first occurrence of the name of Sibbes therein, it will be observed, is long posterior to his death.

1. Hannah Sibbs, the daughter of Thomas Sibbs (probably a grand-nephew), and Elizabeth his wife, was baptized the 6th day of January 1679.

2. Francis, ye daughter of Thomas Sibbes and Elizabeth his wife, was baptized ye 5th of June 1683.
₊ See an entry from Thurston 'Register,' of her marriage.

3. Richard, the son of Thomas Sibbs and Elizabeth his wife, was baptized May ye 1st 1688.

From the 'deaths' we find 'Thomas Sibbes was buried January ye 18th 1690,' and 'Elizabeth Sibbes, widow, was buried, August 9th 1706.'

4. John Nunn and Sarah Sibbes (probably a grand-neice), both of this parish, were married, April 12. 1697.

Of this marriage were born :—
(1.) Mary, 'baptized December ye 30th 1702.'
(2.) John, 'baptized January ye 9th 1706.' (Died in a few days.)
(3.) Esther, 'baptized May ye 26th 1708.'

* Qu. 'Vile litigations?'—Ed.

Of 'Sarah Sibbes' = Mrs Nunn, we read, 'Sarah, the wife of John Nunn of Thurston, was buried here, April 28th 1719.' A 'Frances Nunn of Rattlesden, was buried, Feb. 18. 1725.'

A third branch is as follows :—

5. 'John Limner of Chevington, and Elizabeth Sibbes (probably another grand-niece), of this town, were married, August ye 23d 1700.'

There was issue :—

'Esther, daughter of John Limner and Elizabeth his wife, . . baptized Octob. ye 15th 1701.'

III. Thurston 'Registers,' as Tostock.

Only two occurrences of the name of Sibbes are found :—

1. Titulus Matrimonii, 1707.

'Robert Steggles of Tostock, and Frances Sibbes of Thurston, married, Ap. 23.' (See under Tostock, No. 2.)

2. 'Mr Richard Sibbes, clerk, rector of Gedding 65 years, aged 93, Feb. 2. 1737.'

This was doubtless the 'Richard' of the Cambridge list (*supra* No. 2). He was probably non-resident. In the 'registers' of Gedding, only one entry during the whole period of his incumbency, bears his signature as 'rector.'

IV. Bright's 'Brights of Suffolk' (*ante* pp. lxxxv-vi).

In the family papers of 'the Netherhall Family,' John Sibbes, no doubt the Doctor's nephew, appears as a 'witness' in a dispute about a 'meadow' (page 127). On the back of a letter (January ye 6th 1703), is a memorandum by Thomas Bright, relating to accounts and rents, under the heads of Thurston, Pakenham, Barton, and Tostock, in which, among others, occur the names of 'John, Robert, and Thomas Sibbes,' perhaps 'tenants' on the estate. Finally, in a letter, 'June 10. 1729,' a Mr Howard writes to the famous beauty, 'Mary Bright,' that 'yesterday he view^d Mr Sibbs' copyhold lands, held of her manor.'

C, page cxxvi.—SUCCESSORS OF SIBBES IN HIS OFFICES.

1. 'Preacher,' Gray's Inn.

13th November 1635. Hannibal Potter, Dr of Divinity, chose preacher.

9th February 1641. Mr Jackson is chose lecturer, to preach twice of a Sunday.

28th May 1647. Mr Horton chose preacher.

13th January 1662. Mr Caley, preacher and lect^r of this Society, if he please to accept thereof.

12th November 1662. Mr Cradock chose lect^r, wth same allowance as Mr Wilkins.

2. 'Master,' Catherine Hall, Cambridge.

There was a keen contest for the 'Mastership.' The subsequently celebrated Bishop Brownrig was appointed. For interesting notice, with references, of Brownrig, and for the papers relating to the disputes, consult Mr Mayor's 'Autobiography of Matthew Robinson' (pp. 130–146); also 'Garrard's Letter to Strafford (September 1. 1635, Strafford's Letters, vol. i. p. 462).

A DESCRIPTION OF CHRIST.

A DESCRIPTION OF CHRIST.

NOTE.

The title-page, which is given below,* of the original and only early edition of the 'Description of Christ' bears, it will be observed, that it consists of the 'leading—*i. e.*, introductory—sermons to that treatise called the Bruised Reed.' Hence its position in our reprint. It seemed proper to place the two together.

The 'Description,' as having been published posthumously, will not compare in finish with the more famous 'Bruised Reed,' and, indeed, occasionally (as at p 6, line 10 from bottom, p. 13, line 8 from bottom), partakes very much of the nature of those 'notes . . . . by some who had not perfectly taken them,' to which Sibbes deprecatingly refers in his address to the 'Christian reader,' prefixed to the latter. Still, in substance, if not in composition, the 'Description' is valuable; and having been published in the 'Beams of Divine Light' according 'to the doctor, his own appointment,' it carries his authority. It is to be hoped that in no after-reprints will the 'Description' and 'Bruised Reed' be disjoined.   G. †

* Original Title page—

A
DESCRIPTION
OF CHRIST,
In { His neerenesse to God,
His calling,
His qualification,
His execution of his calling.
In three Sermons.
Being the leading Sermons to that Treatise called the Bruised Reed, preached
upon the precedent words.
By the late Reverend and learned Divine, Richard Sibs,
Doctor in Divinitie, Master of Katherine Hall in
Cambridge, and sometimes Preacher at
Grayes Inne.
Isa. 61, 1.
The Spirit of the Lord God is upon me, because the Lord hath annoynted
me to preach good tidings unto the meeke.
London.
Printed by G. M. for N. Bourne and R. Harford, and are to be sold at the south
entrance of the Royall Exchange, and at the guilt Bible in Queenes-head-
Alley in Pater-noster-row. MDCXXXIX.

† Throughout the present edition of Sibbes, those foot-notes without any signature or initial belong to the author or his original editors. For all others prefixed or subjoined to the several treatises, &c., having G. attached, the Editor is responsible.

A DESCRIPTION OF CHRIST.

Behold my servant, whom I have chosen ; my beloved, in whom my soul is well pleased: I will put my Spirit upon him, and he shall shew judgment to the Gentiles. He shall not strive, nor cry; neither shall any man hear his voice in the streets, &c.—MATT. XII. 18.

THE words are the accomplishment of a prophecy, taken out of Isaiah xlii. 1, 2, as we may see by the former verse, 'that it might be fulfilled.' Now the occasion of bringing them in here in this verse, it is a charge that Christ gives, verse 16, that they should not discover and make him known for the miracles he did. He withdraws himself; he was desirous to be concealed, he would not live to the view over much, for he knew the rebellious disposition of the Jews, that were willing to change their government, and to make him king; therefore, he laboured to conceal himself all kind of ways. Now, upon this charge, that they should tell nobody, he brings in the prophet Isaiah prophesying of him, 'Behold my servant, &c.; he shall not strive nor cry, neither shall any man hear his voice in the streets.' Other kings labour that their pomp and magnificence may be seen; but he shall not mind ostentation, he shall not be contentious nor clamorous. For these three things are meant when he saith, 'he shall not strive, nor cry, neither shall his voice be heard in the streets;' he shall not yield to any ostentation, for he came in an abased state to work our salvation; he shall not be contentious, nor yet clamorous in matter of wrong; there shall be no boasting any kind of way, as we shall see when we come to the words. You see, then, the inference here.

The inference in the prophet Isaiah is to comfort the people, and to direct them how to come to worship the true God, after he had declaimed against their idolatry, as we see in the former chapter, 'Behold my servant,' &c. Great princes have their ambassadors, and the great God of heaven hath his Son, his servant in whom he delights, through whom, and by whom, all intercourse between God and man is.

It is usual in the prophecies, especially of Isaiah, that evangelical prophet, when he foretells anything comfortable to the people, in the promise of temporal things, he riseth to stablish their faith in better things, by adding thereto a prophecy, and promise of Christ the Messiah, to insinuate thus much, I will send you the Messiah, that is a greater gift than this that I have promised you; therefore you may be sure of the less, as the apostle reasons excellently, 'If he spared not his own son, but delivered him to death for us all, how shall he not with him give us all things?' Rom. viii. 32. So here, I have promised you deliverance out of Babylon, and this and that; do you doubt of the performance? Alas! what is that in comparison of a greater favour I intend you in Christ, that shall deliver you out of another manner of Babylon? 'Behold my servant whom I have chosen;' and in Isaiah vii. 14, 'Behold a virgin shall conceive, and bear a son,' &c. I will send you the Messiah; God shall become man; therefore, I will not stand for any outward favour or deliverance whatsoever. So he goes to the grand promise, that they might reason from the greater to the less.

There is another end, why in other promises there is mention of the promise of the Messiah, to uphold their faith. Alas! we are unworthy of these promises, we are laden with sin and iniquity. It is no matter, I will send you the Messiah. 'Behold my servant in whom my soul delighteth,' and for his sake I will delight in you. I am well pleased with you, because I am well pleased in him; therefore, be not discouraged. 'All the promises are yea and amen in Jesus Christ,' 2 Cor. i. 19; for all the promises that be, though they be for the things of this life, they are made for Christ, they are yea in him, and they are performed for his sake, they are amen in him. So much for the occasion of the inference in the evangelist St Matthew, and likewise in the prophet Isaiah.

To come more directly to the words, 'Behold my servant whom I have chosen, my beloved in whom my soul is well pleased,' &c.

In the words you have *a description of Christ, his nearness to God:* 'Behold my servant whom I have chosen, my beloved in whom my soul is well pleased.' And then his *calling and qualification:* 'I will put my Spirit upon him.' And the *execution of that calling:* 'He shall shew judgment to the Gentiles.' Then the *quiet and peaceable manner* of the execution of his calling: 'He shall not strive nor cry, neither shall any man hear his voice in the streets,' &c.

Behold!—This word is as it were a beacon lighted up to all the rest. In all the evangelists you have this word often repeated, and the prophets likewise when they speak of Christ; there is no prophecy almost but there is this word, 'Behold.'

Why? Not to spend time in the variety of acceptions' (= acceptations), but to speak of it as may serve for the present purpose. The use of it in the prophet, especially out of which these words are taken, was to present Christ to the hearts of the people of God then; therefore, he saith, 'Behold,' for Christ was present to the believers then; he did profit before he was, he did good before he was exhibited, because he was 'the Lamb of God slain from the beginning of the world,' Rev. xiii. 8; he was yesterday as well as to-day, and to-morrow as well as to-day, 'yesterday, to-day, and the same for ever,' Heb. xiii. 8; he was present to their faith, and present to them in types and sacrifices, and present in God's acceptation of him for them; therefore, the prophets mount up with the wing of prophecy, and in regard of the certainty of the things to come, they speak as if they were present, as if they had looked on Christ present, 'Behold my servant,' and 'Behold a virgin,' &c.

But that is not all. Another use of this word 'behold,' was to call the people's minds from their miseries, and from other abasing objects that dejected them, and might force despair. Why do you dwell upon your unworthiness and sin? raise up your mind, 'Behold my servant whom I have chosen,' &c. This is an object worth beholding and admiration, especially of a distressed soul that may see in Christ whatsoever may comfort it.

A third end of it is to raise the mind from any vulgar, common, base contents.* You look on these things, and are carried away with common trivial objects, as the poor disciples when they came to the temple; they stood wondering at the stones. What wondrous stones! what goodly building is here! Mark xiii. 1. So shallow-minded men, they see any earthly excellency, they stand gazing. Alas, saith Christ, do you wonder at these things? So the prophet here raiseth up the minds of men to look on an object fit to be looked on, 'Behold my servant,' &c. So that the Holy Ghost would have them from this saving object, Christ, to raise satisfaction to their souls every way. Are you dejected? here is comfort; are you sinful? here is righteousness; are you led away with present contentments? here you have honours, and pleasures, and all in Christ Jesus. You have a right to common pleasures that others have, and besides them you have interest to others that are everlasting pleasures that shall never fail, so that there is nothing that is dejecting and abasing in man, but there is comfort for it in Christ Jesus; he is a salve for every sore, a remedy for every malady; therefore, 'Behold my servant.'

This word 'behold,' it is a word of wonderment, and, indeed, in Christ there are a world of wonders, everything is wonderful in him. Things new and wonderful, and things rare, and things that are great, that transcend our capacity, are wonderful, that stop our understanding that it cannot go through them. Vulgar things, we see through them quickly, but when we see things that stay our understandings, that raise our understandings higher, and that are more capacious than our understandings, here is matter of admiration and wonder. Now whatsoever may make wonderment is in Jesus Christ, whose name is Wonderful, as it is in Isa. ix. 7; therefore the prophet saith, 'Behold.'

My servant.—Christ is called a servant, first, in respect of his creation, because being a man, as a creature he was a servant. But that is not all.

He was a servant in respect of his condition. Servant implies a base and low condition, Philip. ii. 7. Christ took upon him the form of a servant; he emptied himself; he was the lowest of all servants in condition: for none was ever so abased as our glorious Saviour.

And then, it is a name of office, as well as of base condition. There are ordinary servants and extraordinary, as great kings have their servants of state. Christ besides his abasement, he was a servant of state, he was an ambassador sent from the great God; a prophet, a priest, and a king, as we shall see afterwards; an extraordinary servant, to do a piece of service that all the angels in heaven, and all the men on the earth joined together, could not perform. This great master-piece of service was to bring God and man together again, that were at variance, as it is, 1 Peter iii. 18, 'to bring us to God.' We were severed and scattered from God. His office was to gather us together again, to bring us all to one head again, to bring us to himself, and so to God, to reconcile us, as the Scripture phrase is, Col. i. 20. Now, it being the greatest work and service that ever was, it required the greatest servant; for no creature in the world could perform it. All the angels of heaven would have sunk under this service, to have undergone satisfaction to divine justice; for the angels themselves, when they sinned, they could not recover themselves, but sunk under their own

* That is, 'contentments.—ED.

sin eternally. Thus we see how he is God's servant, who set him apart, and chose him to this service.

And then he was a servant to us; for the Son of man came to minister, not to be ministered unto, Matt. xx. 28. He washed his disciples' feet. He was a servant to us, because he did our work and suffered our punishment; we made him serve by our sins, as the prophet saith, Isa. xliii. 24. He is a servant that bears another man's burden. There was a double burden—of obedience active, and obedience passive. He bore them both. He came under the law for us, both doing what we should have done, and indeed far more acceptably, and suffering that we should have suffered, and far more acceptably. He being our surety, being a more excellent person, he did bear our burden, and did our work, therefore he was God's servant, and our servant; and God's servant, because he was our servant, because he came to do a work behoveful to us.

Herein appears the admirable love and care of God to us wretched creatures, here is matter of wonderment.

If we look to him that was a servant;

If we look to that in God and him, that made him stoop to be a servant;

If we look to the manner of the performance of this service;

If we look to the fruit of that service; they are all matter of wonderment.

If we look to the person that was this servant; the apostle, in Philip. ii. 6, will tell you, he thought it not robbery to be equal with God, yet he took upon him the shape of a servant. Was not this wonderful, for God to become man, the glorious God to abase himself, to be a servant? God-man, glorious God, and base servant; for the living God to die, for the incomprehensible God to be enclosed in the womb of a virgin, for glory itself to be abased, for riches to become poor, what matter of wonderment is here! The very angels stand at a gaze and wonder, they pry into these things, 1 Peter i. 12; his name may well be wonderful.

There are four notable conjunctions that are especially wonderful, two in us, and two above us.

One in us, is the conjunction of so excellent a thing as the soul breathed in by God. The soul of man is an admirable thing. The world is not worth it in the judgment of him that gave himself for it. That this should be joined to a piece of earth (indeed, I am wonderfully made, saith David, Ps. cxxxix. 14) in regard of his body, but the conjunction of the soul and body together, so excellent a substance to so base a thing as earth, to a piece of red, well-coloured earth (*a*),* to a lump of flesh, it is a wondrous conjunction.

But there is a more supernatural conjunction of man when all of us, sinners as we are, are knit to Christ our head, and head and members make one Christ. Here is a wondrous conjunction. St Paul calls it a mystery, Eph. v. 32. These conjunctions in us are wonderful.

But now, to go higher, in Christ there are more wonderful conjunctions; for the greatest and the meanest to join together, for God and man to come together, the Lord of all and a servant, and such a servant as should be under a curse, for the Highest of all to come to the deepest abasement. For there was no abasement ever so deep as Christ's was, in a double regard.

First, None ever went so low as he, for he suffered the wrath of God, and bore upon him the sins of us all; none ever was so low.

And then in another respect his abasement was greatest, because he

* The letters *a*, *b*, *c*, &c., in the text, refer to notes appended to the respective treatise, &c.—G.

descended from the highest top of glory; and for him to be man, to be a servant, to be a curse, to suffer the wrath of God, to be the lowest of all—Lord, whither dost thou descend? Here is a wonder in these conjunctions.

Next to Christ's abasement was Adam's; because he was the most excellent, being in the state of innocency, and carrying the image of God, and being familiar with God. For him presently to come into that fearful condition, it was the greatest abasement; because it was from the greatest dignity that made the abasement of Christ so great. For lordship to submit to service, for God to be man, the blessed God to become a curse, here is matter of wonder indeed.

In Christ, again, there was a conjunction of perfect body, perfect soul, and perfect God, and all make one Christ. In the Trinity there is a conjunction of three persons in one nature. That is a wondrous conjunction, but it belongs not to our present purpose. Here you see there is matter of wonder in the person, that Christ should be a servant.

There is matter of wonder likewise in that from whence he is a servant. Whence comes it that Christ is a servant? It is from the wondrous love of God, and the wondrous love of Christ. To be so abased, it was wondrous love in God to give him to us to be so abased, and the wondrous misery we were in, that we could not otherwise be freed from; for such was the pride of man, that he, being man, would exalt himself to be like God. God became man, he became a servant to expiate our pride in Adam, so that it is wondrous in the spring of it. There was no such love as Christ's to become a servant, there was no such misery as we were in, out of which we were delivered by this abasement of Christ becoming a servant; so it is wondrous in that regard, springing from the infinite love and mercy of God, which is greater in the work of redemption and reconciliation than in the creation of the world, for the distance between nothing and something was less than the distance between sin and happiness. For nothing adds no opposition; but to be in a sinful state there is opposition. Therefore it was greater love and mercy for God, when we were sinful, and so obnoxious to eternal destruction, to make us of sinners, not only men, but to make us happy, to make us heirs of heaven out of a sinful and cursed estate, than to make us of nothing something, to make us men in Adam, for there God prevailed over nothing, but here his mercy triumphed over that which is opposite to God, over sinfulness and cursedness. To shew that the creature cannot be so low but there is somewhat in God above the misery of the creature, his mercy shall triumph over the basest estate where he will shew mercy. Therefore there is mercy above all mercy and love above all love, in that Christ was a servant.

Thirdly, It is wondrous in regard of the fruit we have by this service of Christ, the work of our redemption, to be translated from the kingdom of Satan to the glorious liberty of the sons of God, Rom. viii. 21, to be brought out of darkness into marvellous light. It is a marvellous matter of wonder, the good we have by this abasement of Christ, 'Behold what love the Father hath shewed us, that we should be called the sons of God!' 1 John iii. 1. Now, all this comes from Christ's being a servant. Our liberty comes from his service and slavery, our life from his death, our adoption and sonship and all comes from his abasement. Therefore it is a matter of wonderment for the great things we have by it, O the depth, O the depth, saith St Paul, Rom. xi. 33. Here are all dimensions in this excellent work that Christ hath wrought by his abasement, by his incarnation, and taking upon him the form of a servant, and dying for us; here is the height and breadth, and length and depth of the love of God in Christ. O the riches of God's mercy! The apostles they stand in a wonder and admiration of this, and indeed, if anything be to be admired, it is Christ, that wondrous conjunction, the wondrous love that wrought it, and the wondrous fruit we have by it.

It is the baseness of our nature we can wonder at shallow things. There cannot be foolery, but there will be many about it presently, and stand admiring every empty idle thing that the nature of man is carried away with; whereas indeed there is nothing worthy of admiration but the wonderful love of God. O how wonderful are thy works, saith David, of the works of creation, Ps. viii. 1. The work of creation and of providence whereby God guides the world are wonderful, and the psalmist cries out of the folly of men, that do not regard the work of the Lord, 'Fools regard not this' Ps. xiv 1; 'The works of the Lord are worthy to be considered, they are known of all that delight in them,' Ps. cxi. 2. But if these things be so wonderful, and to be regarded and delighted in, alas! what is all the work of redemption! Great is the mystery of godliness, God manifested in the flesh, &c., 1 Tim. iii. 16. There are mysteries, matters of admiration, but carnal men think these trival matters, they can hear matters of more rarity; and when they speak of these things, alas! they are too wise to wonder, tush, they know the gospel well enough, whereas indeed, as we see here, they are things that deserve the admiration of angels; and as they deserve it, so the angels pry into these excellent secrets in Jesus Christ, 1 Pet. i. 12.

Christ was a servant by office and by condition. We must not rest in this base condition; for he took upon him the form of a servant that he might be an excellent servant. There is both baseness and excellency in the word servant; for his humiliation was a degree of his exaltation, and a part of his advancement. If we regard his human nature, it was an advancement for man's nature to be grafted into God by conception and incarnation; but if we regard his Godhead, for him to conceal himself, and lay aside the beams and rays of majesty, and clothe himself with man's flesh, this was the first degree of humiliation. It was an advancement to his flesh, but it was a concealing and hiding to his Godhead. For God to become a servant this was an abasement: but then consider the excellency of the service, how God delighted in it, and how useful it was to us, and we shall see that he was a servant by way of excellency. There was first in Christ human flesh, abased flesh, and then glorious flesh. Abasement was first necessary for Christ; for he could not have performed the office of a servant, unless he had undertaken the condition of a servant. He must first be abased and then glorious, our ill must be his before his good could be ours; and how could he undergo our ill, our sin and misery, and the curse due to us, but he must be abased? Our sins must be imputed to him, and then his righteousness and whatsoever is good is ours; so here is both the abasement of his condition, and the excellency of his office to be a king, priest, and prophet to his church, as we shall see afterwards.

Is the Lord Christ a servant? This should teach us not to stand upon any terms. If Christ had stood upon terms, if he had refused to take upon him the shape of a servant, alas! where had we and our salvation been? And yet wretched creatures, we think ourselves too good to do God and our brethren any service. Christ stood not upon his greatness, but, being equal with God, he became a servant. Oh! we should dismount from the tower of our conceited excellency. The heart of man is a proud creature, a proud piece of flesh. Men stand upon their distance. What! shall I stoop to him? I am thus and thus. We should descend from the heaven of our conceit, and take upon us the form of servants, and abase ourselves to do good to others, even to any, and account it an honour to do any good to others in the places we are in. Christ did not think himself too good to leave heaven, to conceal and veil his majesty under the veil of our flesh, to work our redemption, to bring us out of the cursed estate we were in. Shall we think ourselves too good for any service? Who for shame can be proud when he thinks of this, that God was abased? Shall God be abased, and man proud? Shall God become a servant, and shall we that are servants think much to serve our fellow-servants? Let us learn this lesson, to abase ourselves; we cannot have a better pattern to look unto than our blessed Saviour. A Christian is the greatest freeman in the world; he is free from the wrath of God, free from hell and damnation, from the curse of the law; but then, though he be free in these respects, yet, in regard of love, he is the greatest servant. Love abaseth him to do all the good he can; and the more the Spirit of Christ is in us, the more it will abase us to anything wherein we can be serviceable.

Then, again, here is comfort for us, that Christ, in whatsoever he did in our redemption, is God's servant. He is appointed by God to the work; so, both God and Christ meet together in the work. Christ is a voluntary in it, for he emptied himself, he took upon him the form of a servant, Phil. ii. 6, he came from heaven voluntarily. And then withal the Father joins with him, the Father appointed him and sent him, the Father laid him as the corner-stone, the Father sealed him, as it is, John vi. 27, the Father set him out, as it is, Rom. iii. 25. 'He hath set him out as the propitiatory.' Therefore, when we think of reconciliation and redemption, and salvation wrought by Christ, let us comfort ourselves in the solidity of the work, that it is a service perfectly done. It was done by Christ, God-man. It is a service accepted of God, therefore God cannot refuse the service of our salvation wrought by Christ. Christ was his servant in the working of it. We may present it to God, it is the obedience of thy servant, it is the satisfaction of thy servant. Here is that will give full content and satisfaction to conscience, in this, that whatsoever Christ did, he was God's servant in it. But we shall better understand the intent of the Holy Ghost when we have gone over the rest of the words, 'Behold my servant whom I have chosen.'

Christ was chosen before all worlds to be the head of the elect. He was predestinate and ordained by God. As we are ordained to salvation, so Christ is ordained to be the head of all that shall be saved. He was chosen eternally, and chosen in time. He was singled out to the work by God; and all others that are chosen are chosen in him. There had been no choosing of men but in him; for God saw us so defiled, lying in our filth, that he could not look upon us but in his Son. He chose him, and us in him.

Here is meant, not only choosing by eternal election to happiness, but a choosing to office. There is a choosing to grace and glory, and a choosing to office. Here, it is as well meant, a choosing to office, as to grace and glory. God, as he chose Christ to grace and glory, so he chose him to the office of Mediatorship. Christ did not choose himself; he was no usurper. No man calls himself to the office, as it is in Heb. v. 4; but Christ was called and appointed of God. He was willing, indeed, to the work, he took it voluntary upon him; but as Mediator, God chose him, God the Father and he joining together.

If we respect eternal salvation, or grace, or office, Christ was chosen in respect of his manhood; for, as it is well observed by divines, Christ is the head of all that are predestinate; and the human nature of Christ could not merit its choice, it could not merit its incarnation, it could not merit union with the Godhead, it was merely from grace. How could Christ's manhood deserve anything of God before it was? Things must have a subsistence before they can work: our blessed Saviour is the pattern of all election, and his manhood could not merit to be knit to the second person; as how could it, being a creature? Therefore the knitting of the human nature of Christ to his divine, it is called the grace of union. The choosing of the human nature of Christ to be so gracious and glorious, it was of grace.

Christ he was both a chosen servant and a choice servant. In calling him a chosen servant, it implies his excellency, as a chosen vessel, Acts ix. 15, a chosen arrow in God's quiver, Lament. iii. 13, so a chosen servant, every way excellent.

This adds to our comfort, that whatsoever Christ did for us, he did it as chosen; he is a chosen stone, as St Peter saith, 1 Peter ii. 6, 'a precious corner-stone;' though refused of the builders, yet precious in God's sight!

Was Christ a chosen servant of God, and shall not we take God's choice? Is not God's choice the best and the wisest? Hath God chosen Christ to work our salvation, and shall we choose any other? Shall we run to saints' mediation, to the virgin Mary, and others, for intercession, which is a part of Christ's office? Who chose Mary, and Peter, and Paul to this work? There is no mention in Scripture of them for this purpose, but behold *my servant*, whom I have chosen.

God in paradise did choose a wife for Adam, so God hath chosen a husband for his church; he hath chosen Christ for us: therefore it is intolerable sacrilegious rebellion and impudency to refuse a Saviour and Mediator of God's choosing, and to set up others of our own, as if we were wiser to choose for ourselves than God is. We may content ourselves well enough with God's choice, because he is the party offended.

Besides, it is folly to go out from Christ, where there is all fulness and content, to leave God's chosen servant, and to go to any other servant, to any broken vessel. God rests in this servant as Pharaoh did in Joseph, the second person in the kingdom, Gen. xli. 40, 43. Therefore let God's choice and ours agree.

And this directs us also, in our devotions to God, how to carry ourselves in our prayers and services, to offer Christ to God. Behold, Lord, thy chosen servant, that thou hast chosen to be my Mediator, my Saviour, my all in all to me, he is a mediator and a Saviour of thine own choosing, thou canst not refuse thy own choice; if thou look upon me, there is nothing but matter of unworthiness, but look upon him whom thou hast chosen, my head and my Saviour!

Again, if Christ be a chosen servant, O let us take heed how we neglect Christ. When God hath chosen him for us, shall not we think him worthy to be embraced and regarded; shall we not kiss the Son with the kiss of love, and faith, and subjection? He is a Saviour of God's own choosing, refuse him not. What is the reason that men refuse this chosen stone? They will not be laid low enough to build upon this corner stone, this hidden stone. The excellency of Christ is hidden, it appears not to men, men will not be squared to be built upon him. Stones for a building must be framed, and made even, and flat. Men stick out with this and that lust, they will not be pared and cut and fitted for Christ. If they may have their lusts and wicked lives, they will admit of Christ. But we must make choice of him as a stone to build upon him; and to be built on him, we must be made like him. We like not this laying low and abasing, therefore we refuse this corner stone, though God hath made him the corner of building to all those that have the life of grace here, or shall have glory hereafter.

The papists admit him to be a stone, but not the only stone to build on, but they build upon him and saints, upon him and works, upon him and traditions. But he is the only corner stone. God hath chosen him only, and we must choose him only, that we may be framed and laid upon him to make up one building. So much for that, 'Behold my servant whom I have chosen.'

My Beloved, in whom my soul is well pleased.—How do we know that these words in the prophet Isaiah are fitly appliable to Christ? By the greatest authority that ever was from the beginning of the world, by the immediate voice of God the Father from heaven, who applies these words in Isaiah to Christ, Matt. iii. 17, in his inauguration when he was baptized, 'This is my beloved Son, in whom I am well pleased,' this is that my Son, that beloved, ὁ ἀγαπητὸς, the beloved Son, so beloved that my soul delights in him, he is capable of my whole love, I may pour out my whole love upon him. 'In whom I am well pleased,' it is the same with that here, 'in whom my soul delighteth,' the one expresseth the other.

How, and in what respect is Christ thus beloved of God?

First as he is God, the Son of God, the engraven image of his Father, so he is *primum amabile*, the first lovely thing that ever was. When the Father loves him, he loves himself in him, so he loves him as God, as the second person, as his own image and character.

And as man he loves him, for as man he was the most excellent creature in the world, he was conceived, fashioned, and framed in his mother's womb by the Holy Ghost. It is said, Heb. x. 5, God gave him a body. God the Father by the Holy Ghost fashioned and framed and fitted him with a body, therefore God must needs love his own workmanship.

Again, there was nothing in him displeasing to God, there was no sin found in his life any way, therefore as man he was well pleasing to God. He took the manhood and ingrafted it into the second person, and enriched it there; therefore he must needs love the manhood of Christ, being taken into so near a union with the Godhead.

As God and man mediator especially, he loves and delights in him. In regard of his office, he must needs delight in his own ordinance and decree. Now he decreed and sealed him to that office, therefore he loves and delights in him as a mediator of his own appointing and ordaining, to be our king, and priest, and prophet.

Again, he loved and delighted in him, in regard of the execution of his office both in doing and suffering. In doing, the evangelist saith, 'He did all things well,' Mark vii. 37. When he healed the sick, and raised the dead, and cured all diseases, whatsoever he did was well done. And for his suffering, God delighted in him for that, as it is in John x. 17, 'My Father loves me, because I lay down my life;' and so in Isa. liii. 12, 'He shall divide him a portion with the great, because he poured out his soul unto death;' and in Phil. ii. 9, 'Because he abased himself to the death of the cross, 'God gave him a name above all names:' therefore God loves and delights in him for his suffering and abasement.

It is said of Noah, Gen. viii. 21, that he offered a sacrifice after the flood, and 'the Lord smelled a sweet savour of his sacrifice,' and thereupon he saith, 'I will not curse the earth again.' So God loves and delights in Christ as he offered himself a sacrifice of a sweet smelling savour wherein God rests; he felt such a sweet savour in the sacrifice of Christ, he is so delighted in it, that he will never destroy mankind, he will never destroy any that believe in Christ. The sacrifice of Noah was a type of Christ's sacrifice.

Now, that Christ's sacrifice was so acceptable to God, there is a direct place for it in Eph. v. 2, 'Walk in love, as Christ hath loved us, and hath given himself an offering and a sacrifice to God of a sweet smell.' And indeed how many sweet savours were there in the sacrifice of Christ offered on the cross! Was there not the sweet savour of obedience? he was 'obedient to the death of the cross,' Phil. ii. 8. There was the sweet savour of patience, and of love to mankind. Therefore God delighted in him, as God, as man, as mediator God-man, in his doings, in his sufferings, every way.

Doth God delight thus in Christ, in his person, or considered mystically? I answer; both. God loves and delights in Christ mystical, that is, in Christ and his members, in whole Christ. 'This is my beloved Son, in whom I am well pleased,' not only with whom alone by himself, but 'in whom,' in him as God, in him in body and soul, in him as head of the church, in him mystically, in all that are under him any kind of way. God delights in him, and all his.

Is it possible that he should delight in the head, and refuse the members? that he should love the husband, and mislike the spouse? O no; with the same love that God loves Christ, he loves all his. He delights in Christ and all his, with the same delight. There is some difference in the degree, 'that Christ in all things may have the pre-eminence,' Col. i. 18, but it is the same love; therefore our Saviour sets it down excellently in his own prayer, he desires 'that the same love wherewith his Father loved him may be in them that are his,' John xvii. 20, that they may feel the love wherewith his Father loves him, for he loved him and his members, him and his spouse, with all one love.

This is our comfort and our confidence, that God accepts us, because he accepts his beloved; and when he shall cease to love Christ, he shall cease to love the members of Christ. They and Christ make one mystical Christ. This is our comfort in dejection for sin. We are so and so indeed, but Christ is the chosen servant of God, 'in whom he delighteth,' and delights in us in him. It is no matter what we are in ourselves, but what we are in Christ when we are once in him and continue in him. God loves us with that inseparable love wherewith he loves his own Son. Therefore St Paul triumphs, Rom. viii. 35, 'What shall separate us from the love of God in Christ Jesus?' This love, it is founded in Christ, 'therefore neither things present, nor things to come (as he goes on there gloriously), shall be able to separate us.' You see what a wondrous confidence and comfort we have hence, if we labour to be in Christ, that then God loves and delights in us, because he loves and delights in Christ Jesus.

And here is a wondrous comfort, that God must needs love our salvation and redemption when he loves Christ, because 'he poured out his soul to death to save us.' Doth not God delight that we should be saved, and our sins should be forgiven, when he loves Christ because he abased himself for that purpose? What a prop and foundation of comfort is this, when the devil shall present God to us in a terrible hideous manner, as an avenging God, 'and consuming fire,' &c., Heb. xii. 29; indeed out of Christ he is so. Let us present to ourselves thoughts of God as the Scripture sets forth God to us; and as God sets forth himself, not only in that sweet relation as a Father to Christ, but our father, 'I go to my Father and your Father, to my God and your God,' John xx. 17, having both one God, and love and care. There is none of us all but the devil will have a saying to us, either in the time of our life, in some terrible temptation, especially when any outward abasement comes, or at the hour of death; and all the cordials we have gathered out of the word will then be little enough to support the drooping soul, especially in the hour of temptation. O beloved, what a wondrous stay and satisfaction to a distressed conscience doth this yield, that Christ in all that he hath wrought for us is God's chosen servant, 'whom he loves and delights in,' and delights in him for this very work, that he abased himself and gave himself for us, that he wrought God's work, because he wrought reconciliation for us! If we can believe in Christ, we see here what ground of comfort we have, that God loves and delights in us, as he doth in his own Son.

And what a comfort is it now, in our daily approach to God, to minister boldness to us in all our suits, that we go to God in the name of one that he loves, 'in whom his soul delights,' that we have a friend in court, a friend in heaven for us, that is at the right hand of God, and interposeth himself there for us in all our suits, that makes us acceptable, that perfumes our prayers and makes them acceptable. His intercession is still by virtue of his service, dying for us. He intercedes by virtue of his redemption. If God love him for the work of redemption, he loves him for his intercession, therefore God must needs regard the prayers made by him, by virtue of his dying for us, when he loves him for dying for us. Be sure therefore, in all our suits to God, to take along our elder brother, to take our beloved brother, take Benjamin with us, offer all to God in him, our persons to be accepted in him, our prayers, our hearing, our works, and all that we do, and we shall be sure to speed; for he is one in whom the soul of God delights. There must be this passage and repassage, as God looks upon us lovely in him, and delights in us as we are members of him. All God's love and the fruits of it come to us as we are in Christ, and are one with him. Then in our passage to God again we must return all, and do all, to God in Christ. Be sure not to go to a naked God; for so he is 'a consuming fire,' but go to him in the mediation of him whom he loves, 'and in whom his soul delighteth.'

And shall God love him and delight in him, and shall not our soul delight in Christ? This therefore should stir up our affections to Christ, to be faithful in our conjugal affection as the spouse of Christ, to say, 'My beloved is mine and I am my beloved's,' Cant. ii. 16. Christ calls his church, 'My love and my dove,' Cant. vi. 9. Doth Christ delight in us, and God delight in Christ, and shall not we delight in Christ that delights in us, and in whom God delights? In the 1 Cor. xvi. 22, the apostle is bold to pronounce a bitter curse, 'Anathema Maran-atha,' upon him that loves not the Lord Christ Jesus, a most bitter curse. When Christ shall become a servant to do our work for us, to suffer for us, to bear the burden of our sins upon the tree, to become our husband, to bestow his riches upon us, to raise us to the same condition with himself, and withal to be such a one as God hath chosen out to love and delight in as the best object of his love, and most capable of it, and for us not to solace and delight ourselves in him that God delights in, when God delights in him for our sake. God loves and delights in him for the work of salvation and redemption by his blood, and shall not we love and embrace him for his love which is for our good? What good hath God by it but only the glory of his mercy, in saving our souls through Christ? Therefore if God love him for the good he doth to us, much more should we love him for the fruit of it that we receive ourselves.

It should shame us therefore when we find dulness and coldness upon us, that we can hear of anything better than of Christ; and arguments concerning Christ are cold to us. Alas! where is our love, and joy, and delight; and when we can make no better but a carnal use of the incarnation and other benefits by Christ! We should therefore desire God to shed the love of Christ into our hearts more and more, that we may feel in our souls the love that he bears to us, and may love God and Christ again, for that that he hath done for us.

Hence we have also a ground of estimation of Christians to be excellent persons. Doth God value poor sinful souls so much as to give Christ for them to become a Saviour? doth he delight in Christ for giving himself for them? and shall not we love one another whom God and Christ so loves?

But if God love and delight in those that are in Christ, with the same love and delight that he hath in him, how shall I know that I am in Christ, and that God thus delights in me?

Briefly, a man may know that he is in Christ, if he find the Spirit of Christ in him; for the same Spirit when Christ took our nature, that sanctified that blessed mass whereof he was made, when there was a union between him and the second person, the same Spirit sanctifies our souls and bodies. There is one Spirit in the head and in the members. Therefore if we find the Spirit of Christ in us, we are in Christ and he in us. Now this Spirit is renewing, 'Whosoever is in Christ is a new creature,' 2 Cor. v. 17; all is new, 'old things are done away,' the old manner of language, the old disposition, old affections, old company, all old things are past, all is new; and if a man be a new creature, he hath right and title to 'the new heaven and new earth,' 2 Pet. iii. 18. Let us examine the work of grace in us. If there be no change in us we have no present interest in Christ. We have to do with him because he is still wooing us to be in him, but as yet we have no title to him.

The very beholding of Christ is a transforming sight. The Spirit that makes us new creatures, and stirs us up to behold this servant, it is a transforming beholding. If we look upon him with the eye of faith, it will make us like Christ; for the gospel is a mirror, and such a mirror, that when we look into it, and see ourselves interested in it, we are changed from glory to glory, 2 Cor. iii. 18. A man cannot look upon the love of God and of Christ in the gospel, but it will change him to be like God and Christ. For how can we see Christ, and God in Christ, but we shall see how God hates sin, and this will transform us to hate it as God doth, who hated it so that it could not be expiated but with the blood of Christ, God-man. So, seeing the holiness of God in it, it will transform us to be holy. When we see the love of God in the gospel, and the love of Christ giving himself for us, this will transform us to love God. When we see the humility and obedience of Christ, when we look on Christ as God's chosen servant in all this, and as our surety and head, it transforms us to the like humility and obedience. Those that find not their dispositions in some comfortable measure wrought to this blessed transformation, they have not yet those eyes that the Holy Ghost requireth here. 'Behold my servant whom I have chosen, my beloved in whom my soul delighteth.'

I will put my Spirit upon him.—Now we come to the qualification of Christ for his calling, in these words, I will put my Spirit upon him—that is, I will clothe him with my Spirit, I will put it, as it were, upon him as a garment.

Now there were divers degrees of Christ's receiving the Spirit at several times. For he was conceived by the Holy Ghost. The Holy Ghost did sanctify that blessed mass whereof his body was framed in the womb of the virgin, he was quickened in the womb in his conception by the Holy Ghost, and he was graced by the Holy Ghost, and led by the Spirit in all things before his baptism. But afterward, when he came to set upon his office, to be the prophet and priest and king of his church, that great office of saving mankind, which he did not solemnly set upon till he was thirty years old, then God poured upon him a special portion of the Spirit, answerable to that great calling, then the Spirit lighted upon him, Matt. iii. 16. Christ was ordained to his office by the greatest authority that ever any was ordained from the beginning of the world. For at his baptism, when he was ordained and set apart to his office, there was the Father from heaven uttered an audible voice, 'This is my beloved Son, in whom I am well pleased,' Mat. iii. 17; and there was Christ, the party baptized and installed into that great office; then there was the Holy Ghost, in the form and shape of a dove. It being a matter of the greatest consequence that ever was in the world, greater than the creation, it was fit it should be done with the greatest authority; and so it was, the Father, Son, and Holy Ghost being present at the admission of Christ into his office. This is especially here intended, though the other be included, I will put my Spirit upon him—that is, I will anoint him, as it is in Isa. lxi. 1, 'The Spirit of the Lord is upon me,' saith Christ, 'because the Lord hath anointed me to preach good tidings to the meek, to bind up the broken-hearted, to proclaim liberty to the captives, to open the prison for them that are bound, to proclaim the acceptable year of the Lord'—that is, the year of jubilee, for that was a type of Christ, to preach the gospel deliverance to all that are in captivity, servitude, and thraldom under Satan and sin. This was accomplished when Christ, at his baptism, entered upon his office. God put his Spirit upon him, to set him apart, to ordain him, and to qualify him with abundance of grace for the work; for there are these three things especially meant by putting the Spirit upon him, separation or setting apart, and ordaining, and enriching with the gifts of the Spirit.

When any one is called to great place, there is a setting apart from others, and an ordaining to that particular, and a qualifying. If it be a calling of God, he qualifies where he ordains always.

But Christ had the Spirit before. What doth he mean, then, when he saith he will put the Spirit upon him now?

I answer, he had the Spirit before, answerable to that condition he was in. Now he received the Spirit answerable to that condition he was to undertake. He was perfect then for that condition. Now he was to be made perfect for that office he was to set upon. He was always perfect. He had abundance of Spirit for that estate he was in, but now he was to enter upon another condition, to preach the gospel, to be a prophet, and after to be a priest. Therefore he saith now especially, I will put my Spirit upon him.

Now, this putting of the Spirit, it is expressed in Isa. lxi. 1, and other places, by anointing. There were three sorts of persons that were anointed before Christ, prophets, priests, and kings. Now Christ was to be a prophet, a priest, and a king. Therefore he was to be anointed with the Spirit, to enable him to these three offices.

I might here take occasion to enlarge myself in the offices of Christ, but I will only speak of them as the text ministereth just occasion.

There are three main defects in man since the fall.

There is ignorance and blindness.

There is rebellion in the will and affections.

And in regard of his condition, by reason of the sins of nature and life, a subjection to a cursed estate, to the wrath of God and eternal damnation.

Now, answerable to these three grand ills, whosoever shall be ordained a saviour must provide proportionable remedies for these. Hereupon comes a threefold office in Christ, that is ordained to save man, to cure this threefold mischief and malady.

As we are ignorant and blind, he is a prophet to instruct us, to convince us of the ill state we are in, and then to convince us of the good he intends us, and hath wrought for us, to instruct us in all things concerning our everlasting comfort. He is such a prophet as teacheth not only the outward, but the inward man. He openeth the heart, he teacheth to do the things he teacheth. Men teach what we should do, but they teach not the doing of them. He is such a prophet as teacheth us the very things; he teacheth us to love and to obey, &c.

And answerable to the rebellion and sinfulness of our dispositions, he is a king to subdue whatsoever is ill in us, and likewise to subdue all opposite power without us. By little and little he will trample all enemies under his feet, and under our feet, too, ere long.

Now, as we are cursed by reason of our sinful condition, so he is a priest to satisfy the wrath of God for us. He was made a curse for us, Gal. iii. 13. He became a servant, that, being so, he might die, and undergo the cursed death of the cross; not only death, but a cursed death, and so his blood might be an atonement as a priest. So, answerable to the threefold ill in us, you see here is a threefold office in Christ.

Now Christ performs these three offices in this order.

First of all he is a prophet. When he was baptized the Spirit was put upon him, as in Isa. lxi. 1, to preach deliverance to the captives. First, he preached wherefore he came into the world, why God sent him, and discovered to the world the state they were in; and when he had preached as a prophet, then as a priest, he died, and offered himself a sacrifice.

After death his kingly office was most apparent. For then he rose again as a triumphant king over death and all our enemies, and ascended in his triumphant chariot to heaven, and there he sits gloriously as a king in his throne at the right hand of God. So that however at his baptism, and before, when he was sanctified in his mother's womb, he was both king, priest, and prophet, yet in regard of the order of manifestation, he manifested himself first to be a prophet, secondly a priest, and thirdly to be a king. For his kingly office brake forth but seldom in the time of his abasement. Sometimes it did, to shew that he was ruler and commander of earth and sea, and devils, and all. He wrought miracles, but the glorious manifestation of his kingly office, it was after his resurrrection.

Now, the fundamental, the chief office to which he was anointed by the Spirit, upon which the rest depends, it was his priestly office; for wherefore was his teaching, but to instruct us what he must do and suffer for us, and what benefit we have by his sacrifice—reconciliation with God, and freedom from the wrath of God, and right unto life everlasting, by his obedience to the cursed death of the cross? And how comes he to be a king to rule over us by his Holy Spirit, and to have a right unto us, but because as a priest he died for us first? He washed us with his blood, he purged us with his blood, and then he made us kings and priests, Rev. i. 5. All other benefits came from this—he washed our souls in his blood first. Whatsoever we have from God, is especially from the great work of Christ as a priest abasing himself, and dying for us; and thereupon he comes to be a prophet and a king. Thus we see the order of Christ's offices, how they come to be fruitful to us, the rest especially, by virtue of his priestly office.

Note this by the way: Christ's priestly office, his sacrificing himself for us, includes two branches. A priest was to offer sacrifice and to pray for the people. Our Saviour Christ did both in the days of his humiliation, in his prayer in John xvii. There, as a priest, he commends his sacrifice to God before he died; and now he is in heaven making intercession for us, to the end of the world. He appears for us there. We see, then, to what purpose God put the Spirit upon Christ, to enable him to be a prophet, a priest, and a king, and thereupon to take away those mischiefs and evils that we were subject and enthralled to; so that we have a supply for all that may any way abase us and cast us down, in the all-sufficiency that is in Christ Jesus, who was anointed with the Spirit for this end.

It may be objected, Christ was God himself; he had the Spirit, and gives the Spirit; therefore, how could the Spirit be put upon him?

I answer, Christ is both God and man. Christ, as God, gives the Spirit to his human nature; so he communicates his Spirit. The Spirit is his Spirit as well as the Father's. The Spirit proceeds from them both. Christ, as man, receives the Spirit. God the Father and the Son put the Spirit upon the manhood of Christ; so Christ both gives and receives the Spirit in diverse respects. As God, he gives and sends the Spirit. The spiration and breathing of the Spirit is from him as well as from the Father, but as man he received the Spirit.

And this is the reason of it: next under the Father, Son, and Holy Ghost, Christ the Mediator, was to be the spring and original of all comfort and good. Therefore, Christ's nature must not only be sanctified and ordained by the Spirit; but he must receive the Spirit to enrich it, for whatsoever is wrought in the creature is by the Spirit. Whatsoever Christ did as man, he did by the Spirit. Christ's human nature, therefore, must be sanctified, and have the Spirit put upon it. God the Father, the first person in Trinity, and God the Son, the second, they work not immediately, but by the Holy Ghost, the third person. Therefore, whatsoever is wrought upon the creature, it comes from the Holy Ghost immediately. So Christ received the Holy Ghost as sent from the Father and the Son. Now as the Holy Spirit is from the Father and the Son, so he works from the Father and the Son. He sanctifieth and purifieth, and doth all from the Father and the Son, and knits us to the Father and the Son; to the Son first, and then to the Father. Therefore it is said, 'The grace of our Lord Jesus Christ, the love of God the Father, and the communion of the Holy Ghost,' 2 Cor. xiii. 14; because all the communion we have with God is by the Holy Ghost. All the communion that Christ as man had with God was by the Holy Ghost; and all the communion that God hath with us, and we with God, is by the Holy Ghost: for the Spirit is the bond of union between Christ and us, and between God and us. God communicates himself to us by his Spirit, and we communicate with God by his Spirit. God doth all in us by his Spirit, and we do all back again to God by the Spirit. Because Christ, as a head, as the second Adam, was to be the root of all that are saved, as the first Adam was the root of all that are damned, he was therefore to receive the Spirit, and to have it put upon him in a more excellent and rich manner: for we must know that all things are first in Christ, and then in us.

God chose him first, and then he chose us. God singled him out to be the Saviour, the second Adam, and he calls us in Christ.

God justified Christ from our sins, being our surety, taking our sins upon him. We are justified, because he by his resurrection quit himself from the guilt of our sins, as having paid the debt.

Christ is the first fruits of them that rise again, 1 Cor. xv. 20. We rise again because he is risen. Christ first ascended; we ascend in Christ. Christ is first loved; we are loved in the Beloved. Christ is first blessed; we are blessed with all spiritual blessings in Jesus Christ, Eph. i. 3. So, whatsoever is in us, we have it at the second hand. We have the Spirit in us, but he is first in Christ; God hath put the Spirit in Christ, as the spring, as the second Adam, as a public person, that should receive the Spirit for us all. He is first in all things; Christ must have the pre-eminence. He hath the pre-eminence in all, both before time, in time, and after time, in election, in whatsoever is done here in this world, and in glorification. All is first in Christ, and then in us. He is the elder brother.

We must understand this, to give Christ his due honour and respect, and to know whence we have all we have. Therefore the Spirit is said here, first, to be 'put upon Christ.' We have not the Holy Ghost immediately from God, but we have him as sanctifying Christ first, and then us; and whatsoever the Holy Ghost doth in us, he doth the same in Christ first, and he doth it in us because in Christ. Therefore, in John xvi. 14, 15, Christ saith, He shall take of mine. Whatsoever the Holy Ghost works in us, he takes of Christ first. How is that?

Thus: the Holy Ghost comforts us with reasons from Christ. He died, and hath reconciled us to God; therefore, now God is at peace with thee. Here the Holy Ghost takes a ground of comfort from the death of Christ. When the Holy Ghost would raise a man up to holiness of life, he tells him, Christ thy Saviour and head is quickened, and is now in heaven, therefore we ought to rise to holiness of life. If the Holy Ghost be to work either comfort or grace, or anything, he not only doth the same thing that he did first in Christ, but he doth it in us by reasons from Christ, by grounds fetched from Christ. The Holy Ghost tells our souls that God loves Christ first, and he loves us in Christ, and that we are those that God gave Christ for, that we are those that Christ makes intercession for in heaven. The Holy Ghost witnesseth to us the love of the Father and the Son, and so he fetcheth from Christ whatsoever he works.

And hence the work of the Holy Ghost is distinguished from illusions and delusions, that are nothing but frantic conceits of comfort that are groundless. The Holy Ghost fetcheth all from Christ in his working and comfort, and he makes Christ the pattern of all; for whatsoever is in Christ, the Holy Ghost, which is the Spirit of Christ, works in us as it is in Christ. Therefore, in John i. 13, it is said, 'of his fulness we receive grace for grace'—that is, grace answerable to his grace. There are three things that we receive answerable to Christ by the Spirit.

We receive grace—that is, the favour of God answerable to the favour

God shews his Son. He loves his Son, he is graciously disposed to him, and he loves us.

So grace habitual. We have grace in us answerable to the grace in Christ. We have love answerable to his love, patience answerable to his patience, obedience and humility answerable to that in Christ. The Spirit works a conformity to Christ in all things.

Likewise, in the third place, the Spirit assures us of the same privileges that issue from grace. Christ is a Son; the Spirit tells us we are sons. Christ is an heir; the Spirit tells us we are heirs with Christ. Christ is the king of heaven and earth; the Spirit tells us that we are kings, that his riches are ours. Thus we have ' grace for grace,' both favour and grace in us, and privileges issuing from grace, we have all as they are in Christ. Even as in the first Adam we receive of his emptiness, curse for curse, ill for ill; for his blindness and rebellion we are answerable; we are born as he was after his fall: so in the second Adam, by his Spirit, we receive grace for grace.

Hence issues this, that our state now in Christ is far more excellent than our state in Adam was.

How doth it spring hence?

Thus, Christ is God-man. His nature was sanctified by the Spirit; he was a more excellent person, he gives and sends the Spirit. Adam was only a mere man, and therefore his goodness could not be so derived to his posterity; for, however the Holy Ghost was in Adam, yet the Holy Ghost did not so fill him, he was not so in him as in Christ. The Holy Ghost is in Christ in a more excellent manner; for Christ being equal with God, he gave the Holy Ghost; the Holy Ghost comes from Christ as God. Now the second Adam being a more excellent person, we being in Christ the second Adam, we are in a more excellent, and in a more safe estate; we have a better keeper of our happiness than Adam. He being a mere man, he could not keep his own happiness, but lost himself and all his posterity. Though he were created after the image of God, yet being but a mere man, he shewed himself to be a man—that is, a changeable creature; but Christ being God and man, having his nature sanctified by the Spirit, now our happiness is in a better keeping, for our grace hath a better spring. The grace and sanctification we have, it is not in our own keeping, it distils into us answerable to our necessities; but the spring is indeficient, it never fails, the spring is in Christ. So the favour that God bears us, it is not first in us, but it is first in Christ; God loves him, and then he loves us; he gives him the Spirit, and us in him. Now, Christ is the keeper both of the love of God towards us and the grace of God; and whatsoever is good he keeps all for us, he receives all for himself and for us; he receives not only the Spirit for himself, but he receives it as Mediator, as head: for ' we all of his fulness receive grace for grace.' He receives it as a fountain to diffuse it, I say. This shews us our happy and blessed condition in Jesus Christ, that now the grace and love of God and our happiness, and the grace whereby we are sanctified and fitted for it, it is not in our own keeping originally, but in our head Christ Jesus.

These be comfortable considerations, and, indeed, the life and soul of a Christian's life and comfort. If we conceive them aright, they will quicken us to obedience, and we shall know what the gospel is. To come to make some use of it.

I might observe this, that none should take that office upon them to which they are not called of God, nor qualified by his Spirit, especially ministers, because Christ did not set upon his office, till the Spirit was put upon him. The Spirit must enable us and fit us for everything. But I leave that, and come to that which concerns us all.

First, then, hath God put the Spirit upon Christ, as the evangelist saith in John iii. 34, 'He whom God hath sent'—that is Christ—'he speaketh the word of God: for God gives him not the Spirit by measure.' God doth not stand measuring grace out to Christ, but he pours it out upon him, full measure, running over, because he receives it not for himself alone, but for us. We receive the Spirit by measure, Eph. iv. 7, 'according to the measure of the gift of Christ.' Christ gives us all a measure of sanctifying knowledge and of every grace, till we 'grow to be a perfect man in Christ,' Eph. iv. 13. Therefore it is called the 'first fruits of the Spirit,' Rom. viii. 23, as much as shall fit us for heaven, and grace sufficient, though it be not that measure we shall have hereafter, or that we would have here. Christ had a full measure, the fulness of a fountain, diffusive, not only abundance for himself, but redundance, and overflowing for the good of others; he being the head of the church, not only a head of eminence, but of influence to bestow and convey all grace in him to all his members, proportionable to the service of every member. Therefore he received not the Spirit according to measure—that is, sparingly—but it was showered upon him; he was filled and clothed with the Holy Ghost. Is it so?

Let us labour, then, to see where to have supply in all our wants. We have a full treasury to go to. All treasure is hid in Christ for us. What a comfort is this in anything we want! If we want the favour of God, go to his beloved Christ, desire God to love us in his beloved, and to accept us in his gracious Son, in him whom he hath made his servant, and anointed with his Spirit for that purpose.

If we want particular graces, go to the well-head Christ, consider of Christ now filled for us, as it was in Aaron. The oil that was poured on Aaron's head ran down to his beard, and to the skirts of his clothing, Ps. cxxxiii. 2, the meanest parts of his garment were bedewed with that oil: so the graces of God's Spirit poured upon our head Christ, our Aaron, our High Priest, run down upon us, upon all ranks of Christians, even upon the skirts, the weakest and lowest Christians. Every one hath grace for grace; we all partake of the oil and anointing of our spiritual Aaron, our High Priest. If we want anything, therefore, let us go to him. I can do all, saith St Paul, in Christ that strengtheneth me, Philip. iv. 13. Go to him for patience, for comfort, for everything, because God hath put his Spirit upon him, to supply all our wants; he hath the oil of gladness above his fellows, Ps. xlv. 7; but for his fellows he hath the oil of grace more than any, but it is not only for him, but for us all. Therefore, let us have comfortable meditations of the fulness of Christ, and make use of it, all this is for me. In Col. ii. 9, St Paul sets it out, 'in him the fulness of the Godhead dwells personally;' for that is meant by σωματικῶς, and it follows after, 'in him we are complete.' Wherefore is all the fulness that is in him? to shew that in him we are complete. So, in 1 John v. 20, 21, to shew how the spirits of the apostles agree, in this saith he, 'we know that the Son of God is come in the flesh, and hath given us an understanding to know him that is true, and we are in him that is true, even in his Son Jesus Christ. This is true God and eternal life.' Christ is true God and eternal life for us all; for our comfort, 'we know that the Son of God is come, and hath given us an understanding, &c. Little children, keep yourselves from idols.' How doth this depend upon the other? Thus;

will you go to idols, stocks and stones, devices of men's brain, for supply of grace and comfort? Christ, whom God hath sent, he is come into the world; he is God and eternal life. 'God hath given eternal life, and this life is in his Son,' 1 John v. 11; therefore, why should you go to idols?

What is the ground of popish idolatries and abominations? They conceive not aright of the fulness of Christ, wherefore he was ordained, and sent of God; for if they did, they would not go to idols and saints, and leave Christ. Therefore let us make this use of it, go out of Christ for nothing. If we want favour, go not to saints, if we want instruction, go not to traditions of men. He is a prophet wise enough, and a priest full enough to make us accepted of God. If we want any grace, he is a king able enough, rich enough, and strong enough to subdue all our rebellions in us, and he will in time by his Spirit overcome all, 'Stronger is he that is in us than he that is in the world,' 1 John iv. 4. The spirit in the world, the devil and devilish-minded men, they are not so strong as the Spirit of Christ; for by little and little the Spirit of Christ will subdue all. Christ is a king, go not out of him therefore for anything. 'Babes, keep yourselves from idols,' 1 John v. 21. You may well enough, you know whom to go to.

Therefore let us shame ourselves. Is there such a store-house of comfort and grace every way in Christ? Why are we so weak and comfortless? Why are we so dejected as if we had not such a rich husband? All our husband's riches are ours for our good, we receive of it in our measure, why do we not go to the fountain and make use of it? Why, in the midst of abundance, are we poor and beggarly? Here we may see the misery of the world. Christ is a prophet to teach us the way to heaven, but how few be there that will be directed by him! Christ is a king to subdue all our spiritual and worst enemies, to subdue those enemies that kings tremble at, to subdue death, to subdue the fear of judgment and the wrath of God, and yet how few will come under his government! 'Christ is the light of the world,' John ix. 5, yet how few follow him! Christ is the way, yet how few tread in his steps! Christ is our wisdom and our riches, yet how few go to him to fetch any riches, but content themselves with the transitory things of this life! Men live as if Christ were nothing, or did nothing concern them, as if he were a person abstracted from them, as if he were not a head or husband, as if he had received the Spirit only for himself and not for them, whereas all that is in Christ is for us. I beseech you therefore let us learn to know Christ better, and to make use of him.

Again, if Christ hath 'the Spirit put upon him for us all,' then in our daily slips and errors make this use, to offer Christ to God with this argument. Take an argument from God himself to bind him. God will be bound with his own arguments. We cannot bind him with ours, but let us go to him and say, Lord, though I be thus and thus sinful, yet for Christ Jesus' sake thy servant, whom thou lovest and hast put thy Spirit upon him to be a priest, and to make intercession for me, for his sake pardon, for his sake accept. Make use of God's consecration of Christ by the Spirit to God himself, and bind him with his own mediator, and with his own priest of his own ordaining. Thou canst not, Lord, refuse a Saviour and mediator of thine own, sanctified by thine own Spirit, whom thou hast set apart, and ordained and qualified every way for this purpose. Let us go to God in the name of this mediator Jesus Christ every day, and this is to make a good use of this, that God hath 'put his Spirit upon him.'

But to make a use of trial, how shall we know that this comfort belongs to us, that Christ hath the Spirit put upon him for us or no, whether he be ordained a king, priest, and prophet for us? That which I said before will give light to this. We must partake of the same Spirit that Christ hath, or else we are none of his members. As we partake of his name, so we must also of his anointing. Thereupon we are called Christians, because we partake of the anointing and Spirit of Christ, and if we have the Spirit of Christ, it will work the same in us as it did in Christ, it will convince us of our own ill, of our rebellions, and cursed estate, and it will convince us likewise of the good we have in him. And then, he is a Spirit of union, to knit us to Christ, and make us one with him, and thereupon to quicken us, to lead us, and guide us, and to dwell in us continually, to stir up prayers and supplications in us, to make us cry familiarly to God as to a Father, to comfort and support us in all our wants and miseries, as he did Christ, 'to help our infirmities,' as the apostle at large, in Rom. viii. 20, sets down the excellent office of the Holy Ghost, what he doth in those that are Christ's. Let us therefore examine ourselves, what the Spirit doth in us, if Christ be set apart to redeem us as a priest. Surely all his offices go together. He doth by the same Spirit rule us, Rev. i. 5, 'He hath washed us in his blood, and made us kings and priests.' Whosoever he washeth in his blood he maketh him a king and a priest, he makes him by the power of his Spirit able to rule over his base corruptions. We may know then, whether we have benefit by Christ by his Spirit, not only by the Spirit witnessing that we are the sons of God, but by some arguments whereby the Spirit may witness without delusion. For though the Spirit of Christ tells us that we are Christ's, yet the proof must be from guiding and leading, and comforting and conforming us to Jesus Christ, in making us kings and prophets, enlightening our understandings to know his will, and conforming us to be like him. The Spirit of Christ is a Spirit of power and strength. It will enable us to perform duties above nature, to overcome ourselves and injuries, it will make us to want and to abound, it will make us able to live and to die, as it enabled Christ to do things that another man could not do. So a Christian can do that, and suffer that that another man cannot do and suffer, because he hath the Spirit of Christ.

At the least, whosoever hath the Spirit of Christ, he shall find that Spirit in him striving against that which is contrary, and by little and little getting ground. Where there is no conflict, there is no Spirit of Christ at all. I will not be large in the point, only I speak this by way of trial, to know whether we have the Spirit of Christ in us or no. If not, we have nothing to do with Christ; for Christ saves us not as he is out of us only. Christ was to do something of himself that we have no share in, only the good of it is ours. He was to redeem us by his blood, to be a sacrifice. The title to heaven and salvation was wrought by Christ out of us. But there is somewhat that he doth not only for us, but he works in us by his Spirit, that is, the fitting of us for that he hath given us title to, and the applying of that that he hath done for us. Whosoever therefore hath any benefit by Christ, he hath the Spirit to apply that to himself and to fit and qualify him to be a member of such a head, and an heir of such a kingdom. Whosoever Christ works anything for, he doth also work in them. There is a Spirit of application, and that Spirit of application, if it be true, it is a Spirit of sanctification and renovation fitting us every way for our condition.

Let us not abuse ourselves, as the world commonly doth, concerning Christ. They think God is merciful, and Christ is a Saviour. It is true, but what hath he wrought in thee by his Spirit? hast thou the Spirit of Christ?

or 'else thou art none of his,' Rom. viii. 9. Wherever Christ is, he goes with his Spirit to teach us to apply what Christ hath done for us, and to fit us to be like him. Therefore, let those that live in any sins against conscience, think it a diabolical illusion to think God and Christ is merciful. Aye, but where is the work of the Spirit? All the hope thou hast is only that thou art not in hell as yet, [only] for the time to come; but for the present I dare not say thou hast anything to do with Christ, when there is nothing of the Spirit in thee. The Spirit of Christ conforms the spouse to be like the husband, and the members to be like the head. Therefore, beg of Christ that he would anoint himself king in our hearts, and prophet and priest in our hearts, to do that that he did, to know his will as a prophet, to rule in us as a king, and to stir up prayers in us as a priest, to do in some proportion that that he doth, though it be in never so little a measure, for we receive it in measure, but Christ beyond measure. We must labour for so much as may manifest to us the truth of our estate in Christ, that we are not dead but living branches.

Now Christ gives and conveys his Spirit especially, and most of all since his ascension and sitting at the right hand of God, for after his resurrection he declared his victory over all his enemies, and therefore was able to give the Spirit without opposition, and upon his resurrection, death and hell and the anger of God were overcome, and our sins were satisfied for. Now Christ was head indeed, having trod all his enemies under his feet; now he was enabled to give the Spirit. But upon his ascension into heaven, and his sitting there, he was more enabled. For even as the sun being so high above the earth, doth convey his light and heat and influence upon the inferior bodies, so Christ being so highly advanced, is fitter to infuse his Spirit and grace here below since his exaltation. Therefore, the church is fuller of grace, and grace hath been more spread and diffused since the ascension of Christ than before, and the evangelist gives it as a reason, 'The Spirit was not yet given, because Christ was not ascended,' John vii. 39; intimating that, after his ascension, there was a more full portion of the Spirit given, God being fully appeased by the death of Christ, and Christ staying the advantage that was fittest, to give the Spirit. Now God the Father gives the Spirit with the Son, so in both regards there was a greater fulness of the Spirit. Therefore, the prophets speaking of the times of Christ, especially of his exaltation, shew that then they should be filled with the Spirit, that the Spirit should be poured upon all flesh more abundantly than before. And that is the reason that the apostles so differed from themselves, before and after Christ's ascension. What a wondrous alteration was there! Peter before, he flies even at the voice of a maid, and they were full of contention and vainglory: but after we see, when the Spirit, the Holy Ghost, came down after Christ's ascension into heaven, how courageous and valorous they were, that they accounted it a matter of glory to suffer anything; and, indeed, we have more or less valour and courage, the more or less Spirit we have. Now they having received more abundance of Spirit, hereupon they were more courageous and undaunted at one time than another. And this abundance of the Spirit comes especially since Christ's advancement.

But how or by what means doth Christ give his Spirit to us? This Spirit that is so necessary for us, it is given by the ministry of the gospel, which is the ministry of the Spirit. 'Received ye the Holy Ghost by the works of the law, or by the hearing of faith preached?' Gal. iii. 2. When the love of God in Christ, and the benefits by Christ, are laid open in the preaching of the gospel to us, God gives his holy Spirit, the Spirit of Christ. Now God in Christ would save us by a triumphant and abundant love and mercy, and the Spirit of God never goes but where there is a magnifying of the love and mercy of God in Christ; therefore the ministry of the gospel, which only discovers the amity and love of God to mankind, being now reconciled in Christ, it is accompanied with the Spirit, to assure us of our part and portion in those benefits, for the Spirit is the fruit of God's love as well as Christ. Christ is the first gift, and the Spirit is the second, therefore that part of the word that discovers God's exceeding love to mankind, leaving angels when they were fallen, in their cursed estate, and yet giving his Son to become man, and 'a curse for us:' the discovery of this love and mercy of God, and of his Son Christ to us, is joined with the Spirit. For by the Spirit we see our cursed estate without the love and mercy of God in Christ, and likewise we are convinced of the love of God in Christ, and thereupon we love God again, and trust to his mercy, and out of love to him perform all cheerful obedience. Whatsoever we do else, if it be not stirred by the Spirit, apprehending the love of God in Christ, it is but morality. A man shall never go to heaven but by such a disposition and frame and temper of soul as is wrought by the Holy Ghost, persuading the soul first of the love and favour of God in Christ. What are all our performances if they be not out of love to God? and how shall we love God except we be persuaded that he loves us first? Therefore the gospel breeds love in us to God, and hath the Spirit together with it, working a blessed frame of sanctification, whereby we are disposed to every good duty. Therefore if we would have the Spirit of God, let us attend upon the sweet promises of salvation, upon the doctrine of Christ; for together with the knowledge of these things, the Holy Ghost slides and insinuates and infuseth himself into our souls.

Therefore the ministers of the gospel should be much in laying open the riches of God in Christ. In unfolding Christ, all other things will follow, as St Paul in Titus ii. 11, 12,' 'The grace of God hath shined, hath appeared gloriously, teaching us to deny all ungodliness and worldly lusts, and to live holily and soberly in this present world.' Where the grace and love of God is persuaded and shed into the soul, all will follow.

What is the reason that former times were called dark times (and so they were), the times of popery a dark age? Christ was veiled, the gospel was veiled, there was no preaching of salvation by Christ' alone, people were sent to stocks and stones, and to saints, and instead of the word, they were sent to legends and such things. Christ was obscured, thereupon they were dark ages. Those ages wherein the Spirit of God is most, is where Christ is most preached, and people are best always where there is most Spirit; and they are most joyful and comfortable and holy, where Christ is truly laid open to the hearts of people. The preaching of mere morality, if men be not careful to open Christ, to know how salvation is wrought by Christ, and how all good comes by Christ, it will never make a man perfectly good and fit him for heaven. It may make a man reform many abuses, like a philosopher, which hath its reward and respect amongst men, but nothing to give comfort at the hour of death and the day of judgment. Only that whereby the Spirit is conveyed, is the knowledge and preaching of Christ in his state and offices.

Again, the Spirit of Christ is given in obedience to this gospel, Acts v. 32. He gives the Holy Ghost to them that obey him. Now, there is the obedience of faith, and the obedience of life. When the soul is wrought to obedience, to believe, and to be directed by God, then the Holy Spirit is given in a further measure still. The Holy Ghost is given to them that obey, to them that do not resist the Spirit of God. For in the ministry of the gospel the Spirit is given in some degree to reprobates. It is offered, it knocks at the hearts of the vilest persons, that live in filthy and false courses of life, whose tongues and bodies are all instruments of an unsanctified soul to offend God. They have gracious motions offered them, but then they do not obey them. Therefore the Spirit seizeth not upon them, to rule in them. They have the Spirit knocking upon them; he doth not dwell in them, and take up his lodging in them. The Spirit is given to them that obey the sweet motions of it. Now, who is it that hears the blessed word of God, the blessed tidings of salvation, but he hath sweet motions of the Spirit to be in love with God, and the mercy of God, and to hate sin a little for a time, then presently upon it corruption joins and swells against those motions, and they only rest in the bare motion, and never come to any perfection. This is the state of reprobates in the church. They have many motions by the Holy Ghost, but their hearts are not subdued to obedience, not to constant obedience. Therefore, if we would have the Spirit of Christ, let us labour to subject ourselves unto it. When we have any good motion by the ministry of the word, or by conference, or by reading of good things (as holy things have a savour in them, the Spirit breathes in holy exercises), Oh give way to the motions of God's Spirit. We shall not have them again perhaps, turn not back those blessed messengers, let us entertain them, let the Spirit dwell and rule in us. It is the most blessed lodger that ever we entertained in all our lives. If we let the Spirit guide and rule us, it will lead us and govern and support us in life and death, and never leave us till it have raised our bodies (the Spirit of Christ in us at length will quicken our dead bodies), Rom. viii. 11, it will never leave us till it have brought us to heaven. This is the state of those that belong to God, that give way to the motions of God's Spirit to rule and guide them. Therefore, if we would have the Spirit of Christ, let us take heed of rebelling against it.

This is the state of many of us,—the Lord be merciful to us, and cure us, —that we do not only not receive the motions of the Spirit deeply into us, but if they be such as cross us in our pleasures and profits, though the word and Spirit join together, there is a rising of the proud spirit of man against so much of the Spirit and the motions of it, and against such parts of the word as crosseth us. This will be laid heavy to our charge one day, that we would bring the Spirit of God to our corruptions, and not bring our hearts to God's Spirit; and hereupon be those phrases in the Scripture of tempting the Spirit. Ananias and Sapphira tempted the Spirit, Acts v. 9 —that is, when men will do that which is naught, and try whether God will forgive them, and put it off or no. How many are there that tempt the Spirit, that put it off, 'Perhaps I shall have the like motions another time,' 'I shall have better occasion when I can gain no more, when I can have my pleasure no more.' Thus men resist the Spirit, as St Stephen saith, Acts vii. 51—that is, when the Spirit discovers to them what they should believe, and what they should do, and they see it crosseth their resolution to be naught. Hereupon they resist the work of the Spirit, that else would close with their souls, and sanctify them, and fit them for heaven, if they would give way to it. And there is a quenching of the Spirit—that is, when men have sweet motions of the Spirit, and presently by some ill language or course of life they defile their vessels, and quench the sweet motions of the Spirit. Let us take heed of all these, of tempting, of resisting, and quenching the Spirit. For undoubtedly, living in the bosom of the church, we have many heavenly motions, especially those that have so much goodness in them as to attend upon God's ordinances. They have those motions at those times that they never have after perhaps, but they either resist them or quench them, and wrong and grieve the Spirit, as St Paul saith, 'Grieve not the Spirit of God, whereby you are sealed to the day of redemption,' Eph. iv. 30. Men speak or do somewhat that grieves the Spirit of God in them, their conscience being enlightened by the Spirit, tells them that they have done that which is naught; yet notwithstanding, for this or that advantage, to please this or that company, they will speak or do that which is ill, and then the Spirit that was given in some measure before is grieved at this carnal and sinful liberty. Therefore, if ye would be guided by the Spirit of Christ, take heed of all these, and of such like courses.

Another means whereby we may come to obtain the Spirit is prayer. To be guided by the Spirit of Christ, next to Christ himself, our Saviour, is the most excellent thing in the world, therefore it is worth the begging and getting. 'How much more shall your heavenly Father give his Holy Spirit to them that ask him?' Luke xi. 13, insinuating that we can ask nothing greater than the Spirit. A man that hath a sanctified judgment, next the forgiveness of his sins through Christ, he begs nothing more than the Spirit to witness the favour of God in Christ, and to fit him for other favours, especially to fit us for the world to come. God can give nothing greater, nor can we beg nothing greater, if we have sanctified judgments, than the Spirit of God. Therefore let us have an high esteem of the Holy Spirit, of the motions of it, and out of an high esteem in our hearts beg of God the guidance of the Spirit, that he would lead us by his Spirit, and subdue our corruptions, that we may not be led by our own lusts, and so consequently by Satan, that leads us by our own lusts in the way that leads to perdition. So much for that, 'I will put my Spirit,' &c.

And he shall shew judgment to the Gentiles.—After Christ was fully furnished, as he was furnished with the Spirit of God, and with a commission from heaven, from Father, Son, and Holy Ghost, having this high commission, and gifts for it by the Spirit, he falls upon his office presently. We are never fit for anything till we have the Spirit, and when we have the Spirit it is active and vigorous and working. 'He shall shew judgment to the Gentiles.'

What is meant by judgment here?

By judgment is meant laws. He shall declare his laws, his truth, and, together with declaring the truth of the gospel, which is his evangelical law, he shall declare it in the soul, and bow the neck of the inward man to the obedience of this his judgment. Christ then, by himself and his apostles and ministers, shall declare his truth, which is the sceptre of his government, to the Gentiles; and not only declare it as princes do their laws, by proclamations and statutes, &c., but he shall declare it to the heart by his Spirit.

Now, in the Hebrew language, ordinarily, wise government is called judgment (*b*). He shall declare judgment, that is, his manner of government, he shall declare it by his Spirit, and cause our spirits to submit to it.

And, indeed, grace is called judgment, in the phrase of Scripture, the grace of sanctification, because it is agreeable to judgment, to God's law. It is agreeable to it, and wrought by it in the soul, and it is the best judgment. For grace whereby the soul is subject to the judgment and law and rule of God, it must needs be the best judgment, because it is agreeable to God's judgment. Grace judgeth aright of things, and subdues all things, the affections and inward man to itself.

But why is the word of God called judgment?

It is called so frequently in the Psalms, and in other places of Scripture, because the truth of God shews what God doth judge. Judgment is originally in God, who is the first truth and the first good. The first truth judgeth best of truths; what is light and what is darkness, what is truth and what is error, what is good and what is ill, what is safe and what is dangerous. All will grant that God is the first light and the first truth; therefore, he doth originally judge of the difference of things; for even as in the creation he put an eternal difference between light and darkness, and severed things that were in the confused chaos, and established an orderly world, that heaven should be above, and earth below, that one thing should be above another, and all in judgment; so in the governing of mankind, he shews his judgment by his word, and that word shews how God judgeth of things. Laws shew judgment, what is to be done, and what is not to be done. The gospel shews God's judgment, what he will have us believe and hope for, and how we must carry ourselves in way of thankfulness. If we do this, then the gospel, the word of God, judgeth what shall become of us; 'we shall be saved,' Mark xvi. 16. If we do the contrary, the word again judgeth what our state shall be, 'we shall be damned,' *ibid*. So it is called judgment, because it judgeth what is good and what is ill, and because it determineth what shall become of us if we obey or disobey.

Hereupon it is that the word of God is a glass wherein we may see our own condition infallibly, what will become of us. The word of God judgeth thus: he that lives in such and such sins shall come to this end, God will inflict these and these judgments upon him. Judgment, in the first place, is, You shall do this and this, because it is good. Judgment, in the second place, is, Because you have not done this, this shall befall you. So the evangelical judgment of the gospel is this, 'He that repents and believes shall not perish, but have everlasting life,' John iii. 15; but he that arms and furnisheth his heart to rebellion, he shall perish in his sins, 'He that believeth not is condemned already, the wrath of God hangs over his head,' John iii. 18. So from this, that God's truth is called judgment, we may know how to judge of ourselves, even as God judgeth in his word. We may see our own faces and conditions there. He that is a man of death may see it in the word, and he that is appointed for happiness may there see his condition.

Again, not only the word of God, the gospel, which is out of us in the book of God, is called judgment, but the work of God in the soul, sanctification, is called judgment. Hence, we may observe what is the most judicious course in the world, the most judicious frame of soul, when it is framed to the judgment and truth of God, being the first truth. When a man is sanctified and set in a holy frame, it is from a sanctified judgment. The flesh is subject to the Spirit. Here is all in a gracious order. The baser part doth not rule the higher, but the higher part of the soul, a sanctified judgment, rules all, because the whole is in right judgment. Therefore, sanctification is called judgment, and other courses, though they be never so fashionable, are but madness and folly and disorder in the censure in the Scripture. Nothing is judgment and true wisdom, but sanctification and obedience flowing from sanctification. Therefore, saith Moses, in Deut. iv. 6, 'Then shall you be known to be a wise people when you obey the laws that I have given you.' Only that, shews a wise, judicious man to be obedient to God's truth by the Spirit sanctifying him. Without the truth of God and the Spirit in us, framing our souls answerable to the truth, we are out of all good order; for then the affections that should be ruled, rule us ; then the body and the lusts of the body rule the soul ; and the devil rules by both. What a shameful disorder is this, when a man shall be ruled by the devil and his own lusts, that he should tread under feet and trample upon ! And this is the state of all that have not this judgment in them, that have not the word of God written in their hearts, bowing and bending them by the Spirit of God to spiritual obedience. To prove this, I will name but one place among many, Tit. iii. 8 ; he shews the state of all men that are not brought into subjection by this judgment, by the word and Spirit of truth. We, ourselves, saith he, 'were sometimes foolish and disobedient ;' till this judgment is set up in us, we are foolish in our understandings, and disobedient in our wills and affections, deceived and misled by the devil and our own lusts : for that follows upon folly. Those that are foolish and disobedient are deceived and led away to eternal destruction. 'There is a way that seems good in a man's own eyes, but the issues of it are death,' saith Solomon, Prov. xiv. 12. This is the state of all men that are not led with the judgment of God's truth and Spirit, sanctifying and framing their souls to obedience, they are foolish and disobedient and deceived, and so it will prove with them in the end, 'serving diverse lusts, and pleasures, living in malice and envy, hating one another,' Titus iii. 3. Now when God by his blessed truth and Spirit sets up his rule in the heart, it brings all into captivity ; as St Paul saith, it brings all the inner man into subjection : ' The word of God is the weapon of God ; these judgments are mighty in operation, together with the Spirit, to beat down all strongholds and to set up another judgment there ; it brings all into captivity to the truth and command of God, and to the motions of the Spirit, 2 Cor. x. 4, 5 (c). The word and Spirit beat down all the strongholds that are raised up in the heart by Satan, and our corruptions. So we see here what is meant by this phrase, 'he shall declare judgment to the Gentiles.' It is a militant word, therefore I have stood somewhat the longer in unfolding of it.

Now this is wrought by the preaching of the gospel, 'he shall declare judgment to the Gentiles.' All grace comes by declaring ; 'The gospel is the power of God to salvation,' Rom. i. 16. Let but the gospel (which is God's judgment how men shall be saved, and how they shall walk in obedience by way of thankfulness to God) be declared, and all that belong to God shall come in, and yield homage to it, and be brought in subjection. The devil in the antichristian state knows this well enough. Therefore he labours to hinder the declaration of judgment by all means ; he will not have God's judgments but men's traditions declared. He knows the declaring of God's judgments will breed an alteration quickly in men's dispositions : For when he saith, he shall declare judgment to the Gentiles, he means the consequent as well as the thing, he shall so declare judgment that they shall yield spiritual obedience and come in and be saved.

Let the devil do his worst, let all seducers of souls do their worst, if they would but give way to the preaching of the gospel, let but judgment be declared, let God's arm be stretched forth in delivering the truth, he would soon gain souls out of the captivity and bondage of Satan. They know it well enough ; therefore by all the ways they can, they stop the preaching of the gospel, and disgrace and hinder it, and set up men's traditions instead of the gospel. But I will not enlarge myself farther upon these words, but go on to the next.

He shall not strive nor cry, neither shall any man hear his voice in the streets.—These words set down the mild and sweet and amiable manner of Christ's carriage upon earth. Here, in his first coming to work the great work of our redemption, he did not carry the matter in an outward glorious manner, in pomp; but he would have his miracles concealed ofttimes and himself hidden. His Godhead was hid under the veil of his manhood. He could not have wrought our salvation else. If the devil and the world had known Christ to be as he was, they would never have made those attempts against him. Therefore, considering he had such a dispensation to work our salvation as a king, priest, and prophet, he would not cry and contend and strive, he would not come with any great noise.

Now, here is an opposition to the giving of the law, and likewise to the coming and carriage of civil princes. You know when the law was given all the mount was on fire, and the earth thereabout quaked and trembled, and the people fled. They could not endure to hear the voice of God speaking in the mount; there was such a terrible smoke and fire, they were all afraid. Thus came Moses. Now, did Christ come as Moses? Was the gospel delivered by Christ as the law was, in terrors and fears? Oh, no. Christ came not in such a terrible manner, in thunder and lightning; but the gospel, it came sweetly. A dove, a mild creature, lit upon the head of Christ when he was baptized, to shew his mild manner of carriage; and he came with blessing in his mouth in his first sermon of all: 'Blessed are the poor in spirit, blessed are they that mourn, blessed are they that hunger and thirst after righteousness,' Matt. v. 3, 4, 6. The law came with curses: ' Cursed is every one that continueth not in all things written in the law to do them,' Gal. iii. 10. Christ came in another manner; the gospel was delivered in a mild, sweet manner. Christ, as an ambassador, came sweetly to entreat and beseech. There is a crying, indeed, but it is a crying out of love and entreaty, not a shouting in a terrible manner as was at the giving of the law, no, nor as at the coming of other civil princes into a city, with shouting and noise of trumpets, with pomp, and state, and great attendants. Christ came not into the world to execute his kingdom and office in such pomp and noise as it is said of Agrippa, Acts xxv. 23, ' He came with great pomp.' So worldly princes carry things thus, and it is needful in some sort. People must have shows and pomp; the outward man must have outward things to astonish it withal. It is a policy in state so to do. But Christ came in another manner. He came not to make men quake and tremble that came to speak and deal with him. He came not with clamour and fierceness; for who would have come to Christ then? But he came in a mild, and sweet, and amiable manner. We see a little before the text (ver. 16), upon occasion of the inference of these words, he commands and chargeth them that they should not discover him and make him known. When he had done a good work he would not have it known.

Now, there are three things especially insinuated in this description, ' He shall not strive nor cry, neither shall any man hear his voice in the street.' That Christ should not be outwardly glorious to publish his own excellency, nor contentious; he should not cry nor quarrel, nor he should not be clamorous, if he had any wrong, to be all on fire presently, but he should be as a meek lamb, he should make no noise, he should not come in vainglory or clamour, &c.

But here we must know that Christ was a wise discerner of the fitness of times; for sometimes he would have things published, sometimes he would not; sometimes he would be known, sometimes he would not. Christ, in his second coming, shall come all in majesty and glory with his angels, and all the earth shall appear before him; but now his wisdom told him, now he came to save the world as a prophet, priest, and king, to work man's salvation, that he must hide and conceal himself; and so he ordered all his courses by discretion. Every sacrifice must be salted with salt, everything should be seasoned with the salt of discretion. This is the steward of all our actions, to know what is fit. Christ knew it was fittest to conceal himself now at this time.

Now, by Christ's example we should learn this, not to be vainglorious, not to make a great noise. You have some, if they do anything that is good, presently all the world must know it. This was not Christ's disposition. It is a disposition that is hardly wrought out of man's heart without an exceeding great measure of the Spirit of God; for we see good men have been given this way. David would number the people, that it might be known what a great monarch he was, what a great number of people he had, 2 Sam. xxiv. He was a good man, yet vainglorious. He smarted for it. So good Hezekiah. Ambassadors were sent to him from the king of Babylon, and that they should know that Hezekiah was no beggarly prince, out must come the vessels of the temple and all his treasures, to shew what a rich king the king of Judah was, 2 Kings xx. 13, *et seq.* His vainglory cost him all his riches, as the prophet told him. So the disciples. Before they received a great measure of the Spirit, how vainglorious were they! They contended for the higher place; therefore they advise Christ to go up to Jerusalem, that he might be known. As Jehu said to Jonadab, 'Come up and see my zeal for the Lord of hosts,' 2 Kings x. 16, he accounts it nothing unless it be seen. So flesh and blood. If there be anything done that is good, all the world must know it presently. Christ chargeth them that no noise should be made, but that they should conceal him.

What should we learn hence?

To be of Christ's disposition, that is, to have no more care of the knowledge of things than the light of the things themselves will discover, to do works of light, and if the things themselves will break forth to men's eyes and they must see our light shine, then let them, and imitate our good works; but for us to blazon them abroad ourselves, it is not the spirit of Christ.

Let us labour to have humility of spirit, that that may grow up with us in all our performances, that all things that we speak and do may savour of a spirit of humility, that we may seek the glory of God in all things more than our own.

And let us commit the fame and credit of what we are or do to God. He will take care of that. Let us take care to be and to do as we should, and then for noise and report, let it be good or ill as God will send it. We know ofttimes it falls out that that which is precious in man's eye is abominable in God's. If we seek to be in the mouths of men, to dwell in the talk and speech of men, God will abhor us, and at the hour of death it will not comfort us what men speak or know of us, but sound comfort must be from our own conscience and the judgment of God. Therefore, let us labour to be good in secret. Christians should be as minerals, rich in the depth of the earth. That which is least seen is his riches. We should have our treasure deep. For the discovery of it we should be ready when we are called to it, and for all other accidental things, let them fall out as God in his wisdom sees good. So let us look through good report and bad report to heaven; let us do the duties that are pleasing to God and our own conscience, and God will be careful enough to get us applause. Was it not sufficient for Abel, that though there was no great notice taken what faith he had, and how good a man he was, yet that God knew it and discovered it? God sees our sincerity and the truth of our hearts, and the graces of our inward man, he sees all these, and he values us by these, as he did Abel. As for outward things there may be a great deal of deceit in them, and the more a man grows in grace, the less he cares for them. As much reputation as is fit for a man will follow him in being and doing what he should. God will look to that. Therefore we should not set up sails to our own meditations, that unless we be carried with the wind of applause, to be becalmed and not go a whit forward; but we should be carried with the Spirit of God and with a holy desire to serve God, and our brethren, and to do all the good we can, and never care for the speeches of the world, as St Paul saith of himself: 'I care not what ye judge of me, I care not what the world judgeth, I care not for man's judgment,' 1 Cor. iv. 3. This is man's day. We should, from the example of Christ, labour to subdue this infirmity which we are sick of naturally. Christ concealed himself till he saw a fitter time. We shall have glory enough, and be known enough to devils, to angels, and men ere long. Therefore, as Christ lived a hidden life, that is, he was not known what he was, that so he might work our salvation, so let us be content to be hidden men. A true Christian is hidden to the world till the time of manifestation comes. When the time came, Christ then gloriously discovered what he was; so we shall be discovered what we are. In the mean time, let us be careful to do our duty that may please the Spirit of God, and satisfy our own conscience, and leave all the rest to God. Let us meditate, in the fear of God, upon these directions for the guidance of our lives in this particular.

NOTES.

(a) P. 6.—'Red, well-coloured earth.' The allusion is to the name of Adam, or man—אָדָם, red, ruddy—and to his derivation, as recorded in Gen. ii. 7.

(b) P. 26.—'In the Hebrew language ordinarily wise government is called judgment.' This holds of various Hebrew terms. In the passage explained (Isa. xlii. 1), the term rendered judgment, is מִשְׁפָּט, which is equivalent to תּוֹרָה, *law*.

(c) P. 28.—2 Cor. x. 4, 5. Sibbes's translation of this somewhat difficult passage may be profitably compared with Alford, Stanley, Hodge, and others, *in loc.* It is surprising how many of these unpretending and almost incidental renderings anticipate the results of the highest scholarship of our time. He may not be—who is?—invariably accurate critically, but he rarely fails in his insight into the 'mind of the Spirit.' G.

THE BRUISED REED AND SMOKING FLAX.

NOTE.

The editions of the 'Bruised Reed and Smoking Flax' known to the editor are, with the letters used to designate those collated for the present publication, as follows:—

(*a*) The Brvised Reede, and Smoaking Flax. Some Sermons contracted out of the 12. of Matth. 20. At the desire, and for the good of wcaker Christians. By R. Sibbes, D.D. Zach. 4, 10, Who hath despised the day of small things? London. Printed for R. Dawlman, dwelling at the signe of the Brazen Serpent in Paul's Church-yard. 1630. 18mo. A.

This is the *first* edition.

(*b*) 'The second Edition, enlarged.' 1631. 18mo. B.
(*c*) 3d edition 1631. 18mo.
(*d*) 4th „ 1632. 18mo.
(*e*) 5th „ 'corrected,' 1635. 18mo. E
(*f*) 6th „ 1638. 18mo.
(*g*) 6th „ [so designated] 'corrected, and divided into chapters.' 1658. 18mo. G.

The text of our reprint is E, as having been the last issued during the lifetime of Sibbes. The 'corrections' and 'enlargements' of B, and the original readings of A, are noted. These will shew the watchful pains which Sibbes took in the matter even of style. It also deepens the regret that so many of his writings labour under the disadvantage of posthumous publication.

The division 'into chapters,' which we probably owe to the celebrated John Goodwin, who also prefixed an admirable 'Epistle' to another of Sibbes's volumes (Exposition of Philippians, c. iii., &c., &c., 4to, 1639), it has been deemed advisable to retain. It is the form in which all subsequent editions have appeared.

The 'various readings,' are given as foot-notes.

G

TO THE RIGHT HONOURABLE

SIR HORATIO VERE, KNIGHT,

LORD VERE OF TILBURY, AND GENERAL OF THE ENGLISH FORCES
UNDER THE HIGH AND MIGHTY LORDS
THE STATES GENERAL OF THE UNITED PROVINCES IN THE NETHERLANDS : *

AND TO HIS PIOUS CONSORT,

THE LADY MARY VERE,†

INCREASE OF GRACE, ETC.

RIGHT HONOURABLE,
Soldiers that carry their lives in their hands had need, above all others, to carry grace in their hearts, that so having made peace with God, they may be fit to encounter with men; and having by faith in Christ disarmed death before they die, they may sacrifice their life with the more

---

* Sir Horatio Vere was the youngest son of Geffrey de Vere, Esq., who again was son of John Vere, 15th Earl of Oxford. He was born at Kirkby Hall, Essex, in 1565. As the titles of the present 'Epistle Dedicatory' shew, he was a military commander of note, only second to his illustrious brother Sir Francis. Returning from a campaign in Bohemia, in 1622–3, the king (James I.), according to Camden, 'received him so graciously and thankfully, that forgetting himself, he stood bare to him.' On the accession of Charles I., in 1625, he was, in consideration of his eminent services, raised to the peerage, by the title of Lord Vere, Baron Tilbury. He was the first peer created by Charles. He died, May 2. 1635, only three months before Sibbes himself. Besides the tribute of the author of the 'Bruised Reed,' to the worth of Sir Horatio, Fuller has burnished his name as of one renowned for piety, meekness, and valour. A volume of poems, now rarely to be met with, was published on his death. It is entitled, 'Elegies, celebrating the happy memory of Horatio Vere.' (London, 1642, 8vo.) For full 'Memoirs' of him, consult the *Extinct Peerage* books. G.

† Lady Mary Vere.—Anderson in his 'Memorable Women of the Puritan Times,' (2 vols., 1862, *just issued*,) has given a singularly interesting, and on the whole, accurate account of this remarkable Lady. (See vol. i. pp. 31-85.) It was to her the Parliament entrusted the care of the children of Charles I. She died on the 25th of December 1671, in the ninety-first year of her age. Gurnall preached her funeral sermon. G.

courage and comfort, which to neglect, being a matter of eternity, is not valour, but desperate madness, because in this business, as in oversights of war, there is no place for a second repentance, the first error being unrecoverable. In evils above the strength of man to prevail against[*] and his patience to endure, there God hath planted the affection of fear, which might stir us up to avoid the danger by flying to him in Christ, who being our friend, it is no matter who is our enemy: we may be killed, but cannot be hurt; so safe it is to be under his command that hath command over death, hell, judgment, and all that we most fear. Yet such is our nature, that by familiarity with danger, we grow by degrees insensibly to be hardened against it, and to look no further than death, as if to die were only to give up the ghost, and then an end of all. And hereupon it is, that they that follow the wars are generally taken to be men not most religious; the more respect those of that profession deserve, that have learned upon what terms to live and die, that are sure of a better life before they leave this, that have laid up their life in Christ; amongst whom, Right Honourable, the world hath a long time taken notice of you, in whom both religion and military employment, meekness of spirit with height of courage, humility with honour, by a rare and happy combination have met together. Whereby you have much vindicated your profession from common imputation, and shewed that piety can enter into tents, and follow after camps, and that God hath his Joshuas and his Corneliuses in all ages. But I will not use many words of yourself to yourself, because though you have done much that may and will be spoken, yet you love not to hear or speak of what you have done.

It may seem to some unbefitting to offer a discourse of a 'bruised reed' to such a strong and flourishing cedar. But experience sheweth that the strongest plants in God's house are exposed sometimes to strong winds of temptation, and thereupon meet with bruisings, that they may the better know by whose strength they stand, and that the greatest may learn to go out of themselves to the same common rock and fountain of strength with the meanest. David was a valiant man; yet upon experience of his oft failings and recoveries, he became towards God as a weaned child. Lowliness of mind to Godward and greatness of spirit against His enemies may well stand together; for the way to be above all other things is to submit to God first. Besides, this text speaketh of the prevailing government of Christ in his church and in his children, which may be an encouragement to your Lordship still, not only to own the cause of Christ in these times, wherein men are ashamed of what they should glory in, and glory in their shame; but likewise to fight the Lord's battles, when called to it, and help him against the mighty, for victory attendeth Christ's side in the end. Though God, to revenge the quarrel of his covenant, suffer his enemies to prevail yet for a time, to harden them the more, yet they have undertaken a damned cause; and howsoever the church hath justly provoked God, yet the cause shall stand impregnable against all created

---

[*] 'Against,' added first in B.

power of devils and men. We naturally desire victory, and many desire it more than truth or goodness, which only are victorious; and so out of a depraved judgment they cross their own desires, seeking to overcome in that wherein it were safer for them to be overcome. These* are sure to meet with shame in the conclusion instead of victory; or else we must deny Christ to be King of his church and Judge of the world. Proceed on still, Honourable Lord, to stand for Christ both in peace and war, and this shall be found to your honour when Christ shall come ' to be glorious in his saints,' 2 Thess. i. 10, that he thought you worthy to honour himself by, when others, that oppose or betray the cause of Christ for base ends, shall not dare to hold up their heads.

I would not divide you from your Honourable Lady, being obliged to both, and both being one, as in other bands, so in that above nature, in love to the best things; both exemplary in all religious courses; both in your places, likewise, having been employed in great services for the common good, so that not only this but foreign States are bound to bless God for you both. Going on in these ways, you will find God making his promise good of honouring them that honour him.

I do not so far overvalue this poor work as to think it worthy of your Honours, but thus I thought meet to witness my deserved respect to you both. If I be to blame for suffering these sermons, long since preached, thus to come forth, others must divide the fault with me, who had brought it to that pass that it was almost necessary for me to take this course. The Lord continue to bless your Honours, with all your branches, and to maintain his grace in you, ' until he hath brought forth judgment unto victory,' Mat. xii. 20.

Your Honours' to command in the Lord,

RICHARD SIBBES.

* 'They,' in A.

TO THE GENERAL READER.

To prevent a further inconvenience, I was drawn to let these notes pass with some review, considering there was an intendment of publishing them, by some who had not perfectly taken them; and these first, as being next at hand: and having had occasion lately of some fresh thoughts concerning this argument, by dealing with some, the chief ground of whose trouble was the want of considering of the gracious nature and office of Christ; the right conceit of which is the spring of all service to Christ, and comfort from him. God hath laid up all grace and comfort in Christ for us, and planted a wonderful sweetness of pity and love in his heart towards us. As God his father hath *fitted him with a body*, Heb. x. 7, so with a heart to be a merciful Redeemer. What do* the Scriptures speak but Christ's love and tender care over those that are humbled? and besides the mercy that resteth in his own breast, he works the like impression in his ministers and others, *to comfort the feeble-minded, and to bear with the weak*, 1 Thess. v. 14. Ministers by their calling are friends of the Bride, and to bring Christ and his Spouse together, and therefore ought, upon all good occasions, to lay open all the excellencies of Christ, and amongst others, as that he is highly born, mighty, One 'in whom all the treasures of wisdom are hid,' Col. ii. 3, &c., so likewise gentle, and of a good nature, and of a gracious disposition. It cannot but cheer the heart of the spouse, to consider, in all her infirmities and miseries she is subject to,† that she hath a husband of a kind disposition, that knows how to give the honour of mild usage to the weaker vessel, that will be so far from rejecting her, because she is weak, that he will pity her the more. And as he is kind at all times, so especially when it is most seasonable; he will speak to her heart, 'especially in the wilderness,' Hos. ii. 24. The more glory to God, and the more comfort to a Christian soul, ariseth from the belief and application of these things, the more the enemy of God's glory and man's comfort labours to breed mispersuasions of them, that if he cannot keep men from heaven, and bring them into that cursed condition he is in himself, yet he may trouble them in their passage; some and none of the worst, Satan prevails withal so far as to neglect the means, upon fear they should, being so sinful, dishonour God and increase their sins; and so they lie smothering under this temptation, as it were bound hand and foot by Satan, not daring to make out to Christ, and yet are secretly upheld by a spirit of faith, shewing itself in hidden sighs and groans unto God. These are abused by false representations of Christ; all whose ways to such being ways of mercy, and all his thoughts, thoughts of love. The more Satan is malicious

* 'Doth,' in A and B. † 'Unto,' in A and B.

in keeping the soul in darkness, the more care is to be had of establishing the soul upon that which will stay it. Amongst other grounds to build our faith on, as the free offer of grace to all that will receive it, Rev. xxii.17; the gracious invitation of all that are weary and heavy laden, Matt. xi. 28; those that have nothing to buy withal, Isa. lv. 1; the command binding to believe, 1 John. iii. 23; the danger of not believing, being shut up prisoners thereby under the guilt of all other sins, John xvi. 9; the sweet entreaty to believe, and ordaining ambassadors to desire peace, 2 Cor. v. 20; putting tender affections into them, answerable to their calling, ordaining sacraments for the sealing of the covenant. Besides these, I say, and such moving inducements, this is one infusing vigour and strength into all the rest, that they proceed from Christ, a person authorised, and from those bowels that moved him not only to become a man, but a curse for us; hence it is, that he '*will not quench the smoking wick or flax.*' It adds strength to faith to consider, that all expressions of love issue from nature in Christ, which is constant. God knows that, as we are prone to sin, so, when conscience is thoroughly awaked, we are as prone to despair for sin; and therefore he would have us know, that he setteth himself in the covenant of grace to triumph in Christ over the greatest evils and enemies we fear, and that his thoughts are not as our thoughts are, Isa. v. 8; that he is God, and not man, Hos. xi. 9; that there are heights, and depths, and breadths of mercy in him above all the depths of our sin and misery, Eph. iii. 18; that we should never be in such a forlorn condition, wherein there should be ground of despair, considering our sins be the sins of men, his mercy the mercy of an infinite God. But though it be a truth clearer than the sunbeams, that a broken-hearted sinner ought to embrace mercy so strongly enforced; yet there is no truth that the heart shutteth itself more against than this, especially in sense of misery, when the soul is fittest for mercy, until the Holy Spirit sprinkleth the conscience with the blood of Christ, and sheddeth his love into the heart, that so the blood of Christ in the conscience may cry louder than the guilt of sin; for only God's Spirit can raise the conscience with comfort above guilt, because he only is greater than the conscience. Men may speak comfort, but it is Christ's Spirit that can only comfort. Peace is the *fruit of the lips*, but yet *created* to be so, Isa. lvii. 19. No creature can take off wrath from the conscience, but he that set it on, though all the prevailing arguments be used that can be brought forth, till the Holy Ghost effectually persuadeth, by a divine kind of rhetoric, which ought to raise up our hearts to him who is the comforter of his people, that he would seal them to our souls. Now God dealing with men as understanding creatures, the manner which he useth in this powerful work upon their consciences, is by way of friendly intercourse, as entreaty and persuasion, and discovery of his love in Christ, and Christ's gracious inclination thus even to the weakest and lowest of men. *Laquitur Deus ad modum nostrum, agit ad modum suum.* And, therefore, because he is pleased by such like motives to enter into the heart and settle a peace there, we ought with reverence to regard all such sanctified helps, and among the rest this of making use of this comfortable description of Christ by God the Father, in going boldly in all necessities to the throne of grace. But we must know this comfort is only the portion of those that give up themselves to Christ's government, that are willing in all things to be disposed of by him. For here we see in this Scripture both joined together, mercy to bruised reeds, and yet government prevailing by degrees over corruptions. Christ so favoureth weak ones, as that he frameth their souls to a better condition than they are in. Neither can it be otherwise, but that a soul looking for mercy should submit itself at the same time to be guided. Those relations of husband, head, shepherd, &c., imply not only meekness and mercy, but government likewise. When we become Christians to purpose, we live not exempt from all service, but only we change our Lord. Therefore, if any in an ill course of life snatch comforts before they are reached out unto them, let them know they do it at their own perils. It is as if some ignorant man should come into an apothecary's shop, stored with variety of medicines of all sorts, and should take what comes next to hand, poison perhaps, instead of physic. There is no word of comfort in the whole book of God intended for such *as regard iniquity in their hearts*, Ps. lxvi. 18; though they do not act it in their lives. Their only comfort is, that the sentence of damnation is not executed, and thereupon there is yet opportunity of safer thoughts and resolutions, otherwise they stand not only convicted but condemned by the word; and Christ *that rideth on the white horse*, Rev. vi. 2, will spend all his arrows upon them, and wound them to death. If any shall bless himself in an ill way, God's wrath shall burn to hell against such. There is no more comfort to be expected from Christ, than there is care to please him. Otherwise to make him an abettor of a lawless and loose life, is to transform him into a fancy, nay, into the likeness of him whose works he came to destroy, 1 John iii. 8, which is the most detestable idolatry of all. One way whereby the Spirit of Christ prevaileth in his, is to preserve them from such thoughts; yet we see people will frame a divinity to themselves, pleasing to the flesh, suitable to their own ends, which, being vain in the substance, will prove likewise vain in the fruit, and as a building upon the sand.

The main scope of all, is, to allure us to the entertainment of Christ's mild, safe, wise, victorious government, and to leave men naked of all pretences, why they will not have Christ to rule over them, when we see salvation not only strongly wrought, but sweetly dispensed by him. His government is not for his own pleasure, but for our good. We are saved by a way of love, that love might be kindled by this way in us to God again; because this affection melteth the soul, and mouldeth it to all duty and acceptable manner of performance of duty. It is love in duties that God regards, more than duties themselves. This is the true and evangelical disposition arising from Christ's love to us, and our love to him again; and not to fear to come to him, as if we were to take an elephant by the tooth. It is almost a fundamental mistake, to think that God delights in slavish fears, whenas the fruits of Christ's kingdom are peace and joy in the Holy Ghost: for from this mistake come weak, slavish, superstitious conceits.

Two things trouble the peace of Christians very much (1), their weaknesses hanging upon them, and (2) fear of holding out for time to come. A remedy against both is in this text, for Christ is set out here as a mild Saviour to weak ones; and, for time to come, his powerful care and love is never interrupted, until he bring forth judgment to victory. And thereupon it is that both the means of salvation and grace wrought by means, and glory the perfection of grace, come all under one name of the KINGDOM OF GOD so oft; because whom by means he brings to grace, he will by grace bring to glory.

This makes * the thoughts of the latter judgment comfortable unto us, that he who is then to be our judge, cannot but judge for them who have been ruled by him here; for whom he guides by his counsel, those he

* 'Maketh,' in A and B.

brings to glory, Ps. lxxiii. 24. If our faith were but as firm as our state in Christ is secure and glorious, what manner of men should we be?

If I had gone about to affect writing in a high strain, I should have missed of mine end, and crossed the argument in hand. For shall we that are servants quench those weak sparks which our Lord himself is pleased to cherish? I had rather hazard the censure of some, than hinder the good of others; which, if it be any ways furthered by these few observations, I have what I aimed at. I intended not a treatise, but opening of a text; what I shall be drawn to do in this kind must be by degrees, as leisure in the midst of many interruptions will permit: the Lord guide our hearts, tongues, and pens for his glory and the good of his people.

RICHARD SIBBES.

THE BRUISED REED AND SMOKING FLAX.

A bruised reed shall he not break, and smoking flax shall he not quench, till he send forth judgment unto victory.—MATT. xii. 20.

[CHAPTER I.—*The Text opened and divided. What the Reed is, and what the Bruising.*]

THE prophet Isaiah being lifted up, and carried with the wing of prophetical spirit, passeth over all the time between him and the appearing of Jesus Christ in the flesh, and seeth with the eye of prophecy, and with the eye of faith, Christ as present, and presenteth him, in the name of God, to the spiritual eye of others, in these words : ' Behold my servant whom I have chosen,' &c., Isa. xliii. 10. Which place is alleged by Saint Matthew as fulfilled now in Christ, Matt. xii. 18. Wherein is propounded—
    First, the calling of Christ to his office.
    Secondly, the execution of it.

    I. For his calling : God styleth him here his righteous servant, &c. Christ was God's servant in the greatest piece of service that ever was ; a chosen, and a choice servant : he did and suffered all by commission from the Father : wherein we may see the sweet love of God to us, that counts the work of our salvation by Christ his greatest service ; and that he will put his only beloved Son to that service. He might well prefix *Behold*, to raise up our thoughts to the highest pitch of attention and admiration. In time of temptation, misgiving consciences look so much to the present trouble they are in, that they need be roused up to behold him in whom they may find rest for their distressed souls. In temptations it is safest to behold nothing but Christ the true brazen serpent, the true *Lamb of God that taketh away the sins of the world*, John i. 29. This saving object hath a special influence of comfort into the soul, especially if we look not only on Christ, but upon the Father's authority and love in him. For in all that Christ did and suffered as Mediator, we must see *God in him reconciling the world unto himself*, 2 Cor. v. 19.
    What a support to our faith is this, that God the Father, the party offended by our sins, is so well pleased with the work of redemption ! And what a comfort is this, that seeing God's love resteth on Christ, as well

pleased in him, we may gather that he is as well pleased with us, if we be in Christ! For his love resteth in whole Christ, in Christ mystical, as well as Christ natural, because he loveth him and us with one love. Let us, therefore, embrace Christ, and in him God's love, and build our faith safely on such a Saviour, that is furnished with so high a commission.

See here, for our comfort, a sweet agreement of all three persons: the Father giveth a commission to Christ; the Spirit furnisheth and sanctifieth to it; Christ himself executeth the office of a Mediator. Our redemption is founded upon the joint agreement of all three persons of the Trinity.

II. For the execution of this his calling, it is set down here to be modest, without making a noise, or raising dust by any pompous coming, as princes use to do. '*His voice shall not be heard.*' His voice indeed was heard, but what voice? '*Come unto me, all ye that are weary and heavy laden,*' Mat. xi. 28. He cried, but how? '*Ho, every one that thirsteth, come,*' &c., Isa. lv. 1. And as his coming was modest, so it was mild, which is set down in these words: The bruised reed shall he not break, &c. Wherein we may observe these three things:—

First, The condition of those that Christ had to deal withal. (1.) They were *bruised reeds;* (2.) *smoking flax.*

Secondly, Christ's carriage toward* them. He *brake not* the bruised reed, nor *quenched* the smoking flax: where more is meant than spoken; for he will not only not break the bruised reed, nor quench, &c., but he will cherish them.

Thirdly, The constancy and progress of this his tender care, '*until judgment come to victory*'—that is, until the sanctified frame of grace begun in their hearts be brought to that perfection, that it prevaileth over all opposite corruption.

1. For the *first,* the condition of men whom he was to deal withal is, that they were bruised reeds, and smoking flax; not trees, but reeds; and not whole, but bruised reeds. The church is compared to weak things; to a dove amongst the fowls; to a vine amongst the plants; to sheep amongst the beasts; to a woman, which is the weaker vessel: and here God's children are compared to bruised reeds and smoking flax. First,† we will speak of them as they are bruised reeds, and then as smoking flax.

They are bruised reeds before their conversion, and oftentimes after: before conversion all (except such as being bred up in the church, God hath delighted to shew himself gracious unto from their childhood), yet in different degrees, as God seeth meet; and as difference is in regard of temper, parts, manner of life, &c., so in God's intendment of employment for the time to come; for usually he empties such of themselves, and makes them nothing, before he will use them in any great services.

(1.) This bruised reed is a man that for the most part is in some misery, as those were that came to Christ for help, and (2) by misery is brought to see sin the cause of it; for whatsoever pretences sin maketh, yet bruising or breaking is the end of it; (3) he is sensible of sin and misery, even unto bruising; and (4), seeing no help in himself, is carried with restless desire to have supply from another, with some hope, which a little raiseth him out of himself to Christ, though he dareth not claim any present interest of mercy. This spark of hope being opposed by doubtings, and fears rising from corruption, maketh him as smoking flax; so that both these together, a *bruised* reed and *smoking* flax, make up the state of a poor dis-

* 'Towards,' in A and B.   † 'And first,' in A and B.

tressed man. Such an one as our Saviour Christ termeth poor in spirit, Mat. v. 3, who seeth a want, and withal seeth himself indebted to divine justice, and no means of supply from himself or the creature, and thereupon mourns, and upon some hope of mercy from the promise and examples of those that have obtained mercy, is stirred up to hunger and thirst after it.

[CHAPTER II.—*Those that Christ hath to do withal are Bruised.*]

This bruising is required [1] before conversion (1), that so the Spirit may make way for itself into the heart by levelling all proud, high thoughts, and that we may understand ourselves to be what indeed we are by nature. We love to wander from ourselves and to be strangers at home, till God bruiseth us by one cross or other, and then we *bethink ourselves*, and come home to ourselves with the prodigal (Luke xv. 17.)

A marvellous hard thing it is to bring a dull and a shifting heart to cry with feeling for mercy. Our hearts, like malefactors, until they be beaten from all shifts, never cry for the mercy of the Judge. Again (2), this bruising maketh us set a high price upon Christ. The gospel is the gospel indeed then; then the fig-leaves of morality will do us no good. And (3) it maketh us more thankful, and (4) from thankfulness more fruitful in our lives; for what maketh many so cold and barren, but that bruising for sin never endeared God's grace unto them? Likewise (5), this dealing of God doth establish us the more in his ways, having had knocks and bruisings in our own ways. This is the cause oft of relapses and apostasies, because men never smarted for sin at the first; they were not long enough under the lash of the law. Hence this inferior work of the Spirit in *bringing down high thoughts*, 2 Cor. x. 5, is necessary before conversion. And, for the most part, the Holy Spirit, to further the work of conviction, joineth some affliction, which, sanctified, hath a healing and purging power.

Nay, [2] after conversion we need bruising, that (1) reeds may know themselves to be reeds, and not oaks; even reeds need bruising, by reason of the remainder of pride in our nature, and to let us see that we live by mercy. And (2) that weaker Christians may not be too much discouraged when they see stronger shaken and bruised. Thus Peter was bruised when he wept bitterly, Matt. xxvi. 75. This reed, till he met with this bruise, had more wind in him than pith. 'Though all forsake thee, I will not,' &c., Matt. xxvi. 35. The people of God cannot be without these examples. The heroical deeds of those great worthies do not comfort the church so much as their falls and bruises do. Thus David was bruised, Ps. xxxii. 3–5, until he came to a free confession, without guile of spirit; nay, his sorrows did rise in his own feeling unto the exquisite pain of breaking of bones, Ps. li. 8. Thus Hezekiah complains that God had 'broken his bones' as a lion, Isa. xxxviii. 13. Thus the chosen vessel St Paul needed the messenger of Satan to buffet him, lest he should be lifted up above measure, 2 Cor. xii. 7.

Hence we learn that we must not pass too harsh judgment upon ourselves or others when God doth exercise us with bruising upon bruising; there must be a conformity to our head, Christ, who 'was bruised for us,' Isa. liii. 5, that we may know how much we are bound unto him. Profane spirits, ignorant of God's ways in bringing his children to heaven, censure broken-hearted Christians for desperate persons, whenas God is about a gracious good work with them. It is no easy matter to bring a man from nature to grace, and from grace to glory, so unyielding and untractable are our hearts.

[CHAPTER III.—*Christ will not Break the Bruised Reed.*]

2. The second point is, that Christ will not '*break the bruised reed.*' Physicians, though they put their patients to much pain, yet they will not destroy nature, but raise it up by degrees. Chirurgeons* will lance and cut, but not dismember. A mother that hath a sick and froward child will not therefore cast it away. And shall there be more mercy in the stream than in the spring? Shall we think there is more mercy in ourselves than in God, who planteth the affection of mercy in us? But for further declaration of Christ's mercy to all bruised reeds, consider the comfortable relations he hath taken upon him of husband, shepherd, brother, &c., which he will discharge to the utmost; for shall others by his grace fulfil what he calleth them unto, and not he that, out of his love, hath taken upon him these relations, so thoroughly founded upon his Father's assignment, and his own voluntary undertaking? Consider his borrowed names from the mildest creatures, as lamb, hen, &c., to shew his tender care; consider his very name Jesus, a Saviour, given him by God himself; consider his office answerable to his name, which is that he should 'heal the broken-hearted,' Isa. lxi. 1. At his baptism the Holy Ghost sate on him in the shape of a dove, to shew that he should be a dove-like, gentle Mediator. See the gracious manner of executing his offices. As a prophet, he came with blessing in his mouth, 'Blessed be the poor in spirit,' &c., Matt. v. 3, and invited those to come to him whose hearts suggested most exceptions against themselves, 'Come unto me, all ye that are weary and heavy laden,' Matt. xi. 28. How did his bowels yearn when 'he saw the people as sheep without a shepherd!' Matt. ix. 36. He never turned any back again that came unto him, though some went away of themselves. He came to die as a priest for his enemies. In the days of his flesh he dictated a form of prayer unto his disciples, and put petitions unto God into their mouths, and his Spirit to intercede in their hearts; and now makes intercession in heaven for weak Christians, standing between God's anger and them; and shed tears for those that shed his blood. So he is a meek King; he will admit mourners into his presence, a king of poor and afflicted persons: as he hath beams of majesty, so he hath bowels of mercies and compassion; 'a prince of peace,' Isa. ix. 6. Why was he 'tempted, but that he might succour those that are tempted,' Heb. ii. 18. What mercy may we not expect from so gracious a mediator, 1 Tim. ii. 5, that took our nature upon him that he might be gracious. He is a physician good at all diseases, especially at the binding up of a broken heart; he died that he might heal our souls with a plaster of his own blood, and by that death save us, which we were the procurers of ourselves, by our own sins; and hath he not the same bowels in heaven? 'Saul, Saul, why persecutest thou me?' Acts ix. 4, cried the head in heaven, when the foot was trodden on, on earth. His advancement hath not made him forget his own flesh; though it has freed him from passion, yet not from compassion towards us. The lion of the tribe of Judah will only tear in pieces those that 'will not have him rule over them,' Luke xix. 17. He will not shew his strength against those that prostrate themselves before him.

* 'Surgeons,' in A and B.

Use 1. What should we learn from hence, but 'to come boldly to the throne of grace,' Heb. iv. 16, in all our grievances? Shall our sins discourage us, when he appears there only for sinners? Art thou bruised? Be of good comfort, he calleth thee; conceal not thy wounds, open all before him, keep not Satan's counsel. Go to Christ though trembling; as the poor woman, if we can but 'touch the hem of his garment,' Matt. ix. 20, we shall be healed and have a gracious answer. Go boldly to God in our flesh; for this end that we might go boldly to him, he is flesh of our flesh, and bone of our bone. Never fear to go to God, since we have such a Mediator with him, that is not only our friend, but our brother and husband. Well might the angels proclaim from heaven, 'Behold, we bring you tidings of joy,' Luke ii. 10. Well might the apostle stir us up to 'rejoice in the Lord again and again,' Phil. iv. 4: he was well advised upon what grounds he did it. Peace and joy are two main fruits of his kingdom. Let the world be as it will, if we cannot rejoice in the world, yet we may rejoice in the Lord. His presence maketh any condition comfortable. 'Be not afraid,' saith he to his disciples, when they were afraid as if they had seen a ghost, 'it is I,' Matt. xiv. 27, as if there were no cause of fear where he is present.

Use 2. Let this stay us when we feel ourselves bruised. Christ his course is first to wound, then to heal. No sound, whole soul shall ever enter into heaven. Think in temptation, Christ was tempted for me; according to my trials will be my graces and comforts. If Christ be so merciful as not to break me, I will not break myself by despair, nor yield myself over to the roaring lion Satan, to break me in pieces.

Use 3. Thirdly, See the contrary disposition of Christ, and Satan and his instruments. Satan setteth upon us when we are weakest, as Simeon and Levi upon the 'Shechemites, when they were sore,' Gen. xxxiv. 25; but Christ will make up in us all the breaches sin and Satan have made; he 'binds up the broken-hearted,' Isa. lxi. 1. And as a mother tendereth most the most diseased and weakest child, so doth Christ most mercifully incline to the weakest, and likewise putteth an instinct into the weakest things to rely upon something stronger than themselves for support. The vine stayeth itself upon the elm, and the weakest creatures have oft the strongest shelters. The consciousness of the church's weakness makes her willing to lean on her beloved, and to hide herself under his wing.

[CHAPTER IV.—*Signs of one truly bruised.—Means and measure of bruising, and comfort to such.*]

Objection. But how shall we know whether we are such as those that may expect mercy?

Answer 1. By bruising here is not meant those that are brought low only by crosses, but such as by them are brought to see their sin, which bruiseth most of all. When conscience is under the guilt of sin, then every judgment brings a report of God's anger to the soul, and all less* troubles run into this great trouble of conscience for sin. As all corrupt humours run to the diseased and bruised part of the body, and as every creditor falls upon the debtor when he is once arrested, so when conscience is once awaked, all former sins and present crosses join together to make the bruise the more painful. Now, he that is thus bruised will be content with nothing

* 'Lesser,' in A and B.

but with mercy from him that hath bruised him. 'He hath wounded, and he must heal,' Isa. lxi. 1. Lord, thou hast bruised me deservedly for my sins, bind up my heart again,* &c. 2. Again, a man truly bruised judgeth sin the greatest evil, and the favour of God the greatest good. 3. He had rather hear of mercy than of a kingdom. 4. He hath mean conceits of himself, and thinketh he is not worth the earth he treads on. 5. Towards others he is not censorious, as being taken up at home, but is full of sympathy and compassion to those that are under God's hand. 6. He thinketh those that walk in the comforts of God's Spirit the happiest men of the world. 7. 'He trembleth at the word of God,' Isa. lxvi. 2, and honoureth the very feet of those blessed instruments that bring peace unto him, Rom. x. 15. 8. He is more taken up with the inward exercises of a broken heart than with formality, and yet careful to use all sanctified means to convey comfort.

Question. But how shall we come to have this temper?

Answer. First, we must conceive of bruising either as a state into which God bringeth us, or as a duty to be performed by us. Both are here meant. We must join with God in bruising of ourselves. When he humbles us, let us humble ourselves, and not stand out against him, for then he will redouble his strokes; and let us justify Christ in all his chastisements, knowing that all his dealing towards us is to cause us to return into our own hearts. His work in bruising tendeth to our work in bruising ourselves. Let us lament our own untowardness, and say, Lord, what an heart have I that needs all this, that none of this could be spared! We must lay siege to the hardness of our own hearts, and aggravate sin all we can. We must look on Christ, who was bruised for us, look on him whom we have pierced with our sins. But all directions will not prevail, unless God by his Spirit convinceth us deeply, setting our sins before us, and driving us to a stand. Then we will make out for mercy. Conviction will breed contrition, and this humiliation. Therefore desire God that he would bring a clear and a strong light into all the corners of our souls, and accompany it with a spirit of power to lay our hearts low.

A set measure of bruising ourselves cannot be prescribed; yet it must be so far, as 1, we may prize Christ above all, and see that a Saviour must be had; and 2, until we reform that which is amiss, though it be to the cutting off our right hand, or pulling out our right eye. There is a dangerous slighting of the work of humiliation, some alleging this for a pretence for their overly dealing with their own hearts, that Christ will not break the bruised reed; but such must know that every sudden terror and short grief is not that which makes us bruised reeds; not a *little hanging down our heads like a bulrush*, Isa. lviii. 5, but a working our hearts to such a grief as will make sin more odious unto us than punishment, until we offer an holy violence against it; else, favouring ourselves, we make work for God to bruise us, and for sharp repentance afterwards. It is dangerous, I confess, in some cases with some spirits, to press too much and too long this bruising, because they may die under the wound and burden before they be raised up again. Therefore it is good in mixed assemblies to mingle comfort, that every soul may have its due portion. But if we lay this for a ground, that there is more mercy in Christ than sin in us, there can be no danger in thorough dealing. It is better to go bruised to heaven than sound to hell. Therefore let us not take off ourselves too soon, nor pull off the plaster before the cure be wrought, but keep ourselves under

* 'Lord . . . . again,' not in A and B, but in E.

this work till sin be the sourest, and Christ the sweetest, of all things. And when God's hand is upon us in any kind, it is good to divert our sorrow for other things to the root of all, which is sin. Let our grief run most in that channel, that as sin bred grief, so grief may consume sin.

Quest. But are we not bruised unless we grieve more for sin than we do for punishment?

Ans. Sometimes our grief from outward grievances may lie heavier upon the soul than grief for God's displeasure; because in such cases the grief works upon the whole man, both outward and inward, and hath nothing to stay it, but a little spark of faith: which, by reason of the violent impression of the grievance, is suspended in the exercises of it: and this is most felt in sudden distresses which come upon the soul as a torrent or land-flood, and especially in bodily distempers, which by reason of the sympathy between the soul and the body, work upon the soul so far as they hinder not only the spiritual, but often the natural acts. Hereupon St James wisheth in affliction to pray ourselves, but in case of sickness to *send for the elders*, James v. 14; that may, as those in the gospel, offer up the sick person to God in their prayers, being unable to present their own case. Hereupon God admitteth of such a plea from the sharpness and bitterness of the grievance, as in David, Ps. vi., &c. 'The Lord knoweth whereof we are made, he remembereth we are but dust,' Ps. ciii. 14; that our strength is not the strength of steel. It is a branch of his faithfulness unto us as his creatures, whence he is called 'a faithful Creator,' 1 Pet. iv. 19; 'God is faithful, who will not suffer us to be tempted above that we are able,' 1 Cor. x. 13. There were certain commandments which the Jews called the hedges of the law: as to fence men off from cruelty, he commanded they should 'not take the dam with the young, nor seethe the kid in the mother's milk,' Exod. xxiii. 19; 'nor muzzle the mouth of the ox,' 1 Cor. ix. 9. Hath God care of beasts, and not of his more noble creature? And therefore we ought to judge charitably of the complaints of God's people which are wrung from them in such cases. Job had the esteem with God of a patient man, notwithstanding those passionate complaints. Faith overborne for the present will get ground again; and grief for sin, although it come short of grief for misery in violence, yet it goeth beyond it in constancy; as a running stream fed with a spring holdeth out, when a sudden swelling brook faileth.

For the concluding of this point, and our encouragement to a thorough work of bruising, and patience under God's bruising of us, let all know that none are fitter for comfort than those that think themselves furthest off. Men, for the most part, are not lost enough in their own feeling for a Saviour. A holy despair in ourselves is the ground of true hope, Hos. xiv. 3. In God the fatherless find mercy: if men were more fatherless, they should feel more God's fatherly affection from heaven; for God that dwelleth in highest heavens, Isa. lxvi. 2, dwelleth likewise in the lowest soul. Christ's sheep are weak sheep, and wanting in something or other; he therefore applieth himself to the necessities of every sheep. 'He seeks that which was lost, and brings again that which was driven out of the way, and binds up that which was broken, and strengthens the weak,' Ezek. xxxiv. 16; his tenderest care is over the weakest. The lambs he carrieth in his bosom, Isa. xl. 11; 'Peter, feed my lambs,' John xxi. 15. He was most familiar and open to the troubled souls. How careful was he that Peter and the rest of the apostles should not be too much dejected after his resurrection! 'Go, tell the disciples, and tell Peter,' Mark xvi. 7.

Christ knew that guilt of their unkindness in leaving of him had dejected their spirits. How gently did he endure Thomas his unbelief! and stooped so far unto his weakness, as to suffer him to thrust his hand into his side (*a*).

[CHAPTER V.—*Grace is little at first.*]

For the second branch, God will not quench the smoking flax, or wick, but will blow it up till it flameth. In smoking flax there is but a little light, and that weak, as being not able to flame, and this little mixed with smoke.

The observations hence are, first, *That in God's children, especially in their first conversion, there is but a little measure of grace, and that little mixed with much corruption, which, as smoke, is offensive.* Secondly, *That Christ will not quench this smoking flax.*

Obs. 1. For the first, *Grace is little at the first.* There are several ages in Christians, some babes, some young men: grace is as 'a grain of mustard seed,' Matt. xvii. 20. Nothing so little as grace at first, and nothing more glorious afterward: things of greatest perfection are longest in coming to their growth. Man, the perfectest creature, comes to perfection by little and little; worthless things, as mushrooms and the like, like Jonah's gourd, soon spring up, and soon vanish. A new creature is the most excellent frame in all the world, therefore it groweth up by degrees; we see in nature that a mighty oak riseth of an acorn. It is with a Christian as it was with Christ, who sprang out of the dead stock of Jesse, out of David's family, Isa. liii. 2, when it was at the lowest, but he grew up higher than the heavens. It is not with the trees of righteousness as it was with the trees of paradise, which were created all perfect at the first. The seeds of all the creatures in this goodly frame of the world were hid in the chaos, in that confused mass at the first, out of which God did command all creatures to arise; in the small seeds of plants lie hid both bulk and branches, bud and fruit. In a few principles lie hid all comfortable conclusions of holy truth. All these glorious fireworks of zeal and holiness in the saints had their beginning from a few sparks.

Let us not therefore be discouraged at the small beginnings of grace, but look on ourselves, as 'elected to be blameless and without spot,' Eph. i. 4. Let us only look on our imperfect beginning to enforce further strife to perfection, and to keep us in a low conceit. Otherwise, in case of discouragement, we must consider ourselves, as Christ doth, who looks on us as such as he intendeth to fit for himself. Christ valueth us by what we shall be, and by that we are elected unto. We call a little plant a tree, because it is growing up to be so. 'Who is he that despiseth the day of little things?' Zech. iv. 10. Christ would not have us despise little things.

The glorious angels disdain not attendance on little ones; little in their own eyes, and little in the eyes of the world.

Grace, though little in quantity, yet is much in vigour and worth.

It is Christ that raiseth the worth of little and mean places and persons. Bethlehem the least, Micah v. 2, Mat. ii. 6, and yet not the least; the least in itself, not the least in respect Christ was born there. The second temple, Hag. ii. 9, came short of the outward magnificence of the former; yet more glorious than the first, because Christ came into it. The Lord of the temple came into his own temple. The pupil of the eye is very little, yet seeth a great part of the heaven at once. A pearl, though little, yet is of much esteem: nothing in the world of so good use, as the least dram of grace.*

[CHAPTER VI.—*Grace is mingled with Corruption.*]

Obs. 2. But grace is not only little, but mingled with corruption; whereof it is, that a Christian is said to be smoking flax. Whence we see, that *grace doth not waste corruption all at once, but some is left to conflict withal.* The purest actions of the purest men need Christ to perfume† them, and so is his office. When we pray, we need to pray again for Christ to pardon the defects of them. See some instances of this smoking flax. Moses at the Red Sea, being in a great perplexity, and knowing not what to say, or which way to turn him, groaned to God: no doubt this was a great conflict in him. In great distresses we know not what to pray, but the Spirit makes request with sighs that cannot be expressed, Rom. viii. 26. Broken hearts can yield but broken prayers.

When David was before the king of Gath, 1 Sam. xxi. 13, and disfigured himself in an uncomely manner, in that smoke there was some fire also; you may see what an excellent psalm he makes upon that occasion, Ps. xxxiv.; wherein, upon experience, ver. 18, he saith, 'The Lord is near unto them that are of a contrite spirit.' Ps. xxxi. 22, 'I said in my haste, I am cast out of thy sight; there is smoke: yet thou heardest the voice of my prayer; there is fire.' 'Master, carest thou not that we perish?' Mat. viii. 25, cry the disciples; here is smoke of infidelity, yet so much light of faith as stirred them up to pray to Christ. 'Lord, I believe:' there is light; ' but help my unbelief,' Mark ix. 24: there is smoke.

Jonah cries, ii. 4, 'I am cast out of thy sight:' there is smoke; 'yet will I look again to thy holy temple:' there is light.

'O miserable man that I am,' Rom. vii. 24, saith St Paul upon sense of his corruption; but yet breaks out into thanks to God through Jesus Christ our Lord.

'I sleep,' saith the Church in the Canticles, 'but my heart wakes,' Cant. v. 2. In the seven Churches, which for their light are called ' seven golden candlesticks,' Rev. ii. iii., most of them had much smoke with their light.

The ground of this mixture is, that we carry about us a double principle, grace and nature. The end of it is especially to preserve us from those two dangerous rocks which our natures are prone to dash upon, security and pride; and to force us to pitch our rest on justification, not sanctification, which, besides imperfection, hath some soil.

Our spiritual fire is like our ordinary fire here below, that is, mixed; but fire is most pure in its own element above; so shall all our graces be when we are where we would be, in heaven, which is our proper element.

Use. From this mixture it is, that the people of God have so different judgments of themselves, looking sometimes at the work of grace, sometimes at the remainder of corruption, and when they look upon that, then they think they have no grace; though they love Christ in his ordinances and children, yet dare not challenge so near acquaintance as to be his. Even as a candle in the socket sometimes sheweth its light, and sometimes the show of light is lost; so sometimes well persuaded they are of themselves, sometimes at a loss.

---

* 'As the least dram of grace *is*,' in A and B.   † 'Perform,' in A and B.

[CHAPTER VII.—*Christ will not quench small and weak beginnings.*]

Doct. Now for the second observation, *Christ will not quench the smoking flax.* First, because this spark is from heaven, it is his own, it* is kindled by his own spirit. And secondly, it tendeth to the glory of his powerful grace in his children, that he preserveth light in the midst of darkness,—a spark in the midst of the swelling waters of corruption.

There is an especial blessing in that little spark; 'when wine is found in a cluster, one saith, Destroy it not; for there is a blessing in it,' Isa. lxv. 8. We see how our Saviour Christ bore with Thomas in his doubting, John xx. 27; with the two disciples that went to Emmaus, who staggered 'whether he came to redeem Israel or no,' Luke xxiv. 21: he quenched not that little light in Peter, which was smothered: Peter denied him, but he denied not Peter, Mat. xxvi. 'If thou wilt, thou canst,' said one poor man in the gospel, Mat. viii. 2; 'Lord, if thou canst' said another, Mark ix. 22; both were this smoking flax, neither of both were quenched. If Christ had stood upon his own greatness, he would have rejected him that came with his *if*, but Christ answers his *if* with a gracious and absolute grant, 'I will, be thou clean.' The woman that was diseased with an issue did but touch, and with a trembling hand, and but the hem of his garment, and yet went away both healed and comforted. In the seven churches, Rev. ii. and iii., we see he acknowledgeth and cherisheth anything that was good in them. Because the disciples slept of infirmity, being oppressed with grief, our Saviour Christ frameth a comfortable excuse for them, 'The spirit is willing, but the flesh is weak,' Mat. xxvi. 41.

If Christ should not be merciful, he would miss of his own ends; 'there is mercy with thee that thou mayest be feared,' Ps. cxxx. 4. Now all are willing to come under that banner of love which he spreadeth over his: 'therefore to thee shall all flesh come,' Ps. lxv. 2. He useth moderation and care, 'lest the spirit should fail before him, and the souls which he hath made,' Isa. lvii. 16. Christ's heart yearned, the text saith, 'when he saw them without meat, lest they should faint,' Mat. xv. 32; much more will he have regard for the preventing of our spiritual faintings.

Here see the opposite disposition between the holy nature of Christ, and the impure nature of man. Man for a little smoke will quench the light; Christ ever we see cherisheth even the least beginnings. How bare he with the many imperfections of his poor disciples. If he did sharply check them, it was in love, and that they might shine the brighter. Can we have a better pattern to follow than this of him by whom we hope to be saved? 'We that are strong ought to bear with the infirmities of them that are weak,' Rom. xv. 1. 'I become all things to all men, that I may win some,' 1 Cor. ix. 22. O that this gaining and winning disposition were more in many! Many, so far as in us lieth, are lost for want of encouragement. See how that faithful fisher of men, St Paul, labours to catch his judge, 'I know thou believest the prophets,' Acts xxvi. 27; and then wisheth all saving good, but not bonds; he might have added them too, but he would not discourage one that made but an offer, he would therefore wish Agrippa only that which was good in religion. How careful was our blessed Saviour of little ones that they might not be offended, Mat. xii. xiii. How doth he defend his disciples from malicious imputations of the Pharisees! How careful not to put new wine into old vessels, Mat. ix. 17, not to alienate new beginners

* 'That,' in A.

with the austerities of religion (as some indiscreetly). O, saith he, they shall have time to fast when I am gone, and strength to fast when the Holy Ghost is come upon them.

It is not the best way to fall foul presently with young beginners for some lesser vanities, but shew them a more excellent way, and breed them up in positive grounds, and other things will be quickly out of credit with them. It is not amiss to conceal their wants, to excuse some failings, to commend their performances, to cherish their towardness, to remove all rubs out of their way, to help them every way to bear the yoke of religion with greater ease, to bring them in love with God and his service, lest they distaste it before they know it. For the most part we see Christ planteth in young beginners a love which we call 'the first love,' Rev. ii. 4, to carry them through their profession with more delight, and doth not expose them to crosses before they have gathered strength; as we breed up young plants, and fence them from the weather, until they be rooted.* Mercy to others should move us to deny ourselves in our lawful liberties oftentimes, in case of offence of weak ones; it is the 'little ones that are offended,' Matt. xviii. 6. The weakest are aptest to think themselves despised, therefore we should be most careful to give them content.

It were a good strife amongst Christians, one to labour to give no offence, and the other to labour to take none. The best men are severe to themselves, tender over others.

Yet people should not tire and wear out the patience of others: nor should the weaker so far exact moderation from others, as to bear out themselves upon their indulgence, and so to rest in their own infirmities, with danger to their own souls, and scandal to the church.

Neither† hereupon must they set light by the gifts of God in others, which grace teacheth to honour wheresoever they are found, but know their parts and place, and not enterprise anything above their measure, which may make their persons and their case obnoxious to scorn. When blindness and boldness, ignorance and arrogance, weakness and wilfulness, meet together in one, it renders men odious to God, it maketh men burdensome in society, dangerous in their counsels, troublers of better designs, untractable and uncapable of better direction, miserable in the issue: where Christ sheweth his gracious power in weakness, he doth it by letting men understand themselves so far as to breed humility, and magnifying of God's love to such as they are: he doth it as a preservative against discouragements from weakness, seeing it bringeth men into a less distance from grace, as being an advantage to poverty of spirit, than greatness of condition and parts, which yield to corrupt nature fuel for pride. Christ refuseth none for weakness of parts, that none should be discouraged; accepteth of none for greatness, that none should be lifted up with that which is of so little reckoning with God. It is no great matter how dull the scholar be, when Christ taketh upon him to be the teacher: who as he prescribeth what to understand, so he giveth understanding itself even to the simplest.

The church suffereth much from weak ones, therefore we may challenge liberty to deal with them, as mildly, so oftentimes directly. The scope of true love is to make the party better, which by concealment oftentimes is hindered; with some a spirit of meekness prevaileth most, but with some a rod. Some must be 'pulled out of the fire,' Jude 23, with violence, and they will bless God for us in the day of their visitation. We see our Saviour multiplies woe upon woe when he was to deal with hard-hearted

* 'Well-rooted,' in A.   † 'Neither . . . simplest.' This paragraph first added in B

hypocrites, Mat. xxiii. 13, for hypocrites need* stronger conviction than gross sinners, because their will is nought, and thereupon usually their conversion is violent. An hard knot must have an answerable wedge, else in a cruel pity we betray their souls. A sharp reproof sometimes is a precious pearl, and a sweet balm. The wounds of secure sinners will not be healed with sweet words. The Holy Ghost came as well in fiery tongues, as in the likeness of a dove, and the same Holy Spirit will vouchsafe a spirit of prudence and discretion, which is the salt to season all our words and actions. And such wisdom will teach us 'to speak a word in season,' Isa. l. 4, both to the weary, and likewise to the secure soul. And, indeed, he had need have 'the tongue of the learned,' Isa. l. 4, that shall either raise up or cast down; but in this place I speak of mildness towards those that are weak and are sensible of it. These we must bring on gently, and drive softly, as Jacob did his cattle, Gen. xxxiii. 14, according to their pace, and as his children were able to endure.

Weak Christians are like glasses which are hurt with the least violent usage, otherwise if gently handled will continue a long time. This honour of gentle use we are to give to 'the weaker vessels,' 1 Pet. iii. 7, by which we shall both preserve them, and likewise make them useful to the church and ourselves.

In unclean bodies if all ill humours be purged out, you shall purge life and all away. Therefore though God saith, that 'he will fine them as silver is fined,' Zech. xiii. 9; yet, Isa. xlviii. 10, he said, 'he hath fined them, but not as silver,' that is, so exactly as that no dross remaineth, for he hath respect to our weakness. Perfect refining is for another world, for the world of the souls of perfect men.

[CHAPTER VIII.—*Tenderness required in ministers toward young beginners.*]

1. Divines had need to take heed therefore how they deal with these in divers particulars: as first let them be careful they strain not things too high (*b*), making those general and necessary evidences of grace, which agree not to the experience of many a good Christian, and lay salvation and damnation upon those things that are not fit to bear so great a weight, whereupon men are groundlessly cast down lower by them, than they can hastily be raised up again by themselves or others. The ambassadors of so gentle a Saviour should not be over-masterly, setting up themselves in the hearts of people where Christ alone should sit as in his own temple. Too much† respect to man was one of the inlets of popery. 'Let a man account of us as of the ministers of Christ,' 1 Cor. iv. 1, neither more nor less, just so much. How careful was St Paul in cases of conscience not to lay a snare upon any weak conscience.

They should take heed likewise that they hide not their meaning in dark speeches, speaking in the clouds. Truth feareth nothing so much as concealment, and desireth nothing so much as clearly to be laid open to the view of all: when it is most naked, it is most lovely and powerful.

Our blessed Saviour, as he took our nature upon him, so he took upon him our familiar manner of speech, which was part of his voluntary abasement. St Paul was a profound man, yet became as a nurse to the weaker sort, 1 Thess. ii. 7.

That spirit of mercy that was in Christ should move his servants to be

* 'Do need,' in A and B.   † 'Too much . . . . just so much,' added first in B.

content to abase themselves for the good of the meanest. What made the 'kingdom of heaven suffer violence,' Matt. xi. 22, after John the Baptist's time, but that comfortable truths were with that plainness and evidence laid open, that the people were so affected with them, as they offered a holy violence to them?

Christ chose those to preach mercy, which had felt most mercy, as St Peter and St Paul; that they might be examples of what they taught. St Paul 'became all things to all men,' 1 Cor. ix. 2, stooping unto them for their good. Christ came down from heaven, and emptied himself of majesty in tender love to souls; shall we not come down from our high conceits to do any poor soul good? shall man be proud after God hath been humble? We see the ministers of Satan turn themselves into all shapes to 'make proselytes,' Matt. xxiii. 15. A Jesuit will be every man. We see ambitious men study accommodation of themselves to the humours of those by whom they hope to be raised;* and shall not we study application of ourselves to Christ, by whom we hope to be advanced, nay, are already sitting with him in heavenly places? After we are gained to Christ ourselves, we should labour to gain others to Christ. Holy ambition and covetousness will move us to put upon ourselves the disposition of Christ: but we must put off ourselves first.

We should not, thirdly, rack their wits with curious or 'doubtful disputes,' Rom. xiv 1; for so we shall distract and tire them, and give occasion to make them cast off the care of all. That age of the church which was most fertile in nice questions, was most barren in religion: for it makes people think religion to be only a matter of wit, in tying and untying of knots; the brains of men given that way are hotter usually than their hearts.

Yet notwithstanding, when we are cast into times and places wherein doubts are raised about main points, here people ought to labour to be established. God suffereth questions oftentimes to arise for trial of our love and exercise of our parts. Nothing is so certain as that which is certain after doubts. *Nil tam certum quâm quod ex dubio certum.* Shaking settles and roots. In a contentious age, it is a witty thing to be a Christian, and to know what to pitch their souls upon; it is an office of love here to take away the stones, and to smooth the way to heaven. Therefore, we must take heed that, under pretence of avoidance of disputes, we do not suffer an adverse party to get ground upon the truth; for thus may we easily betray both the truth of God and souls of men.

And likewise those are failing that, by overmuch austerity, drive back troubled souls from having comfort by them; for by this carriage many smother their temptations, and burn inwardly, because they have none into whose bosom they may vent their grief and ease their souls.

We must neither bind where God looseth, nor loose where God bindeth, nor open where God shutteth, nor shut where God openeth; the right use of the keys is always successful. In personal application there must be great heed taken; for a man may be a false prophet, and yet speak the truth. If it be not a truth to the person to whom he speaketh; if he 'grieve those whom God hath not grieved,' Lam. iii. 33, by unseasonable truths, or by comforts in an ill way, the hearts of the wicked may be strengthened. One man's meat may be another's bane.

If we look to the general temper of these times, rousing and waking Scriptures are fittest; yet there be many broken spirits need soft and oily words. Even in the worst time the prophets mingled sweet comfort for

* 'To raise themselves,' in A and B.

the hidden remnant of faithful people. God hath comfort; 'Comfort ye my people,' Isa. xl. 1, as well as ' lift up thy voice as a trumpet,' Isa. lviii. 1.

And here likewise there needs a caveat. Mercy doth not rob us of our right judgment, as that we should take stinking* fire-brands for smoking flax. None will claim mercy more of others, than those whose portion is due severity. This example doth not countenance lukewarmness, nor too much indulgence to those that need quickening. Cold diseases must have hot remedies. It made for the just commendations of the church of Ephesus, 'that it could not bear with them which are evil,' Rev. ii. 2. We should so bear with others, as we discover withal a dislike of evil. Our Saviour Christ would not forbear sharp reproof, where he saw dangerous infirmities in his most beloved disciples. It bringeth under a curse ' to do the work of the Lord negligently,' Jer. xlviii. 10 ; even where it is a work of just severity, as when it is sheathing the sword in the bowels of the enemy. And those whom we suffer to be betrayed by their worst enemies, their sins, will have just cause to curse us another day.

It is hard to preserve just bounds of mercy and severity, without a spirit above our own ; which we ought to desire to be led withal in all things. That ' wisdom which dwelleth with prudence,' Prov. viii. 12, will guide us in these particulars, without which virtue is not virtue, truth not truth. The rule and the case must be laid together ; for if there be not a narrow insight, seeming likeness in conditions will be the breeder of errors in our opinions of them. Those fiery, tempestuous, and destructive spirits in popery, that seek to promote their religion by cruelty, shew that they are strangers to that wisdom which is from above, which maketh men gentle, peaceable, and ready to shew that mercy they have felt before themselves. It is a way of prevailing, as agreeable to Christ, so likewise to man's nature, to prevail by some forbearance and moderation.

And yet oft we see a false spirit in those that call for moderation. It is but to carry their own projects with the greater strength ; and if they prove of the prevailing hand, they will hardly shew that moderation to others they now call for from others. And there is a proud kind of moderation likewise, when men will take upon them to censure both† parties, as if they were wiser than both, although,‡ if the spirit be right, a looker on may see more than those that are in conflict.

[CHAPTER IX.—*Governors should be tender of weak ones, and also private Christians.*]

2. So in the censures of the church, it is more suitable to the spirit of Christ to incline to the milder part, and not to kill a fly on the forehead with a beetle (c), nor shut men out of heaven for a trifle. The very snuffers of the tabernacle were made of pure gold, to shew the purity of those censures, whereby the light of the church is kept bright. That power that is given to the church is given for edification, not destruction. How careful was St Paul, that the incestuous Corinthian, 2 Cor. ii. 7, repenting, should not be swallowed up with too much grief.

As for civil magistrates, they, for civil exigences and reasons of state, must let the law have its course ; yet thus far they should imitate this mild king, as not to mingle bitterness and passion with authority derived from God. Authority is a beam of God's majesty, and prevaileth most where

* 'Smoking,' in A and B.   † 'Either party,' in A.   ‡ 'Though,' in A and B.

there is least mixture of that which is man's. It requireth more than ordinary wisdom to manage it aright. This string must not be too much strained up, nor too much let loose. Justice is an harmonical thing. Herbs hot or cold beyond a certain degree, kill. We see even contrary elements preserved in one body by a wise contemperation. Justice in rigour is oft extreme injustice, where some considerable circumstances should incline to moderation; and the reckoning will be easier for bending rather to moderation than rigour.

Insolent carriage toward miserable persons, if humbled, is unseemly in any who look for mercy themselves. Misery should be a loadstone of mercy, not a footstool for pride to trample on.

Sometimes it falleth out that those that are under the government of others, are most injurious by waywardness and harsh censures, herein disparaging and discouraging the endeavours of superiors for public good. In so great weakness of man's nature, and especially in this crazy age of the world, we ought to take in good part any moderate happiness we enjoy by government; and not be altogether as a nail in the wound, exasperating things by misconstruction. Here love should have a mantle to cast upon lesser errors of those above us. Oftentimes the poor man is the oppressor by unjust clamours. We should labour to give the best interpretation to the actions of governors that the nature of the actions will possibly bear.

In the last place, there is something for private Christians, even for all of us in our common relations, to take notice of: we are debtors to the weak in many things.

1. Let us be watchful in the use of our liberty, and labour to be inoffensive in our carriage, that our example compel them not. There is a commanding force in an example, as Peter, Gal. ii. Looseness* of life is cruelty to ourselves, and to the souls of others. Though we cannot keep them from perishing which will perish, in regard of the event; yet if we do that which is apt of itself to destroy the souls of others, their ruin is imputable to us.

2. Let men take heed of taking up Satan's office, in depraving the good actions of others, as he did Job's, 'doth he serve God for nought?' Job i. 9, or slandering their persons, judging of them according to the wickedness that is in their own hearts. The devil getteth more by such discouragements, and these reproaches that are cast upon religion, than by fire and fagot. These, as unseasonable frosts, nip all gracious offers in the bud; and as much as in them lieth, with Herod, labour to kill Christ in young professors. A Christian is a hallowed and a sacred thing, Christ's temple; 'and he that destroyeth his temple, him will Christ destroy,' 1 Cor. iii. 17.

3. Amongst the things that are to be taken heed of, there is amongst private Christians a bold usurpation of censure towards others, not considering their temptations. Some will unchurch and unbrother in a passion. But distempers do not alter true relations; though the child in a fit should disclaim the mother, yet the mother will not disclaim the child.

There is therefore in these judging times good ground of St James's caveat, that there should not 'be too many masters,' James iii. 1; that we should not smite one another by hasty censures, especially in things of an indifferent nature; some things are as the mind of him is that doth them, or doth them not; for both may be unto the Lord.

A holy aim in things of a middle nature makes the judgments of men,

* 'A looseness,' in A.

although seemingly contrary, yet not so much blameable. Christ, for the good aims he seeth in us, overlooketh any ill in them, so far as not to lay it to our charge.

Men must not be too curious in prying into the weaknesses of others. We should labour rather to see what they have that is for eternity, to incline our heart to love them, than into that weakness which the Spirit of God will in time consume, to estrange us. Some think it strength of grace to endure nothing in the weaker, whereas the strongest are readiest to bear with the infirmities of the weak.

Where most holiness is, there is most moderation, where it may be without prejudice of piety to God and the good of others. We see in Christ a marvellous temper of absolute holiness, with great moderation, in this text. What had become of our salvation, if he had stood upon terms, and not stooped thus low unto us? We need not affect to be more holy than Christ; it is no flattery to do as he doth, so it be to edification.

The Holy Ghost is content to dwell in smoky, offensive souls. O that that Spirit would breathe into our spirits the like merciful disposition! We endure the bitterness of wormwood, and other distasteful plants and herbs, only because we have some experience of some wholesome quality in them; and why should we reject men of useful parts and graces, only for some harshness of disposition, which, as it is offensive to us, so grieveth themselves?

Grace whilst we live here is in souls, which as they are unperfectly renewed, so they dwell in bodies subject to several humours, which will incline the soul sometimes to excess in one passion, sometimes to excess in another.

Bucer was a deep and a moderate divine; upon long experience he resolved to refuse none in whom he saw, *aliquid Christi*, something of Christ.

The best Christians in this state of imperfection are like gold that is a little too light, which needs some grains of allowance to make it pass. You must grant the best their allowance. We must supply out of our love and mercy, that which we see wanting in them.

The church of Christ is a common hospital, wherein all are in some measure sick of some spiritual disease or other; that we should all have ground of exercising mutually the spirit of wisdom and meekness.

1. This that we may the better do, let us put upon ourselves the spirit of Christ. The spirit of God carrieth a majesty with it. Corruption will hardly yield to corruption in another. Pride is intolerable to pride. The weapons of this warfare must not be carnal, 2 Cor. x. 4. The great apostles would not set upon the work of the ministry, until they were 'clothed as it were with power from on high,' Luke xxiv. 49. The Spirit will only work with his own tools. And we should think what affection Christ would carry to the party in this case. That great physician, as he had a quick eye and a healing tongue, so had he a gentle hand, and a tender heart.*

2. And secondly, put upon us the condition of him whom we deal withal: we are, or have been, or may be such: make the case our own, and withal consider in what near relation a Christian standeth unto us, even as a brother, a fellow-member, heir of the same salvation. And therefore let us take upon ourselves a tender care of them every way; and especially in cherishing the peace of their consciences. Conscience is a tender and

* Nil sic spiritualem virum indicat quam alieni peccati tractatio.—*Aug*[*ustine*] in Gal. vi.

delicate thing, and so must be used, It is like a lock, if the wards be troubled, it will be troublesome to open.*

[CHAPTER X.—*Rules to try whether we be such as Christ will not quench.*]

For trial, to let us see whether we be this smoking flax which Christ will not quench. In this trial remember these:—1. *Rules.* 2. *Signs.*

1. We must have two eyes, one to see imperfections in ourselves and others; the other to see what is good. 'I am black,' saith the church, 'but yet comely,' Cant. i. 5. Those ever want comfort that are much in quarrelling with themselves, and through their infirmities are prone to feed upon such bitter things, as will most nourish that distemper they are sick of. These delight to be looking on the dark side of the cloud only.

2. We must not judge of ourselves always according to present feeling; for in temptations we shall see nothing but smoke of distrustful thoughts. Fire may be raked up in the ashes, though not seen; life in the winter is hid in the root.

3. Take heed of false reasoning; as because our fire doth not blaze out as others, therefore we have no fire at all; and by false conclusions come to sin against the commandment in bearing false witness against ourselves. The prodigal would not say he was no son, but that he was not worthy to be called a son, Luke xv. 19. We must neither trust to false evidence, nor deny true; for so we should dishonour the work of God's Spirit in us, and lose the help of that evidence which would cherish our love to Christ, and arm us against Satan's discouragements. Some are so faulty this way, as if they had been hired by Satan, the 'accuser of the brethren,' Rev. xii. 10, to plead for him, in accusing themselves.

4. Know, for a ground of this, that in the covenant of grace, God requires the truth of grace, not any certain measure; and a spark of fire is fire as well as the whole element. Therefore we must look to grace in the spark as well as in the flame. All have not the like strong, yet the like precious faith, 2 Pet. i. 1, whereby they lay hold, and put on, the perfect righteousness of Christ. A weak hand may receive a rich jewel; a few grapes will shew that the plant is a vine, and not a thorn. It is one thing to be wanting in grace, and another thing to want grace altogether. God knoweth we have nothing of ourselves, therefore in the covenant of grace he requireth no more than he giveth, and giveth what he requireth, and accepteth what he giveth: 'He that hath not a lamb may bring a pair of turtle doves,' Lev. xii. 6. What is the gospel itself but a merciful moderation, in which Christ's obedience is esteemed ours, and our sins laid upon him, and wherein God of a judge becometh the father, pardoning our sins and accepting our obedience, though feeble and blemished! We are now brought to heaven under the covenant of grace by a way of love and mercy.

It will prove a special help to know distinctly the difference between the covenant of works and the covenant of grace, between Moses and Christ; Moses without all mercy breaketh all bruised reeds, and quencheth all smoking flax. For the law requireth, 1, personal; 2, perpetual; 3, perfect obedience; 4, and from a perfect heart; and that under a most terrible curse, and giveth no strength, a severe task-master, like Pharaoh's requiring the whole tale, and yet giving no straw. Christ cometh with blessing

* Nil magis ad misericordiam inclinat quam proprii periculi cogitatio.—*August*[*ine*].

after blessing even upon those whom Moses had cursed, and with healing balm for those wounds which Moses had made.

The same duties are required in both covenants; as, 'to love the Lord with all our hearts, with all our souls,' &c., Deut. vi. 5. In the* covenant of works, this must be taken in the rigour; but under the covenant of grace, as it is a sincere endeavour proportionable to grace received (and so it must be understood of Josias, and others, when it is said, 'they loved God with all their hearts,' &c.), it must have an evangelical mitigation.

The law is sweetened by the gospel, and becometh delightful to the inner man, Rom. vii. 22. Under this gracious covenant sincerity is perfection. This is the death in the pot in the Roman religion,† that they confound two covenants; and it deads the comfort of drooping ones, that they cannot distinguish them. And thus they suffer themselves to be held under bondage,' Isa. lxi. 1, 2, when Christ hath set them free; and stay themselves in the prison, when Christ hath set open the doors before them.

5. Grace sometimes is so little as is undiscernible to us; the Spirit sometimes hath secret operations in us, which we know not for the present; but Christ knoweth. Sometimes in bitterness of temptation, when the Spirit struggles with sense of God's anger, we are apt to think God an enemy; and a troubled soul is like troubled water,‡ we can see nothing in it; and so far as it is not cleansed, it will cast up mire and dirt. It is full of objections against itself, yet for the most part we may discern something of the hidden life, and of these smothered sparks.

In a gloomy day there is so much light whereby we may know it to be day, and not night; so there is something in a Christian under a cloud, whereby he may be discerned to be a true believer, and not a hypocrite. There is no mere darkness in the state of grace, but some beam of light, whereby the kingdom of darkness wholly prevaileth not.

[CHAPTER XI.—*Signs of smoking flax which Christ will not quench.*]

These things premised, let us know for a trial, 1. First, *if there be any holy fire in us, it is kindled from heaven* by the 'Father of lights, who commandeth light to shine out of darkness,' 2 Cor. iv. 6. As it is kindled in the use of means, so it is fed. The light in us, and the light in the word, spring one from the other, and both from one Holy Spirit; and, therefore, those that regard not the word, it is because there 'is no light in them,' Isa. viii. 20. Heavenly truths must have a heavenly light to discern them. Natural men see heavenly things, but not in their own proper light, but by an inferior light. God in every converted man putteth a light into the eye of his soul, proportionable to the light of truths revealed unto him. A carnal eye will never see spiritual things.

2. Secondly, *the least divine light hath heat with it in some measure;* light in the understanding breedeth heat of love in the affections. *Claritas in intellectu parit ardorem in affectu.* In what measure the sanctified understanding seeth a thing to be true, or good, in that measure the will embraces it. Weak light breeds weak inclinations; a strong light, strong inclinations. A little spiritual light is of strength enough to answer strong objections of flesh and blood, and to look through all earthly allurements and opposing§ hindrances, presenting them as far inferior to those heavenly objects it eyeth.

---

* 'This,' in A and B.
† Roman religion = Popery.—G.
‡ 'Waters,' in A and B.
§ 'And all,' in A and B.

All light that is not spiritual, because it wanteth the strength of sanctifying grace, yieldeth* to every little temptation, especially when it is fitted and suited to personal inclinations. This is the reason why Christians that have light little for quantity, but yet heavenly for quality, hold out, when men of larger apprehensions sink.

This prevailing of light in the soul is because, together with the spirit of illumination, there goeth, in the godly, a spirit of power, 2 Tim. i. 7, to subdue the heart to truth revealed, and to put a taste and relish into the will, suitable to the sweetness of the truths; else a mere natural will will rise against supernatural truths, as having an antipathy and enmity against them. In the godly, holy truths are conveyed by way of a taste; gracious men have a spiritual palate as well as a spiritual eye. Grace altereth the relish.

3. Thirdly, where this heavenly light is kindled, *it directeth in the right way*. For it is given for that use, to shew us the best way, and to guide in the particular passages of life; if otherwise, it is but common light, given only for the good of others. Some have light of knowledge, yet follow not that light, but are guided by carnal reason and policy; such as the prophet speaks of, 'All you that kindle a fire, walk in the light of your own fire, and in the sparks that you have kindled; but this you shall have of mine hand, ye shall lie down in sorrow,' Isa. l. 11. God delights to confound carnal wisdom, as enmity to him, and robbing him of his prerogative, who is God only wise. We must, therefore, walk by his light, and not the blaze of our own fire. God must light our candle, Ps. xviii. 28, or else we are like to abide in darkness. Those sparks that are not kindled from heaven, are not strong enough to keep us from lying down in sorrow, though they make a greater blaze and show than the light from above, as madmen do greater things than sober, but by a false strength: so the excess of these men's joy ariseth from a false light, 'the candle of the wicked shall be put out,' Job xviii. 6.

The light that some men have, it is like lightning, which after a sudden flash leaveth them more in darkness. They can love the light as it shines, but hâte it as it discovers and directs. A little holy light will enable to keep the word, and not betray religion, and deny Christ's name, as Christ speaketh of the church of Philadelphia, Rev. iii. 8.

4. Fourthly, where this fire is, *it will sever things of diverse natures, and shew a difference between things, as gold and dross*. It will sever between flesh and spirit, and shew that this is of nature, this of grace. All is not ill in a bad action, or good in a good action. There is gold in ore, which God and his Spirit in us can distinguish. A carnal man's heart is like a dungeon, wherein is nothing to be seen but horror and confusion; this light maketh us judicious and humble, upon clearer sight of God's purity, and our own uncleanness; and maketh us able to discern of the work of the Spirit in another.

5. Fifthly, so far as a man is spiritual, *so far is light delightful unto him*, as willing to see anything amiss, that he may reform, and any further service discovered that he may perform, because he truly hateth ill and loveth good; if he goeth against light discovered, he will soon be reclaimed, because light hath a friendly party within him. Whereupon, at a little sight of his error he is soon counselable, as David in his intendment to kill Nabal, and blessed God afterwards, when he is stopped in an ill way, 1 Sam. xxv. 32.

* 'It yieldeth,' in A and B.

In a carnal man, the light breaks in upon him, but he labours to shut the passages, he hath no delight to come to the light. It is impossible before the Spirit of grace hath subdued the heart, but that it should sin against the light, either by resisting of it, or keeping it prisoner under base lusts, and burying it, as it were, in the earth ; or perverting of it, and so making it an agent and factor for the flesh, in searching out arguments to plead for it, or abusing that little measure of light they have, to keep out a greater, higher, and more heavenly light ; and so, at length, make that light they have a misleading guide to utter darkness. And the reason is, because it hath no friend within, the soul is in a contrary frame ; and light always hindereth that sinful peace that men are willing to speak to themselves : whence we see it oft enrages men the more, as the sun in the spring breedeth aguish distempers, because it stirreth humours, and doth not waste them. There is nothing in the world more unquiet than the heart of a wicked man, that sitteth under means of knowledge, until, like a thief, he hath put out the candle, that he may sin with the less check. Spiritual light is distinct, it seeth spiritual good, with application to ourselves ; but common light is confused, and lets sin lie quiet. Where fire is in any degree, it will fight against the contrary matter. God hath put irreconcilable hatred between light and darkness at first, so between good and ill, flesh and spirit, Gal. v. 17 ; grace will never join with sin, no more than fire with water. Fire will mingle with no contrary, but preserveth its own purity, and is never corrupted as other elements are. Therefore, those that plead and plot for liberties of the flesh, shew themselves strangers from the life of God. Upon this strife, gracious men oft complain that they have no grace, but they contradict themselves in their complaints ; as if a man that seeth should complain he cannot see, or complain that he is asleep, when the very complaint, springing from a displeasure against sin, sheweth that there is something in him opposite to sin. Can a dead man complain ? Some things, though bad in themselves, yet discover good ; as smoke discovers some fire. Breaking out in the body shews strength of nature. Some infirmities discover more good than some seeming beautiful actions. Excess of passion in opposing evil, though not to be justified, yet sheweth a better spirit than a calm temper, where there is just cause of being moved. Better it is that the water should run something muddily, than not at all. Job had more grace in his distempers, than his friends in their seeming wise carriage. Actions soiled with some weaknesses, are more accepted than complemental performances.

6. Sixthly, fire, where it is in the least measure, *is in some degree active*; so the least measure of grace is *working*, as springing from the Spirit of God, which, from the working nature of it, is compared to fire. Nay, in sins, when there seemeth nothing active, but corruption, yet there is a contrary principle, which breaks the force of sin, so that it is not out of measure sinful, as in those that are carnal, Rom. vii. 13.

7. Seventhly, fire maketh metals *pliable and malleable, so doth grace, where it is begun;* it worketh the heart to be pliable and ready for all good impressions. Untractable spirits shew that they are not so much as smoking flax.

8. Eighthly, fire turneth all, as much as it can, to fire ; so grace *laboureth to breed the like impression in others, and make as many good as it can.* Grace likewise maketh a gracious use even of natural and civil things, and doth spiritualise them. What another man doth only civilly, a gracious man will do holily. Whether he eateth or drinketh, or whatsoever

he doth, he doth all to the glory of God, 1 Cor. x. 81, making everything serviceable to the last end.

9. Ninthly, *sparks by nature fly upwards; so the Spirit of grace carrieth the soul heaven-ward, and setteth before us holy and heavenly aims.* As it was kindled from heaven, so it carries us back to heaven. The part followeth the whole: fire mounteth upward, so every spark to its own element. Where the aim and bent of the soul is God-wards, there is grace, though opposed. The least measure of it is holy desires springing from faith and love, for we cannot desire anything which we do not believe first to be, and the desire of it issues from love. Hence desires are counted a part of the thing desired, in some measure; but then they must be, *first, constant,* for constancy shews that they are supernaturally natural, and not enforced; *secondly,* they must be *carried to spiritual things,* as to believe, to love God, &c.: not out of a special exigent, because, if now they had grace, they think they might escape some danger, but as a loving heart is carried to the thing loved for some excellency in itself; and *thirdly,* with desire there is grief when it is hindered, which stirs up to prayer: 'Oh that my ways were so directed, that I might keep thy statutes!' Ps. cxix. 5; O miserable man that I am, who shall deliver? &c., Rom. vii. 24; *fourthly,* desires put us onward still: O that I might serve God with more liberty; O that I were more free from these offensive, unsavoury, noisome lusts!

10. Tenthly, *fire worketh itself, if it hath any matter to feed on, into a larger compass, and mounteth higher and higher, and the higher it riseth, the purer is the flame;* so where true grace is, it groweth in measure and purity. Smoking flax will grow to a flame; and as it increaseth, so it worketh out the contrary, and refineth itself more and more. *Ignis, quo magis lucet, eo minus fumat.* Therefore, it argueth a false heart to set ourselves a measure in grace, and to rest in beginnings, alleging that Christ will not quench the smoking flax. But this merciful disposition in Christ is joined with perfect holiness, shewed in perfect hatred to sin; for rather than sin should not have its deserved punishment, himself became a sacrifice for sin, wherein his Father's holiness and his own most of all shined. And besides this, in the work of sanctification, though he favours his work in us, yet favours he not sin in us; for he will never take his hand from his work, until he hath taken away sin, even in its very being, from our natures. The same Spirit that purified that blessed mass whereof he was made, cleanseth us by degrees to be suitable to so holy a head, and frameth the judgment and affection of all to whom he sheweth mercy, to concur with his own, in labouring to further his ends, in abolishing of sin out of our nature.

[CHAPTER XII.—*Scruples hindering comfort removed.*]

Use. From the meditation of these rules and signs, much comfort may be brought into the souls of the weakest; which, that it may be in the more abundance, let me add something for the helping them over some few ordinary objections and secret thoughts against themselves, which getting within the heart, oftentimes keep them under.

1. Some think they have no faith at all, because they have no full assurance; whenas the fairest fire that can be will have some smoke. The best actions will smell of the smoke. The mortar wherein garlic hath been stamped, will always smell of it; so all our actions will savour something of the old man.

2. In weakness of body some think grace dieth, because their performances are feeble, their spirits, being the instruments of their souls' actions, being wasted; not considering that God regards those hidden sighs of those that want abilities to express them outwardly. He that pronounceth them blessed that consider the poor, will have a merciful consideration of such himself.

3. Some again are haunted with hideous representations to their fantasies, and with vile and unworthy thoughts of God, of Christ, of the word, &c., which, as busy flies, disquiet and molest their peace; these are cast in like wildfire by Satan, as may be discerned by the, 1, strangeness; 2, strength and violence; 3, horribleness of them even unto nature corrupt. *Vellem servari Domine, sed cogitationes non patiuntur.* A pious soul is no more guilty of them, than Benjamin of Joseph's cup put into his sack. Amongst other helps prescribed by godly writers, as abomination of them, and diversion from them to other things, &c., let this be one, to complain unto Christ against them, and to fly under the wings of his protection, and to desire him to take our part against his and our enemy. Shall every sin and blasphemy of man be forgiven, and not these blasphemous thoughts, which have the devil for their father, when Christ himself was therefore molested in this kind, that he might succour all poor souls in the like case?

But* there is a difference betwixt Christ and us in this case, by reason that Satan had nothing of his own in Christ, his suggestions left no impression at all in his holy nature; but, as sparks falling into the sea, were presently quenched. Satan's temptations of Christ were only suggestions on Satan's part, and apprehensions of the vileness of them on Christ's part. To apprehend ill suggested by another, is not ill. It was Christ's grievance, but Satan's sin. But thus he yielded himself to be tempted, that he might both pity us in our conflicts, and train us up to manage our spiritual weapons as he did. Christ could have overcome him by power, but he did it by argument. But when Satan cometh to us, he findeth something of his own in us, which holdeth correspondency and hath intelligence with him; there is the same enmity in our nature to God and goodness in some degree, that is in Satan himself; whereupon his temptations fasten for the most part some taint upon us. And if there wanted a devil to suggest, yet sinful thoughts would arise from within us; though none were cast in from without, we have a mint of them within: these thoughts, *morosa cogitatio,* if the soul dwell on them so long as to suck or draw from and by them any sinful delight, then they leave a more heavy guilt upon the soul, and hinder our sweet communion with God, and interrupt our peace, and put a contrary relish into the soul, disposing of it to greater sins. All scandalous breakings out are but thoughts at the first. Ill thoughts are as little thieves, which, creeping in at the window, open the door to greater; thoughts are seeds of actions. These, especially when they are helped forward by Satan, make the life of many good Christians almost a martyrdom. In this case it is an unsound comfort that some minister, that ill thoughts arise from nature, and what is natural is excusable; but we must know, that nature, as it came out of God's hands at the first, had no such risings out of it: the soul, as inspired of God, had no such unsavoury breathings; but since that by sin it betrayed itself, it is in some sort natural to it to forge sinful imaginations, and to be a furnace of such sparks; and this is an aggravation

* 'But' . . . . to 'subjection in himself.' This long paragraph first introduced in B.

of the sinfulness of natural corruption, that it is so deeply rooted, and so generally spread in our nature.

It furthereth humiliation to know the whole breadth and depth of sin; only this, that our nature now, so far as it is unrenewed, is so unhappily fruitful in ill thoughts, ministers this comfort, that it is not our case alone, as if our condition herein were severed from others, as some have been tempted to think, even almost to despair; none, say they, have such a loathsome nature as I have. This springs from ignorance of the spreading of original sin, for what can come from an unclean thing, but that which is unclean? 'As in the water face answers face, so the polluted heart of one man answereth to the heart of another,' Prov. xxvii 19, where grace hath not made some difference. As in annoyances from Satan, so here, the best way is to lay open our complaints to Christ, and cry with St Paul, *Domine sim patior*, 'O miserable man that I am, who shall deliver me from this body of death?' Rom. vii. 24, 25: upon this venting of his distressed soul, he presently found comfort; for he breaketh into thanksgiving, 'Thanks be to God,' &c. And it is good to take advantage from hence to hate this noisome body of death the more, and to draw nearer unto God, as that holy man after his 'foolish and beastly thoughts,' Ps. lxxiii. 22 and 28, did, and to keep our hearts closer to God, seasoning them with heavenly meditations in the morning, storing up good matter that our heart may be a good treasury, and begging of Christ his Holy Spirit to stop that cursed issue, and to be a living spring of better thoughts in us. Nothing more abaseth the spirits of holy men that desire to delight in God after they have escaped the common defilements of the world, than these unclean issues of spirit, as being most contrary to God, who is a pure Spirit: but the very irksomeness of them yields matter of comfort against them; they force the soul to all spiritual exercises, to watchfulness, and a more near walking with God, and to raise itself to thoughts of a higher nature, which the truth of God, works of God, communion of saints, the mystery of godliness, the consideration of the terror of the Lord, of the excellency of the state of a Christian, and conversation suitable, do abundantly minister. They discover to us a necessity of daily purging and pardoning grace, and of seeking to be found in Christ, and so bring the best often upon their knees.

But our chief comfort is, that our blessed Saviour, as he bade Satan avaunt from himself after he had given way awhile to his impudency, Mat. iv. 10; so he will command him to be gone from us, when it shall be good for us; he must be gone at a word. And he can and will likewise in his due time rebuke the rebellious and extravagant stirrings of our hearts, and bring all the thoughts of the inner man in subjection to himself.

4. Some think, when they begin once to be troubled with the smoke of corruption more than they were before, therefore they are worse than they were. It is true, that corruptions appear now more than before, but they are less.

For, first, sin, the more it is seen the more it is hated, and thereupon is the less. Motes are in a room before the sun shines, but they then only appear.

Secondly, contraries, the nearer they are one to another, the sharper is the conflict betwixt them: now of all enemies the spirit and the flesh are nearest one to another, being both in the soul of a regenerate man, and in faculties of the soul, and in every action that springeth from those faculties, and therefore it is no marvel the soul, the seat of this battle, thus divided in itself, be as smoking flax.

Thirdly, the more grace, the more spiritual life, and the more spiritual life, the more antipathy to the contrary; whence none are so sensible of corruption, as those that have the most living souls.

And fourthly, when men give themselves to carnal liberties, their corruptions trouble them not, as not being bound* and tied up; but when once grace suppresseth their extravagant and licentious excesses, then the flesh boileth, as disdaining to be confined; yet they are better now than they were before. That matter which yields smoke was in the torch before it was lighted; but it is not offensive till the torch begins to burn. Let such know, that if the smoke be once offensive to them, it is a sign that there is light. It is better to enjoy the benefit of light, though with smoke, than to be altogether in the dark.

Neither is smoke so offensive, as light is comfortable to us, it yielding an evidence of truth of grace in the heart; therefore, though it be cumbersome in the conflict, yet it is comfortable in the evidence. It is better corruption should offend us now, than by giving way to it to redeem a little peace with loss of comfort afterwards. Let such therefore as are at variance and odds with their corruptions, look upon this text as their portion of comfort.

[CHAPTER XIII.—*Set upon Duties notwithstanding Weaknesses.*]

Here is an use of encouragement to duty, that Christ will not quench the smoking flax, but blow it up. Some are loath to perform good duties, because they feel their hearts rebelling, and duties come off untowardly. We should not avoid good actions for the infirmities cleaving unto them. Christ looketh more at the good in them that he meaneth to cherish, than the ill in them that he meaneth to abolish. A sick man, though in eating he something increaseth the disease, yet he will eat, that nature may get strength against the disease; so though sin cleaveth to what we do, yet let us do it, since we have to deal with so good a Lord, and the more strife we meet withal, the more acceptance. Christ loveth to taste of the good fruits that come from us, although they will always relish of the old stock. A Christian complaineth he cannot pray. O I am troubled with so many distracting thoughts, and never more than now. But hath he put into thine heart a desire to pray? He will hear the desires of his own Spirit in thee. 'We know not what to pray for as we ought' (nor do anything else as we ought), 'but the Spirit helpeth our infirmities, with inexpressible sighs and groans,' Rom. viii. 26, which are not hid from God. 'My groanings are not hid from thee,' Ps. xxxviii. 9. God can pick sense out of a confused prayer. These desires cry louder in his ears than thy sins. Sometimes a Christian hath such confused thoughts, he can say nothing, but as a child crieth, O Father, not able to shew what it needs, as Moses at the Red Sea.

These stirrings of spirit touch the bowels of God, and melt him into compassion towards us, when they come from the spirit of adoption, and from a striving to be better.

Object. Oh, but is it possible, thinketh the misgiving heart, that so holy a God should accept such a prayer?

Ans. Yes, he will accept that which is his own, and pardon that which is ours. 'Jonah prayed in the whale's belly,' Jonah ii. 1, being burdened with the guilt of sin, yet God heareth him. Let not, therefore, infirmities discourage us. St James takes away this objection, v. 17. Some might object, If I were as holy as Elias, then my prayers might be regarded;

* 'Bounded,' in G.

but, saith he, 'Elias was a man of like passions to us,' he had his passions as well as we; for do we think that God heard him because he was without fault? No, surely. But look we to the promises: 'Call upon me in the day of trouble, and I will hear thee,' Ps. l. 15; 'Ask and ye shall receive,' Matt. vii. 7; and such like. God accepteth our prayers, though weak. 1. Because we are his own children, they come from his own Spirit. 2. Because they are according to his own will. 3. Because they are offered in Christ's mediation, and he takes them, and mingleth them with his own odours, Rev. viii. 3. There is never a holy sigh, never a tear we shed, lost. And as every grace increaseth by exercise of itself, so doth the grace of prayer. By prayer we learn to pray. So, likewise, we should take heed of a spirit of discouragement in all other holy duties, since we have so gracious a Saviour. Pray as we are able, hear as we are able, strive as we are able, do as we are able, according to the measure of grace received. God in Christ will cast a gracious eye upon that which is his own. Would St Paul do nothing, because 'he could not do the good he would?' Phil. iii. 14. Yes, he 'pressed to the mark.' Let us not be cruel to ourselves when Christ is thus gracious.

There is a certain meekness of spirit whereby we yield thanks to God for any ability at all, and rest quiet with the measure of grace received, seeing it is God's good pleasure it should be so, who giveth the will and the deed, yet so as we rest not from further endeavours. But when, upon faithful endeavour, we come short of that we would be, and short of that others are, then know for our comfort, Christ will not quench the smoking flax, and that sincerity and truth, as before was said, with endeavour of growth, is our perfection. It is comfortable what God saith, 'He only shall go to his grave in peace, because there is some goodness,' 1 Kings xiv. 13, though but some goodness. 'Lord, I believe,' Mark ix. 24, with a weak faith, yet with faith; love thee with a faint love, yet with love; endeavour in a feeble manner, yet endeavour. A little fire is fire, though it smoketh. Since thou hast taken me into thy covenant to be thine of an enemy, wilt thou cast me off for these infirmities, which, as they displease thee, so are they the grief of my own heart?

[CHAPTER XIV.—*The Case of Indisposition Resolved, and Discouragements.*]

1. From what hath been spoken, with some little addition, it will not be difficult to resolve that case which some require help in, namely, whether we ought to perform duties, our hearts being altogether indisposed. For satisfaction we must know, 1, Our hearts of themselves do linger after liberty, and are hardly brought under the yoke of duty; and the more spiritual the duty is, the more is their untowardness. Corruption getteth ground, for the most part, in every neglect. It is as in rowing against the tide, one stroke neglected will not be gained in three; and therefore it is good to keep our hearts close to duty, and not to hearken unto the excuses they are ready to frame.

2. In the setting upon duty, God strengtheneth his own party that he hath in us. We find a warmness of heart, and increase of strength, the Spirit going along with us, and raising us up by degrees, until it leaveth us as it were in heaven. God often delighteth to take the advantage of our indisposition, that he may manifest his work the more clearly, and that all the glory of the work may be his, whose all the strength is.

3. Obedience is most direct when there is nothing else to sweeten the action. Although the sacrifice be imperfect, yet the obedience with which it is offered hath acceptance.

4. That which is won as a spoil from our corruptions will have such a degree of comfort afterwards, as for the present it hath of cumber. Feeling and freeness of spirit is oft reserved until duty be discharged; reward followeth work. In and after duty we find that experience of God's presence which, without obedience, we may long wait for, and yet go without. This hindereth not the Spirit's freedom in blowing upon our souls when it listeth, John iii. 8. For we speak only of such a state of soul as is becalmed, and must row, as it were, against the stream. As in sailing, the hand must be to the stern, and the eye to the star; so here, put forth that little strength we have to duty, and look up for assistance, which* the Spirit, as freely, so seasonably will afford.

Caution. (1.) Yet in these duties, that require as well the body as the soul, there may be a cessation till strength be repaired. Whetting doth not let (*d*), but fit. (2.) In sudden passions there should be a time to compose and calm the soul, and to put the strings in tune. The prophet would have a minstrel to bring his soul into frame, 1 Sam. xvi. 16, 17.

So likewise we are subject to discouragements in suffering, by reason of impatience in us. Alas! I shall never get through such a cross. But if God bring us into the cross, he will be with us in the cross, and at length bring us out more refined; we shall lose nothing but dross, Zech. xiii. 9. Of our own strength we cannot bear the least trouble, and by the Spirit's assistance we can bear the greatest. The Spirit will join his shoulders to help us to bear our infirmities. 'The Lord will put his hand to heave us up,' Ps. xxxvii. 24. 'You have heard of the patience of Job,' saith James, chap. v. 11. We have heard likewise of his impatiency too; but it pleased God mercifully to overlook that. It yields us comfort also in desolate conditions, as contagious sicknesses, and the like, wherein we are more immediately under God's hand. Then Christ hath a throne of mercy at our bed's side, and numbers our tears and our groans. And, to come to the matter we are now about, the Sacrament,† it was ordained not for angels, but for men; and not for perfect men, but for weak men; and not for Christ, who is truth itself, to bind him, but because we are ready, by reason of our guilty and unbelieving hearts, to call truth itself into question. Therefore it was not enough for his goodness to leave us many precious promises, but he giveth us seals to strengthen us; and, what though we are not so prepared as we should, yet let us pray as Hezekiah did: 'The Lord pardon every one that prepareth his heart to seek the Lord God of his fathers, though he be not cleansed according to the purification of the sanctuary,' 2 Chron. xxx. 19. Then we come comfortably to this holy sacrament, and with much fruit. This should carry us through all duties with much cheerfulness, that, if we hate our corruptions, and strive against them, they shall not be counted ours. It is not I, saith St Paul, but 'sin that dwelleth in me,' Rom. vii. 17; for what displeaseth us shall never hurt us, *quod non placet, non nocet*, and we shall be esteemed of God to be that we love, and desire, and labour to be. What we desire to be we shall be, and what we desire truly to conquer we shall conquer; for God will fulfil the desire of them that fear him, Ps. cxlv. 19. The desire is an earnest of the thing desired. How little encouragement will carry us to the affairs of

---

* 'Which . . . . afford,' not in A, B, but in E.

† Marginal note—This was preached at the Sacrament.

this life! And yet all the helps God offers will hardly prevail with our backward natures. Whence are, then, discouragements? 1. Not from the Father, for he hath bound himself in covenant 'to pity us as a father pitieth his children,' Ps. ciii. 13, and to accept as a father our weak endeavours; and what is wanting in the strength of duty, he giveth us leave to take up in his gracious indulgence, whereby we shall honour that grace wherein he delights, as much as in more perfect performances. *Possibilitas tua mensura tua.*

2. Not from Christ, for he oy office will not quench the smoking flax. We see* how Christ bestoweth the best fruits of his love upon persons, for condition mean, for parts weak, for infirmities, nay, for grosser falls, offensive: *first*, thus it pleaseth him to confound the pride of flesh, which usually taketh measure of God's love by some outward excellency. *Secondly*, thus he is delighted to shew the freedom of his grace and his prerogative royal, that 'whosoever glorieth, may glory in the Lord,' 1 Cor. i. 31.

In the eleventh to the Hebrews, among that cloud of witnesses, we see Rahab, Gideon, and Samson, ranked with Abraham the father of the faithful, Heb. xi. 31, 32. Our blessed Saviour, as he was the image of his Father, so in this he was of the same mind, glorifying his Father for revealing the mystery of the gospel to simple men, neglecting those that carried the chief reputation of wisdom in the world, Heb. xi. 31, 32.

It is† not unworthy of the remembering that which Saint Augustine speaketh‡ of a silly man in his time, destitute almost altogether of the use of reason, who when he was most patient of all injuries done to himself, yet from a reverence of religion he would not endure any injury done to the name of Christ; insomuch that he would cast stones at those that blasphemed, and would not in that case spare his own governors; which sheweth that the parts of none are so low, as that they are beneath the gracious regard of Christ; where it pleaseth him to make his choice, and to exalt his mercy, he passeth by no degree of wit, though never so plain.

3. Neither do discouragements come from the Spirit;§ he helps our infirmities, and by office is a comforter, Rom. viii. 26. If he convinceth of sin, and so humbleth us, it is that he may make way to shew his office of comforting us. Discouragements, then, must come from ourselves and Satan, who laboureth to fasten on us a loathing of duty.

[CHAPTER XV.—*Of infirmities. No cause of discouragement. In whom they are. And how to recover peace lost.*]

And among other causes of discouragement, some are much vexed with scruples, even against the best duties; partly by distemper of body, helped by Satan's malice, casting dust in their eyes, in their way to heaven; and partly from some remainder of ignorance, which like darkness breedeth fears; and as ignorance of other things, so especially of this merciful disposition in Christ, the persuasion of which would easily banish false fears, they conceive of him as one sitting at a catch for all advantages against them; wherein they may see how they wrong not only themselves but his goodness. This scrupulosity, for the most part, is a sign of a godly soul,

---

* 'We see' .... to 'wisdom in the world.' This paragraph added first in B.
† 'It is' ... to 'never so plain.' This paragraph not in A, B, but in E.
‡ Aug. de peccatorum meritis et remiss., lib. i. cap. 14.
§ 'Not from the Spirit,' in A.

as some weeds are of a good soil : therefore are they the more to be pitied, for it is a heavy affliction, and the ground of it in most is not so much from trouble of conscience, as from sickness of fantasy. The end of Christ's coming was to free us from all such groundless fears.

There is still in some, such ignorance of that comfortable condition we are in under the covenant of grace, as by it they are much discouraged. Therefore we must know, 1, That weaknesses do not break covenant with God. They do not between husband and wife; and shall we make ourselves more pitiful than Christ, who maketh himself a pattern of love to all other husbands ? 2. Weaknesses do not debar us from mercy, nay, they incline God the more, Ps. lxxviii. 39. Mercy is a part of the church's jointure, 'Christ marries her in mercy,' Hos. ii. 19. The husband is bound to bear with the wife, as 'being the weaker vessel,' 1 Pet. iii. 7; and shall we think he will exempt himself from his own rule, and not bear with his weak spouse?

3. If Christ should not be merciful to our infirmities, he should not have a people to serve him.

Put case therefore we be very weak, yet so long as we are not found amongst malicious opposers and underminers of God's truth, let us not give way to despairing thoughts ; we have a merciful Saviour. But lest we flatter ourselves without ground, we must know that weaknesses are accounted either, 1, Imperfections cleaving to our best actions; or, 2, Such actions as proceed from want of age in Christ, whilst we are babes; or, 3, From want of strength, where there hath been little means; or, 4, They are sudden indeliberate breakings out, contrary to our general bent and purpose, whilst our judgment is overcast with the cloud of a sudden temptation. After which, 1, we are sensible of our infirmity; 2, We grieve for it; 3, And from grief, complain; and 4, With complaining strive and labour to reform; and 5, In labouring get some ground of our corruption.

Weaknesses* so considered, howsoever they be matter of humiliation, and the object of our daily mortification, yet may stand with boldness with God, neither is a good work either extinguished by them, or tainted so far as to lose all acceptance with God. But to plead for an infirmity is more than an infirmity; to allow ourselves in weaknesses is more than a weakness. The justification of evil sealeth up the lips, so that the soul cannot call God Father with that child-like liberty, or enjoy sweet communion with him, until peace be made by shaming ourselves, and renewing our faith. Those that have ever been bruised for sin, if they fall they are soon recovered. Peter was recovered with a gracious look of Christ; David by Abigail's words. Tell a thief or a vagrant that he is out of the way, he regards it not, because his aim is not to walk in any certain way, but as it serveth his own turn.

For the further clearing of this, we must conceive, 1, That wheresoever sins of infirmity are, there in that person must be the life of grace begun. There can be no weakness, where there is no life. 2. There must be a sincere and general bent to the best things; though for a sudden a godly man be drawn or driven aside in some particulars, yet by reason of that interest the Spirit of Christ hath in him, and because his aims are right for the main, he will either recover of himself, or yield to the counsel of others. 3. There must be a right judgment allowing of the best ways, or else the heart is rotten, and infuseth corruption into the whole conversation, so that all their actions become infected at the spring-head; they justify looseness, and condemn God's ways, as too much strictness; their principles whereby they work are not good. 4. There must be a conjugal love to Christ, so

* 'Weaknesses' . . to 'perfecteth his strength.' This paragraph first added in B.

as upon no terms they will change their Lord and husband, and yield themselves absolutely over to be ruled by their own lusts, or the lusts of others.

A Christian's carriage towards Christ may in many things be very offensive, and cause some strangeness; yet he will own Christ, and Christ him; he will not resolve upon any way wherein he knows he must break with Christ.

Where the heart is thus in these respects qualified, there we must know this, that Christ counteth it his honour to pass by many infirmities, nay, in infirmities he perfecteth his strength. There be some almost invincible infirmities,* as forgetfulness, heaviness of spirit, sudden passions, fears, &c., which though natural, yet are for the most part tainted with sin; of these,† if the life of Christ be in us, we are weary, and would fain shake them off, as a sick man his ague; otherwise it is not to be esteemed weakness so much as wilfulness, and the more will, the more sin; and little sins, when God shall awake the conscience, and 'set them in order before us,' Ps. l. 21, will prove great burdens, and not only bruise a reed, but shake a cedar. Yet God's children never sin with full will, because there is a contrary law of the mind, whereby the dominion of sin is broken, which always hath some secret working against the law of sin. Notwithstanding‡ there may be so much will in a sinful action, as may wonderfully waste our comfort afterward, and keep us long upon the rack of a disquieted conscience, God in his fatherly dispensation suspending the sense of his love. So much as we give way to our will in sinning, in such a measure of distance we set ourselves from comfort. Sin against conscience is as a thief in the candle, which wasteth our joy, and thereby weakeneth our strength. We must know, therefore, that wilful breeches in sanctification will much hinder the sense of our justification.

Quest. What course shall such take to recover their peace?

Ans. Such must give a sharp sentence against themselves, and yet cast themselves upon God's mercy in Christ, as at their first conversion. And now they had need to clasp about Christ the faster, as they see more need in themselves, and let them remember the mildness of Christ here, that will not quench the smoking flax. Ofttimes we see that, after a deep humiliation, Christ speaks more peace than before, to witness the truth of this reconciliation, because he knows Satan's enterprises in casting down such, lower, and because such are most abased in themselves, and are ashamed to look Christ in the face, by reason of their unkindness. We see God did not only pardon David, but after much bruising gave him wise Solomon to succeed him in the kingdom. We see in the Canticles, chap. vi. 44, that the church, after she had been humbled for her slighting of Christ, Christ sweetly entertains her again, and falleth into commendation of her beauty. We must know for our comfort that Christ was not anointed to this great work of the mediator for lesser sins only, but for the greatest, if we have but a spark of true faith to lay hold on him. Therefore, if there be any bruised reed, let him not except himself, when Christ doth not except him; 'Come unto me, all ye that are weary and heavy laden,' &c., Matt. xi. 28. Why should we not make use of so gracious a disposition? we are only therefore poor, because we know not our riches in Christ. In time of temptation, rather believe Christ than the devil, believe truth from truth itself, hearken not to a liar, an enemy, and a murderer.

---

* A necessitatibus meis libera me Domine.—*Aug* [*ustine*].
† 'If .... in us,' added in B. ‡ 'Yet,' in A.

[CHAPTER XVI.—*Satan not to be believed, as he representeth Christ unto us.*]

Since Christ is thus comfortably set out unto us, let us not believe Satan's representations of him. When we are troubled in conscience for our sins, his manner is then to present him to the afflicted soul as a most severe judge armed with justice against us. But then let us present him to our souls, as thus offered to our view by God himself, as holding out a sceptre of mercy, and spreading his arms to receive us. When we think of Joseph, Daniel, John the Evangelist, &c., we frame conceits of them with delight, as of mild and sweet persons; much more when we think of Christ, we should conceive of him as a mirror of all meekness. If the sweetness of all flowers were in one, how sweet must that flower needs be? In Christ all perfections of mercy and love meet; how great then must that mercy be that lodgeth in so gracious a heart? whatsoever tenderness is scattered in husband, father, brother, head, all is but a beam from him, it is in him in the most eminent manner. We are weak, but we are his; we are deformed, but yet carry his image upon us. A father looks not so much at the blemishes of his child, as at his own nature in him; so Christ finds matter of love from that which is his own in us. He sees his own nature in us: we are diseased, but yet his members. Who ever neglected his own members because they were sick or weak? none ever hated his own flesh. Can the head forget the members? can Christ forget himself? we are his fulness, as he is ours. He was love itself clothed with man's nature, which he united so near to himself, that he might communicate his goodness the more freely unto us; and took not our nature when it was at the best, but when it was abased, with all natural and common infirmities it was subject unto. Let us therefore abhor all suspicious thoughts, as either cast in or cherished by that damned spirit, who as he laboured to divide between the Father and the Son by jealousies, 'If thou be the Son of God,' &c., Matt. iv. 6, so his daily study is, to divide betwixt the Son and us, by breeding mispersuasions in us of Christ, as if there were not such tender love in him to such as we are. It was his art from the beginning to discredit God with man, by calling God's love into question, with our first father Adam; his success then makes him ready at that weapon still.

Object. But for all this, I feel not Christ so to me, saith the smoking flax, but rather the clean contrary; he seemeth to be an enemy unto me, I see and feel evidences of his just displeasure,

Ans. Christ may act the part of an enemy a little while, as Joseph did, but it is to make way for acting his own part of mercy in a more seasonable time; he cannot hold in his bowels long. He seemeth to wrestle with us, as with Jacob, but he supplies us with hidden strength, at length to get the better. Faith pulls off the vizard from his face, and sees a loving heart under contrary appearances. *Fides Christo larvam detrahit.* At first he answers the woman of Canaan crying after him not a word; 2, Then gives her a denial; 3, Gives an answer tending to her reproach, calling her dog, as being without the covenant; yet she would not be so beaten off, for she considered the end of his coming. As his Father was never nearer him in strength to support him, than when he was furthest off in sense of favour to comfort him; so Christ is never nearer us in power to uphold us, than when he seemeth most to hide his presence from us. The influence of the Sun of righteousness pierceth deeper than his light. In such cases, whatsoever Christ's present carriage is towards us, let us oppose his nature and office against it; he cannot deny himself, he cannot but discharge tne office his Father hath laid upon him. We see here the Father hath undertaken that he shall not 'quench the smoking flax;' and Christ again undertaking for us to the Father, appearing before him for us, until he presents us blameless before him, John xvii. 6, 11. The Father hath given us to Christ, and Christ giveth us back again to the Father.

Object. This were good comfort, if I were but as smoking flax.

Ans. It is well that thy objection pincheth upon thyself, and not upon Christ; it is well thou givest him the honour of his mercy towards others, though not to thyself: but yet do not wrong the work of his Spirit in thy heart. Satan, as he slandereth Christ to us, so he slandereth us to ourselves. If thou beest not so much as smoking flax, then why dost thou not renounce thy interest in Christ, and disclaim the covenant of grace? This thou darest not do. Why dost thou not give up thyself wholly to other contents? This thy spirit will not suffer thee. Whence come these restless groanings and complaints? lay this thy present estate, together with this office of Christ to such, and do not despise the consolation of the Almighty, nor refuse thy own mercy. Cast thyself into the arms of Christ, and if thou perishest, perish there; if thou dost not, thou art sure to perish. If mercy be to be found anywhere, it is there.

Herein appears Christ's care to thee, that he hath given thee a heart in some degree sensible: he might have given thee up to hardness, security and profaneness of heart, of all spiritual judgments the greatest. He that died for his enemies, will he refuse those, the desire of whose soul is towards him? He that by his messengers desires us to be reconciled, will he put us off when we earnestly seek it at his hand? No, doubtless, when he prevents us by kindling holy desires in us, he is ready to meet us in his own ways. When the prodigal set himself to return to his father, his father stays not for him, but meets him in the way. 'When he prepares the heart to seek, he will cause his ear to hear,' Ps. x. 17. He cannot find in his heart to hide himself long from us. If God should bring us into such a dark condition, as that we should see no light from himself, or the creature, then let us remember what he saith by the prophet Isaiah, 'He that is in darkness, and seeth no light,' Isa. l. 10, no light of comfort, no light of God's countenance, 'yet let him trust in the name of the Lord.' We can never be in such a condition, wherein there will be just cause of utter despair; therefore let us do as mariners do, cast anchor in the dark. Christ knows how to pity us in this case; look what comfort he felt from his Father in his breakings, Isa. liii. 5, the like we shall feel from himself in our bruising.

The sighs of a bruised heart carry in them some report, as of our affection to Christ, so of his care to us. The eyes of our souls cannot be towards him, but that he hath cast a gracious look upon us first. The least love we have to him is but a reflection of his love first shining upon us. As Christ did in his example whatsoever he gives us in charge to do, so he suffered in his own person whatsoever he calleth us to suffer, that he might the better learn to relieve and pity us in our sufferings. In his desertion in the garden, and upon the cross, he was content to want that unspeakable solace in the presence of his Father, both to bear the wrath of the Lord for a time for us, and likewise to know the better how to comfort us in our greatest extremities. God seeth it fit we should taste of that cup of which his Son drank so deep, that we might feel a little what sin is, and what his Son's love was; but our comfort is, that Christ drank the dregs of the cup for us, and will succour us, that our spirits utterly fail not under that little

taste of his displeasure which we may feel. He became not only a man, but a curse, a man of sorrows for us. He was broken, that we should not be broken; he was troubled, that we should not be desperately troubled; he became a curse, that we should not be accursed. Whatsoever may be wished for in an all-sufficient comforter, is all to be found in Christ,
1. Authority from the Father, all power was given him,' Matt. xxviii. 18.
2. Strength in himself, as having his name the mighty God, Isa. ix. 6.
3. Wisdom, and that from his own experience, how and when to help.
4. Willingness, as being flesh of our flesh, and bone of our bone, Isa. ix. 6.

[CHAPTER XVII.—*Reproof of such as sin against this merciful disposition in Christ. Of quenching the Spirit.*]

We are now to take notice of divers sorts of men that offend deeply against this merciful disposition of Christ: as, 1, Such as go on in all ill courses of life upon this conceit, as if it were in vain to go to Christ, their lives have been so ill; whenas so soon as we look to heaven, all encouragements are ready to meet us and draw us forward. Amongst others this is one allurement, that Christ is ready to welcome us, and lead us further. None are damned in the church but those that will. Such as either enforce upon themselves hard conceits of Christ, that they may have some show of reason to fetch contentment from other things: as that unprofitable servant, Matt. xxv. 30, that would needs take up a conceit, that his master was a hard man; hereby to flatter himself in his unfruitful courses, in not improving that talent which he had.

2. Such as take up a hope of their own, that Christ will suffer them to walk in the ways to hell, and yet bring them to heaven: whereas all comfort should draw us nearer to Christ, else it is a lying comfort, either in itself or in our application of it.

And 3. Those that will cast water themselves upon those sparks which Christ labours to kindle in them, because they will not be troubled with the light of them.

Such must know that the Lamb can be angry, and they that will not come under his sceptre of mercy, shall be crushed in pieces by his sceptre of power, Ps. ii. 9. Though he will graciously tender and maintain the least spark of true grace, yet where he findeth not the spark of grace, but opposition to his Spirit striving with them, his wrath once kindled shall burn to hell. There is no juster provocation than when kindness is churlishly refused.

When God would have cured Babylon, and she would not be cured, then she was given up to destruction, Jer. li. 9.

When Jerusalem would not be gathered under the wing of Christ, then their habitation is left desolate, Matt. xxiii. 37, 38.

When wisdom stretcheth out her hand and men refuse, then wisdom will laugh at men's destruction, Prov. i. 26. Salvation itself will not save those that spill the potion, and cast away the plaster. A pitiful case, when this merciful Saviour shall delight in destruction: when he that made men shall have no mercy on them, Isa. xxvii. 11.

O, say the rebels of the time, God hath not made us to damn us. Yes, if you will not meet Christ in the ways of his mercy, it is fit you should 'eat the fruit of your own ways, and be filled with your own devices,' Prov. i. 31.

This will be the hell of hell, when men shall think, that they have loved their sins more than their souls; when they shall think, what love and mercy hath been almost enforced upon them, and yet they would perish. The more accessary we are in pulling a judgment upon ourselves, the more the conscience will be confounded in itself, when they shall acknowledge Christ to be without all blame, themselves without excuse.

If men appeal to their own consciences, they will tell them, the Holy Spirit hath often knocked at their hearts, as willing to have kindled some holy desires in them. How else can they be said to resist the Holy Ghost, but that the Spirit was readier to draw them to a further degree of goodness than stood with their own wills? whereupon those in the church that are damned are self-condemned before. So that here we need not rise to higher causes, when men carry sufficient cause* in their own bosoms.

4. And the best of us all may offend against this merciful disposition, if we be not watchful against that liberty our carnal disposition will be ready to take from it. Thus we reason, if Christ will not quench the smoking flax, what need we fear that any neglect on our part can bring us under a comfortless condition? If Christ will not do it, what can?

Ans. You know the apostle's prohibition notwithstanding, 1 Thess. v. 19, 'Quench not the Spirit.' These cautions of not quenching are sanctified by the Spirit as means of not quenching. Christ performeth his office in not quenching, by stirring up suitable endeavours in us; and none more solicitous in the use of the means than those that are most certain of the good success. The ground is this: the means that God hath set apart for the effecting of any thing, fall under the same purpose that he hath to bring that thing to pass; and this is a principle taken for granted, even in civil matters; as who, if he knew before it would be a fruitful year, would therefore hang up his plough and neglect tillage?

Hence the apostle stirs up from the certain expectation of a blessing, 1 Cor. xv. 57, 58, and this encouragement here from the good issue of final victory is intended to stir us up, and not to take us off. If we be negligent in the exercise of grace received, and use of means prescribed, suffering our spirits to be oppressed with multitudes and variety of cares of this life, and take not heed of the damps of the times, for such miscarriage God in his wise care suffereth us oft to fall into a worse condition for feeling, than those that were never so much enlightened. Yet in mercy he will not suffer us to be so far enemies to ourselves, as wholly to neglect these sparks once kindled. Were it possible that we should be given up to give over all endeavour wholly, then we could look for no other issue but quenching; but Christ will tend this spark, and cherish this small seed, so as he will preserve in the soul always some degree of care. If we would make a comfortable use of this, we must consider all those means whereby Christ doth preserve grace begun; as *first*, holy communion, whereby one Christian heateth another; 'two are better than one,' &c., Eccles. iv. 9. 'Did not our hearts burn?' Luke xxiv. 32, said the disciples. *Secondly*, much more communion with God in holy duties, as meditation and prayer, which doth not only kindle, but addeth a lustre to the soul. *Thirdly*, we feel by experience the breath of the Spirit to go along with the ministerial breath, whereupon the apostle knits these two together: 'Quench not the Spirit;' 'despise not prophecies,' 1 Thess. v. 19, 20. Nathan by a few words blew up the decaying sparks in David. Rather than God will suffer his fire in us to die, he will send some Nathan or other, and something always is left

* 'Of their own damnation,' in A and B.

in us to join with the word as connatural to it ; as a coal that hath fire in it will quickly catch more to it : smoking flax will easily take fire. *Fourthly*, grace is strengthened by the exercise of it; 'Up and be doing, and the Lord be with thee,' 1 Chron. xxii. 16, said David to his son Solomon : stir up the grace that is in thee, for so holy motions turn to resolutions, resolutions to practice, and practice to a prepared readiness to every good work.

Caution. Yet let us know that grace is increased in the exercise of it, not by virtue of the exercise itself, but as Christ by his Spirit floweth into the soul, and bringeth us nearer unto himself the fountain, and instilleth such comfort in the act, whereby the heart is further enlarged. The heart of a Christian is Christ's garden, and his graces are as so many sweet spices and flowers, which his Spirit blowing upon makes* them to send forth a sweet savour : therefore keep the soul open for entertainment of the Holy Ghost, for he will bring in continually fresh forces to subdue corruption, and this most of all on the Lord's day. John was in the Spirit on the Lord's day, even in Patmos, the place of his banishment, Rev. i. 10 ; then the gales of the Spirit blow more strongly and sweetly. As we look, therefore, for the comfort of this doctrine, let us not favour our natural sloth, ' but exercise ourselves to godliness,' 1 Tim. iv. 7, and labour to keep this fire always burning upon the altar of our hearts, and dress our lamps daily, and put in fresh oil, and wind up our souls higher and higher still : resting in a good condition is contrary to grace, which cannot but promote itself to a further measure ; let none turn this ' grace into wantonness,' Jude 4. Infirmities are a ground of humility, not a plea for negligence, not an encouragement to presumption. We should be so far from being ill, because Christ is good, as that those coals of love should melt us ; therefore those may well suspect themselves in whom the consideration of this mildness of Christ doth not work that way : surely where grace is, corruption is as ' smoke to their eyes, and vinegar to their teeth,' Prov. x. 29. And therefore they will labour in regard of their own comfort, as likewise for the credit of religion and the glory of God, that their light may break forth. If a spark of faith and love be so precious, what an honour will it be to be rich in faith ! Who would not rather walk in the light, and in the comforts of the Holy Ghost, than to live in a dark, perplexed estate ? and not rather to be carried with full sail to heaven, than to be tossed always with fears and doubts ? The present trouble in conflict against a sin is not so much as that disquiet which any corruption favoured will bring upon us afterward ; true peace is in conquering, not in yielding. The comfort in this text intended is for those that would fain do better, but find their corruptions clog them ; that are in such a mist, that ofttimes they cannot tell what to think of themselves ; that fain would believe, and yet oft fear they do not believe, and think that it cannot be that God should be so good to such sinful wretches as they are ; and yet they allow not themselves in these fears and doubts.

5. And among others, how do they wrong themselves and him, that will have other mediators to God for them than he ? Are any more pitiful than he, who became man to that end, that he might be pitiful to his own flesh ? Let all at all times repair to this meek Saviour, and put up all our suits in his prevailing name. What need we knock at any other door ? can any be more tender over us than Christ ? What encouragement have we to commend the state of the church in general, or of any broken-hearted Christian, unto him by our prayers ? Of whom we may speak unto Christ, as they of Lazarus, Lord, the church which thou lovest, and gavest thyself

* 'Maketh,' in A and B.

for, is in distress : Lord, this poor Christian, for whom thou wert bruised, Isa. liii. 5, is bruised and brought very low. It cannot but touch his bowels when the misery of his own dear bowels is spread before him.

6. Again, considering this gracious nature in Christ, let us think with ourselves thus : when he is so kind unto us, shall we be cruel against him in his name, in his truth, in his children ? how shall those that delight to be so terrible ' to the meek of the earth,' Zech. ii. 3, hope to look so gracious a Saviour in the face ? they that are so boisterous towards his spouse, shall know one day they had to deal with himself in his church. So it cannot but cut the heart of those that have felt this love of Christ, to hear him wounded who is the life of their lives, and the soul of their souls : this maketh those that have felt mercy weep over Christ, whom they have pierced with their sins. There cannot but be a mutual and quick sympathy between the head and the members. When we are tempted to any sin, if we will not pity ourselves, yet we should spare Christ, in not putting him to new torments. The apostle could not find out a more heart-breaking argument to enforce a sacrificing ourselves to God, than to conjure us by the mercies of God in Christ, Rom. xii. 1.

7. This mercy of Christ likewise should move us to commiserate the state * of the poor church, torn by enemies without, and rending itself by divisions at home. It cannot but work upon any soul that ever felt comfort from Christ, to consider what an affectionate entreaty the apostle useth to mutual agreement in judgment and affection. 'If any consolation in Christ, if any comfort of love, if any fellowship of the Spirit, if any bowels and mercies, fulfil my joy, be like-minded,' Phil. ii. 1 ; as if he should say, Unless you will disclaim all consolation in Christ, &c., labour to maintain the unity of the Spirit in the bond of peace. What a joyful spectacle is this to Satan and his faction, to see those that are separated from the world fall in pieces among themselves ! Our discord is our enemy's melody.

The more to blame those that for private aims affect differences from others, and will not suffer the wounds of the church to close and meet together. Which must not be understood, as if men should dissemble their judgment in any truth where there is just cause of expressing themselves; for the least truth is Christ's and not ours, and therefore we are not to take liberty to affirm or deny at our pleasures. There is a due in a penny as well as in a pound, therefore we must be faithful in the least truth, when season calleth for it. Then our ' words are like apples of gold with pictures of silver,' Prov. xxv. 11. One word spoken in season, will do more good than a thousand out of season. But in some cases peace, by 'keeping our faith to ourselves,' Rom. xiv. 22, is of more consequence than the open discovery of some things we take to be true ; considering the weakness of man's nature is such that there can hardly be a discovery of any difference in opinion, without some estrangement of affection. So far as men are not of one mind, they will hardly be of one heart, except where grace and the peace of God, Col. iii. 15, bear great rule in the heart : therefore open show of difference is never good but when it is necessary ; howsoever some, from a desire to be somebody, turn into by-ways, and yield to a spirit of contradiction in themselves ; yet, if St Paul may be judge, ' are they not carnal ? ' 1 Cor. iii. 3 ; if it be wisdom, it is wisdom from beneath : for the wisdom from above, as it is pure, so it is *peaceable*, James iii. 17. Our blessed Saviour, when he was to leave the world, what doth he press upon his disciples more than peace and love ? And in his

* 'Estate,' in A and B.

last prayer, with what earnestness did he beg of his Father that 'they might be one, as he and the Father were one!' John xvii. 21. But what he prayed for on earth, we shall only enjoy perfectly in heaven. Let this make the meditation of that time the more sweet unto us.

8. And further, to lay open offenders in this kind, what spirit shall we think them to be of, that take advantages of the bruisedness and infirmities of men's spirits to relieve them with false peace for their own worldly ends? A wounded spirit will part with anything. Most of the gainful points of popery, as confession, satisfaction, merit, purgatory, &c., spring from hence, but they are physicians of no value, or rather tormentors than physicians at all. It is a greater blessing to be delivered from the 'sting of these scorpions,' Rev. ix. 5, than we are thankful for. Spiritual tyranny is the greatest tyranny, and then especially when it is where most mercy should be shewed; yet even there some, like cruel surgeons, delight in making long cures, to serve themselves upon the misery of others. It bringeth men under a terrible curse, 'when they will not remember to shew mercy, but persecute the poor and needy man, that they might even slay the broken in heart,' Ps. cix. 16.

Likewise, to such as raise temporal advantage to themselves out of the spiritual misery of others, join such as raise estates by betraying the church, and are unfaithful in the trust committed unto them: when the children shall cry for the bread of life, and there is none to give them, bringing thus upon the people of God that heavy judgment of a spiritual famine, starving Christ in his members; shall we so requite so good a Saviour, who counteth the love and mercy shewed 'in feeding his lambs,' John xxi. 15, as shewed to himself?

Last of all, they carry themselves very unkindly towards Christ, who stumble at this his low stooping unto us in his government and ordinances, that are ashamed of the simplicity of the gospel, that count preaching foolishness.

They, out of the pride of their heart, think they may do well enough without the help of the word and sacraments, and think Christ took not state enough upon him; and therefore they will mend the matter with their own devices, whereby they may give the better content to flesh and blood, as in popery. What greater unthankfulness can there be than to despise any help that Christ in mercy hath provided for us? In the days of his flesh, the proud Pharisees took offence at his familiar conversing with sinful men, who only did so as a physician to heal their souls. What defences was St Paul driven to make for himself, for his plainness in unfolding the gospel? The more Christ, in himself and in his servants, shall descend to exalt us, the more we should, with all humility and readiness, entertain that love, and magnify the goodness of God, that hath put the great work of our salvation, and laid the government upon so gentle a Saviour, that will carry himself so mildly in all things wherein he is to deal betwixt God and us, and us and God. The lower Christ comes down to us, the higher let us lift him up in our hearts: so will all those do that have ever found the experience of Christ's work in their heart.

[CHAPTER XVIII.—*Of Christ's judgment in us, and his victory, what it is.*]

We come to the third part, the constant progress of Christ's gracious power, until he hath set up such an absolute government in us, which shall prevail over all corruptions. It is said here, he will cherish his beginnings of grace in us, until he bring forth judgment unto victory. By judgment here, is meant the kingdom of grace in us, that government whereby Christ sets up a throne in our hearts. Governors among the Jews were first called judges, then kings : whence this inward rule is called judgment ; as likewise, because it agrees unto the judgment of the word, which the psalmist oft calleth judgment, Ps. lxxii. 1, 2, because it agreeth to God's judgment. Men may read their doom in God's word, what it judgeth of them God judgeth of them. By this judgment set up in us, good is discerned, allowed, and performed ; sin is judged, condemned, and executed. Our spirit being under the Spirit of Christ, is governed by him, and so far as it is governed by Christ, it governs us graciously.

Christ and we are of one judgment, and of one will. He hath his will in us ; and his judgments are so invested into us, as that they are turned into our judgment, we carrying 'his law in our hearts, written by his Spirit,' Jer. xxxi. 33. The law in the inner man and the law written, answer as counterpanes each other.

The meaning then is, that the gracious frame of holiness set up in our hearts by the Spirit of Christ, shall go forward until all contrary power be brought under. The spirit of judgment will be a spirit of burning, Isa. iv. 4, to consume whatsoever opposed corruption like rust eats into the soul. If God's builders fall into errors, and build stubble upon a good foundation, God's Spirit, as a spiritual 'fire, will reveal this in time, 1 Cor. iii. 13,' and waste it. They shall, by a spirit of judgment, condemn their own errors and courses. The whole work of grace in us is set out under the name of judgment, and sometimes wisdom, because judgment is the chief and leading part in grace ; whereupon that gracious work of repentance is called a change of the mind,* and an after-wisdom. As on the other side, in the learned languages, the words that do express wisdom imply likewise the general relish and savour of the whole soul,† and rather more the judgment of taste than of sight, or any other sense, because taste is the most necessary sense, and requireth the nearest application of the object of all other senses. So in spiritual life, it is most necessary that the Spirit should alter the taste of the soul, so as that it might savour the things of the Spirit so deeply, that all other things should be out of relish.

And as it is true of every particular Christian, that Christ's judgment in him shall be victorious, so likewise of the whole body of Christians—the church. The government of Christ, and his truth, whereby he ruleth as by a sceptre, shall at length be victorious in spite of Satan, antichrist, and all enemies. Christ 'riding on his white horse,' Rev. vi. 2, hath a bow, and goeth forth conquering, Rev. xix. 11, in the ministry, that he may overcome either to conversion or to confusion. But yet I take judgment for Christ's kingdom and government within us principally. 1. Because God especially requireth the subjection of the soul and conscience as his proper throne. 2. Because if judgment should prevail in all other ‡ about us and not in our own hearts, it would not yield comfort to us ; hereupon it is the first thing that we desire when we pray, ' Thy kingdom come,' that Christ would come and rule in our hearts. The kingdom of Christ in his ordinances serves but to bring Christ home into his own place, our hearts.

The words being thus explained, that judgment here includeth the government of both mind, will, and affections, there are divers conclusions that naturally do spring from them.

* μετάνοια.   † φρονεῖν, sapere.   ‡ 'Others,' in A and B.

[CHAPTER XIX.—*Christ is so mild that yet he will govern those that enjoy the comfort of his mildness.*]

The first conclusion from the connection of this part of the verse with the former is, that Christ is upon those terms mild, so that he will set up his government in those whom he is so gentle and tender over. He so pardons as he will be obeyed as a king; he so taketh us to be his spouse, as he will be obeyed as a husband. The same Spirit that convinceth us of the necessity of his righteousness to cover us, convinceth us also of the necessity of his government to rule us. His love to us moveth him to frame us to be like himself, and our love to him stirreth us up to be such as he may take delight in, neither have we any more faith, or hope than care to be purged as he is pure; he maketh us subordinate governors, yea, kings under himself, giving us grace not only to set against, but to subdue in some measure our base affections. It is one main fruit of Christ's exaltation that he may turn every one of us from our wickedness, Acts iii. 26. 'For this end Christ died and rose again and liveth, that he should be Lord of the dead and living,' Rom. xiv. 9. God hath bound himself by an oath that he would grant us, that 'without fear we might serve him in holiness and righteousness in his sight,' Luke i. 75, not only in the sight of the world.

1. This may serve for a trial to discern who may lay just claim to Christ's mercy; only those that will take his yoke, and count it a greater happiness to be under his government, than to enjoy any liberty of the flesh; that will take whole Christ, and not single out of him what may stand with their present contentment; that will not divide Lord from Jesus, and so make a Christ of their own: none ever did truly desire mercy pardoning, but desired mercy healing. David prayeth for a new spirit, as well as for sense of pardoning mercy, Ps. li. 10.

2. This sheweth that those are misled, that make Christ to be only righteousness to us, and not sanctification, except by imputation: whereas it is a great part of our happiness to be under such a Lord, who was not only born for us, and given unto us, but 'hath the government likewise upon his shoulders,' Isa. ix. 6, 7, that is our Sanctifier as well as our Saviour, our Saviour as well by the effectual power of his Spirit from the power of sin, as by the merit of his death from the guilt thereof; so that this, 1, Be remembered, that the first and chief ground of our comfort is, that Christ as a priest offered himself as a sacrifice to his Father for us. The guilty soul flieth first to Christ crucified, made a curse for us. Thence it is that Christ hath right to govern us, thence it is that he giveth us his Spirit as our guide to lead us home.

2. In the course of our life, after that we are in state of grace, and be overtaken with any sin, we must remember to have recourse first unto Christ's mercy to pardon us, and then to the promise of his Spirit to govern us.

3. And when we feel ourselves cold in affection and duty, it is the best way to warm ourselves at this fire of his love and mercy in giving himself for us.

4. Again, remember this, that Christ, as he ruleth us, so it is by a spirit of love from a sense of his love, whereby his commandments are easy to us. He leadeth us by his free Spirit, a Spirit of liberty: his subjects are voluntaries. The constraint that he layeth upon his subjects is that of love: he

draweth us with the cords of love sweetly. Yet remember withal, that he draweth us strongly by a Spirit of power, for it is not sufficient that we have motives and encouragements to love and obey Christ from that love of his, whereby he gave himself for us to justify us; but Christ's Spirit must likewise subdue our hearts, and sanctify them to love him, without which all motives would be ineffectual. Our disposition must be changed, we must be new creatures; they seek for heaven in hell that seek for spiritual love in an unchanged heart. When a child obeys his father, it is so from reasons persuading him, as likewise from a child-like nature which giveth strength to these reasons: it is natural for a child of God to love Christ so far as he is renewed, not only from inducement of reason so to do, but likewise from an inward principle and work of grace, whence those reasons have their chief forces; first, we are made partakers of the divine nature, and then we are easily induced and led by Christ's Spirit to spiritual duties.

[CHAPTER XX.—*The spiritual government of Christ is joined with judgment and wisdom.*]

The second conclusion is, that Christ's government in his church and in his children is a wise and well-ordered government, because it is called judgment, and judgment is the life and soul of wisdom. Of this conclusion there are two branches: 1. That the spiritual government of Christ in us is joined with judgment and wisdom. 2. Wheresoever true spiritual wisdom and judgment is, there likewise the Spirit of Christ bringeth in his gracious government. For the first, a well-guided life by the rules of Christ standeth with the strongest and highest reason of all; and therefore holy men are called the 'children of wisdom,' Luke vii. 81, and are able to justify, both by reason and experience, all the ways of wisdom. Opposite courses are folly and madness. Hereupon St Paul saith, that a 'spiritual man judgeth all things,' 1 Cor. ii. 15, that appertain to him, and is judged of none that are of an inferior rank, because they want spiritual light and sight to judge; yet this sort of men will be judging, 'and speaking ill of what they know not,' 2 Pet. ii. 12; they step from ignorance to prejudice and rash censure, without taking right judgment in their way, and therefore their judgment comes to nothing. But the judgment of a spiritual man, so far forth as he is spiritual, shall stand, because it is agreeable to the nature of things: as things are in themselves, so they are in his judgment. As God is in himself infinite in goodness and majesty, &c., so he is to him; he ascribes to God in his heart his divinity and all his excellencies. As Christ is in himself the only mediator, and all in all in the church, Col. iii. 11, so he is to him, by making Christ so in his heart. 'As all things are dung in comparison of Christ,' Phil. iii. 8, so they are to Paul, a sanctified man. As the very worst thing in religion, 'the reproach of Christ is better than the pleasure of sin for a season,' Heb. xi. 26; so it is to Moses, a man of a right esteem. 'As one day in the courts of God is better than a thousand elsewhere,' Ps. lxxxiv. 10, so it is to David, a man of a reformed judgment. There is a conformity of a good man's judgment to things as they are in themselves, and according to the difference or agreement put by God in things, so doth his judgment differ or agree.

Truth is truth, and error, error, and that which is unlawful is unlawful, whether men think so or no. God hath put an eternal difference betwixt light and darkness, good and ill, which no creature's conceit can alter; and therefore no man's judgment is the measure of things further than it agrees to truth stamped upon things themselves by God. Hereupon, because a wise man's judgment agrees to the truth of things, a wise man may in some sense be said to be the measure of things; and the judgment of one holy wise man to be preferred before a thousand others. Such men usually are immoveable as the sun in its course, because they think, and speak, and live by rule. 'A Joshua and his house will serve God,' Josh. xxiv. 15, whatsoever others do, and will run a course contrary to the world, because their judgments lead them a contrary way. Hence it is that Satan hath a spite at the eye of the soul, the judgment, to put out that by ignorance and false reason, for he cannot rule in any until either he hath taken away or perverted judgment: he is a prince of darkness, and ruleth in darkness of the understanding. Therefore he must first be cast out of the understanding by the prevailing of truth, and planting it in the soul. Those therefore that are enemies of knowledge help Satan and antichrist, whose kingdom, like Satan's, is a kingdom of darkness, to erect their throne. Hence it is promised by Christ, that 'the Holy Ghost shall convince the world of judgment,' John xvi. 8; that is, that he is resolved to set up a throne of government, because the great lord of misrule, 'Satan, the prince of the world,' is judged by the gospel, and the Spirit accompanying it, his impostures are discovered, his enterprises laid open; therefore when the gospel was spread, the oracles ceased, 'Satan fell from heaven like lightning,' Luke x. 18; men were 'translated out of his kingdom into Christ's,' Col. i. 13. Where prevailing is by lies, there discovery is victory; 'they shall proceed no further, for their folly shall be manifest to all,' 2 Tim. iii. 9. So that manifestation of error giveth a stop to it, for none will willingly be deceived. Let truth have full scope without check or restraint, and let Satan and his instruments do their worst, they shall not prevail; as Jerome saith of the Pelagians in his time.* The discovery of your opinions is the vanquishing of them, your blasphemies appear at the first blush.

Use. Hence we learn the necessity, that the understanding be principled with supernatural knowledge, for the well managing of a Christian conversation.

There must be light to discover a further end than nature, for which we are Christians, and a rule suitable directing to that end, which is the will of God in Christ, discovering his good pleasure toward us, and our duty towards him; and in virtue of this discovery we do all that we do, that any way may further our reckoning: 'The eye must first be single, and then the whole body and frame of our conversation will be light,' Matt. vi. 22; otherwise both we and our course of life are nothing but darkness. The whole conversation of a Christian is nothing else but knowledge digested into will, affection, and practice. If the first concoction in the stomach be not good, that in the liver cannot be good; so if there be error in the judgment, it mars the whole practice, as an error in the foundation doth the building: God will have 'no blind sacrifices, no unreasonable services,' Mal. i. 13, but will have us to 'love him with all our mind,' Rom. xii. 1, that is, wih our understanding part, as well as 'with all our hearts,' Luke x. 27, that is, the affecting part of the soul.

This order of Christ's government by judgment is agreeable unto the soul, and God delighteth to preserve the manner of working peculiar unto man, that is, to do what he doth out of judgment: as grace supposeth

---

* Sententias vestras prodidisse, superasse est.—Hieron. in Epist. ad Ctesiphon: rima fronte apparent blasphemiæ.

nature as founded upon it, so the frame of grace preserveth the frame of nature in man. And, therefore Christ bringeth all that is good in the soul through judgment, and that so sweetly, that many out of a dangerous error think, that that good which is in them and issueth from them is from themselves, and not from the powerful work of grace. As in evil, the devil so subtilly leadeth us according to the stream of our own nature, that men think that Satan had no hand in their sin; but here a mistake is with little peril, because we are ill of ourselves, and the devil doth but promote what ill he findeth in us. But there are no seeds of supernatural goodness at all in us. God findeth nothing in us but enmity; only he hath engraven this in our nature to incline in general to that which we judge to be good. Now when he shall clearly discover what is good in particular, we are carried to it; and when convincingly he shall discover that which is ill, we abhor it as freely as we embraced it before.

From whence we may know, when we work as we should do or no, that is, when we do what we do out of inward principles, when we fall not upon that which is good, only because we are so bred, or because such or such whom we respect do so, or because we will maintain a side, so making religion a faction; but out of judgment, when what we do that is good, we first judge it in ourselves so to be; and what we abstain from that is ill, we first judge it to be ill from an inward judgment. A sound Christian, as he enjoyeth the better part, so hath first made choice of it with Mary, Luke x. 42; he established all his thoughts by counsel, Prov. xx. 18. God indeed useth carnal men to very good service, but without a thorough altering and conviction of their judgment.* He worketh by them, but not in them, therefore they do neither approve the good they do, nor hate the evil they abstain from.

[CHAPTER XXI.—*Where true wisdom and judgment is, there Christ sets up his government.*]

The second branch is, that wheresoever true wisdom and judgment is, there Christ hath set up his government; because where wisdom is, it directs us not only to understand, but to order our ways aright. Where Christ by his Spirit as a prophet teaches, he likewise as a king by his Spirit subdueth the heart to obedience of what is taught. This is that teaching which is promised of God, when not only the brain, but the heart itself, is taught: when men do not only know what they should do, but are taught the very doing of it; they are not only taught that they should love, fear, and obey, but they are taught love itself, and fear and obedience itself. Christ sets up his chair in the very heart, and alters the frame of that, and makes his subjects good, together with teaching of them to be good. Other princes can make good laws, but they ' cannot write them in their people's hearts,' Jer. xxxii. 40. This is Christ's prerogative, he infuseth into his subjects his own Spirit, ' Upon him there doth not only rest the spirit of wisdom and understanding, but likewise the spirit of the fear of the Lord,' Isa. xi. 2. The knowledge which we have of him from himself, is a transforming knowledge, 2 Cor. iii. 18. The same Spirit that enlighteneth the mind, inspireth gracious inclinations into the will and affections, and infuseth strength into the whole man. As a gracious man judgeth as he should, so he affecteth and doth as he judgeth, his life is a commentary of his inward

* 'Judgments,' in A and B.

man; there is a sweet harmony betwixt God's truth, his judgment, and his whole conversation. The heart of a Christian is like Jerusalem when it was at the best, a city compact within itself, Psa. cxii. 3; where are set up the thrones of judgment, Ps. cxxii. 5. Judgment should have a throne in the heart of every Christian. Not that judgment alone will work a change, there must be grace to alter the bent and sway of the will, before it will yield to be wrought upon by the understanding. But God hath so joined these together, as that whensoever he doth savingly shine upon the understanding, he giveth a soft and pliable heart; for without a work upon the heart by the Spirit of God, it will follow its own inclination to that which it affecteth, whatsoever the judgment shall say to the contrary: there is no connatural proportion betwixt an unsanctified heart and a sanctified judgment. For the heart unaltered will not give leave to the judgment coldly and soberly to conclude what is best: as the sick man whilst his aguish distemper corrupteth his taste, is rather desirous to please that, than to hearken what the physician shall speak. Judgment hath not power over itself where the will is unsubdued, for the will and affections bribe it to give sentence for them, when any profit or pleasure shall come in competition with that which the judgment in general only shall think to be good; and, therefore, it is for the most part in the power of the heart, what the understanding shall judge and determine in particular things. Where grace hath brought the heart under, there unruly passions do not cast such a mist before the understanding, but that in particular it seeth that which is best; and base respects, springing from self-love, do not alter the case, and bias the judgment into a contrary way; but that which is good in itself shall be good unto us, although it cross our particular worldly interests.

Use. The right conceiving of this hath an influence into practice, which hath drawn me to a more full explanation: this will teach us the right method of godliness, to begin with judgment, and then to beg of God, together with illumination, holy inclinations of our will and affections, that so a perfect government may be set up in our hearts, and that our 'knowledge may be with all judgment,' Phil. i. 9, that is, with experience and feeling. When the judgment of Christ is set up in our judgments, and thence, by the Spirit of Christ, brought into our hearts, then it is in its proper place and throne; and until then, truth doth us no good, but helpeth to condemn us. The life of a Christian is a regular life, and he that walketh by the rule, Gal. vi. 16, of the new creature, peace shall be upon him: 'he that despiseth his way and loveth to live at large, seeking all liberty to the flesh, shall die,' Prov. xix. 16. And it is made good by St Paul, 'If we live after the flesh, we shall die,' Rom. viii. 13.

We learn likewise, that men of an ill governed life have no true judgment: no wicked man can be a wise man. And that without Christ's Spirit the soul is in confusion, without beauty and form, as all things were in the chaos before the creation. The whole soul is out of joint till it be set in again by him whose office is to 'restore all things.' The baser part of the soul which should be subject, ruleth all, and keepeth under that little truth that is in the understanding, holding it captive to base affections; and Satan by corruption getteth all the holds of the soul, till Christ, stronger than he, cometh, and driveth him out, and taketh possession of all the powers and parts of soul and body, to be weapons of righteousness, to serve him, and then new lords new laws. Christ as a new conqueror changeth the fundamental laws of old Adam, and establisheth a government of his own.

[CHAPTER XXII.—*Christ's government is victorious.*]

The third conclusion is, that this government is victorious. The reasons are:—

1. Because Christ hath conquered all in his own person first, and he is God over all, blessed for evermore; and therefore over 'sin, death, hell, Satan, the world,' &c., Rom. ix. 5. And as he hath overcome them in himself, so he overcomes them in our hearts and consciences. We use to say, conscience maketh a man a king or a caitiff, because it is planted in us to judge for God, either with us or against us. Now if natural conscience be so forcible, what will it be when besides its own light it hath the light of divine truth put into it? It will undoubtedly prevail, either to make us hold up our heads with boldness, or abase us beneath ourselves. If it subject itself by grace to Christ's truth, then it boldly overlooks death, hell, judgment, and all spiritual enemies, because then Christ sets up his kingdom in the conscience, and makes it a kind of paradise.

The sharpest conflict which the soul hath is between the conscience and God's justice: now if the conscience, sprinkled with the blood of Christ, hath prevailed over assaults fetched from the justice of God as now satisfied by Christ, it will prevail over all other opposition whatsoever.

2. We are to encounter with accursed and damned enemies; therefore, if they begin to fall before the Spirit in us, they shall fall: if they rise up again, it is to have the greater fall.

3. The Spirit of truth, to whose tuition Christ hath committed his church, and the truth of the Spirit, which is the sceptre of Christ, abide for ever; therefore the soul begotten by the immortal seed of the Spirit, 1 Pet. i. 23, and this truth, must not only live for ever, but likewise prevail over all that oppose it, for both the word and Spirit are mighty in operation, Heb. iv. 12; and if the ill spirit be never idle in those whom God delivereth up to him, we cannot think that the Holy Spirit will be idle in those whose leading and government is committed to him. No; as he dwelleth in them, so he will drive out all that rise up against him, until he be all in all.

What is spiritual is eternal. Truth is a beam of Christ's Spirit, both in itself and as it is ingrafted into the soul, therefore it, and the grace, though little, wrought by it, will prevail. A little thing in the hand of a giant will do great matters. A little faith strengthened by Christ will work wonders.

4. 'To him that hath shall be given,' Matt. xxv. 29; the victory over any corruption or temptation is a pledge of final victory. As Joshua said when he set his foot upon the five kings which he conquered, 'Thus God shall do with all our enemies,' Josh. x. 25; heaven is ours already, only we strive till we have full possession.

5. Christ as king brings in a commanding light into the soul, and bows the neck, and softens the iron sinew of the inner man; and where he begins to rule, he rules for ever, 'his kingdom hath no end,' Luke i. 33.

6. The end of Christ's coming was to destroy the works of the devil, both for us and in us; and the end of the resurrection was, as to seal unto us the assurance of his victory; so, 1, To quicken our souls from death in sin; 2, To free our souls from such snares and sorrows of spiritual death as accompany the guilt of sin; 3, To raise them up more comfortable, as the sun breaks forth more gloriously out of a thick cloud; 4, To raise us out of particular slips and failings, stronger; 5, To raise us out of all troublesome and dark conditions of this life; and, 6, At length to raise our

bodies out of the dust. For the same power that the Spirit shewed in raising Christ, our head, from the sorrows of death, and the lowest degree of his abasement; the same power obtained by the death of Christ from God, now appeased by that sacrifice, will the Spirit shew in the church, which is his body, and in every particular member thereof.

And this power is conveyed by faith, whereby, after union with Christ in both his estates of humiliation and exaltation, we see ourselves not only 'dead with Christ, but risen and sitting together with him in heavenly places,' Eph. ii. 6. Now we, apprehending ourselves to be dead and risen, and thereupon victorious over all our enemies in our head, and apprehending that his scope in all this is to conform us to himself, we are by this faith changed into his likeness, 2 Cor. iii. 18, and so become conquerors over all our spiritual enemies, as he is, by that power which we derive from him who is the storehouse of all spiritual strength for all his. Christ at length will have his end in us, and faith resteth assured of it, and this assurance is very operative, stirring us up to join with Christ in his ends.

And so for the church in general, by Christ it will have its victory: Christ is 'that little stone cut out of the mountain without hands, that breaketh in pieces that goodly image,' Dan. ii. 35, that is, all opposite government, until it become 'a great mountain, and filleth the whole earth.' So that the stone that was cut out of the mountain, becomes a mountain itself at length. Who art thou, then, O mountain, that thinkest to stand up against this mountain? All shall lie flat and level before it: he will bring down all mountainous, high, exalted thoughts, and lay the pride of all flesh low. When chaff strives against the wind, stubble against the fire, when the heel kicks against the pricks, when the potsherd strives with the potter, when man strives against God, it is easy to know on which side the victory will go. The winds may toss the ship wherein Christ is, but not overturn it. The waves may dash against the rock, but they do but break themselves against it.

Object. If this be so, why is it thus with the church of God, and with many a gracious Christian? the victory seemeth to go with the enemy.

Ans. For answer, remember, 1, God's children usually in their troubles overcome by suffering; here lambs overcome lions, and doves eagles, by suffering, that herein they may be conformable to Christ, who conquered most when he suffered most; together with Christ's kingdom of patience there was a kingdom of power.

2. This victory is by degrees, and therefore they are too hasty-spirited that would conquer so soon as they strike the first stroke, and be at the end of their race at the first setting forth; the Israelites were sure of their victory in their voyage *(f)* to Canaan, yet they must fight it out. God would not have us presently forget what cruel enemies Christ hath overcome for us; 'Destroy them not, lest the people forget it, saith the Psalmist, Ps. lix. 11. That so by the experience of that annoyance we have by them, we might be kept in fear to come under the power of them.

3. That God often worketh by contraries: when he means to give victory, he will suffer us to be foiled at first; when he means to comfort, he will terrify first; when he means to justify, he will condemn us first; whom he means to make glorious, he will abase first. A Christian conquers, even when he is conquered; when he is conquered by some sins, he gets victory over others more dangerous, as spiritual pride, security, &c.

4. That Christ's work, both in the church and in the hearts of Christians, often goeth backward, that it may go the better forward. As seed rots in

the ground in the winter time, but after comes better up, and the harder the winter the more flourishing the spring, so we learn to stand by falls, and get strength by weakness discovered—*virtutis custos infirmitas*—we take deeper root by shaking; and, as torches flame brighter by moving, thus it pleaseth Christ, out of his freedom, in this manner to maintain his government in us. Let us herein labour to exercise our faith, that it may answer Christ's manner of carriage towards us; when we are foiled, let us believe we shall overcome; when we are fallen, let us believe we shall rise again. Jacob, after he had a ' blow upon which he halted, yet would not give over wrestling,' Gen. xxxii. 24, till he had gotten the blessing; so let us never give over, but in our thoughts knit the beginning, progress, and end together, and then we shall see ourselves in heaven out of the reach of all enemies. Let us assure ourselves that God's grace, even in this imperfect estate, is stronger than man's free will in the state of first perfection, being* founded now in Christ, who, as he is the author, so will be ' the finisher, of our faith,' Heb. xii. 2; we are under a more gracious covenant.

That† which some say of faith rooted, *fides radicata*, that it continueth, but weak faith may come to nothing, seemeth to be crossed by this Scripture; for, as the strongest faith may be shaken, so the weakest where truth is, is so far rooted, that it will prevail. Weakness with watchfulness will stand out, when strength with too much confidence faileth. Weakness, with acknowledging of it, is the fittest seat and subject for God to perfect his strength in; for consciousness of our infirmities driveth us out of ourselves to him in whom our strength lieth.

Hereupon it followeth that weakness may stand with the assurance of salvation; the disciples, notwithstanding all their weaknesses, are bidden to rejoice, Luke x. 20, that their names are written in heaven. Failings, with conflict, in sanctification should not weaken the peace of our justification, and assurance of salvation. It mattereth not so much what ill is in us, as what good; not what corruptions, but how we stand affected to them; not what our particular failings be, so much as what is the thread and tenor of our lives; for Christ's mislike of that which is amiss in us, redounds not to the hatred of our persons,‡ but to the victorious subduing of all our infirmities.

Some have, after conflict, wondered at the goodness of God, that so little and shaking faith should have upheld them in so great combats, when Satan had almost catched them. And, indeed, it is to be wondered how much a little grace will prevail with God for acceptance, and over our enemies for victory, if the heart be upright. Such is the goodness of our sweet Saviour, that he delighteth still to shew his strength in our weakness.

Use 1. First, therefore, for the great consolation of poor and weak Christians, let them know, that a spark from heaven, though kindled under greenwood that sobs (*g*) and smokes, yet it will consume all at last. Love once kindled is strong as death, much water cannot quench it, and therefore it is called a vehement flame, or flame of God, Cant. viii. 6, kindled in the heart by the Holy Ghost; that little that is in us is fed with an everlasting spring. As the fire that came down from heaven in Elias his time, 1 Kings xviii. 38, licked up all the water, to shew that it came from God, so will this fire spend all our corruption; no affliction without, or corruption within, shall quench it. In the morning we see oft clouds gather about the sun, as if they would hide it, but the sun wasteth them by little and little, till it come to its full strength. At the first, fears and doubts hinder

* 'And it is,' in A.   † 'That ... lieth,' added first in B.   ‡ 'Person,' in A and B.

the breaking out of this fire, until at length it gets above them all, and Christ prevails; and then he backs his own graces in us. Grace conquers us first, and we by it conquer all things else; whether it be corruptions within us, or temptations without us.

The church of Christ, begotten by the word of truth, hath the doctrine of the apostles for her crown, and tramples the moon, that is, the world, and all worldly things, 'under her feet,' Rev. xii. 1; 'every one that is born of God overcometh the world,' 1 John v. 4. Faith, whereby especially Christ rules, sets the soul so high, that it overlooks all other things as far below, as having represented to it, by the Spirit of Christ, riches, honour, beauty, pleasures of a higher nature.

Now that we may not come short of the comfort intended, there are two things especially to be taken notice of by us: 1. Whether there be such a judgment or government set up in us, to which this promise of victory is made. 2. Some rules or directions how we are to carry ourselves, that the judgment of Christ in us may indeed be victorious.

The evidences whereby we may come to know that Christ's judgment in us is such as will be victorious, are, 1, If we be able from experience to justify all Christ's ways, let flesh and blood say what it can to the contrary, and can willingly subscribe to that course which God hath taken in Christ, to bring us to heaven, and still approve a further measure of grace than we have attained unto, and project and forecast for it. No other men can justify their courses, when their conscience is awaked. 2. When reasons of religion be the strongest reasons with us, and prevail more than reasons fetched from worldly policy. 3. When we are so true to our ends and fast to our rule, as no hopes or fears can sway us another way, but still we are looking what agrees or differs from our rule. 4. When we 'can do nothing against the truth, but for the truth,' 2 Cor. xiii. 8, as being dearer to us than our lives; truth hath not this sovereignty in the heart of any carnal man. 5. When if we had liberty to choose under whose government we would live, yet out of a delight in the inner man to Christ's government we would make choice of him only to rule us before any other, for this argues, that we are like-minded to Christ, a free and a voluntary people, and not compelled unto Christ's service, otherwise than by the sweet constraint of love. When we are so far in liking with the government of Christ's Spirit, that we are willing to resign up ourselves to him in all things, for then his kingdom is come unto us, when our wills are brought to his will. It is the bent of our wills that maketh us good or ill.

6. A well ordered uniform life, not by fits or starts, shews a well ordered heart a in a clock; when the hammer strikes well, and the hand of the dial points well, it is a sign that the wheels are right set. 7. When Christ's will cometh in competition with any earthly loss or gain, yet if then, in that particular case, the heart will stoop to Christ, it is a true sign; for the truest trial of the power of grace is in such particular cases which touch us nearest, for there our corruption maketh the greatest head. When Christ came near home to the young man, Matt. x. 22, in the gospel, he lost a disciple of him. 8. When we can practise duties pleasing to Christ, though contrary to flesh, and the course of the world, and when we can overcome ourselves in that evil to which our nature is prone, and standeth so much inclined unto, and which agreeth to the sway of the times, and which others lie enthralled under, as desire of revenge, hatred of enemies, private ends, &c., then it appears that grace is in us above nature, heaven above earth, and will have the victory.

For the further clearing of this and helping of us in our trial, we must know there be three degrees of victory. 1. When we resist though we be foiled. 2. When grace gets the better though with conflict. 3. When all corruption is perfectly subdued. Now we have strength but only to resist, yet we may know Christ's government in us will be victorious, because what is said of the devil is said of all our spiritual enemies, 'If we resist, they shall in time fly from us,' James iv. 7; because 'stronger is he that is in us,' that taketh part with his own grace, 'than he that is in the world,' 1 John iv. 4. And if we may hope for victory upon bare resistance, what may we not hope for when the Spirit hath gotten the upper hand?

[CHAPTER XXIII.—*Means to make Grace victorious.*]

For the second, that is, directions.

We must know, though Christ hath undertaken this victory, yet he accomplisheth it by training us up to fight his battles; he overcometh in us, by making us 'wise to salvation,' 2 Tim. iii. 15; and in what degree we believe Christ will conquer, in that degree we will endeavour by his grace that we may conquer; for faith is an obedient and a wise grace. Christ maketh us wise to ponder and weigh things, and thereupon to rank and order them so as we may make the fitter choice of what is best. Some rules to help us in judging are these:

(1.) To judge of things as they help or hinder the main; (2.) as they further or hinder our reckoning; (3.) as they make us more or less spiritual, and so bring us nearer to the fountain of goodness, God himself; (4.) as they bring us peace or sorrow at the last; (5.) as they commend us more or less to God, and wherein we shall approve ourselves to him most; (6.) likewise to judge of things now, as we shall do hereafter when the soul shall be best able to judge, as when we are under any public calamity, or at the hour of death, when the soul gathereth itself from all other things to itself. (7.) Look back to former experience, see what is most agreeable unto it, what was best in our worst times. If grace is or was best then, it is best now. And (8.) labour to judge of things as he doth who must judge us, and as holy men judge, who are led by the* Spirit; more particularly, (9.) what those judge, that have no interest in any benefit that may come by the thing which is in question: for outward things blind the eyes even of the wise; we see papists are most corrupt in those things where their honour, ease, or profit is engaged; but in the doctrine of the Trinity, which doth not touch upon these things, they are sound. But it is not sufficient that judgment be right, but likewise ready and strong.

1. Where Christ establisheth his government, he inspireth care to keep the judgment clear and fresh, for whilst the judgment standeth straight and firm, the whole frame of the soul continueth strong and impregnable. True judgment in us advanceth Christ, and Christ will advance it. All sin is either from false principles, or ignorance, or mindlessness, or unbelief of true. By inconsideration and weakness of assent, Eve lost her hold at first, Gen. iii. 6. It is good, therefore, to store up true principles in our hearts, and to refresh them often, that in virtue of them our affections and actions may be more vigorous. When judgment is fortified, evil finds no entrance, but good things have a side within us, to entertain them. Whilst true convincing light continueth, we will not do the least ill of sin for the greatest

* 'His.' in A and B.

ill of punishment. 'In vain is the net spread in the eyes of that which hath wings,' Prov. i. 17. Whilst the soul is kept aloft, there is little danger of snares below; we lose our high estimation of things before we can be drawn to any sin.

And because knowledge and affection mutually help one another, it is good to keep up our affections of love and delight, by all sweet inducements and divine encouragements; for what the heart liketh best, the mind studieth most. Those that can bring their hearts to delight in Christ know most of his ways. Wisdom loveth him* that loves her. Love is the best entertainer of truth; and when it is not 'entertained in the love of it,' 2 Thess. ii. 10, being so lovely as it is, it leaveth the heart, and will stay no longer. It hath been a prevailing way to begin by withdrawing the love to corrupt the judgment; because as we love, so we use to judge; and therefore it is hard to be affectionate and wise in earthly things; but in heavenly things, where there hath been a right information of the judgment before, the more our affections grow, the better and clearer our judgments will be, because our affections, though strong, can never rise high enough to the excellency of the things. We see in the martyrs, when the sweet doctrine of Christ had once gotten their hearts, it could not be gotten out again by all the torments the wit of cruelty could devise. If Christ hath once possessed the affections, there is no dispossessing of him again. A fire in the heart overcometh all fires without.

3. Wisdom likewise teacheth us wherein our weakness lieth, and our enemy's strength, whereby a jealous fear is stirred up in us, whereby we are preserved; for out of this godly jealousy we keep those provocations which are active and working, from that which is passive and catching in us, as we keep fire from powder. They that will hinder the generation of noisome creatures will hinder the conception first, by keeping male and female asunder. This jealousy will be much furthered by observing strictly what hath helped or hindered a gracious temper in us; and it will make us take heed that we consult not with flesh and blood in ourselves or others. How else can we think that Christ will lead us out to victory, when we take counsel of his and our enemies?

4. Christ maketh us likewise careful to attend all means whereby fresh thoughts and affections may be stirred up and preserved in us. Christ so honoureth the use of means, and the care he putteth into us, that he ascribeth both preservation and victory unto our care of keeping ourselves. 'He that is begotten of God keepeth himself,' 1 John v. 18, but not by himself, but by the Lord, in dependence on him on the use of means. We are no longer safe than wise to present ourselves to all good advantages of acquaintance, &c. By going out of God's walks we go out of his government, and so lose our frame, and find ourselves overspread quickly with a contrary disposition. When we draw near to Christ, James iv. 8, in his ordinances, he draws near unto us.

5. Keep grace in exercise. It is not sleepy habits, but grace in exercise, that preserveth us. Whilst the soul is in some civil or sacred employment, corruptions within us are much suppressed, and Satan's passages stopped, and the Spirit hath a way open to enlarge itself in us, and likewise the guard of angels then most nearly attends us; which course often prevails more against our spiritual enemies than direct opposition. It stands upon Christ's honour to maintain those that are in his work.

6. Sixthly, in all directions we must look up to Christ the quickening

* 'Them,' in A and B.

Spirit, and resolve in his strength. Though we are exhorted to 'cleave to the Lord with full purpose of heart,' Acts xi. 23, yet we must pray with David, 'Lord, for ever keep it in the thoughts of our hearts, and prepare our hearts unto thee,' 1 Chron. xxix. 18. Our hearts are of themselves very loose and unsettled, 'Lord, unite our hearts unto thee to fear thy name,' Ps. lxxxvi. 11, or else, without him, our best purposes will fall to the ground. It is a pleasing request, out of love to God, to beg such a frame of soul from him, wherein he may take delight; and therefore in the use of all the means we must send up our desires and complaints to heaven to him for strength and help, and then we may be sure that 'he will bring forth judgment unto victory.'

7. Lastly, it furthers the state of the soul, to know what frame it should be in, that so we may order our souls accordingly. We should always be fit for communion with God, and be heavenly-minded in earthly business, and be willing to be taken off from them, to redeem time for better things. We should be ready at all times to depart hence, and to live in such a condition as we would be content to die in. We should have hearts prepared for every good duty, open to all good occasions, and shut to all temptations, keeping our watch, and being always ready armed. So far as we come short of these things, so far we have just cause to be humbled, and yet press forward, that we may gain more upon ourselves, and make these things more familiar and lovely unto us; and when we find our souls any ways falling downwards, it is best to raise them up presently by some waking meditations, as of the presence of God, of the strict reckoning we are to make, of the infinite love of God in Christ, and the fruits of it, of the excellency of a Christian's calling, of the short and uncertain time of this life; how little good all those things that steal away our hearts will do us ere long, and how it shall be for ever with us thereafter, as we spend this little time well or ill, &c. The more we give way for such considerations to sink into our hearts, the more we shall rise nearer to that state of soul which we shall enjoy in heaven. When we grow regardless of keeping our souls, then God recovers our taste of good things again by sharp crosses. Thus David, Solomon, Samson, &c., were recovered. It is much easier kept than recovered.

Object. But, notwithstanding my striving, I seem to stand at a stay.

Ans. 1. Grace, as the seed in the parable, grows, we know not how, yet at length, when God seeth fittest, we shall see that all our endeavour hath not been in vain. The tree falleth upon the last stroke, yet all the former strokes help it forward.

Ans. 2. Sometimes victory is suspended because some Achan is not found out, Judges xx. 26, or because we are not humble enough, as Israel had the worst against the Benjamites till they fasted and prayed; or because we betray our helps, and stand not upon our guard, and yield not presently to the motions of the Spirit, which mindeth us always of the best things, if we would regard it. Our own consciences will tell us, if we give them leave to speak, that some sinful favouring of ourselves is the cause. The way in this case to prevail is, 1, To get the victory over the pride of our own nature, by taking shame to ourselves, in humble confession to God; and then, 2, To overcome the unbelief of our hearts, by yielding to the promise of pardon; and then, 3, In confidence of Christ's assistance, to set ourselves against those sins which have prevailed over us; and then prevailing over ourselves, we shall easily prevail over all our enemies, and conquer all conditions we shall be brought into.

[CHAPTER XXIV.—*All should side with Christ.*]

Use 2. If Christ will have the victory, then it is the best way for nations and states to 'kiss the Son,' Ps. ii. 12, and to embrace Christ and his religion, to side with Christ, and to own his cause in the world. His side will prove the stronger side at last. Happy are we if Christ honour us so much as to use our help 'to fight his battle against the mighty,' Judges v. 23. True religion in a state is as the main pillar of a house, and staff of a tent that upholds all. 2. So for families, let Christ be the chief governor of the family; and 3, Let every one be as a house of Christ, to dwell familiarly in, and to rule. Where Christ is, all happiness must follow. If Christ goeth, all will go. Where Christ's government in his ordinances and his Spirit is, there all subordinate government will prosper. Religion inspireth life and grace into all other things; all other virtues, without it they are but as a fair picture without a head. Where Christ's laws are written in the heart, there all other good laws are best obeyed. None despise man's law but those that despise Christ's first. *Nemo humanam authoritatem contemnit, nisi qui divinam prius contempsit.* Of all persons, a man guided by Christ is the best; and of all creatures in the world, a man guided by will and affection, next the devil, is the worst. The happiness of weaker things stands in being ruled by stronger. It is best for a blind man to be guided by him that hath sight, it is best for sheep, and such like shiftless creatures, to be guided by man, and it is happiest for man to be guided by Christ, because his government is so victorious that it frees us from the fear and danger of our greatest enemies, and tends to bring us to the greatest happiness that our nature is capable of. This should make us to joy when Christ reigneth in us. When 'Solomon was crowned, the people shouted,' so that the earth rang,' 1 Kings i. 39, 40. Much more should we rejoice in Christ our king.

And likewise for those whose souls are dear unto us, our endeavour should be that Christ may reign in them also, that they may be baptized by Christ with this fire, Matt. iii. 11, that these sparks may be kindled in them. Men labour to cherish the spirit and mettle, as they term it, of those they train up, because they think they will have use of it in the manifold affairs and troubles of this life. Oh, but let us cherish the sparks of grace in them; for a natural spirit in great troubles will fail, but these sparks will make them conquerors over the greatest evils.

Use 3. If Christ's judgment shall be victorious, then popery, being an opposite frame, set up by the wit of man to maintain stately idleness, must fall. And it is fallen already in the hearts of those upon whom Christ hath shined. It is a lie, and founded upon a lie, upon the infallible judgment of a man subject to sin and error. When that which is taken for a principle of truth becomes a principle of error, the more relying upon it, the more danger.

[CHAPTER XXV.—*Christ's government shall be openly victorious.*]

It is not only said, *judgment shall be victorious, but that Christ will bring it openly forth to victory.* Whence we observe that grace shall be glory, and run into the eyes of all. Now Christ doth conquer, and hath his own ends, but it is in some sort invisibly. His enemies within and without us seem to have the better. But he will bring forth judgment unto victory, to the view of all. The wicked that now shut their eyes shall see it to their torment. It shall not be in the power of subtle men to see or not see what they would. Christ will have power over their hearts; and as his wrath shall immediately seize upon their souls against their wills, so will he have power over the eyes of their souls, to see and know what will increase their misery. Grief shall be fastened to all their senses, and their senses to grief.

Then all the false glosses which they put upon things shall be wiped off. Men are desirous to have the reputation of good, and yet the sweetness of ill; nothing so cordially opposed by them as that truth which layeth them open to themselves, and to the eyes of others, their chief care being how to daub with the world and their own consciences. But the time will come when they shall be driven out of this fools' paradise, and the more subtle their conveyance of things hath been, the more shall be their shame. Christ, whom God hath chosen to set forth the chief glory of his excellencies, is now veiled in regard of his body the church, but will come ere long to be glorious in his saints, 2 Thess. i. 10, and not lose the clear manifestation of any of his attributes; and will declare to all the world what he is, when there shall be no glory but that of Christ and his spouse. Those that are as smoking flax now shall then 'shine as the sun in the firmament,' Matt. xiii. 43, and their 'righteousness break forth as the noon-day,' Ps. xxxvii. 6.

The image of God in Adam had a commanding majesty in it, so that all creatures reverenced him; much more shall the image of God in the perfection of it command respect in all. Even now there is a secret awe put into the hearts of the greatest, towards those in whom they see any grace to shine, from whence it was that Herod feared John Baptist; but what will this be in their day of bringing forth, which is called 'the day of the revelation of the sons of God?' Rom. viii. 19.

There will be more glorious times when 'the kingdoms of the earth shall be the Lord Jesus Christ's,' Rev. xi. 10, and he shall reign for ever; then shall judgment and truth have its victory; then Christ will plead his own cause; truth shall no longer be called heresy and schism, nor heresy catholic doctrine; wickedness shall no longer go masked and disguised; goodness shall appear in its own lustre, and shine in its own beams; things shall be what they are, 'nothing is hidden but shall be laid open,' Matt. x. 26; iniquity shall not be carried in a mystery any longer; deep dissemblers that think to hide their counsels from the Lord shall walk no longer invisible as in the clouds. As * Christ will not quench the least spark kindled by himself, so will he damp the fairest blaze of goodly appearances which are not from above.

Use. If this were believed, men would make more account of sincerity, which will only give us boldness, and not seek for covershames; the confidence whereof, as it maketh men now more presumptuous, so it will expose them hereafter to the greater shame.

If judgment shall be brought forth to victory, then those that have been ruled by their own deceitful hearts and a spirit of error, shall be brought forth to disgrace; that God that hath joined grace and truth with honour, hath joined sin and shame together at last; all the wit and power of man can never be able to sever what God hath coupled. Truth and piety may be trampled upon for a time, but as the two witnesses, Rev. xi. 11, after

* 'As Christ .... above,' not in A, B, but in E.

they were slain rose again, and stood upon their feet, so whatsoever is of God shall at length stand upon its own bottom. There shall be a resurrection not only of bodies but of credits. Can we think that he that threw the angels out of heaven will suffer dust and worms' meat to run a contrary course, and to carry it away always so? No; as verily as Christ is 'King of kings and Lord of lords,' Rev. xix. 16, so will he dash all those pieces of earth 'which rise up against him, as a potter's vessel,' Ps. ii. 9. Was there ever any fierce against God and prospered? Job ix. 4. No; doubtless the rage of man shall turn to Christ's praise, Ps. lxxvi. 10. What was said of Pharaoh shall be said of all heady enemies, who had rather lose their souls than their wills, that they are but raised up for Christ to get himself glory in their confusion.

Let us, then, take heed that we follow not the ways of those men, whose ends we shall tremble at; there is not a more fearful judgment can befal the nature of man, than to be given up to a reprobate judgment of persons and things, because it cometh under a woe 'to call ill good, and good ill,' Isa. v. 20.

How will they be laden with curses another day, that abuse the judgment of others by sophistry and flattery, deceivers and being deceived? 2 Tim. iii. 13. Then the complaint of our first mother Eve will be taken up but fruitlessly, Gen. xiii. 3; the serpent hath deceived me; Satan in such and such hath deceived me; sin hath deceived me; a foolish heart hath deceived me. It is one of the highest points of wisdom to consider upon what grounds we venture our souls. Happy men will they be, who have by Christ's light a right judgment of things, and suffer that judgment to prevail over their hearts.

The soul of most men is drowned in their senses and carried away with weak opinions, raised from vulgar mistakes and shadows of things. And Satan is ready to enlarge the imagination of outward good and outward ill, and make it greater than it is, and spiritual things less, presenting them through false glasses. And so men, trusting in vanity, vanquish themselves in their own apprehensions. A woful condition, when both we and that which we highly esteem shall vanish together, which will be as truly as Christ's judgment shall come to victory; and in what measure the vain heart of man hath been enlarged, to conceive a greater good in things of this world than there is, by so much the soul shall be enlarged to be more sensible of misery when it sees its error. This is the difference betwixt a godly wise man and a deluded worldling; that which the one doth now judge to be vain, the other shall hereafter feel to be so when it is too late. But this is the vanity of our natures, that though we shun above all things to be deceived and mistaken in present things, yet in the greatest matters of all we are willingly ignorant and misled.

[CHAPTER XXVI.—*Christ alone advanceth this government.*]

The fifth conclusion is, that this government is set up and advanced by Christ alone; he bringeth judgment to victory. We both fight and prevail 'in the power of his might,' Eph. vi. 10; we overcome by the Spirit, obtained by 'the blood of the Lamb,' Rev. xii. 11.

It is he alone that 'teacheth our hands to war and fingers to fight,' Ps. cxliv. 1. Nature, as corrupted, favours its own being, and will maintain itself against Christ's government. Nature, simply considered, cannot raise itself above itself to actions spiritual of a higher order and nature; therefore the divine power of Christ is necessary to carry us above all our own strength, especially in duties wherein we meet with greater opposition; for there not only nature will fail us, but ordinary grace, unless there be a stronger and a new supply. In taking up a burden that is weightier than ordinary, if there be not a greater proportion of strength than weight, the undertaker will lie under it; so to every strong encounter there must be a new supply of strength, as in Peter, Matt. xxvi. 69, when he was assaulted with a stronger temptation, being not upheld and shored up with a mightier hand, notwithstanding former strength, foully fell. And being fallen, in our raisings up again it is Christ that must do the work, 1, By removing; or 2, Weakening; or 3, Suspending opposite hinderances; 4, And by advancing the power of his grace in us, to a further degree than we had before we fell; therefore when we are fallen, and by falls have gotten a bruise, let us go to Christ presently to bind us up again.

Use. Let us know, therefore, that it is dangerous to look for that from ourselves which we must have from Christ. Since the fall, all our strength lies in him, as Samson's in his hair, Judges xvi. 17; we are but subordinate agents, moving as we are moved, and working as we are first wrought upon, free so far forth as we are freed, no wiser nor stronger than he makes us to be for the present in anything we undertake.* It is his Spirit that actuates and enliveneth, and applieth that knowledge and strength we have, or else it faileth and lieth as useless in us; we work when we work upon a present strength; therefore dependent spirits are the wisest and the ablest. Nothing is stronger than humility, that goeth out of itself; or weaker than pride, that resteth upon its own bottom, *Frustra nititur qui non innititur;* and this should the rather be observed, because naturally we affect a kind of divinity, *affectatio divinitatis,* in setting upon actions in the strength of our own parts; whereas Christ saith, 'Without me you,' apostles that are in a state of grace, ' can do nothing,' John xv. 5, he doth not say you can do a little, but nothing. Of ourselves,† how easily are we overcome! how weak to resist! we are as reeds shaken with every wind; we shake at the very noise and thought of poverty, disgrace, losses, &c., we give in presently, we have no power over our eyes, tongues, thoughts, affections, but let sin pass in and out. How soon are we overcome of evil! whereas we should overcome evil with good. How many good purposes stick in the birth, and have no strength to come forth! all which shews how nothing we are without the Spirit of Christ. We see how weak the apostles themselves were, till they were endued with strength from above, Matt. xxvi. 69. Peter was blasted with the speech of a damsel, but after the Spirit of Christ fell upon them, the more they suffered, the more they were encouraged to suffer; their comforts grew with their troubles; therefore in all, especially difficult encounters, let us lift up our hearts to Christ, who hath Spirit enough for us all, in all our exigencies, and say with good Jehoshaphat, 'Lord, we know not what to do, but our eyes are towards thee,' 2 Chron. xx. 12; the battle we fight is thine, and the strength whereby we fight must be thine. If thou goest not out with us, we are sure to be foiled. Satan knows nothing can prevail against Christ, or those that rely upon his power; therefore his study is, how to keep us in ourselves, and in the creature: but we must carry this always in our minds, that that which is begun in self-confidence will end in shame.

* Sic se habent mortalium corda: quæ scimus, cum necesse non est, in necessitate nescimus.—*Ber*[*nard*] *de consid.*

† ' Of ourselves . . . . troubles,' added first in B.

The manner of Christ's *bringing forth judgment to victory*, is by letting us see a necessity of dependence upon him; hence proceed those spiritual desertions wherein he often leaveth us to ourselves, both in regard of grace and comfort, that we may know the spring head of these to be out of ourselves. Hence it is that in the mount, that is, in extremities, God is most seen, Gen. xxii. 18. Hence it is that we are saved by the grace of faith, that carrieth us out of ourselves to rely upon another; and that faith worketh best alone, when it hath least outward support. Hence it is, that we often fail in lesser conflicts, and stand out in greater, because in lesser we rest more in ourselves, in greater we fly to the rock of our salvation, which is higher than we, Ps. lxi. 2. Hence likewise it is, that we are stronger after foils, because hidden corruption, undiscerned before, is now discovered, and thence we are brought to make use of mercy pardoning, and power supporting. One main ground of this dispensation is, that we should know it is Christ that giveth both the will and the deed, and that as a voluntary work* according to his own good pleasure. And therefore we should 'work out our salvation in a jealous fear and trembling,' Phil. ii. 12, lest by unreverent and presumptuous walking, we give him cause to suspend his gracious influence, and to leave us to the darkness of our own heart.

Those that are under Christ's government have the spirit of revelation, whereby they see and feel a divine power sweetly and strongly enabling them for to preserve faith, when they feel the contrary, and hope in a state hopeless, and love to God under signs of his displeasure, and heavenly-mindedness in the midst of worldly affairs and allurements, drawing a contrary way. They feel a power preserving patience, nay, joy in the midst of causes of mourning, inward peace in the midst of assaults. Whence † is it that, when we are assaulted with temptation, and when compassed with troubles, we have stood out, but from a secret strength upholding us? To make so little grace so victorious over so great a mass of corruption, this requireth a spirit more than human; this is as to preserve fire in the sea, and a part of heaven even as it were in hell. Here we know where to have this power, and to whom to return the praise of it. And it is our happiness, that it is so safely hid in Christ for us, in one so near unto God and us. Since the fall, God will not trust us with our own salvation, but it is both purchased and kept by Christ for us, and we for it through faith, wrought by the power of God, and laying hold of the same: which power is gloriously set forth by St Paul, 1, To be a great power; 2, An exceeding power; 3, A working and a mighty power; 4, Such a power as was wrought in raising Christ from the dead, Eph. i. 19. That grace which is but a persuasive offer, and in our pleasure to receive or refuse, is not that grace which brings us to heaven; but God's people feel a powerful work of the Spirit, not only revealing unto us our misery, and deliverance through Christ, but emptying us of ourselves as being redeemed from ourselves, and infusing new life into us, and after strengthening us, and quickening of us when we droop and hang the wing, and never leaving us till perfect conquest.

[CHAPTER XXVII.—*Victory not to be had without fighting.*]

The sixth conclusion is, that this prevailing government shall not be without fighting. There can be no victory where there is no combat. In

* 'Worker,' in A and B.   † 'Whence . . . us,' added in B.

Isaiah it is said, 'He shall bring judgment in truth,' Is. xlii. 3 ; here it is said, he shall send forth judgment unto victory. The word 'send forth' hath a stronger sense in the original (*h*), to send forth with force ; to shew, that where his government is in truth, it will be opposed, until he getteth the upper hand. Nothing is so opposed as Christ and his government, both within us and without us. And within us most in our conversion, though corruption prevails not so far as to make void the powerful work of grace, yet there is not only a possibility of opposing, but a proneness to oppose, and not only a proneness, but an actual withstanding the working of Christ's Spirit, and that in every action, but yet no prevailing resistance so far as to make void the work of grace, but corruption in the issue yields to grace.

There is much ado to bring Christ into the heart, and to set a tribunal for him to judge there ; there is an army of lusts [in] mutiny against him. The utmost strength of most men's endeavours and parts is to keep Christ from ruling in the soul ; the flesh still laboureth to maintain its own regency, and therefore it cries down the credit of whatsoever crosseth it, as God's blessed ordinances, &c., and highly prizeth anything, though never so dead and empty, if it give way to the liberty of the flesh.

And no marvel if the spiritual government of Christ be so opposed : 1. Because it is government, and that limits the course of the will, and casteth a bridle upon its wanderings ; everything natural resists what opposeth it ; so corrupt will labours to bear down all laws, and counteth it a generous thing not to be awed, and an argument of a low spirit to fear any, even God himself, until unavoidable danger seizeth on men, and then those that feared least out of danger fear most in danger, as we see in Belshazzar, Dan. v. 6.

2. It is spiritual government, and therefore the less will flesh endure it. Christ's government bringeth the very thoughts and desires, which are the most immediate and free issue of the soul, into obedience. Though a man were of so composed a carriage, that his whole life were free from outward offensive breaches, yet with Christ to be 'carnally or worldly-minded is death,' Rom. viii. 6 : he looketh on a worldly mind with a greater detestation than any one particular offence.*

But Christ's Spirit is in those who are in some degree earthly-minded.

Truth it is, but not as an allower and maintainer, but as an opposer, subduer, and in the end as a conqueror. Carnal men would fain bring Christ and the flesh together, and could be content with some reservation to submit to Christ ; but Christ will be no underling to any base affection ; and therefore, where there is allowance of ourselves in any sinful lust, it is a sign the keys were never given up to Christ to rule us.

3. Again,† this judgment is opposed, because it is judgment, and men love not to be judged and censured. Now Christ, in his truth, arraigneth them, giveth sentence against them, and bindeth them over to the latter judgment of the great day. And therefore they take upon them to judge that truth that must judge them ; but truth will be too good for them. Man hath a day now, which St Paul calls 'man's day,' 1 Cor. iv. 33, wherein he getteth upon his bench, and usurpeth a judgment over Christ and his ways ; but God hath a day wherein he will set all straight, and his judgment shall stand. And the saints shall have their time, when they shall

---

* Gravius est peccatum diligere quam perpetrare, &c.—*Greg*[*ory*]. *Moral.*, lib. xxv. cap. 11.

† 'Again . . . . opposed,' added in B.

sit in judgment upon them that judge them now, 1 Cor. vi. 2. In the mean time, Christ will rule in the midst of his enemies, Ps. cx. 3, even in the midst of our hearts.

Use. It is therefore no sign of a good condition to find all quiet, and nothing at odds; for can we think that corruption, which is the elder in us, and Satan, the strong man that keepeth many holds in us, will yield possession quietly? No; there is not so much as a thought of goodness discovered by him, but he joineth with corruption to kill it in the birth. And as Pharaoh's cruelty was especially against the male children, so Satan's malice is especially against the most religious and manly resolutions.

This, then, we are always to expect, that wheresoever Christ cometh, there will be opposition. When Christ was born, all Jerusalem was troubled; so when Christ is born in any man, the soul is in an uproar, and all because the heart is unwilling to yield up itself to Christ to rule it.

Wheresoever Christ cometh he breedeth division, not only, 1, between man and himself; but, 2, between man and man; and 3, between church and church: of which disturbance Christ is no more the cause than physic is of trouble in a distempered body, of which noisome humours are the proper cause; for the end of physic is the peace of humours. But Christ thinketh it fit that the thoughts of men's hearts should be discovered, and he is as well for the falling as the rising of many in Israel, Luke ii. 34.

Thus the desperate madness of men is laid open, that they had rather be under the guidance of their own lusts, and by consequence of Satan himself, to their endless destruction, than put their feet into Christ's fetters, and their necks under his yoke; whereas, indeed, Christ's service is the only true liberty. His yoke is an easy yoke, his burden but as the burden of wings to a bird, that maketh her fly the higher. Satan's government is rather a bondage than a government, unto which Christ giveth up those that shake off his own, for then he giveth Satan and his factors power over them, since they will not 'receive the truth in love,' 2 Thess. ii. 20: take him, Jesuit, take him, Satan, blind him and bind him and lead him to perdition. Those that take the most liberty to sin are the most perfect slaves, because most voluntary slaves. The will in everything is either the best or the worst; the further men go on in a wilful course, the deeper they sink in rebellion; and the more they cross Christ, doing what they will, the more they shall one day suffer what they would not. In the mean time, they are prisoners in their own souls, bound over in their consciences to the judgment of him after death, whose judgment they would none of in their lives. And is it not equal that they should feel him a severe judge to condemn them, whom they would not have a mild judge to rule them?

[CHAPTER XXVIII.—*Be encouraged to go on cheerfully, with confidence of prevailing.*]

For conclusion and general application of all that hath been spoken, unto ourselves. We see the conflicting, but yet sure and hopeful state of God's people. The victory lieth not upon us, but upon Christ, who hath taken upon him, as to conquer for us, so to conquer in us. The victory lieth neither in our own strength to get, nor in our enemies to defeat it. If it lay upon us, we might justly fear. But Christ will maintain his own government in us, and take our part against our corruptions; they are his enemies as well as ours. 'Let us therefore be strong in the Lord, and in the power of his might,' Eph. vi. 10. Let us not look so much who are our enemies, as who is our judge and captain, nor what they threaten, but what he promiseth. We have more for us than against us. What coward would not fight when he is sure of victory? None are here overcome, but he that will not fight. Therefore, when any base fainting seizeth upon us, let us lay the blame where it is to be laid.

Discouragement* rising from unbelief and ill report, brought upon the good land by the spies, moved God to swear in his wrath, that they should not enter into his rest. Let us take heed a spirit of faint-heartedness, rising from seeming difficulty and disgrace, cast upon God's good ways, provoke not God to keep us out of heaven. We see here what we may look for from heaven. O beloved, it is a comfortable thing to conceive of Christ aright, to know what love, mercy, strength we have laid up for us in the breast of Christ. A good conceit of the physician, we say, is half the cure; let† us make use of this his mercy and power every day, in our daily combats. Lord Jesus, thou hast promised not to quench the smoking flax, not to break the bruised reed; cherish thine own grace in me, leave me not to myself, the glory shall be thine. Let us not suffer Satan to transform Christ unto us, to be otherwise than he is to those that are his. Christ will not leave us, till he hath made us like himself, 'all glorious within and without, and presented us blameless before his Father,' Jude 24. What a comfort is this in our conflicts with our unruly hearts, that it shall not always be thus! Let us strive a little while, and we shall be happy for ever. Let us think when we are troubled with our sins, that Christ hath this in charge of his Father, 'that he shall not quench the smoking flax,' until he hath subdued all. This putteth a shield into our hands to beat back all 'the fiery darts of Satan,' Eph. vi. 16. He will object, (1.) thou art a great sinner; we may answer, Christ is a strong Saviour; but he will object, (2.) thou hast no faith, no love; yes, a spark of faith and love; but (3.) Christ will not regard that; yes, 'he will not quench the smoking flax;' but (4.) this is so little and weak, that it will vanish and come to nought: nay, but Christ will cherish it, until he hath brought judgment to victory. And thus much for our comfort we have already, that even when we first believed, we overcame God himself, as it were, by believing the pardon of all our sins; notwithstanding the guilt of our own consciences, and his absolute justice, Now having been prevailers with God, what shall stand against us if we can learn to make use of our faith?

O what a confusion is this to Satan, that he should labour to blow out a poor spark, and yet should not be able to quench it; that a grain of mustard seed should be stronger than the gates of hell; that it should be able to remove mountains of oppositions and temptations cast up by Satan and our rebellious hearts between God and us. Abimelech could not endure that it should be said, 'a woman had slain him,' Jud. ix. 54; and it must needs be a torment to Satan, that a weak child, a woman, and decrepit old man should, by a spirit of faith, put him to flight.

Since there is such comfort where there is a little truth of grace, that it will be so victorious, let us oft try what God hath wrought in us, search our good as well as our ill, and be thankful to God for the least measure of grace, more than for any outward thing; it will be of more use and comfort than all this world, which passeth away and cometh to nothing. Yea, let us be thankful for that promised and assured victory, which we may rely on without presumption, as St Paul doth; 'thanks be to God, that hath given us

---

* 'Discouragement . . . . heaven,' added in B.

† 'Let . . . thine,' a transposition of A and B here.

victory in Jesus Christ,' 1 Cor. xv. 57. See a flame in a spark, a tree in a seed; see great things in little beginnings; look not so much to the beginning, as to the perfection, and so we shall be in some degree joyful in ourselves, and thankful unto Christ.

Neither* must we reason from a denial of a great measure of grace, to a denial of any at all in us; for faith and grace stand not in an indivisible point, so as he that hath not such and such a measure hath none at all; but as there is a great breadth between a spark and a flame, so there is a great wideness between the least measure of grace and the greatest; and he that hath the least measure, is within the compass of God's eternal favour; though he be not a shining light, yet he is a smoking wick, which Christ's tender care will not suffer him to quench.

And let all this that hath been spoken allure those that are not yet in state of grace, to come under Christ's sweet and victorious government, for though we shall have much opposition, yet if we strive, he will help us; if we fail, he will cherish us; if we be guided by him, we shall overcome; if we overcome, we are sure to be crowned. And for the present state of the church, we see now how forlorn it is, yet let us comfort ourselves, that Christ's cause shall prevail; ' Christ will rule, till he hath made his enemies his footstool,' Ps. cx. 1, not only to trample upon, but to help him up to mount higher in glory. ' Babylon shall fall, for strong is the Lord who hath condemned her,' Rev. xviii. 8. Christ's judgment not only in his children, but also against his enemies, shall be victorious, for he is ' King of kings and Lord of lords,' Rev. xix. 1. God will not always† suffer antichrist and his supports to revel and ruffle in the church as they do.

If we look to the present state of the church of Christ, it is as Daniel in the midst of lions, as a lily amongst thorns, as a ship not only tossed, but almost covered with waves. It is so low, that the enemies think they have buried Christ, in regard of his gospel, in the grave, and there they think to keep him from rising; but Christ as he rose in his person, so he will roll away all stones, and rise again in his church. How little support hath the church and cause of Christ at this day! how strong a conspiracy is against it! the spirit of antichrist is now lifted up, and marcheth furiously; things seem to hang on a small and invisible thread. But our comfort is, that Christ liveth and reigneth and standeth on Mount Sion in defence of them that stand for him, Rev. xiv. 1; and when States and kingdoms shall dash one against another, Christ will have care of his own children and cause, seeing there is nothing else in the world that he much esteemeth. At this very time the delivery of his church, and the ruin of his enemies, is in working; we see no things in motion till Christ hath done his work, and then we shall see that the Lord reigneth.

Christ and his church, when they are at the lowest, are nearest rising: his enemies at the highest are nearest a downfall.

The Jews are not yet come in under Christ's banner; but God, that hath persuaded Japhet to come into the tents of Shem, will persuade Shem to come into the tents of Japhet, Gen. ix. 27. The ' fulness of the Gentiles is not yet come in,' Rom. xi. 25, but Christ, that hath the ' utmost parts of the earth given him for his possession,' Ps. ii. 8, will gather all the sheep his Father hath given him into one fold, that there may be one sheepfold and one shepherd, John x. 16.

The faithful Jews rejoiced to think of the calling of the Gentiles; and why should not we joy to think of the calling of the Jews?

* ' Neither . . . quench,' not in A, B, but in E. † ' God will not,' &c., added in B.

The gospel's course hath hitherto been as that of the sun, from east to west, and so in God's time may proceed yet further west (*i*). No creature can hinder the course of the sun, nor stop the influence of heaven, nor hinder the blowing of the wind, much less hinder the prevailing power of divine truth, until Christ hath brought all under one head, and then he will present all to his Father; these are they thou hast given unto me; these are they that have taken me for their Lord and King, that have suffered with me; my will is that they be where I am, and reign with me. And then he will deliver up the kingdom even to his Father, and put down all other rule, and authority, and power, 1 Cor. xv. 24.

Let us then bring our hearts to holy resolutions, and set ourselves upon that which is good, and against that which is ill, in ourselves or others, according to our callings, upon this encouragement, that Christ's grace and power shall go along with us. What had become of that great work of reformation of religion in the latter-spring of the gospel, if men had not been armed with invincible courage to outstride all lets, upon this faith, that the cause was Christ's, and that he would not be wanting to his own cause. Luther ingenuously confessed, that he carried matters often inconsiderately, and with mixture of passion; but upon acknowledgment, God took not advantage of his errors, but the cause being God's, and his aims being holy, to promote the truth, and being a mighty man in prayer, and strong in faith, God by him kindled that fire which all the world shall never be able to quench. According to our faith, so is our encouragement to all duties, therefore let us strengthen faith, that it may strengthen all other graces. This very belief, that faith shall be victorious, is a means to make it so indeed. Believe it, therefore, that though it be often as smoking flax, yet it shall prevail. If it prevail with God himself in trials, shall it not prevail over all other opposition? 'Let us wait a while, and we shall see the salvation of the Lord,' Exod. iv. 13.

The Lord reveal himself more and more unto us in the face of his Son Jesus Christ. and magnify the power of his grace in cherishing those beginnings of grace in the midst of our corruptions, and sanctify the consideration of our own infirmities to humble us, and of his tender mercy to encourage us; and persuade us, that since he hath taken us into the covenant of grace, he will not cast us off for those corruptions; which as they grieve his Spirit, so they make us vile in our own eyes. And because Satan labours to obscure the glory of his mercy, and hinder our comfort by discouragements, the Lord add this to the rest of his mercies, that, since he is so gracious to those that yield to his government, we may make the right use of this grace, and not lose any portion of comfort that is laid up for us in Christ. And [may] he vouchsafe to let the prevailing power of his Spirit in us be an evidence of the truth of grace begun, and a pledge of final victory, at that time when he will be all in all, in all his, for all eternity. Amen. Finis.*

---

* Added here to G is the following couplet:—
>   Quassatâ (Lector) quid arundine vilius, aut te?
>   At non frangeris, si pius, Unctus ait—   G. J.
> It may be thus rendered:
>   Than shaken reed what can more worthless be?
>   Reader, just such thou art:
>   But hast thou faith?
>   Then take good heart;
>   The Anointed saith,
>   Nor it nor thou by him shall broken be.
> The initials are probably those of John Goodwin reversed.   G.

NOTES.

(a) P. 49.—' Stooped so far . . . . as to suffer him to thrust his hand into his side.' It is questionable if Thomas really did this. His early faith recovered itself in presence of the Lord, and the narrative seems rather to indicate that he did not avail himself of the tenderly-forgiving offer of his Master. See Archbishop Whately's lecture on the apostle Thomas in his Lectures on the Apostles, (2d ed. 1853).

(b) P. 53.—' Strain not things too high, making those general and necessary evidences of grace which agree not,' &c. This characteristically gentle warning reminds us of an anecdote of the excellent Ebenezer Erskine, one of the founders of what is now the United Presbyterian Church. He had been delivering a course of sermons on '*Marks* of Grace,' and had spent much time in shewing how many things men might possess and nevertheless be 'hypocrites.' Chancing some time after to be on a visit to a very saintly but lowly 'aged' believer, who was apparently dying, the good man was startled by an exclamation, 'Oh! Mr Erskine, if I were just as good as one of your —— hypocrites, I would be happy.' The words struck home, and Erskine was wont to tell it, and to add that the remark opened his eyes to the danger by over-high 'marks' of causing God's own dearest children to 'write bitter things against themselves' without cause. This anecdote, related by one whose grandfather attended Mr Erskine at Stirling, strikingly enforces Sibbes's counsel.

(c) P. 55.—' Kill a fly on the forehead with a beetle.' ' Beetle ' = mallet. In the margin opposite the passage in A, B, and E, is 'As Parisien.' Query, Peter Lombard?

(d) P. 67.—' Let ' [= hinder]. Few words present such a curious example of utter reversal of meaning as this. Formerly to let was to 'hinder,' now it means to 'permit.' It occurs in the former sense both in O. T. and N. T., *e. g.*, Isa. xliii. 13, and Rom. i. 13 ; 2 Thess. ii. 7. It is here referred to once for all.

(e) P. 68.—' Catch ' = on the watch. This supplies Richardson's lack (in his great Dictionary), of an example of 'catch' in the meaning here.

(f) P. 85.—' Voyage ' = a travel, a journey ; but now limited to *travel* by sea. Milton uses it repeatedly in the earlier sense. See *P. L.*, ii., 426, 919 ; vii. 431. *P. R.* i., 103.

(g) P. 86.—' Sobs.' To 'sob' means to 'sop' or 'soak,' and 'sobs,' as applied to kindled 'greenwood,' is vividly descriptive.

(h) P. 96.—' Send forth hath a stronger sense in the original.' Consult and compare Dr J. A. Alexander on the passage in his commentary on Isaiah (ed. by Eadie, 1848).

(i) P. 100.—' The gospel's course hath hitherto been as that of the sun, from east to west, and so in God's time may proceed further west.' This remarkable anticipation may be placed side by side with the better known but much later, and admittedly grander, vaticination of Berkeley :—

> '*Westward* the course of empire takes its way ;
> The four first acts already past,
> A fifth shall close the drama with the day ;
> Time's noblest offspring is the last.

The 'Priest' of Bemerton, George Herbert, may have had his equally memorable couplet suggested by Sibbes's words, the 'Bruised Reed' having preceded 'The Temple' by three years :—

> ' Religion stands a-tiptoe in our land,
> Ready to pass to the American strand.'
> *Church Millitant.*

Sibbes and his Puritan contemporaries turned with wistful eye to '*New* England,' and read in the light of the present position of America among the nations of the earth, it is curious to note the mingled hope and dread with which the mighty unknown continent was regarded. John Cotton, John Davenport, Thomas Hooker, and many other of Sibbes's personal friends, became fugitives thither. For various curious *memorabilia* on the subject of this note (Sibbes's being an addition thereto), consult Mayor's Nicholas Ferrar, pp. 52–3. G.

THE SWORD OF THE WICKED.

THE SWORD OF THE WICKED.

NOTE.

The title-page, a copy of which is given below [*], will, as in the case of 'The Description of Christ,' in its relation to 'The Bruised Reed,' explain the position of 'The Sword of the Wicked' in the present publication. It will be observed that it consists of the *leading*, *i.e.*, introductory sermons to that treatise, called 'The Soule's Conflict.' As such, it falls to be associated therewith. The 'Sword of the Wicked' forms a small portion of one of the posthumously-published quartos of Sibbes, entitled 'Evangelicall Sacrifices' [1640]. It labours under the same disadvantage with the 'Description,' as compared with its companion treatise, the 'Soul's Conflict,' being even more unfinished; but abounds with pungent and vigorous writing.

G.

[*] Title-page—

The
SWORD
of
THE WICKED.
In two Sermons.
Being the leading Sermons to that Treatise called
The Soules Conflict.
By
The late Learned and Reverend Divine,
Rich. Sibbs:
Doctor in Divinity, Mr of Katherine Hall
in Cambridge, and sometimes Preacher
to the Honourable Society of
Grayes-Inne.
Psal. 57. 4.
Their Tongue is a sharpe Sword.
London,
Printed by E. P. for N. B. and R. H. 1639. 4to.

THE SWORD OF THE WICKED.

As with a sword in my bones, mine enemies reproach me; while they say unto me daily, Where is thy God?—PSALM XLII. 10.

THE Psalms are, as it were, the anatomy of a holy man; they lay the inside of a true devout man outward, even to the view of others. If the Scriptures be compared to a body, the Psalms may well be the heart, they are so full of sweet and holy affections and passions. In other portions of Scripture, God speaks to us; in the Psalms, holy men (especially David, who was the penman of most of them), speak to God, wherein we have the passages of a broken, humble soul to God. Among the rest, in this Psalm David lays open variety of passions. His condition at this time was such, as that he was an exiled man, from his own house and his own friends, and which grieved him worst of all, from the tabernacle, the house of God. It was upon the occasion of Saul's persecution, or of Absalom's, his son; but I take it rather of Saul's, that hunted him as a partridge in the wilderness. Hereupon you have a discovery, how this holy man of God stood affected with this case and condition of his. First he lays open his grief. His grief ariseth from his desire. He that loves most and desireth most, he always grieves most; and all other affections have their scantling (*a*) from love, which is the firstborn affection of the soul. Therefore, before he lays out his grief, he sets out his desire to the house of God, the want whereof grieved him most of all. 'As the hart panteth after the water brooks, so panteth my soul after thee, O God,' ver. 1. As the chased hart panteth after water, so the soul thirsteth for God, for the living God, 'O when shall I come and appear before God?' ver. 2.*

Then after his desire, he lays forth his grief, 'My tears have been my meat day and night, while they continually say unto me, Where is thy God?' ver. 3. Grievances never come alone, but as Job's messengers, they come one after another, even to God's children. When he is disposed to correct them, they are multiplied. Therefore, here is not only a grief of want, that he was debarred of those sweet comforts which he had before in the tabernacle, but here is likewise a grief from the reproach of his enemies, that took occasion from his disconsolate estate to upbraid him, 'Where is thy

---

* This opening paragraph is very nearly identical with the commencement of the 'Soul's Conflict.'—G.

God?' 'My tears have been my meat day and night, while they continually say unto me, Where is thy God?' He dissolves the cloud of his grief into the shower of tears, 'My tears have been my meat.' They were so plentiful that they did feed his soul as it were.

Then he sets down another ground of his grief, from the remembrance of his former happiness; as usually, that doth make the grief raw and more sensible, for *felix miser, maxime miser*, he that hath been happy in former time and now is miserable, is most miserable of all, because his former happiness makes him most sensible. Therefore, of all men in hell, the torment of great men is most, because they had most sense of comfort in this world; mighty men shall be mightily tormented, that is all the privilege they shall have in hell. Therefore, to aggravate his grief, O, saith he, when I remember what comfort I had formerly in the house of God, I pour out my soul. It was not enough that he poured out his tears, or words, but I pour out my soul, for in former times, 'I went with the multitude to the house of God,' ver. 4, and led a goodly train to the house of God, the picture of a good magistrate, and a good master of a family; he goes not alone to the house of God, but he leads his train, he is attended on by his servants. David went not alone into the house of God, but with the multitude, 'with the voice of them that kept holiday,' ver. 4. Well, he had grief enough, his heart was full of grief. Now in the next verse he takes up his soul, and expostulates with himself, 'Why art thou so sad, O my soul? and why art thou disquieted in me? hope thou in God, for I shall yet praise him for the help of his countenance,' ver. 5. So you see here, he is not so flat in his grief that he gives over-long way to it, but he even falls a chiding of his soul, 'Why art thou cast down, O my soul? why art thou disquieted within me?' O! but yet grief will not be so stilled! affliction is not quelled at the first, nor grief stilled and stayed at the first. Therefore it gathers upon him again in the next verse, 'O my God, my soul is cast down within me, when I remember thee from the land of Jordan, and of the Hermonites, from the hill Mizar.' When I remember thee from these places, my soul is cast down again, and my afflictions are multiplied; though he had fallen out with his soul before, for his impatience. 'One deep calls to another,' deep calls upon deep, 'as the noise of the water-spouts,' ver. 7. He compares affliction to water-spouts, as it is in Scripture. 'All thy waves and billows have gone over me,' ver. 7. Even as one deep calls to another, so one affliction calls to another. Then when he had given a little way again to his grief, and complained to God, he takes up his soul another time; yet, saith he, 'The Lord will command his lovingkindness in the day time, and in the night his song shall be with me, and I will pray to the God of my life,' ver. 8. He presents to himself the goodness of God, to comfort his soul. And he presents to him in the next verse his own resolution, 'I will say to God (for the time to come) my rock, why hast thou forgotten me? and why go I mourning, for the oppression of the enemy,' ver. 9. So here he stays his soul once again; he presents to his soul the lovingkindness of God, with renewing his resolution to seek God: an effectual way to stay the soul, by considering God's love and mercy, and by renewing our resolutions and purposes to cleave to God, 'I will say to God my rock, why hast thou forgotten me?'

Aye, but here is a third assault of grief again, for there is a spring of corruption in us, and such a principle in us as will yield murmurings and discontent again and again; therefore in the verse I have read to you, he comes again to complain, 'As with a sword in my bones, mine enemies reproach me; while they say unto me daily, Where is thy God?' ver. 10. He had complained once of this before, but it had a fresh working with his thoughts again, 'As with a sword in my bones,' &c. Hereupon, he is forced the third time to expostulate, and to fall out with his soul, ' Why art thou cast down, O my soul? and why art thou disquieted? hope thou in God, for I shall yet praise him, who is the health of my countenance, and my God,' ver. 11. He comes to his former remedy, he had stilled his grief once before with the same meditation and upbraiding of his own soul, and chiding himself; but he comes to it here as a *probatum est*, as a tried remedy, he takes up his soul very short, 'Why art thou so cast down, O my soul? why art thou disquieted within me?' You see how David's passions here are interlaced with comforts, and his comforts with passions, till at last he gets the victory of his own heart. Beloved, neither sin, nor grief for sin, are stilled and quieted at the first. You have some short-spirited Christians, if all be not quiet at the first, all is lost with them; but it is not so with a true Christian soul, with the best soul living. It was not so with David: when he was in distemper, he checks himself; the distemper was not yet stilled, he checks himself again; then the distemper breaks out again, then he checks himself again; and all little enough to bring his soul to a holy, blessed, quiet temper, to that blessed tranquillity and rest that the soul should be in, before it can enjoy its own happiness, and enjoy sweet communion with God. As you see in physic, perhaps one purge will not carry away the peccant humour, then a second must be added; perhaps that will not do it, then there must be a third; so when the soul hath been once checked, perhaps it will not do, we must fall to it again, go to God again. And then it may be there will be breaking out of the grief and malady again; we must to it again, and never give over; that is the right temper of a Christian.

Before I come to the words, observe in general this, *that a living soul, the soul that is alive in grace, that hath the life of grace quickening it, is most sensible of all, in the want of spiritual means.* As here, the grief of griefs was (which he begins with), that he was banished from the tabernacle.

What shall we think therefore of those that excommunicate themselves from God's assembly, where there is the Father, Son, and Holy Ghost, all the Trinity dispensing their bounty, and where the prayers of God's people meet together in one as it were, and bind God? What shall we think of them that prefer their private devotions, as they say, before God's assemblies? Surely they are not of David's mind; and it is a shrewd argument, that they never had the life of grace in them yet: for where life is, there will be hunger and thirst. *Acrius urgent quæ ad naturam.* It is a true aphorism, those things press upon nature hardest that touch upon the necessities of nature, rather than those that touch upon delight. We can want delights, but necessities of nature we cannot; therefore hunger and thirst, they are such passions as will not be quiet. Delicacies and novelties the soul of a hungry man can be content to want, but not spiritual food for the soul. We see how famine wrought upon the patriarchs, it made them go down into Egypt for food. I note it only by the way, that men may know how to judge of themselves, when they can very well be content, without a blessed supply of holy means. Holy David, when the means was but dark and obscure, when the canon was not enlarged, when all was in types and clouds, yet he felt that comfort in the tabernacle and in the ordinances of God, that he could not endure the want of them; but as the hart brayeth after the water-brooks, so his soul panted after God. But to come to the words themselves,

' As with a sword in my bones, mine enemies reproach me, when they say unto me daily, where is thy God ?'

Here are two things considerable in the words.

The carriage and disposition and expression of others to David.

And *David's affection towards it, how he was disposed towards it, how he did bear it.*

For their disposition, they were enemies, *mine enemies, &c.*

The expression of it, *they reproach me.*

The specialty of that expression, how they reproached him, they said unto him, ' *Where is thy God ?*' They do reproach him in his religion.

The aggravation of that specialty is, they say, openly to his face, they go not behind my back, they esteem so slightly of me, they say it to my face. And continually too, they are never weary, they say daily, Where is thy God ? They are enemies, they reproach, they reproach in this, ' Where is thy God ?' and they do it impudently, and daily.

How doth David entertain this usage ? how doth he carry himself all this while ? He must needs be sensible of it, and therefore he expresseth it in most significant words. Oh, saith he, these things were as *a sword in my bones.* There be diverse readings of the words; but we will take them as they are laid down, being very well, *as with a sword in my bones* (or as it is in the margin, (*b*) *as killing in my bones*), mine enemies reproach me. It was as killing to him, it did go to his heart, it cut him to the quick. As a sword is to the body and bones, so are their words to my soul, I cannot endure it, it is death to me. It is a most emphatical manner of expressing the enemies' disposition and carriage. Thus you have the words unfolded. I will but touch some particulars ; those that I think most needful for us to take notice of, I will dwell more upon. *Mine enemies*, saith he, *reproach me.*

Mine enemies. There hath been contrary seeds from the beginning of the world, and will be while Satan is in the world. Till he be cast into the ' burning lake,' and be there in perpetual chains adjudged to torment, he will raise up men alway that shall be of his side. And as long as that grand enemy is, and as long as men are that will be subject to his government, as alway there will be, he will have a great faction in the world. And by reason that he hath a party in us, the flesh, he will have the greatest party in the world. The most go the broad way, so that *God's children,* even David himself, *shall not want enemies.*

Mine enemies. It is strange that he should have enemies, that was so harmless a man, that when they were sick and distressed, he prayed for them, and put on sackcloth for them, as it is Ps. xli. This compassionate, sweet-natured man, yet notwithstanding you see he had enemies, and enemies that would discover themselves to reproach him, and that bitterly ; in the bitterest manner, they reproach him in his religion. It is a large point, if I should give myself liberty in it. I do but touch it, that we may be armed by this observation, against the scandal of opposition, that if we meet with enemies in the world, we should not be much offended at it ; grieve we may, but wonder we need not. Was there ever any that did more good than our Saviour Christ ? ' He went about doing good,' Acts x. 38. He did never a miracle that was harmful (but only of the swine that were drowned in the sea, and that was their own fault), but he went about doing all the good he could ; yet, notwithstanding, we see what malicious opposites he had. That that is true of the head must be true in the members. Therefore, we should rejoice in our conformity to Christ, if it be in a good cause, that we find enemies and opposition. *O imperator,*

&c., saith he, O the emperor is become a Christian. It was a blessed time. Oh! but the devil is not made a Christian yet, and he will never be made good: for he is *in termino*, as we say, he is in his bounds, his nature is immoveable; he is in hell in regard of his estate, though he be loose to do mischief. Now, until the devil be good, God's children shall never want enemies; and he will never be good. Therefore, though there were good kings and good governors over all the world, yet good men shall never want enemies as long as the devil is alive, as long as he hath any thing to do in the world. Enemies therefore we must look for, and such enemies as will not conceal their malice neither: for that were something if they would suffer their malice to boil and concoct in their own hearts, but that will not be, but ' out of the abundance of the heart the mouth will speak.' Where there is a bad treasury, there will be a bad vent;* therefore we see here, they reproach him, ' *mine enemies.*'

Reproach me. It is the proper expression of malice, reproach; and it is that that the nature of man can least endure of all. The nature of man can endure an outward wrong, a loss or a cross, but a reproach, especially if it be a scornful reproach, the nature of man is most impatient of. For there is no man, but he thinks himself worthy of some respect. Now a reproachful scorn shews a disrespect, and when the nature of man sees itself disrespected, it grows to terms of impatience. There is not the meanest man living but he thinks himself worthy of some regard. Therefore I cannot blame David, even out of the principle of nature, to be affected here when they reproached him, and gave him vile terms, ' mine enemies *reproach me.*' Their tongues were tipt from hell, and they did but utter that that was in their hearts. If the tongues of wicked men, as St James saith, be a world of mischief, what is the whole man? what is the heart, and tongue, and life, and all of wicked men?

Now this reproach of wicked men, it is a grievous persecution, as Ishmael persecuted Isaac in that manner, as it is, Gal. iv., taken out of the story in Genesis. I will not enter into the commonplace of reproach; it is taken by the by here.

Only by the way, let it be a support to us. If we be reproachfully used in the world, let us not be much cast down. It is no credit for a man to do that that the devil and his instruments do; nor it is no discredit for us to suffer that that David suffered. Let this satisfy thee, there is not the vilest man living but hath this weapon to serve the devil with, a reproachful tongue. He that sits upon the ale bench, that rakes in the channel,† the basest wretch in the world, hath a tongue to serve the devil with in reproaches. It is no credit for them to do that that the vilest person in the world can do; and it is no shame for thee to suffer that that the best man that ever lived did suffer. So much for that, *mine enemies reproach me.*

But what is the specialty of this reproach? To come to that more particularly. *They say unto me, Where is thy God?*

They touch him in his religion. They saw him persecuted by Saul, scorned by Saul's courtiers; they see him driven up and down, as a partridge in the wilderness; they saw him banished from the sanctuary, destitute of friends; they saw him in this disconsolate estate, and they judge by sense and appearance, that they thought he was a man that God regarded not at all: therefore say they, *Where is thy God?*

God's children are impatient, as far as they are men, of reproaches; but so far as they are Christian men, they are impatient of reproaches in reli-

* That is, 'out-going.'—Ed.   † That is, 'the kennel' or sewer.—Ed.

gion: *Where is now thy God?* They were not such desperate atheists as to think there was no God, to call in question whether there were a God or no, though indeed they were little better; but they rather reproach and upbraid him with his singularity, *Where is thy* God? You are one of God's darlings; you are one that thought nobody served God but you; you are one that will go alone—*your* God.

So this is an ordinary reproach, an ordinary part for wicked men, to cast at the best people, especially when they are in misery. What is become of your profession now? What is become of your forwardness and strictness now? What is become of your much reading and hearing now; and your doing such things now? What is become of your God that you bragged so of, and thought yourselves so happy in, as if he had been nobody's God but yours? We may learn hence the disposition of wicked men. It is a character of a poisonful, cursed disposition to upbraid a man with his religion.

But what is the scope? The scope is worse than the words, *Where is thy God?* The scope is to shake his faith, and his confidence in God; and this is that that touched him so nearly while they upbraided him, *Where is thy God?* Indeed, they had some probability and show of truth; for now God seemed opposite to him, when he was banished from his house, from that blessed communion with him that he had. Their purpose was therefore to shake his faith and affiance in God; and herein they shewed themselves right, the children of the devil, whose scope is to shake the faith and affiance of God's people, in all his temptations, and by his instruments. For the devil knows well enough, that as long as God and the soul join together, it is in vain to trouble any man; therefore he labours to put jealousies, to accuse God to man, and man to God. He knows there is nothing in the world can stand against God. As long as we make God our confidence, all his enterprises are in vain. His scope is therefore to shake our affiance in God: *Where is thy God?* So he dealt with the Head of the church, our blessed Saviour himself, when he came to tempt him. 'If thou be the Son of God, command these stones to be made bread,' Matt. iv. 3. He comes with an *if;* he laboured to shake him in his sonship. The devil, since he was divided from God himself eternally, is become a spirit of division; he labours to divide the Son from the Father; he labours to divide even God the Father from his own Son: *If thou be the Son of God.* So he labours to sever Christians from their head, Christ; subjects from their princes, and princes from their subjects; friends from friends, and one from another;—he is a spirit of division: *Where is thy God?* There was his scope, to breed division, if he could, between his heart and God, that he might call God into jealousy, as if he had not regarded him: thou hast taken a great deal of pains in serving thy God; thou seest how he regards thee now: *Where is thy God?*

We should labour to make this use of it, to counter-work Satan; to strengthen that most of all, that the devil labours to shake most of all. Shall the devil labour to shake our faith and affiance in God above all other things, and shall we not labour to strengthen that? Above all things, let us look to our head, as the serpent winds about and keeps his head. Keep faith, and keep all. If faith be safe, all is safe; let us strengthen that, and strengthen all; weaken that, and we weaken all. What cares Satan for other sins that we fall into? He aims at our assurance, that we may doubt of God's love, whom we have been so bold as to sin against. That is it he aims at, to make weak faith in the particular acts of sin we commit. He knows that sin naturally breeds doubts, as flesh breeds worms.

Where sin is, if it be in never such a little degree, he knows it will breed doubts and perplexities, and where they are, he hath that he would have. He labours to hinder that sweet communion that should be between the soul and God: *Where is now thy God?* You see wicked men are the children of the devil right in this.

Again, they instance here in matter of religion against him. You see how ready wicked and devilish-minded men are, to tread over the hedge where it is lowest, as the proverb is, to add affliction to affliction, especially in that that may touch a man nearest. They could not touch him nearer than in this, *Where is thy God?* They knew it well enough, where is now your religion? This, they thought, would anger him to the heart. Here is a devilish disposition. You have a terrible psalm for it, Ps. cix., of those that add affliction to the afflicted; *they are cursed persons.* This is the disposition of wicked men, they have no mercy. Malice, we say, is unsatiable. One would think that our Saviour Christ, when he was upon the cross, racked there in all his parts, a man exposed to so much misery and scorn as he was, that they should have had pity upon him; but upon the cross they reproached him, Aha, he saved others, himself he cannot save; let him come from the cross, and we will believe in him. What a bitter sarcasm was this, that came from hell itself! Nay, when he was dead, one would have thought their malice should have been buried with his body. Malice is ordinarily among men living, not the dead; but when he was dead, *This impostor said, &c.,* Matt. xxvi. 61. They laboured to bury his good name, that nothing tending to his honour might remain of him. Indeed, it is the nature of malice to wish the not being of the thing it maliceth, no, not the name. *Let his name perish from the earth,* Ps. xli. 5. It was extremity of malice to work upon this disadvantage, when they see him thus afflicted, to vex him with that he was most affected with, *Where is thy God?*

Therefore, let those that feel and feed that devilish disposition in themselves to insult over God's people, especially in matters of religion to vex them, and when there is a wound already, to make the affliction greater, to add affliction to affliction, let them judge of what disposition they are.

They say unto me. You see here another circumstance, *they say unto me.* They are so impudent that they are not afraid to reproach him to his face; *they say unto him,* as if they would stand to their reproach. This is one circumstance of aggravation. Indeed malice is very impudent, when it is come to the extremity. I only observe it, that if we meet with such insolency of malice, not to be discouraged; it hath been thus before, and thus it will be to the end of the world.

And, then, they are not wearied, their malice is unwearied; they say to me, *Daily.* Day by day their malice is fed with a spring, with a malicious heart. A malicious heart and a slanderous tongue alway go well together. The devil, that was the first grand slanderer, hath communion with a malicious heart, and he foments malice, and cherisheth that malicious, poisonful disposition; and a malicious disposition never wants malicious words. As one saith of anger and fury, it ministereth weapons (*c*), so we may say of malice and hatred, it ministereth words alway. A malicious heart will never want words: they say to me, *daily.* These are but circumstances, but yet they are somewhat considerable, for they tend to the aggravation of the disconsolate estate of this holy man, that he should meet with such wretched men, that had no pity at all on him, but say to him daily,

Where is now thy God? You see then from hence that God is a God, as the prophet saith, ofttimes hiding himself, Isa. xlv. 15, that God vails himself ofttimes to his children. Not only from the eyes of wicked men, that they think godly men deserted of God, but sometimes from the very sense and feeling of God's children themselves. They are in such desertions that they are fain to complain that God hath hid himself, and is as a stranger to them. This is the state of God's children in this world. Though God love them dearly, 'as the apple of his eye, and as the signet on his hand,' Zech. ii. 8, and Jer. xxii. 24, yet notwithstanding his carriage to them is ofttimes so strange, that those that look upon their estate in this world think they are men, as it were, forlorn and destitute of God. And this estate must needs be, because of necessity there must be a conformity between us and our Saviour. It was so with our Saviour, 'My God, my God, why hast thou forsaken me?' Matt. xxvii. 46. God was never nearer him in all his life than then, and yet he cries out, 'My God, my God, why hast thou forsaken me?' And as he spake, so the rest thought of him, as if he had been a man forsaken; and so here they say to this holy man, *Where is thy God?*

Therefore let us lay up this likewise for the strengthening of our faith in the like case, that we be not overmuch discouraged. If God hide himself, if others think our estates miserable, and ourselves think ourselves so, it is no strange matter. It was thus with David. He was so neglected of God that they thought God had clean forsaken him. *Where is thy God?*

Our life is now hid with Christ, as the apostle saith, Col. iii. 8. We have a blessed and glorious life, but it is hid in our Head. Even as in winter time the trees have a life, but it is hid in the root, so a Christian hath a blessed condition at all times, but his glory and happiness is hid in his Head, and there is a cloud between him and his happiness.

Therefore let us support ourselves with this in all times, was God gone from David indeed when they said, 'Where is thy God?' Oh no; God was as near David now as ever he was, nay, rather nearer. God was never nearer Moses than when he was sprawling upon the water in that ark they had made for him, Ex. ii. 3. He was never nearer Daniel than when he was in the lion's den, Dan. vi. 19. God came between the lion's teeth and Daniel. And, as I said, he was never nearer our Saviour than when he was on the cross. And he was never nearer to David than when they said, 'Where is thy God?' When trouble is near, God is never far off. That is an argument to make God near, *Lord, be not far off, for trouble is near.* And extremity and danger and trouble, it is God's best opportunity to be with his children, however he do not help for the present ofttimes. '*Where is thy God?*'

David might rather have said to them, Where are your eyes? where is your sight? for God is not only in heaven, but in me. Though David was shut from the sanctuary, yet David's soul was a sanctuary for God; for God is not tied to a sanctuary made with hands. God hath two sanctuaries, he hath two heavens: the heaven of heavens and a broken spirit. God dwelt in David as in his temple. God was with David and in him; and he was never more with him, nor never more in him, than in his greatest afflictions. They wanted eyes, he wanted not God. Though sometimes God hide himself, not only from the world, but from his own children, yet he is there; howsoever their sorrow is such that it dims their sight (as we see in Hagar), so that they cannot see him for the present, Gen. xxi. 19. He sometimes looks in their face, as we see Mary. She could not see Christ distinctly, but thought him to be the gardener. There is a kind of concealment a while in heavenly wisdom, yet, notwithstanding, God is with his children always, and they know it by faith, though not by feeling always. As we know what Jacob said, 'God was in this place, and I was not aware,' Gen. xxviii. 16, when he slept upon the stone, and had that heavenly vision; so it is with God's people in their trouble. God is with his church and children, and wicked men are not aware of it. Christ is in them, and they are not aware of it. Christ was in the saints when Saul persecuted them, and Paul was not aware of it, 'Saul, Saul, why persecutest thou me? Who art *thou*, Lord?' saith he. Alas! he dreamed not of Christ. However wicked men of the world think, yet God is near his own children, in the most disconsolate condition that can be. It is, when they say, '*Where is thy God?*' as if a man should ask what is become of the moon between the old and the new, when the dark side is towards us, when we see no moon at all for a time, till the new come? The moon is near, and more enlightened with the sun then than at other times, and is nearer to him. So in afflictions. However the dark side of God's children be toward the world, that they cannot see them, yet their light side is towards God. God shines upon them, and enlightens them more then at that time with solid comfort, that keeps them from sinking, than at other times. Therefore it was an ignorant question of them to ask, *Where is thy God?* It shewed they were ignorant of the passages of God's dealing with his children, as indeed none are greater atheists than your scoffers. *Where is thy God?* as if God had been only a God of observation, to be observed outwardly in all his passages towards his children, whereas, as I said, he is a God hiding himself ofttimes; and he shews himself in contrary conditions most of all, most comfortably. His work is by contraries. But these carnal men were ignorant of the mysteries of religion, and the mysteries of divine providence towards God's children. Therefore their question savours of their disposition, *Where is now thy God?* Thus briefly I have gone over their disposition and carriage towards the holy man David, that they were enemies of hostile nature and disposition, and they reproached him, and daily, and that in his religion, *Where is thy God?*

I beseech you let us look to it in time, that it may not be truly said to us, by way of upbraiding, *Where is now thy God?* God may be strange to us indeed; let us so carry ourselves as that God may own us in the worst times. If they had said this truly, how grievous had it been to David! but it was more malice than truth. For David found experience of God. He might rather have upbraided them, *Where is your God?* and there is no wicked man, but a man may in his greatest extremity upbraid him, and that in truth, Where is your God? your riches, honour, and estate? where is all this that you supported yourself with, and bore yourself so big on, that you despised all others? what has become of all now? A man cannot stand in a thing that stands not itself. A man cannot build on that that hath no good foundation. Now all men that are not truly religious, they have some idol or other that will deceive them. Therefore a man may truly say to them, that which they falsely and maliciously say to God's people, *Where is your God?*

So much for their disposition and carriage. Now how stands David affected with this? that is the second part.

As with a sword in my bones. It was as a sword to his bones. Now that that toucheth the bones is the most exquisite grief. That that we call the grief of the teeth, you see what an exquisite grief it is in that little member. When the bones are cut or touched, it is a most exquisite grief. *As with a sword in my bones, my enemies reproach me.* What was the matter that this reproach, *Where is thy God?* touched him so to the quick? What was the cause? The causes were diverse.

First of all concerning God: for when they said to him, 'Where is thy God?'

First, It tended to the reproach of God, as if God were so fickle a friend as to desert his best friends in the time of misery. This touched upon God by way of disparagement, therefore it must needs touch David, who was God's friend.

Then, again, it touched God in another thing, in his manner of providence, as if he had been a God of the hills and not of the valleys; as if he had been a God for one time and not for another. Where is now thy God? What is become of him?

Again, in the third place, it touched upon him in this, as if he had favoured them, being cursed, formal hypocrites, more than David; as if he had favoured their formal, hypocritical, base, dead courses, that were most abominable to God. For these persecutors were Saul's courtiers, and other enemies. Wicked men, they thought to justify their own ways by this reproach, You see we are as good as you. God respects us; we fall not into such miseries; we have recourse to Saul, though he have cast out you and others, &c. So it tended to God's reproach in that, as if God had justified their course, as if they had been dearer to him that were most abominable.

And this is to make an idol of God, to make God justify those courses that he most abhors, as it is in Ps. l., 'Thou thoughtest I was like unto thee.' Because God lets a wicked man alone, thou thoughtest that I was a companion for thee, and would take thee by the hand; whereas God will not do so.

In these three respects, especially, God was wronged when they said, 'Where is thy God?' as if he had not been a true and faithful friend to his children; and, besides, as if he had not a providence over his children in the worst condition; as if he had allowed and liked of the base carriage, and condition, and profession of these wretched men as well as of David's. '*Where is now thy God?*' You see God respects us as well as you. But there was no such matter; he respected David more than a thousand of them.

Again, this touched upon religion itself, this reproach, 'Where is now thy God?' where is your goodly profession? as if it were in vain to serve God, a horrible reproach to religion. It is not in vain altogether to serve the devil; he bestows somewhat upon his servants. This was a base thought, to think that God would do no good to them that serve him. That is the fountain of all good, that doeth good to his enemies, that suffers his sun to shine upon his enemies, Mat. v. 45. For him to desert his friends, for a man to be truly religious and get nothing by it, this tended to the reproach of religion; and through David's sides they strike at God and religion, as if it were in vain to serve God, as they said in Malachi's time, Mal. iii. 14. And, indeed, this is in the hearts of men now-a-days. If they see a man that makes care and conscience of his ways, under a cloud, or that he doth not so prosper in the world as others do, they begin to have weak conceits of the profession of religion, as if that were the cause, as if there was nothing gotten by serving of God. But we may be loose professors, and go in a libertine course, and please God as well as others. This is a great grief to God's children. They know well enough it is not in vain to serve God. God is not a barren wilderness, Jer. ii. 31, to those that serve him; they are not barren ground that are careful in his service. So you see upon what ground he was thus affected, because God and religion were touched in it.

Take away a godly man's religion, and his God whom he serves in religion, you take away his life; touch him in that, you touch him in his best freehold. Therefore, when these malicious enemies say, *Where is thy God?* they could not more touch David than so. Profane men of the world come and tell them of religion and such things. Alas! they turn it off with scorn, for they would have the world know that they are not very religious; they never speak of God and of religion but in scorn, or by way of discourse. But a man that is religious to purpose, and makes it his trade, makes it that whereby he hopes to be saved, he takes to heart any thing that is spoken against religion, their words are *as a sword in his bones*, while they say unto him, *Where is thy God?* It is better to be distempered than not to be moved, when God and religion are touched. The Holy Ghost that appeared in the shape of a dove, Matt. iii. 16, appeared at another time in fiery tongues, Acts ii. 8, to shew that the meek spirit of God is zealous other whiles in his children. This was another reason he was thus affected.

And, *thirdly*, in this reproach of theirs, thus violent, 'Where is now thy God?' here was a damping of the spirits of all good men in those times, that should hear of this reproach. Words affect strangely; they have a strange force with men, especially in weak fancies, that are not grounded in their judgment and faith. The spies made a shrewd oration, and brought an ill report on the land: Oh! it is a land that devours the inhabitants, Num. xiii. 32. It was a speech discomfortable, and it wrought so, that it made them all murmur and be discouraged. It is not to be thought what mischief comes from speech cunningly handled. This malicious speech, 'Where is thy God?' and what is become of all thy devotion at the tabernacle, that thou didst frequent so, and drewest others, a great train with thee, what is become of all now? When weak men, that had the beginnings of goodness in them, should see a man reproached for this, questionless it would damp the beginnings of goodness. O would not this go to the heart of David, to see insolent men to quench good things in good men with reproaches! Well, we see what reason the holy man David had to be so sensible of this reproach, for they said unto him daily, 'Where is thy God?'

Now, therefore, to make some use of it to ourselves, let us enter into our own souls, and examine with what spirits and feeling we hear God reproached, and religion reproached, and hindered, and disgraced any kind of way. If we be not sensible of this, and sensible to the quick, we may suspect we are not of David's spirit, that was a man after God's own heart, 1 Samuel xiii. 14; Acts xiii. 22. It was a cutting of his bones, when they came to disparage his religion, and profession, and to touch him in that. Shall a man see men forsake religion, and go backward, and desert the cause of God, and see it oppressed, and not be affected with all this? Certainly he hath a dead soul. That which hath no grief, when there is cause of grief, certainly it is to be accounted but as dead flesh. That heart is but dead flesh that is not touched with the sense of religion.

And to come a little nearer to our times, when we can hear of the estate of the church abroad, the poor church in the Palatinate, in Bohemia, (*d*) and those places, you see how like a canker, superstition is grown up amongst them; when we hear of these things and are not affected, and do not send up a sigh to God, it is a sign we have hollow and dead hearts. No question but if we were there among those malignant spirits that are there, their speeches are daily such, as these wicked men's were to David, What is become of your reformation? What is become of your new religion? Where is that now, I pray? You that do upbraid us with idolatry, what is become of your religion? No question but they have these sarcasms and bitter speeches daily; and those that have the Spirit of God, they are grieved to the heart. If we have the Spirit of God and of Christ in our breasts, and anything of the spirit of David and of holy men, we will grieve at this.

The apostle St Paul, when Elymas laboured to stop, when one was to be converted, he breaks out, 'Thou child of the devil, and enemy of all good, why dost thou not cease to pervert the right ways of God?' Acts xiii. 10. A man that is not fired in this case, hath nothing at all in him. When we see wicked men go about to pervert religion, and overturn all, and we are not stirred at it, it is an ill sign.

Let us, therefore, take a trial of ourselves, how we stand affected in case of religion. He that hath no zeal in him hath no love. By an antiperistasis, an opposition of the contrary increaseth the contrary; if a man have any goodness, if it be environed with opposition, it will intend (*e*) the goodness and increase it. Lot shewed his goodness in Sodom the more, because of the wickedness of the Sodomites. When a man is in vile company, and hears religion disgraced, and good persons scoffed at, and will not have a word to justify good causes and good persons, he hath no life at all of religion; for if he had, he would then have more religion than ordinary, the contrary would then intend, and increase the contrary. There was a blessed mixture of many affections in this grief of the holy man David, when he said, 'their words were as a sword in his bones.' There was great grief, not only for himself, as a man being sensible of reproaches, for men are men; and not out of corrupt nature, but out of the principles of nature, they are sensible of reproaches. Here was grief in respect of God, and in respect of himself; and here was the love of God and the love of religion in this grief. Here was zeal in this, and a sweet mixture of blessed affections; a sweet temper in this, when he saith, 'their words were as a sword in my bones.'

Let us make a use of trial, bring ourselves to this pattern, and think, if we do come short of this, then we come short of that that should be in us. But especially let us consider with what hearts we entertain those doleful and sad reports of foreign churches, and with what consideration and view we look upon the present estate of the church, whether we be glad or no. There are many false spirits that either are not affected at all, or else they are inwardly glad of it; they are of the same disposition that those cursed Edomites were of, 'Down with it, down with it, even unto the ground,' Ps. cxxxvii. 7. I hope that there are but few such amongst us here, therefore I will not press that. But if we be dead-hearted, and are not affected with the cause of the church, let us suspect ourselves, and think all is not well. The fire from heaven is not kindled in our hearts. Our hearts are not yet the altar where God hath kindled that heavenly fire, if we can hear religion disgraced, and good causes go backward, and not be affected. 'Curse ye Meroz.' Why? Because 'they went not out to help the Lord,' Jud. v. 23. If those be cursed that do not help, as they can, by their prayers, then surely they are cursed that are dead-hearted, that are not affected at all, that join with the persecutors, that cry, 'Down with it even to the ground,' and say, 'Aha, so we would have it.' If those be cursed that help not forward the cause of the church, at least by their prayers, and strive and contend for 'the faith once given,' Jude 3, what shall we think of those that are not affected at all ? nay, which is worst of all, that hinder good causes, that are scorners of religion and good causes, what shall we think of those wretched spirits ? How opposite are they to the spirit of David !

To add one thing more, we may learn hence the extent of the commandments, how to enlarge the commandments. Our Saviour, Christ, when he came to preach the gospel, he began with the enlargement of the commandments, shewing the spiritual meaning and extent of the law, 'He that calleth his brother Raca, or fool, is in danger of hell fire,' and 'He that looks on a woman to lust after her, hath committed adultery with her in his heart,' Mat. v. 22, 28. You see here the prophet David, when he speaks of their reproach, he speaks of it as if they had a murderous intention; and in the event and issue it is a kind of murder. *As with a sword in my bones, my enemies reproach me*, &c. This sword were but words. He is a murderer in God's esteem, and so it will prove if he repent not, that wounds another man with his tongue. For what doth the Holy Ghost here in David ? Doth he not set out words by swords ? Is it not oft in the Psalms, 'Their words are as swords, the poison of asps is under their lips ?' Rom. iii. 13. There is an excellent place you have for this in Prov. xii. 18, 'There is that speaks like the piercing of a sword, but the tongue of the wise is health.' A good man hath a healing tongue, he hath a medicinal, salving tongue; but a wicked man, his words are as swords, and, as he saith here, their speaking is as the piercing of a sword. Therefore, hence let us learn not to think ourselves free from murder when we have killed nobody, or free from adultery when we are free from the gross act. This is but a pharisaical gloss upon the commandments; but if we will understand the commandments of God as they are to be understood, we must enlarge them as the Scripture enlargeth them. He that prejudiceth the life and comfort of any man, he is a murderer of him in God's esteem; and he that labours to cut another man to the heart with sharp, piercing words, in God's esteem he is a murderer. Those that, though among men, they cannot say black is their eye, and pride themselves, as if they were very religious men; yet, notwithstanding, they are men that are not wanting of their tongues, men that care not to speak bitterly and sharply of others. If they did consider of this, it would take them down, and make them think a little meaner of themselves, when, indeed, in God's construction, they are little better than murderers. 'As with a sword in my bones, mine enemies reproach me, while they say to me daily, Where is thy God ?' So much for these words.

NOTES.

(a) P. 105.—'Scantling' = a proportion, or simply, portion. This is a somewhat peculiar use of a not very common word. It occurs in Shakspeare once in the same sense with that here:

'. . . . . Trust to me, Ulysses,
Our imputation shall be oddly pois'd
In this wild action : for the success,
Although particular, shall give a *scantling*
Of good or bad unto the general.'—*Troilus and Cressida*, i. 3.

See also Locke, Human Understanding, b. ii., c. 21.

(*b*) P. 108.—'As killing in my bones.' The strong impression 'killing,' or even as it might be rendered, murder, is a literal equivalent of the original (רָצַח), which is intended to express excruciating pain. Compare Ezekiel xxi. 22, rendered 'slayeth' in auth. version.

(*c*) P. 111.—'As one saith of anger.' The reference is to Virgil, Æn., lib. i., v. 150:

'. . . . . . . *Furor arma ministrat ;*
Tum pietate gravem ac meritis, si forte virum quem
    Conspexere,' &c.

(*d*) P. 115.—'The poor church in the Palatinate.' Our memoir shews the deep interest Sibbes, in common with the 'Puritans,' took in the persecuted Protestants of Bohemia.

(*e*) P. 116.—'Intend' = stretch, and so augment. Richardson illustrates the word from Barrow.

G.

THE SOUL'S CONFLICT WITH ITSELF,

AND VICTORY OVER ITSELF BY FAITH.

A TREATISE OF THE INWARD DISQUIETMENTS OF DISTRESSED

SPIRITS, WITH COMFORTABLE REMEDIES

TO ESTABLISH THEM.

THE SOUL'S CONFLICT, AND VICTORY OVER ITSELF BY FAITH.

NOTE.

The several editions of the 'Soul's Conflict,' known to the Editor, and collated for the present publication, are, with the letters used to designate them, as follows :—

(*a*) The Sovles Conflict with it selfe, and Victorie over it selfe by Faith. A Treatise of the inward disquietments of distressed spirits, with comfortable remedies to establish them. '*Returne unto thy rest, O my soule, for the Lord hath dealt bountifully with thee.*'

By R. Sibbs, D.D., Master of Katherine Hall, in Cambridge, and Preacher at Grayes Inne, London.

Printed at London, by M. Flesher, for R. Dawlman, at the Brazen Serpent, in Paul's Churchyard. 1635. 12mo. A.

⁎ This is the *first* edition.

(*b*) There was a re-issue in same year—1635—of A. It is distinguishable from it by having 'Victory' for 'Victorie' in title-page, and by certain corrections, and one alteration. The chief interest attaching to it rests on the latter, upon which Bishop Patrick makes his charge against the Puritans of 'falsification.' See note at end of treatise.

(*c*) 2d edition, 1635. 12mo. C.
(*d*) Another called '2d edition,' 1636. 12mo. ' D.
(*e*) 3d edition, 1636. 12mo. E.
(*f*) 4th edition, 1638. 12mo. F.
(*g*) Another called '4th edition,' 1651. 12mo. G.
(*h*) 5th edition, 1658. 12mo, H.

The text of our reprint is A (see title-page *supra*), with collations from B; C to H consist simply of reproductions of C, and which, except in the addition of the 'Verses' by Benlowes and Quarles, follows B. I have preferred A as our text, from its having been published by Sibbes himself, but have carefully noted the 'corrections' and alteration *supra* as unquestionably made by his authority. The division into chapters of C has been retained, as facilitating perusal.

G.

TO THE RIGHT WORSHIPFUL

SIR JOHN BANKES, KNIGHT,
THE KING'S MAJESTY'S ATTORNEY-GENERAL,*

SIR EDWARD MOSELY, KNIGHT,
HIS MAJESTY'S ATTORNEY OF THE DUCHY [OF LANCASTER],†

SIR WILLIAM DENNY, KNIGHT,
ONE OF THE KING'S LEARNED COUNCIL,‡

SIR DUDLEY DIGGES, KNIGHT,
ONE OF THE MASTERS OF THE CHANCERY;‖

AND THE REST OF THE WORSHIPFUL,

READERS AND BENCHERS, WITH THE ANCIENTS,
BARRISTERS, STUDENTS,

AND ALL OTHERS BELONGING TO THE HONOURABLE SOCIETY OF GRAY'S INN,

R[ICHARD] SIBBES

DEDICATETH THESE SERMONS, PREACHED AMONGST THEM, IN TESTIMONY

OF HIS DUE OBSERVANCE, AND DESIRE OF THEIR

SPIRITUAL AND ETERNAL GOOD.

---

* Sir John Bankes was a man of mark in his generation. He was constituted Lord Chief Justice of the Common Pleas, from being attorney, as above described, in 1640–41. He adhered to Charles I; and was employed against Hampden the patriot, in the case of ship-money. His wife's noble defence of Corfe Castle, and its fall by treachery in the next year, has been well told by a descendant in a volume dedicated to the story of Corfe Castle. He died in 1644, at Oxford.—Consult Foss's admirable Judges of England, vol. vi.; also Lloyd's 'Memoires,' pp. 586–7, 1668.

† Sir Edward Mosely or Mosley was of the family of Ancoats, near Manchester, now represented by Sir Oswald Mosley, Bart.

‡ Sir William Denny was of Cambridgeshire and Ireland.—See *Burke*.

‖ Sir Dudley Digges, like Bankes, is a historical character. After fulfilling various senatorial and diplomatic appointments, and suffering imprisonment more than once, he was admitted Master in Chancery in 1631, and received a grant of the reversion of the office of Master of the Rolls after the death of Sir Julius Cæsar. He obtained possession of it at Sir Julius's death, in April 1636, and held it till his own, in March 18. 1639. He is one of Fuller's 'Worthies.'—See Foss, as *supra*.

G.

TO THE CHRISTIAN READER.

THERE be two sorts of people always in the visible church, one that Satan keeps under with false peace, whose life is nothing but a diversion to present contentments, and a running away from God and their own hearts, which they know can speak no good unto them; these speak peace to themselves, but God speaks none. Such have nothing to do with this Scripture, Ps. xlii. 11; the way for these men to enjoy comfort, is to be soundly troubled. True peace arises from knowing the worst first, and then our freedom from it. It is a miserable peace that riseth from ignorance of evil. The angel 'troubled the waters,' John v. 4, and then it* cured those that stepped in. It is Christ's manner to trouble our souls first, and then to come with healing in his wings.

But there is another sort of people, who being drawn out of Satan's kingdom and within the covenant of grace, whom Satan labours to unsettle and disquiet: being the 'god of the world,' 2 Cor. iv. 4, he is vexed to see men in the world, walk above the world. Since he cannot hinder their estate, he will trouble their peace, and damp their spirits, and cut asunder the sinews of all their endeavours. These should take themselves to task as David doth here, and labour to maintain their portion and the glory of a Christian profession. For whatsoever is in God or comes from God, is for their comfort. Himself is the *God of comfort*, Rom. xv. 5; his Spirit most known by that office, John xiv. 26. Our blessed Saviour was so careful that his disciples should not be too much dejected, that he forgat his own bitter passion to comfort them, whom yet he knew would all forsake him: 'Let not your hearts be troubled,' saith he, John xiv. 1, 27. And his own soul was troubled to death, that we should not be troubled: 'whatsoever is written is written for this end,' 2 Cor. ii. 9; every article of faith hath a special influence in comforting a believing soul. They are not only food, but cordials; yea, he put himself to his oath, that we might not only have consolation, but *strong consolation*, Heb. vi. 18. The sacraments seal unto us all the comforts we have by the death of Christ. The exercise of religion, as prayer, hearing, reading, &c., is, that 'our joy may be full,' 2 John 12. The communion of saints is chiefly ordained to comfort the feeble-minded and to strengthen the weak, 1 Thess. v. 14. God's government of his church tends to this. Why doth he sweeten our pilgrimage, and let us see so many comfortable days in the world, but that we should serve him with cheerful and good hearts? As for crosses, he doth but cast us down, to raise us up, and empty us that he may fill us, and

* 'It,' removed in C.

melt us that we may be 'vessels of glory,' Rom. ix. 23, loving us as well in the furnace, as when we are out, and standing by us all the while. 'We are troubled, but not distressed; perplexed, but not in despair; persecuted but not forsaken,' 2 Cor. iv. 8. If we consider from what fatherly love afflictions come, how they are not only moderated but sweetened and sanctified in the issue to us, how can it but minister matter of comfort in the greatest seeming discomforts? How then can we let the reins of our affections loose to sorrow without being injurious to God and his providence? as if we would teach him how to govern his church.

What unthankfulness is it to forget our consolation, and to look only upon matter of grievance! to think so much upon two or three crosses, as to forget a hundred blessings! to suck poison out of that from which we should suck honey! What folly is it to straiten and darken our own spirits! and indispose ourselves from doing or taking good! A limb out of joint can do nothing without deformity and pain; dejection takes off the wheels of the soul.

Of all other, Satan hath most advantage of discontented persons, as most agreeable to his disposition, being the most discontented creature under heaven; he hammers all his dark plots in their brains. The discontentment of the Israelites in the wilderness provoked God to 'swear that they should never enter into his rest,' Ps. xcv. 11. There is 'another spirit in my servant Caleb,' saith God, Num. xiv. 24. The spirit of God's people is an encouraging spirit. Wisdom teaches them, if they feel any grievances, to conceal them from others that are weaker, lest they be disheartened. God threatens it as a curse to give a trembling heart, and sorrow of mind, Deut. xxviii. 65; whereas on the contrary, joy is as oil to the soul, it makes duties come off cheerfully and sweetly from ourselves, graciously to others, and acceptably to God. A prince cannot endure it in his subjects, nor a father in his children, to be lowering at their presence. Such usually have stolen waters, Prov. ix 17, to delight themselves in.

How many are there, that upon the disgrace that follows religion, are frighted from it? But what are discouragements, to the encouragements religion brings with it? which are such as the very angels themselves admire at. Religion indeed brings crosses with it, but then it brings comforts above those crosses. What a dishonour is it to religion to conceive that God will not maintain and honour his followers; as if his service were not the best service! what a shame is it for an heir of heaven to be cast down for every petty loss and cross! to be afraid of a man whose breath is in his nostrils, Isa. ii. 22, in not standing to a good cause, when we are sure God will stand by us, assisting and comforting us, whose presence is able to make the greatest torments sweet! *Tua presentia, Domine, Laurentio ipsam craticulam dulcem fecit.*

My discourse tends not to take men off from all grief and mourning; 'Light for the righteous is sown in sorrow,' Ps. xcvii. 11. Our state of absence from the Lord, and living here in a vale of tears, our daily infirmities, and our sympathy with others, requires it; and where most grace is there is most sensibleness, as in Christ. But we must distinguish between grief and that sullenness and dejection of spirit, which is with a repining and taking off from duty. When Joshua was overmuch cast down at Israel's turning their backs before their enemies, God reproves him, 'Get thee up, Joshua, why liest thou upon thy face?' Josh. vii. 10.

Some would have men, after the committing of gross sins, to be presently comfortable, and believe, without humbling themselves at all. Indeed, when we are once in Christ, we ought not to question our state in him, and if we do, it comes not from the Spirit; but yet a guilty conscience will be clamorous and full of objections, and God will not speak peace unto it till it be humbled. God will let his best children know what it is to be too bold with sin, as we see in David and Peter, who felt no peace till they had renewed their repentance. The way to rejoice ' with joy unspeakable and glorious,' 1 Pet. i. 8, is to stir up sighs 'that cannot be uttered,' Rom. viii. 26. And it is so far, that the knowledge of our state in grace should not humble us, that very ingenuity considering God's love to us, out of the nature of the thing itself, worketh sorrow and shame in us, to offend his Majesty.

One main stop that hinders Christians from rejoicing is, that they give themselves too much liberty to question their grounds of comfort and interest in the promises. This is wonderful, comfortable say they, but what is it to me, the promise belongs not to me? This ariseth from want of giving all 'diligence to make their calling sure,' 2 Pet. i. 10, to themselves. In watchfulness and diligence we sooner meet with comfort than in idle complaining. Our care, therefore, should be to get sound evidence of a good estate, and then likewise to keep our evidence clear; wherein we are not to hearken to our own fears and doubts, or the suggestion of our enemy, who studies to falsify our evidence, but to the word, and our own consciences enlightened by the Spirit; and then it is pride and pettishness to stand out against comfort to themselves. Christians should study to corroborate their title. We are never more in heaven, before we come thither, than when we can read our evidences. It makes us converse much with God, it sweetens all conditions, and makes us willing to do and suffer anything. It makes us have comfortable and honourable thoughts of ourselves, as too good for the service of any base lust, and brings confidence in God both in life and death.

But what if our condition be so dark that we cannot read our evidence at all?

Here look up to God's infinite mercy in Christ, as we did at the first, when we found no goodness in ourselves, and that is the way to recover whatsoever we think we have lost. By honouring God's mercy in Christ, we come to have the Spirit of Christ; therefore, when the waters of sanctification are troubled and muddy, let us run to the witness of blood. God seems to walk sometimes contrary to himself; he seems to discourage, when secretly he doth encourage, as the 'woman of Canaan,' Matt. xv. 21–23; but faith can find out these ways of God, and untie these knots, by looking to the free promise and merciful nature of God. Let our sottish and rebellious flesh murmur as much as it will, Who art thou? and what is thy worth? yet a Christian 'knows whom he believes,' 2 Tim. i. 12. Faith hath learned to set God against all.

Again, we must go on to add grace to grace. A growing and fruitful Christian is always a comfortable Christian; the oil of grace brings forth the oil of gladness. Christ is first a king of righteousness, and then a king of peace, Heb. vii. 2; the righteousness that he works by his Spirit brings a peace of sanctification, whereby though we are not freed from sin, yet we are enabled to combat with it, and to get the victory over it. Some degree of comfort follows every good action, as heat accompanies fire, and as beams and influences issue from the sun; which is so true, that very heathens, upon the discharge of a good conscience, have found comfort and peace answerable; this is a reward before our reward, *præmium ante præmium.*

Another thing that hinders the comfort of Christians is, that they forget what a gracious and merciful covenant they live under, wherein the perfection that is required is to be found in Christ. Perfection in us is sincerity; what is the end of faith but to bring us to Christ? Now imperfect faith, if sincere, knits us* to Christ, in whom our perfection lies.

God's design in the covenant of grace is to exalt the riches of his mercy above all sin and unworthiness of man; and we yield him more glory of his mercy by believing, than it would be to his justice to destroy us. If we were perfect in ourselves, we should not honour him so much, as when we labour to be found in Christ, having his righteousness upon us, Philip. iii. 9.

There is no one portion of Scripture oftener used to fetch up drooping spirits than this: '*Why art thou cast down, O my soul?*' It is figurative, and full of rhetoric, and all little enough to persuade the perplexed soul quietly *to trust in God;* which, without this retiring into ourselves and checking our hearts, will never be brought to pass. Chrysostom brings in a man loaden with troubles, coming into the church, where, when he heard this passage read, he presently recovered himself, and becomes another man, (Homil. in Genes. xxix.). As David, therefore, did acquaint himself with this form of dealing with his soul, so let us, demanding a reason of ourselves, Why we are cast down; which will at least check and put a stop to the distress, and make us fit to consider more solid grounds of true comfort.

Of necessity the soul must be something calmed and stayed before it can be comforted. Whilst the humours of the body rage in a great distemper, there is no giving of physic; so when the soul gives way to passion, it is unfit to entertain any counsel, therefore it must be stilled by degrees, that it may hear reason; and sometimes it is fitter to be moved with ordinary reason (as being more familiar unto it), than with higher reasons fetched from our supernatural condition in Christ, as from the condition of man's nature subject to changes, from the uncomeliness of yielding to passion for that which it is not in our power to mend, &c.; these and such like reasons have some use to stay the fit for a while, but they leave the core untouched, which is sin, the trouble of all troubles. Yet when such considerations are made spiritual by faith on higher grounds, they have some operation upon the soul, as the influence of the moon having the stronger influence of the sun mingled with it becomes more effectual upon these inferior bodies. A candle light being ready at hand is sometimes as useful as the sun itself.

But our main care should be to have evangelical grounds of comfort near to us, as reconciliation with God, whereby all things else are reconciled to us, adoption and communion with Christ, &c., which is never sweeter than under the cross. Philip Lansgrave of Hesse, being a long time prisoner under Charles the Fifth, was demanded what upheld him all that time? who answered that 'he felt the divine comfort of the martyrs.' *Respondit divinas consolationes martyrum se sensisse.* There be divine comforts which are felt under the cross, and not at other times.

Besides personal troubles, there are many much dejected with the present state of the church, seeing the blood of so many saints to be shed, and the enemies oft to prevail; but God hath stratagems, as Joshua at Ai, Josh. vii. He seems sometimes to retire, that he may come upon his enemies with the greater advantage. The end of all these troubles will no doubt be the ruin of the antichristian faction; and we shall see the church in her more perfect beauty when the enemies shall be in that place which is fittest

* 'Us,' omitted in O.

for them, the lowest, that is, the footstool of Christ, Ps. cx. 1. The church, as it is highest in the favour of God, so it shall be the highest in itself. 'The mountain of the Lord shall be exalted above all mountains,' Isa. ii. 2. In the worst condition, the church hath two faces, one towards heaven and Christ, which is always constant and glorious; another towards the world, which is in appearance contemptible and changeable. But God will in the end give her beauty for ashes, and glory double to her shame, Isa. lxi. 3, and she shall in the end prevail; in the mean time, the power of the enemies is in God's hand, *robur hostium apud Deum*. The church of God conquers when it is conquered, even as our head Christ did, who overcame by patience as well as by power. Christ's victory was upon the cross. The spirit of a Christian conquers when his person is conquered.

The way is, instead of discouragement, to search all the promises made to the church in these latter times, and to turn them into prayers, and press God earnestly for the performance of them. Then we shall soon find God both cursing his enemies and blessing his people out of Zion, by the faithful prayers that ascend up from thence.

In all the promises we should have special recourse to God in them. In all storms there is sea room enough in the infinite goodness of God for faith to be carried with full sail.

And it must be remembered that in all places where God is mentioned, we are to understand God in the promised Messiah, typified out so many ways unto us. And to put the more vigour into such places in the reading of them, we in this latter age of the church must think of God shining upon us in the face of Christ, and our Father in him. If they had so much confidence in so little light, it is a shame for us not to be confident in good things, when so strong a light shines round about us, when we profess we believe 'a crown of righteousness is laid up for all those that love his appearing,' 2 Tim. iv. 8. Presenting these things to the soul by faith, setteth the soul in such a pitch of resolution, that no discouragements are able to seize upon it. 'We faint not,' saith St Paul. Wherefore doth he not faint? Because 'these light and short afflictions procure an exceeding weight of glory,' 2 Cor. iv. 17.

Luther, when he saw Melancthon, a godly and learned man, too much dejected for the state of the church in those times, falls a chiding of him, as David doth here his own soul: 'I strongly hate those miserable cares,' saith he, 'whereby thou writest thou art even spent. It is not the greatness of the cause, but the greatness of our incredulity. If the cause be false, let us revoke it. If true, why do we make God in his rich promises a liar? Strive against thyself, the greatest enemy. Why do we fear the conquered world, that have the conqueror himself on our side?' '*Ego miserrimas curas, quibus te consumi scribis, vehementer odi. Quod sic regnant in corde tuo, non est magnitudo causæ, sed magnitudo incredulitatis nostræ. Si causa falsa est revocemus. Si vera, cur facimus illum tantis promissis mendacem; luctare contra teipsum maximum hostem.*'*

Now, to speak something concerning the publishing of this treatise. I began to preach on the text about twelve years since in the city, and afterwards finished the same at Gray's Inn. After which, some having gotten imperfect notes, endeavoured to publish them without my privity. Therefore, to do myself right, I thought fit to reduce them to this form. There

---

* These remarkable words of a remarkable man are found in letters addressed to Melancthon during the Diet of Augsburg, A.D. 1530. They are effectively quoted by D'Aubigné, Hist. of Reformation, b. xiv., § x., c. 6.—G.

is a pious and studious gentleman of Gray's Inn, that hath of late published observations upon the whole psalm,* and another upon this very verse† very well; and many others, by treatises of faith,‡ and such like, have furthered the spiritual peace of Christians much. It were to be wished that we would all join to do that which the apostles gloried in, ' to be helpers of the joy of God's people,' 2 Cor. i. 24. By reason of my absence while the work was in printing, some sentences were mistaken. Some will be ready to deprave the labours of other men; but, so good may be done, let such ill-disposed persons be what they are, and what they will be, unless God turn their hearts. And so I commend thee and this poor treatise to God's blessing.

R. SIBBES.

Gray's Inn, *July* 1. 1635.

* 'Whole psalm.' This probably refers to William Bloy's 'Meditations on the 42d Psalm.' 1632.
† 'Very verse.' Query, Dr John Reading's 'David's Soliloquy; being the Substance of Several Sermons on Psalm xlii. 11. 1630?'
‡ 'Faith.' Sibbes had himself prefaced Ball, and Preston, and Culverwell on 'Faith.'
*** Sir Egerton Brydges, in his Restituta, iii. p. 500, has this note :—' One of these (on 'Faith'), was written by the Rev. John Rogers, minister of Dedham in Essex; but I cannot point out the two writers previously alluded to.' G.

IN OPUS POSTHUMUM ADMODUM REVERENDI,

MIHIQUE MULTIS NOMINIBUS COLENDI,
RICHARDI SIBBES, S. T. PROFESSORIS, AULÆ
SANCTÆ. CATH. PRÆFECTI DIGNISSIMI.

VADE, liber, pie dux animæ, pie mentis Achates·
  Te relegens, fructu ne pereunte legat;
Quam fœlix prodis! Præ sacro codice sordent,
  Bartole, sive tui; sive, Galene, tui.

Fidu præco Dei, cœlestis cultor agelli,
  Assidui pretium grande laboris habet:
Quo mihi nec vitâ melior, nec promptior ore,
  Gratior aut vultu, nec fuit arte prior.

Nil opus ut nardum caro combibat uncta Sabæum,
  Altáve marmoreus sydera tangat apex:
Non eget hic urnâ, non marmore; nempe volumen
  Stat sacrum, vivax marmor, et urna, pio.

Qui Christo vivens incessit tramite cœli,
  Æthercúmque obiit munus, obire nequit:
Ducit hic angelicis æqualia sæcula lustris,
  Qui verbo studium contulit omne suum.

Perlegat hunc legum cultrix veneranda senectus,
  Et quos plena Deo mens super astra vehit:
Venduntur (quanti!) circum palatia fumi!
  Hic sacer altaris carbo minoris erit?

Heu! pietas ubi prisca? profana ô tempora! mundi
  Fæx! vesper! prope nox! ô mora! Christe veni.
Si valuere preces unquam, et custodia Christi,
  Nunc opus est precibus, nunc ope, Christe, tuâ.

Certat in humanis vitiorum infamia rebus,
  Hei mihi! nulla novis sufficit herba malis?
Probra referre pudet; nec enim decet: exprobret illa
  Qui volet; est nostrum flere, silendo queri.

Flere? Tonabo tuas, pietas neglecta, querelas:
  Quid non schisma, tepor, fastus, et astus agunt?
Addo—Sed historicus Tacitus fuit optimus. Immo
  Addam—sphærarum at musica muta placet.

EDV. BENLOSIO.*

CRESSINGÆ TEMPLARIORUM,
Prid. Cal. Febr. MDCXXXV.†

---

* Edward Benlowes, Esq. He was of Brenthall, Essex. Consult Brydges's Restituta, iii. 41, 42; and Wood's Fasti Oxon. (ed. by Bliss), ii. 358. His principal book is his 'Theophila.' Samuel Butler, Pope, and Bishop Warburton, have satirized his poetry. It is to be feared his tribute to Sibbes will not neutralize the general condemnation. He was a good man, and the friend of good men, to his own impoverishment.

† Sibbes died *July* 5. 1635, and yet this poem, dated '*February* 1635,' is *in memoriam*. The explanation is that prior to 1752, the year in England was reckoned not from 1st January, but from 25th March. All those days, therefore, intervening between the 31st of December and the 25th of March, which we should now date as belonging to a particular year, were then dated as belonging to the year preceding that. Hence while Benlowes wrote according to our reckoning in 1636, he still dates 1635.
G.

ON THE WORK OF MY LEARNED FRIEND DOCTOR SIBBES.

Fool that I was! to think my easy pen
Had strength enough to glorify the fame
Of this known author, this rare man of men,
Or give the least advantage to his name.
    Who think by praise to make his name more bright,
    Shew the sun's glory by dull candle-light.*

Blest saint! thy hallow'd pages do require
No slight preferment from our slender lays;
We stand amazed at what we most admire:
Ah, what are saints the better for our praise!
    He that commends this volume does no more
    Than warm the fire or gild the massy ore.*

Let me stand silent, then. O may that Spirit
Which led thine hand direct mine eye, my breast,
That I may read and do, and so inherit
(What thou enjoy'st and taught'st) eternal rest!
    Fool that I was! to think my lines could give
    Life to that work, by which they hope to live.

                       Fra[ncis] Qua[rles].†

---

* Sir Egerton Brydges, in his Restituta, annotates here.—'This is much in unison with Shakespeare's thought :—

      " To gild refined gold, to paint the lily,
      To seek the beauteous eye of heaven to garnish,
      Is wasteful and ridiculous excess." '

Aristotle might haply here have been introduced by the Commentators, *e. g.*, 'They who demonstrate plain things, light a candle to see the sun,' iii. p. 499.

† Francis Quarles. There is no doubt that this was the quaint poet of the 'Emblems,' and many other volumes not so well known as they deserve to be. It was common to contract names thus, formerly. The 'Garden of Spiritual Flowers,' (1622) is worded on title-page, 'A Garden of Spirituall Flowers, planted by Ri. Ro., Will. Per., Ri. Gree., M. M., and Geo. Web.,' designating severally, Richard Rogers, William Perkins, Richard Greene, &c., &c., and so in many other instances.   G.

THE SOUL'S CONFLICT WITH ITSELF.

Why art thou cast down, O my soul? and why art thou disquieted within me? hope thou in God; for I shall yet praise him, who is the health of my countenance, and my God.—PSALM XLII. 11.

THE Psalms are, as it were, the anatomy of a holy man, which lay the inside of a truly devout man outward to the view of others. If the Scriptures be compared to a body, the Psalms may well be the heart, they are so full of sweet affections and passions. For in other portions of Scripture God speaks to us; but in the Psalms holy men speak to God and their own hearts, as

In this Psalm we have *the passionate passages of a broken and troubled spirit.*

At this time David was a banished man, banished from his own house, from his friends, and, which troubled him most, from the house of God, upon occasion of Saul's persecution, who hunted him as a partridge upon the mountains. See how this works upon him.

1. *He lays open his desire springing from his love;* love being the prime and leading affection of the soul, from whence grief springs, from being crossed in that we love. For the setting out of which his affection to the full, he borroweth an expression from the hart. No hart, being chased by the hunters, panteth more after the waters than my heart doth after thee, O God, ver. 1. Though he found God present with him in exile, yet there is a sweeter presence of him in his ordinances, which now he wanted and took to heart. Places and conditions are happy or miserable as God vouchsafeth his gracious presence more or less; and, therefore, 'When, O when shall it be that I appear before God?' ver. 2.

2. Then, after his strong desire, *he lays out his grief*, which he could not contain, but must needs give a vent to it in tears; and he had such a spring of grief in him as fed his tears day and night, ver. 3. All the ease he found was to dissolve this cloud of grief into the shower of tears.

Quest. But why gives he this way to his grief?

Ans. Because, together with his exiling from God's house, he was upbraided by his enemies with his religion, 'Where is now thy God?' ver. 3. Grievances come not alone, but, as Job's messengers, Job i., follow one another. These bitter taunts, together with the remembrance of his former happiness in communion with God in his house, made deep impressions in his soul, when he 'remembered how he went with the multitude into the house of God,' ver. 4, and led a goodly train with him, being willing, as a good magistrate and master of a family, not to go to the house of God alone, nor to heaven alone, but to carry as many as he could with him. Oh! the remembrance of this made him pour forth, not his words or his tears only, but his very soul. Former favours and happiness make the soul more sensible of all impressions to the contrary. Hereupon, finding his soul over sensible, he expostulates with himself, 'Why art thou cast down, O my soul? and why art thou disquieted within me?' &c.

But though the remembrance of the former sweetness of God's presence did somewhat stay him, yet his grief would not so be stilled, and therefore it gathers upon him again. One grief called upon another, ver. 7, as one deep wave follows another, without intermission, until his soul was almost overwhelmed under these waters; yet he recovers himself a little with looking up to God, who he expected would with speed and authority send forth his lovingkindness, with command to raise him up and comfort him, and give him matter of 'songs in the night,' ver. 8. For all this, his unruly grief will not be calmed, but renews assaults upon the return of the reproach of his enemies. Their words were as swords, ver. 10, unto him, and his heart being made very tender and sensible of grief, these sharp words enter too deep; and thereupon he hath recourse to his former remedy, as being the most tried, to chide his soul, and charge it to trust in God.

CHAPTER I.—*General Observations upon the Text.*

Obs. 1. Hence in general we may observe that *grief gathered to a head will not be quieted at the first.* We see here passions intermingled with comforts, and comforts with passions; and what bustling there is before David can get the victory over his own heart. You have some short-spirited Christians that, if they be not comforted at the first, they think all labour with their hearts is in vain, and thereupon give way to their grief. But we see in David, as distemper ariseth upon distemper, so he gives check upon check and charge upon charge to his soul, until at length he brought it to a quiet temper. In physic, if one purge will not carry away the vicious humour, then we add a second; if that will not do it, we take a third. So should we deal with our souls. Perhaps one check, one charge will not do it, then fall upon the soul again; send it to God again, and never give over until our souls be possessed of our souls again.

Again, in general observe in David's spirit that *a gracious and living soul is most sensible of the want of spiritual means.*

Reason. The reason is because spiritual life hath answerable taste, and hunger and thirst after spiritual helps.

We see in nature that those things press hardest upon it that touch upon the necessities of nature, rather than those that touch upon delights; for these further only our comfortable being, but necessities uphold our being itself, *acrius urgent quæ necessitatis sunt, quam quæ spectant ad voluptatem.* We see how famine wrought upon the patriarchs to go into Egypt: where we may see what to judge of those who willingly excommunicate themselves from the assemblies of God's people, where the Father, Son, and Holy Ghost are present, where the prayers of holy men meet together in one, and, as it were, bind God, and pull down God's blessing. No private devotion hath that report of acceptance from heaven.

Obs. 3. A third general point is, that *a godly soul, by reason of the life of grace, knows when it is well with it and when it is ill, when it is a good day with it and when a bad.* When God shines in the use of means, then the soul is, as it were, in heaven; when God withdraws himself, then it is in darkness for a time. Where there is but only a principle of nature, without sanctifying grace, there men go plodding on and keep their rounds, and are at the end, where they were at the beginning; not troubled with changes, because there is nothing within to be troubled; and, therefore, dead means, quick means, or no means, all is one with them, an argument of a dead soul. And so we come particularly and directly to the words, '*Why art thou cast down, O my soul? and why art thou disquieted within me?*' &c.

The words imply, 1, *David's state wherein he was;* and 2, express his *carriage in that state.*

His estate was such that in regard of outward condition, he was in variety of troubles; and that in regard of inward disposition of spirit, he was first *cast down,* and then *disquieted.*

Now for his carriage of himself in this condition, and disposition, he dealeth roundly with himself. David reasoneth the case with David, and first checketh himself for being too much *cast down,* and then for being too much *disquieted.*

And then layeth a charge upon himself *to trust in God;* wherein we have the duty he chargeth upon himself, which is to *trust in God,* and the grounds of the duty:

First, from confidence of better times to come, which would yield him matter of *praising God.*

And then by a representation of God unto him, as a saving God in all troubles, nay, as salvation itself, an open glorious Saviour in the view of all, *The salvation of my countenance.* And all this enforced from David's interest in God, *He is my God.*

Obs. 1. Whence observe first, from the state he was now in, that *since guilt and corruption hath been derived by the fall, into the nature of man, it hath been subjected to misery and sorrow, and that in all conditions, from the king that sitteth on the throne to him that grindeth on the mill.* None ever have* been so good or so great, as could raise themselves so high as to be above the reach of troubles.

1. And that choice part of mankind, the first-fruits and excellency of the rest, which we call the church, more than others; which appears by consideration both of the head, the body, and members of the church. For the *head* Christ, he took our flesh as it was subject to misery after the fall, and was, in regard of that which he endured, both in life and death, a man of sorrows.

2. For the *body*, the church, it may say from the first to the last, as it is, Ps. cxxix. 1, 'From my youth up they have afflicted me.' The church began in blood, hath grown up by blood, and shall end in blood, as it was redeemed by blood.

3. For the *members*, they are all predestinated to a conformity to Christ their head, as in grace and glory, so in abasement, Rom. viii. 29. Neither is it a wonder for those that are born soldiers to meet with conflicts, for travellers to meet with hard usage, for seamen to meet with storms, for strangers in a strange country, especially amongst their enemies, to meet with strange entertainment.

A Christian is a man of another world, and here from home, which he

* 'Hath,' in C.

would forget, if he were not exercised here, and would take his passage for his country. But though all Christians agree and meet in this, that 'through many afflictions we must enter into heaven,' Acts xiv. 22, yet according to the diversity of place, parts, and grace, there is a different cup measured to every one.

Use. And therefore it is but a plea of the flesh, to except against the cross, 'never was poor creature distressed as I am.' This is but self-love, for was it not the case both of head, body, and members, as we see here in David a principal member? when he was brought to this case, thus to reason the matter with himself, 'Why art thou cast down, O my soul? and why art thou disquieted within me?'

Obs. 2. From the frame of David's spirit under these troubles, we may observe, that as the case is thus with all God's people, to be exercised with troubles, *they are sensible of them oftentimes, even to casting down and discouraging.* And the reason is (1), they are flesh and blood, subject to the same passions, and made of the same mould, subject to the same impressions from without as other men. And (2) their nature is upheld with the same supports and refreshings as others, the withdrawing and want of which affecteth them. And (3) besides those troubles they suffer in common with other men, by reason* of their new advancement and their new disposition they have in and from Christ their head, they are more sensible in a peculiar manner of those troubles that any way touch upon that blessed condition, from a new life they have in and from Christ; which will better appear if we come more particularly to a discovery of the more special causes of this distemper, some of which are, 1. Without us. 2. Some within us.

CHAPTER II.—*Of Discouragements from without.*

I. *Outward causes of discouragement.*

1. *God himself:* who sometimes withdraws the beams of his countenance from his children, whereupon the soul even of the strongest Christian is disquieted; when together with the cross, God himself seems to be an enemy unto them. The child of God, when he seeth that his troubles are mixed with God's displeasure, and perhaps his conscience tells him that God hath a just quarrel against him, because he hath not renewed his peace with his God, then this anger of God puts a sting into all other troubles, and adds to the disquiet. There were some ingredients of this divine temptation, as we call it, in holy David at this time; though most properly a divine temptation be, when God appears unto us as an enemy, without any special guilt of any particular sin, as in Job's case.

And no marvel if Christians be from hence disquieted, whenas the Son of God himself, having always enjoyed the sweet communion with his Father, and now feeling an estrangement, that he might be a curse for us, complained in all his torments of nothing else, but 'My God, my God, why hast *thou* forsaken me? Matt. xxvii. 46. It is with the godly in this case as with vapours drawn up by the sun, which, when the extracting force of the sun leaves them, fall down again to the earth from whence they are drawn. So when the soul, raised up and upheld by the beams of his countenance, is left of God, it presently begins to sink. We see when the body of the sun is partly hid from us, for totally it cannot, in an eclipse by the body of the moon, that there is a drooping in the whole frame of nature;

* 'By reason,' added in B.

so it is in the soul, when there is anything that comes between God's gracious countenance and it.

2. Besides, if we look down to inferior causes, the soul is oft cast down by Satan, who is all for casting down, and for disquieting. For being a cursed spirit, cast and tumbled down himself from heaven, where he is never to come again, [he] is hereupon full of disquiet, carrying a hell about himself; whereupon all that he labours for is to cast down and disquiet others, that they may be, as much as he can procure, in the same cursed condition with himself. He was not ashamed to set upon Christ himself with this temptation of casting down, and thinks Christ's members never low enough, till he can bring them as low as himself.

By his envy and subtilty we were driven out of paradise at the first, and now he envies us the paradise of a good conscience; for that is our paradise until we come to heaven, into which no serpent shall ever creep to tempt us. When Satan seeth a man strongly and comfortably walk with God, he cannot endure that a creature of meaner rank by creation than himself should enjoy such happiness. Herein, like some peevish men which are his instruments, men too contentious and bred up therein, as the salamander in the fire, who when they know the cause to be naught, and their adversaries to have the better title, yet, out of malice, they will follow them with suits and vexations, though they be not able to disable their opposites' title. If their malice have not a vent in hurting some way, they will burst for anger.

It is just so with the devil; when he seeth men will to heaven, and that they have good title to it, then he follows them with all dejecting and uncomfortable temptations that he can. It is his continual trade and course to seek his rest in our disquiet, he is by beaten practice and profession a tempter in this kind.

3. Again, what Satan cannot do himself by immediate suggestions, that he labours to work by his instruments, who are all for casting down of those who stand in their light, as those in the psalm, who cry, 'Down with him, down with him, even to the ground,' Ps. cxxxvii. 7; a character and stamp of which men's dispositions we have in the verse before this text; 'Mine enemies,' saith David, 'reproach me.' As sweet and as compassionate a man as he was, to pray and put on sackcloth for them, Ps. xxxv. 13, yet he had enemies, and such enemies, as did not suffer their malice only to boil and concoct in their own breasts, but out of the abundance of their hearts, they reproached him in words. There is nothing the nature of man is more impatient of than of reproaches; for there is no man so mean but thinks himself worthy of some regard, and a reproachful scorn shews an utter disrespect, which issues from the very superfluity of malice.

Neither went they behind his back, but were so impudent to say it to his face. A malicious heart and a slandering tongue go together, and though shame might have suppressed the uttering of such words, yet their insolent carriage spake as much in David's heart, Ps. xxxix. 1. We may see by the language of men's carriage what their heart saith, and what their tongue would vent if they dared.

And this their malice was unwearied, for they said daily unto him, as if it had been fed with a continual spring. Malice is an unsatiable monster, it will minister words, as rage ministers weapons. But what was that they said so reproachfully, and said daily? 'Where is now thy God?' ver. 3. They upbraid him with his singularity, they say not now, Where is God, but Where is thy God, that thou dost boast so much on, as if thou hadst some special interest in him? where we see that the scope of the devil and wicked men is to shake the godly's faith and confidence in their God. As Satan laboured to divide betwixt Christ and his Father, 'If thou beest the Son of God, command that these stones be made bread,' Matt. iv. 3, so he labours to divide betwixt Father and Son and us. They labour to bring God in jealousy with David, as if God had neglected him bearing himself so much upon God. They had some colour of this, for God at this time had vailed himself from David, as he does oft from his best children, for the better discovery of the malice of wicked men; and doth not Satan tip the tongues of the enemies of religion now, to insult over the church now lying a bleeding!* What's become† of their reformation, of their gospel? Nay, rather what's become of your eyes, we may say unto them? For God is nearest to his children when he seems farthest off. 'In the mount of the Lord it shall be seen,' Gen. xxii. 14; God is with them, and in them, though the wicked be not aware of it; it is all one, as if one should say betwixt the space of the new and old moon, Where is now the moon? whenas it is never nearer the sun than at that time.

Quest. Where is now thy God?

Ans. In heaven, in earth, in me, everywhere but in the heart of such as ask such questions, and yet there they shall find him too in his time, filling their consciences with his wrath; and then, where is their God? where are their great friends, their riches, their honours, which they set up as a god? what can they avail them now?

But how was David affected with these reproaches? Their words were as swords, 'as with a sword in my bones,' &c., ver. 10, they spake daggers to him, they cut him to the quick when they touched him in his God, as if he had neglected his servants, whenas the devil himself regards those who serve his turn. Touch a true godly man in his religion, and you touch his life and his best freehold; he lives more in his God than in himself; so that we may see here, there is a murder of the tongue, a wounding tongue as well as a healing tongue. Men think themselves freed from murder if they kill none, or if they shed no blood, whereas they cut others to the heart with bitter words. It is good to extend the commandment to awake the conscience the more, and breed humility, when men see there is a murdering of the tongue. We see David, therefore, upon this reproach, to be presently so moved, as to fall out with himself for it, 'Why art thou so cast down and disquieted, O my soul?' This bitter taunt ran so much in his mind, that he expresseth it twice in this psalm; he was sensible that they struck at God through his sides; what they spake in scorn and lightly, he took heavily. And indeed, when religion suffers, if there be any heavenly fire in the heart, it will rather break out, than not discover itself at all. We see by daily experience, that there is a special force in words uttered from a subtle head, a false heart and a smooth tongue, to weaken the hearts of professors, by bringing an evil report upon the strict profession of religion; as the cunning and false spies did upon the good land, Num. xiii. 27, as if it were not only in vain, but dangerous to appear for Christ in evil times. If the example of such as have faint spirits will discourage in an army, as we see in Gideon's history, Judges vii., then what will speech enforced both by example and with some show of reason do?

4. To let others pass, we need not go further than ourselves, for to find causes of discouragement; there is a seminary of them within us. Our flesh, an enemy so much the worse, by how much the nearer, will be ready

* This was preached in the beginning of the troubles of the church. [1623. G.]
† 'What becomes,' in C.

to upbraid us within us, 'Where is now thy God?' why shouldst thou stand out in a profession that finds no better entertainment?

CHAPTER III.—*Of Discouragements from within.*

But to come to some particular causes *within* us. There is cause oft in the body of those in whom a melancholy temper prevaileth. Darkness makes men fearful. Melancholy persons are in a perpetual darkness, all things seem black and dark unto them, their spirits, as it were, dyed black. Now to him that is in darkness, all things seem black and dark; the sweetest comforts are not lightsome enough unto those that are deep in melancholy. It is, without great watchfulness, Satan's bath; which he abuseth as his own weapon to hurt the soul, which, by reason of its sympathy with the body, is subject to be misled. As we see where there is a suffusion of the eye by reason of distemper of humours, or where things are presented through a glass to the eye, things seem to be of the same colour; so whatsoever is presented to a melancholy person, comes in a dark way to the soul. From whence it is that their fancy being corrupted, they judge amiss, even of outward things, as that they are sick of such and such a disease, or subject to such and such a danger, when it is nothing so; how fit are they then to judge of things removed from sense, as of their spiritual estate in Christ?

II. *Causes privative, of discouragement in ourselves.*

1. To come to causes more near the soul itself, as when there is want of that which should be in it, as of *knowledge in the understanding,* &c. Ignorance, being darkness, is full of false fears. In the night time men think every bush a thief. Our forefathers in time of ignorance were frighted with everything; therefore it is the policy of popish tyrants, taught them from the prince of darkness, to keep the people in darkness, that so they might make them fearful, and then abuse that fearfulness to superstition; that they might the better rule in their consciences for their own ends; and that so having entangled them with false fears, they might heal them again with false* cures.

2. Again, though the soul be not ignorant, yet if it be *forgetful and mindless,* if, as the apostle saith, 'you have forgot the consolation that speaks unto you,' &c., Heb. xii. 5. We have no more present actual comfort than we have remembrance; help a godly man's memory, and help his comfort; like unto charcoal, which, having once been kindled, is the more easy to take fire. He that hath formerly known things, takes ready acquaintance of them again, as old friends; things are not strange to him.

3. And further, *want of setting due price upon comforts;* as the Israelites were taxed for setting nothing by the pleasant land. It is a great fault when, as they said to Job, 'the consolation of the Almighty seem light and small unto us,' Job xv. 11, unless we have some outward comfort which we linger after.

4. Add unto this, *a childish kind of peevishness;* when they have not what they would have, like children, they throw away all; which, though it be very offensive to God's Spirit, yet it seizeth often upon men otherwise gracious. Abraham himself, wanting children, Gen. xv. 2, undervalued all other blessings. Jonah, because he was crossed of his gourd, was weary of his life. The like may be said of Elias, flying from Jezebel. This peevishness is increased by a too much flattering of their grief, so far as to justify

* 'False' is misprinted 'safe' in A and B. 'False,' the correction, is from C.

it; like Jonas, 'I do well to be angry even unto death,' Jonah iv. 9; he would stand to it. Some, with Rachel, are so peremptory, that they 'will not be comforted,' Jer. xxxi. 15, as if they were in love with their grievances. Wilful men are most vexed in their crosses. It is not for those to be wilful that have not a great measure of wisdom to guide their wills; for God delights to have his will of those that are wedded to their own wills, as in Pharaoh. No men more subject to discontentments than those who would have all things after their own way.

5. Again, one main ground is, *false reasoning, and error in our discourse*, as that we have no grace when we feel none. Feeling is not always a fit rule to judge our states by, that God hath rejected us, because we are crossed in outward things, whenas this issues from God's wisdom and love. How many imagine their failings to be fallings, and their fallings to be fallings away; infirmities to be presumptions; every sin against conscience, to be the sin against the Holy Ghost; unto which misapprehensions, weak and dark spirits are subject. And Satan, as a cunning rhetorician, here enlargeth the fancy, to apprehend things bigger than they are. Satan abuseth confident spirits another contrary way; to apprehend great sins as little, and little as none. Some also think that they have no grace, because they have not so much as grown Christians; whereas there be several ages in Christ. Some, again, are so desirous and enlarged after what they have not, that they mind not what they have. Men may be rich, though they have no millions, and be not emperors.

6. Likewise, some are much troubled, because they proceed by *a false method and order* in judging of their estates. They will begin with election, which is the highest step of the ladder; whereas they should begin from a work of grace wrought within their hearts, from God's calling them by his Spirit, and their answer to his call, and so raise themselves upwards to know their election by their answer to God's calling. 'Give all diligence,' saith Peter, 'to make your calling and election sure,' 2 Pet. i. 10, your election by your calling. God descends down unto us from election to calling, and so to sanctification; we must ascend to him, beginning where he ends. Otherwise it is as great folly as in removing of a pile of wood, to begin at the lowest first, and so, besides the needless trouble, to be in danger to have the rest to fall upon our heads. Which, besides ignorance, argues pride, appearing in this, that they would bring God to their conceits, and be at an end of their work before they begin.

This great secret of God's eternal love to us in Christ is hidden in his breast, and doth not appear to us, until in the use of means God by his Spirit discovereth the same unto us; the Spirit letteth into the soul so much life and sense of God's love in particular to us, as draweth the soul to Christ, from whom it draweth so much virtue as changeth the frame of it, and quickeneth it to duty, which duties are not grounds of our state in grace, but issues, springing from a good state before; and thus far they help us in judging of our condition, that though they be not to be rested in, yet as streams they lead us to the spring-head of grace from whence they arise.

And of signs, some be more apt to deceive us, as being not so certain, as 'delight and joy in hearing the word,' Mat. xiii. 20, as appeareth in the third ground; some are more constant and certain, as love to those that are truly good, and to all such, and because they are such, &c. These as they are wrought by the Spirit, so the same Spirit giveth evidence to the soul of the truth of them, and leadeth us to faith from whence they come, and faith leads us to the discovery of God's love made known to us in hearing the word opened. The same Spirit openeth the truth to us, and our understandings to conceive of it, and our hearts to close with it by faith, not only as a truth, but as a truth belonging to us.

Now this faith is manifested, either by itself reflecting upon itself the light of faith, discovering both itself and other things, or by the cause of it, or by the effect, or by all. Faith is oft more known to us in the fruit of it, than in itself, as in plants, the fruits are more apparent than the sap and root. But the most settled knowledge is from the cause, as when I know I believe, because in hearing God's gracious promises opened and offered unto me, the Spirit of God carrieth my soul to cleave to them as mine own portion, Eph. i. 13. Yet the most familiar way of knowledge of our estates is from the effects to gather the cause, the cause being oftentimes more remote and spiritual, the effects more obvious and visible. All the vigour and beauty in nature which we see, comes from a secret influence from the heavens which we see not; in a clear morning we may see the beams of the sun shining upon the top of hills and houses before we can see the sun itself.

Things in the working of them, do issue from the cause, by whose force they had their being; but our knowing of things ariseth from the effect, where the cause endeth. We know God must love us before we can love him, and yet we oft first know that we love him, 1 John iv. 19; the love of God is the cause why we love our brother, and yet we know we love our brother whom we see more clearly, than God whom we do not see, ver. 20.

It is a spiritual peevishness that keeps men in a perplexed condition, that they neglect these helps to judge of their estates by, whereas God takes liberty to help us sometime to a discovery of our estate by the effects, sometimes by the cause, &c. And it is a sin to set light by any work of the Spirit, and the comfort we might have by it, and therefore we may well add this as one cause of disquietness in many, that they grieve the Spirit, by quarrelling against themselves and the work of the Spirit in them.

7. Another cause of disquiet is, that men by a natural kind of popery *seek for their comfort too much sanctification*, neglecting justification, relying too much upon their own performances. St Paul was of another mind, accounting all but dung and dross, compared to the righteousness of Christ, Philip. iii. 8, 9. This is that garment, wherewith being decked, we please our husband, and wherein we get the blessing. This giveth satisfaction to the conscience, as satisfying God himself, being performed by God the Son, and approved therefore by God the Father. Hereupon the soul is quieted, and faith holdeth out this as a shield against the displeasure of God and temptations of Satan. Why did the apostles in their prefaces join grace and peace together,* but that we should seek for our peace in the free grace and favour of God in Christ?

No wonder why papists maintain doubting, who hold salvation by works, because Satan joining together with our consciences will always find some flaw even in our best performances; hereupon the doubting and misgiving soul comes to make this absurd demand, as, Who shall ascend to heaven? Ps. xxiv. 3, which is all one as to fetch Christ from heaven, and so bring him down to suffer on the cross again. Whereas if we believe in Christ we are as sure to come to heaven as Christ is there. Christ ascending and

* Grace and peace. See 1 Cor. i. 3; 2 Cor. i. 2; Gal. i. 3; Eph. i. 2; 1 Peter i. 2; Rev. i. 4, &c., &c.—G.

descending, with all that he hath done, is ours. So that neither height nor depth can separate us from God's love in Christ, Rom. viii. 39.

But we must remember, though the main pillar of our comfort be in the free forgiveness of our sins, yet if there be a neglect in growing in holiness, the soul will never be soundly quiet, because it will be prone to question the truth of justification, and it is as proper for sin to raise doubts and fears in the conscience, as for rotten flesh and wood to breed worms.

8. And therefore we may well join this as a cause of disquietness, *the neglect of keeping a clear conscience.* Sin, like Achan, or Jonah in the ship, is that which causeth storms within and without. Where there is not a pure conscience, there is not a pacified conscience; and therefore though some, thinking to save themselves whole in justification, neglect the cleansing of their natures and ordering of their lives, yet in time of temptation they will find it more troublesome than they think. For a conscience guilty of many neglects, and of allowing itself in any sin, to lay claim to God's mercy, is to do as we see mountebanks sometimes do, who wound their flesh to try conclusions upon their own bodies, how sovereign the salve is; yet oftentimes they come to feel the smart of their presumption, by long and desperate wounds. So God will let us see what it is to make wounds to try the preciousness of his balm; such may go mourning to their graves. And though, perhaps, with much wrestling with God they may get assurance of the pardon of their sins, yet their conscience will be still trembling, like-as David's, though Nathan had pronounced unto him the forgiveness of his sin, Ps. li., till God at length speaks further peace, even as the water of the sea after a storm is not presently still, but moves and trembles a good while after the storm is over. A Christian is a new creature and walketh by rule, and so far as he walketh according to his rule, peace is upon him, Gal. vi. 16. Loose walkers that regard not their way, must think to meet with sorrows instead of peace. Watchfulness is the preserver of peace. It is a deep spiritual judgment to find peace in an ill way.

9. Some again reap the fruit of their *ignorance of Christian liberty*, by unnecessary scruples and doubts. It is both unthankfulness to God and wrong to ourselves, to be ignorant of the extent of Christian liberty. It makes melody to Satan to see Christians troubled with that they neither should or need. Yet there is danger in stretching Christian liberty beyond the bounds. For a man may condemn himself in that he approves, as in not walking circumspectly in regard of circumstances, and so breed his own disquiet, and give scandal to others.

10. Sometimes also, God suffers men to be disquieted for *want of employment*, who, in shunning labour, procure trouble to themselves; and by not doing that which is needful, they are troubled with that which is unnecessary. An unemployed life is a burden to itself. God is a pure act, always working, always doing; and the nearer our soul comes to God, the more it is in action and the freer from disquiet. Men experimentally feel that comfort, in doing that which belongs unto them, which before they longed for and went without; a heart not exercised in some honest labour works trouble out of itself.

11. Again, *omission of duties and offices of love* often troubles the peace of good people; for even in time of death, when they look for peace and desire it most, then looking back upon their former failings, and seeing opportunity of doing good wanting to their desire (the parties perhaps being deceased to whom they owed more respect), are hereupon much disquieted, and so much the more because they see now hope of the like advantages cut off.

A Christian life is full of duties, and the peace of it is not maintained without much fruitfulness and looking about us. Debt is a disquieting thing to an honest mind, and duty is debt. Hereupon the apostle layeth the charge, 'that we should owe nothing to any man but love,' Rom. xiii. 8.

12. Again, one special cause of too much disquiet is, *want of firm resolution in good things*. The soul cannot but be disquieted when it knows not what to cleave unto, like a ship tossed with contrary winds. Halting is a deformed and troublesome gesture ; so halting in religion is not only troublesome to others and odious, but also disquiets ourselves. 'If God be God, cleave to him,' 1 Kings xviii. 21. If the duties of religion be such as will bring peace of conscience at the length, be religious to purpose, practise them in the particular passages of life. We should labour to have a clear judgment, and from thence a resolved purpose ; a wavering-minded man is inconsistent in all his ways, James i. 6. God will not speak peace to a staggering spirit that hath always its religion and its way to choose. Uncertain men are always unquiet men : and giving too much way to passion maketh men in particular consultations unsettled. This is the reason why, in particular cases, when the matter concerns ourselves, we cannot judge so clearly as in general truths, because Satan raiseth a mist between us and the matter in question.

III. *Positive causes.*

May be, 1. *When men lay up their comfort too much on outward things*, which, being subject to much inconstancy and change, breed disquiet. Vexation always follows vanity, when vanity is not apprehended to be where it is. In that measure we are cast down in the disappointing of our hopes, as we were too much lifted up in expectation of good from them. Whence proceed these complaints : Such a friend hath failed me ; I never thought to have fallen into this condition ; I had settled my joy in this child, in this friend, &c. But this is to build our comfort upon things that have no firm foundation, to build castles in the air, as we use to say. Therefore it is a good desire of the wise man Agur to desire God 'to remove from us vanity and lies,' Prov. xxx. 8 ; that is, a vain and false apprehension pitching upon things that are vain and lying, promising that* contentment to ourselves from the creature which it cannot yield. Confidence in vain things makes a vain heart, the heart becoming of the nature of the thing it relies on. We may say of all earthly things as the prophet speaketh, 'here is not our rest,' Mic. ii. 10.

It is no wonder, therefore, that worldly men are oft cast down and disquieted, when they walk in a vain shadow, Ps. xxxix. 6, as likewise that men given much to recreations should be subject to passionate distempers, because here, things fall out otherwise than they looked for ; recreations being about matters that are variable, which especially falls out in games of hazard, wherein they oft spare not divine providence itself, but break out into blasphemy.

Likewise men that grasp more businesses than they can discharge, must needs bear both the blame and the grief of losing or marring many businesses, it being almost impossible to do many things so well as to give content to conscience ; hence it is that covetous and busy men trouble both their hearts and their houses. Though some men, from a largeness of parts and a special dexterity in affairs, may turn over much, yet the most capacious heart hath its measure, and when the cup is full, a little drop may

* 'a,' in C.

cause the rest to spill. There is a spiritual surfeit, when the soul is overcharged with business; it is fit the soul should have its meet burden and no more.

2. As likewise, those that *depend too much upon the opinions of other men.* A very little matter will refresh, and then again discourage, a mind that rests too much upon the liking of others—*Sic leve sic parvum est animum quod laudis avarum subruit aut reficit.* Men that seek themselves too much abroad, find themselves disquieted at home. Even good men many times are too much troubled with the unjust censures of other men, specially in the day of their trouble. It was Job's case; and it is a heavy thing to have affliction added to affliction. It was Hannah's case, who, being troubled in spirit, was censured by Eli for distemper in brain, 1 Sam. i. 14; but for vain men who live more to reputation than to conscience, it cannot be that they should long enjoy settled quiet, because those in whose good opinion they desire to dwell, are ready often to take up contrary conceits upon slender grounds.

3. It is also a ground of overmuch trouble, when *we look too much and too long upon the ill in ourselves and abroad.* We may fix our eyes too long even upon sin itself, considering that we have not only a remedy against the hurt by sin, but a commandment to rejoice always in the Lord, Philip. iv. 4. Much more may we err in poring too much upon our afflictions; wherein we may find always in ourselves upon search, a cause to justify God, and always something left to comfort us; though we naturally mind more one cross than a hundred favours, dwelling over long upon the sore.

So likewise, our minds may be too much taken up in consideration of the miseries of the times at home and abroad, as if Christ did not rule in the midst of his enemies, and would not help all in due time; or as if the condition of the church in this world were not for the most part in an afflicted and conflicted condition. Indeed there is a perfect rest both for the souls and bodies of God's people, but that is not in this world, but is kept for hereafter; here we are in a sea, where what can we look for but storms?

To insist upon no more, one cause is, that we do usurp upon God, and take his office upon us, by troubling ourselves in forecasting the event of things, whereas our work is only to do our work and be quiet, as children when they please their parents take no further thought; our trouble is the fruit of our folly in this kind.

Use 1. That which we should observe from all that hath been said is, that we be not over hasty in censuring others, when we see their spirits out of temper, for we see how many things there are that work strongly upon the weak nature of man. We may sin more by harsh censure than they by overmuch distemper; as, in Job's case, it was a matter rather of just grief and pity, than great wonder or heavy censure.

Use 2. And, for ourselves, if our estate be calm for the present, yet we should labour to prepare our hearts, not only for an alteration of estate, but of spirit, unless we be marvellous careful beforehand, that our spirits fall not down with our condition. And if it befalls us to find it otherwise with our souls than at other times, we should so far labour to bear it, as that we do not judge it our own case alone, when we see here David thus to complain of himself, 'Why art thou cast down, O my soul?' &c.

CHAPTER IV.—*Of casting down ourselves, and specially by sorrow—evils thereof.*

To return again to the words, 'Why art thou cast down, O my soul?' &c., or, Why dost thou cast down thyself?' or, Art cast down by thyself?

Obs. 1. Whence we may further observe, *that we are prone to cast down ourselves,* we are accessory to our own trouble, and weave the web of our own sorrow, and hamper ourselves in the cords of our own twining. God neither loves nor wills that we should be too much cast down. We see our Saviour Christ, how careful he was that his disciples should not be troubled, and therefore he labours to prevent that trouble which might arise by his suffering and departure from them, by a heavenly sermon; 'Let not your hearts be troubled,' &c., John xiv. 1. He was troubled himself that we should not be troubled. The ground, therefore, of our disquiet is chiefly from ourselves, though Satan will have a hand in it. We see many, like sullen birds in a cage, beat themselves to death. This casting down of ourselves is not from humility, but from pride; we must have our will, or God shall not have a good look from us, but as pettish and peevish children, we hang our heads in our bosom, because our wills are crossed.

Use. Therefore, in all our troubles we should look first *home to our own hearts,* and stop the storm there; for we may thank our own selves, not only for our troubles, but likewise for overmuch troubling ourselves in trouble. It was not the troubled condition that so disquieted David's soul, for if he had had a quiet mind, it would not have troubled him. But David yielded to the discouragements of the flesh, and the flesh, so far as it is unsubdued, is like the sea that is always casting mire and dirt of doubts, discouragements, and murmurings in the soul; let us, therefore, lay the blame where it is to be laid.

Obs. 2. Again, we see, *it is the nature of sorrow to cast down, as of joy to lift up.* Grief is like lead to the soul, heavy and cold; it sinks downwards, and carries the soul with it. The poor publican, to shew that his soul was cast down under the sight of his sins, hung down his head, Luke xviii. 13; the position of his body was suitable to the disposition of his mind, his heart and head were cast down alike. And it is Satan's practice to go over the hedge where it is lowest; he adds more weights to the soul by his temptations and vexations. His sin cast him out of heaven, and by his temptations he cast us out of our paradise, and ever since, he labours to cast us deeper into sin, wherein his scope is, to cast us either into too much trouble for sin, or presumption in sin, which is but a lifting up, to cast us down into deep despair at length, and so at last, if God's mercy stop not his malice, he will cast us as low as himself, even into hell itself.

Reason. The ground hereof is because, *as the joy of the Lord doth strengthen, so doth sorrow weaken the soul.* How doth it weaken?

1. By weakening the execution of the functions thereof, because it drinketh up the spirits, which are the instruments of the soul.

2. Because it contracteth, and draweth the soul into itself from communion of that comfort it might have with God or man. And then the soul being left alone, if it falleth, hath none to raise it up, Eccl. iv. 10.

Use. Therefore, if we will prevent casting down, let us prevent grief the cause *of it,* and sin the cause of that. Experience proves that true which the wise man says, 'Heaviness in the heart of a man makes it stoop, but a good word makes it better,' Prov. xii. 25. It bows down the soul, and therefore our blessed Saviour inviteth such unto him, 'Come unto me, ye who are heavy laden with the burden of your sins,' Matt. xi. 28. The body bends under a heavy burden, so likewise the soul hath its burden, 'Why art thou cast down, O my soul? why so disquieted?' &c.

Obs. 3. Whence we see, 1, that casting down breeds disquieting : because it springs from pride, which is a turbulent passion, whenas men cannot stoop to that condition which God would have them in; this proceeds from discontentment, and that from pride. As we see a vapour enclosed in a cloud causeth a terrible noise of thunder, whilst it is pent up there, and seeketh a vent ; so all the noise within proceeds from a discontented swelling vapour. It is air enclosed in the bowels of the earth which shakes it, which all the four winds cannot do.

No creature under heaven so low cast down as Satan, none more lifted up in pride, none so full of discord. The impurest spirits are the most disquiet and stormy spirits, troublesome to themselves and others ; for when the soul leaves God once, and looks downwards, what is there to stay it from disquiet? Remove the needle from the pole-star, and it is always stirring and trembling, never quiet till it be right again. So, displace the soul by taking it from God, and it will never be quiet. The devil cast out of heaven and out of the church, keeps ado ; so do unruly spirits led by him.

Now I come to the remedies.
1. *By expostulation with himself*, Why art, &c.
2. *By laying a charge upon himself*, Trust in God.

Trust in God. It is supposed here, that there is no reason, which the wisdom from above allows to be a reason, why men should be discouraged; although the wisdom from beneath, which takes part with our corruption, will seldom want a plea. Nay, there is not only no reason for it, but there are strong reasons against it, there being a world of evil in it.

For, 1. *It indisposes a man to all good duties*, it makes him like an instrument out of tune, and like a body out of joint, that moveth both uncomely and painfully. It unfits to duties to God, who loves a cheerful giver, and especially a thanksgiver. Whereupon the apostle joins them both together, 'In all things be thankful, and rejoice evermore,' 1 Thess. v. 17, 18. In our communion with God in the sacraments, joy is a chief ingredient. So in duties to men, if the spirit be dejected, they are unwelcome, and lose the greatest part of their life and grace ; a cheerful and a free spirit in duty is that which is most accepted in duty. We observe not so much what, as from what affection a thing is done.

2. *It is a great wrong to God himself*, and it makes us conceive black thoughts of him, as if he were an enemy. What an injury is it to a gracious father that such whom he hath followed with many gracious evidences of his favour and love should be in so ill a frame as once to call it into question!

3. So *it makes a man forgetful of all former blessings*, and stops the influence of God's grace for the time present and for that to come.

4. So, again, *for receiving of good*, it makes us unfit to receive mercies. A quiet soul is the seat of wisdom; therefore, meekness is required for the receiving of that 'engrafted word which is able to save our souls,' James i. 21. Till the Spirit of God meekens the soul, say what you will, it minds nothing; the soul is not empty and quiet enough to receive the seed of the word. It is ill sowing in a storm; so a stormy spirit will not suffer the word to take place. Men are deceived when they think a dejected spirit to be an humble spirit. Indeed, it is so when we are cast down in the

sense of our own unworthiness, and then as much raised up in the confidence of God's mercy. But when we cast ourselves down sullenly, and neglect our comforts, or undervalue them, it proceeds from pride; for it controls, as much as in us lies, the wisdom and justice of God, when we think with ourselves, Why should it be so with us? as if we were wiser to dispose of ourselves than God is. It disposeth us for entertaining any temptation. Satan hath never more advantage than upon discontent.

5. Besides, *it keeps off beginners from coming in*, and entering into the ways of God, bringing an ill report upon religion, causing men to charge it falsely for an uncomfortable way, whenas men never feel what true comfort meaneth till they give up themselves to God. And it damps, likewise, the spirits of those that walk the same way with us, whenas we should, as good travellers, cheer up one another both by word and example. In such a case the wheels of the soul are taken off, or else, as it were, want oil, whereby the soul passeth on very heavily, and no good action comes off from it as it should, which breeds not only uncomfortableness, but unsettledness in good courses. For a man will never go on comfortably and constantly in that which he heavily undertakes. That is the reason why uncheerful spirits seldom hold out as they should. St Peter knew this well, and therefore he willeth that there should be 'quietness and peace betwixt husband and wife, that their prayers be not hindered,' 1 Pet. iii. 7, insinuating that their prayers are hindered by family breaches; for by that means those two that should be one flesh and spirit are divided, and so made two, and when they should mind duty their mind is taken up with wrongs done by the one to the other.

There is nothing more required for the performing of holy duties than uniting of spirits, and therefore God would not have the sacrifice brought to the altar before reconciliation with our brother, Matt. v. 24. He esteems peace so highly, that he will have his own service stay for it. We see when Moses came to deliver the Israelites out of bondage, Exod. ix., their mind was so taken up with their grief that there was nobody within to give Moses an answer; their souls went altogether after their ill usage.

Use. Therefore, we should all endeavour and labour for a calmed spirit, that we may the better serve God in praying to him and praising of him; and serve one another in love, that we may be fitted to do and receive good, that we may make our passage to heaven more easy and cheerful, without drooping and hanging the wing. So much as we are quiet and cheerful upon good grounds, so much we live, and are, as it were, in heaven. So much as we yield to discouragement, we lose so much of our life and happiness, cheerfulness being, as it were, that life of our lives and the spirit of our spirits by which they are more enlarged to receive happiness and to express it.

CHAPTER V.—*Remedies of casting down: to cite the soul, and press it to give an account.*

Obs. 1. But to come to some helps:

First, in that he expostulates with himself, we may observe that one way to raise a dejected soul is *to cite it before itself, and, as it were, to reason the case.* God hath set up a court in man's heart, wherein the conscience hath the office both of informer, accuser, witness, and judge; and if matters were well carried within ourselves, this prejudging would be a prevention of future judging. It is a great mercy of God that the credit and comfort of man are so provided for that he may take up matters in himself, and so prevent public disgrace. But if there be not a fair dispatch and transaction in this inferior court within us, there will be a review in a higher court. Therefore, by slubbering over our matters we put God and ourselves to more trouble than needs. For a judgment must pass first or last, either within us or without us, upon all unwarrantable distempers. We must not only be ready to give an account of our faith, upon what grounds we believe; but of all our actions, upon what grounds we do what we do; and of our passions, upon what grounds we are passionate; as in a well-governed state, uproar and sedition is never stirred, but account must be given. Now in a mutiny, the presence and speech of a venerable man composeth the minds of the disordered multitude; so likewise in a mutiny of the spirit, the authority that God hath put into reason, as a beam of himself, commands silence, and puts all in order again.

Reason. And there is good reason for it, for man is an understanding creature, and hath a rule given him to live by, and therefore is to be countable of every thought, word, action, passion. Therefore the first way to quiet the soul, is, to ask a reason of the tumult raised, and then many of our distempers for shame will not appear, because though they rage in silent darkness, yet they can say nothing for themselves, being summoned before strength of judgment and reason. Which is the reason why passionate men are loth that any court should be kept within them; but labour to stop judgment all they can. If men would but give themselves leave to consider better of it, they would never yield to such unreasonable motions of the soul; if they could but gain so much of their unruly passions, as to reason the matter within themselves, to hear what their consciences can tell them in secret, there would not be such offensive breakings out. And therefore, if we be ashamed to hear others upbraiding us, let us for shame hear ourselves; and if no reason can be given, what an unreasonable thing is it for a man endowed with reason to contrary his own principles! and to be carried as a beast without reason; or if there be any reason to be given, then this is the way to scan it, see whether it will hold water or not. We shall find some reasons, if they may be so called, to be so corrupt and foul, that if the judgment be not corrupted by them, they dare not be brought to light, but always appear under some colour and pretext; for sin, like the devil, is afraid to appear in its own likeness, and men seek out fair glosses for foul intentions. The hidden, secret reason is one, the open is another; the heart being corrupt sets the wit awork, to satisfy corrupt will; such kind of men are afraid of their own consciences, as Ahab of Micaiah, 1 Kings xxii. 16, because they fear it would deal truly with them; and therefore they take either present order for their consciences, or else, as Felix put off Paul, Acts xxiv. 25, they adjourn the court for another time. Such men are strangers at home, afraid of nothing more than themselves, and therefore in a fearful condition, because they are reserved for the judgment of the great day, if God doth not before that set upon them in this world. If men, carried away with their own lusts, would give but a little check, and stop themselves in their posting to hell, and ask, What have I done? What am I now about? Whither will this course tend? How will it end? &c., undoubtedly men would begin to be wise. Would the blasphemer give away his soul for nothing (for there is no engagement of profit or pleasure in this as in other sins, but it issues merely out of irreverence, and a superfluity of profaneness), would he, I say, draw so heavy a guilt upon himself for nothing, if he would but make use of his reason? Would an old man, when he is very near his journey's end, make longer provision for a short way, if he would ask himself a reason? But, indeed, covetousness is an unreasonable vice.

If those also of the younger sort would ask of themselves, why God should not have the flower and marrow of their age? and why they should give their strength to the devil? it might a little take them off from the devil's service. But sin is a work of darkness, and therefore shuns not only the light of grace, but even the light of reason. Yet sin seldom wants a seeming reason. Men will not go to hell without a show of reason. But such be sophistical fallacies, not reasons; and, therefore, sinners are said to play the sophisters with themselves. Satan could not deceive us, unless we deceived ourselves first, and are willingly deceived. Wilful sinners are blind, because they put out the light of reason, and so think God, like themselves, blind too, Ps. l. 21, and, therefore, they are deservedly termed madmen and fools; for, did they but make use of that spark of reason, it would teach them to reason thus: I cannot give an account of my ways to myself; what account shall I, or can I, give then to the Judge of all flesh ere it be long.

And as it is a ground of repentance in stopping our course to ask, What have I done? so likewise of faith and new obedience, to ask, What shall I do for the time to come? and then upon settling, the soul in way of thanks will be ready to ask of itself, 'What shall I return to the Lord?' &c. So that the soul, by this dealing with itself, promoteth itself to all holy duties till it come to heaven.

1. The reason why we are thus backward to the keeping of this court in ourselves is *self-love*. We love to flatter our own affections, but this self-love is but self-hatred in the end. As the wise man says, he that regards not this part of wisdom, ' hates his own soul, and shall eat the fruits of his own ways,' Prov. i. 31.

2. As likewise it issues from an *irksomeness of labour*, which makes us rather willing to seem base and vile to ourselves and others, than to take pains with our own hearts to be better, as those that are weary of holding the reins give them up unto the horse neck, and so are driven whither the rage of the horse carrieth them. Sparing a little trouble at first, doubles it in the end; as he who will not take the pains to cast up his books, his books will cast up him in the end. It is a blessed trouble that brings sound and long peace. This labour saves God a labour, for therefore he judgeth us, because we would not take pains with ourselves before, 1 Cor. xi. 31.

3. And *pride* also, with a desire of liberty, makes men think it to be a diminishing of greatness and freedom either to be curbed, or to curb ourselves. We love to be absolute and independent; but this, as it brought ruin upon our nature in Adam, so it will upon our persons. Men, as Luther was wont to say, are born with a pope in their belly, they are loath to give an account, although it be to themselves, their wills are, instead of a kingdom to them, *mens mihi pro regno*.

Let us, therefore, when any lawless passions begin to stir, deal with our souls as God did with Jonah, ' Doest thou well to be angry?' Jonah iv. 4, to fret thus. This will be a means to make us quiet; for, alas! what weak reasons have we often of strong motions. Such a man gave me no respect, such another looked more kindly upon another man than upon me, &c. You have some of Haman's spirit, Esth. v. 13, that for a little neglect would ruin a whole nation. Passion presents men that are innocent as guilty to us, *facit ira nocentes ;* and because we will not seem to be mad without reason, pride commands the wit to justify anger, and so one passion maintains and feeds another.

Obs. 2. Neither is it sufficient to *cite the soul before itself ; but it must be pressed to give an account,* as we see here David doubles and trebles the expostulation ; as oft as any distemper did arise, so oft did he labour to keep it down. If passions grow too insolent, Eli's mildness will do no good, 1 Sam. ii. 24. It would prevent much trouble in this kind to subdue betimes, in ourselves and others, the first beginnings of any unruly passions and affections ; which, if they be not well tutored and disciplined at the first, prove as headstrong, unruly, and ill nurtured children, who, being not chastened in time, take such a head, that it is oft above the power of parents to bring them in order. A child set at liberty, saith Solomon, 'breeds shame, at length, to his parents,' Prov. xxix. 15. Adonijah's example shews this. The like may be said of the affections set at liberty ; it is dangerous to redeem a little quiet by yielding to our affections, which is never safely gotten but by mortification of them.

Those that are in great place are most in danger, by yielding to themselves, to lose themselves ; for they are so taken up with the person for a time put upon them, that they, both in look and speech and carriage, often shew that they forget both their natural condition as men, and much more their supernatural as Christians ; and therefore are scarce counselable by others or themselves in those things that concern their severed condition, that concerneth another world. Whereas it were most wisdom so to think of their place they bear, whereby they are called gods, Ps. lxxxii. 6, 7, as not to forget they must lay their person aside, and ' die like men,' 2 Sam. xxiv. 4. David himself that in his afflicted condition could advise with himself, and check himself, yet in his free and flourishing estate neglected the counsel of his friends. Agur was in jealousy of a full condition, and lest instead of saying, what have I done ? why am I thus cast down, &c., he should say, ' Who is the Lord ?' Prov. xxx. 9.

Meaner men in their lesser sphere often shew what their spirits would be, if their compass were enlarged.

It is a great fault in breeding youth, for fear of taking down of their spirits, not to take down their pride, and get victory of their affections : whereas a proud unbroken heart raiseth us more trouble often than all the world beside. Of all troubles, the trouble of a proud heart is the greatest. It was a great trouble to Haman to lead Mordecai's horse, Esth. vi. 1, which another man would not have thought so ; the moving of a straw is troublesome to proud flesh. And therefore it is good to ' bear the yoke from our youth,' Lam. iii. 27 ; it is better to be taken down in youth, than to be broken in pieces by great crosses in age. First or last, self-denial and victory over ourselves is absolutely necessary ; otherwise faith, which is a grace that requireth self-denial, will never be brought into the soul, and bear rule there.

Quest. But, what if pressing upon our souls will not help ?

Ans. Then speak to God, to Jesus Christ by prayer, that as he rebuked the winds and the waves, and went upon the sea, so he would walk upon our souls, and command a calm there. It is no less power to settle a peace in the soul, than to command the seas to be quiet. It is God's prerogative to rule in the heart, as likewise to give it up to itself, which, next to hell is the greatest judgment ; which should draw us to the greater reverence and fear of displeasing God. It was no ill wish of him,* that desired God to free him from an ill man, himself. *Domine, libera me a malo homine, meipso.*

CHAPTER VI.—*Other observations of the same nature.*

Obs. 3. Moreover we see that *a godly man can cast a restraint upon himself*, as David here stays himself in falling. There is a principle of grace, that stops the heart, and pulls in the reins again when the affections are loose. A carnal man, when he begins to be cast down, sinks lower and lower, until he sinks into despair, as lead sinks into the bottom of the sea. 'They sunk, they sunk, like lead in the mighty waters,' Exod. xv. 5. A carnal man sinks as a heavy body to the centre of the earth, and stays not if it be not stopped: there is nothing in him to stay him in falling, as we see in Ahithophel and Saul, 2 Sam. xvii. 23, who, wanting a support, found no other stay but the sword's point. And the greater their parts and places are, the more they entangle themselves; and no wonder, for they are to encounter with God and his deputy, conscience, who is King of kings, and Lord of lords. When Cain was cast out of his father's house, his heart and countenance was always cast down, for he had nothing in him to lift it upwards. But a godly man, though he may give a little way to passion, yet, as David, he recovers himself. Therefore as we would have any good evidence that we have a better spirit in us than our own, greater than the flesh or the world, let us, in all troubles we meet with, gather up ourselves, that the stream of our own affections carry us not away too far.

There is an art or skill of bearing troubles, if we could learn it, without overmuch troubling of ourselves, as in bearing of a burden there is a way so to poise it that it weigheth not over heavy: if it hangs all on one side, it poises the body down. The greater part of our troubles we pull upon ourselves, by not parting our care so, as to take upon us only the care of duty, and leave the rest to God; and by mingling our passions with our crosses, and like a foolish patient, chewing the pills which we should swallow down. We dwell too much upon the grief, when we should remove the soul higher. We are nearest neighbours unto ourselves. When we suffer grief, like a canker, to eat into the soul, and like a fire in the bones, to consume the marrow and drink up the spirits, we are accessory to the wrong done both to our bodies and souls: we waste our own candle, and put out our light.

Obs. 4. We see here again, that *a godly man can make a good use of privacy*. When he is forced to be alone he can talk with his God and himself; one reason whereof is, that his heart is a treasury and storehouse of divine truths, whence he can speak to himself, by way of check, or encouragement of himself: he hath a Spirit over his own spirit, to teach him to make use of that store he hath laid up in his heart. The Spirit is never nearer him than when by way of witness to his spirit he is thus comforted; wherein the child of God differs from another man, who cannot endure solitariness, because his heart is empty; he was a stranger to God before, and God is a stranger to him now, so that he cannot go to God as a friend. And for his conscience, that is ready to speak to him that which he is loth to hear: and therefore he counts himself a torment to himself, especially in privacy.

We read of great princes, who after some bloody designs were as terrible

* Augustine.—ED.

to themselves,* as they were formerly to others, and therefore could never endure to be awaked in the night, without music or some like diversion. It may be, we may be cast into such a condition, where we have none in the world to comfort us; as in contagious sickness, when none may come near us, we may be in such an estate wherein no friend will own us. And therefore let us labour now to be acquainted with God and our own hearts, and acquaint our hearts with the comforts of the Holy Ghost; then, though we have not so much as a book to look on, or a friend to talk with, yet we may look with comfort into the book of our own heart, and read what God hath written there by the finger of his Spirit. All books are written to amend this one book of our heart and conscience. *Ideo scribuntur omnes libri, ut emendetur unus.* By this means we shall never want a divine to comfort us, a physician to cure us, a counsellor to direct us, a musician to cheer us, a controller to check us, because, by help of the word and Spirit, we can be all these to ourselves.

Obs. 5. Another thing we see here, that God hath made *every man a governor over himself.* The poor man, that hath none to govern, yet may he be a king in himself. It is the natural ambition of man's heart to desire government, as we see in the bramble, Judges ix. Well then, let us make use of this disposition to rule ourselves. Absalom had high thoughts. O, if I were a king, I would do so and so! so our hearts are ready to promise, if I were as such and such a man in such and such a place, I would do this and that.

But how dost thou manage thine own affections? How dost thou rule in thine house, in thyself? Do not passions get the upper hand, and keep reason under foot? When we have learned to rule over our own spirits well, then we may be fit to rule over others. 'He that is faithful in a little, shall be set over more,' Matt. xxv. 21. 'He that can govern himself,' in the wise man's judgment, 'is better than he that can govern a city,' Prov. xvi. 32. He that cannot, is like a city without a wall, where those that are in may go out, and the enemies without may come in at their pleasure. So where there is not a government set up, there sin breaks out, and Satan breaks in without control.

Obs. 6. See again, the *excellency of the soul, that can reflect upon itself, and judge of whatsoever comes from it.* A godly man's care and trouble is especially about his soul, as David here looks principally to that, because all outward troubles are for to help that. When God touches our bodies, our estates, or our friends, he aims at the soul in all. God will never remove his hand, till something be wrought upon the soul, as 'David's moisture was as the drought in summer,' Ps. xxxii. 4, so that he roared, and carried himself unseemly for so great and holy a man, till his heart was subdued to deal without all guile with God in confessing his sin; and then God forgave him the iniquity thereof, and healed his body too. In sickness, or in any other trouble, it is best the divine should be before the physician, and that men begin where God begins. In great fires, men look first to their jewels, and then to their lumber; so our soul is our best jewel. A carnal, worldly man is called, and well called, a fleshly man, because his very soul is flesh, and there is nothing but the world in him. And therefore, when all is not well within, he cries out, My body is troubled, my state is broken, my friends fail me, &c.; but all this while, there is no care for the poor soul, to settle a peace in that.

* As Charles IX. after the massacre in France. Thuanus, lib. 57. Somnum post casum Sanbartholomæum nocturni horrores plerumque interrumpebant et rursus adhibiti symphoniaci expergefacto conciliabant.

The possession of the soul is the richest possession, no jewel so precious. The account for our own souls, and the souls of others, is the greatest account, and therefore the care of souls should be the greatest care. What an indignity is it, that we should forget such souls to satisfy our lusts! to have our wills! to be vexed with any, who by their judgment, example, or authority, stop, as we suppose, our courses! Is it not the greatest plot in the world, first, to have their lusts satisfied; secondly, to remove, either by fraud or violence, whatsoever standeth in their way; and, thirdly, to put colours and pretences upon this to delude the world and themselves, employing all their carnal wit and worldly strength for their carnal aims, and fighting for that which fights against their own souls? For, what will be the issue of this but certain destruction?

Of this mind are not only the dregs of people, but many of the more refined sort, who desire to be eminent in the world; and to have their own desires herein, give up the liberty of their own judgments and consciences to the desires and lusts of others. To be above others, they will be beneath themselves, having those men's persons in admiration for hope of advantage, whom otherwise they despise; and so, substituting in their spirits man in the place of God, lose heaven for earth, and bury that divine spark, their souls, capable of the divine nature, and fitter to be a sanctuary and temple for God to dwell in, than by closing with baser things to become base itself. We need not wonder that others seem base to carnal men, who are base both in and to themselves. It is no wonder they should be cruel to the souls of others, who are cruel to their own souls; that they should neglect and starve others, that give away their own souls in a manner for nothing. Alas! upon what poor terms do they hazard that, the nature and worth whereof is beyond man's reach to comprehend! Many are so careless in this kind, that if they were thoroughly persuaded that they had souls that should live for ever, either in bliss or torment, we might the more easily work upon them. But as they live by sense, as beasts, so they have no more thoughts of future times than beasts, except at such times as conscience is awaked by some sudden judgment, whereby God's wrath is revealed from heaven against them. But happy were it for them, if they might die like beasts, whose misery dies with them.

To such an estate hath sin brought the soul, that it willingly drowneth itself in the senses, and becomes, in some sort, incarnate with the flesh.

We should therefore set ourselves to have most care of that, which God cares most for, which he breathed into us at first, set his own image upon, gave so great a price for, and values above all the world besides. Shall all our study be to satisfy the desires of the flesh, and neglect this?

Is it not a vanity to prefer the casket before the jewel, the shell before the pearl, the gilded potsherd before the treasure? and is it not much more vanity to prefer the outward condition before the inward? The soul is that which Satan and his hath most spite at, for in troubling our bodies or estates, he aims at the vexation of our souls. As in Job (ch. i.) his aim was to abuse that power God had given him over his children, body, and goods, to make him, out of a disquieted spirit, blaspheme God. It is an ill method to begin our care in other things, and neglect the soul, as Ahithophel, who set his house in order, when he should have set his soul in order first, 2 Sam. xvii. 23. Wisdom begins at the right end. If all be well at home, it comforts a man, though he meets with troubles abroad. Oh, saith he, I shall have rest at home; I have a loving wife and dutiful children: so whatsoever we meet withal abroad, if the soul be quiet, thither we can retire with comfort. See that all be well within, and then all troubles from without cannot much annoy us.

Grace will teach us to reason thus—God hath given mine enemies power over my liberty and condition, but shall they have power and liberty over my spirit? It is that which Satan and they most seek for; but never yield, O my soul! and thus a godly man will become more than a conqueror; when in appearance he is conquered, the cause prevails, his spirit prevails, and is undaunted. A Christian is not subdued till his spirit is subdued. Thus Job prevailed over Satan and all his troubles, at length. This tormenteth proud persons, to see godly men enjoy a calm and resolute frame of mind in the midst of troubles; when their enemies are more troubled in troubling them, than they are in being troubled by them.

Obs. 7. We see likewise here, *how to frame our complaints.* David complains not of God, nor of his troubles, nor of others, but of his own soul; he complains of himself to himself, as if he should say, Though all things else be out of order, yet, O my soul, thou shouldst not trouble me too, thou shouldst not betray thyself unto troubles, but rule over them. A godly man complains to God, yet not of God, but of himself. A carnal man is ready to justify himself and complain of God, he complains not to God, but of God, at the least, in secret murmuring, he complains of others that are but God's vials; he complains of the grievance that lies upon him, but never regards what is amiss in himself within; openly he cries out upon fortune, yet secretly he striketh at God, under that idol of fortune, by whose guidance all things come to pass; whilst he quarrels with that which is nothing, he wounds him that is the cause of all things; like a gouty man that complains of his shoe, and of his bed, or an aguish man of his drink, when the cause is from within. So men are disquieted with others, when they should rather be disquieted and angry with their own hearts.

We condemn Jonah for contending with God, and justifying his unjust anger, but yet the same risings are in men naturally, if shame would suffer them to give vent to their secret discontent; their heart speaks what Jonah his tongue spake. Oh! but here we should lay our hand upon our mouth, and adore God, and command silence to our souls.

No man is hurt but by himself first. We are drawn to evil, and allured from a true good to a false by our own lusts, 'God tempts no man,' James i. 13. Satan hath no power over us further than we willingly lie open to him. Satan works upon our affections, and then our affections work upon our will. He doth not work immediately upon the will. We may thank ourselves in willingly yielding to our own passions, for all that ill Satan or his instruments draws us unto. Saul was not vexed with an evil spirit, 1 Sam. xvi., till he gave way to his own evil spirit of envy first. The devil entered not into Judas, Mat. xxvii. 3, until his covetous heart made way for him. The apostle strengtheneth his conceit against rash and lasting anger from hence, that by this we give way to the devil, Eph. iv. 27. It is a dangerous thing to pass from God's government, and come under Satan's.

Satan mingleth himself with our own passions, therefore we should blame ourselves first, be ashamed of ourselves most, and judge ourselves most severely. But self-love teacheth us a contrary method, to translate all upon others; it robs us of a right judgment of ourselves. Though we desire to know all diseases of the body by their proper names, yet we will conceive of sinful passions of the soul under milder terms; as lust under love, rage under just anger, murmuring under just displeasure, &c. Thus whilst we flatter our grief, what hope of cure! Thus sin hath not only made all the creatures enemies to us, but ourselves the greatest enemies to ourselves ; and therefore we should begin our complaints against ourselves, and discuss ourselves thoroughly. How else shall we judge truly of other things without us, above us, or beneath us? The sun when it rises, enlightens first the nearest places, and then the more remote ; so where true light is set up, it discovers what is amiss within first.

Obs. 8. Hence also we see, that *as in all discouragements a godly man hath most trouble with his own heart, so he knows how to carry himself therein,* as David doth here.

For the better clearing of this, we must know there be divers kinds and degrees of conflicts in the soul of man whilst it is united to the body.

1. First, between one corrupt passion and another, as between covetousness and pride ; pride calls for expense, covetousness for restraint. Oft passions fight not only against God and reason, to which they owe a homage, but one against another ; sin fights against sin, and a lesser sin is oftentimes overcome by a greater. The soul in this case is like the sea tossed with contrary winds : and like a kingdom divided, wherein the subjects fight both against their prince, and one against another.

2. Secondly, there is a natural conflict in the affections, whereby nature seeks to preserve itself, as betwixt anger and fear ; anger calls for revenge, fear of the law binds the soul to be quiet. We see in the creatures, fear makes them abstain from that which their appetites carry them unto. A wolf comes to the* flock with an eagerness to prey upon it, but seeing the shepherd standing in defence of his sheep, returns and doth no harm ; and yet for all this, as he came a wolf, so he returns a wolf.

A natural man may oppose some sin from an obstinate resolution against it,† not from any love of God, or hatred of sin, as sin, but because he conceives it a brave thing to have his will ; as one hard weapon may strike at another, as a stone wall may beat back an arrow. But this opposition is not from a contrariety of nature, as is betwixt fire and water.

3. Thirdly, there is a conflict of a higher nature, as between some sins and the light of reason helped by a natural conscience. The heathen could reason from the dignity of the soul, to count it a base thing to prostitute themselves to beastly lusts, so as it were degrading and unmanning themselves. *Major sum et ad majora natus quam ut corporis mei sim mancipium.* (Seneca, Ep. 65). Natural men, desirous to maintain a great opinion of themselves, and to awe the inferior sort by gravity of deportment in carriage, will abstain from that which otherwise their hearts carry them unto, lest yielding should render them despised, by laying themselves too much open ; as because passion discovers a fool as he is, and makes a wise man thought meaner than he is ; therefore a prudent man will conceal his passion. Reason refined and raised by education, example, and custom, doth break in some degree the force of natural corruption, and brings into the soul, as it were, another nature, and yet no true change ; as we see in such as have been inured to good courses, they feel conscience checking them upon the first discontinuance and alteration of their former good ways, but this is usually from a former impression of their breeding, as the boat moves some little time upon the water by virtue of the former stroke ; yet at length we see corruption prevailing over education, as in Jehoash, who was awed by the

---

* 'A,' in C.

† 'A natural . . . . love. In A reads, 'a natural man may oppose an obstinate resolution to commit some sin not from love.' Corrected in B as above.—G.

reverent respect he bare to his uncle Jehoiada, he was good 'all his uncle's days,' 2 Kings xii. 2. And in Nero, in whom the goodness of his education prevailed over the fierceness of his nature, for the first five years (*a*).

4. Fourthly, but in the church, where there shineth a light above nature, as there is a discovery of more sins, and some strength, with the light to perform more duty; so there is a further conflict than in a man that hath no better than nature in him. By a discovery of the excellent things of the gospel, there may be some kind of joy stirred up, and some degree of obedience: whence there may be some degree of resistance against the sins of the gospel, as obstinate unbelief, desperation, profaneness, &c. A man in the church may do more than another out of the church, by reason of the enlargement of his knowledge; whereupon such cannot sin at so easy a rate as others that know less, and, therefore, meet with less opposition from conscience.

5. Fifthly, There is yet a further degree of conflict betwixt the sanctified powers of the soul and the flesh, not only as it is seated in the baser parts, but even in the best faculties of the soul, and as it mingles itself with every gracious performance: as in David, there is not only a conflict between sin and conscience, enlightened by a common work of the Spirit; but between the commanding powers of the soul sanctified, and itself unsanctified, between reasons of the flesh and reasons of the Spirit, between faith and distrust, between the true light of knowledge and false light. For it is no question but the flesh would play its part in David, and muster up all the strength of reason it had. And usually flesh, as it is more ancient than the spirit, we being first natural, then spiritual, so it will put itself first forward in devising shifts, as Esau comes out of the womb first before Jacob, Gen. xxv. 25; yet hereby the spirit is stirred up to a present examination and resistance, and in resisting, as we see here, at length the godly gets the victory. As in the conflict between the higher parts of the soul with the lower, it clearly appears that the soul doth not rise out of the temper of the body, but is a more noble substance, commanding the body by reasons fetched from its own worth; so in this spiritual conflict, it appears there is something better than the soul itself, that hath superiority over it.

CHAPTER VII.—*Difference between good men and others in conflicts with sin.*

Quest. But how doth it appear that this combat in David was a *spiritual combat?*

Ans. 1. First, *A natural conscience is troubled for sins against the light of nature only*, but David for inward and secret corruptions, as discouragement and disquietness arising from faint-trusting in God.

David's conflict was not only with the sensual, lower part of his soul, which is carried to ease and quiet and love of present things, but he was troubled with a mutiny in his understanding between faith and distrust; and therefore he was forced to rouse up his soul so oft to trust in God; which shews that carnal reason did solicit him to discontent, and had many colourable reasons for it.

2. Secondly, *A man endued with common grace is rather a patient than an agent in conflicts;* the light troubles him against his will, as discovering and reproving him, and hindering his sinful contentments; his heart is more biassed another way if the light would let him; but a godly man labours to help the light, and to work his heart to an opposition against

sin; he is an agent as well as a patient. As David here doth not suffer disquieting, but is disquieted with himself for being so. A godly man is an agent in opposing his corruption, and a patient in enduring of it, whereas a natural man is a secret agent in and for his corruptions, and a patient in regard of any help against them; a good man suffers evil and doth good, a natural man suffers good and doth evil.

3. Thirdly, *A conscience guided by common light withstands distempers most by outward means;* but David here fetcheth help from the Spirit of God in him, and from trust in God. Nature works from within, so doth the new nature. David is not only something disquieted, and something troubled for being disquieted, but sets himself thoroughly against his distempers; he complains and expostulates, he censures and chargeth his soul. The other, if he doth anything at all, yet it is faintly; he seeks out his corruption as a coward doth his enemy, loath to find him, and more loath to encounter him.

4. Fourthly, *David withstands sin constantly, and gets ground.* We see here he gives not over at the first, but presseth again and again. Nature works constantly, so doth the new nature. The conflict in the other is something forced, as taking part with the worser side in himself; good things have a weak, or rather no party in him, bad things a strong; and therefore he soon gives over in this holy quarrel.

5. Fifthly, *David is not discouraged by his foils,* but sets himself afresh against his corruptions, with confidence to bring them under.* Whereas he that hath but a common work of the Spirit, after some foils, lets his enemy prevail more and more, and so despairs of victory, and thinks it better to sit still than to rise and take a new fall; by which means his latter end is worse than his beginning; for beginning in the spirit, he ends in the flesh. A godly man, although upon some foil, he may for a time be discouraged, yet by holy indignation against sin he renews his force, and sets afresh upon his corruptions, and gathers more strength by his falls, and groweth into more acquaintance with his own heart and Satan's malice, and God's strange ways in bringing light out of darkness.

6. Sixthly, An ordinary Christian may be disquieted for being disquieted, as David was, but then it is only as disquiet hath vexation in it; but David here striveth against the unquietness of his spirit, not only as it brought vexation with it, but *as it hindered communion with his God.*

In sin there is not only a guilt binding over the soul to God's judgment, and thereupon filling the soul with inward fears and terrors; but in sin likewise there is—1, A contrariety to God's holy nature; and, 2, A contrariety to the divine nature and image stamped upon ourselves; 3, A weakening and disabling of the soul from good; and, 4, A hindering of our former communion with God, sin being in its nature a leaving of God, the fountain of all strength and comfort, and cleaving to the creature. Hereupon the soul, having tasted the sweetness of God before, is now grieved, and this grief is not only for the guilt and trouble that sin draws after it, but from an inward antipathy and contrariety betwixt the sanctified soul and sin. It hates sin as sin, as the only bane and poison of renewed nature, and the only thing that breeds strangeness betwixt God and the soul. And this hatred is not so much from discourse and strength of reason, as from nature itself rising presently against its enemy; the lamb presently shuns the wolf from a contrariety: antipathies wait not for any strong reason, but are exercised upon the first presence of a contrary object.

* That is, 'defeats.'—ED.

7. Seventhly, Hereupon ariseth the last difference, that because the soul hateth sin as sin, therefore it *opposeth it universally and eternally, in all the powers of the soul; and in all actions, inward and outward, issuing from those powers.* David regarded no iniquity in his heart, but hated every evil way, Ps. lxvi. 18; the desires of his soul were, that it might be so directed that he might keep God's law, Ps. cxix. 5. And if there had been no binding law, yet there was such a sweet sympathy and agreement betwixt his soul and God's truth, that he delighted in it above all natural sweetness; hence it is that St John saith, 'He that is born of God cannot sin,' 1 John iii. 9; that is, so far forth as he is born of God, his new nature will not suffer him; he cannot lie, he cannot deceive, he cannot be earthly-minded, he cannot but love and delight in the persons and things that are good. There is not only a light in the understanding, but a new life in the will, and all other faculties of a godly man; what good his knowledge discovereth, that his will makes choice of, and his heart loveth; what ill his understanding discovers, that his will hateth and abstains from. But in a man not thoroughly converted, the will and affections are bent otherwise; he loves not the good he doth, nor hates the evil he doth not.

Use. Therefore let us make a narrow search into our souls upon what grounds we oppose sin, and fight God's battles. A common Christian is not cast down because he is disquieted in God's service, or for his inward failings that he cannot serve God with that liberty and freedom he desires, &c. But a godly man is troubled for his distempers, because they hinder the comfortable intercourse betwixt God and his soul, and that spiritual composedness and sabbath of spirit, which he enjoyed before, and desires to enjoy again. He is troubled that the waters of his soul are troubled so that the image of Christ shines not in him as it did before. It grieves him to find an abatement in affection, in love to God, a distraction or coldness in performing duties, any doubting of God's favour, any discouragement from duty, &c. A godly man's comforts and grievances are hid from the world; natural men are strangers to them. Let this be a rule of discerning our estates, how we stand affected to the distempers of our hearts; if we find them troublesome, it is a ground of comfort unto us that our spirits are ruled by a higher Spirit; and that there is a principle of that life in us, which cannot brook the most secret corruption, but rather casts it out by a holy complaint, as strength of nature doth poison, which seeks its destruction. And let us be in love with that work of grace in us, which makes us out of love with the least stirrings that hinder our best condition.

Obs. 9. See again, *We may be sinfully disquieted for that which is not a sin to be disquieted for.* David had sinned if he had not been somewhat troubled for the banishment from God's house, and the blasphemy of the enemies of the church; but yet, we see, he stops himself, and sharply takes up his soul for being disquieted. He did well in being disquieted, and in checking himself for the same; there were good grounds for both. He had wanted spiritual life if he had not been disquieted, [but] he abated the vigour and liveliness of his life by being overmuch disquieted.

CHAPTER VIII.—*Of unfitting dejection, and when it is excessive. And what is the right temper of the soul herein.*

Quest. § I. Then, how shall we know when a man is cast down and disquieted, otherwise than is befitting?

Ans. There is a threefold miscarriage of inward trouble.

1. *When the soul is troubled for that it should not be vexed for,* as Ahab, when he was crossed in his will for Naboth's vineyard, 1 Kings xxi. 1, 2, seq.

2. *In the ground,* as when we grieve for that which is good, and for that which we should grieve for; but it is with too much reflecting upon our own particular.

As in the troubles of the state or church, we ought to be affected; but not because these troubles hinder any liberties of the flesh, and restrain pride of life, but from higher respects; as that, by these troubles God is dishonoured, the public exercises of religion hindered, and the gathering of souls thereby stopped, as the states and commonwealths, which should be harbours of the church, are disturbed, as lawless courses and persons prevail, as religion and justice are triumphed over and trodden under. Men usually are grieved for public miseries from a spirit of self-love only, because their own private is embarked in the public. There is a depth of deceit of the heart in this matter.

3. So for the *measure,* when we trouble ourselves, though not without cause, yet without bounds.

The spirit of man is like unto moist elements, as air and water, which have no bounds of their own to contain them in, but those of the vessel that keeps them. Water is spilt and lost without something to hold it, so it is with the spirit of man, unless it be bounded with the Spirit of God. Put the case, a man be disquieted for sin, for which not to be disquieted is a sin, yet we may look too much, and too long upon it; for the soul hath a double eye, one to look to sin, another to look up to God's mercy in Christ. Having two objects to look on, we may sin in looking too much on the one, with neglect of the other.

Quest. § II. *Seeing then, disquieting and dejection for sin is necessary, how shall we know when it exceeds measure?*

Ans. 1. First, *when it hinders us from holy duties, or in the performance of them,* by distraction or otherwise; whereas they are given to carry us to that which is pleasing to God, and good to ourselves.

Grief is ill when it taketh off the soul from minding that it should, and so indisposeth us to the duties of our callings. Christ upon the cross was grieved to the utmost, yet it did not take away his care for his mother, John xix. 26, 27: so the good thief, Luke xxiii. 42, in the midst of his pangs laboured to gain his fellow, and to save his own soul, and to glorify Christ. If this be so in grief of body, which taketh away the free use of reason and exercise of grace more than any other grief, then much more in grief from more remote causes; for in extremity of body the sickness may be such as all that we can perform to God is a quiet submission and a desire to be carried unto Christ by the prayers of others; we should so mind our grief as not to forget God's mercy, or our own duty.

2. Secondly, *when we forget the grounds of comfort,* and suffer our mind to run only upon the present grievance. It is a sin to dwell on sin and turmoil our thoughts about it, when we are called to thankfulness. A physician in good discretion forbids a dish at some times to prevent the nourishment of some disease, which another time he gives way unto. So we may and ought to abstain from too much feeding our thoughts upon our corruptions in case of discouragement, which at other times is very necessary. It should be our wisdom in such cases to change the object, and

labour to take off our minds, and give them to that which calls more for them. Grief oft passeth unseasonably upon us, when there is cause of joy, and when we are called to joy; as Joab justly found fault with David for grieving too much, when God had given him the victory, and rid him and the state of a traitorous son, 2 Sam. xix. 5, *seq.* God hath made some days for joy, and joy is the proper work of those days. 'This is the day which the Lord hath made,' Ps. cxviii. 24. Some in a sick distemper desire that which increaseth their sickness; so some that are deeply cast down, desire a weakening* ministry, and whatever may cast them down more, whereas they should meditate upon comforts, and get some sweet assurance of God's love. Joy is the constant temper which the soul should be in. 'Rejoice evermore,' 1 Thes. v. 16, saith the apostle. If a sink be stirred, we stir it not more, but go into a sweeter room. So we should think of that which is comfortable, and of such truths as may raise up the soul, and sweeten the spirit.

3. Thirdly, Grief is too much, *when it inclines the soul to any inconvenient courses*: for if it be not looked to, it is an ill counsellor, when either it hurts the health of our bodies, or draws the soul, for to ease itself, to some unlawful liberty. When grief keeps such a noise in the soul, that it will not hear what the messengers of God, or the still voice of the Spirit saith. As in combustions, loud cries are scarce heard, so in such cases the soul will neither hear itself nor others. The fruit of this overmuch trouble of spirit is increase of trouble.

Quest. § III. Another question may be, *What that sweet and holy temper is the soul should be in, that it may neither be faulty in the defect, nor too much abound in grief and sorrow?*

Ans. 1. The soul must be raised *to a right grief.*

2. The grief that is raised, though it be right, yet it must be *bounded.* Before we speak of raising grief in the godly, we must know there are some who are altogether strangers to any kind of spiritual grief or trouble at all; such must consider, that the way to prevent everlasting trouble, is to desire to be troubled with a preventing trouble. Let those that are not in the way of grace think with themselves what cause they have not to take a minute's rest while they are in that estate. For a man to be in debt both body and soul, subject every minute to be arrested and carried prisoner to hell, and not to be moved; for a man to have the wrath of God ready to be poured out upon him, and hell gape for him, nay, to carry a hell about him in conscience, if it were awake, and to have all his comfort here hanging upon a weak thread of this life, ready to be cut and broken off every moment, and to be cursed in all those blessings that he enjoys; and yet not to be disquieted, but continually treasuring up wrath against the day of wrath, by running deeper into God's books: for a man to be thus, and not to be disquieted, is but the devil's peace, whilst the strong man holds possession. A burning ague is more hopeful than a lethargy. The best service that can be done to such men, is to startle and rouse them, and so with violence to pull them out of the fire, as Jude speaks, ver. 23, or else they will another day curse that cruel mercy that lets them alone now. In all their jollity in this world, they are but as a book fairly bound, which when it is opened is full of nothing but tragedies. So when the book of their consciences shall be once opened, there is nothing to be read but lamentations and woes. Such men were in a way of hope, if they had but so much

* 'Weakening.' In A and B 'wakening,' but corrected in C as above.

apprehension of their estates, as to ask themselves, ' What have I done ?' If this be true that there are such fearful things prepared for sinners, why am I not cast down ? why am I no more troubled and discouraged for my wicked courses ? Despair to such is the beginning of comfort ; and trouble the beginning of peace. A storm is the way to a calm, and hell the way to heaven.

(1.) But for raising of a right grief in the soul of a holy man, *look what is the state of the soul in itself, in what terms it is with God:* whether there be any sin hanging on the file (*b*) unrepented of. If all be not well within us, then here is place for inward trouble, whereby the soul may afflict itself.

God saw this grief so needful for his people, that he appointed certain days for afflicting them, Lev. xvi. 29 ; because it is fit that sin contracted by joy should be dissolved by grief; and sin is so deeply invested into the soul, that a separation betwixt the soul and it cannot be wrought without much grief. When the soul hath smarted for sin, it sets then the right price upon reconciliation with God in Christ, and it feeleth what a bitter thing sin is, and therefore it will be afraid to be too bold with it afterward ; it likewise aweth the heart so, that it will not be so loose towards God as it was before ; and certainly that soul that hath felt the sweetness of keeping peace with God, cannot but take deeply to heart, that there should be any thing in us that should divide betwixt us and the fountain of our comfort, that should stop the passage of our prayers and the current of God's favours both towards ourselves and others ; it is such an ill as is the cause of all other ill, and damps all our comforts.

(2.) *We should look out of ourselves also,* considering whether for troubles at home and abroad, God calls not to mourning or troubling of ourselves ; grief of compassion is as well required as grief of contrition.

It is a dead member that is not sensible of the state of the body. Jeremiah, for fear he should not weep enough for the distressed state of the church, desired of God, ' that his eyes might be made a fountain of tears,' Jer. ix. 1. A Christian, as he must not be proud flesh, so neither must he be dead flesh ; none more truly sensible either of sin or of misery, so far as misery carries with it any sign of God's displeasure, than a true Christian ; which issues from the life of grace, which, where it is in any measure, is lively. and therefore sensible ; for God gives motion and senses for the preservation of life. As God's bowels are tender towards us, so God's people have tender bowels towards him, his cause, his people, and his church. The fruit of this sensibleness, is earnest prayer to God. As Melancthon said well, If I cared for nothing, I would pray for nothing, *Si nil curarem nil orarem.**

Grief being thus raised, must, as we said before, be *bounded and guided.*

(1.) God hath framed the soul, and planted such affections in it, as may answer all his dealing towards his children ; that when he enlargeth himself towards them, then the soul should enlarge itself to him again ; when he opens his hand, we ought to open our hearts ; when he shews any token of displeasure, we should grieve ; when he troubles us, we should trouble and grieve ourselves. As God any way discovereth himself, so the soul should be in a suitable pliableness. Then the soul is as it should be, when it is ready to meet God at every turn, to joy when he calls for it, to mourn when he calls for that, to labour to know God's meaning in every thing.

* Melancthon. . . The following is the exact saying :—' Ad alium, qui à curis eum dehortabatur : Si *nihil,* inquit, *curarem, nihil orarem.*'—Dicta Melancthonis, in his Life in Melchior Adam's *Vitæ* Germ. Theolog. ed. Frankfort, 1653, p. 358.—G.

(2.) Again, God hath made the soul for a communion with himself, which communion is especially placed in the affections, which are the springs of all spiritual worship. Then the affections are well ordered, when we are fit to have communion with God, to love, joy, trust, to delight in him above all things. The affections are the inward movings of the soul, which then move best when they move us to God, not from him. They are the feet of the soul, whereby we walk with, and before God. When we have our affections at such command, that we can take them off from any thing in the world, at such times as we are to have more near communion with God in hearing or prayer, &c., as Abraham when he was to sacrifice left whatsoever might hinder him at the 'bottom of the mount,' Gen. xxii. 5. When we let our affections so far into the things of the world, as we cannot taken them off when we are to deal with God, it is a sign of spiritual intemperancy. It is said of the Israelites that they brought Egypt with them into the wilderness; so many bring the world into their hearts with them when they come before God.

(3.) But because our affections are never well-ordered without judgment, as being to follow, not to lead, it is an evidence that the soul is in a fit temper, when there is such a harmony in it, as that we judge of things as they are, and affect as we judge, and execute as we affect. This harmony within breeds uniformity and constancy in our resolutions, so that there is, as it were, an even thread drawn through the whole course and tenor of our lives, when we are not off and on, up and down. It argues an ill state of body when it is very hot, or very cold, or hot in one part, and cold in another; so unevenness of spirit argues a distemper. A wise man's life is of one colour, like itself. The soul bred from heaven, so far as it is heavenly-minded, desires to be, like heaven, above all storms, uniform, constant; not as things under the sun, which are always in changes, constant only in inconstancy. Affections are as it were the wind of the soul, and then the soul is carried as it should be, when it is neither so becalmed that it moves not when it should, nor yet tossed with tempests to move disorderly; when it is so well balanced that it is neither lift up nor cast down too much, but keepeth a steady course. Our affections must not rise to become unruly passions, for then as a river that overfloweth the banks, they carry much slime and soil with them. Though affections be the wind of the soul, yet unruly passions are the storms of the soul, and will overturn all, if they be not suppressed. The best, as we see in David here, if they do not steer their hearts aright, are in danger of sudden gusts. A Christian must neither be a dead sea, nor a raging sea.

(4.) Our affections are then in best temper, when they become so many graces of the Spirit, as when love is turned to a love of God, joy, to a delight in the best things, fear, to a fear of offending him more than any creature, sorrow, to a sorrow for sin, &c.

(5.) They are likewise in good temper, when they move us to all duties of love and mercy towards others; when they are not shut where they should be open, nor open where they should be shut.

Yet there is one case where exceeding affection is not over-exceeding, as in an ecstasy of zeal upon a sudden apprehension of God's dishonour, and his cause trodden under foot. It is better in this case, rather scarce to be our own men, than to be calm or quiet. It is said of Christ and David, that their hearts were eaten up with a holy zeal for God's house, Ps. lxix. 9, cxix. 139, Isa. lix. 19. In such a case, Moses, unparalleled for meekness, was turned into a holy rage, Exod. xxxii. 19. The greatness of the provocation, the excellency of the object, and the weight of the occasion, bears out the soul, not only without blame, but with great praise, in such seeming distempers. It is the glory of a Christian to be carried with full sail, and as it were with a spring-tide of affection. So long as the stream of affection runneth in the due channel, and if there be great occasions for great motions, then it is fit the affections should rise higher, as to burn with zeal, to be 'sick of love,' Cant. ii. 5., to be more vile for the Lord, as David, 2 Sam. vi. 22, to be counted out of our wits, 2 Cor. v. 13, with St Paul, to further the cause of Christ and the good of souls.

Thus we may see the life of a poor Christian in this world. 1. He is in great danger, if he be not troubled at all. 2. When he is troubled, he is in danger to be over-troubled. 3. When he hath brought his soul in tune again, he is subject to new troubles. Betwixt this ebbing and flowing there is very little quiet. Now because this cannot be done without a great measure of God's Spirit, our help is to make use of that promise of giving 'the Holy Ghost to them that ask it,' John. xi. 13. To teach us when, how long, and how much to grieve; and when, and how long, and how much to rejoice, the Spirit must teach the heart this, who as he moved upon the waters before the creation, so he must move upon the waters of our souls, for we have not the command of our own hearts. Every natural man is carried away with his flesh and humours, upon which the devil rides, and carries him whither he list; he hath no better counsellors than flesh and blood, and Satan counselling with them. But a godly man is not a slave to his carnal affections, but as David here, labours to bring into captivity the first motions of sin in his heart.

CHAPTER IX.—*Of the soul's disquiets, God's dealings, and power to contain ourselves in order.*

Obs. 1. Moreover we see, that *the soul hath disquiets proper to itself, besides those griefs of sympathy that arise from the body;* for here the soul complains of the soul itself, as when it is out of the body it hath torments and joys of its own. And if those troubles of the soul be not well cured, then by way of fellowship and redundance they will affect the outward man, and so the whole man shall be enwrapt in misery.

Obs. 2. From whence we further see, that *God, when he will humble a man, need not fetch forces from without.* If he let but our own hearts loose, we shall have trouble and work enough, though we were as holy as David; God did not only exercise him with a rebellious son out of his own loins, but with rebellious risings out of his own heart. If there were no enemy in the world, nor devil in hell, we carry that within us, that, if it be let loose, will trouble us more than all the world besides. Oh that the proud creature should exalt himself against God, and run into a voluntary course of provoking him, who can not only raise the humours of our bodies against us, but the passions of our minds also to torment us! Therefore it is the best wisdom not to provoke the great God, for 'are we stronger than he,' 1 Cor. x. 22, that can raise ourselves against ourselves? and work wonders not only in the great world, but also in the little world, our souls and bodies, when he pleases?

Obs. 3. We see likewise hence a *necessity of having something in the soul above itself.* It must be partaker of a diviner nature than itself; otherwise, when the most refined part of our souls, the very spirit of our minds, is out of frame, what shall bring it in again? Therefore we must conceive in a godly man, a double self, one which must be denied, the other which must deny; one that breeds all the disquiet, and another that stilleth what the other hath raised. The way to still the soul, as it is under our corrupt self, is not to parley with it, and divide government for peace sake, as if we should gratify the flesh in something, to redeem liberty to the spirit in other things; for we shall find the flesh will be too encroaching. We must strive against it, not with subtlety and discourse, so much as with peremptory violence silence it and vex it. An enemy that parleys will yield at length. Grace is nothing else but that blessed power, whereby as spiritual we gain upon ourselves as carnal. Holy love is that which we gain of self-love; and so joy, and delight, &c. Grace labours to win ground of the old man, until at length it be all in all; indeed we are never ourselves perfectly, till we have wholly put off ourselves; nothing should be at a greater distance to us than ourselves. This is the reason why carnal men, that have nothing above themselves but their corrupt self, sink in great troubles, having nothing within to uphold them, whereas a good man is wiser than himself, holier than himself, stronger than himself; there is something in him more than a man. There be evils that the spirit of man alone, out of the goodness of nature, cannot bear; but the spirit of man, assisted with an higher Spirit, will support and carry him through. It is a good trial of a man's condition to know what he esteems to be himself. A godly man counts the inner man, the sanctified part, to be himself, whereby he stands in relation to Christ and a better life. Another man esteems his contentment in the world, the satisfaction of his carnal desires, the respect he finds from men by reason of his parts, or something without him, that he is master of; this he counts himself, and by this he values himself, and to this he makes his best thoughts and endeavours serviceable: and of crosses in these things he is most sensible, and so sensible, that he thinks himself undone if he seeth not a present issue out of them.

That which most troubles a good man in all troubles is himself, so far as he is unsubdued; he is more disquieted with himself than with all troubles out of himself; when he hath gotten the better once of himself, whatsoever falls from without is light. Where the spirit is enlarged, it cares not much for outward bondage; where the spirit is lightsome, it cares not much for outward darkness; where the spirit is settled, it cares not much for outward changes; where the spirit is one with itself, it cannot* bear outward breaches; where the spirit is sound, it can bear outward sickness. Nothing can be very ill with us, when all is well within. This is the comfort of a holy man, that though he be troubled with himself, yet by reason of the spirit in him, which is his better self, he works out by degrees whatever is contrary, as spring-water, being clear of itself, works itself clean, though it be troubled by something cast in, as the sea will endure no poisonous thing, but casts it upon the shore. But a carnal man is like a spring corrupted, that cannot work itself clear, because it is wholly tainted; his eye and light is darkness, and therefore no wonder if he seeth nothing. Sin lieth upon his understanding, and hinders the knowledge of itself; it lies close upon the will, and hinders the striving against itself.

True self that is worth the owning, is when a man is taken into a higher condition, and made one with Christ, and esteems neither of himself nor others, as happy for anything according to the flesh. 1. He is under the law and government of the Spirit, and so far as he is himself, works accord-

* Qu. 'can?'—ED.

ing to that principle. 2. He labours more and more to be transformed into the likeness of Christ, in whom he esteemeth that he hath his best being. 3. He esteems of all things that befall him, to be good or ill, as they further or hinder his best condition. If all be well for that, he counts himself well, whatsoever else befalls him.

Another man, when he doth anything that is good, acts not his own part; but a godly man, when he doth good, is in his proper element; what another man doth for by-ends and reasons, that he doth from a new nature, which, if there were no law to compel, yet would move him to that which is pleasing to Christ. If he be drawn aside by passion or temptation, that he judgeth not to be himself, but taketh a holy revenge on himself for it, as being redeemed and taken out from himself; he thinks himself no debtor, nor to owe any service to his corrupt self. That which he plots and projects and works for is, that Christ may rule everywhere, and especially in himself, for he is not his own but Christ's, and therefore desires to be more and more emptied of himself, that Christ might be all in all in him.

Thus we see what great use there is of dealing with ourselves, for the better composing and settling of our souls. Which, though it be a course without glory and ostentation in the world, as causing a man to retire inwardly into his own breast, having no other witness but God and himself; and though it be likewise irksome to the flesh, as calling the soul home to itself, being desirous naturally to wander abroad and be a stranger at home; yet it is a course both good in itself, and makes the soul good.

For by this means the judgment is exercised and rectified, the will and affections ordered, the whole man put into an holy frame fit for every good action. By this the tree is made good, and the fruit cannot but be answerable; by this the soul itself is set in tune, whence there is a pleasant harmony in our whole conversation. Without this, we may do that which is outwardly good to others, but we can never be good ourselves. The first justice begins within, when there is a due subjection of all the powers of the soul to the spirit, as sanctified and guided by God's Spirit; when justice and order is first established in the soul, it will appear from thence in all our dealings. He that is at peace in himself, will be peaceable to others, peaceable in his family, peaceable in the church, peaceable in the state. The soul of a wicked man is in perpetual sedition; being always troubled in itself, it is no wonder if it be troublesome to others. Unity in ourselves is before union with others.

To conclude this first part, concerning intercourse with ourselves. As we desire to enjoy ourselves, and to live the life of men and of Christians, which is, to understand our ways; as we desire to live comfortably, and not to be accessory of yielding to that sorrow which causeth death; as we desire to answer God and ourselves, when we are to give an account of the inward tumults of our souls; as we desire to be vessels prepared for every good work, and to have strength to undergo any cross; as we desire to have healthy souls, and to keep a sabbath within ourselves; as we desire not only to do good, but to be good in ourselves: so let us labour to quiet our souls, and often ask a reason of ourselves, why we should not be quiet?

CHAPTER X.—*Means not to be overcharged with sorrow.*

To help us further herein, besides that which hath been formerly spoken, 1. *We must take heed of building an ungrounded confidence of happiness for time to come*, which makes us when changes come, 1, Unacquainted with them; 2, Takes away expectation of them; 3, And preparation for them. When any thing is strange and sudden, and lights upon us unfurnished and unfenced, it must needs put our spirits out of frame. It is good therefore to make all kind of troubles familiar to us, in our thoughts at least, and this will break the force of them. It is good to fence our souls beforehand against all assaults, as men use to keep out the sea, by raising banks; and if a breach be made, to repair it presently.

We had need to maintain a strong garrison of holy reasons against the assaults of strong passions; we may hope for the best, but fear the worst, and prepare to bear whatsoever. We say that a set diet is dangerous, because variety of occasions will force us upon breaking of it; so in this world of changes we cannot resolve upon any certain condition of life, for upon alteration the mind is out of frame. We cannot say this or that trouble shall not befall; yet we may, by help of the Spirit, say, nothing that doth befall shall make me do that which is unworthy of a Christian.

That which others make easy by suffering, that a wise man maketh easy by thinking of beforehand. *Quæ alii diu patiendo levia faciunt, sapiens levia facit diu cogitando.* If we expect the worst, when it comes, it is no more than we thought of; if better befalls us, then it is the sweeter to us, the less we expected it. Our Saviour foretells the worst, ' In the world you shall have tribulation,' John xvi. 33; therefore look for it; but then He will not leave us. Satan deludes with fair promises; but when the contrary falls out, he leaves his followers in their distresses. We desire peace and rest, but we seek it not in its own place; ' there is a rest for God's people,' Heb. iv. 9, but that is not here, nor yet; but it remains for them; ' they rest from their labours,' Rev. xiv. 13, but that is after they ' are dead in the Lord.' There is no sound rest till then. Yet this caution must be remembered, that we shape not in our fancies such troubles as are never likely to fall out. It comes either from weakness or guiltiness, to fear shadows. We shall not need to make crosses; they will, as we say of foul weather, come before they be sent for. How many evils do people fear, from which they have no further hurt than what is bred only by their causeless fears! Nor yet, if they be probable, must we think of them so as to be altogether so affected, as if undoubtedly they would come, for so we give certain strength to an uncertain cross, and usurp upon God, by anticipating that which may never come to pass. It was rashness in David to say, ' I shall one day perish by the hand of Saul,' 1 Sam. xxvii. 1.

If they be such troubles as will certainly come to pass, as parting with friends and contentments, at least, by death; then, 1. Think of them so as not to be much dismayed, but furnish thy heart with strength beforehand, that they may fall the lighter. 2. Think of them so as not to give up the bucklers to passion, and lie open as a fair mark for any uncomfortable accident to strike to the heart; nor yet so think of them as to despise them, but to consider of God's meaning in them, and how to take good by them. 3. Think of the things we enjoy, so as to moderate our enjoying of them, by considering there must be a parting, and therefore how we shall be able to bear it when it comes.

2. If we desire not to be overcharged with sorrow when that which we fear is fallen upon us, we must then beforehand look *that our love to any thing in this world shoot not so far as that, when the time of severing cometh, we part with so much of our hearts by that rent.* Those that love too much will always grieve too much. It is the greatness of our affections which causeth

the sharpness of our afflictions. He that cannot abound without pride and high-mindedness, will not want without too much dejectedness. Love is planted for such things as can return love, and make us better by loving them; wherein we shall satisfy our love to the full. It is pity so sweet an affection should be lost. So sorrow is for sin, and for other things, as they make sin the more bitter to us. The life of a Christian should be a meditation how to unloose his affections from inferior things. He will easily die that is dead before in affection. But this will never be, unless the soul seeth something better than all things in the world, upon which it may bestow itself. In that measure our affections die in their excessive motion to things below, as they are taken up with the love and admiration of the best things. He that is much in heaven in his thoughts is free from being tossed with tempests here below. The top of those mountains that are above the middle region are so quiet as that the lightest things, as ashes, lie still, and are not moved. The way to mortify earthly members, that bestir themselves in us, is to mind things above, Col. iii. 1, 5. The more the ways of wisdom lead us on high, the more we avoid the snares below.

In the uncertainty of all events here, labour to frame that contentment in and from our own selves which the things themselves will not yield; frame peace by freeing our hearts from too much fear, and riches by freeing our hearts from covetous desires. Frame a sufficiency out of contentedness. If the soul itself be out of tune, outward things will do no more good than a fair shoe to a gouty foot.

And seek not ourselves abroad out of ourselves in the conceits of other men. A man shall never live quietly that hath not learned to be set lightby of others. He that is little in his own eyes will not be troubled to be little in the eyes of others. Men that set too high a price upon themselves, when others will not come to their price, are discontent. Those whose condition is above their worth, and their pride above their condition, shall never want sorrow; yet we must maintain our authority, and the image of God in our places, for that is God's and not ours; and we ought so to carry ourselves as we approve ourselves to their consciences, though we have not their good words. 'Let none despise thy youth,' saith St Paul to Timothy, 1 Tim. iv. 12—that is, walk so before them as they shall have no cause. It is not in our own power what other men think or speak, but it is in our power, by God's grace, to live so that none can think ill of us, but by slandering, and none believe ill but by too much credulity.

3. When anything seizeth upon us, we must take heed we *mingle not our own passions with it;* we must neither bring sin to, nor mingle sin with, the suffering; for that will trouble the spirit more than the trouble itself. We are more to deal with our own hearts than with the trouble itself. We are not hurt till our souls be hurt. God will not have it in the power of any creature to hurt our souls, but by our own treason against ourselves.

Therefore we should have our hearts in continual jealousy, for they are ready to deceive the best. In sudden encounters some sin doth many times discover itself, the seed whereof lieth hid in our natures, which we think ourselves very free from. Who would have thought the seeds of murmuring had lurked in the meek nature of Moses? that the seeds of murder had lurked in the pitiful heart of David? 2 Sam. xii. 9, that the seeds of denial of Christ, Matt. xxvi. 72, had lien hid in the zealous affection of Peter towards Christ? If passions break out from us, which we are not naturally inclined unto, and over which by grace we have got a great conquest, how watchful need we be over ourselves in those things, which, by temper, custom, and company we are carried unto! and what cause have we to fear continually that we are worse than we take ourselves to be!

There are many unruly passions lie hid in us, until they be drawn out by something that meeteth with them ; either—

(1.) *By way of opposition,* as when the truth of God spiritually unfolded meets with some beloved corruption, it swelleth bigger. The force of gunpowder is not known until some spark light on it; and oftentimes the stillest natures, if crossed, discover the deepest corruptions. Sometimes it is drawn out by dealing with the opposite spirits of other men. Oftentimes retired men know not what lies hid in themselves.

(2.) *Sometimes by crosses,* as many people, whilst the freshness and vigour of their spirits lasteth, and while the flower of age, and a full supply of all things continueth, seem to be of a pleasing and calm disposition; but afterwards, when changes come, like Job's wife, they are discovered, Job ii. 9. Then that which in nature is unsubdued, openly appears.

(3.) *Temptations likewise have a searching power to bring that to light in us which was hidden before.* Satan hath been a winnower and a sifter of old, Luke xxii. 3. He thought if Job had been but touched in his body, he would have cursed God to his face, Job i.

Some men, out of policy, conceal their passion until they see some advantage to let it out, as Esau smothered his hatred until his father's death. *Aperta perdunt odia vindictæ locum.* When the restraint is taken away, men, as we say, shew themselves in their pure naturals. Unloose a tiger or a lion, and you know what he is. *Solve leonem et senties.*

(4.) Further, *let us see more every day into the state of our own souls.* What a shame is it that so nimble and swift a spirit as the soul is, that can mount up to heaven, and from thence come down into the earth in an instant, should, whilst it looks over all other things, overlook itself! that it should be skilful in the story almost of all times and places, and yet ignorant of the story of itself! that we should know what is done in the court and country, and beyond the seas, and be ignorant of what is done at home in our own hearts! that we should live known to others, and yet die unknown to ourselves! that we should be able to give account of anything better than of ourselves to ourselves! This is the cause why we stand in our own light, why we think better of ourselves than others, and better than is cause ; this is that which hindereth all reformation, for how can we reform that which we are not willing to see, and so we lose one of the surest evidences of our sincerity, which is, a willingness to search into our hearts, and to be searched by others. A sincere heart will offer itself to trial.

And therefore let us sift our actions, and our passions, and see what is flesh in them, and what is spirit, and so separate the precious from the vile. It is good likewise to consider what sin we were guilty of before, which moved God to give us up to excess in any passion, and wherein we have grieved his Spirit. Passion will be more moderate when thus it knows it must come to the trial and censure. This course will either make us weary of passion, or else passion will make us weary of this strict course. We shall find it the safest way to give our hearts no rest till we have wrought on them to purpose, and gotten the mastery over them.

When the soul is inured to this dealing with itself, it will learn the skill to command, and passions will be soon commanded, as being inured to be examined and checked ; as we see dogs, and such like domestical creatures, that will not regard a stranger, yet will be quieted in brawls presently by the voice of their master, to which they are accustomed. This fits us for service. Unbroken spirits are like unbroken horses, unfit for any use until they be thoroughly subdued.

(5.) And it were best to prevent, as much as in us lieth, *the very first risings*, before the soul be overcast. Passions are but little motions at the first, but grow as rivers do, greater and greater, the farther they are carried from their spring. The first risings are the more to be looked unto, because there is most danger in them, and we have least care over them. Sin, like rust, or a canker, will by little and little eat out all the graces of the soul. There is no staying when we are once down the hill, till we come to the bottom. No sin but is easier kept out than driven out. If we cannot prevent wicked thoughts, yet we may deny them lodging in our hearts. It is our giving willing entertainment to sinful motions that increaseth guilt, and hindereth our peace. It is that which moveth God to give us up to a further degree of evil affections. Therefore what we are afraid to do before men, we should be afraid to think before God. It would much further our peace to keep our judgments clear, as being the eye of the soul, whereby we may discern in every action and passion what is good and what is evil; as likewise to preserve tenderness of heart, that may check us at the first, and not brook the least evil being discovered. When the heart begins once to be kindled, it is easy to smother the smoke of passion, which otherwise will fume up into the head, and gather into so thick a cloud as we shall lose the sight of ourselves, and what is best to be done. And therefore David here labours to take up his heart at the first; his care was to crush the very first insurrections of his soul, before they came to break forth into open rebellion. Storms we know rise out of little gusts. Little risings neglected cover the soul before we are aware. If we would check these risings, and stifle them in their birth, they would not break out afterwards to the reproach of religion, to the scandal of the weak, to the offence of the strong, to the grief of God's Spirit in us, to the disturbance of our own spirits in doing good, and to the disheartening of us in troubling of our inward peace, and thereby weakening our assurance. Therefore let us stop beginnings as much as may be; and so soon as they begin to rise, let us begin to examine what raised them, and whither they are about to carry us, Ps. iv. 4. The way to be still is to examine ourselves first, and then censure what stands not with reason. As David doth, when he had given way to unbefitting thoughts of God's providence, ' So foolish,' saith he, ' was I, and as a beast before thee,' Ps. lxxiii. 22.

Especially then, look to these sinful stirrings when thou art to deal with God. I am to have communion with a God of peace, what then do turbulent thoughts and affections in my heart? I am to deal with a patient God, why should I cherish revengeful thoughts? Abraham drove away the birds from the sacrifice, Gen. xv. 11. Troublesome thoughts, like birds, will come before they be sent for, but they should find entertainment accordingly.

(6.) In all our grievance let us look to something that may *comfort us, as well as discourage;* look to that we enjoy, as well as that we want. As in prosperity God mingles some crosses to diet us, so in all crosses there is something to comfort us. As there is a vanity lies hid in the best worldly good, so there is a blessing lies hid in the worst worldly evil. God usually maketh up that with some advantage in another kind, wherein we are inferior to others. Others are in greater place, so they are in greater danger. Others be richer, so their cares and snares be greater: the poor in the world may be richer in faith than they, James ii. 5. The soul can better digest and master a low estate than a prosperous, and under some abasement, it is in a less distance from God. Others are not so afflicted as we, then they have less experience of God's gracious power than we. Others may have more healthy bodies, but souls less weaned from the world. We would not change conditions with them, so as to have their spirits with their condition. For one half of our lives, the meanest are as happy and free from cares, as the greatest monarch, that is, while both sleep; and usually the sleep of the one is sweeter than the sleep of the other. What is all that the earth can afford us, if God deny health? and this a man in the meanest condition may enjoy. That wherein one man differs from another, is but title, and but for a little time; death levelleth all.

There is scarce any man, but the good he receives from God is more than the ill he feels, if our unthankful hearts would suffer us to think so. Is not our health more than our sickness? do we not enjoy more than we want, I mean, of the things that are necessary? are not our good days more than our evil? but we would go to heaven upon roses, and usually one cross is more taken to heart, than a hundred blessings. So unkindly we deal with God. Is God indebted to us? doth he owe us any thing? those that deserve nothing, should be content with any thing.

We should look to others as good as ourselves, as well as to ourselves, and then we shall see it is not our own case only. Who are we that we should look for an exempted condition from those troubles which God's dearest children are addicted unto?

Thus when we are surprised contrary to our looking for and liking, we should study rather how to exercise some grace, than give way to any passion. Think, now is a time to exercise our patience, our wisdom, and other graces. By this means we shall turn that to our greatest advantage, which Satan intendeth greatest hurt to us by. Thus we shall not only master every condition, but make it serviceable to our good. If nature teach bees, not only to gather honey out of sweet flowers, but out of bitter, shall not grace teach us to draw even out of the bitterest condition something to better our souls? we learn to tame all creatures, even the wildest, that we may bring them to our use: and why should we give way to our own unruly passions?

(7.) It were good to have in our eye *the beauty of a well-ordered soul*, and we should think that nothing in this world is of sufficient worth to put us out of frame. The sanctified soul should be like the sun in this, which though it worketh upon all these inferior bodies, and cherisheth them by light and influence, yet is not moved nor wrought upon by them again, but keepeth its own lustre and distance; so our spirits, being of a heavenly breed, should rule other things beneath them, and not be ruled by them. It is a holy state of soul to be under the power of nothing beneath itself. Are we stirred? then consider, is this matter worth the loss of my quiet? What we esteem, that we love; what we love, we labour for; and therefore let us esteem highly of a clear, calm temper, whereby we both enjoy our God and ourselves, and know how to rank all things else. It is against nature for inferior things to rule that which the wise Disposer of all things hath set above them. We owe the flesh neither suit nor service; we are no debtors to it.

The more we set before the soul that quiet estate in heaven which the souls of perfect men now enjoy, and itself ere long shall enjoy there, the more it will be in love with it, and endeavour to attain unto it. And because the soul never worketh better, than when it is raised up by some strong and sweet affection—*anima nunquam melius agit, quam ex imperio alicujus insignis affectus*—let us look upon our nature, as it is in Christ, in whom it is pure, sweet, calm, meek, every way lovely. This sight is a changing sight; love is an affection of imitation; we affect a likeness to him we love. Let us 'learn of Christ to be humble and meek,' and then we 'shall find rest to our souls,' Mat. xi. 29. The setting of an excellent idea and platform before us, will raise and draw up our souls higher, and make us sensible of the least moving of spirit, that shall be contrary to that, the attainment whereof we have in our desires. He will hardly attain to mean things, that sets not before him higher perfection. Naturally we love to see symmetry and proportion, even in a dead picture, and are much taken with some curious piece. But why should we not rather labour to keep the affections of the soul in due proportion? seeing a meek and well ordered soul is not only lovely in the sight of men and angels, but is much set by, by the great God himself. But now the greatest care of those that set highest price upon themselves is, how to compose their outward carriage in some graceful manner, never studying how to compose their spirits; and rather how to cover the deformity of their passions than to cure them. Whence it is that the foulest inward vices are covered with the fairest vizards, and to make this the worse, all this is counted the best breeding.

The Hebrews placed all their happiness in peace, and when they would comprise much in one word, they would wish peace. This was that the angels brought news of from heaven, at the birth of Christ, Luke ii. 14. Now peace riseth out of quietness and order, and God that is 'the God of peace, is the God of order' first, 1 Cor. xiv. 33. What is health, but when all the members are in their due positure,* and all the humours in a settled quiet? Whence ariseth the beauty of the world, but from that comely order wherein every creature is placed; the more glorious and excellent creatures above, and the less below? So it is in the soul; the best constitution of it is when by the Spirit of God it is so ordered, as that all be in subjection to the law of the mind. What a sight were it for the feet to be where the head is, and the earth to be where the heaven is, to see all turned upside down? And to a spiritual eye it seems as great a deformity, to see the soul to be under the rule of sinful passions.

Comeliness riseth out of the fit proportion of divers members to make up one body, when every member hath a beauty in itself, and is likewise well suited to other parts. A fair face and a crooked body, comely upper parts, and the lower parts uncomely, suit not well; because comeliness stands in oneness, in a fit agreement of many parts to one. When there is the head of a man, and the body of a beast, it is a monster in nature; and is it not as monstrous for to have an understanding head, and a fierce untamed heart? It cannot but raise up a holy indignation in us against these risings, when we consider how unbeseeming they are. What do these base passions in a heart dedicated to God, and given up to the government of his Spirit? what an indignity is it for princes to go afoot, and servants on horseback? for those to rule, whose place is to be ruled? as being good attendants, but bad guides. It was Ham's curse to be a 'servant of servants,' Gen. ix. 25.

(8.) This must be strengthened with a strong *self-denial*, without which there can be no good done in religion.

There be two things that most trouble us in the way to heaven, corruption within us, and the cross without us: that which is within us must be denied, that that which is without us may be endured. Otherwise we

* That is, 'position.'—Ed.

cannot follow him by whom we look to be saved. The gate, the entrance of religion, is narrow; we must strip ourselves of ourselves before we can enter; if we bring any ruling lust to religion, it will prove a bitter root of some gross sin, or of apostasy and final desperation.

Those that sought the praise of men more than the praise of God, John xii. 43, could not believe, because that lust of ambition would, when it should be crossed, draw them away. The young man thought it better for Christ to lose a disciple than that he should lose his possession, and therefore went away as he came, Mat. xix. 22. The 'third ground,' Mat. xiii. 25, came to nothing; because the plough had not gone deep enough to break up the roots, whereby their hearts were fastened to earthly contentments. This self-denial we must carry with us through all the parts of religion, both in our active and passive obedience; for in obedience there must be a subjection to a superior; but corrupt self neither is subject, nor can be, Rom. viii. 7. It will have an oar in everything, and maketh everything, yea, religion, serviceable to itself. It is the idol of the world, or rather the god that is set highest of all in the soul; and so God himself is made but an idol. It is hard to deny a friend who is another self, harder to deny a wife that lieth in the bosom, but most hard to deny ourselves. Nothing so near us as ourselves to ourselves, and yet nothing so far off. Nothing so dear, and yet nothing so malicious and troublesome. Hypocrites would part with the fruit of their body, Mic. vi. 7, sooner than the sin of their souls.

CHAPTER XI.—*Signs of victory over ourselves, and of a subdued spirit.*

Quest. But how shall we know whether we have by grace got the victory over ourselves or not?

Ans. I answer, 1. *If in good actions we stand not so much upon the credit of the action as upon the good that is done.* What we do as unto God, we look for acceptance from God. It was Jonah his fault to stand more upon his own reputation than the glory of God's mercy. It is a prevailing sign when, though there be no outward encouragements, nay, though there be discouragements, yet we can rest in the comfort of a good intention. For usually inward comfort is a note of inward sincerity. Jehu must be seen, or else all is lost, 2 Kings x. 16.

2. It is a good evidence of some prevailing when, *upon religious grounds, we can cross ourselves in those things unto which our hearts stand most affected.* This sheweth we reserve God his own place in our hearts.

3. When, being privy to our own inclination and temper, we have gotten such *a supply of Spirit as that the grace which is contrary to our temper appears in us.* As oft we see none more patient than those that are naturally inclined to intemperancy of passion, because natural proneness makes them jealous over themselves. Some, out of fear of being overmuch moved, are not moved so much as they should be. This jealousy stirreth us up to a careful use of all helps. Where grace is helped by nature, there a little grace will go far; but where there is much untowardness of nature, there much grace is not so well discerned. Sour wines need much sweetening. And that is most spiritual which hath least help from nature, and is won by prayer and pains.

4. When we are not *partial when the things concern ourselves.* David could allow himself another man's wife, and yet judgeth another man

worthy of death for taking away a poor man's lamb, 2 Sam. xii. 4. Men usually favour themselves too much when they are chancellors in their own cause, and measure all things by their private interest. He hath taken a good degree in Christ's school that hath learned to forget himself here.

5. It is a good sign when, upon discovery of self-seeking, *we can gain upon our corruption;* and are willing to search and to be searched, what our inclination is, and where it faileth. That which we favour we are tender of, it must not be touched. A good heart, when any corruption is discovered by a searching ministry, is affected as if it had found out a deadly enemy. Touchiness and passion argues guilt.

6. This is a sign of a man's victory over himself, when he loves health and peace of body and mind, with a supply of all needful things, chiefly for this end, *that he may with more freedom of spirit serve God in doing good to others.* So soon as grace entereth into the heart, it frameth the heart to be in some measure public; and thinks it hath not its end in the bare enjoying of anything, until it can improve what it hath for a further end. Thus to seek ourselves is to deny ourselves, and thus to deny ourselves is truly to seek ourselves. It is no self-seeking when we care for no more than that, without which we cannot comfortably serve God. When the soul can say unto God, Lord, as thou wouldst have me serve thee in my place, so grant me such a measure of health and strength, wherein I may serve thee.

Object. But what if God thinks it good that I shall serve him in weakness, and in want and suffering?

Ans. Then it is a comfortable sign of gaining over our own wills, when we can yield ourselves to be disposed of by God, as knowing best what is good for us. There is no condition but therein we may exercise some grace, and honour God in some measure. Yet because some enlargement of condition is ordinarily that estate wherein we are best able to do good in, we may in the use of means desire it, and upon that resign up ourselves wholly unto God, and make his will our will, without exception or reservation, and care for nothing more than we can have with his leave and love. This Job had exercised his heart unto; whereupon in that great change of condition he sinned not, Job ii. 10; that is, fell not into the sins incident to that dejected and miserable state; into sins of rebellion and discontent. He carried his crosses comely, with that staidness and resignedness which became a holy man.

7. It is further a clear evidence of a spirit subdued, when *we will discover the truth of our affection towards God and his people, though with censure of others.* David was content to endure the censure of neglecting the state and majesty of a king, out of joy for settling the ark, 2 Sam. vi. 22. Nehemiah could not dissemble his grief for the ruins of the church, though in the king's presence, Neh. ii. 3. It is a comfortable sign of the wasting of self-love, when we can be at a point what becomes of ourselves, so it go well with the cause of God and the church.

Now the way to prevail still more over ourselves, as when we are to do or suffer anything, or withstand any person in a good cause, &c., is, not to think that we are to deal with men, yea, or with devils, so much as with ourselves. The saints resisted their enemies to death, by resisting their own corruptions first. If we once get the victory over ourselves, all other things are conquered to our ease. All the hurt Satan and the world do us, is by correspondency with ourselves. All things are so far under us, as we are above ourselves. *Te vince, et mundus tibi victus est,* &c.

For the further subduing of ourselves, it is good to follow sin to the first hold and castle, which is corrupt nature; the streams will lead us to the spring head. Indeed, the most apparent discovery of sin is in the outward carriage; we see it in the fruit before in the root, as we see grace in the expression before in the affection. But yet we shall never hate sin thoroughly until we consider it in the poisoned root from whence it ariseth.

That which least troubles a natural man doth most of all trouble a true Christian. A natural man is sometimes troubled with the fruit of his corruption, and the consequents of guilt and punishment that attend it; but a true-hearted Christian with corruption itself. This drives him to complain, with St Paul, 'O wretched man that I am, who shall deliver me,' not from the members only, but 'from this body of death?' Rom. vii. 24, which is as noisome to my soul as a dead carrion is to my senses, which, together with the members, is marvellously nimble and active, and hath no days, nor hours, or minutes of rest; always laying about it to enlarge itself, and like spring water, which, the more it issueth out, the more it may.

It is a good way, upon any particular breach of our inward peace, presently to have recourse to that which breeds and foments all our disquiet. Lord! what do I complain of this my unruly passion? I carry a nature about me subject to break out continually upon any occasion. Lord! strike at the root, and dry up the fountain in me. Thus David doth arise from the guilt of those two foul sins of murder and adultery, Ps. li. 5, to the sin of his nature, the root itself; as if he should say, Lord, it is not these actual sins that defile me only, but if I look back to my first conception, I was tainted in the spring of my nature.

This is that which put David's soul so much out of frame; for from whence was this contradiction? and whence was this contradiction so unwearied in making head again and again against the checks of the Spirit in him? Whence was it that corruption would not be said nay? Whence were these sudden and unlooked for objections of the flesh? but from the remainder of old Adam in him, which, like a Michal within us, is either scoffing at the ways of God, or, as a Job's wife, fretting and thwarting the motions of God's Spirit in us; which prevails the more because it is homebred in us, whereas holy motions are strangers to most of our souls. Corruption is loath that a new comer-in should take so much upon him as to control, as the Sodomites thought much that Lot, being a stranger, should intermeddle amongst them, Gen. xix. 9. If God once leave us, as he did Hezekiah, to try what is in us, what should we find but darkness, rebellion, unruliness, doubtings, &c., in the best of us. This flesh of ours hath principles against all God's principles, and laws against all God's laws, and reasons against all God's reasons. Oh, if we could but one whole hour seriously think of the impure issue of our hearts, it would bring us down upon our knees in humiliation before God! But we can never whilst we live, so thoroughly as we should, see into the depth of our deceitful hearts, nor yet be humbled enough for what we see; for though we speak of it and confess it, yet we are not so sharpened against this corrupt flesh of ours as we should. How should it humble us that the seeds of the vilest sin, even of the sin against the Holy Ghost, is in us? And no thank to us that they break not out. It should humble us to hear of any great enormous sin in another man, considering what our own nature would proceed unto if it were not restrained (c). We may see our own nature in them as face answering face, Prov. xxvii. 19. If God should take his Spirit from us, there is enough in us to defile a whole world; and although we be ingrafted into Christ, yet we carry about us a relish of the old stock still. David was a man of a good natural constitution, and, for grace, a man after God's own heart, and had got the better of himself in a great measure, and had learned to overcome himself in matter of revenge, as in Saul's case, 1 Sam. xxiv. 6; yet now we see the vessel is shaken a little, and the dregs appear that were in the bottom before. Alas! we know not our own hearts till we plough with God's heifer, till his Spirit bringeth a light into our souls. It is good to consider how this impure spring breaks out diversely in the diverse conditions we are in. There is no estate of life, nor no action we undertake, wherein it will not put forth itself to defile us; it is so full of poison that it taints whatsoever we do, both our natures, conditions, and actions. In a prosperous condition, like David, we think we shall never be moved, Ps. xxx. 6. Under the cross the soul is troubled, and drawn to murmur, and to be sullen, and sink down in discouragement, to be in a heat almost to blasphemy, to be weary of our callings, and to quarrel with everything in our way. See the folly and fury of most men in this, for us silly worms to contradict the great God. And to whose peril is it? Is it not our own? Let us gather ourselves with all our wit and strength together; alas! what can we do but provoke him, and get more stripes? We may be sure he will deal with us as we deal with our children. If they be froward and unquiet for lesser matters, we will make them cry and be sullen for something. Refractory, stubborn horses are the more spurred, and yet shake not off the rider.

CHAPTER XII.—*Of original righteousness, natural corruption, Satan's joining with it, and our duty thereupon.*

Object. § I. But here mark a plot of spiritual treason. Satan, joining with our corruption, setteth the wit on work to persuade the soul that this inward rebellion is not so bad, because it is natural to us, as a condition of nature rising out of the first principles in our creation, and was curbed in by the bridle of original righteousness, which they would have accessary and supernatural, and therefore allege that concupiscence is less odious and more excusable in us, and so no great danger in yielding and betraying our souls unto it, and by that means persuading us that that which is our deadliest enemy hath no harm in it, nor meaneth any to us.*

Ans. This rebellion of lusts against the understanding is not natural, as our nature came out of God's hands at the first, Gen. i. 27; for this, being evil and the cause of evil, could not come from God, who is good and the cause of all good, and nothing but good, who, upon the creation of all things, pronounced them good, and, after the creation of man, pronounced of all things that they were very good, ver. 31. Now, that which is ill and very ill cannot be seated at the same time in that which is good and very good. God created man at the first right; he of himself 'sought out many inventions,' Eccles. vii. 29. As God beautified the heaven with stars, and decked the earth with variety of plants, and herbs, and flowers, so he adorned man, his prime creature here below, with all those endowments that were fit for a happy condition; and original righteousness was fit and due

* Most of the most dangerous opinions of popery, as justification by works, state of perfection, merit, satisfaction, supererogation, &c., spring from hence, that they have slight conceits of concupiscence as a condition of nature. Yet some of them, as Michael Bayns, professor at Louvain, &c., are sound in the point.

to an original and happy condition. Therefore, as the angels were created with all angelical perfections, and as our bodies were created in an absolute temper of all the humours, so the soul was created in that sweet harmony wherein there was no discord, as an instrument in tune, fit to be moved to any duty; as a clean, neat glass, the soul represented God's image and holiness.

§ II. Therefore it is so far, that concupiscence should be natural, that the contrary to it, namely, righteousness, wherein Adam was created, was natural to him; though it were planted in man's nature by God, and so in regard of the cause of it, was supernatural; yet because it was agreeable to that happy condition, without which he could not subsist, in that respect it was natural, and should have been derived, if he had stood, together with his nature, to his posterity. As heat in the air, though it hath its first impression from the heat of the sun, yet is natural, because it agreeth to the nature of that element; and though man be compounded of a spiritual and earthly substance, yet it is natural that the baser earthly part should be subject to the superior, because where there is different degrees of worthiness, it is fit there should be a subordination of the meaner to that which is in order higher. The body naturally desires food and bodily contentments, yet in a man endued with reason, this desire is governed so as it becomes not inordinate. A beast sins not in its appetite, because it hath no power above to order it. A man that lives in a solitary place, far remote from company, may take his liberty to live as it pleaseth him; but if he comes to live under the government of some well-ordered city, then he is bound to submit to the laws and customs of that city, under penalty upon any breach of order; so the risings of the soul, howsoever in other creatures they are not blameable, having no commander in themselves, above them, yet in man they are to be ordered by reason and judgment.

Therefore it cannot be, that concupiscence should be natural, in regard of the state of creation. It was Adam's sin; which had many sins in the womb of it, that brought this disorder upon the soul. Adam's person first corrupted our nature, and nature being corrupted, corrupts our persons, and our persons being corrupted, increase the corruption of our nature, by custom of sinning, which is another nature in us. As a stream, the farther it runs from the spring head, the more it enlargeth its channel, by the running of lesser rivers into it, until it emptieth itself into the sea; so corruption, till it be overpowered by grace, swelleth bigger and bigger, so that though this disorder was not natural, in regard of the first creation, yet since the fall it has become natural, even as we call that which is common to the whole kind, and propagated from parents to their children, to be natural; so that it is both natural and against nature, natural now, but against nature in its first perfection.

And because corruption is natural to us, therefore, 1, We delight in it; whence it comes to pass, that our souls are carried along in an easy current, to the committing of any sin without opposition. 2. Because it is natural, therefore it is unwearied and restless, as light bodies are not wearied in their motion upwards, nor heavy bodies in their motion downwards, nor a stream in its running to the sea, because it is natural: hence it is that the 'old man,' Eph. iv. 22, is never tired in the 'works of the flesh,' Gal. v. 19, nor never drawn dry. When men cannot act sin, yet they will love sin, and act it over again by pleasing thoughts of it, and by sinful speculations suck out the delight of sin; and are grieved, not for their sin, but because they want strength and opportunity to commit it; if sin would not leave them, they would never leave sin. This corruption of our nature is not wrought in us by reason and persuasions, for then it might be satisfied with reasons, but it is in us by way of a natural inclination, as iron is carried to the loadstone; and till our natures be altered, no reason will long prevail, but our sinful disposition, as a stream stopped for a little while, will break out with greater violence. 8. Being natural, it needs no help, as the earth needs no tillage to bring forth weeds. When our corrupt nature is carried contrary to that which is good, it is carried of itself, as when Satan lies or murders, it comes from his own cursed nature; and though Satan joineth with our corrupt nature, yet the proneness to sin, and the consent unto it, is of ourselves.

Quest. § III. But how shall we know that Satan joins with our nature, in those actions unto which nature itself is prone?

Ans. Then Satan adds his help, when our nature is carried more eagerly than ordinary to sin; as when a stream runs violently, we may know that there is not only the tide, but the wind that carrieth it.

So in sudden and violent rebellions, it is Satan that pusheth on nature left to itself of God. A stone falls downwards by its own weight, but if it falls very swiftly, we know it is thrown down by an outward mover. Though there were no devil, yet our corrupt nature would act Satan's part against itself; it would have a supply of wickedness, as a serpent doth poison, from itself, it hath a spring to feed it. *Nemo se palpet de suo, Satan est, &c.* (Augustine).

But that man, whilst he lives here, is not altogether excluded from hope of happiness, and hath a nature not so large and capable of sin as Satan's; whereupon he is not so obstinate in hating God and working mischief as he, &c. Otherwise there is, for kind, the same cursed disposition, and malice of nature against true goodness in man, which is in the devils and damned spirits themselves.

It is no mitigation of sin, to plead it is natural; for natural diseases, as leprosies, that are derived from parents, are most dangerous, and least curable. Neither is this any excuse, for because as it is natural, so it is voluntary, not only in Adam, in whose loins we were, and therefore sinned, but likewise in regard of ourselves, who are so far from stopping the course of sin either in ourselves or others, that we feed and strengthen it, or at least give more way to it, and provide less against it than we should, until we come under the government of grace; and by that means we justify Adam's sin, and that corrupt estate that followeth upon it, and shew, that if we had been in Adam's condition ourselves, we would have made that ill choice which he made. And though this corruption of our nature be necessary to us, yet it is no violent necessity from an outward cause, but a necessity that we willingly pull upon ourselves, and therefore ought the more to humble us; for the more necessarily we sin, the more voluntarily, and the more voluntarily, the more necessarily, the will putting itself voluntarily into these fetters of sin.* Necessity is no plea, when the will is the immediate cause of any action. *Quicquid sibi imperavit animus, obtinuit* (Seneca). Men's hearts tell them they might rule their desires if they would; for tell a man of any dish which he liketh, that there is poison in it, and he will not meddle with it: so tell him that death is in that sin which he is about to commit, and he will abstain, if

---

* 'Fetters of sin.' Margin-note in C—Suspirabam ligatus, non ferro aliquo, sed mea ferrea voluntate, vellem meum tenebat inimicus, et inde mihi catenam fecerit. Augustine, Conf.

he believe it to be so ; if he believe it not, it is his voluntary unbelief and atheism.

If the will would use that sovereignty it should, and could, at the first, we should be altogether freed from this necessity. Men are not damned because they cannot do better, but because they will do no better ; if there were no will, there would be no hell, *Cesset voluntas propria et non erit infernus.* For men willingly submit to the rule and law of sin, they plead for it, and like it so well, as they hate nothing so much as that which any way withstandeth those lawless laws.

Those that think it their happiness to do what they will, that they might be free, cross their own desires, for this is the way to make them most perfect slaves. When our will is the next immediate cause of sin, and our consciences bear witness to us that it is so, then conscience is ready to take God's part in accusing ourselves ; our consciences tell us to our faces that we might do more than we do to hinder sin, and that when we sin, it is not through weakness, but out of the wickedness of our nature.

Our consciences tell us that we sin not only willingly, but often with delight, so far forth as we are not subdued by grace, or awed by something above us, and that we esteem any restraint to be our misery. And where by grace the will is strengthened, so that it yields not a full consent, yet a gracious soul is humbled even for the sudden risings of corruption that prevent deliberation. As here David, though he withstood the risings of his heart, yet he was troubled, that he had so vile a heart that would rise up against God, and therefore takes it down. Who is there that hath not cause to be humbled, not only for his corruption, but that he doth not resist with that strength, nor labour to prevent it with that diligence which his heart tells him he might?

We cannot have too deep apprehensions of this breeding sin, the mother and nurse of all abominations ; for the more we consider the height, the depth, the breadth, and length of it, the more shall we be humbled in ourselves, and magnify the height, the depth, the breadth, and the length of God's mercy in Christ, Eph. iii. 18. The favourers of nature are always the enemies of grace. This, which some think and speak so weakly and faintly of, is a worse enemy to us than the devil himself ; a more near, a more restless, a more traitorous enemy, for by intelligence with it the devil doth us all the hurt he doth, and by it maintains forts in us against goodness. This is that which, either by discouragement or contrariety, hinders us from good ; or else, by deadness, tediousness, distractions, or corrupt aims, hinders us in doing good. This putteth us on to evil, and abuseth what is good in us, or from us, to cover or colour sin, and furnishes us with reasons either to maintain what is evil, or shifts to translate it upon false causes, or fences to arm us against whatsoever shall oppose us in our wicked ways ; though it neither can nor will be good, yet it would be thought to be so by others, and enforces a conceit upon itself that it is good. It imprisons and keeps down all light that may discover it, both within itself and without itself, if it lie in its power ; it flatters itself, and would have all the world flatter it too, which, if it doth not, it frets, especially if it be once discovered and crossed. Hence comes all the plotting against goodness, that sin may reign without control. Is it not a lamentable case that man, who, out of the very principles of nature, cannot but desire happiness and abhor misery, yet should be in love with eternal misery in the causes of it, and abhor happiness in the ways that lead unto it ? This sheweth us what a wonderful deordination and disorder is brought upon man's nature; for every other creature is naturally carried to that which is helpful unto it, and shunneth that which is any way hurtful and offensive. Only man is in love with his own bane, and fights for those lusts that fight against his soul.

§ IV. Our duty is, 1. To labour to see this sinful disposition of ours, not only as it is discovered in the Scriptures, but as it discovers itself in our own hearts. This must be done by the light and teaching of God's Spirit, who knows us and all the turnings and windings and byways of our souls, better than we know ourselves. We must see it as the most odious and loathsome thing in the world, making our natures contrary to God's pure nature, and of all other duties making us most indisposed to spiritual duties, wherein we should have nearest communion with God, because it seizeth on the very spirits of our minds.

2. We should look upon it as worse than any of those filthy streams that come from it; nay, than all the impure issues of our lives together. There is more fire in the furnace than in the sparkles; there is more poison in the root than in all the branches. For if the stream were stopped, and the branches cut off, and the sparkles quenched, yet there would be a perpetual supply. As in good things, the cause is better than the effect, so in ill things the cause is worse. Every fruit should make this poisonous root more hateful to us, and the root should make us hate the fruit more, as coming from so bad a root, as being worse in the cause than in itself; the affection is worse than the action, which may be forced or counterfeited. We cry out upon particular sins, but are not humbled as we should be for our impure dispositions, without the sight of which there can be (1.) no sound repentance arising from the deep and thorough consideration of sin; (2.) no desire to be new moulded, without which we can never enter into so holy a place as heaven; (3.) no self-denial, till we see the best things in us are enmity against God; (4.) no high prizing of Christ, without whom our natures, our persons, and our actions are abominable in God's sight; (5.) nor any solid peace settled in the soul, which peace ariseth not from the ignorance of our corruption, or compounding with it, but from sight and hatred of it, and strength against it.

3. Consider the spiritualness and large extent of the law of God, together with the curse annexed, which forbids not only particular sins, but all the kinds, degrees, occasions, and furtherances of sin in the whole breadth and depth of it, and our very nature itself, so far as it is corrupted; for want of which we see many 'alive without the law,' Rom. vii. 9, jovial and merry from ignorance of their misery, who, if they did but once see their natures and lives in that glass, it would take away that liveliness and courage from them, and make them vile in their own eyes. Men usually look themselves in the laws of the state wherein they live, and think themselves good enough, if they are free from the danger of penal statutes; this glass discovers only foul spots, gross scandals, and breakings out; or else they judge of themselves by parts of nature, or common grace, or by outward conformity to religion, or else by that light they have to guide themselves in the affairs of this life, by their fair and civil carriage, &c.; and thereupon live and die without any sense of the power of godliness, which begins in the right knowledge of ourselves, and ends in the right knowledge of God. The spiritualness and purity of the law should teach us to consider the purity and holiness of God; the bringing of our souls into whose presence will make us to abhor ourselves, with Job, 'in dust

and ashes,' Job xlii. 6. Contraries are best seen by setting one near the other; whilst we look only on ourselves, and upon others amongst whom we live, we think ourselves to be somebody. It is an evidence of some sincerity wrought in the soul, not to shun that light which may let us see the foul corners of our hearts and lives.

4. The consideration of this likewise should enforce us to carry a double guard over our souls. David was very watchful, yet we see here he was surprised unawares by the sudden rebellion of his heart. We should observe our hearts as governors do rebels and mutinous persons. Observation awes the heart. We see to what an excess sin groweth in those that deny themselves nothing, nor will be denied in anything; who, if they may do what they will, will do what they may; who turn liberty into licence, and make all their abilities and advantages to do good, contributary to the commands of overruling and unruly lusts.

Were it not that God partly by his power suppresseth, and partly by his grace subdueth the disorders of man's nature for the good of society, and the gathering of a church upon earth, corruption would swell to that excess, that it would overturn and confound all things together with itself. Although there be a common corruption that cleaves to the nature of all men in general, as men (as distrust in God, self-love, a carnal and worldly disposition, &c.), yet God so ordereth it, that in some there is an ebb and decrease, in others, God justly leaving them to themselves, a flow and increase of sinfulness, even beyond the bounds of ordinary corruption, whereby they become worse than themselves, either like beasts in sensuality, or like devils in spiritual wickedness. Though all be blind in spiritual things, yet some are more blinded; though all be hard-hearted, yet some are more hardened; though all be corrupt in evil courses, yet some are more corrupted; and sink deeper into rebellion than others.

Sometimes God suffers this corruption to break out in civil men, yea even in his own children, that they may know themselves the better, and because sometimes corruption is weakened not only by smothering, but by having a vent, whereupon grace stirs up in the soul a fresh hatred and revenge against it; and lets us see a necessity of having whole Christ, not only to pardon sin, but to purge and cleanse our sinful natures.

Caution. But yet that which is ill in itself, must not be done for the good that comes by it by accident; this must be a comfort after our surprisals, not an encouragement before.

5. And because the divine nature, wrought in us by divine truth, together with the Spirit of God, is the only counter-poison against all sin, and whatsoever is contrary to God in us, therefore we should labour that the truth of God may be grafted in our hearts, that so all the powers of our souls may relish of it, that there may be a sweet agreement betwixt the soul and all things that are spiritual, that truth being engrafted in our hearts, we may be engrafted into Christ, and grow up in him, and put him on more and more, and be changed into his likeness. Nothing in heaven or earth will work out corruption, and change our dispositions, but the Spirit of Christ, clothing divine truths with a divine power to this purpose.

6. When corruption rises, pray it down, as St Paul did, 2 Cor. xii. 8, and to strengthen thy prayer, claim the promise of the new covenant, that God would ' circumcise our hearts,' and ' wash us with clean water,' that he would ' write his law in our hearts, and give us his Holy Spirit when we beg it,' Ezek. xxxvi. 25–27 ; and look upon Christ as a public ' fountain open for Judah and Jerusalem to wash in,' Zech. xiii. 1. Herein consists our com-

fort, 1, that Christ hath all fulness for us, and that our nature is perfect in him; 2, That Christ in our nature hath satisfied divine justice, not only for the sin of our lives, but for the sin of our nature. And, 3, That he will never give over until by his Spirit he hath made our nature holy and pure as his own, till he hath taken away not only the reign, but the very life and being of sin out of our hearts. 4, That to this end he leaves his Spirit and truth in the church to the end of the world, that the seed of the Spirit may subdue the seed of the serpent in us, and that the Spirit may be a never-failing spring of all holy thoughts, desires, and endeavours in us, and dry up the contrary issue and spring of corrupt nature.

And Christians must remember, when they are much annoyed with their corruptions, that it is not their particular case alone, but the condition of all God's people, lest they be discouraged by looking on the ugly deformed visage of old Adam, which affrighteth some so far that it makes them think, no man's nature is so vile as theirs; which were well if it tended to humiliation only; but Satan often abuseth it towards discouragement and desperation. Many out of a misconceit think that corruption is greatest when they feel it most, whereas indeed, the less we see it and lament it, the more it is. Sighs and groans of the soul are like the pores of the body, out of which in diseased persons sick humours break forth and so become less. The more we see and grieve for pride, which is an immediate issue of our corrupted nature, the less it is, because we see it by a contrary grace; the more sight the more hatred, the more hatred of sin, the more love of grace, and the more love the more life, which the more lively it is, the more it is sensible of the contrary. Upon every discovery and conflict corruption loses some ground, and grace gains upon it.

CHAPTER XIII.—*Of imagination, sin of it, and remedies for it.*

§ I. And amongst all the faculties of the soul, most of the disquiet and unnecessary trouble of our lives arises from the vanity and ill government of that power of the soul which we call *imagination* and *opinion*, bordering between the senses and our understanding; which is nothing else but a shallow apprehension of good or evil taken from the senses. Now because outward good or evil things agree or disagree to the senses, and the life of sense is in us before the use of reason, and the delights of sense are present, and pleasing and suitable to our natures, thereupon the imagination setteth a great price upon sensible good things; and the judgment itself since the fall, until it hath a higher light and strength, yieldeth to our imagination. Hence it comes to pass that the best things, if they be attended with sensible inconveniences, as want, disgrace in the world, and such like, are misjudged for evil things; and the very worst things, if they be attended with respect in the world, and sensible contentments, are imagined to be the greatest good; which appears not so much in men's words (because they are ashamed to discover their hidden folly and atheism), but the lives of people speak as much, in that particular choice which they make. Many there are who think it not only a vain but a dangerous thing to serve God, and a base thing to be awed with religious respect; they count the ways that God's people take no better than madness, and that course which God takes in bringing men to heaven by a plain publishing of heavenly truths, to be nothing but foolishness; and those people that regard it, are esteemed, as the Pharisees esteemed them that heard Christ, ignorant, base, and despicable persons. Hence arise all those false prejudices against the ways of holiness, as they in the Acts were shy in entertaining the truth, because it was 'a way everywhere spoken against,' Acts xxviii. 22. The doctrine of the cross hath the cross always following it, which imagination counteth the most odious and bitter thing in the world.

This imagination of ours is become the seat of vanity, and thereupon of vexation to us, because it apprehends a greater happiness in outward good things than there is, and a greater misery in outward evil things than indeed there is; and when experience shews us that there is not that good in those things which we imagine to be, but, contrarily, we find much evil in them which we never expected, hereupon the soul cannot but be troubled. The life of many men, and those not the meanest, is almost nothing else but a fancy; that which chiefly sets their wits awork and takes up most of their time is how to please their own imagination, which setteth up an excellency, within itself, in comparison of which it despiseth all true excellency and those things that are of most necessary consequence indeed. Hence springs ambition and the vein of being great in the world; hence comes an unmeasurable desire of abounding in those things which the world esteems highly of. There is in us naturally a competition and desire of being equal or above others in that which is generally thought to make us happy and esteemed amongst men. If we be not the only men, yet we will be somebody in the world; something we will have to be highly esteemed for, wherein if we be crossed, we count it the greatest misery that can befall us.

And, which is worse, a corrupt desire of being great in the opinion of others creeps into the profession of religion, if we live in those places wherein it brings credit or gain. Men will sacrifice their very lives for vainglory. It is an evidence a man lives more to opinion and reputation of others than to conscience, when his grief is more for being disappointed of that approbation which he expects from men, than for his miscarriage towards God. It mars all in religion when we go about heavenly things with earthly affections, and seek not Christ in Christ, but the world. What is popery but an artificial frame of man's brain to please men's imaginations by outward state and pomp of ceremonies, like that golden image of Nebuchadnezzar, wherein he pleased himself so, that, to have uniformity in worshipping the same, he compelled all, under pain of death, to fall down before it, Dan. iii. 6. This makes superstitious persons always cruel, because superstitious devices are the brats of our own imagination, which we strive for more than for the purity of God's worship. Hence it is, likewise, that superstitious persons are restless (as the woman of Samaria) in their own spirits, as having no bottom, but fancy instead of faith.

§ II. Now, the reason why imagination works so upon the soul is, because it stirs up the affections answerable to the good or ill which it apprehends, and our affections stir the humours of the body, so that oftentimes both our souls and bodies are troubled hereby.

Things work upon the soul in this order: 1. Some object is presented. 2. Then it is apprehended by imagination as good and pleasing, or as evil and hurtful. 3. If good, the desire is carried to it with delight; if evil, it is rejected with distaste, and so our affections are stirred up suitably to our apprehension of the object. 4. Affections stir up the spirits. 5. The spirits raise the humours, and so the whole man becomes moved, and oftentimes distempered; this falleth out by reason of the sympathy between the soul and body, whereby what offendeth one redoundeth to the hurt of the other.

And we see conceived* troubles have the same effect upon us as true. Jacob was as much troubled with the imagination of his son's death as if he had been dead indeed. Imagination, though it be an empty, windy thing, yet it hath real effects. Superstitious persons are as much troubled for neglecting any voluntary service of man's invention, as if they had offended against the direct commandment of God. Thus superstition breeds false fears, and false fear brings true vexation. It transforms God to an idol, imagining him to be pleased with whatsoever pleases ourselves, whenas we take it ill that those who are under us should take direction from themselves and not from us in that which may content us. Superstition is very busy, but all in vain. 'In vain they worship me,' Mat. xv. 9, saith God. And how can it choose but vex and disquiet men, when they shall take a great deal of pains in vain, and, which is worse, to displease most in that wherein they think to please most. God blasteth all devised service with one demand, 'Who required these things at your hands?' Isa. i. 12. It were better for us to ask ourselves this question beforehand, Who required this? Why do we trouble ourselves about that which we shall have no thank for? We should not bring God down to our own imaginations, but raise our imaginations up to God.

Now, imagination hurteth us, 1. By false representations. 2. By preventing reason, and so usurping a censure of things before our judgments try them, whereas the office of imagination is to minister matter to our understanding to work upon, and not to lead it, much less mislead it, in anything. 3. By forging matter out of itself without ground; the imaginary grievances of our lives are more than the real. 4. As it is an ill instrument of the understanding to devise vanity and mischief.

§ III. The way to cure this malady in us is, 1. *To labour to bring these risings of our souls into the obedience of God's truth and Spirit*, 2 Cor. x. 5. For imagination, of itself, if ungoverned, is a wild and a ranging thing; it wrongs not only the frame of God's work in us, setting the baser part of a man above the higher, but it wrongs likewise the work of God in the creatures and everything else, for it shapes things as itself pleaseth; it maketh evil good if it pleaseth the senses, and good evil if it be dangerous and distasteful to the outward man, which cannot but breed an unquiet and an unsettled soul. As if it were a god, it can tell good and evil at its pleasure; it sets up and pulls down the price of what it listeth. By reason of the distemper of imagination, the life of many is little else but a dream. Many good men are in a long dream of misery, and many bad men in as long a dream of happiness, till the time of awaking come, and all because they are too much led by appearances. And as in a dream men are deluded with false joys and false fears, so here; which cannot but breed an unquiet and an unsettled soul. Therefore, it is necessary that God, by his word and Spirit, should erect a government in our hearts to captivate and order this licentious faculty.

2. Likewise, it is good *to present real things to the soul*, as the true riches and true misery of a Christian, the true honour and dishonour, true beauty and deformity, the true nobleness and debasement, of the soul. Whatever is in the world are but shadows of things in comparison of those true realities which religion affords. And why should we vex ourselves about a vain shadow? Ps. xxxix. 6.

* That is, 'apprehended.'—ED.

The Holy Ghost, to prevent further mischief by these outward things, gives a dangerous report of them, calling them vanity, unrighteous mammon, Luke xvi. 9, uncertain riches, thorns, yea, nothing, Prov. xxiii. 5; because, though they be not so in themselves, yet, our imagination overvaluing them, they prove so to us upon trial. Now, knowledge that is bought by trial is often dear bought; and therefore God would have us prevent this by a right conceit of things beforehand, lest trusting to vanity we vanish ourselves, and trusting to nothing we become nothing ourselves, and, which is worse, worse than nothing.

3. Oppose *serious consideration against vain imagination;* and because our imagination is prone to raise false objects, and thereby false conceits and discourses in us, our best way herein is to propound true objects of the mind to work upon, as, 1. To consider the greatness and goodness of Almighty God and his love to us in Christ. 2. The joys of heaven and the torments of hell. 3. The last and strict day of account. 4. The vanity of all earthly things. 5. The uncertainty of our lives, &c. From the meditation of these truths the soul will be prepared to have right conceits of things, and discourse upon true grounds of them, and think with itself that if these things be so indeed, then I must frame my life suitable to these principles. Hence arise true affections in the soul, true fear of God, true love and desire after the best things, &c. The way to expel wind out of our bodies is to take some wholesome nourishment, and the way to expel windy fancies from the soul is to feed upon serious truths.

4. Moreover, to the well ordering of this unruly faculty, it is necessary that *our nature itself should be changed;* for as men are, so they imagine; as the 'treasure of the heart is,' Mat. xii. 35, such is that which comes from it. *Mala mens, malus animus,* an evil heart cannot think well. Before the heart be changed, our judgment is depraved in regard of our last end; we seek our happiness where it is not to be found. 'Wickedness comes from the wicked,' 1 Sam. xxiv. 13, as the proverb is. If we had as large and as quick apprehensions as Satan himself, yet if the relish of our will and affections be not changed, they will set the imaginations awork, to devise satisfaction to themselves. For there is a mutual working and reflux betwixt the will and the imagination; the imagination stirs up the will, and as the will is affected, so imagination worketh.

When the law of God by the Spirit is so written in our hearts, that the law and our hearts become agreeable one to the other, then the soul is inclined and made pliable to every good thought. When the heart is once taught of God to love, it is the nature of this sweet affection, as the apostle saith, to 'think no evil,' 1 Cor. xiii. 5, either of God or man; and not only so, but it carries the bent of the whole soul with it to good, so that we love God not only with all our heart, but with all our mind, Mat. xxii. 37, that is, both with our understanding and imagination. Love is an affection full of inventions, and sets the wit awork to devise good things; therefore our chief care should be, that our hearts may be circumcised and purified, so as they may be filled with the love of God, and then we shall find this duty not only easy, but delightful unto us. The prophet healed the waters by casting salt into the spring, 2 Kings ii. 20, so the seasoning of the spring of our actions seasons all. And indeed, what can be expected from man, whilst he is vanity, but vain imaginations? What can we look for from a viper but poison? A man naturally is either weaving spiders' webs, or hatching cockatrices' eggs, Isa. lix. 5, that is, his heart is exercised either in vanity or mischief; for not only the frame of the heart, but what the heart frameth, is evil continually, Gen. vi. 5. A wicked man that is besotted with false conceits, will admit of no good thoughts to enter.

5. Even when we are good, and devise good things, yet there is still some sickness of fancy remaining in the best of us, whereby we work trouble to ourselves; and therefore it is necessary we should labour *to restrain and limit our fancy*, and stop these waters at the beginning, Prov. vii. 14, giving no not the least way thereunto. If it begins to grow wanton, tame the wildness of it by fastening it to the cross of Christ (whom we have pierced with our sins, Zech. xii. 10; and amongst other, with these sins of our spirits), who hath redeemed us from our vain thoughts and conversations, 1 Peter i. 18; set before it the consideration of the wrath of God, of death, and judgment, and the woful estate of the damned, &c., and take it not off till thy heart be taken off from straying from God. When it begins once to run out to impertinences, confine it to some certain thing, and then upon examination we shall find it bring home some honey with it; otherwise it will bring us nothing but a sting from the bitter remembrance of our former misspent thoughts and time, which we should redeem and fill up with things that most belong to our peace, Luke xix. 47. Idleness is the hour of temptation, wherein Satan joins with our imagination, and sets it about his own work, to grind his grease;* for the soul as a mill, either grinds that which is put into it, or else works upon itself. Imagination is the first wheel of the soul, and if that move amiss, it stirs all the inferior wheels amiss with it. It stirs itself, and other powers of the soul are stirred by its motion; and therefore the well ordering of this is of the greater consequence. For as the imagination conceiveth, so usually the judgment concludeth, the will chooseth, the affections are carried, and the members execute.

If it break loose, as it will soon run riot, yet give no consent of the will to it. Though it hath defiled the memory, yet let it not defile the will. Though it be the first-born of the soul, yet let it not, as Reuben, ascend unto the father's bed—that is, our will,—and defile that which should be kept pure for the Spirit of Christ.† Resolve to act nothing upon it, but cross it before it moves to the execution and practice of anything. As in sickness, many times we imagine, by reason of the corruption of our taste, physic to be ill for us, and those meats which nourish the disease to be good, yet care of health makes us cross our own conceits, and take that which fancy abhors; so if we would preserve sound spirits, we must conclude against groundless imagination, and resolve that whatsoever it suggests cannot be so, because it crosses the grounds both of religion and reason. And when we find imagination to deceive us in sensible things, as melancholy persons are subject to mistake, we may well gather that it will much more deceive us in our spiritual condition; and indeed, such is the incoherence, impertinency, and unreasonableness of imagination, that men are oft ashamed and angry with themselves afterwards, for giving the least way to such thoughts; and it is good to chastise the soul for the same, that it may be more wary for time to come. Whilst men are led

* Qu. 'grist?'—ED.

† Bernard. The following is the reference of Sibbes *supra*:—'Plane exclamandum nobis est cum Sancto Jacobo atque dicendum Reuben primogenitus, &c. Rubea enim et carnalis atque sanguinea hujusmodi concupiscentia est, quæ tunc cubile nostrum ascendit, cum non solum memoriam tangit cogitatione, sed et ipsum voluntatis stratum ingreditur, et polluit prava dilectione. Bene autem primogenitus noster dicitur appetitus ille carnalis,' &c. &c.—Sermo de triplici genere cogitationum nostrarum. Edn. Antwerp, 1616, p. 411. G.

with imagination, they work not according to right rules prescribed to men, but as other baser creatures, in whom phantasy is the chief ruling power; and therefore, those whose will is guided by their fancies, live more like beasts than men.

We allow a horse to prance and skip in a pasture, which if he doth when he is once backed by the rider, we count him an unruly and unbroken jade; so howsoever in other creatures we allow liberty of fancy, yet we allow it not in man to frisk and rove at its pleasure, because in him it is to be bridled with reason.

6. Especially take heed of those *cursed imaginations out of which, as of mother roots, others spring forth;* as questioning God's providence, and care of his children, his justice, his disregarding of what is done here below, &c., thoughts of putting off our amendment for time to come, and so blessing ourselves in any evil way, thoughts against the necessity of exact and circumspect walking with God, &c., Eph. v. 15. When these and such like principles of Satan's and the flesh's divinity take place in our hearts, they block up the soul against the entrance of soul-saving truths, and taint our whole conversation, which is either good or evil, as the principles are by which we are guided, and as our imagination is, which lets in all to the soul.

The Jews in Jeremiah's time were forestalled with vain imaginations against sound repentance, and therefore his counsel is, 'Wash thine heart, O Jerusalem! how long shall vain thoughts lodge within thee?' Jer. iv. 14.

7. Fancy will the better be kept within its due bounds, *if we consider the principal use thereof.* Sense and imagination is properly to judge what is comfortable or uncomfortable, what is pleasing or displeasing to the outward man, not what is morally or spiritually good or ill; and thus far by the laws of nature and civility we are bound to give fancy contentment both in ourselves and others, as not to speak or do anything uncomely, which may occasion a loathing or distaste in our converse with men; and it is a matter of conscience to make our lives as comfortable as may be. As we are bound to love, so we are bound to use all helps that may make us lovely, and endear us into the good affections of others. As we are bound to give no offence to the conscience of another, so to no power or faculty either of the outward or inward man of another. Some are taken off in their affection by a fancy, whereof they can give but little reason; and some are more careless in giving offence in this kind, than stands with that Christian circumspection and mutual respect which we owe one to another. The apostle's rule is of large extent, 'Whatsoever things are not only true, and honest, and just, but whatsoever things are lovely and of good report, &c., think of these things,' Phil. iv. 8. Yet our main care should be to manifest ourselves rather to men's *consciences* than to their *imaginations.*

8. It should be our wisdom, likewise, *to place ourselves in the best conveniency of all outward helps, which may have a kind working upon our fancy; and to take heed to the contrary, as time, place, and objects,* &c. There be good hours and good messengers of God's sending, golden opportunities wherein God uses to give a meeting to his children, and breathes good thoughts into them. Even the wisest and holiest men, as David and Solomon, &c., had no further safety than they were careful of well-using all good advantages, and sequestering themselves from such objects as had a working power upon them. By suffering their souls to be led by their fancies, and their hearts to run after their eyes, they betrayed and robbed themselves of much grace and comfort, thereupon Solomon cries out with

grief and shame from his own experience, 'Vanity of vanities,' &c. Eccles. i. 2. Fancy will take fire before we be aware. Little things are seeds of great matters. Job knew this, and therefore made a 'covenant with his eyes,' Job xxxi. 1; but a 'fool's eyes are in the corners of the earth,' saith Solomon, Prov. xvii. 24.

Sometimes the ministering of some excellent thought—*præclara cogitatio*—from what we hear or see, proves a great advantage of spiritual good to the soul. Whilst St Augustine out of curiosity delighted to hear the eloquence of St Ambrose, he was taken with the matter itself, sweetly sliding together with the words into his heart.* Of later times, whilst Galeaceus Caracciolus, an Italian marquis, and nephew to Pope Paul V., was hearing Peter Martyr reading upon 1 Corinthians, and shewing the deceivableness of man's judgment in spiritual things, and the efficacy of divine truth in those that belong unto God, and further using a similitude to this purpose: 'If a man be walking afar off, and see people dancing together, and hear no noise of the music, he judges them fools and out of their wits; but when he comes nearer and hears the music, and sees that every motion is exactly done by art, now he changes his mind, and is so taken up with the sweet agreement of the gesture and the music, that he is not only delighted therewith, but desirous to join himself in the number. So it falls out, saith he, with men: whilst they look upon the outward carriage and conversation of God's people, and see it differing from others, they think them fools; but when they look more narrowly into their courses, and see a gracious harmony betwixt their lives and the word of God, then they begin to be in love with the "beauty of holiness," and join in conformity of holy obedience with those they scorned before.' This similitude wrought so with this nobleman, that he began, from that time forward, to set his mind to the study of heavenly things.†

One seasonable truth falling upon a prepared heart, hath oftentimes a sweet and strong operation. Luther confesseth that having heard a grave divine, Staupicius, say 'that that is kind repentance which begins from the love of God,' ever after that time the practice of repentance was sweeter to him. This speech of his likewise took well with Luther, that in doubts of predestination we should begin from the wounds of Christ, *doctrina prædestinationis incipit a vulneribus Christi*,—that is, from the sense of God's love to us in Christ, we should arise to the grace given us in election before the world was, 2 Tim. i. 9.

The putting of lively colours upon common truths hath oft a strong working both upon the fancy and our will and affections. The spirit is refreshed with fresh things, or old truths refreshed. This made the preacher seek to find out pleasing and acceptable words, Eccl. xii. 10: and our Saviour Christ's manner of teaching was by a lively representation to men's fancies, to teach them heavenly truths in an earthly, sensible man-

---

* See the memorable 'confession' in 'The Confessions' of Augustine, Book V., xiii. 23; xiv. 24. A few words may interest:—'Though I took no pains to learn *what* he spake, but only to hear *how* he spake...... yet together with the words which I would choose, came also into my mind the things which I would refuse; for I could not separate them. And while I opened my heart to admit "how eloquently he spake," there also entered, "how truly he spake;" but this by degrees.'

† The authority given in the margin is 'Beza in his life.' This is a translation from the Italian, and was published in 1596. No less than two translations into English are extant: one, 4to, 1608, and another, 4to, 1612. Sibbes's quotations are from c. iii. The whole passage is given from the quaint translation of 1608, in Note *d*.

ner; and indeed, what do we see or hear but will yield matter to a holy heart to raise itself higher?

We should make our fancy serviceable to us in spiritual things, and take advantage by any pleasure, or profit, or honour which it presents our thoughts withal, to think thus with ourselves, 'what is this to the true honour, and to those enduring pleasures,' &c.? And seeing God hath condescended to represent heavenly things to us under earthly terms, we should follow God's dealing herein. God represents heaven to us under the term of a banquet, and of a kingdom, &c., Luke x. 32; our union with Christ under the term of a marriage, yea, Christ himself, under the name of whatsoever is lovely or comfortable in heaven or earth. So the Lord sets out hell to us by whatsoever is terrible or tormenting. Here is a large field for our imagination to walk in, not only without hurt, but with a great deal of spiritual gain. If the wrath of a king be as the roaring of a lion, Prov. xix. 12, what is the wrath of the King of kings? If fire be so terrible, what is hell fire? If a dark dungeon be so loathsome, what is that eternal dungeon of darkness? If a feast be so pleasing, what is the 'continual feast of a good conscience?' Prov. xv. 15. If the meeting of friends be so comfortable, what will our meeting together in heaven be? The Scripture, by such like terms, would help our faith and fancy both at once. A sanctified fancy will make every creature a ladder to heaven. And because childhood and youth are ages of fancy, therefore it is a good way to instil into the hearts of children betimes, the loving of good and the shunning of evil, by such like representations as agree with their fancies, as to hate hell under the representation of fire and darkness, &c. Whilst the soul is joined with the body, it hath not only a necessary but a holy use of imagination, and of sensible things whereupon our imagination worketh. What is the use of the sacraments but to help our souls by our senses, and our faith by imagination? As the soul receives much hurt from imagination, so it may have much good thereby.

But yet it ought not to invent or devise what is good and true in religion. Here fancy must yield to faith, and faith to divine revelation. The things we believe are such as neither 'eye hath seen, nor ear heard, neither came into the heart of man,' 1 Cor. ii. 9, by imagination stirred up from anything which we have seen or heard. They are above, not only imagination, but reason itself, in men and angels. But after God hath revealed spiritual truths, and faith hath apprehended them, then imagination hath use while the soul is joined with the body, to colour divine truths, and make lightsome what faith believes; for instance, it doth not devise either heaven or hell; but when God hath revealed them to us, our fancy hath a fitness of enlarging our conceits of them, even by resemblance from things in nature, and that without danger; because the joys of heaven and the torments of hell are so great that all the representations which nature affords us fall short of them.

Imagination hath likewise some use in religion, by putting cases to the soul, as when we are tempted to any unruly action we should think with ourselves, what would I do if some holy, grave person whom I much reverence should behold me? Whereupon the soul may easily ascend higher, God sees me, and my own conscience is ready to witness against me, &c.

It helps us also in taking benefit by the example of other men. Good things are best learned by others expressing of them to our view. The very sight often, nay, the very thought of a good man doth good, as representing to our souls some good thing which we affect—*est aliquid quod ex magno viro vel tacente proficias*—which makes histories and the lively characters and expressions of virtues and vices useful to us. The sight, yea, the very reading of the suffering of the martyrs hath wrought such a hatred of that persecuting church as hath done marvellous good. The sight of justice executed upon malefactors works a greater hatred of sin in men than naked precepts can do. So outward pomp and state in the world doth further that awful respect due to authority, &c.

9. Lastly, it would much avail for the well ordering of our thoughts *to set our souls in order every morning, and to strengthen and perfume our spirits with some gracious meditations*,* especially of the chief end and scope wherefore we live here, and how every thing we do or befalls us may be reduced and ordered to further the main. The end of a Christian is glorious, and the oft thoughts of it will raise and enlarge the soul, and set it on work to study how to make all things serviceable thereunto. It is a thing to be lamented that a Christian born for heaven, having the 'prize of his high calling,' Phil. iii. 14, set before him, and matters of that weight and excellency to exercise his heart upon, should be taken up with trifles, and fill both his head and heart with vanity and nothing, as all earthly things will prove ere long; and yet if many men's thoughts and discourses were distilled, they are so frothy that they would hardly yield one drop of true comfort.

§ IV. *Obj.* Oh, but, say some, thoughts and imaginations are free, and we shall not be accountable for them.

Ans. This is a false plea, for God hath a sovereignty over the whole soul, and his law binds the whole inward and outward man. As we desire our whole man should be saved by Christ, so we must yield up the whole man to be governed by him; and it is the effect of the dispensation of the gospel, accompanied with the Spirit, to captivate whatsoever is in man unto Christ, and to bring down all 'high towering imaginations,' 2 Cor. x. 5, that exalt themselves against God's Spirit. There is a divinity in the word of God, powerfully unfolded, which will convince our souls of the sinfulness of natural imaginations, as we see in the idiot, (*e*) 1 Cor. xiv. 24, 25, who, seeing himself laid open before himself, cried out, that 'God was in the speaker,' 1 Cor. xiv. 25.

There ought to be in man a conformity to the truth and goodness of things, or else, 1, we shall wrong our own souls with false apprehensions; and 2, the creature, by putting a fashion upon it otherwise than God hath made; and 3, we shall wrong God himself, the author of goodness, who cannot have his true glory but from a right apprehension of things as they are. What a wrong is it to men when we shall take up false prejudices against them without ground! and so suffer our conceits to be envenomed against them by unjust suspicions, and by this means deprive ourselves of all that good which we might receive by them; for our nature is apt to judge and accept of things as the persons are, and not of persons according to the things themselves. This faculty exercises a tyranny in the soul, setting up and pulling down whom it will. Job judged his friends altogether vain, Job xxvii. 12, because they went upon a vain imagination and discourse, judging him to be an hypocrite, which could not but add much to his affliction. When men take a toy† in their head against a person or place, they are ready to reason as he did, 'Can any good come out of Nazareth?' John vi. 46.

* 'Meditations. Sibbes himself practised this excellent counsel, as witness his golden little volume of 'Meditations,' first published in 1638, 18mo.
† That is, 'fancy.'—G.

It is an indignity for men to be led with surmises and probabilities, and so to pass a rash judgment upon persons and things. Oftentimes falsehood hath a fairer gloss of probability than truth; and vices go masked under the appearance of virtue, whereupon seeming likeness—*similitudo mater errorum*—breeds a mistake of one thing for another; and Satan oftentimes casts a mist before our imagination, that so we might have a misshapen conceit of things. By a spirit of illusion he makes worldly things appear bigger to us, and spiritual things lesser than indeed they are; and so by sophisticating of things our affections come to be misled. Imagination is the womb, and Satan the father of all monstrous conceptions and disordered lusts, which are well called deceitful lusts, Eph. iv. 22, and lusts of ignorance, 1 Tim. vi. 9, foolish and noisome lusts, because they both spring from error and folly, and lead unto it.

We see, even in religion itself, how the world, together with the help of 'the god of the world,' 2 Cor. iv. 4, is led away, if not to worship images, yet to worship the image of their own fancy. And where the truth is most professed, yet people are prone to fancy to themselves such a breadth of religion as will altogether leave them comfortless when things shall appear in their true colours. They will conceit to embrace truth without hatred of the world, and Christ without his cross, and a godly life without persecutions. They would pull a rose without pricks. Which, though it may stand with their own base ends for a while, yet will not hold out in times of change, when sickness of body and trouble of mind shall come. Empty conceits are too weak to encounter with real griefs.

Some think orthodox and right opinions to be a plea for a loose life, whereas there is no ill course of life but springs from some false opinion. God will not only call us to account how we have believed, disputed, and reasoned, &c., but how we have lived. Our care, therefore, should be to build our profession, not on seeming appearances, but upon sound grounds, that the gates of hell cannot prevail against. The hearts of many are so vain that they delight to be blown up with flattery, because they would have their imaginations pleased, yea, even when they cannot but know themselves abused, and are grieved to have their windy bladder pricked, and so to be put out of their conceited happiness. Others, out of a tediousness in serious and settled thoughts, entertain everything as it is offered to them at the first blush, and suffer their imaginations to carry them presently thereunto without further judging of it. The will naturally loves variety and change, and our imagination doth it service herein, as not delighting to fix long upon anything. Hereupon men are contented, both in religion and in common life, to be misled with prejudices upon shallow grounds; whence it is that the best things and persons suffer much in the world. The power and practice of religion is hated under odious names, and so condemned before it is understood; whence we see a necessity of getting spiritual eye-salve, for without true knowledge the heart cannot be good, Prov. xix. 2.

It is just with God that those who take liberty in their thoughts should be given up to their own imaginations, Rom. i. 28, to delight in them, and to be out of conceit with the best things, and so to reap the fruit of their own ways. Nay, even the best of God's people, if they take liberty herein, God will let loose their imagination upon themselves, and suffer them to be entangled and vexed with their own hearts. Those that give way to their imaginations, shew what their actions should be, if they dared; for if they forbear doing evil out of conscience, they should as well forbear imagining evil, for both are alike open to God and hateful to him ; and, therefore, oft where there is no conscience of the thought, God gives men up to the deed. The greatest and hardest work of a Christian is least in sight, which is the well ordering of his heart. Some buildings have most workmanship under ground. It is our spirits ' that God, who is a Spirit,' John iv. 24, hath most communion withal ; and the less freedom we take to sin here, the more argument of our sincerity, because there is no law to bind the inner man but the law of the Spirit of grace, whereby we are ' a law to ourselves,' Rom. ii. 14. A good Christian begins his repentance where his sin begins, in his thoughts, which are the next issue of his heart. God counts it an honour when we regard his all-seeing eye so much, as that we will not take liberty to ourselves in that which is offensive to him, no, not in our hearts, wherein no creature can hinder us. It is an argument that the Spirit hath set up a kingdom and order in our hearts, when our spirits rise within us against any thing that lifts itself up against goodness.

§ V. *Obj.* Many flatter themselves, from an impossibility of ruling their imaginations, and are ready to lay all upon infirmity and natural weakness, &c.

Ans. But such must know that if we be sound Christians, the Spirit of God will enable us to do all things, evangelically, that we are called unto, if we give way without check to the motions thereof. Where the Spirit is, it is such a light as discovers not only dunghills, but motes themselves, even light and flying imaginations, and abaseth the soul for them, and by degrees purgeth them out ; and if they press, as they are as busy as flies in summer, yet a good heart will not own them, nor allow himself in them, but casts them off, as hot water doth the scum, or as the stomach doth that which is noisome unto it. They find not that entertainment here which they have in carnal hearts, where the scum soaks in, which are stews of unclean thoughts, shambles of cruel and bloody thoughts, exchanges and shops of vain thoughts, a very forge and mint of false, politic, and undermining thoughts, yea often a little hell of confused and black imaginations. There is nothing that more moveth a godly man to renew his interest every day in the perfect righteousness and obedience of his Saviour, than these sinful stirrings of his soul, when he finds something in himself always enticing and drawing away his heart from God, and intermingling itself with his best performances. Even good thoughts are troublesome if they come unseasonably, and weaken our exact performance of duty.

§ VI. But here some misconceits must be taken heed of.

1. As we must take heed that we account not our imaginations to be religion, so we must not account true religion, and the power of godliness, to be a matter of imagination only ; as if holy men troubled themselves more than needs, when they stand upon religion and conscience, seeking to approve themselves 'to God in all things,' 1 Thess. v. 12, and endeavouring, so far as frailty will permit, to ' avoid all appearances of evil,' 1 Thess. v. 22. Many men are so serious in vanities and real in trifles, that they count all which dote not upon such outward excellencies as they do, because the Spirit of God hath revealed to them things of a higher nature, to be fantastics and humorous* people, and so impute the work of the Spirit to the flesh, God's work to Satan, which comes near unto blasphemy. They imagine good men to be led with vain conceits, but good

* That is, 'whimsical.'—G.

men know them to be so led. Not only St Paul, Acts xxvi. 24, but Christ himself, John x. 20, were counted beside themselves, when they were earnest for God and the souls of his people. But there is enough in religion to bear up the soul against all imputations laid upon it: the true children of wisdom are always able to justify their mother, Mat. xi. 19, and the conscionable practice of holy duties, if founded upon such solid grounds as shall hold out when heaven and earth shall vanish.

2. We must know that—as there is great danger in false conceits of the way to heaven, when we make it broader than it is, for by this means we are like men going over a bridge, who think it broader than it is, but being deceived by some shadow, sink down, and are suddenly drowned; so men mistaking the straight way to life, and trusting to the shadow of their own imagination, fall into the bottomless pit of hell before they are aware;—in like manner the danger is great in making the way to heaven narrower than indeed it is, by weak and superstitious imaginations, making more sins than God hath made. The wise man's counsel is, that we should not make ourselves over-wicked, nor be foolisher than we are, Eccl. vii. 17, by devising more sins in our imagination than we are guilty of.

It is good in this respect, to know our Christian liberty, which being one of the fruits of Christ's death, we cannot neglect the same, without much wrong not only to ourselves, but to the rich bounty and goodness of God. So that the due rules of limitation be observed, from authority, piety, sobriety, needless offence of others, &c., we may with better leave, use all those comforts which God hath given to refresh us in the way to heaven, than refuse them. The care of the outward man binds conscience so far, as that we should neglect nothing which may help us in a cheerful serving of God, in our places, and tend to the due honour of our bodies, which are the 'temples of the Holy Ghost,' 1 Cor. iii. 16, 17, and companions with our souls in all performances, so that under this pretence we take not too much liberty to satisfy the lusts of the body. Intemperate use of the creatures is the nurse of all passions; because our spirits, which are the soul's instruments, are hereby inflamed and disturbed. It is no wonder to see an intemperate man transported into any passion.

3. Some out of their high and airy imaginations, and out of their iron and flinty philosophy, will needs think outward good and ill, together with the affections of grief and delight stirred up thereby, to be but opinions and conceits of good and evil only, not true, and really so founded in nature, but taken up of ourselves. But though our fancy be ready to conceit a greater hurt in outward evils than indeed there is, as in poverty, pain of body, death of friends, &c., yet we must not deny them to be evils. That wormwood is bitter, it is not a conceit only, but the nature of the thing itself, yet to abstain from it altogether, for the bitterness thereof, is a hurtful conceit. That honey is sweet, it is not a conceit only, but the natural quality of it is so; yet out of a taste of the sweetness, to think we cannot take too much of it, is a misconceit paid home with loathsome bitterness. Outward good and outward evil, and the affections of delight and sorrow rising thence, are naturally so, and depend not upon our opinion. This were to offer violence to nature, and to take man out of man, as if he were not flesh but steel. Universal experience, from the sensibleness of our nature in any outward grievance, is sufficient to damn this conceit.

The way to comfort a man in grief, is not to tell him that it is only a conceit of evil, and no evil indeed that he suffers. This kind of learning will not down with him, as being contrary to his present feeling. But the way is, to yield unto him that there is cause of grieving, though not of overgrieving, and to shew him grounds of comforts stronger than the grief he suffers. We should weigh the degrees of evil in a right balance, and not suffer fancy to make them greater than they are; so as that for obtaining the greatest outward good, or avoiding the greatest outward ill of suffering, we should give way to the least evil of sin. This is but a policy of the flesh to take away the sensibleness of evil, that so those checks of conscience and repentance for sin, which is oft occasioned thereby, might be taken away; that so men may go on enjoying a stupid happiness, never laying anything to heart, nor afflicting their souls, until their consciences awaken in the place of the damned, and then they feel that grief return upon them for ever, which they laboured to put away when it might have been seasonable to them.

§ VII. I have stood the longer upon this, because Satan and his instruments, by bewitching the imagination with false appearances, misleadeth not only the world, but troubleth the peace of men 'taken out of the world,' James i. 27, 1 John iv. 5, 6, whose estate is laid up safe in Christ, who, notwithstanding, pass their few days here in an uncomfortable, wearisome, and unnecessary sadness of spirit, being kept in ignorance of their happy condition by Satan's juggling and their own mistakes, and so come to heaven before they are aware. Some again pass their days in a golden dream, and drop into hell before they think of it. But it is far better to dream of ill, and when we awake to find it but a dream, than to dream of some great good, and when we awake to find the contrary.

As the distemper of the fancy—*læsa phantasia*—disturbing the act of reason, oftentimes breeds madness in regard of civil conversation; so it breeds, likewise, spiritual madness, carrying men to those things, which, if they were in their right wits, they would utterly abhor. Therefore we cannot have too much care upon what we fix our thoughts. And what a glorious discovery is there of the excellencies of religion that would even ravish an angel, which may raise up, exercise, and fill our hearts! We see our fancy hath so great a force in natural conceptions, that it oft sets a mark and impression upon that which is conceived in the womb. So, likewise, strong and holy conceits of things, having a divine virtue accompanying of them, transform the soul, and breed spiritual impressions answerable to our spiritual apprehensions. It would prevent many crosses, if we would conceive of things as they are. When trouble of mind, or sickness of body, and death itself cometh, what will remain of all that greatness which filled our fancies before? Then we can judge soberly, and speak gravely of things. The best way of happiness, is not to multiply honours or riches, &c., but to cure our conceits of things, and then we cannot be very much cast down with anything that befalls us here.

Therefore, when anything is presented to our souls, which we see is ready to work upon us, we should ask of ourselves upon what ground we entertain such a conceit, whether we shall have the same judgment after we have yielded to it as now we have? and whether we will have the same judgment of it in sickness and death and at the day of reckoning as we have for the present? That which is of itself evil, is always so at one time as well as another. If the time will come when we shall think those things to be vain, which now we are so eagerly set upon, as if there were some great good in them, why should we not think so of them now, whenas the reforming of our judgment may do us good, rather than to be led on with a pleasing error until that time, wherein the sight of our error will fill our hearts with horror and shame, without hope of ever changing our condition?

Here, therefore, is a special use of these soliloquies, to awake the soul and to stir up reason cast asleep by Satan's charms, that so scattering the clouds through which things seem otherwise than they are, we may discern and judge of things according to their true and constant nature. Demand of thy soul, Shall I always be of this mind? Will not the time come when this will prove bitterness in the end? Shall I redeem a short contentment with lasting sorrow? Is my Judge of my mind? Will not a time come when all things shall appear as they are? Is this according to the rule? &c.

To conclude, therefore, whereas there be divers principles of men's actions, as, 1, Natural inclination, inclining us to some courses more than others; 2, Custom, which is another nature in us; 3, Imagination, apprehending things upon shallow grounds, from whence springs affection, whereby we desire glory in things above our own strength and measure, and make show of that, the truth whereof is wanting in us; 4, True judgment, discerning the true reasons of things; 5, Faith, which is a spiritual principle planted in the soul, apprehending things above reason, and raising us up to conceive of all things as God hath discovered them. Now a sound Christian should not be lightly led with those first common grounds of natural inclination, custom, opinion, &c., but by judgment enlightened, advanced, and guided by faith. And we must take heed we suffer not things to pass suddenly from imagination to affection, without asking advice of our judgment, and faith in the way, whose office is to weigh things in God's balance, and, thereupon, to accept or refuse them.

CHAPTER XIV.—*Of help by others. Of true comforters and their graces. Method. Ill success.*

§ I. But because we are subject to favour, and flatter ourselves, it is wisdom to take the benefit of a second self, that is, a well chosen friend, living or dead, books I mean, which will speak truly, without flattery, of our estates. 'A friend is made for the time of adversity,' Prov. xvii. 17; and two are better than one, Eccl. iv. 9, for, by this means, our troubles are divided, and so more easily borne. The very presence of a true-hearted friend yields often ease to our grief. Of all friends, those that by office are to speak a word to a weary soul are most to be regarded, as speaking to us in Christ's stead. Oftentimes, especially in our own case, we are blinded and benighted with passion, and then the judgment of a friend is clearer. Loving friends have a threefold privilege: 1, Their advice is suitable, and fit to our present occasion, they can meet with our grievance, so cannot books so well; 2, What comes from a living friend, comes lively, as helped by his Spirit; 3, In regard of ourselves, what they say is apprehended with more ease, and less plodding and bent of mind. There is scarce anything wherein we see God more in favour towards us, than in our friends, and their seasonable speeches, our hearts being naturally very false and willingly deceived. God often gives us up to be misled by men, not according to his, but our own naughty hearts. As men are, so are their counsellors, for such they will have, and such God lets them have. Men, whose wills are stronger than their wits, who are wedded to their own ways, are more pleased to hear that which complies with their inclinations, than a harsh truth which crosses them. This presages ruin, because they are not counselable. Wherefore God suffers them to be led through a fool's paradise to a true prison, as men that will neither hear themselves nor others who would do them good against their wills. It was a sign God would destroy Eli's sons, when they would hear no counsel, 1 Sam. ii. 25. God fills such men with their own ways, Prov. xiv. 14. Men in great place, often in the abundance of all things else, want the benefit of a true friend, *Ideo amicus deest quia nihil deest*, because, under pretence of service of them, men carry their own ends. As great men* flatter themselves, so they are flattered by others, and so robbed of the true judgment of themselves. Of all spiritual judgments this is the heaviest, for men to be given up to such a measure of self-willness, and to refuse spiritual balm to heal them. Usually such 'perish without remedy,' Prov. xxix. 1, because to be wilfully miserable is to be doubly miserable, for it adds to our misery, that we brought it willingly upon ourselves.

It is a course that will have a blessing attending it, for friends to join in league, one to watch over another, and observe each other's ways. It is a usual course for Christians to join together in other holy duties, as hearing, receiving of the sacrament, prayer, &c.; but this fruit of holy communion which ariseth from a mutual observing one another is much wanting. Whence it is that so many droop, so many are so uncheerful in the ways of God, and lie groaning under the burden of many cares, and are battered with so many temptations, &c., because they are left only to their own spirits. What an unworthy thing is it that we should pity a beast overloaded, and yet take no pity of a brother! *(f)* whereas there is no living member of Christ but hath spiritual love infused into him and some ability to comfort others. Dead stones in an arch uphold one another, and shall not living? It is the work of an angel to comfort; nay, it is the office of the Holy Ghost to be a Comforter, not only immediately, but by breathing comfort into our hearts, together with the comfortable words of others. Thus one friend becomes an angel, nay, a god, to another. And there is a sweet sight of God in the face of a friend; for though the comfort given by God's messengers be ordinarily most effectual, as the blessing of parents, who are in God's room, is more effectual than the blessing of others upon their children, yet God hath promised a blessing to the offices of communion of saints performed by one private man towards another. Can we have a greater encouragement than, under God, to be gainer of a soul, which is as much in God's esteem as if we should gain a world? Spiritual alms are the best alms. Mercy shewed to the souls of men is the greatest mercy, and wisdom in winning of souls is the greatest wisdom in the world, because the soul is especially the man, upon the goodness of which the happiness of the whole man depends. What shining and flourishing Christians should we have if these duties were performed! As we have a portion in the communion of saints, so we should labour to have humility to take good, and wisdom and love to do good. A Christian should have feeding lips and a healing tongue. The leaves, the very words, of the tree of righteousness have a curing virtue in them.

Some will shew a great deal of humanity in comforting others, but little Christianity; for as kind men they will utter some cheerful words, but as Christians they want wisdom from above to speak a gracious word in season, Isa. l. 4, 2 Tim. iv. 2. Nay, some there are who hinder the saving working of any affliction upon the hearts of others by unseasonable and unsavoury discourses, either by suggesting false remedies, or else diverting

* 'Great men' in C, is simply 'as they.'

men to false contentments, and so become spiritual traitors rather than friends, taking part with their worst enemies, their lusts and wills. Happy is he that in his way to heaven meeteth with a cheerful and skilful guide and fellow-traveller, that carrieth cordials with him against all faintings of spirit. It is a part of our wisdom to salvation to make choice of such a one as may further us in our way. An indifferency for any company shews a dead heart. Where the life of grace is, it is sensible of all advantages and disadvantages. How many have been refreshed by one short, apt, savoury speech, which hath begotten, as it were, new spirits in them.

In ancient times, as we see in the story of Job, chap. ii. 12, it was the custom of friends to meet together to comfort those that were in misery, and Job takes it for granted, that 'to him that is afflicted pity should be shewed from his friends,' chap. vi. 14. For besides the presence of a friend, which hath some influence of comfort in it, 1. The discovery of his loving affection hath a cherishing sweetness in it. 2. The expression of love in real comforts and services, by supplying any outward want of the party troubled, prevails much. Thus Christ made way for his comforts to the souls of men by shewing outward kindness to their bodies. Love, with the sensible fruits of it, prepareth for any wholesome counsel. 3. After this, wholesome words carry a special cordial virtue with them, especially when the Spirit of God in the affectionate speaker joins with the word of comfort, and thereby closeth with the heart of a troubled patient. When all these concentre and meet together in one, then is comfort sealed up to the soul. The child in Elizabeth's womb sprang at the presence and salutation of Mary, Luke i. 41. The speech of one hearty friend cannot but revive the spirits of another. Sympathy hath a strange force, as we see in the strings of an instrument, which being played upon, as they say, the strings of another instrument are also moved with it. After love hath once kindled love, then the heart, being melted, is fit to receive any impression. Unless both pieces of the iron be red hot, they will not join together. Two spirits warmed with the same heat will easily solder together.

§ II. In him that shall stay the mind of another there had need to be an excellent temper of many graces, as, 1. Knowledge of the grievance, together with wisdom to speak a word in season, and to conceal that which may set the cure backwards. 2. Faithfulness with liberty, not to conceal anything which may be for his good, though against present liking. The very life and soul of friendship stands in freedom, tempered with wisdom and faithfulness. 3. Love with compassion and patience to bear all, and hope all, and not to be easily provoked by the waywardness of him we deal with. Short-spirited men are not the best comforters. God himself is said to 'bear with the manners of his people in the wilderness,' Acts xiii. 18. It is one thing to bear with a wise sweet moderation that which may be borne, and another thing to allow or approve that which is not to be approved at all, *Non est idem ferre, si quid ferendum non est, et probare si quid probandum non est.* Where these graces are in the speaker, and apprehended so to be by the person distempered, his heart will soon embrace whatsoever shall be spoken to rectify his judgment or affection. A good conceit of the spirit of the speaker is of as much force to prevail as his words. Words especially prevail, when they are uttered more from the bowels than the brain, and from our own experience, which made even Christ himself a more compassionate High Priest. When men come to themselves again they will be the deepest censurers of their own miscarriage.

§ III. Moreover to the right comforting of an afflicted person, special care must be had of discerning the true ground of his grievance; the core must be searched out. If the grief ariseth from outward causes, then it must be carried into the right channel, the course of it must turn another way, as in staying of blood. We should grieve for sin in the first place, as being the evil of all evils. If the ground be sin, then it must be drawn to a head, from a confused grief to some more particular sin, that so we may strike the right vein; but if we find the spirit much cast down for particular sins, then comfort is presently to be applied. But if the grief be not fully ripe, then, as we use to help nature in its offers to purge, by physic, till the sick matter be carried away; so when conscience, moved by the spirit, begins to ease itself by confession, it is good to help forward the work of it, till we find the heart low enough for comfort to be laid upon. When Paul found the jailor cast down almost as low as hell, he stands not now upon further hammering, and preparing of him for mercy, that work was done already, but presently stirs him up to 'believe in the Lord Jesus Christ,' Acts xvi. 31. Here being a fit place for an interpreter to declare unto man his righteousness, and his mercy that belongs unto him, after he hath acknowledged his personal and particular sins, which the natural guilt of the heart is extremely backward to do, and yet cannot receive any sound peace till it be done. If signs of grace be discerned, here likewise is a fit place to declare unto man the saving work of grace in his heart, which Satan labours to hide from him. Men oft are not able to read their own evidences without help.

In case of stiffness and standing out, it is fit the man of God, 1 Tim. vi. 11 and 2 Tim. iii. 17, should take some authority upon him, and lay a charge upon the souls of men in the name of Christ, to give way to the truth of Christ, and to forbear putting off that mercy which is so kindly offered, when we judge it to be their portion; which course will be successful in hearts awed with a reverend fear of grieving God's Spirit. Sometimes men must be dealt roundly withal, as David here deals with his own soul, that so whilst we ask a reason of their dejection, they may plainly see they have no reason to be so cast down. For oftentimes grievances are irrational, rising from mistakes; and counsel, bringing into the soul a fresh light, dissolves those gross fogs, and setteth the soul at liberty. What grief is contracted by false reason, is by true reason removed.* Thus it pleaseth God to humble men, by letting them see in what need they stand one of another, that so the communion of saints may be endeared. Every relation wherein we stand towards others, are so many bonds and sinews whereby one member is fitted to derive comfort to another, 'through love the bond of perfection,' Col. iii. 14; all must be done in this sweet affection. A member out of joint must be tenderly set in again, and bound up, which only men guided by the spirit of love seasoned with discretion are fit to do. They are taught of God to do what they should. The more of Christ is in any man, the more willingness and fitness to this duty; to which this should encourage us, that in strengthening others we strengthen ourselves, and derive upon ourselves the blessing pronounced on those that 'consider the needy,' Ps. xli. 1, which will be our comfort here and crown hereafter, that God hath honoured us, to be instruments of spiritual good to others. It is an injunction to 'comfort the feeble-minded,' 1 Thes. v. 14, and there is an heavy imputation on those that 'comforted not the weak,' Ezek. xxxiv. 4; when men will not own men in trouble, but estrange themselves as the

* 'Removed,' is in B and C 'altered.'

herd of deer forsakes and pushes away* the wounded deer from them. And those that are any ways cast down, must stoop to those ways which God hath sanctified to convey comfort; for though sometimes the Spirit of God immediately comforts the soul, which is the sweetest, yet for the most part the ' Sun of righteousness that hath healing in his wings,' Mal. iv. 2, conveyeth the beams of his comfort by the help of others, in whom he will have much of our comfort to lie hid; and for this very end it pleaseth God to exercise his children, and ministers especially, with trials and afflictions, that so they, having felt what a troubled spirit is in themselves, might be able to comfort others in their distresses with the same comfort wherewith they have been comforted, 2 Cor. vii. 7. God often suspends comfort from us to drive us to make use of our Christian friends, by whom he purposeth to do us good, *Si illatas molestias lingua dicat, a conscientia dolor emanat, vulnera enim clausa plus cruciant.*—Greg. Oftentimes the very opening of men's grievances bringeth ease, without any further working upon them. The very opening of a vein cools the blood. If God in the state of innocency thought it fit man should have a helper, if God thought it fit to send an angel to comfort Christ in his agonies, shall any man think the comfort of another more than needs? Satan makes every affliction, by reason of our corruption, a temptation to us, whereupon we are to encounter not only with our own corruptions, but with our spiritual wickednesses, Eph. vi. 12; and need we not then that others should join forces with us to discover the temptation, and to confirm and comfort us against it? For so reason joining with reason, and affection with affection, we come by uniting of strength to be impregnable. Satan hath most advantage in solitariness, and thereupon sets upon Christ in the wilderness, Mat. iv., and upon Eve single, Gen. iii., and it added to the glory of Christ's victory, that he overcame him in a single combat, and in a place of such disadvantage. Those that will be alone, at such times, do as much as in them lieth to tempt the tempter himself, to tempt them. The preacher gives three reasons why 'two are better than one,' Eccles. iv. 9. 1. Because if one fall, the other may lift him up. As that which is stronger shoreth up that which is weaker, so feeble minds are raised and kept up by the stronger; nay, oftentimes he that is weaker in one grace is stronger in another. One may help by his experience and meekness of love, that needs the help of another for knowledge. 2. If two lie together, one may warm another by kindling one another's spirits. Where two meet together upon such holy grounds and aims, there Christ by his Spirit makes up another, and this threefold cable who shall break? Mat. xviii. 20. While Joash lived, Jehoiada stood upright; while Latimer and Ridley lived, they kept up Cranmer by intercourse of letters and otherwise, from entertaining counsels of revolt. The disciples presently upon Christ's apprehension fainted, notwithstanding he laboured by his heavenly doctrine to put courage and comfort into them. 3. If any give an onset upon them, there is two to withstand it, spirit joining with spirit; and because there is an acquaintance of spirits as well as of persons, those are fittest to lay open our minds unto, in whom upon experience of their fidelity our hearts may most safely rely, *Solatium vitæ, habere cui pectus aperias.*† We lose much of our strength in the loss of a

---

* 'Forsakes and pushes away,' in B and C 'Forsake and push away,' and 'estrange themselves' dropped.
† Ambrose. The reference is to Ambrose de Off. Min. lib. iii. cap. 22, and is more exactly as follows :—' Solatium quippe vitæ hujus est, ut habeas cui pectus aperias tuum.'—G.

true friend; which made David bemoan the loss of his friend Jonathan, 'Woe is me for thee, my brother Jonathan!' 2 Sam. i. 20. He lost a piece of himself, by losing him whom his heart so clave unto. St Paul accounted that God had shewed especial mercy to him, in the recovery of Epaphroditus, Phil. ii. 27.

§ IV. But there are divers miscarriages in those that are troubled, which make the comfort of others of none effect.

1. When the troubled party deals not directly, but doubleth with him that is to help him. Some are ashamed to acknowledge the true ground of their grievance, pretending sorrow for one thing, when their hearts tell them it ariseth from another: like the lapwings, which make greatest noise farthest from their nest, because they would not have it discovered. This deceit moved our blessed Saviour, who knew what was in the hearts of men, to fit his answers many times, rather to the man than to the matter.

2. Some rely too much upon particular men, Oh if they had such a one they should do well, and mislike others, fitter perhaps to deal with them, as having more thorough knowledge of their estates, because they would have their disease rather covered than cured, or if cured, yet with soft words, whereas no plaster worketh better than that which causes smart. Some out of mere humorous fondness must have that which can hardly be got, or else nothing pleases them. David must needs have the 'waters of Bethlehem,' 2 Sam. xxiii. 15, when others were nearer hand. And oftentimes when men have not only whom they desire, but such also who are fit and dexterous in dealing with a troubled spirit, yet their souls feel no comfort, because they make idols of men; whereas men at the best are but conduits of comfort, and such as God freely conveyeth comfort by, taking liberty oft to deny comfort by them, that so he may be acknowledged the 'God of all comfort,' 2 Cor. i. 3.

3. Some delude themselves, by thinking it sufficient to have a few good words spoken to them, as if that could cure them; not regarding to apprehend the same, and mingle it with faith, without which, good words lose their working, even as wholesome physic in a dead stomach.

Besides miscarriages in comforting, times will often fall out in our lives, that we shall have none either to comfort us, or to be comforted by us, and then what will become of us unless we can comfort ourselves? Men must not think always to live upon alms, but lay up something in store for themselves, and provide oil for their own lamps, and be able to draw out something from the treasury of their own hearts. We must not go to the surgeon for every scratch. No wise traveller but will have some refreshing waters about him. Again, we are often driven to retire home to our own hearts, by uncharitable imputations of other men. Even friends sometimes become miserable comforters. It was Job's case, chap. ii.; his friends had honest intentions to comfort him, but erred in their manner of dealing. If he had found no more comfort by reflecting upon his own sincerity, than he received from them, who laboured to take it from him, he had been doubly miserable. We are most privy to our own intentions and aims, whence comfort must be fetched; let others speak what they can to us, if our own hearts speak not with them, we shall receive no satisfaction. Sometimes it may fall out, that those which should unloose our spirits when they are bound up, mistake; the key misses the right wards, and so we lie bound still. Opening of our estate to another is not good but when it is necessary; and it is not necessary, when we can fetch supply from our own store. God would have us tender of our reputations, except in some special cases, wherein we are to give glory to God, Josh. vii. 19, by a free and full confession. Needless discovery of ourselves to others, makes us fear the conscience of another man, as privy to that which we are ashamed he should be privy unto ; and it is neither wisdom nor mercy to put men upon the rack of confession, further than they can have no ease any other way. For by this means we raise in them a jealousy towards us, and oft without cause, which weakeneth and tainteth that love which should unite hearts in one.

CHAPTER XV.—*Of flying to God in disquiets of souls ; eight observations out of the text.*

Quest. What if neither the speech of others to us, nor the rebuke of our own hearts, will quiet the soul ? Is there no other remedy left ?

Ans. Yes ; then look up to God, the father and fountain of comfort, as David doth here ; for the more special means whereby he sought to recover himself was by laying a charge upon his soul to trust in God. For having let his soul run out too much, he begins to recollect himself again, and resign up all to God.

§ I. *Quest.* But how came David to have the command of his own soul, so as to take it off from grief, and to place it upon God ? Could he dispose of his own heart himself ?

Ans. The child of God hath something in him above a man ; he hath the Spirit of God to guide his spirit. This command of David to his soul was under the command of the great commander. God commands David to trust in him, and at the same time infuseth strength into his soul by thinking of God's command, and trusting to God's power, to command itself to trust in God ; so that this command is not only by authority, but by virtue likewise of God's command. As the inferior orbs move as they are moved by a higher, so David's spirit here moves as it is moved by God's Spirit, which inwardly spake to him to speak to himself.

David, in speaking thus to his own soul, was, as every true Christian is, a prophet and an instructor to himself ; it is but as if inferior officers should charge in the name and power of the king. God's children have a principle of life in them from the Spirit of God, by which they command themselves. To give charge belongs to a superior. David had a double superior above him, his own spirit as sanctified, and God's Spirit guiding that. Our spirits are the Spirit's agents, and the Holy Spirit is God's agent, maintaining his right in us. As God hath made man a free agent, so he guides him, and preserves that free manner of working which is agreeable to man's nature.

By this it appears that David's moving of himself did not hinder the Spirit's moving of him, neither did the Spirit's moving of him hinder him from moving himself in a free manner ; for the Spirit of God moveth according to our principles, it openeth our understandings to see that it is best to trust in God ; it moveth so sweetly, as if it were an inbred principle, and all one with our own spirits. If we should hold our will to move itself, and not to be moved by the Spirit, we should make a god of it, whose property is to move other things, and not to be moved by any.*

We are in some sort lords over our own speeches and actions, but yet under a higher lord. David was willing to trust in God, but God wrought

* Ergone ita liberi esse volunt, ut nec Deum volunt habere Dominum ?—Aug. de Spir. et Lit.

that will in him. He first makes our will good, and then works by it. It is a sacrilegious liberty that will acknowledge no dependence upon God. We are wise in his wisdom, and strong in his strength, who saith, 'Without me ye can do nothing,' John xv. 5. Both the bud of a good desire, and the blossom of a good resolution, and the fruit of a good action, all comes ̇from God. Indeed, the understanding is ours whereby we know what to do, and the will is ours whereby we make choice of what is best to be done; but the light whereby we know, and the guidance whereby we choose, that is from a higher agent, which is ready to flow into us with present fresh supply, when by virtue of former strength we put ourselves forward in obedience to God.* Let but David say to his soul being charged of God to trust, I charge thee, my soul, to trust in him, and he finds a present strength enabling to it. Therefore, we must both depend upon God as the first mover, and withal set all the inferior wheels of our souls agoing, according as the Spirit of God ministers motion unto us. So shall we be free from self-confidence, and likewise from neglecting that order of working which God hath established. David hearkened what the Lord said, before he said anything to himself,—so should we. God's commands tend to this, that we should command ourselves. God, and the minister under God, bid us trust in him, but all is to no purpose till grace be wrought in the soul, whereby it bids itself. Our speaking to others doth no good, till they, by entertaining what we say, speak the same to their own souls.

In this charge of David upon his own soul, we may see divers passages and privileges of a gracious heart in trouble.

§ II. *Obs.* 1. As 1. *That a Christian, when he is beaten out of all other comforts, yet hath a God to run unto.* A wicked man beaten out of earthly comforts, is as a naked man in a storm, and an unarmed man in the field, or as a ship tossed in the sea without an anchor, which presently dashes upon rocks, or falleth upon quicksands; but a Christian, when he is driven out of all comforts below, nay, when God seems to be angry with him, he can appeal from God angry to God appeased, he can wrestle and strive with God by God's own strength, fight with him with his own weapons, and plead with God by his own arguments. What a happy estate is this! Who would not be a Christian, if it were but for this, to have something to rely on when all things else fail? The confusion and unquietness which troubles raise in the soul may drive it from resting in itself, but there can never be any true peace settled, until it sees and resolves what to stay upon.

§ III. 2. We see here that *there is a sanctified use of all troubles to God's children.* First, they drive them *out of themselves*, and then draw them nearer to God. Crosses, indeed, of themselves estrange us more from God, but by an overruling work of the Spirit they bring us nearer to him. The soul of itself is ready to misgive, as if God had too many controversies with it, to shew any favour towards it; and Satan helpeth. Because he knows nothing can stand and prevail against God, or a soul that relieth on him, therefore he labours to breed and increase an everlasting division betwixt God and the soul. But let not Christians muse so much upon their trouble, but see whither it carries them, whether it brings them nearer unto God or not. It is a never-failing rule of discerning a man to be in the state of grace, *when he finds every condition draw him nearer to God;* for thus it

---

* Certum est, nos velle cum volumus, sed ille facit ut velimus.—Aug. For the thought, not the words, see Conf., Book VII., iii. 5, and elsewhere repeatedly.—G.

appears that such love God, and are called of him, unto whom 'all things work together for the best,' Rom. viii. 28.

§ IV. 3. Again, hence we see that the Spirit of God by these *inward speeches* doth awake the soul, and keep it in a holy exercise, by stirring up the grace of faith to its proper function. It is not so much the having of grace, as grace in *exercise*, that preserves the soul. Therefore, we should by this and the like means 'stir up the grace of God in us,' 2 Tim. i. 6, that so it may be kept a-working, and in vigour and strength. It was David's manner to awake himself, by bidding both 'heart and harp to awake,' Ps. lvii. 8. It is the waking Christian, that hath his wit and his grace ready about him, who is the safe Christian. Grace dormant, without the exercise, doth not secure us. It is almost all one, in regard of present exigence, for grace not to be and not to work. The soul without action is like an instrument not played upon, or like a ship always in the haven. Motion is a preservative of the purity of things. Even life itself is made more lively by action. The Spirit of God, whereby his children are led, is compared to things of the quickest and strongest actions, as fire and wind, &c. God himself is a pure act, always in acting; and everything, the nearer it comes to God, the more it hath its perfection in working. The happiness of man consists chiefly in a gracious frame of spirit, and actions suitable sweetly issuing therefrom. The very rest of heavenly bodies is in motion in their proper places. By this stirring up the grace of God in us, sparkles come to be flames, and all graces are kept bright. Troubles stir up David;* David being stirred, stirs up himself.

§ V. 4. We see likewise here a further use *of soliloquies or speeches to our own hearts*. When the soul by entering into itself sees itself put out of order, then it enjoins this duty of trusting in God upon it. If we look only on ourselves, and not turn to God, the work of the soul is imperfect. Then the soul worketh as it should, whenas by reflecting on itself, it gathers some profitable conclusion, and leaveth itself with God. David, upon reflecting on himself, found nothing but discouragement; but when he looks upward to God, there he finds rest. This is one end why God suffers the soul to tire and beat itself, that, finding no rest in itself, it might seek to him. David yields not so much to his passion as that it should keep him from God. Therefore, let no man truly religious pretend, for an excuse, his temper or provoking occasions, &c., for grace doth raise the soul above nature. Grace doth not only stop the soul in an evil way, but carries it to a contrary good, and raiseth it up to God. Though holy men be subject to 'like passions with others,' James v. 17, as it is said of Elias, yet they are not so enthralled to them, as that they carry them wholly away from their God; but they hear a voice of the Spirit within them, calling them back again to their former communion with God; and so grace takes occasion, even from sin, to exercise itself.

§ VI. 5. Observe further, that *distrust is the cause of all disquiet*. The soul suffers itself by something here below to be drawn away from God, but can find no rest till it return to him again. As Noah's dove had no place to set her foot upon, Gen. viii. 11, till it was received into the ark from whence it came. And it is God's mercy to us, that when we have let go our hold of God, we should find nothing but trouble and unquietness in any-

* A connective 'and' in C.

thing else, that so we might remember from whence we are fallen, and return home again. That is a good trouble which frees us from the greatest trouble, and brings with it the most comfortable rest. It is but an unquiet quiet, and a restless rest which is out of God. It is a deep spiritual judgment for a man to find too much rest in the creature. The soul that hath had a saving work upon it, will be always impatient until it recovers its former sweetness in God. After God's Spirit hath once touched the soul, it will never be quiet until it stands pointed God-ward.

Obj. But conscience may object, upon any offence is God offended, and therefore not to be trusted?

Ans. It is true, where faith is not above natural conscience; but a conscience 'sprinkled with the blood of Christ,' Heb. x. 22, is not scared from God by its infirmities and failings, but as David here is rather stirred up to run unto God by his distemper; and it had been a greater sin than his distemper not to have gone unto God. Those that have the spirit of sons in their hearts, run not further from God after they have a little strayed from him; but, though it be the nature of sinful passions to breed grief and shame, yet they will repair to God again, and their confidence overcomes their guilt, so well are they acquainted with God's gracious disposition.

Yet we see here, David thinks not of trusting in God, till first he had done justice upon his own soul, in rebuking the unruly motions thereof. Censure for sin goeth before favour in pardoning sin or boldness to ask pardon of God. Those that love God must hate ill, Ps. xcvii. 10. If our consciences condemn us of allowing any sin, we cannot have boldness with God, who is light and can abide no darkness, and 'greater than our consciences,' 1 John iii. 20.

§ VII. 6. Moreover, hence we see *it is no easy thing to bring God and the heart together*. David here as he often checks his heart, so he doth often charge his heart. Doubts and troubles are still gathering upon him, and his faith still gathering upon them. As one striving to get the haven, is driven back by the waves, but recovering himself again, gets forward still, and after often beating back, at length obtains the wished haven, and then is at rest, so much ado there is to bring the soul unto God, the harbour of true comfort. It were an easy thing to be a Christian, if religion stood only in a few outward works and duties, but to take the soul to task, and to deal roundly with our own hearts, and to let conscience have its full work, and to bring the soul into spiritual subjection unto God, this is not so easy a matter, because the soul out of self-love is loath to enter into itself, lest it should have other thoughts of itself than it would have. David must bid his soul trust, and trust, and trust again before it will yield. One main ground of this difficulty is, that contrary which is in the soul by reason of contrary principles. The soul so far as it is gracious commands, so far as it is rebellious resists, which drew holy Austin to a kind of astonishment: 'The soul commands the body and it yields,' saith he, 'it commands itself, and is resisted by itself. It commands the hand to move, and it moveth with such an unperceivable quickness that you can discern no distance betwixt the command and the motion. Whence comes this? but because the soul perfectly wills not, and perfectly enjoins not that which is good, and so far forth that it fully wills not, so far it holds back.'* There should

---

* Unde hoc monstrum et quare istud? . . . . . Non ex toto vult, non ex toto imperat, in tantum non fit quod imperat, in quantum non vult.—Augustine, Confess., Book VIII., ix. 21.

be no need of commanding the soul if it were perfect, for then it would be of itself, what it now commandeth. If David had gotten his soul at perfect freedom at the first, he needed not have repeated his charge so often upon it. But the soul naturally sinks downward, and therefore had need often to be wound up.

§ VIII. 7. We should therefore labour to bring our souls, as David doth here, to a firm and peremptory resolution, and not stand wavering, and as it were equally balanced betwixt God and other things; but enforce our souls. We shall get little ground of infidelity else. Drive your souls, therefore, to this issue, either to rely upon God, or else to yield up itself to the present grievance. If by yielding, it resolves to be miserable, there's an end; but if it desires rest, then let it resolve upon this only way, to trust in God. And well may the soul so resolve, because in God there are grounds of quieting the soul, above all that may unsettle it; in him there is both worth to satisfy, and strength to support the soul. The best way to maintain inward peace, is to settle and fix our thoughts upon that which will make us better, till we found our hearts warmed and wrought upon thereby, and then, as the prophet speaks, 'God will keep us in peace, peace,' that is, 'in perfect and abundant peace,' Isa. xxvi. 3. This resolution stayed Job, that though God should kill him, yet he resolved 'to trust in him,' Job xiii. 15. Answerable to our resolution is our peace, the more resolution the more peace. Irresolution of itself, without any grievance, is full of disquiet. It is an unsafe thing always to begin to live, to be always cheapening and paltering with God; come to this point once, trust God I ought, therefore, trust God I will, come what may or will.

And it is good to renew our resolutions again and again: for every new resolution brings the soul closer to God, and gets further in him, and brings fresh strength from him; which, if we neglect, our corruption joining with outward hindrances will carry us further and further backward, and this will double, yea multiply our trouble and grief to recover ourselves again. We have both wind and tide against us, we are going up the hill, and, therefore, had need to arm ourselves with resolution. Since the fall, the motion of the soul upward, as of heavy bodies, is violent, in regard of corruption which weighs it downward, and, therefore, all enforcement is little enough. Oppose, therefore, with David, an invincible resolution, and then doubt not of prevailing. If we resolve in God's power and not our own, and be 'strong in the Lord,' Eph. vi. 10, and not in ourselves, then it matters not what our troubles or temptations be either from within, or without, for trust in God at length will triumph.

Here is a great mercy, that when David had a little let go his hold of God, yet God would not let go his hold of him, but by a spirit of faith draws him back again to himself. God turns us unto him, and then we return. 'Turn us again,' saith the psalmist, 'cause thy face to shine upon us, and we shall be saved,' Ps. lxxx. 19. When the soul leaves God once, it loses its way and itself; and never returns till God recalls it again. *Animus æger semper errat.* If moral principles, cherished and strengthened by good education, will enable the soul against vicious inclinations, so that, though some influence of the heavens work upon the air, and the air upon the spirits, and the spirits upon the humours, and these incline the temper, and that inclines the soul of a man such and such ways, yet breeding in the refineder sort of civil persons will much prevail to draw them another way. What, then, may we think of this powerful grace of faith which is altogether supernatural? Will not this carry the soul above all natural inclinations whatsoever, though strengthened by outward occasions, if we resolve to put it to it? David was a king of other men, but here he shews that he was a king of himself. What benefit is it for a man to be ruler over all the world, and yet remain a slave to himself?

§ IX. 8. Again, David here doth not only resolve, but *presently takes up his soul, before it strayed too far from God.* The further and the longer the soul wanders from God, the more it entangles itself, and the thicker darkness will cover the soul, yea, the loather it is to come to God again, being ashamed to look God in the face after discontinuing of acquaintance with him; nay, the stronger the league grows betwixt sin and the soul, and the more there groweth a kind of suitableness betwixt the soul and sin. Too long giving way to base thoughts and affections, discovers too much complacency and liking of sin. If we once give way, a little grief will turn into bitter sorrow, and that into a settled pensiveness and heaviness of spirit; fear will grow into astonishment, and discouragement into despair. If ever we mean to trust God, why not now? How many are taken away in their offers and essays, before they have prepared their hearts to cleave unto God! The sooner we give up ourselves to the Lord, the sooner we know upon what terms we stand, and the sooner we provide for our best security, and have not our grounds of comfort to seek when we shall stand most in need of them. Time will salve up grief in the meanest of men; reason, in those that will suffer themselves to be ruled thereby, will cure, or at least stay the fits of it, sooner; but faith, if we stir it up, will give our souls no rest, until it hath brought us to our true rest, that is, to God. Therefore we should press the heart forward to God presently, that Satan make not the rent greater.

§ X. 9. Lastly, here we see, that *though the soul be overborne by passion for a time, yet if grace hath once truly seasoned it, it will work itself into freedom again.* Grace, as oil, will be above. The eye when any dust falls into it, is not more tender and unquiet, till it be wrought out again, than a gracious soul is, being once troubled. The spirit, as a spring, will be cleansing of itself more and more. Whereas the heart of a carnal man is like a standing pool, whatsoever is cast into it, there it rests. Trouble and disquietness in him are in their proper place. It is proper for the sea to rage and cast up dirt. God hath set it down for an eternal rule, that vexation and sin shall be inseparable. Happiness and rest were severed from sin in heaven when the angels fell, and in paradise when Adam fell, Gen. iii., and will remain for ever separated, until the breach be made up by faith in Christ. *Jussisti Domine, et sic est, ut omnis inordinatus affectus sibi sit pœna.* —Aug.

CHAPTER XVI.—*Of trust in God; grounds of it; especially his providence.*

But to come nearer to the unfolding of this trust in God, which David useth here as a remedy against all distempers. Howsoever confidence and trust be an affection of nature, yet by the Spirit's sanctifying and carrying it to the right object, it becomes a grace of wonderful use. In the things of this life, usually he that hopes most is the most unwise man, he being most deceived that hopes most, because he trusts in that which is uncertain;

and therefore deceitful hope is counted but the dream of a waking man. But in religion it is far otherwise; here hope is the main supporting grace of the soul, springing from faith in the promises of God.

Trust and hope are often taken in the same sense, though a distinction betwixt them hath sometimes its use. Faith looks to the word promising, hope to the thing promised in the word; faith looks to the authority of the promiser, hope especially to the goodness of the promise; faith looks upon things as present, hope as to come hereafter. God as the first truth, is that which faith relies on; but God as the chief good is that which hope rests on. Trust or confidence is nothing else but the strength of hope. If the thing hoped for be deferred, then of necessity it enforces waiting, and waiting is nothing else but hope and trust lengthened.

Howsoever there may be use of these and such like distinctions, yet usually they are taken promiscuously, especially in the Old Testament. The nature and use of faith is set out by terms of staying, resting, leaning, rolling ourselves upon God, &c., which come all to one, and therefore we forbear any further curious distinction.

Now, seeing trusting in God is a remedy against all distempers, it is necessary that we should bring the object and the act, God and the soul, together; for effecting of which it is good to know something concerning God and something concerning trust. God only is the fit object of trust. He hath all the properties of that which should be trusted on. A man can be in no condition wherein God is at a loss and cannot help him. If comforts be wanting, he can create comforts, not only out of nothing, but out of discomforts. He made the whale that swallowed up Jonah a means to bring him to the shore, Jonah i. 17. The sea was a wall to the Israelites on both sides, Exod. xiv. 22. The devouring flames were a great refreshing to the three children in the fiery furnace, Dan. iii. That trouble which we think will swallow us up, may be a means to bring us to our haven; 'so mighty is God in power, and so excellent in working,' Isa. xxviii. 29. God then, and God only, is a fit foundation for the soul to build itself upon, for the firmer the foundation is, the stronger will the building be; therefore those that will build high must dig deep. The higher the tree riseth, the deeper the root spreadeth and fasteneth itself below. So it is in faith: if the foundation thereof be not firm, the soul cannot build itself strongly upon it. Faith hath a double principle to build on, either a principle of being, or a principle of knowing. The principle of being is God himself, the principle of knowing is God's word, whereby God cometh forth 'out of that hidden light which none can attain unto,' 1 Tim. vi. 16, and discovereth his meaning towards us for our good.

This then must, 1, be supposed for a ground, *that there is a God*, and that God *is*, that is, hath a full and eternal being, and giveth a being, and an order of being, to all things else. Some things have only a being, some things life and being, some things sense, &c., and some things have a more excellent being, including all the former, as the being of creatures endued with reason. If God had not a being, nothing else could be. In things subordinate one to another, take away the first, and you take away all the rest. Therefore this proposition, God is, is the first truth of all; and if this were not, nothing else should be, as we see if the heavenly bodies do not move, there is no motion here below.

2. In the divine nature or being, there is a subsisting of three persons, every one so set out unto us, as fitted for us to trust in; the Father as a Creator, the Son as a Redeemer, the Holy Ghost as a Comforter, and all

this is in reference to us. God in the first person hath decreed the great work of our salvation, and all things tending to the accomplishment of it. God in the second person hath exactly and fully answered that decree and plot, in the work of our redemption. God in the third person discovers and applies all unto us, and fits us for communion with the Father and the Son, from whom he proceeds.

3. God cannot be comfortably thought upon out of Christ our Mediator, in whom he was 'reconciling the world to himself,' 1 Cor. v. 19, as being a friend both to God and us, and therefore fit to bring God and the soul together, being a middle person in the Trinity. In Christ, God's nature becomes lovely to us, and ours to God; otherwise there is an utter enmity betwixt his pure and our impure nature. Christ hath made up the vast gulf between God and us. There is nothing more terrible to think on, than an absolute God out of Christ.

4. Therefore, for the better drawing of us to trust in God, we must conceive of him under the sweet relation of a Father. God's nature is fatherly now unto us, and therefore lovely.

5. And for further strengthening our faith it is needful to consider what excellencies the Scripture giveth unto God, answerable to all our necessities. What sweet names God is pleased to be known unto us by for our comfort, 'as a merciful, gracious, long-suffering God,' &c. Exod. xxxiv. 6.

When Moses desired to see the glory of God, God thus manifested himself, in the way of goodness: 'I will make all my goodness pass before thee,' Exod. xxxiii. 16.

Whatsoever is good in the creature is first in God as a fountain; and it is in God in a more eminent manner and fuller measure. All grace and holiness, all sweetness of affection, all power and wisdom, &c. as it is in him, so it is from him: and we come to conceive these properties to be in God, 1, by feeling the comfort and power of them in ourselves; 2, by observing these things in their measure to be in the best of the creatures, whence we arise to take notice of what grace and what love, what strength and wisdom, &c., is in God, by the beams of these which we see in his creature, with adding in our thoughts fulness peculiar to God, and abstracting imperfections incident to the creature. For that is in God in the highest degree, the sparkles whereof is but in us.

6. Therefore it is fit that unto all other eminencies in God, we should strengthen our faith by considering those glorious singularities, which are altogether incommunicable to the creature, and which gives strength to his other properties, as that God is not only gracious and loving, powerful, wise, &c., but that he is infinitely, eternally, and unchangeably so. All which are comprised in and drawn from that one name Jehovah, as being of himself, and giving a being to all things else, of nothing; and able, when it pleaseth him, to turn all things to nothing again.

7. As God is thus, so he makes it good by answerable actions and dealing towards us, by his continual providence, the consideration whereof is a great stay to our faith; for by this providence God makes use of all his former excellencies for his people's good, for the more comfortable apprehension of which, it is good to know that God's providence is extended as far as his creation. Every creature, in every element and place whatsoever, receiveth a powerful influence from God, who doth what pleaseth him, both in heaven and earth, in the sea, and all places. But we must know God doth not put things into a frame, and then leave them to their own motion, as we do clocks, after we have once set them right, and ships, after

we have once built them, commit them to wind and waves; but as he made all things, and knows all things, so, by a continued kind of creation, he preserves all things in their being and working, and governs them in their ends. He is the first mover that sets all the wheels of the creature aworking. One wheel may move another, but all are moved by the first. If God moves not, the clock of the creature stands. If God should not uphold things, they would presently fall to nothing, from whence they came. If God should not guide things, Satan's malice, and man's weakness, would soon bring all to a confusion. If God did not rule the great family of the world, all would break and fall to pieces, whereas the wise providence of God keepeth everything on its right hinges. All things stand in obedience to this providence of God, and nothing can withdraw itself from under it. If the creature withdraw itself from one order of providence, it falls into another. If man, the most unruly and disordered creature of all, withdraw himself from God's gracious government of him to happiness, he will soon fall under God's just government of him to deserved misery. If he shakes off God's sweet yoke, he puts himself under Satan's heavy yoke, who, as God's executioner, hardens him to destruction. And so, whilst he rushes against God's will, he fulfils it; and whilst he will not willingly do God's will, God's will is done upon him against his will.

The most casual things fall under providence, yea, the most disordered thing in the world, sin, and, of sins the most horrible that ever the sun beheld, the 'crucifying of the Lord of life,' Acts iii. 15, was guided by a hand of providence to the greatest good. For that which is casual in regard of a second cause, is not so in regard of the first, whose providence is most clearly seen in casual events that fall out by accident, for in these the effect cannot be ascribed to the next cause. God is said to kill him who was unwarily slain by the falling of an axe or some instrument of death, Deut. xix. 5.

And though man hath a freedom in working, and of all men the hearts of kings are most free, yet even these are 'guided by an overruling power,' Prov. xxi. 1, as the rivers of water are carried in their channels whither skilful men list to derive them.

For settling of our faith the more, God taketh liberty in using weak means to great purposes, and setting aside more likely and able means; yea, sometimes he altogether disableth the greatest means, and worketh often by no means at all. It is not for want of power in God, but from abundance and multiplying of his goodness that he useth any means at all. There is nothing that he doth by means but he is able to do without means.

Nay, God often bringeth his will to pass by crossing the course and stream of means, to shew his own sovereignty and to exercise our dependence, and maketh his very enemies the accomplishers of his own will, and so to bring about that which they oppose most. Hence it is that we believe under hope against hope, Ps. cxxxv. 6.

But we must know, God's manner of guiding things is without prejudice to the proper working of the things themselves. He guideth them sweetly according to the instincts he hath put into them; for,

1. He furnishes creatures with a virtue and power to work, and likewise with a manner of working suitable to their own nature; as it is proper for a man, when he works, to work with freedom, and other creatures by natural instinct, &c.

2. God maintaineth both the power and manner of working, and perfecteth and accomplisheth the same by acting of it, being nearer to us in

all we do than we are to ourselves. *Intimior intimo nostro.* 3. He applies and stirs up our abilities and actions to this or that particular as he seeth best. 4. He suspends or removes the hindrances of all actions, and so powerfully, wisely, and sweetly orders them to his own ends. When any evil is intended, God either puts bars and lets to the execution of it, or else limiteth and boundeth the same, both in regard of time and measure, so that our enemies either shall not do the evil at all, or else not so long a time or not in such a height of mischief as their malice would carry them to. The rod of the wicked may light upon the back of the righteous, Ps. cxxv. 3, but it shall not rest there. God knows how to take our enemies off, sometimes by changing or stopping their wills, by offering considerations of some good or ill, danger or profit, to them; sometimes by taking away and weakening all their strength, or else by opposing an equal or greater strength against it. All the strength our enemies have rests in God, who, if he denies concourse and influence, the arm of their power, as Jeroboam's, when he stretched it out against the prophet, shrinks up presently.

God is not only the cause of things and actions, but the cause, likewise, of the cessation of them, why they fall not out at all. God is the cause why things are not, as well as why they are. *Deus est prima causa cujuscunque non esse.* The cause why men favour us not, or, when they do favour us, want present wisdom and ability to help us, is from God's withdrawing the concurrence of his light and strength from them. If a skilful physician doth us no good, it is because it pleaseth God to hide the right way of curing at that time from him. Which should move us to see God in all that befalls us, who hath sufficient reason, as to do what he doth, so not to do what he doth not, to hinder as well as to give way.

The God of spirits hath an influence into the spirits of men, into the principles and springs of all actions; otherwise he could not so certainly foretell things to come. God had a work in Absalom's heart in that he refused the best counsel. There is nothing independent of him who is the mover of all things, and himself unmoveable.

Nothing so high, that is above his providence; nothing so low, that is beneath it; nothing so large, but is bounded by it; nothing so confused, but God can order it; nothing so bad, but he can draw good out of it; nothing so wisely plotted, but God can disappoint it, as Ahithophel's counsel; nothing so simply and unpoliticly carried, but he can give a prevailing issue unto it; nothing so freely carried, in regard of the next cause, but God can make it necessary in regard of the event; nothing so natural, but he can suspend it in regard of operation, as heavy bodies from sinking, fire from burning, &c.

It cannot but bring strong security to the soul, to know that in all variety of changes and intercourse of good and bad events, God, and our God, hath such a disposing hand. Whatsoever befalls us, all serves to bring God's electing love, and our glorification together, God's providence serveth his purpose to save us. All sufferings, all blessings, all ordinances, all graces, all common gifts, nay, our very falls, yea, Satan himself with all his instruments, as over-mastered, and ruled by God, have this injunction upon them, to further God's good intendment to us, and a prohibition to do us no harm. Augustus taxed the world for civil ends, but God's providence used this as a means for Christ to be born at Bethlehem. Ahasuerus could not sleep, and thereupon calls for the chronicles, the reading of which occasioned the Jews' delivery, Esth. vi. 1. God oft disposeth little occasions to great purposes. And by those very ways whereby proud men have gone about to withstand God's counsels, they have fulfilled them, as we see in the story of Joseph and Moses, 'in the thing wherein they dealt proudly, he was above them,' Exod. x. 11. *Divinum consilium, dum devitatur, impletur; humana sapientia, dum reluctatur, comprehenditur.*—Greg.

CHAPTER XVII.—*Of graces to be exercised in respect of Divine Providence.*

We are under a providence that is above our own; which should be a ground unto us, of exercising those graces that tend to settle the soul, in all events. As,

1. Hence to lay our hand upon our mouths, and command the soul an holy silence, not daring to yield to the least rising of our hearts against God. 'I was dumb, and opened not my mouth, because thou didst it,' Ps. xxxix. 9, saith David. Thus Aaron, when he had lost his two sons, both at once, and that by fire, Lev. x. 1, 2, and by fire from heaven, which carried an evidence of God's great displeasure with it, yet held his peace. In this silence and hope is our strength. Flesh and blood is prone to expostulate with God, and to question his dealing, as we see in Gideon, Jeremiah, Asaph, Habakkuk, and others, 'If the Lord be with us, why then is all this befallen us?' Jud. vi. 13; but, after some struggling between the flesh and the spirit, the conclusion will be, yet howsoever matters go, 'God is good to Israel,' Ps. lxxiii. 1. Where a fearful spirit, and a melancholy temper, a weak judgment, and a scrupulous and raw conscience meet in one, there Satan and his, together with men's own hearts, which, like sophisters, are continually cavilling against themselves, breed much disquiet, and makes the life uncomfortable. Such, therefore, should have a special care, as to grow in knowledge, so to stick close to sure and certain grounds, and bring their consciences to the rule. Darkness causeth fears. The more light, the more confidence. When we yield up ourselves to God, we should resolve upon quietness, and if the heart stirs, presently use this check of David, 'Why art thou disquieted?'

God's ways seem oft to us full of contradictions, because his course is to bring things to pass by contrary means. There is a mystery not only in God's decree concerning man's eternal estate, but likewise in his providence, as why he should deal unequally with men otherwise equal. His judgments are a great depth, which we cannot fathom, but they will swallow up our thoughts and understandings. God oft wraps himself in a cloud, and will not be seen till afterward. Where we cannot trace him, we ought with St Paul to admire and adore him. When we are in heaven, it will be one part of our happiness to see the harmony of those things that seem now confused unto us. All God's dealings will appear beautiful in their due seasons, though we for the present see not the contiguity and linking together of one with another.

2. Hence likewise proceeds a holy resigning of ourselves to God, 'who doth all things according to the counsel of his own will,' Dan. xi. 16; Eph. i. 11. *Voluntas Dei, necessitas rei.* His will is a wise will; it is guided by counsel, a sovereign prevailing will. The only way to have our will is to bring it to God's will. If we could delight in him, we should have our heart's desire. Thus David yields up himself to God: 'Here I am; let the Lord deal with me as seemeth good unto him, 2 Sam. xv. 26. And thus Eli, when God foretold by Samuel the ruin of his house, quiets him-

self: 'It is the Lord; let him do what seemeth him good,' 1 Sam. iii. 18. Thus our blessed Saviour stays himself: 'Not my will, but thy will be done.' And thus the people of God, when Paul was resolved to go to Jerusalem, submitted, saying, 'The will of the Lord be done,' Acts xxi. 14, —a speech fit to proceed out of the heart and mouth of a Christian. *Vox vere Christianorum*.

We may desire and long after a change of our condition, when we look upon the grievance itself, but yet remember still that it be with reservation, when we look upon the will of God, as, 'How long, Lord, holy and true,' &c. Rev. vi. 10. Out of inferior reasons we may with our Saviour desire a removal of the cup; but when we look to the supreme reason of reasons, the will of God, here we must stoop and kiss the rod. 'Thus humbling ourselves under his mighty hand,' 1 Peter v. 6, which by murmuring and fretting we may make more heavy, but not take off, still adding new guilt and pulling on new judgments.

3. The way patiently to suffer God's will, is to inure ourselves first to do it. Passive obedience springs from active. He that endures anything will endure it quietly, when he knows it is the will of God, and considers that whatever befalls him comes from his good pleasure. Those that have not inured themselves to the yoke of obedience, will never endure the yoke of suffering; they fume and rage 'as a wild boar in a net,' Isa. li. 20, as the prophet speaks. It is worth the considering, to see two men of equal parts under the same cross, how quietly and calmly the one that establisheth his soul on Christ will bear his afflictions, whereas the other rageth as a fool, and is more beaten.

Nothing should displease us that pleaseth God: neither should anything be pleasing to us that displeaseth him. This conformity is the ground of comfort. Our own will takes away God, as much as in it lies. *Propria voluntas Deum quantum in ipsa eximit.* 'If we acknowledge God in all our ways, he will direct our paths, and lead us the way that we should go,' Prov. iii. 6. The quarrel betwixt God and us is taken up, when his will and our will are one; when we have sacrificed ourselves and our wills unto God; when, as he is highest in himself, so his will hath the highest place in our hearts. We find by experience that, when our wills are so subdued, that we delight to do what God would have us do, and to be what God would have us be, that then sweet peace presently riseth to the soul.

When we can say, Lord, if thou wilt have me poor and disgraced, I am content to be so; if thou wilt have me serve thee in this condition I am in, I will gladly do so. It is enough to me that thou wouldst have it so. I desire to yield readily, humbly, and cheerfully to thy disposing providence. Thus a godly man says amen to God's amen, and puts his *fiat* and *placet* to God's. As the sea turns all rivers into its own relish, so he turns all to his own spirit, and makes whatsoever befalls him an exercise of some virtue. A heathen could say that calamities did rule over men, but a wise man hath a spirit overruling all calamities; much more a Christian. For a man to be in this estate, is to enjoy heaven in the world under heaven. God's kingdom comes where his will is thus done and suffered.

None feel more sweet experience of God's providence than those that are most resolute in their obedience. After we have given glory to God in relying upon his wisdom, power, and truth, we shall find him employing these for our direction, assistance, and bringing about of things to our desired issue, yea, above whatever we looked for, or thought of.

In all cases that fall out, or that we can put to ourselves, as in case of extremity, opposition, strange accidents, desertion, and damps of spirit, &c., here we may take sanctuary, that we are in covenant with him who sits at the stern and rules all, and hath committed the government of all things to his Son, our brother, our Joseph, the second person in heaven. We may be sure that no hurt shall befall us that he can hinder; and what cannot he hinder 'that hath the keys of hell and of death?' Rev. i. 18, unto whom we are so near that he carries 'our names in his breast, and on his shoulders,' Heb. iv. 15, as the high priest did those of the twelve tribes. Though his church seems a widow neglected, ye he will make the world know that she hath a husband will right her in good time.

Quest. But it may be demanded, What course is to be taken for guidance of our lives in particular actions, wherein doubts may arise what is most agreeable to the will of God?

Ans. 1. We must not put all carelessly upon a providence, but first consider what is our part; and, so far as God prevents us with light, and affords us helps and means, we must not be failing in our duty. We should neither outrun nor be wanting to providence. But in perplexed cases, where the reasons on both sides seem to be equally balanced, see whether part make more for the main end, the glory of God, the service of others, and advancement of our own spiritual good. *Summa ratio quæ pro religione facit.* Some things are so clear and even, that there is not a best between them, but one may be done as well as the other, as when two ways equally tend to one and the same place.

2. We are not our own, and therefore must not set up ourselves. We must not consult with flesh and blood either in ourselves or others, for self-love will deprave all our actions, by setting before us corrupt ends. It considers not what is best, but what is safest. By-respects sway the balance the wrong way.

3. When things are clear, and God's will is manifest, further deliberation is dangerous, and for the most part argues a false heart; as we see in Balaam, who, though he knew God's mind, yet would be still consulting, till God in judgment gave him up to what his covetous heart led him unto, 2 Pet. ii. 15. A man is not fit to deliberate till his heart be purged of false aims; for else God will give him to the darkness of his own spirit, and he will be always warping, unfit for any bias. Where the aims are good, there God delighteth to reveal his good pleasure. Such a soul is level and suitable to any good counsel that shall be given, and prepared to entertain it. In what measure any lust is favoured, in that measure the soul is darkened. Even wise Solomon, whilst he gave way to his lust, had like to have lost his wisdom.

We must look to our place wherein God hath set us. If we be in subjection to others, their authority in doubtful things ought to sway with us. It is certain we ought to obey; and if the thing wherein we are to obey be uncertain unto us, we ought to leave that which is uncertain and stick to that which is certain; in this case we must obey those that are gods under God. Neither is it the calling of those that are subjects, to inquire over curiously into the mysteries of government; for that, both in peace and war, breeds much disturbance, and would trouble all designs (*g*).*

The laws under which we live are particular determinations of the law of God [in some duties of the second table. For example, the law of God

---

* See note '*g*' for the charge based on the subsequent alteration of this passage and context.

says, 'Exact no more than what is thy due,' Luke iii. 13. But what in particular is thy due, and what another man's, the laws of men determine],* and therefore ought to be a rule unto us so far as they reach; though it be too narrow a rule to be good only so far as man's law guides unto.† Yet law being the joint reason and consent of many men for public good, hath a use for guidance of all actions that fall under the same. Where it dashes not against God's law, what is agreeable to law is agreeable to conscience.

The law of God in the due enlargement of it, to the least beginning and occasions, is exceeding broad, and allows of whatsoever stands with the light of reason or the bonds of humanity, civility, &c., and whatsoever is against these is so far against God's law. So that higher rules be looked to in the first place, there is nothing lovely or praiseworthy among men but ought to be seriously thought on.

Nature of itself is wild and untamed, and impatient of the yoke; but as beasts that cannot endure the yoke at first, after they are inured awhile unto it bear it willingly, and carry their work more easily by it, so the yoke of obedience makes the life regular and quiet. The meeting of authority and obedience together, maintains the peace and order of the world.

So of that question.‡

5. Though blind enfolded§ obedience, such as our adversaries would have, be such as will never stand with sound peace of conscience, which always looks to have light to direct it; for else a blind conscience would breed blind fears; yet in such doubtful cases wherein we cannot wind out ourselves, we ought to light our candles at others whom we have cause to think, by their place and parts, should see further than we. In matters of outward estate, we will have men skilful of our counsel; and Christians would find more sound peace, if they would advise with their godly and learned pastors and friends. Where there is not a direct word, there is place for the counsel of a prudent man, *sententia boni viri*. And it is a happiness for them whose business is much, and parts not large, to have the benefit of those that can give aim, and see further than themselves. The meanest Christian understands his own way, and knows how to do things with better advantage to his soul than a graceless though learned man; yet is still glad of further discovery. In counsel there is peace, the thoughts being thus established, Prov. xx. 18.

When we have advised and served God's providence in the use of means, then if it fall out otherwise than we look for, we may confidently conclude that God would not have it so, otherwise to our grief we may say it was the fruit of our own rashness.

Where we have cause to think that we have used better means in the search of grounds, and are more free from partial affections than others, there we may use our own advice more safely. Otherwise what we do by consent from others, is more secure and less offensive, as being more countenanced.

In advice with others, it is not sufficient to be generally wise, but experienced and knowing in that we ask, which is an honour to God's gifts where we find them in any kind. When we set about things in passion,

---

* The words in brackets inserted first in B. See note *g*.—G.
† The following margin-note first added in B: 'Nimis angusta innocentia est ad legem bonum esse.'—G.
‡ Inserted first in C.
§ 'Blinde enfolded' in A, and therefore given in text; but 'blindfold' in B and C.—G.

we work not as men or Christians, but in a bestial manner. The more passion, the less discretion; because passion hinders the sight of what is to be done. It clouds the soul, and puts it on to action without advisement. Where passions are subdued, and the soul purged and cleared, there is nothing to hinder the impression of God's Spirit; the soul is fitted as a clean glass to receive light from above. And that is the reason why mortified men are fittest to advise with in the particular cases incident to a Christian life.

After all advice, extract what is fittest, and what our spirits do most bend unto; for in things that concern ourselves God affords a light to discern, out of what is spoken, what best suiteth us. And every man is to follow most what his own conscience, after information, dictates unto him; because conscience is God's deputy in us, and under God most to be regarded, and whosoever sins against it, in his own construction sins against God. God vouchsafeth every Christian in some degree the grace of spiritual prudence, whereby they are enabled to discern what is fittest to be done in things that fall within their compass.

It is good to observe the particular becks* of providence, how things join and meet together. Fit occasions and suiting of things are intimations of God's will. Providence hath a language which is well understood by those that have a familiar acquaintance with God's dealing; they see a train of providence leading one way more than to another.

Take especial heed of not grieving the Spirit when he offers to be our guide, by studying evasions, and wishing the case were otherwise. This is to be lawgivers to ourselves, thinking that we are wiser than God. The use of discretion is not to direct us about the end, whether we should do well or ill (for a single heart always aims at good), but when we resolve upon doing well, and yet doubt of the manner how to perform it. Discretion looks not so much to what is lawful, for that is taken for granted, but what is most expedient. A discreet man looks not to what is best, so much as what is fittest in such and such respects, by eyeing circumstances, which, if they sort not, do vary the nature of the thing itself.

And because it is not in man to know his own ways, we should look up unto Christ, the great Counsellor of his church, to vouchsafe the spirit of counsel and direction to us; that 'make our way plain before us,' by suggesting unto us, 'this is the way, walk in it,' Isa. xxx. 21. We owe God this respect, to depend upon him for direction in the particular passages of our lives, in regard that he is our Sovereign, and his will is the rule, and we are to be accountable to him as our judge. It is God only that can see through businesses, and all helps and lets that stand about.

After we have rolled ourselves upon God, we should immediately take that course he inclines our hearts unto, without further distracting fear. Otherwise it is a sign we 'commit not our way to him,' 1 Pet. iv. 19, when we do not quietly trust him, but remain still as thoughtful as if we did not trust him. After prayer and trust follows 'the peace of God,' Phil. ii. 4, and a heart void of further dividing care. We should therefore presently question our hearts, for questioning his care, and not regard what fear will be ready to suggest, for that is apt to raise conclusions against ourselves, out of self-conceited grounds, whereby we usurp upon God and wrong ourselves.

It was a good resolution of the three young men in Daniel, 'We are not careful to answer thee, O king,' Dan. iii. 16. We know our duty, let God do with us as he pleaseth. If Abraham had hearkened to the voice of nature,

* That is, signals, indications.—G.

he would never have resolved to sacrifice Isaac, but because he cast himself upon God's providing, God in the mount provided a ram instead of his son.

CHAPTER XVIII.—*Other grounds of trusting in God, namely, the Promises, and twelve directions about the same.*

§ I. But for the better settling of our trust in God, a further discovery is necessary than of the nature and providence of God; for though the nature of God be written in the book of the creatures in so great letters, as he that runs may read, and though the providence of God appears in the order and use of things, yet there is another book whereby to know the will of God towards us, and our duty towards him. We must therefore have a knowledge of the promises of God, as well as of his providence, for though God hath discovered himself most graciously in Christ unto us, yet had we not a word of promise, we could not have the boldness to build upon Christ himself. Therefore, from the same grounds, that there is a God, there must be a revealing of the will of God, for else we can never have any firm trust in him further than he offers himself to be trusted. Therefore hath God opened his heart to us in his word, and reached out so many sweet promises for us to lay hold on, and stooped so low, by gracious condescending mixed with authority, as to enter into a covenant with us to perform all things for our good; for promises are, as it were, the stay of the soul in an imperfect condition, and so is faith in them until all promises shall end in performance, and faith in sight, and hope in possession.

Now these promises are, 1, for their spring from whence they proceed, free engagements of God, for if he had not bound himself, who could? and 2, they are for their value precious; and 3, for their extent large, even of all things that conduce to happiness; and 4, for their virtue quickening and strengthening the soul, as coming from the love of God, and conveying that love unto us by his Spirit in the best fruits thereof; and 5, for their certainty, they are as sure as the love of God in Christ is, upon which they are founded, and from which 'nothing can separate us,' Rom. viii. 39. For all promises are either Christ himself, the promised seed, or else they are of good things made to us in him and for him, and accomplished for his sake. They are all made first to him as heir of the promise, as Angel of the Covenant, as head of his body, and as our elder brother, &c. For promises being the fruits of God's love, and God's love being founded first on Christ, it must needs follow that all the promises are both made, and made good to us in and through him, who is 'yesterday, and to-day, and for ever the same,' Heb. xiii. 8.

That we should not call God's love into question, he not only gives us, (1) his word, but a binding word, his promise; and not only (2) a naked promise, but hath (3) entered into a covenant with us, founded upon full satisfaction by the blood of Christ, and unto this covenant sealed by the blood of the Lord Jesus, he hath (4) added the seals of sacraments, and unto this he hath added (5) his oath, that there might be no place left of doubting to the distrustful heart of man. There is no way of securing promises amongst men, but God hath taken the same to himself, and all to this end that we might not only know his mind towards us, but be fully persuaded of it, that as verily as he lives, he will make good whatever he hath promised for the comfort of his children. What greater assurance can there be than for being itself to lay his being in pawn? and for life itself to lay life to pawn, and all to comfort a poor soul?

The boundless and restless desire of man's spirit will never be stayed without some discovery of the chief good, and the way to attain the same. Men would have been in darkness about their final condition and the way to please God, and to pacify and purge their consciences, had not the word of God set down the spring and cause of all evil, together with the cure of it, and directed us how to have communion with God, and to raise ourselves above all the evil which we meet withal betwixt us and happiness, and to make us every way 'wise to salvation,' 2 Tim. iii. 15. Hence it is that the Psalmist prefers the manifestation of God by his word before the manifestation of him in his most glorious works, Ps. xix. 7.

And thus we see the necessity of a double principle for faith to rely on: 1, God; and 2, the Word of God revealing his will unto us, and directing us to make use of all his attributes, relations, and providence for our good; and this word hath its strength from him who gives a being and an accomplishment unto it; for words are as the authority of him that uttereth them is. When we look upon a grant in the word of a king, it stays our minds, because we know he is able to make it good; and why should it not satisfy our souls to look upon promises in the word of God? whose words, as they come from his truth and express his goodness, so they are all made good by his power and wisdom.

By the bare word of God it is that the heavens continue, and the earth, without any other foundation, hangs in the midst of the world; therefore well may the soul stay itself on that, even when it hath nothing else in sight to rely upon. By his word it is that the covenant of day and night, and the preservation of the world from any further overflowing of waters, 2 Peter iii. 7, continueth, which, if it should fail, yet his covenant with his people shall abide firm for ever, though the whole frame of nature were dissolved.

When we have thus gotten a fit foundation for the soul to lay itself upon, our next care must be, by trusting, to build on the same. All our misery is either in having a false foundation, or else in loose building upon a true. Therefore, having so strong a ground as God's nature, his providence, his promise, &c., to build upon, the only way for establishing our souls is, by trust, to rely firmly on him.

Now the reason why trust is so much required, is because, 1, it emptieth the soul; and 2, by emptying enlargeth it; and 3, seasoneth and fitteth the soul to join with so gracious an object; and 4, filleth it by carrying it out of itself unto God, who presently, so soon as he is trusted in, conveys himself and his goodness to the soul; and thus we come to have the comfort, and God the glory of all his excellencies. Thus salvation comes to be sure unto us, whilst faith, looking to the promises, and to God freely offering grace therein, resigns up itself to God, making no further question from any unworthiness of its own.

And thus we return to God by cleaving to him, from whom we fell by distrust, living under a new covenant merely of grace, Jer. xxxi. 3, and no grace fitter than that which gives all to Christ. Considering the fountain of all our good is, out of ourselves, in him, it being safest for us, who were so ill husbands at the first, that it should be so, therefore it is fit we should have use of such a grace that will carry us out of ourselves to the spring head.

The way, then, whereby faith quieteth the soul, is by raising it above all discontentments and storms here below, and pitching it upon God, thereby uniting it to him, whence it draws virtue to oppose and bring under whatsoever troubles its peace. For the soul is made for God, and never finds rest till it returns to him again (*h*). When God and the soul meet, there will follow contentment. God simply considered, is not all our happiness, but God as trusted in; and Christ as we are made one with him. The soul cannot so much as 'touch the hem of Christ's garment,' but it shall find 'virtue coming from him,' Mat. ix. 20, to sanctify and settle it. God in Christ is full of all that is good. When the soul is emptied, enlarged, and opened by faith to receive goodness offered, there must needs follow sweet satisfaction.

§ II. 1. For the better strengthening of our trust, it is not sufficient that we trust in God and his truth revealed, *but we must do it by light and strength from him.* Many believe in the truth by human arguments, but no arguments will convince the soul but such as are fetched from the inward nature, and powerful work of truth itself. No man can know God, but by God; none can know the sun, but by its own light; none can know the truth of God, so as to build upon it, but by the truth itself and the Spirit revealing it by its own light to the soul. That soul which hath felt the power of truth in casting it down, and raising it up again, will easily be brought to rest upon it. It is neither education, nor the authority of others that profess the same truth, or that we have been so taught by men of great parts, &c., will settle the heart, until we find an inward power and authority in the truth itself shining in our hearts by its own beams. Hence comes unsettledness in time of troubles, because we have not a spiritual discerning of spiritual things. Supernatural truths must have a supernatural power to apprehend them, therefore God createth a spiritual eye and hand of the soul, which is faith. In those that are truly converted, all saving truths are transcribed out of the Scripture into their hearts, 'they are taught of God,' Isa. liv. 13, so as they find all truths, both concerning the sinful estate and the gracious and happy estate of man in themselves. They carry a divinity in them and about them, so as from a saving feeling they can speak of conversion, of sin, of grace, and the comforts of the Spirit, &c., and from this acquaintance are ready to yield and give up themselves to truth revealed, and to God speaking by it.

2. Trust is never sound but upon a spiritual conviction of the truth and goodness we rely upon, for the effecting of which the Spirit of God must likewise *subdue the rebellion and malice of our will,* that so it may be suitable and level to divine things, and relish them as they are. We must apprehend the love of God, and the fruits of it, as better than life itself, and then choosing and cleaving to the same will soon follow; for as there is a fitness in divine truths to all the necessities of the soul, so the soul must be fitted by them to savour and apply them to itself; and then from an harmony between the soul and that which it applies itself unto there will follow, not only peace in the soul, but joy and delight surpassing any contentment in the world besides.

3. As there is in God to satisfy the whole soul, so trust *carries the whole soul to God.* This makes trust not so easy a matter, because there must be an exercise of every faculty of the soul, or else our trust is imperfect and lame. There must be a knowledge of him whom we trust, and why we trust, an affiance and love, &c. Only they that know God will trust in him; not that knowledge alone is sufficient, but because the sweetness of

God's love is let into the soul thereby, which draweth the whole soul to him. We are bidden to trust perfectly in God; therefore, seeing we have a God so full of perfection to trust in, we should labour to trust perfectly in him.

4. And it is good for the exercise of trust to *put cases to ourselves of things that probably may fall out*, and then return to our souls to search what strength we have if such things should come to pass. Thus David puts cases. Perfect faith dares put the hardest cases to its soul, and then set God against all that may befall it, Ps. iii. 6; xlvi. 3; xxvii. 3.

5. Again, *labour to fit the promise to every condition thou art in*. There is no condition but hath a promise suitable, therefore no condition but wherein God may be trusted, because his truth and goodness are always the same. And in the promise, look both to the good promised and to the faithfulness and love of the promiser. It is not good to look upon the difficulty of the thing we have a promise against, but who promiseth it, and for whose sake, and so see all good things in Christ made over to us.

6. We should labour likewise *for a single heart to trust in God only*. There is no readier way to fall than to trust equally to two stays, whereof one is rotten, and the other sound; therefore as in point of doctrine we are to rely upon Christ only, and to make the Scriptures our rule only; so in life and conversation, whatever we make use of, yet we should enjoy and rely upon God only; for either God is trusted alone or not at all. Those that trust to others things with God, trust not him but upon pretence to carry their double minds with less check.

7. Again, labour that thy soul may *answer all the relations wherein it stands to God*, by cleaving to him, (1) as a Father, by trusting on his care; (2) as a Teacher, by following his direction; (3) as a Creator, by dependence on him; (4) as a Husband, by inseparable affection of love to him; (5) as a Lord, by obedience, &c. And then we may with comfort expect whatsoever good these relations can yield; all which, God, regarding more our wants and weaknesses than his own greatness, hath taken upon him.

8. Shall these relations *yield comfort from the creature, and not from God himself*, in whom they are in their highest perfection? shall God make other fathers and husbands faithful, and not be faithful himself? All our comfort depends upon labouring to make these relations good to our souls.

And as we must wholly and only trust in God, so likewise we must trust him in all conditions and times, for all things that we stand in need of, until that time comes, wherein we shall stand in need of nothing: for as the same care of God moved him to save us, and to preserve us in the world till we be put in possession of salvation; so the same faith relies upon God for heaven and all necessary provision till we come thither. It is the office of faith to quiet our souls in all the necessities of this life, and we have continual use of trusting while we are here; for even when we have things, yet God still keeps the blessing of them in his own hands, to hold us in a continual dependence upon him. God trains us up this way, by exercising our trust in lesser matters, to fit us for greater. Thus it pleaseth God to keep us in a depending condition until he see his own time; but so good is God that as he intends to give us what we wait for, so will he give us the grace and spirit of faith, to sustain our souls in waiting till we enjoy the same. The unruliness of a natural spirit is never discovered more, than when God defers; therefore we should labour the more not to withdraw our attendance from God.

9. Further, we must know that the condition of a Christian in this life,

is not to see what he trusts God for; 'he lives by faith, and not by sight,' 2 Cor. v. 7; and yet there is such a virtue in faith, which makes evident and present, things to come and unseen; because God, where he gives an eye of faith, gives also a glass of the word to see things in, and by seeing of them in the truth and power of him that promiseth, they become present, not only to the understanding to apprehend them, but to the will to rest upon them, and to the affections to joy in them. It is the nature of faith to work, when it seeth nothing, and oftentimes best of all then, because God shews himself more clearly in his power, wisdom, and goodness, at such times; and so his glory shines most, and faith hath nothing else to look upon then, whereupon it gathers all the forces of the soul together, to fasten upon God.

It should therefore be the chief care of a Christian to strengthen his faith, that so it may answer God's manner of dealing with him in the worst times; for God usually (1, that he might perfectly mortify our confidence in the creature; and 2, that he might the more endear his favours and make them fresh and new unto us; and 3, that the glory of deliverance may be entirely his, without the creatures sharing with him; and 4, that our faith and obedience may be tried to the uttermost, and discovered) suffers his children to fall into great extremities before he will reach forth his hand to help them, as in Job's case, &c. Therefore Christians should much labour their hearts to trust in God in the deepest extremities that may befall them, even when no light of comfort appears either from within or without, yea then especially, when all other comforts fail, Isa. iv. 10. Despair is oft the ground of hope. When the darkness of the night is thickest, then the morning begins to dawn. That which, to a man unacquainted with God's dealings, is a ground of utter despair, the same, to a man acquainted with the ways of God, is a rise of exceeding comfort; for infinite power and goodness can never be at a loss, neither can faith which looks to that, ever be at a stand; whence it is that both God and faith work best alone. In a hopeless estate a Christian will see some door of hope opened, 1, because God shews himself nearest to us, when we stand most in need of him; 'Help, Lord, for vain is the help of man,' Ps. lx. 11. God is never more seen than in the mount. He knows our souls best, and our souls know him best, in adversity. Ps. xxxi. 7; then he is most wonderful in his saints. 2. Because our prayers then are strong cries, fervent and frequent. God is sure to hear of us at such a time, which pleaseth him well, as delighting to hear the voice of his beloved.

10. For our better encouragement in these sad times, and to help our trust in God the more, *we should often call to mind the former experiences, which either ourselves or others have had of God's goodness, and make use of the same for our spiritual good.* 'Our fathers trusted in thee,' saith the head of the church, ' and were not confounded,' Ps. xxii. 14. God's truth and goodness is unchangeable, 'he never leaves those that trust in him,' Ps. ix. 10. So likewise in our own experiences, we should take notice of God's dealings with us in sundry kinds; how many ways he hath refreshed us, and how good we have found him in our worst times. After we have once tried him and his truth, we may safely trust him. God will stand upon his credit, he never failed any yet, and he will not begin to break with us. If his nature and his word and his former dealing hath been sure and square, why should our hearts be wavering? 'Thy word,' saith the Psalmist, 'is very pure (or tried), therefore thy servant loveth it,' Ps. cxix. 140; the word of God is 'as silver tried in the furnace, purified seven times,'

Ps. xii. 6. It is good therefore to observe and lay up God's dealings. Experience is nothing else but a multiplied remembrance of former blessings, which will help to multiply our faith. Tried truth and tried faith unto it, sweetly agree and answer one another. It were a course much tending to the quickening of the faith of Christians, if they would communicate one to another their mutual experiences. This hath formerly been the custom of God's people, 'Come and hear, all ye that fear God, and I will declare what he hath done for my soul,' Ps. lxvi. 16; and David urgeth this as a reason to God for deliverance, that then 'the righteous would compass him about,' Ps. cxlii. 7, as rejoicing in the experience of God's goodness to him. The want of this makes us upon any new trial, to call God's care and love into question, as if he had never formerly been good unto us; whereas every experiment of God's love should refresh our faith upon any fresh onset. God is so good to his children even in this world, that he trains them up by daily renewed experiences of his fatherly care; for besides those many promises of good things to come, he gives us some evidence and taste of what we believe here; that by that which we feel we might be strengthened in that we look for, that so in both (1, sense of what we feel; and 2, certainty of what we look for) we might have full support.

11. But yet we must trust God, *as he will be trusted*, namely, *in doing good*, or else we do not trust him but tempt him. Our commanding of our souls to trust in God, is but an echo of what God commands us first; and therefore in the same manner he commands us, we should command ourselves. As God commands us to trust him in doing good, so should we 'commit our souls to him in well doing,' 1 Pet. iv. 19, and trust him when we are about his own works, and not in the works of darkness. We may safely expect God in his ways of mercy, when we are in his ways of obedience; for religion, as it is a doctrine of what is to be believed, so it is a doctrine according to godliness; and the mysteries of faith are mysteries of godliness, because they cannot be believed but they will enforce a godly conversation. Where any true impression of them is, there is holiness always bred in that soul; therefore a study of holiness must go jointly together with a study of trusting in God. Faith looks not only to promises, but to directions to duty, and breeds in the soul a liking of whatsoever pleaseth God. There is a mutual strengthening in things that are good; trusting stirs to duty, and duty strengthens trusting by increasing our liberty and boldness with God.

12. Again, we must maintain in our souls, *a high esteem of the grace of faith*, the very trial whereof is 'more precious than gold,' 1 Pet. i. 7. What then is the grace of faith itself, and the promises which it layeth hold on? Certainly they transcend in worth whatever may draw us from God; whence it is that the soul sets a high price upon them, and on faith that believes them. It is impossible that anything in the world should come betwixt the heart and those things, if once we truly lay hold on them, to undermine faith or the comfort we have by it. The heart is never drawn to any sinful vanity, or frighted with any terror of trouble, till faith first loseth the sight and estimation of divine things, and forgets the necessity and excellency of them. Our Saviour Christ, when he would stir up a desire of faith in his disciples, Luke xvii. 6, shewed them the power and excellency of the same. Great things stir up faith, and keep it above, and faith keeps the soul that nothing else can take place of abode in it. When the 'great things of God,' Hos. viii. 12, are brought into the heart by faith, what is there in the whole world that can out-bid them? assurance of these

things, upon spiritual grounds, overrules both sense and reason, or whatever else prevails with carnal hearts.

CHAPTER XIX.—*Faith to be prized, and other things undervalued, at least not to be trusted to as the chief.*

That faith may take the better place in the soul, and the soul in God, the heart must continually be taught of what little worth all things else are, as reputation, riches, and pleasures, &c. ; and to see their nothingness in the word of God, and in experience of ourselves and others, that so our heart being weaned from these things, may open itself to God, and embrace things of a higher nature. Otherwise baser things will be nearer the soul than faith, and keep possession against it, so that faith will not be suffered to set up a throne in the heart. There must be an unloosing of the heart, as well as a fastening of it, and God helps us in both ; for, besides the word discovering the vanity of all things else out of God, the main scope of God's dealing with his children in any danger or affliction whatsoever, is to embitter all other things but himself unto them. Indeed it is the power of God properly which makes the heart to trust, but yet the Spirit of God useth this way to bring all things else out of request with us in comparison of those inestimable good things, which the soul is created, redeemed, and sanctified for. God is very jealous of our trust, and can endure no idol of jealousy to be set up in our hearts. Therefore it behoves us to take notice, not only of the deceitfulness of things, but of the deceitfulness of our hearts in the use of them. Our hearts naturally hang loose from God, and are soon ready to join with the creature. Now the more we observe our hearts in this, the more we take them off, and labour to set them where they should be placed ; for the more we know these things, the less we shall trust them.

Obj. But may we not trust in riches, and friends, and other outward helps at all ?

Ans. Yes, so far as they are subordinate to God, our chief stay, with reservation and submission to the Lord ; only so far, and so long as it shall please him to use them for our good. Because God ordinarily conveys his help and goodness to us by some creature, we must trust in God to bless every mercy we enjoy, and to make all helps serviceable to his love towards us. In a word, we must trust and use them in and under God, and so as if all were taken away, yet to think God, being all-sufficient, can do without them, whatsoever he doth by them, for our good. Faith preserves the chastity of the soul, and cleaving to God is a spiritual debt which it oweth to him, whereas cleaving to the creature is spiritual adultery.

It is an error in the foundation to substitute false objects in religion, or in Christian conversation ; for, 1, in religion ; trusting in false objects, as saints, and works, &c., breeds false worship, and false worship breeds idolatry, and so God's jealousy and hatred. 2. In Christian conversation ; false objects of trust breed false comforts and true fears ; for in what measure we trust in anything that is uncertain, in the same measure will our grief be when it fails us. The more men rely upon deceitful crutches, the greater is their fall. God can neither endure false objects, nor a double object, as hath been shewed, for a man to rely upon anything equally in the same rank with himself. For the propounding of a double object, argues a double heart, and a double heart is always unsettled, James i. 8 ;

for it will regard God no longer than it can enjoy that which it joins together with him. Therefore it is said, 'You cannot serve two masters,' Luke xvi. 13, not subordinate one to another; whence it was that our Saviour told those worldly men which followed him, 'that they could not believe in him, because they sought honour one of another,' John v. 44; and in case of competition, if their honour and reputation should come into question, they would be sure to be false to Christ, and rather part with him than their own credit and esteem in the world.

David here, by charging his soul to trust in God, saw there was nothing else that could bring true rest and quiet unto him; for whatsoever is besides God is but a creature; and whatever is in the creature is but borrowed and at God's disposing, and changeable, or else it were not a creature. David saw his error soon, for the ground of his disquiet was trusting something else besides God; therefore when he began to say, 'My hill is strong, I shall not be moved,' &c., Ps. xxx. 6, then presently his soul was troubled. Out of God there is nothing fit for the soul to stay itself upon; for,

1. Outward things are not fitted to the spiritual nature of the soul. They are dead things and cannot touch it, being a lively spirit, unless by way of taint.

2. They are beneath the worth of the soul, and therefore debase the soul, and draw it lower than itself; as a noble woman, by matching with a mean person, much injures herself, especially when higher matches are offered. Earthly things are not given for stays wholly to rest on, but for comforts in our way to heaven. They are no more fit for the soul, than that which hath many angles is fit to fill up that which is round, which it cannot do, because of the unevenness and void places that will remain. Outward things are never so well fitted for the soul, but that the soul will presently see some voidness and emptiness in them, and in itself in cleaving to them; for that which shall be a fit object for the soul, must be, 1, for the nature of it spiritual, as the soul itself is; 2, constant; 3, full and satisfying; 4, of equal continuance with it; and 5, always yielding fresh contents. We cast away flowers, after once we have had the sweetness of them, because there is not still a fresh supply of sweetness. Whatever comfort is in the creature, the soul will spend quickly, and look still for more; whereas the comfort we have in God is 'undefiled and fadeth not away,' 1 Peter i. 4. How can we trust to that for comfort, which by very trusting proves uncomfortable to us? Outward things are only so far forth good, as we do not trust in them. Thorns may be touched, but not rested on, for then they will pierce. We must not set our hearts upon things which are never evil to us, but when we 'set our hearts upon them,' Ps. lxii. 10.

By trusting anything but God, we make it, 1, an idol; 2, a curse, and not a blessing, Jer. xvii. 5; 3; it will prove a lying vanity, not yielding that good which we look for; and 4, a vexation, bringing that evil upon us we look not for.

Of all men Solomon was the fittest to judge of this, because, 1, he had a large heart, able to comprehend the variety of things; and 2, being a mighty king, had advantages of procuring all outward things that might give him satisfaction; and 3, he had a desire answerable, to search out and extract whatever good the creature could yield. And yet, upon the trial of all, he passeth this verdict upon all, that they are but 'vanity,' Eccles. i. 2. Whilst he laboured to find that which he sought for in them, he had like to have lost himself; and seeking too much to strengthen himself by foreign combination, he weakened himself the more thereby, until he came to know where the 'whole of man consists,' Eccles. xii. 13. So that now we need not try further conclusions after the peremptory sentence of so wise a man.

But our nature is still apt to think there is some secret good in the forbidden fruit, and to buy wisdom dearly when we might have it at a cheaper rate, even from former universal experience.

It is a matter both to be wondered at and pitied, that the soul having God in Christ set before it, alluring it unto him, that he might raise it, enlarge it, and fill it, and so make it above all other things, should yet debase and make itself narrower and weaker by leaning to things meaner than itself.

The kingdom, sovereignty, and large command of man continueth while he rests upon God, in whom he reigns, in some sort, over all things under him; but so soon as he removes from God to anything else, he becomes weak, and narrow, and slavish presently; for,

The soul is as that which it relies upon. If on vanity, itself becomes vain; for that which contents the soul must satisfy all the wants and desires of it, which no particular thing can do, and the soul is more sensible of a little thing that it wants than of all other things which it enjoys.

But see the insufficiency of all other things, out of God, to support the soul in their several degrees. 1. First, all outward things can make a man no happier than outward things can do; they cannot reach beyond their proper sphere; but our greatest grievances are spiritual. 2. And as for inward things, whether gifts or graces, they cannot be a sufficient stay for the mind; for (1), Gifts, as policy and wisdom, &c., they are, at the best, very defective, especially when we trust in them, for wisdom makes men often to rebel, and thereupon God delighteth to blast their projects, Isa. xlvii. 10. None miscarry oftener than men of the greatest parts, as none are oftener drowned than those that are most skilful in swimming, because it makes them confident.

And for grace, though it be the beginning of a new creature in us, yet it is but a creature, and therefore not to be trusted in; nay, by trusting in it we imbase it, and make it more imperfect. So far as there is truth of grace, it breeds distrust of ourselves, and carries the soul out of itself to the fountain of strength.

3. And for any works that proceed from grace, by trusting thereunto they prove like the reed of Egypt, which not only deceives us, but hurts us with the splinters. Good works are good, but confidence in them is hurtful; and there is more of our own in them, for the most part, to humble us, than of God's Spirit to embolden us so far as to trust in them. Alas! they have nothing from us but weakness and defilement, and therefore since the fall God would have the object of our trust to be out of ourselves in him, and to that purpose he useth all means to take us out of ourselves and from the creature, that he only might be our trust.

4. Yea, we must not trust itself, but God whom it relies on, who is therefore called our trust. All the glorious things that are spoken of trust are only made good by God in Christ, who, as trusted, doth all for us.

God hath prescribed trust as the way to carry our souls to himself, in whom we should only rely, and not in our imperfect trust, which hath its ebbing and flowing. Neither will trust in God himself for the present suffice us for future strength and grace, as if trusting in God to-day would suffice to strengthen us for to-morrow; but we must renew our trust for fresh supply upon every fresh occasion. So that we see God alone must be the object of our trust.

There is still left in man's nature a desire of pleasure, profit, and of whatever the creature presents as good, but the desire of gracious good is altogether lost, the soul being wholly infected with a contrary taste. Man hath a nature capable of excellency and desirous of it, and the Spirit of God in and by the word reveals where true excellency is to be had; but corrupt nature leaving God seeketh it elsewhere, and so crosseth its own desires, till the Spirit of God discovers where these things are to be had, and so nature is brought to its right frame again by turning the stream into the right current. Grace and sinful nature have the same general object of comfort, only sinful nature seeks it in broken cisterns, and grace in the fountain, Jer. ii. 13. The beginning of our true happiness is from the discovery of true and false objects, so as the soul may clearly see what is best and safest, and then stedfastly rely upon it.

It were an happy way to make the soul better acquainted with trusting in God, to labour to subdue at the first all unruly inclinations of the soul to earthly things, and to take advantage of the first tenderness of the soul to weed out that which is ill, and to plant knowledge and love of the best things in it; otherwise, where affections to anything below get much strength in the soul, it will by little and little be so overgrown that there will be no place left in it either for object or act, God or trust. God cannot come to take his place in the heart by trust, but where the powers of the soul are brought under, to regard him and those great things he brings with him above all things else in the world besides.

In these glorious times wherein so great a light shineth, whereby so great things are discovered, what a shame is it to be so narrow-hearted as to fix upon present things. Our aims and affections should be suitable to the things themselves set before us. Our hearts should be more and more enlarged, as things are more and more revealed to us. We see in the things of this life, as wisdom and experience increaseth, so our aims and desires increase likewise. A young beginner thinks it a great matter if he have a little to begin withal, but as he grows in trading, and seeth further ways of getting, his thoughts and desires are raised higher. Children think as children, but riper age puts away childishness, 1 Cor. xiii. 11, when their understandings are enlarged to see what they did not see before. We should never rest till our hearts, according to the measure of revelation of those excellent things which God hath for us, have answerable apprehension of the same. Oh, if we had but faith to answer those glorious truths which God hath revealed, what manner of lives should we lead!

CHAPTER XX.—*Of the method of trusting in God; and the trial of that trust.*

13. Lastly, to add no more, our trusting in God *should follow God's order in promising.* The first promise is of forgiveness of sin to repentant believers; next, 2, of healing and sanctifying grace; then, 3, the inheritance of the kingdom of heaven to them that are sanctified; 4, and then the promises of all things needful in our way to the kingdom, &c. Now answerably, the soul being enlightened to see its danger, should look first to God's mercy in Christ pardoning sin, because sin only divides betwixt God and the soul; next to the promises of grace for the leading of a Christian life, for true

faith desires healing mercy as well as pardoning mercy, and then to heaven and all things that may bring us thither.

By all this we see that it is not so easy a matter as the world takes it, to bring God and the soul together by trusting on him. It must be effected by the mighty power of God, raising up the soul to himself, to lay hold upon the glorious power, goodness, and other excellencies that are in him, Eph. i. 20. God is not only the object, but the working cause of our trust; for such is our proneness to live by sense and natural reason, and such is the strangeness and height of divine things, such our inclination to a self-sufficiency and contentment in the creature, and so hard a matter is it to take off the soul from false bottoms, by reason of our unacquaintance with God and his ways; besides, such guilt still remains upon our souls for our rebellion and unkindness towards God, that it makes us afraid to entertain serious thoughts of him; and so great is the distance betwixt his infinite majesty, before whom the very angels do cover their faces, and us, by reason of the unspiritualness of our nature, being opposite to his most absolute purity, that we cannot be brought to any familiarity with the Lord, so as to come into his holy presence with confidence to rely upon him, or any comfort to have communion with him, till our hearts be sanctified and lifted up by divine vigour infused into them.

Though there be some inclination, by reason of the remainder of the image of God in us, to an outward moral obedience of the law, yet, alas, we have not only no seeds of evangelical truths and of faith to believe them, but an utter contrariety in our natures, as corrupted, either to this, or any other good. When our conscience is once awaked, we meditate nothing but fears and terrors, and dare not so much as think of an angry God, but rather how we may escape and fly from him. Therefore, together with a deep consideration of the grounds we have of trusting God, it is necessary we should think of the indisposition of our hearts unto it, especially when there is greatest need thereof, that so our hearts may be forced to put up that petition of the disciples to God, 'Lord, increase our faith,' Luke xvii. 5; Lord, help us against our unbelieving hearts, &c. By prayer and holy thoughts stirred up in the use of the means, we shall feel divine strength infused and conveyed into our souls to trust.

The more care we ought to have to maintain our trust in God, because, besides the hardness of it, it is a radical and fundamental grace; it is, as it were, the mother-root and great vein whence the exercise of all graces have their beginning and strength. The decay of a plant, though it appears first from the withering of the twigs and branches, yet it arises chiefly from a decay in the root; so the decay of grace may appear to the view, first in our company, carriage, and speeches, &c.; but the primitive and original ground of the same is weakness of faith in the heart; therefore, it should be our wisdom, especially, to look to the feeding of the root. We must, 1, Look that our principles and foundation be good; and, 2, Build strongly upon them; and, 3, Repair our building every day as continual breaches shall be made upon us, either by corruptions and temptations from within or without; and we shall find that the main breaches of our lives arise either from false principles or doubts, or mindlessness of those that are true. All sin is a turning of the soul from God to some other seeming good, but this proceeds from a former turning of the soul from God by distrust. As faith is the first return of the soul to God, so the first degree of departing from God is by infidelity, and from thence comes a departure by other sins, by which, as sin is of a winding nature, our unbelief more increaseth, and so the rent and breach betwixt our souls and God is made greater still, which is that Satan would have, till at length, by departing further and further from him, we come to have that peremptory sentence of everlasting departure pronounced against us; so that our departure from God now is a degree to separation for ever from him. Therefore, it is Satan's main care to come between God and the soul, that so unloosing us from God, we might more easily be drawn to other things; and if he draws us to other things, it is but only to unloose our hearts from God the more; for he well knows, whilst our souls cleave close to God, there is no prevailing against us by any created policy or power.

It was the cursed policy of Balaam to advise Balak to draw the people from God, by fornication, that so God might be drawn from them. The sin of their base affections crept into the very spirits of their mind, and drew them from God to idolatry. Bodily adultery makes way for spiritual. An unbelieving heart is an ill heart, and a treacherous heart, because it makes us to 'depart from God, the living God,' &c., Heb. iii. 12. Therefore we should especially take heed of it as we love our lives, yea, our best life, which ariseth from the union of our souls with God.

None so opposed as a Christian, and in a Christian nothing so opposed as his faith, because it opposeth whatsoever opposes God, both within and without us. It captivates and brings under whatsoever rises up against God in the heart, and sets itself against whatsoever makes head against the soul.

And because mistake is very dangerous, and we are prone to conceive that to trust in God is an easy matter, therefore it is needful that we should have a right conceit of this trust, what it is, and how it may be discerned, lest we trust to an untrusty trust, and to an unsteady stay.

We may by what hath been said before, partly discern the nature of it, to be nothing else but an exercise of faith, whereby looking to God in Christ through the promises, we take off our souls from all other supports, and lay them upon God for deliverance and upholding in all ill, present or future, felt or feared, and the obtaining of all good, which God sees expedient for us.

1. Now that we may discern the truth of our trust in God the better, we must know, that true trust is willing to be tried and searched, and can say to God as David, 'Now, Lord, what wait I for, my hope is in thee,' Ps. xxxix. 7; and as it is willing to come to trial, so it is able to endure trial, and to hold out in opposition, as appears in David. If faith hath a promise, it will rely and rest upon it, say flesh and blood what it can to the contrary. True faith is as large as the promise, and will take God's part against whatsoever opposes it.

2. And as faith singles not out one part of divine truth to believe and rejects another, so it relies upon God for every good thing, one as well as another; the ground whereof is this, the same love of God that intends us heaven, intends us a supply of all necessaries that may bring us thither.

A child that believes his father will make him heir, doubts not but he will provide him food and nourishment, and give him breeding suitable to his future condition. *Fides non eligit objectum.* It is a vain pretence to believe that God will give us heaven, and yet leave us to shift for ourselves in the way.

3. Where trust is rightly planted, it gives boldness to the soul in going to God; for (1) it is grounded upon the discovery of God's love first to us, and seeth a warrant from him for whatsoever it trusts him for. Though the things themselves be never so great, yet they are no greater than God is willing to bestow. Again, (2) trust is bold because it is grounded upon

the worthiness of a mediator, who hath made way to God's favour for us, and appears now in heaven to maintain it towards us.

4. Yet this boldness is with humility, which carries the soul out of itself; and that boldness which the soul by trust hath with God, is from God himself. It hath nothing to allege from itself but its own emptiness and God's fulness, its own sinfulness and God's mercy, its own humble obedience and God's command; hence it is that the true believer's heart is not lifted up, nor swells with self-confidence; as trust comes in, that goes out. Trust is never planted, and grows but in an humble and low soul. Trust is a holy motion of the soul to God, and motion arises from want. Those, and those only, seek out abroad that want succour at home. *Motus ex indigentia.* Plants move not from place to place, because they find nourishment where they stand; but living creatures seek abroad for their food, and for that end have a power of moving from place to place. And this is the reason why trust is expressed by *going to God.*

5. Hereupon trust is a dependent grace, answerable to our dependent condition. It looks upon all things it hath or desires to have as coming from God and his free grace and power. It desireth not only wisdom, but to be wise in his wisdom, to see in his light, to be strong in his strength. The thing itself contents not this grace of trust, but God's blessing and love in the thing. It cares not for anything further than it can have it with God's favour and good liking.

6. Hence it is that trust is an obsequious* and an observing grace, stirring up the soul to a desire of pleasing God in all things, and to a fear of displeasing him. He that pretends to trust the Lord in a course of offending may trust to this, that God will meet him in another way than he looks for. He that is a tenant at courtesy will not offend his lord. Hence it is that the apostle enforceth that exhortation to work out our salvation with fear and trembling, Phil. ii. 12, 13, because it is God that worketh the will and the deed, and according to his good pleasure, not ours. Therefore faith is an effectual working grace; it works in heaven with God, it works within us, commanding all the powers of the soul; it works without us, conquering whatsoever is in the world on the right hand to draw us from God, or on the left hand to discourage us; it works against hell and the powers of darkness; and all by virtue of trusting, as it draweth strength from God. It stirs up all other graces, and keeps them in exercise, and thereupon the acts of other graces are attributed to faith, as Heb. xi. It breeds a holy jealousy over ourselves, lest we give God just cause to stop the influence of his grace towards us, so to let us see that we stand not by our own strength. Those that take liberty in things they either know or doubt will displease God, shew they want the fear of God; and this want of fear shews their want of dependency, and therefore want of trust. Dependency is always very respective;† it studieth contentment and care to comply. This was it made 'Enoch walk with God, and study how to please him,' Heb. xi. 5. When we know nothing can do us good or hurt but God, it draws our chief care to approve ourselves to him. Obedience of faith and obedience of life will go together; and therefore he that commits his soul to God to save, will commit his soul to God to sanctify and guide in a way of well pleasing, 1 Peter iv. 19. Not only the tame, but most savage creatures, will be at the beck of those that feed them, though they are ready to fall violently upon others. Disobedience, therefore, is against the principles of nature.

* That is, complying, yielding.—G.   † That is, 'respectful.'—ED.

7. This dependency is either in the use of means, or else when means fail us. True dependency is exactly careful of all means. When God hath set down a course of means, we must not expect that God should alter his ordinary course of providence for us; deserved disappointment is the fruit of this presumptuous confidence. The more we depend on a wise physician, the more we shall observe his directions, and be careful to use what he prescribes; yet we must use the means as means, and not set them in God's room, for that is the way to blast our hopes. The way to have anything taken away and not blest, is to set our heart too much upon it. Too much grief in parting with anything, shews too much trust in the enjoying of it; and therefore he that uses the means in faith, will always join prayer unto God, from whom, as every good thing comes, so likewise doth the blessing and success thereof. Where much endeavour is and little seeking to God, it shews there is little trust. The widow that trusted in God, continued likewise 'in prayers day and night,' 1 Tim. v. 5.

The best discovery of our not relying too much on means is, when all means fail, if we can still rely upon God, as being still where he was, and hath ways of his own for helping of us, either immediately from himself, or by setting awork other means, and those perhaps very unlikely, such as we think not of. God hath ways of his own. Abraham never honoured God more than when he trusted in God for a son against the course of nature; and when he had a son, was ready to sacrifice him, upon confidence that God would raise him from the dead again, Gen. ii. 2. This was the ground upon which Daniel, with such great authority, reproved Belshazzar, that he had not a care to glorify God, in whose hands 'his breath was, and all his ways,' Dan. v. 23. The greatest honour we can do unto God, is when we see nothing, but rather all contrary to that we look for, then to shut our eyes to inferior things below, and look altogether upon his all-sufficiency. God can convey himself more comfortably to us when he pleaseth, without means than by means. True trust, as it sets God highest in the soul, so in danger and wants it hath present recourse to him, as the conies to the rocks, Prov. xxx. 26.

8. And because God's times and seasons are the best, it is an evidence of true trust when we can wait God's leisure and not make haste, and so run before God; for else the more haste the worse speed. God seldom makes any promise to his children but he exerciseth their trust in waiting long before, as David for a kingdom, Abraham for a son, the whole world for Christ's coming, &c.

9. One main evidence of true trust in God is here in the text; we see here it hath a quieting and stilling virtue, for it stays the soul upon the fulness of God's love, joined with his ability to supply our wants and relieve our necessities, though faith doth not, at the first especially, so stay the soul as to take away all suspicious fears of the contrary. There be so many things in trouble that press upon the soul, as hinder the joining of God and it together, yet the prevailing of our unbelief is taken away, the reign of it is broken. If the touch of Christ in his abasement on earth drew virtue from him, Mark v. 30, certain it is that faith cannot touch Christ in heaven but it will draw a quieting and sanctified virtue from him, which will in some measure stop the issues of an unquiet spirit. The needle in the compass will stand north, though with some trembling.

A ship that lies at anchor may be something tossed, but yet it still remains so fastened, that it cannot be carried away by wind or weather. The soul, after it hath cast anchor upon God, may, as we see here in David, be disquieted awhile, but this unsettling tends to a deeper settling. The more we believe, the more we are established. Faith is an establishing grace, by faith we stand, and stand fast, and are able to withstand whatsoever opposeth us. For what can stand against God, upon whose truth and power faith relies? The devil fears not us, but him whom we fly unto for succour; it is the ground we stand on secures us, not ourselves.

As it is our happiness, so it must be our endeavour, to bring the soul close to God, that nothing get between, for then the soul hath no sure footing. When we step from God, Satan steps in by some temptation or other presently. It requires a great deal of self-denial to bring a soul either swelling with carnal confidence, or sinking by fear and distrust, to lie level upon God and cleave fast to him. Square will lie fast upon square, but our hearts are so full of unevenness, that God hath much ado to square our hearts fit for him, notwithstanding the soul hath no rest without this.

The use of trust is best known in the worst times, for naturally in sickness we trust to the physician, in want to our wit and shifts, in danger to policy and the arm of flesh, in plenty to our present supply, &c.; but, when we have nothing in view, then indeed should God be God unto us. In times of distress, when he shews himself in the ways of his mercy and goodness, then we should especially magnify his name, which will move him to discover his excellencies the more, the more we take notice of them. And, therefore, David strengthens himself in these words, that he hoped for better times, wherein God would shew himself more gracious to him, because he resolved *to praise him*.

This trusting joints the soul again, and sets it in its own true resting-place, and sets God in his own place in the soul, that is, the highest; and the creature in its place, which is to be under God, as in its own nature, so in our hearts. This is to ascribe 'honour due unto God,' Ps. xxix. 2; the only way to bring peace into the soul. Thus, if we can bring our hope and trust to the God of hope and trust, we shall stand impregnable in all assaults, as will best appear in these particulars.

CHAPTER XXI.—*Of quieting the spirit in troubles for sin; and objections answered.*

To begin with troubles of the spirit, which indeed are the spirit of troubles, as disabling that which should uphold a man in all his troubles. A spirit set in tune and assisted by a higher spirit, will stand out against ordinary assaults, but when God, the God of the spirits of all flesh, shall seem contrary to our spirits, whence then shall we find relief?

Here all is spiritual, God a Spirit, the soul a spirit, the terrors spiritual, the devil, who joins with these, a spirit, yea that which the soul fears for the time to come, is spiritual, and not only spiritual, but eternal, unless it pleaseth God at length to break out of the thick cloud wherewith he covers himself, and shine upon the soul, as in his own time he will.

In this state,* comforts themselves are uncomfortable to the soul. It quarrels with everything. The better things it hears of, the more it is vexed. Oh! what is this to me, what have I to do with these comforts? the more happiness may be had, the more is my grief. As for comforts from God's inferior blessings, as friends, children, estate, &c., the soul is ready to misconstrue God's end in all, as not intending any good to him thereby.

In this condition God doth not appear in his own shape to the soul, but

* 'Estate,' in C.

in the shape of an enemy; and, when God seems against us, who shall stand for us? Our blessed Saviour in his agony had the angels to comfort him; but had he been a mere man, and not assisted by the Godhead, it was not the comfort, no not of angels that could have upheld him, in the sense of his Father's withdrawing his countenance from him. Alas! then, what will become of us in such a case, if we be not supported by a spirit of power and the power of an almighty Spirit?

If all the temptations of the whole world and hell itself were mustered together, they were nothing to this, whereby the great God sets himself contrary to his poor creature.* None can conceive so, but those that have felt it. If the hiding of his face will so trouble the soul, what will his frown and angry look do? Needs must the soul be in a woeful plight, whenas God seems not only to be absent from it, but an enemy to it. When a man sees no comfort from above, and looks inward and sees less; when he looks about him, and sees nothing but evidences of God's displeasure; beneath him, and sees nothing but desperation; clouds without, and clouds within, nothing but clouds in his condition here, he had need of faith to break through all, and see sun through the thickest cloud.

Upon this, the distressed soul is in danger to be set upon by a temptation, called the temptation of blasphemy, *tentatio blasphemiarum*, that is, to entertain bitter thoughts against God, and especially against the grace and goodness of God, wherein he desires to make himself most known to his creature. In those that have wilfully resisted divine truths made known unto them, and, after taste, despised them, a persuasion that God hath forsaken them, set on strongly by Satan, hath a worse effect. It stirs up a hellish hatred against God, carrying them to a revengeful desire of opposing whatsoever is God's, though not always openly, for then they should lose the advantage of doing hurt, yet secretly and subtilly, and under pretence of the contrary. To this degree of blasphemy God's children never fall, yet they may feel the venom of corruption stirring in their hearts, against God and his ways which he takes with them; and this adds greatly to the depth of their affliction, when afterward they think with themselves what hellish stuff they carry in their souls. This is not so much discerned in the temptation, but after the fit is somewhat remitted.

In this kind of desertion, seconded with this kind of temptation, the way is to call home the soul, and to check it, and charge it to trust in God, even though he shews himself an enemy; for it is but a show, he doth but put on a mask, with a purpose to reveal himself the more graciously afterward. His manner is to work by contraries. In this condition God lets in some few beams of light, whereby the soul casts a longing look upon God, even when he seems to forsake it. It will, with Jonah in the belly of hell, look back to the holy temple of God, Jonah ii. 4, it will steal a look unto Christ. Nothing more comfortable in this condition, than to fly to him, that by experience knew what this kind of forsaking meant, for this very end that he might be the fitter to succour us in the like distress, Heb. iv. 15, 16.

Learn, therefore, to appeal from God to God, oppose his gracious nature, his sweet promises to such as 'are in darkness, and see no light,' Isa. l. 10, inviting them to trust in him, though there appear to the eye of sense and reason nothing but darkness. Here make use of that sweet relation of God in Christ becoming a Father to us. 'Doubtless thou art our Father,' Isa.

* Nihil est tentatio vel universi mundi et totius inferni in unum constata, ad eam qua Deus contrarius homini ponitur.—*Luther.*

lxiii. 16. Flesh would make a doubt of it, and thou seemest to hide thy face from us, yet *doubtless* thou art our Father, and hast in former time shewed thyself to be so; we will not leave thee till we have a blessing from thee, till we have a kinder look from thee. This wrestling will prevail at length, and we shall have such a sight of him, as shall be an encouragement for the time to come, when 'we shall be able to comfort others, with those comforts whereby we have been refreshed ourselves,' 2 Cor. i. 4. With the saint's case remember the saint's course, which is to trust in God. So Christ the Head of the church commits himself to that God, whose favour for the present he felt not; so Job resolves upon trust, though God should kill him, Job xiii. 15.

Obj. But these holy persons were not troubled with the guilt of any particular sin, but I feel the just displeasure of God kindled against me for many and great offences.

Ans. True it is, that sin is not so sweet in the committing, as it is heavy and bitter in the reckoning. When Adam had once offended God, paradise itself was not paradise to him. The presence of God, which was most comfortable before, was now his greatest terror, had not God, out of his free, infinite, and preventing mercy, come betwixt him and hell, by the promise of the blessed seed. This seed was made sin to satisfy for sin; sin passive in himself to satisfy for sin active in us, 1 Cor. v. 21.

When God once charges sin upon the soul, alas! who shall take it off? when the great God shall frown, the smiles of the creature cannot refresh us. Sin makes us afraid of that which should be our greatest comfort; it puts a sting into every other evil. Upon the seizing of any evil, either of body, soul, or condition, the guilty soul is embittered and enraged; for from that which it feels, it fore-speaks to itself worse to come, it interprets all that befalls as the messengers of an angry God, sent in displeasure to take revenge upon it. This weakeneth the courage, wasteth the spirits, and blasteth the beauty even of God's dearest ones, Ps. xxxix. 11. There is not the stoutest man breathing, but if God sets his conscience against him it will pull him down, and lay him flat, and fill him with such inward terrors, as he shall be more afraid of himself, than of all the world beside. This were a doleful case, if God had not provided in Christ a remedy for this great evil of evils, and if the Holy Spirit were not above the conscience, able as well to pacify it by the sense of God's love in Christ, as to convince it of sin, and the just desert thereby.

Obj. But my sins are not the sins of an ordinary man, my spots are not as the spots of the rest of God's children.

Conceive of God's mercy as no ordinary mercy, and Christ's obedience as no ordinary obedience. There is something in the very greatness of sin, that may encourage us to go to God, for the greater our sins are, the greater the glory of his powerful mercy pardoning, and his powerful grace in healing will appear. The great God delights to shew his greatness in the greatest things. Even men glory, when they are put upon that, which may set forth their worth in any kind. God 'delighteth in mercy,' Mic. vii. 18. It pleaseth him, nothing so well, as being his chief name, which then we take in vain, when we are not moved by it to come unto him.

That which Satan would use as an argument to drive us from God, we should use as a strong plea with him. Lord, the greater my sins are, the greater will be the glory of thy pardoning mercy. David, after his heinous sins, cries not for mercy, but for 'abundance of mercy;' 'according to the multitude of thy mercies, do away mine offences,' Ps. li. 1. His mercy is not only above his own works, but above ours too. If we could sin more than he could pardon, then we might have some reason to despair. Despair is a high point of atheism, it takes away God and Christ both at once. Judas, in betraying our Saviour, was an occasion of his death as man, but in despairing he did what lay in him to take away his life as God.

When, therefore, conscience, joining with Satan, sets out the sin in its colours, labour thou by faith to set out God in his colours, infinite in mercy and lovingkindess. Here lies the art of a Christian; it is divine rhetoric thus to persuade and set down the soul. Thy sins are great, but Adam's was greater, who being so newly advanced above all the creatures, and taken into so near an acquaintance with God, and having ability to persist in that condition if he would, yet willingly overthrew himself and all his whole posterity, by yielding to a temptation, which though high, as being promised to be like unto God, yet such as he should and might have resisted. No sin we can commit, can be a sin of so tainting and spreading a nature; yet, as he fell by distrust, so he was recovered by trusting, and so must we by relying on a second Adam, whose obedience and righteousness from thence reigns, Rom. v. 17, to the taking away not only of that one sin of Adam, and ours in him, but of all, and not only to the pardon of all sin, but to a right of everlasting life. The Lord thinks himself disparaged, when we have no higher thoughts of his mercy than of our sins, when we bring God down to our model, whenas 'the heavens are not so much higher than the earth, than his thoughts of love and goodness are above the thoughts of our unworthiness,' Isa. lv. 9. It is a kind of taking away the Almighty to limit his boundless mercy in Christ, within the narrow scantling* of our apprehension; yet infidelity doth this, which should stir up in us a loathing of it above all other sins. But this is Satan's fetch,† when once he hath brought us into sins against the law, then to bring us into sins of a higher nature, and deeper danger, even against the blessed gospel, that so there may be no remedy, but that mercy itself might condemn us.

Al lthe aggravations that conscience, and Satan helping it, are able to raise sin unto, cannot rise to that degree of infiniteness, that God's mercy in Christ is of. If there be a spring of sin in us, there is a spring of mercy in him, and a fountain open daily to wash ourselves in, Zech. xiii. 1. If we sin oft, let us do as St Paul, who prayed oft 'against the prick of the flesh,' 2 Cor. xii. 7, 8. If it be a devil of long continuance, yet fasting and prayer will drive him out at length, Mat. xvii. 21.

Nothing keeps the soul more down than sins of long continuance, because corruption of nature hath gotten such strength in them, as nature is added to nature, and custom doth so determine and sway the soul one way, that men think it impossible to recover themselves. They see one link of sin draw on another, all making a chain to fasten them to destruction. They think of necessity they must be damned, because custom hath bred a necessity of sinning in them, and conceive of the promise of mercy, as only made to such as turn from their sinful courses, in which they see themselves so hardened that they cannot repent.

Certain it is, the condition is most lamentable, that yielding unto sin brings men unto. Men are careful to prevent dangerous sicknesses of body, and the danger of law concerning their estates; but seldom consider into what a miserable plight their sins, which they so willingly give themselves up unto, will bring them. If they do not perish in their sins, yet their yielding will bring them into such a doleful condition, that they would give

* That is, 'small portion.'—G.   † That is, 'artifice.'—G.

the whole world, if they were possessors of it, to have their spirits at freedom from this bondage and fear.

To such as bless themselves in an ill way upon hope of mercy, we dare not speak a word of comfort, because God doth not, but threatens his wrath shall burn to hell against them. Yet because while life continues there may be, as a space, so a place and grace for repentance, these must be dealt withal in such a manner, as they may be stayed and stopped in their dangerous courses ; there must be a stop before a turn.

And when their consciences are thoroughly awaked with sense of their danger, let them seriously consider whither sin, and Satan by sin, is carrying of them, and lay to heart the justice of God, standing before them as an angel with a drawn sword, ready to fall upon them if they post on still.

Yet to keep them from utter sinking, let them consider withal, the unlimited mercy of God, as not limited to any person, or any sin, so not to any time. There is no prescription of time can bind God. His mercy hath no certain date that will expire, so as those that fly unto it shall have no benefit. Invincible mercy will never be conquered, and endless goodness never admits of bounds or end.*

What kind of people were those that followed Christ ? Were they not such as had lived long in their sinful courses ? He did not only raise them that were newly dead, but Lazarus, that had lien ' four days in the grave,' John xi. 39. They thought Christ's power in raising the dead had reached to a short time only, but he would let them know that he could as well raise those that had been long as lately dead. If Christ be the physician, it is no matter of how long continuance the disease be. He is good at all kind of diseases, and will not endure the reproach of disability to cure any. Some diseases are the reproaches of other physicians, as being above their skill to help, but no conceit more dangerous when we are to deal with Christ.

' The blessed martyr Bilney was much offended when he heard an eloquent preacher inveighing against sin, saying thus, Behold, thou hast lien rotten in thy own lusts, by the space of sixty years, even as a beast in his own dung, and wilt thou presume in one year to go forward towards heaven, and that in thine old age, as much as thou wentest backward from heaven to hell in sixty years ?' ' Is not this a goodly argument ?' saith Bilney. ' Is this preaching of repentance in the name of Jesus ? It is as if Christ had died in vain for such a man, and that he must make satisfaction for himself. If I had heard, saith he, such preaching of repentance in times past, I had utterly despaired of mercy.' We must never think the door of hope to be shut against us, if we have a purpose to turn unto God. As there is nothing more injurious to Christ, so nothing more foolish and groundless than to distrust, it being the chief scope of God in his word to draw our trust to him in Christ, in whom is always open a breast of mercy for humbled sinners to fly unto.

But thus far the consideration of our long time spent in the devil's service should prevail with us, as to take more shame to ourselves, so to resolve more strongly for God and his ways, and to account it more than sufficient that we have spent already so much precious time to so ill purposes ; and the less time we have, to make the more haste to work for God, and bring all the honour we can to religion in so little a space. Oh, how doth it grieve those that have felt the gracious power of Christ in converting their souls, that ever they should spend the strength of their parts in the work of his and their enemy ! and might they live longer, it is their

* Bonitas invicti non vincitur, et infinita misericordia non finitur.—*Fulgent*[*ius*].

full purpose for ever to renounce their former ways. There is bred in them an eternal desire of pleasing God, as in the wicked there is an eternal desire of offending him, which eternity of desires God looks to in both of them, and rewards them accordingly, though he cuts off the thread of their lives.

But God in wisdom will have the conversions of such as have gone on in a course of sinning, especially after light revealed, to be rare and difficult. Births in those that are ancienter, are with greater danger than in the younger sort. *Cavendum est vulnus quod dolore curatur.* God will take a course, that his grace shall not be turned into wantonness. He oft holds such upon the rack of a troubled conscience, that they and others may fear to buy the pleasure of sin at such a rate. Indeed, where sin abounds, there grace superabounds; but then it is where sin, that abounded in the life, abounds in the conscience in grief and detestation of it, as the greatest evil. Christ groaned at the raising of Lazarus, which he did not at others, because that although to an almighty power all things are alike easy, yet he will shew that there be degrees of difficulties in the things themselves, and make it appear to us that it is so. Therefore, those that have enjoyed long the sweet of sin, may expect the bitterest sorrow and repentance for sin.

Yet never give place to thoughts of despair, as coming from him that would overturn the end of the gospel, which lays open the riches of God's mercy in Christ; which riches none set out more than those that have been 'the greatest of sinners,' 1 Tim. i. 15, as we see in Paul. We cannot exalt God more than by taking notice, and making use of that great design of infinite wisdom in reconciling justice and mercy together, so as now he is not only merciful, but 'just in pardoning sins,' Rom. iii. 26. Our Saviour, as he came towards the latter age of the world, when all things seemed desperate; so he comes to some men in the latter part of their days. The mercy shewed to Zaccheus and the good thief was personal, but the comfort intended by Christ was public, therefore still trust in God.

In this case, we must go to God, with whom all things are possible, to put forth his almighty power, not only in the pardoning, but in subduing our iniquities. He that can make a camel go through a needle's eye, can make a high conceited man lowly, a rich man humble. Therefore, never question his power, much less his willingness, when he is not only ready to receive us when we return, but persuades and entreats us to come in unto him, yea, after backsliding and false dealing with him, wherein he allows no mercy to be shewed by man, yet he will take liberty to shew mercy himself, Jer. iii. 2.

Obj. But I have often relapsed and fallen into the same sin again and again.

Ans. If Christ will have us pardon our brother seventy-seven times,* can we think that he will enjoin us more than he will be ready to do himself, when in case of shewing mercy he would have us think his thoughts to be far above ours? Adam lost all by once sinning, but we are under a better covenant, a covenant of mercy, and are encouraged by the Son to go to the Father every day for the sins of that day.

Where the work of grace is begun, sin loses strength by every new fall; for hence issues deeper humility, stronger hatred, fresh indignation against ourselves, more experience of the deceitfulness of our hearts, renewed resolutions until sin be brought under. That should not drive us from God, which God would have us make use of to fly the rather to him. Since there is a throne of grace set up in Jesus Christ, we may boldly make use of it, and let us be ashamed to sin, and not be ashamed to glorify God's mercy in

* Qu. 'seventy times seven times?'—ED.

begging pardon for sin. Nothing will make us more ashamed to sin than thoughts of so free and large mercy. It will grieve an ingenuous spirit to offend so good a God. Ah, that there should be such a heart in me as to tire the patience of God, and dam up his goodness as much as in me lies! But this is our comfort, that the plea of mercy from a broken spirit to a gracious Father will ever hold good. When we are at the lowest in this world, yet there are these three grounds of comfort still remaining:—1. That we are not yet in the place of the damned, whose estate is unalterable. 2. That whilst we live, there is time and space for recovering of ourselves. 3. That there is grace offered, if we will not shut our hearts against it.

Obj. Oh, but every one hath his time; my good hour may be past.

Ans. That is counsel to thee; it is not past if thou canst raise up thy heart to God, and embrace his goodness. Shew by thy yielding unto mercy, that thy time of mercy is not yet out, rather than by concluding uncomfortably, willingly betray thyself to thy greatest enemy, enforcing that upon thyself, which God labours to draw thee from. As in the sin against the Holy Ghost, fear shews that we have not committed it; so in this, a tender heart fearing lest our time be past, shews plainly that it is not past.

Look upon examples; when the prodigal in his forlorn condition was going to his father, his father stayed not for him, but 'meets him' in the way, Luke xv. 20; he did not only go, but ran to meet him. God is more willing to entertain us than we are to cast ourselves upon him; as there is 'a fountain opened for sin, and for uncleanness,' Zech. xiii. 1, so it is a living fountain of living water, that runs for ever, and can never be drawn dry.

Caution. Here remember, that I build not a shelter for the presumptuous, but only open a harbour for the truly humbled soul to put himself into.

CHAPTER XXII.—*Of sorrow for sin, and hatred for sin, when right and sufficient. Helps thereto.*

Obj. Ah! there's my misery; If I could be humbled for sin, I might hope for mercy, but I never yet knew what a broken heart meant; this soul of mine was never as yet sensible of the grief and smart of sin. How then can I expect any comfort?

Ans. 1. *It is one of Satan's policies to hold us in a dead and barren condition, by following us with conceits, that we have not sorrowed in proportion to our offences.* True it is, we should labour that our sorrow might in some measure answer to the heinousness of our sins; but we must know sorrow is not required for itself in that degree as faith is. If we could trust in God without much sorrow for our sins, then it would not be required, for God delights not in our sorrow as sorrow. God in mercy both requires it and works it, as thereby making us capable vessels of mercy, fit to acknowledge, value, and walk worthy of Christ. He requires it as it is a means to embitter sin, and the delightful pleasures thereof unto us, and by that means bring us to a right judgment of ourselves, and the creature, with which sin commits spiritual adultery, that so we may recover our taste before lost. And then when with the prodigal we return unto ourselves, having lost ourselves before, we are fit to judge of the baseness of sin, and of the worth of mercy; and so upon grounds of right reason, be willing to alter our condition, and embrace mercy upon any terms it shall please Christ to enjoin.

Ans. 2. Secondly, if we could grieve and cast down ourselves beneath the earth, as low as the nethermost pit, *yet this would be no satisfaction to God for sin;* of itself, it is rather an entrance, and beginning of hell.

Ans. 3. Thirdly, we must search what is *the cause of this want of grief which we complain of*, whether it be not a secret cleaving to the creature, and too much contentment in it, which oft stealeth away the heart from God, and brings in such contentment as is subject to fail and deceive us; whereupon from discontentment we grieve, which grief, being carnal, hinders grief of a better kind.

Usually the causes of our want of grief for sin are these :—*First*, a want of serious consideration, and dwelling long enough upon the cause of grief, which springs either from an unsettledness of nature, or distractions from things without. Moveable dispositions are not long affected with anything. One main use of crosses is to take the soul from that it is dangerously set upon, and to fix our running spirits. For though grief for crosses hinders spiritual grief, yet worldly delights hinder more. That grief is less distant from true grief, and therefore nearer to be turned into it.

And *secondly*, put case we could call off our minds from other things, and set them on grief for our sins, yet it is only God's Spirit that can work our hearts to this grief; and for this end, perhaps, God holds us off from it, to teach us that he is the teacher of the heart to grieve. And thereupon it is our duty to wait till he reveal ourselves so far to ourselves, as to stir up this affection in us.

Thirdly, Another cause may be a kind of *doubleness of heart*, whereby we would bring two things together that cannot suit. We would grieve for sin so far as we think it an evidence of a good condition; but then because it is an irksome task, and because it cannot be wrought without severing our heart from those sweet delights it is set upon; hence we are loath God should take that course to work grief, which crosseth our disposition. The soul must therefore, by self-denial, be brought to such a degree of sincerity and simplicity as to be willing to give God leave to work this 'sorrow, not to be sorrowed for,' 2 Cor. vii. 10, by what way he himself pleaseth. But here we must remember again that this self-denial is not of ourselves, but of God, who only can take us out of ourselves, and if our hearts were brought to a stooping herein to his work, it would stop many a cross, and continue many a blessing which God is forced to take from us, that he may work that grief in us which he seeth would not otherwise be kindly wrought.

Ans. 4. God giveth some *larger spirits*, and so their sorrows become larger. Some upon quickness of apprehension, and the ready passages betwixt the brain and the heart, are quickly moved. Where the apprehension is deeper, and the passages slower, there sorrow is long in working, and long in removing. The deepest waters have the stillest motion. Iron takes fire more slowly than stubble, but then it holds it longer.

Ans. 5. Again, *God that searcheth and knows our hearts* better than ourselves, *knows when and in what measure it is fit for to grieve.* He sees it is fitter for some dispositions to go on in a constant grief. We must give that honour to the wisdom of the great physician of souls to know best how to mingle and minister his potions. And we must not be so unkind to take it ill at God's hands when he, out of gentleness and forbearance, ministers not to us that churlish physic he doth to others, but cheerfully embrace any potion that he thinks fit to give us.

Some holy men have desired to see their sin in the most ugly colours, and God hath heard them in their requests. But yet his hand was so heavy upon them that they went always mourning to their very graves, and thought it fitter to leave it to God's wisdom to mingle the potion of sorrow than to be their own choosers.* For a conclusion, then, of this point, if we grieve that we cannot grieve, and so far as it is sin, make it our grief; then put it amongst the rest of our sins, which we beg pardon of, and help against, and let it not hinder us from going to Christ, but drive us to him. For herein lies the danger of this temptation, that those who complain in this kind think it should be presumption to go to Christ, whenas he especially calleth the 'weary and heavy laden sinner to come unto him,' Mat. xi. 28, and therefore such as are sensible that they are not sensible enough of their sin must know, though want of feeling be quite opposite to the life of grace, yet sensibleness of the want of feeling shews some degree of the life of grace. The safest way in this case is from that life and light that God hath wrought in our souls, to see and feel this want of feeling, to cast ourselves and this our indisposition upon the pardoning and healing mercy of God in Christ.

Caution. We speak only of those that are so far displeased with themselves for their ill temper, as they do not favour themselves in it, but are willing to yield to God's way in redressing it, and do not cross the Spirit, moving them thus with David to check themselves, and to trust in God. Otherwise, an unfeeling and careless state of spirit will breed a secret shame of going to God, for removing of that we are not hearty in labouring against, so far as our conscience tells us we are enabled.

The most constant state the soul can be in, in regard of sin, is, upon judgment, to condemn it upon right grounds, and to resolve against it. Whereupon repentance is called an after wisdom and change of the mind. † And this disposition is in God's children at all times. And for affections, love of that which is good, and hatred of that which is evil, these likewise have a settled continuance in the soul. But grief and sorrow rise and fall as fresh occasions are offered, and are more lively stirred up upon some lively representation to the soul of some hurt we receive by sin, and wrong we do to God in it. The reason hereof is, because till the soul be separated from the body, these affections have more communion with the body, and therefore they carry more outward expressions than dislike or abomination in the mind doth. We are to judge of ourselves more by that which is constant than by that which is ebbing and flowing.

Quest. But what is the reason that the affections do not always follow the judgment, and the choice or refusal of the will?

Ans. 1. Our soul being a finite substance, is carried with strength but one way at one time.

2. Sometimes God calls us to joy as well as to grieve, and then no wonder if grief be somewhat to seek.

3. Sometimes when God calleth to grief, and the judgment and will goeth along with God, yet the heart is not always ready, because, it may be, it hath run out so far that it cannot presently be called in again.

4. Or the spirits, which are the instruments of the soul, may be so wasted

---

* Here in margin is placed a name, thus, 'Mr Leaver.' Probably the reference is to the excellent but despondent Thomas Leaver, chaplain to Edward VI., and subsequently one of the refugees at Frankfort. See Fuller's 'Worthies' (i. 547, ed. 1811. 2 vols. 4to); and Bale, de Scrip. Brit. (Cent. ix. 86). There were various eminent Nonconformists of the same name, descendants of Thomas Leaver, contemporary with Sibbes. See Nonconf. Memorial by Palmer (ii. 358; iii. 58, 78, ed. 3 vols. 8vo, 1802).—G. † 'Change of the mind = $\mu\epsilon\tau\acute{a}\nu o\iota a$.—G.

that they cannot hold out to feed a strong grief; in which case the conscience must rest in settled judgment and hatred of ill, which is the surest and never failing character of a good soul.

5. Ofttimes God in mercy takes us off from grief and sorrow, by refreshing occasions, because sorrow and grief are affections very much afflicting both of body and soul.

Quest. When is godly sorrow in that degree wherein the soul may stay itself from uncomfortable thoughts about its condition?

Ans. 1. When we find strength against that sin which formerly we fell into, and ability to walk in a contrary way; for this answers God's end in grief, one of which is a prevention from falling for the time to come. For God hath that affection in him which he puts into parents, which is by smart to prevent their children's boldness of offending for the time to come.

Ans. 2. When that which is wanting in grief is made up in fear. Here there is no great cause of complaint of the want of grief, for this holy affection is the awe-band of the soul, whereby it is kept from starting from God and his ways.

Ans. 3. When after grief we find inward peace; for true grief being God's work in us, he knows best how to measure it. Therefore, whatsoever frame God brings my soul into, I am to rest in his goodness, and not except against his dealing. That peace and joy which riseth from grief in the use of means, and makes the soul more humble and thankful to God, and less censorious and more pitiful to others, is no illusion nor false light.

Ans. 4. The main end of grief and sorrow is to make us value the grace and mercy of God in Christ, above all the contentments which sin feeds on. Which, where it is found, we may know that grief for sin hath enough possessed the soul before. The sufficiency of things is to be judged by an answerableness to their use and ends. God makes sin bitter, that Christ may be sweet. That measure of grief and sorrow is sufficient which brings us and holds us to Christ.

Ans. 5. Hatred, being the strongest, deepest, and steadiest affection of the soul against that which is evil, grief for sin is then right, when it springs from hatred, and increaseth further hatred against it.

1. Now the soul may be known to hate sin when it seeks the utter abolishing of it; for hatred is an implacable and irreconcileable affection.

2. True hatred is carried against the whole kind of sin, without respect of any wrong done to us, but only out of a mere antipathy and contrariety of disposition to it, as the lamb hateth the whole kind of wolves, and man hateth the whole kind of serpents. A toad does us no harm, but yet we hate it.

3. That which is hateful to us, the nearer it is the more we shun and abhor it, as venomous serpents and hurtful creatures, because the nearness of the object affects us more deeply. Therefore, if our grief spring from true hatred of sin, it will make no new league with it, but grieve for all sin, especially for our own particular sins, as being contrary to the work of God's grace in us, then is grief an affection of the new creature, and every way of the right breed.

4. But for fuller satisfaction in this case, we must know there is sometimes grief for sin in us, when we think there is none. It wants but stirring up by some quickening word. The remembrance of God's favours and our unkindness, or the awaking of our consciences by some cross, will raise up this affection feelingly in us. As in the affection of love many think that they have no love to God at all; yet let God be dishonoured in

his name, truth, or children, and their love will soon stir, and appear in just anger.

In want of grief for sin, we must remember, first, that we must have this affection from God, before we can bring it unto God.

And, therefore, in the second place, our chief care should be not to harden our hearts against the motions of the Spirit stirring us to seasonable grief, for that may cause a judicial hardness from God. God oft inflicteth some spiritual judgment as a correction upon men, for not yielding to his Spirit at the first; they feel a hardness of heart growing upon them. This made the church complain, 'Why hast thou hardened our hearts from thy fear?' Isa. lxiii. 17. Which if Christians did well consider, they would more carefully entertain such impressions of sorrow, as the Spirit in the use of the means, and observation of God's dealing towards themselves or others, shall work in them, than they do. It is a saying of Austin, 'Let a man grieve for his sin, and joy for his grief.' Though we can neither love, nor grieve, nor joy of ourselves, as we should, yet our hearts tell us, we are often guilty of giving a check to the Spirit's stirring these affections in us, which is a main cause of the many sharp afflictions we endure in this life, though God's love in the main matter of salvation be most firm unto us.

Third, We must not think to have all this grief at first, and at once, for oftentimes it is deeper after a sight and feeling of God's love than it was before. God is a free agent, and knows every man's several mould, and the several services he is to use them in, and oft takes liberty afterwards to humble men more, when he hath enabled them better to bear it, than in their first entrance into religion. Grief before springs commonly from self-love and fear of danger. Let no man suspect his estate, because God spares him in the beginning. For Christians many times meet with greater trial after their conversion than ever they thought on. When men take little fines, they mean to take the greater rent. God will have his children, first or last, to feel what sin is; and how much they are beholden to him for Christ.

This grief doth not always arise from poring on sin, but by oft considering of the infinite goodness of God in Christ, and thereby reflecting on our own unworthiness, not only in regard of sin past, but likewise of the sin that hangeth upon us, and issues daily from us. The more holy a man is, the more he sees the holiness of God's nature, with whom he desires to have communion, the more he is grieved that there should be anything found in him displeasing to so pure a Majesty.

And as all our grief comes not at first, so God will not have it come all at once, but to be a stream always running, fed with a spring, yet within the banks, though sometimes deeper, sometimes shallower. Grief for sin is like a constant stream; grief for other things is like a torrent, or swelling waters, which are soon up, soon down; what it wants in greatness is made up in continuance.

Fourth, Again, if we watch not our nature, there will be a spice of popery, which is a natural religion, in this great desire of more grief; as, if we had that, then we had something to satisfy God withal, and so our minds will run too much upon works. This grief must not only be wrought by God revealing our sin, and his mercy unto us in Christ; but when it is wrought, we must altogether rest, in a sense of our own emptiness, upon the full satisfaction and worthiness of Christ our Saviour.

All this that hath been said tends not to the abating of our desire to have a tender and bleeding heart for sin ; but that in the pursuit of this desire, we be not cast down so as to question our estates, if we feel not that measure of grief which we desire and endeavour after, or to refuse our portion of joy which God offers us in Christ, considering grief is no further good than it makes way for joy; which caused our Saviour to join them together: blessed are the mourners, for they shall be comforted.' Being thus disposed, we may commit our souls to God in peace, notwithstanding Satan's troubling of us in the hour of temptation.

CHAPTER XXIII.—*Other spiritual causes of the soul's trouble discovered and removed; and objections answered.*

Another thing that disquiets and casts down the soul very much is, that inward conflict betwixt grace and corruption. This makes us most work, and puts us to most disquietment. *Proximorum odia sunt acerbissima.* It is the trouble of troubles to have two inhabitants so near in one soul, and these to strive one against another, in every action, and at all times in every part and power in us: the one carrying us upward, higher and higher still, till we come to God; the other pulling us lower and lower, further from him. This cannot but breed a great disquiet, when a Christian shall be put on to that which he would not, and hindered from that which he would do, or troubled in the performance of it, Rom. vii. 21–23. The more light there is to discern, and life of grace to be sensible hereof, and the more love of Christ, and desire from love to be like to him, the more irksome will this be. No wonder then that the apostle cried out, 'O wretched man that I am,' &c., Rom. vii. 24.

Here is a special use of trust in the free mercy of God in justification, considering all is stained that comes from us. It is one main end of God's leaving us in this conflicting condition, that we may live and die by faith in the perfect righteousness of Christ, whereby we glorify God more than if we had perfect righteousness of our own. Hereby likewise we are driven to make use of all the promises of grace, and to trust in God for the performance of them, in strengthening his own party in us, and not only to trust in God for particular graces, but for his Spirit, which is the spring of all graces, which we have through and from Christ, who will help us in this fight until he hath made us like himself. We are under the government of grace; sin is deposed from the rule it had, and shall never recover the right it had again. It is left in us for matter of exercise, and ground of triumph.

Obj. Oh, say some, I shall never hold out, as good give over at first as at last; I find such strong inclination to sin in me, and such weakness to resist temptation, that I fear I shall but shame the cause ; I shall one day perish, by the hand of Satan strengthening my corruption.

Ans. Why art thou thus troubled? 'Trust in God,' grace will be above nature ; God above the devil, the spirit above the flesh. Be strong in the Lord, the battle is his, and the victory ours beforehand. If we fought in our own cause and strength, and with our weapons, it were something ; but as we fight in the power of God, so are ' we kept by that mighty power through faith unto salvation,' 1 Pet. i. 5. It lies upon the faithfulness of Christ, to put us into that possession of glory which he hath purchased for us ; therefore charge the soul to make use of the promises, and rely upon God for perfecting the good work that he hath begun in thee.

Corruptions be strong, but stronger is he that is in us than that corruption that is in us. When we are weak in our own sense, then are we strong in him who perfecteth strength in our weakness, felt and acknowledged. Our corruptions are God's enemies as well as ours, and, therefore, in trusting to him and fighting against them, we may be sure he will take our part against them.

Obj. But I have great impediments and many discouragements in my Christian course.

Ans. What if our impediments be mountains, faith is able to remove them. 'Who art thou, O mountain?' Zech. iv. 7, saith the prophet. What a world of impediments were there betwixt Egypt and the land of Canaan, betwixt the return out of Babylon and Jerusalem; yet faith removed all by looking to God's power and truth in his promise. The looking too much to the Anakims and giants, and too little to God's omnipotency, shut the Israelites out of Canaan, and put God to his oath that they should 'never enter into his rest,' Ps. xcv. 11; and it will exclude our souls from happiness at length, if, looking too much upon these Anakims within us and without us, we basely despair and give over the field, considering all our enemies are not only conquered for us by our Head, but shall be conquered in us, so that in strength of assistance we fight against them. God gave the Israelites' enemies into their hands, but yet they must fight it out; and what coward will not fight when he is sure of help and victory?

Obj. But I carry continually about me a corrupt heart; if that were once changed, I could have some comfort.

A new heart is God's creature, and he hath promised to create it in us, Ps. li. 10, Eph. ii. 10. A creating power can, not only bring something out of nothing, but contrary out of contrary. Where we are sure of God's truth, let us never question that power to which all things are possible. If our hearts were as ill as God is powerful and good, there were some ground of discouragement. In what measure we give up our hearts to God, in that measure we are sure to receive them better. That grace which enlargeth the heart to desire good is therefore given that God may increase it, being both a part and a pledge of further grace, Ezek. xxxvi. 25. There is a promise of pouring clean water upon us which faith must sue out. Christ hath taken upon him to purge his spouse, and make her fit for himself, Eph. v. 26, 27.

Obj. But I have many wants and defects to be supplied.

Ans. It pleaseth him that in Christ 'all fulness shall dwell,' Col. i. 19, from whose fulness grace sufficient is dispensed to us answerable to the measure of our faith, whereby we fetch it from the fountain. The more we trust, the more we have. When we look, therefore, to our own want, we should look withal to Christ's fulness and his nearness to us, and take advantage from our misery to rest upon his all-sufficiency whose fulness is ours, as himself is. Our fulness, with our life, is hid in Christ, and distilled into us in such measure as his wisdom thinketh fit and as sheweth him to be a free agent, and yet so as the blame for want of grace lieth upon us, seeing he is beforehand with us in his offers of grace; and our own consciences will tell us that our failings are more from cherishing of some lust than from unwillingness in him to supply us with grace.

Obj. But God is of pure eyes, and cannot endure such services as I perform.

Ans. Though God be of pure eyes, yet he looks upon us in 'Him who is blameless and without spot,' Heb. ix. 14, who, by virtue of his sweet-smelling sacrifice, appears for us in heaven, and mingles his odours with our services;

and in him will God be known to us by the name of a kind Father, not only in pardoning our defects, but accepting our endeavours. We offer our services to God, not in our own name, but in the name of our High Priest, who takes them from us, and presents them to his Father as stirred up by his Spirit and perfumed by his obedience. Jonah's prayer was mingled with a great deal of passion and imperfection, yet God could discern something of his own in it, and pity and pardon the rest.

CHAPTER XXIV.—*Of outward troubles disquieting the spirit, and comforts in them.*

As for the outward evils that we meet withal in this life, they are either such, 1, As deprive us of the comforts our nature is supported withal; or else, 2, They bring such misery upon our nature or condition that hinders our well-being in this world.

1. For the first, trust in God, and take out of his all-sufficiency whatsoever we want. Sure we are by his promise that we shall want nothing that is good. What he takes away one way, he can give another; what he takes away in one hand, he can give another; what he withholds one way, he can supply in a better.* Whatsoever comfort we have in goods, friends, health, or any other blessings, it is all conveyed by him, who still remains, though these be taken from us. And we have him bound in many promises for all that is needful for us. We may sue him upon his own bond. Can we think that he who will give us a kingdom, will fail us in necessary provision to bring us thither, who himself is our portion?

2. As for those miseries which our weak nature is subject to, they are all under Christ. They come and go at his command; they are his messengers, sent for our good, and called back again when they have done what they came for. Therefore, look not so much upon them as to Him for strength and comfort in them, mitigation of them, and grace to profit by them.

To strengthen our faith the more in God, he calleth himself a buckler for defence from ill, and an ' exceeding great reward,' Gen. xv. 1, for a supply of all good; a sun for the one, and a shield for the other. Trust him, then, with health, wealth, good name, all that thou hast. It is not in man to take away that from us which God will give us and keep for us. It is not in man's power to make others conceive what they please of us.

Among crosses this is that which disquieteth not the mind least, to be deceived in matter of trust, whenas if we had not trusted we had not been deceived. The very fear of being disappointed made David in his haste think ' all men were liars,' Ps. cxvi. 11. But as it is a sharp cross, so nothing will drive us nearer unto God, who never faileth his.

Friends often prove as the ' reed of Egypt, as a broken staff,' Ezek. xxix. 6, ' and as a deceitful brook,' Job vi. 15, that fails the weary passenger in summer time, when there is most need of refreshing; and it is the unhappiness of men, otherwise happy in the world, that during their prosperous condition, they know not who be their friends; for when their condition declines, it plainly appears, that many were friends of their estates, and not of their persons. But when men will know us least, God will know us most. He knows our souls in adversity, and knows them so as to support and comfort them, and that from the spring-head of comfort, whereby the sweetest comforts are fetched. What God conveyed before by friends, that he doth now instil immediately from himself. The immediate comforts are

* In Margin, ' Amaziah.'

the strongest comforts. Our Saviour Christ told his disciples, that they would 'leave him alone; yet, saith he, I am not alone, but the Father is with me,' John xvi. 32. At St Paul's first appealing 'all forsook him, but the Lord stood by him,' 2 Tim. iv. 16. He wants no company that hath Christ for his companion, *Solus non est cui Christus comes est.*—Cypr[ian.] 'I looked for some to take pity,' saith David, 'but there was none, Ps. lxix. 20. This unfaithfulness of man is a foil to set out God's truth, who is never nearer than when trouble is nearest. There is not so much as a shadow of change in him or his love.

It is just with God when we lay too much weight of confidence upon any creature, to let us have the greater fall. Man may fail us .and yet be a good man, but God cannot fail us and be God, because he is truth itself. Shall God be so true to us, and shall not we be true to him and his truth?

The like may be said in the departure of our friends. Our life is oft too much in the life of others, which God takes unkindly. How many friends have we in him alone! who rather than we shall want friends, can make our enemies our friends. A true believer is to Christ as his mother, brother, and sister, because he carries that affection to them, as if they were mother, brother, and sister, to him indeed, Mat. xii. 50. As Christ makes us all to him, so should we make him all in all to ourselves. If all comforts in the world were dead, we have them still in the living Lord.

Sicknesses are harbingers of death, and in the apprehension of many they be the greatest troubles, and tame great spirits, that nothing else could tame. Herein we are more to deal with God than with men, which is one comfort sickness yieldeth above other troubles. It is better to be troubled with the distempers of our own bodies, than with the distempers of other men's souls; in which we have not only to deal with men, but with the devil himself, that ruleth in the humours of men.

The example of Asa, 2 Chron. xvi. 12, teaches us in this case not to lay too much trust upon the physician, but with Hezekiah first look up to God, and then use the means, 2 Kings xix. 14, 15. If God will give us a *quietus est*, and take us off from business by sickness, then we have a time of serving God by patient subjection to his will. If he means to use our service any further, he will restore our health and strength to do that work he sets us about. Health is at his command, and sickness stays at his rebuke. In the mean, the time of sickness is a time of purging from that defilement we gathered in our health, till we come purer out; which should move us the rather willingly to abide God's time. Blessed is that sickness that proves the health of the soul. We are best, for the most part, when we are weakest, *Optimi sumus dum infirmi sumus.* Then it appears what good proficients we have been in time of health.

Carnal men are oft led along by false hopes suggested by others, and cherished by themselves, that they shall live still and do well till death comes and cuts off their vain confidence and their life both at once, before ever they are acquainted what it is to trust in God aright, in the use of means. We should labour to learn of St Paul in desperate cases, to receive the sentence of death, and not to trust in ourselves, but in God 'that raiseth the dead,' 2 Cor. i. 9. He that raiseth our dead bodies out of the grave, can raise our diseased bodies out of the bed of sickness, if he hath a pleasure to serve himself by us.

In all kind of troubles, it is not the ingredients that God puts into the cup so much afflicts us, as the ingredients of our distempered passions mingled with them. The sting and core of them all is sin. When that is not only pardoned, but in some measure healed, and the proud flesh eaten out, then a healthy soul will bear anything. After repentance, that trouble that before was a correction, becomes now a trial and exercise of grace. 'Strike, Lord,' saith Luther, 'I bear anything willingly, because my sins are forgiven.' We should not be cast down so much about outward troubles, as about sin, that both procures them and envenoms them. We see by experience, when conscience is once set at liberty, how cheerfully men will go under any burden; therefore labour to keep out sin, and then let come what will come.

It is the foolish wisdom of the world to prevent trouble by sin, which is the way indeed to pull the greatest trouble upon us. For sin dividing betwixt God and us, moveth him to leave the soul to entangle itself in its own ways. When the conscience is clear, then there is nothing between God and us to hinder our trust. Outward troubles rather drive us nearer unto God, and stand with his love. But sin defileth the soul, and sets it further from God. It is well-doing that enables us to commit our souls cheerfully unto him, 1 Pet. iii. 21. Whatsoever our outward condition be, 'if our hearts condemn us not, we may have boldness with God,' 1 John. iii. 21. In any trouble our care should be, not to avoid the trouble, but sinful miscarriage in and about the trouble, and so trust God. It is a heavy condition to be under the burden of trouble, and under the burden of a guilty conscience both at once. When men will 'walk in the light of their own fire, and the sparks which they have kindled themselves, it is just with God that they should lie down in sorrow,' Isa. l. 11.

Whatsoever injuries we suffer from those that are ill affected to us, let us commit our cause to the 'God of vengeance,' Isa. lix. 17, and not meddle with his prerogative. He will revenge our cause better than we can, and more perhaps than we desire. The wronged side is the safer side.* If, instead of meditating revenge, we can so overcome ourselves as to pray for our enemies, and deserve well of them, we shall both sweeten our own spirits, and prevent a sharp temptation which we are prone unto; and have an undoubted argument that we are sons of that Father that doth good to his enemies, and members of that Saviour that prayed for his persecutors, Luke xxiii. 34. And withal by 'heaping coals,' Rom. xii. 20, upon our enemies, shall melt them either to conversion or to confusion.

But the greatest trial of trust is in our last encounter with death, wherein we shall find not only a deprivation of all comforts in this life, but a confluence of all ill at once; but we must know, God will be the God of his unto death, and not only unto death, but in death. We may trust God the Father with our bodies and souls which he hath created; and God the Son with the bodies and souls which he hath redeemed; and the Holy Spirit with those bodies and souls that he hath sanctified. We are not disquieted when we put off our clothes and go to bed, because we trust God's ordinary providence to raise us up again. And why should we be disquieted when we put off our bodies and sleep our last sleep, considering we are more sure to rise out of our graves than out of our beds? Nay, we are raised up already in Christ our Head, 'who is the resurrection and the life,' John xi. 25, in whom we may triumph over death, that triumpheth over the greatest monarchs, as a disarmed and conquered enemy. Death is the death of itself, and not of us. If we would have faith ready to die by, we must exercise it well in living by it, and then it will no more fail

* Melior est tristitia iniqua patientis, quam lœtitia iniqua facientis.—*Aug.*

us than the good things we lay hold on by it, until it hath brought us into heaven, where that office of it is laid aside. Here is the prerogative of a true Christian above an hypocrite and a worldling, whenas their trust, and the thing they trust in, fails them, then a true believer's trust stands him in greatest stead.

In regard of our state after death, a Christian need not be disquieted, for the angels are ready to do their office in carrying his soul to paradise, those 'mansions prepared for him,' John xiv. 2. His Saviour will be his judge, and the Head will not condemn the members; then he is to receive the fruit and end of his faith, the reward of his hope; which is so great and so sure, that our trusting in God for that, strengtheneth the heart to trust him for all other things in our passage; so that the refreshing of our faith in these great things, refreshes its dependence upon God for all things here below. And how strong helps have we to uphold our faith in those great things which we are not able to conceive of, till we come to possess them! Is not our husband there? and hath he not taken possession for us? Doth he not keep our place for us? Is not our flesh there in him? and his Spirit below with us? Have we not some first-fruits and earnest of it before hand? Is not Christ now fitting and preparing of us daily, for what he hath prepared and keeps for us? Whither tends all we meet with in this world, that comes betwixt us and heaven, as desertions, inward conflicts, outward troubles, and death at last, but to fit us for a better condition hereafter, and by faith therein to stir up a strong desire after it? 'Comfort one another with these things,' saith the apostle, 1 Thes. iv. 18; these be the things will comfort the soul.

CHAPTER XXV.—*Of the defects of gifts, disquieting the soul; as also the afflictions of the church.*

Among other things, there is nothing more disquiets a Christian, that is called to the fellowship of Christ and his church here, and to glory hereafter, than that he sees himself unfurnished with those gifts that are fit for the calling of a saint; as likewise for that particular standing and place wherein God hath set him in this world, by being a member of a body politic.

For our Christian calling, we must know that Christianity is a matter rather of grace than of gifts, of obedience than of parts. Gifts may come from a more common work of the Spirit; they are common to castaways, and are more for others than for ourselves. Grace comes from a peculiar favour of God, and especially for our own good. In the same duty, where there is required gifts and grace, as in prayer, one may perform it with evidence of greater grace than another of greater parts. Moses, a man not of the best speech, was chosen before Aaron to speak to God, Exod. vii. 11; and to strive with him by prayer, whilst Israel fought with Amalek with the sword, Exod. xvii 11. It is a business more of the heart than of the tongue, more of groans than of words, which groans and sighs the spirit will always stir up even in the worst condition. Yet for parts there is no member, but it is fitted with some abilities to do service in the body, and by faith may grow up to a greater measure. For God calls none to that high condition, but whom in some measure he fits to be an useful member, and endows with a public spirit.

But that is the measure which Christ thinks fit; who will make up that in the body which is wanting in any particular member. God will increase the measure of our gifts as occasion shall be offered to draw them forth;

for there is not the greatest but may have use both of the parts and graces of the meanest in the church. And here the soul may by a spirit of faith go to God in this manner: Lord, the state* of Christianity unto which thy love in Christ hath called and advanced me, is a high condition; and there is need of a great measure of grace to uphold the credit and comfort of it. Whom thou callest unto it, thou dost in some measure furnish to walk worthy of it. Let this be an evidence to my soul of the truth of thy call, that I am enabled by the Spirit for those duties that are required; in confidence of which assistance I will set upon the work: 'Thou hast promised to give wisdom to them that ask it, and to upbraid none with their unworthiness. Nay, 'thou hast promised the Spirit of all grace to those that beg it,' James i. 5. It is that which I need, and it is no more than thou hast promised.

Caution. Only it must be remembered, that we do not walk above our parts and graces, the issue whereof will be discouragement in ourselves and disgrace from others.

The like may be said for our particular calling, wherein we are to express the graces of our Christian calling, and 'serve one another in love,' Gal. v. 13, as members of the state as well as of the church. Therefore every one must have, 1, a calling; 2, a lawful; 3, a useful calling; 4, a calling fitted for his parts, that he may be even for his business, *pares negotio;* 5, a lawful entrance and calling thereunto; 6, and a lawful demeanour in the same. Though the orb and sphere we walk in be little, yet we must keep within the bounds of it, because for our carriage in that, we must give a strict account; and there is no calling so mean but a man shall find enough to give a good account for (*i*). Our care must be to know our work, and then to do it; and so to do it as if it were unto God, with conscience of moderate diligence; for over-doing and over-working anything comes either from ostentation or distrust in God; and negligence is so far from getting any blessing, that it brings us under a 'curse for doing God's work negligently,' Jer. xlviii. 10. For we must think our callings to be services of God, who hath appointed us our standing therein.

That which belongs to us in our calling is care of discharging our duty; that which God takes upon him is assistance, and good success in it. Let us do our work, and leave God to do his own. Diligence and trust in him is only ours, the rest of the burden is his. In a family the father's and the master's care is the greatest; the child's care is only to obey, and the servant's to do his work; care of provision and protection doth not trouble them. Most of our disquietness in our calling is, that we trouble ourselves about God's work. Trust God and be doing, and let him alone with the rest. He stands upon his credit so much, that it shall appear we have not trusted him in vain, even when we see no appearance of doing any good. Peter fished all night and catched nothing, yet upon Christ's word he casts in his net again, and caught so many fish as break his net, Luke v. 6. Covetousness, when men will be richer than God would have them, troubles all; it troubles the house, the whole family, and the house within us, our precious soul, which should be a quiet house for God's spirit to dwell in, whose seat is a quiet spirit. If men would follow Christ's method, and 'seek first the kingdom of heaven,' Mat. vi. 33, all other things would be cast upon them. If thoughts of insufficiency in our places discourage us, remember what God saith to Moses, when he pretended disability to speak, 'Who hath made man's mouth, have not I the Lord?' Exod. iv. 11. All our sufficiency for every calling is from God.

* 'Estate,' in C.

Obj. But you will say, though by God's blessing my particular condition be comfortable, yet the state of God's people abroad, and the miseries of the times, disquiet me.

Ans. We complain of the times, but let us take heed we be not a part of the misery of the times: that they be not the worse for us. Indeed he is a dead member that takes not to heart the ill of the times, yet here is place for that complaint, 'Help, Lord,' Ps. xii. 1. In these tempests do as the disciples did, cry to Christ to rebuke the tempests and storms, Mat. viii. 25. This is the day of Jacob's trouble, let it also be the day of Jacob's trust; let the body do as the head did in the like case, and in time it shall be with the body as it is with the head.

In this case it is good to lay before God all the promises made to his church, with the examples of his presence in it, and deliverance of the same in former times. God is never nearer his church than when trouble is near. When in earth they conclude an utter overthrow, God is in heaven concluding a glorious deliverance. Usually after the lowest ebb, follows the highest spring-tide. Christ stands upon Mount Zion. There is a counsel in heaven, that will dash the mould of all contrary counsels on earth; and which is more, God will work the raising of the church, by that very means by which his enemies seek to ruin it. 'Let us stand still and behold the salvation of the Lord,' Exod. xiv. 13. God gave too dear a price for his church, to suffer it long in the hands of merciless enemies.

As for the seeming flourishing of the enemies of God's church, it is but for a time, and that a short time, and a measured time. 'The wicked plot against the just,' Ps. xxxvii. 12; they 'are plotters and ploughers of mischief,' Job iv. 8; they are skilful and industrious in it, but they reap their own ruin. 'Their day is a coming,' Ps. xxxvii. 12, and 'their pit is in digging,' Ps. xciv. 13; take heed therefore of fretting, Ps. xxxvii. 7; because of the man 'that bringeth wicked devices to pass, for the arms of the wicked shall be broken,' Ps. xxxvii. 17.* We should help our faith by observing God's executing of judgment in this kind. It cannot but vex the enemies of the church, to see at length a disappointing of their projects; but then to see the mould of all their devices turned upon their own heads, will more torment them.

In this case, it will much comfort to go into the sanctuary, for there we shall be able to say, 'Yet God is good to Israel,' Ps. lxxiii. 17. God hath an ark for his. There is no condition so ill, but there is balm in Gilead, comfort in Israel. The depths of misery are never beyond the depths of mercy. God oft for this very end, strips his church of all helps below, that it may only rely upon him: and that it may appear that the church is ruled by a higher power than it is opposed by. And then is the time when we may expect great deliverances of the church, when there is a great faith in the great God.

From all that hath been said, we see that the only way to quiet the soul is, to lay a charge upon it to trust God, and that unquietness and impatiency are symptoms and discoveries of an unbelieving heart.

CHAPTER XXVI.—*Of divine reasons in a believer. Of his minding to praise God, more than to be delivered.*

To go on. '*I shall yet praise him.*'

In these words David expresseth the reasons and grounds of his trust,

* Read Psalms x., xxxvii., xciv., cxxix., &c.

namely, from the interest he had in God by experience and special covenant: wherein in general we may observe, *that those who truly trust in God, labour to back their faith with sound arguments.* Faith is an understanding grace; it knows whom it trusts, and for what, and upon what grounds it trusts. Reason of itself cannot find what we should believe, yet when God hath discovered the same, faith tells us there is great reason to believe it. Faith useth reason, though not as a ground, yet as a sanctified instrument to find out God's grounds, that it may rely upon them. He believes best, that knows best why he should believe. Confidence, and love, and other affections of the soul, though they have no reason grafted in them, yet thus far they are reasonable, as that they are in a wise man raised up, guided, and laid down with reason; or else men were neither to be blamed nor praised for ordering their affections aright; whereas not only civil virtue, but grace itself is especially conversant in ruling the affections by sanctified reason.

The soul guides the will and affections otherwise than it doth the outward members of the body. It sways the affections of confidence, love, joy, &c., as a prince doth his wiser subjects, and as counsellors do a well ordered state, by ministering reasons to them; but the soul governs the outward members by command, as a master doth a slave,—his will is enough. The hand and foot move upon command, without regarding any reason; but we will not trust and rejoice in God without reason, or a show of reason at the least.

Sin itself never wanted a reason, such as it is, but we call it unreasonable, because it hath no good reason for it; for reason being a beam of God, cannot strengthen any work of darkness. God having made man an understanding creature, guides him by a way suitable to such a condition, and that is the reason why God in mercy yields so far to us in his word, as to give us so many reasons of our affiance in him. What is encouragement and comfort but a demonstration to us of greater reasons to raise us up, than there are to cast us down?

David's reasons here, are drawn partly from some promise of deliverance, and partly from God's nature and dealing with him, whom, as he had formerly found a healing and a saving God, so he expects to find him still; and partly from the covenant of grace, *He is my God.*

The chief of his reasons are fetched from God, what he is in himself, and what he is and will be to his children, and what to him in particular. Though godly men have reasons for their trust, yet those reasons be divine and spiritual, as faith itself is; for as naturally as beams come from the sun, and branches from the root, even so by divine discourse one truth issueth from another. And as the beams and the sun, as the root and branches are all of one nature, so the grounds of comfortable truths, and reasons taken from those grounds, are both of the same divinity and authority, though in time of temptation discourse is oft so troubled, that it cannot see how one truth riseth from another. This is one privilege of heaven, that our knowledge there shall not be so much discoursive, proving one thing by another, as definitive, seeing things in their grounds with a more present view; the soul being then raised and enlarged to a present conceiving of things, and there being no flesh and blood in us to raise objections that must be satisfied with reasoning.

Sometimes in a clearer state of the soul, faith hath not so much use of reasons, but upon near and sweet communion with God, and by reason of some likeness between the soul that hath a divine nature stamped upon it, and God, it presently, without any long discourse, runneth to God, as it were, by a supernatural instinct, as by a natural instinct a child runneth to his father in any distress. Yea, and from that common light of nature, which discovereth there is a God, even natural men in extremities will run to God, and God as the author of nature will sometimes hear them, as he doth the young ravens that cry unto him; but comfortably, and with assurance, only those have a familiar recourse unto him, that have a sanctified suitable disposition unto God, as being well acquainted with him.

Sometimes again faith is put to it to use reasons to strengthen itself, and therefore the soul studieth arguments to help itself by, either from inward store laid up in the soul, or else it hearkeneth and yields to reasons suggested by others; and there is no gracious heart but hath a frame suitable and agreeable to any holy and comfortable truth that shall be brought and enforced upon it. There is something in his spirit that answers whatever comes from the Spirit of God. Though perhaps it never heard of it before, yet it presently claims kindred of it, as coming from the same blessed spring, the Holy Spirit; and, therefore, a gracious heart sooner takes comfort than another, as being prepared to close with it.

The reasons here brought by David, are not so much arguments to convince his judgment, as motives and inducements to incline his will to trust in God; for trusting being a holy relying upon God, carrieth especially the will to him. Now the will is led with the goodness of things, as the understanding is led with truth. The heart must be sweetened with consideration of love and mercy in him whom we trust, as well as convinced of his ability to do us good. The cords that draw the heart to trust are the cords of love, and the cords of love are especially the love of him to us whom we love; and, therefore the most prevailing reasons that carry the whole heart, are such as are drawn from the sweetness of God, whereby the heart is opened and enlarged to expect all good, and nothing but good from him.

But we must remember that neither reasons from the truth and power of God, nor inducements or allurements from the goodness of God, will further prevail with the soul, than it hath a fresh light and relish brought into it by the Spirit of God, to discern of those reasons, and answer the contrary.

I shall yet praise him,* or I will yet praise him, I shall because I will, and I will praise him because I shall have occasion to praise him. When God by grace enlarges the will, he intends to give the deed. God's children, wherein their wills are conformable to God's will, shall have their wills fulfilled. God intends his own glory in every mercy, and he that praises him glorifies him, Ps. l. 23. When our wills, therefore, carry us to that which God wills above all, we may well expect he will grant us what we will.

'I shall praise him,' because I have prayed unto him. It is God's direction, to call upon him in trouble, Ps. l. 15, and it is his promise to deliver, and then both his direction and promise that we shall glorify him. When troubles stir up prayer, God's answer to them will stir up praises. David, when he says I shall praise God, pre-supposes that God will deliver him, that he may have ground of praising his name; and he knew God would deliver him, because as from faith he had prayed for deliverance, so he knew that it was God's order in his dealing, to revive after drooping, and to

---

* 'I shall yet,' to 'fail before him.' This very sweet paragraph, by a strange oversight, was omitted in B, and has slipped out from every subsequent edition. Probably it was displaced in B to allow of the additions referred to in Note *g*. The paragraph, 'David minds,' &c., that immediately follows, is twice printed in B, and the closing sentence of the one omitted *above*, occurs at page 531, without any connection with what precedes.—G.

refresh after fainting. God knows otherwise that our spirits would fail before him.

I will praise him. David* minds praising of God more than his own delivery, because he knew his own delivery was intended on God's part, that he might be glorified. It is an argument of an excellent spirit, when all self-respects are drowned in the glory of God: and there is nothing lost therein, for our best being is in God. A Christian begins with loving God for himself; but he ends in loving himself in and for God: and so his end, and God's end, and the end of all things else, concentre and agree in one. We may aim at our own good, so we bring our hearts to refer it to the chief good, as a less circle may well be contained in a greater, so that the lines drawn from both circles, meet in one middle point. It is an excellent ground of sincerity to desire the favour of God, not so much out of self-aims, as that God may have the more free and full praise from us, considering the soul is never more fit for that blessed duty, than when it is in a cheerful plight.

It rejoiced David more that he should have a large heart to serve God, than that he should have enlargement of condition. Holy dispositions think not so much of the time to come, that it will be sweet to them, as that it will further God's praise. True grace raiseth the soul above self-respects, and resteth not till it comes to the chief end wherein its happiness consists.

God is glorified in making us happy, and we enjoying happiness, must glorify God. Although God condescend so low unto us, as not only to allow us, but to enjoin us to look to our own freedom from misery, and enjoyment of happiness, yet a soul thoroughly seasoned with grace, mounteth higher, and is carried with pure respects to advance God's glory; yea, sometimes so far as to forget its own happiness. It respects itself for God, rather than God for itself. A heavenly soul is never satisfied, until it be as near God as is attainable. And the nearer a creature comes to God, the more it is emptied of itself, and all self-aims. Our happiness is more in him, than in ourselves. We seek ourselves most when we deny ourselves most. And the more we labour to advance God, the more we advance our own condition in him.

I will praise. David thinks of his own duty in praising God more than of God's work in delivering him. Let us think of what is our duty, and God will think of what shall be for our comfort. We shall feel God answering what we look for from him, in doing what he expects from us. Can we have so mean thoughts of him as that we should intend his glory, and he not much more intend our good?

This should be a strong plea unto us, in our prayers to prevail with God, when we engage ourselves, upon the revelation of his mercy to us, to yield him all the praises. Lord, as the benefit and comfort shall be mine, so the praises shall be thine!

It is little less than blasphemy to praise God for that which by unlawful shifts we have procured; for besides the hypocrisy of it, in seeming to sacrifice to him, when we sacrifice, indeed, to our own wits and carnal helps, we make him a patron of those ways which he most abhors; and it is idolatry in the highest degree to transform God so in our thoughts, as to think he is pleased with that which comes from his greatest enemy. And there is a gross mistake to take God's curse for a blessing. To thrive in an ill way is a spiritual judgment, extremely hardening in the heart.

* 'Here,' inserted in B.

It is an argument of David's sincerity here that he meant not to take any indirect course for delivering himself, because he intended to praise God, which as no guilty conscience can offer, being afraid to look God in the face, so God would abhor such a sacrifice were it offered to him. St Paul was stirred up to praise God, but withal he was assured 'God would preserve him from every evil work,' 2 Tim. iv. 18.

Sometimes, indeed, where there is no malicious intention, God pardons some breakings out of flesh and blood, endeavouring to help ourselves in danger, so far as not to take advantage of them to desert us in trouble; as in David, who escaped from Achish by counterfeiting, 1 Sam. xxvii. 10; and this yields a double ground of thankfulness, partly for God's overlooking our miscarriage, and partly for the deliverance itself. Yet this indulgence of God will make the soul more ashamed afterward for these sinful shifts; therefore, it must be no precedent to us. There can neither be grace nor wisdom in setting upon a course wherein we can neither pray to God for success in, nor bless God when he gives it. In this case God most blesseth where he most crosseth, and most curseth where the deluded heart thinks he blesseth most.

CHAPTER XXVII.—*In our worst condition we have cause to praise God; still ample cause in these days.*

'I shall yet praise him, or yet I will praise God;' that is, however it goeth with me, yet, as I have cause, so I have a spirit to praise God. When we are at the lowest, yet it is a mercy that we are not consumed. We are never so ill but it might be worse with us. Whatsoever is less than hell is undeserved. It is a matter of praise that yet we have time and opportunity to get into a blessed condition. 'The Lord hath afflicted me sore, but he hath not delivered me to death,' saith David, Ps. xviii. 18.

In the worst times there is a presence of God with his children.

1. In moderating the measure of the cross, that it be not above their strength.

2. In moderating the time of it, 'The rod of the wicked shall not rest long upon the lot of the righteous,' Ps. cxxv. 3. God limits both measure and time.

3. He is present in mixing some comfort, and so allaying the bitterness of a cross.

4. Yea, and he supports the soul by inward strength, so as though it faint, yet it shall not utterly fail.

5. God is present in sanctifying a cross for good, and at length, when he hath perfected his own work in his, he is present for a final deliverance of them. A sound-hearted Christian hath always a God to go to, a promise to go to, former experience to go to, besides some present experiences of God's goodness which he enjoys. For the present he is a child of God, a member of Christ, an heir of heaven. He dwells in the love of God in the cross as well as out of it. He may be cast out of his happy condition in the world, but never out of God's favour.

Obj. If God's children have cause to praise God in their worst condition, what difference is there betwixt their best estate and their worst?

Ans. Howsoever God's children have continual occasion to praise God, yet there be some more especial seasons of praising God than others; there be days of God's own making of purpose to rejoice in, wherein we may say,

'This is the day which the Lord hath made, let us rejoice therein,' Ps. cxviii. 24. And this I think is chiefly intended here. David comforts himself with this, that however it was now with him, yet God would deal so graciously with him hereafter that he should have cause to bless his name.

Though in evil times we have cause to praise God, yet so we are, and such are our spirits, for the most part, that affliction straitens our hearts. Therefore, the apostle thought it the fittest duty in affliction to pray. 'Is any afflicted? let him pray,' saith James; 'is any joyful? let him sing psalms,' James v. 13; shewing that the day of rejoicing is the fittest day of praising God. Every work of a Christian is beautiful in its own time. The graces of Christianity have their several offices at several seasons. In trouble, prayer is in its season. 'In the evil day call upon me,' saith God, Ps. xci. 15. In better times praises should appear and shew themselves. When God manifests his goodness to his, he gives them grace with it to manifest their thankfulness to him. Praising of God is then most comely, though never out of season, when God seems to call for it by renewing the sense of his mercies in some fresh favour towards us. If a bird will sing in winter, much more in the spring. If the heart be prepared in the wintertime of adversity to praise God, how ready will it be when it is warmed with the glorious sunshine of his favour!

Our life is nothing but as it were a web woven with interminglings of wants and favours, crosses and blessings, standings and fallings, combat and victory, therefore there should be a perpetual intercourse of praying and praising in our hearts. There is always a ground of communion with God in one of these kinds, till we come to that condition wherein all wants shall be supplied, where indeed is only matter of praise. Yet praising God in this life hath this prerogative, that here we praise him 'in the midst of his enemies,' Ps. cx. 2. In heaven all will be in concert with us. God esteems it an honour in the midst of devils, and wicked men, whose life is nothing but a dishonour of him, to have those that will make his name, as it is in itself, so great in the world.

David comforts himself in this, that he should praise God, which shews he had inured himself well before to this holy exercise, in which he found such comfort, that he could not but joy in the forethoughts of that time, wherein he should have fresh occasion of his former acquaintance with God. Thoughts of this nature enter not into a heart that is strange to God.

It is a special art, in time of misery to think of matter of joy, if not for the present, yet for the time to come; for joy disposeth to praise, and praise again stirs up joy; these mutually breed one another, even as the seed brings forth the tree, and the tree brings forth the seed. It is wisdom, therefore, to set faith on work, to take as much comfort as we can from future promises, that we may have comfort and strength for the present, before we have the full possession of them. It is the nature of faith to antedate blessings, by making them that are to be performed hereafter, as present now, because we have them in the promise. If God had not allowed us to take many things in trust for the time to come, both for his glory and our good, he would never have left such rich promises to us. For faith doth not only give glory to God, for the present, in a present believing of his truth, and relying upon him, but as it looks forward, it sees an everlasting ground of praising God, and is stirred up to praise him now, for that future matter of praise, which it is sure to have hereafter. The very hopes of future good made David praise God for the present. If the happy condition we look for were present, we would embrace it with present praises. Now, 'faith is the evidence of things not seen,' Heb. xi. 1, and gives a being to that which is not; whereupon a true believing soul cannot but be a praising soul. For this end God reveals beforehand what we shall have, that beforehand we should praise him, as if we possessed it. For that is a great honour to his truth, when we esteem of what he speaks as done, and what he promiseth as already performed. Had we not a perpetuity confidence in the perpetuity of his love to us, how is it possible we should praise him?

Obj. But we want those grounds for the time to come which David had; he had particular promises, which we want.

Ans. 1. Though we want Urim and Thummim and the prophets, to foretell us what the times to come shall be, yet we have the canon of Scripture enlarged; we live under a more glorious manifestation of Christ, and under a more plentiful shedding of the Spirit, whereby that want is abundantly supplied. We have general promises for the time to come, that 'God will never fail nor forsake us,' Deut. xxxi. 6; 'that he will be with us in fire and in water, that he will give an issue to the temptation, and that the issue of all things shall be for our good, that we shall reap the quiet fruit of righteousness,' Heb. xii. 11; 'and no good thing will he withhold from them that lead a godly life,' &c., Ps. lxxxiv. 11. If we had a spirit of faith to apply these generals, we should see much of God's goodness in particular.

2. Besides general promises, we have some particular ones for the time to come; of the confusion of antichrist, of the conversion of the Jews, and fulness of the Gentiles, &c., which, though we perhaps shall never live to see, yet we are members of that body, which hereafter shall see the same; which should stir up our hearts to praise God, as if we did enjoy the present fulfilling of them ourselves, for faith can present them to the soul as if they were now present.

3. Some that have a more near communion with God, may have a particular faith of some particular deliverances, whereupon they may ground particular prayer. Luther praying for a sick friend [Frederick Myco] who was very comfortable and useful to him, had a particular answer for his recovery, whereupon he was so confident, that he sent word to his friend, that he should certainly recover. Latimer prayed with great zeal for three things. 1. That Queen Elizabeth might come to the crown. 2. That he might seal the truth with his heart's blood. 3. And that the gospel might be restored 'once again, once again,' which he expressed with great vehemency of spirit; all which three, God heard him in. But the privileges of a few must not be made a general rule for all. Privileges go not out of the persons, but rest there. Yet if men would maintain a nearer communion with God, there is no doubt but he would reveal himself in more familiar manner to them, in many particulars, than usually he doth. Those particular promises in the 91st Psalm and other places, are made good to such as have a particular faith, and to all others, with those limitations annexed to promises of that nature, so far forth as God seeth it will conduce* to their good and his own glory, and so far forth as they depend upon him in the use of means; and is not this sufficient to stay a gracious heart?

But not to insist upon particular promises and revelations, the performance whereof we enjoy here in this present life, we have rich and precious promises of final and full deliverance from all evil, and perfect enjoying of

* 'Induce, in C.

all good in that life which is to come; yet not so to come, but that we have the earnest and first fruits of it here; all is not kept for heaven. We may say with David, 'Oh how great is thy goodness, which thou hast laid up for them that fear thee,' Ps. xxxi. 19; and not only so, but how great is that goodness which thou hast wrought in them that trust in thee, even before the sons of men! God treasures not up all his goodness for the time to come, but lays much of it out daily before such as have eyes to behold it.

Now God's main end in revealing such glorious promises of the life to come is, that they might be a ground of comfort to us, and of praise to him even in this life; and indeed what can be grievous in this world to him that hath heaven in his eye? What made our blessed Saviour ' endure the cross, and despise the shame, but the joy of glory to come, set before him?' Heb. xii. 2.

The duty that David brought his heart to, before he had a full enjoyment of what he looked for, was patient waiting, it being God's use to put a long date oftentimes to the performances of his promises. David after he had the promise of a kingdom, was put off a long time ere he was invested to it; Abraham was an old man before he enjoyed his son of the promise; Joseph stayed a long time before he was exalted; our blessed Saviour himself was thirty-four years old before he was exalted up into glory.

God defers, but his deferring is no empty space, wherein no good is done, but there is in that space a fitting for promises. Whilst the seed lieth hid in the earth, time is not lost, for winter fits for spring, yea, the harder the winter, the more hopeful the spring; yet were it a mere empty space, we should hold out, because of the great things to come; but being only a preparing time, we should pass it with the less discouragement. Let this support us in all the thwartings of our desire. It is a folly to think, that we should have physic and health both at once. We must endure the working of God's physic. When the sick humour is carried away and purged, then we shall enjoy desired health. God promiseth forgiveness of sin, but thou findest the burden of it daily on thee. Cheer up thyself: when the morning is darkest, then comes day; after a weary week comes a sabbath, and after a fight victory will appear. God's time is best, therefore resolve upon waiting his leisure. For the better demeaning of ourselves herein, we must know we must so wait, that we provoke not in the mean time his patience on whom we depend, by putting forth our hand to any evil, which indeed is a crossing of our hopes. Therefore, *waiting upon God* is always joined with *doing good*. There is an influence in the thing hoped for, in the spirit of him that truly hopes, stirring him up to a suitable conformity, by purging himself of whatsoever will not stand with the holiness of that condition. Waiting implies all graces, as patience, perseverance, long-suffering in holding out, notwithstanding the tediousness of time deferred, courage, and breaking through all difficulties that stand between. For what is waiting, indeed, but a continuing in a gracious inoffensive course, till the accomplishment of our desires?

Whence we may discern a main difference betwixt a Christian and a carnal man, who is short-spirited, and all for the present. He will have his good here, whereas a saint of God continues still waiting, though all things seem contrary to what he expects. The presence of things to come is such to faith, as it makes it ' despise the pleasure of sin for a season,' Heb. xi. 25. What evidence of goodness is it for a man to be good only upon the apprehension of something that contents him? Here is the glory of faith, that it can upon God's bare promise, cross itself in things pleasing to nature, and raise up the soul to a disposition some ways answerable to that blessed estate which, though yet it enjoys not, yet it is undoubtedly persuaded of, and looks for. What can encourage us more to wait than this, that the good we wait for is greater than we are able to conceive, yea, greater than we can desire or hope for?

This was no presumptuous resolution of David's own strength, but it issued from his present truth of heart, so far as he knew the same; together with an humble dependence upon God, both for deliverance, and a heart to praise him for it; because God's benefits are usually entire, and are sweetened with such a sense of his love, as causeth a thankful heart, which to a true Christian, is a greater blessing than the deliverance itself, as making the soul better. David doth acknowledge with humble admiration, that a heart enlarged comes from God, 'Who am I,' saith he, 'and who are my people?' 1 Chron. xxix. 14.

He mentioneth here praising God, instead of deliverance, because a heart enlarged to praise God is indeed the greatest part of the deliverance; for by it the soul is delivered out of its own straits and discontent.

CHAPTER XXVIII.—*Divers qualities of the praise due to God, with helps therein; and notes of God's hearing our prayers.*

Though this be God's due and our duty, and itself a delightful thing, yet it is not so easy a matter to praise God, as many imagine. Music is sweet, but the setting of the strings in tune is unpleasing. Our souls will not be long in tune, and it is harsh to us to go about the setting them in order. Like curious clocks, a little thing will hinder the motion; especially passion, which disturbs not only the frame of grace in us, but the very frame of nature, putting man out of the power and possession of himself; and therefore David here, when he had thoughts of praising God, was fain to take up the quarrel betwixt him and his soul first. Praising sets all the parts and graces of the soul awork; and therefore the soul had need gather itself and its strength together to this duty.

It requires especially self-denial, from a conscience* of our own wants, weaknesses, and unworthiness; it requires a giving up of ourselves, and all ours to be at God's dispose.† The very ground and the fruit which it yields are both God's; and they never gave themselves truly up to God, that are not ready to give all they have to him whensoever he calls for it. Thankfulness is a sacrifice, and in sacrifices there must be killing before offering, otherwise the sacrifice will be as the offering up some unclean creature. Thanksgiving is an incense, and there must be fire to burn that incense. Thanksgiving requires not only affections, but the heat of affections. There must be some assurance of the benefit we praise God for; and it is no easy matter to maintain assurance of our interest in the best things.

Yet in this case, if we feel not sense of assurance, it is good we should praise God for what we have. We cannot deny but God offers himself in mercy to us, and that he intends our good thereby, for so we ought to construe his merciful dealing towards us, and not have him in jealousy without ground. If we bring our hearts to be willing to praise God, for that we cannot but acknowledge comes from him, he will be ready in his time to shew himself more clearly to us. We taste of his goodness many ways, Rom. ii. 4, and it is accompanied with much patience; and these in

* That is, 'consciousness.'—ED. † That is, 'disposal.'—G.

their natures lead us not only to repentance, but likewise to thankful acknowledgment; and we ought to follow that which God leads us unto, though he hath not yet acquainted us with his secrets.

It is good in this case to help the soul with a firm resolution, and to back resolution with a vow, not only in general that we will praise, but particularly of something within our own power, provided it prove no snare to us. For by this means the heart is perfectly gained, and the thing is as good as done in regard of God's acceptance and our comfort; because strong resolutions discover sincerity without any hypocritical reservation and hollowness. Always so much sincerity as a man hath, so much will his inward peace be. Resolution as a strong stream bears down all before it. Little good is done in religion without this, and with it, all is as good as done.

So soon as we set upon this work we shall feel our spirits to rise higher and higher, as the waters in the sanctuary, Ezek. xlvii., as the soul grows more and more heated. See how David riseth by degrees. Be glad in the Lord, Ps. xxxii. 11, and then, rejoice, ye righteous, and then, shout for joy all ye that are upright in heart. The Spirit of God will delight to carry us along in this duty, until it leaves our spirits in heaven, praising God with the saints and glorious angels there. To him that hath and useth it shall be given, Mat. xxv. 29. He that knoweth God aright will honour him by trusting of him; he that honours him by trusting him, will honour him by praying; and he that honours him by prayer, shall honour him by praises; he that honours him by praises here, shall perfect his praises in heaven; and this will quit the labour of setting and keeping the soul in tune. This trading with God is the richest trade in the world. When we return praises to him, he returns new favours to us, and so an everlasting, ever increasing intercourse betwixt God and the soul is maintained. David here resolved to praise God, because he had assurance of such a deliverance as would yield him a ground of praising him.

Praising of God may well be called incense, because, as it is sweet in itself, and sweet to God, so it sweetens all that comes from us. Love and joy are sweet in themselves, though those whom we love and joy in should not know of our affection, nor return the like; but we cannot love and joy in God but he will delight in us. When we neglect the praising of God, we lose both the comfort of God's love and our own too. It is a spiritual judgment to want or lose the sight or sense of God's favours, for it is a sign of want of spiritual life, or at least liveliness; it shews we are not yet in the state of those whom God hath chosen to set forth the riches of his glory upon.

When we consider that, if we answer not kindness and favour shewed unto us by men, we are esteemed unworthy of respect, as having sinned against the bond of human society and love, we cannot but much more take shame to ourselves, when we consider the disproportion of our carriage, and unkind behaviour towards God, when, instead of being temples of his praise, we become graves of his benefits. What a vanity is this in our nature, to stand upon exactness of justice, in answering petty courtesies of men, and yet to pass by the substantial favours of God, without scarce taking notice of them! The best breeding is to acknowledge greatest respects where they are most due, and to think, that if unkindness and rudeness be a sin in civility, it is much more in religion. The greatest danger of unthankfulness is in the greatest matter of all. If we arrogate any spiritual strength to ourselves in spiritual actions, we commit either sacrilege, in robbing God of his due, or mockery, by praising him for that which we hold to be of ourselves. If injustice be to be condemned in man, much more in denying God his due, religion being the first due. It takes much from thankfulness, when we have common conceits of peculiar favours. Praise is not comely in the mouth of fools; God loves no 'blind sacrifice,' Mal. i. 8.

We should, therefore, have wisdom and judgment, not only to know upon what grounds to be thankful, but in what order, by discerning what be the best and first favours whence the rest proceed, and which add a worthiness to all the rest. It is good to see blessings, as they issue from grace and mercy. It much commends any blessing, to see the love and favour of God in it, which is more to be valued than the blessing itself, as it much commends anything that comes from us, when we put a respect of thankfulness, and love to God upon it; and if we observe, we shall find the unkindness of others to us, is but a correction of our unkindness to God.

In praising God it is not good to delay, but take advantage of the freshness of the blessing. What we add to delay, we take from thankfulness; and withal lose the prime and first-fruits of our affections. It is a wise redeeming of time to observe the best seasons of thankfulness. A cheerful heart will best close with a cheerful duty, and therefore it is not good to waste so fit a temper in frivolous things; but after some contentment given to nature, let God have the fruit of his own planting, otherwise it is even no better than the refreshing of him that standeth by a good fire and crieth, 'Ah, ah, I am warm,' Isa. xliv. 16.

David doth not say, 'I will thank God,' but 'I shall praise him,' though he intends that. Thanks is then best when it tends to praising, and there ends; for thanks alone shew respect to our own good only, praises to God's glory; and in particular to the glory of such excellencies whence the benefit comes; and from thence the soul is enlarged to think highly of all God's excellencies.

Hannah, upon particular thanks for her hearing about a child, 1 Sam. ii. 1, takes occasion to set out God's other excellencies, and riseth higher and higher, from one to many, from the present time to that which was to come; from particular favours to herself, she stirs up others to praise God for his mercy to them. So David: 'Deliver me, O God, and my tongue shall sing of thy praises,' Ps. li. 14. He propounds this as an engagement of the Lord to help him, because it should tend to the enlargement of his glory; he was resolved to improve God's favour this way.

The Spirit of God works like new wine, enlarging the spirit from one degree of praising God to another; and because it foresees the eternity of God's love, as far as it can, it endeavours an eternity of God's praise. A gracious heart upon taste of favour shewed to itself, is presently warmed to spread the praise of God to others; and the more it sees the fruit of trusting God, and his truth in performing promise, the more it still honours that trusting, as knowing that it lies upon God's honour to honour those that honour him, 1 Sam. ii. Blessing will procure blessing. The soul hath never such freedom from sin as when it is in a thankful frame; for thankfulness issues from a heart truly humbled and emptied of itself, truly loving and rejoicing in God; and upon any sin the spirit is grieved and straitened, and the lips sealed up in such a heart; for the conscience upon any sin looks upon it not only as disobedience against God's will and authority, but as unthankfulness to his goodness; and this melteth a godly heart most of all. When Nathan told David God had done this and this for him, and was ready to do more, he could not hold in the confession of his sin, but relented and gave in presently, 2 Sam. xii. 8.

We ought not only to give thanks, but to be thankful, to meditate and study the praises of God. Our whole life should be nothing else but a continual blessing of his holy name, endeavouring to bring in all we have, and to lay it out for God and his people, to see where he hath any receivers. Our goodness is nothing to God. We need bring no water to the fountain nor light to the sun. Thankfulness is full of invention, it deviseth liberal things. Though it be our duty to be good stewards of our talents, yet thankfulness adds a lustre, and a more gracious acceptance, as having more of that which God calls for.

Our praising God should not be as sparks out of a flint, but as water out of a spring, natural, ready, free, as God's love to us is. Mercy pleases him, so should praise please us. It is our happiness when the best part in us is exercised about the best and highest work. It was a good speech of him that said, If God had made me a nightingale, I would have sung as a nightingale, but now God hath made me a man, I will sing forth the praises of God, which is the work of a saint only. 'All thy works bless thee, and thy saints praise thee,' Ps. cxlv. 10. All things are either blessings in their nature, or so blessed, as they are made blessings to us by the overruling command of him, who maketh all things serviceable to his. Even the worst things in this sense are made spiritual to God's people against their own nature. How great is that goodness' which makes even the worst things good!

Little favours come from no small love, but even from the same love that God intends the greatest things to us; and are pledges of it. The godly are more thankful for the least favours than worldly men for the greatest. The affection of the giver enhances the gift.

O then let us labour to improve both what we have, and what we are, to his glory. It discovers that we love God, not only with all our understanding, heart, and affection, but, when with all our might and power, so far as we have advantage by any part, relation, or calling whatsoever, we endeavour to do him service. We cannot have a greater honour in the world, than to be honoured of God, to be abundant in this kind.

Our time here is short, and we shall all ere long be called to a reckoning; therefore let us study real praises. God's blessing of us is in deed, and so should ours be of him. Thanks in words is good, but in deeds is better; leaves are good, but fruit is better; and of fruit, that which costs us most. True praise requires our whole man, the judgment to esteem, the memory to treasure up, the will to resolve, the affections to delight, the tongue to speak of, and the life to express the rich favours of God. What can we think of! what can we call to mind! What can we resolve upon! what can we speak! What can we express in our whole course better than the praises of him, ' of whom, and through whom, and to whom we and all things are!' Rom. xi. 36.

Our whole life should speak nothing but thankfulness; every condition and place we are in should be a witness of our thankfulness. This will make the times and places we live in the better for us. When we ourselves are monuments of God's mercy, it is fit we should be patterns of his praises, and leave monuments to others. We should think life is given us, to do something better than live in. We live not to live. Our life is not the end of itself, but the praise of the giver. God hath joined his glory and our happiness together. It is fit that we should refer all that is good to his glory, that hath joined his glory to our best good, in being glorified in our salvation.

David concludes, that he should certainly praise God, because he had prayed unto him. Prayers be the seeds of praises. I have sown, therefore I will reap. What we receive as a fruit of our prayers, is more sweet than what we have by a general providence.

Obj. But how do we know that God hears our prayers?

Ans. 1. If we regard them ourselves, and expect an issue. Prayer is a sure adventure. We may well look for a return.

2. It is a sign that God hath heard our prayers, when he stirs up thankfulness aforehand upon assurance. Thankfulness cannot be without either the grace of God, by which we are thankful, or some taste of the things we are thankful for. God often accepts the prayer, when he doth not grant the thing, and will give us thereby occasion of thanksgiving for his wise care in changing one blessing for another fitter for us. God regards my prayers, when by prayer my heart is wrought to that frame which he requires, that is, an humble subjection to him, from an acknowledgment of my wants, and his fulness. There is nothing stirred up in our hearts by the Spirit, no, not so much as a gracious desire, but God will answer it, if we have a spirit to wait.

3. We may know God hath accepted our prayer, when he makes the way easy and plain after prayer, by a gracious providence; when the course of things begin to change, and we meet with comforts instead of former crosses, and find our hearts quieted and encouraged against what we most feared.

4. Likewise earnestness in prayer is a sign God hears our prayers, as fire kindled from heaven sheweth God accepts the sacrifice. The ground of prevailing by our prayer, is, that they are put up in a gracious name, and for persons in favour, and dictated by God's own Spirit. They work in the strength of the blessed Trinity, not their own, giving God the glory of all his excellencies.

It is God's direction 'to call upon him in trouble,' Ps. l. 15, and it is his promise to deliver; and then both his direction and promise that we shall glorify him. When troubles stir up prayer, God's answer to them will stir up praises. David when he saith, I shall praise God, presupposes God would deliver him, that he might have ground of praising his name. And he knew God would deliver him, because as from faith he had prayed for deliverance, so he knew it was the order of God's dealing, to revive after drooping, and refresh after fainting. God knows otherwise that our spirits would fail before him.

A thankful disposition is a special help in an afflicted condition, for thankfulness springs from love, and 'love rejoiceth in suffering,' Acts xv. 21. Thankfulness raises the soul higher than itself. It is trading with God, whereby, as we by him, so he gains by us. Therefore the saints used this as a motive to God, that he would grant their desires, because the living praise him, and not the dead, Isa. xxxviii. 19. If God expect praise from us, sure he will put us into a condition of praise.

Unthankfulness is a sin detestable both to God and men, and the less punishment it receives from human laws, the more it is punished inwardly by secret shame, and outwardly by public hatred, if once it prove notorious. When God's arrests come forth for denying him his tribute, he chiefly eyes an unthankful heart, and hates all sin the worse, as there is more unthankfulness in it. The neglect of kindness is taken most unkindly. Why should we load God with injuries, that loadeth us with his blessings? Who would requite good with evil? Such men's mercies will prove at last so many indictments against them.

Use. I beseech you therefore labour to be men of praises. If in any duty we may expect assistance, we may in this, that altogether concerns God's glory. The more we praise God, the more we shall praise him. When God by grace enlarges the will, he intends to give the deed. God's children, wherein their wills are conformable to God's will, are sure to have them fulfilled. In a fruitful ground, a man will sow his best seed. God intends his own glory in every mercy, and he that 'praises him, glorifies him,' Ps. l. 23. When our wills therefore carry us to that which God wills above all, we may well expect he will satisfy our desires. The living God is a living fountain, never drawn dry. He hath never done so much for us, but he can and will do more. If there be no end of our praises, there shall be no end of his goodness; no way of thriving like to this. By this means we are sure never to be very miserable. How can he be dejected, that by a sweet communion with God sets himself in heaven? nay, maketh his heart a kind of heaven, 'a temple, a holy of holies,' 2 Cor. vi. 16, wherein incense is offered unto God. It is the sweetest branch of our priestly office, to offer up these daily sacrifices. It is not only the beginning, but a further entrance of our heaven upon earth, and shall be one day our whole employment for ever.

Praise is a just and due tribute for all God's blessings; for what else especially do the best favours of God call for at our hands? How do all creatures praise God, but by our mouths? It is a debt always owing, and always paying; and the more we pay, the more we shall owe. Upon the due discharge of this debt, the soul will find much peace. A thankful heart to God for his blessings, is the greatest blessing of all. Were it not for a few gracious souls, what honour should God have of the rest of the unthankful world? Which should stir us up the more to be trumpets of God's praises in the midst of his enemies, because this, in some sort, hath a prerogative above our praising God in heaven; for there God hath no enemies to dishonour him.

This is a duty that none can except against, because it is especially a work of the heart. All cannot shew their thankfulness in giving, or doing, great matters, but all may express the willingness of their hearts. All *within us* may praise his holy name, Ps. ciii. 1, though we have little or nothing *without* us; and that within us is the thing God chiefly requires. Our heart is the altar on which we offer this incense. God looks not to quantity, but to proportion. He accepts a mite where there is no more to be had.

Quest. But how shall we be enabled to this great duty?

Ans. 1. *Enter into a deep consideration of God's favours, past, present, and to come;* think of the greatness and suitableness of them to our condition, the seasonableness and necessity of them every way unto us. Consider how miserable our life were without them, even without common favours; but as for spiritual favours, that make both our natural and civil condition comfortable, our very life were death, our light were darkness without these. In all favours think not of them so much, as God's mercy and love in Christ, which sweetens them. Think of the freeness of this love, and the smallness of thy own deserts. How many blessings doth God bestow upon us, above our deserts, yea, above our desires, nay, above our very thoughts! He had thoughts of love to us when we had no thoughts ourselves. What had we been if God had not been good unto us! How many blessings hath God bestowed upon us, that we never prayed for! and yet we are not so ready to praise God, as to pray unto him. This more desire of what we want than esteeming of what we have, shews too much prevailing of self-love. But,

2. Secondly, *comparing also ourselves with others*, will add a great lustre to God's favour, considering we are all hewed out of one rock, and differ nothing from the meanest, but in God's free love. Who are we, that God should single us out for the glory of his rich mercy?

3. Considering, likewise, *that the blessings of God to us are such as if none but we had them, and God cares for us as if he had none else to care for in the world besides.* These things well pondered should set the greater price upon God's blessings. What are we in nature and grace but God's blessings?—what is in us, about us, above us? What see we, taste we, enjoy we, but blessings? All we have, or hope to have, are but dead favours to us, unless we put life into them by a spirit of thankfulness. And shall we be as dead as the earth, as the stones we tread on? Shall we live as if we were resolved God should have no praise by us? Shall we make ourselves gods, ascribing all to ourselves? Nay, shall we, as many do, fight against God with his own favours, and turn God's blessings against himself? Shall we abuse peace to security? plenty to ease, promises to presumption, gifts to pride? How can we please the devil better than thus doing? Oh, the wonderful patience of God, to continue life to those whose life is nothing else but a warring against him, the giver of life!

As God hath thoughts of love to us, so should our thoughts be of praises to him, and of doing good in our places to others for his sake. Think with thyself, Is there any I may honour God by relieving, comforting, counselling? Is there any of Jonathan's race? 2 Sam. ix. 1. Is there any of Christ's dear ones? I will do good to them, that they together with me, and for me, may praise God, Psalm cxviii. 1. As David here checks himself for the failing and disquietness of his spirit, and, as a cure thereof, thinks of praising God, so let us, in the like case, stir up our souls as he did, and say, 'Praise the Lord, O my soul, and all that is within me, set forth his holy name,' Psalm ciii. 1. We never use our spirits to better purpose, than when by that light we have from God, we stir them up to look back again to him.

By this it will appear to what good purposes we had a being here in the world, and were brought into communion with Christ by the gospel. The carriage of all things to the right end shews whose we are, and whither we tend. It abundantly appears by God's revealing of himself many ways to us, as by promises, sacraments, sabbaths, &c., that he intended to raise up our hearts to this heavenly duty. The whole gracious dispensation of God in Christ tends to this, that our carriage should be nothing else but an expression of thankfulness to him; that by a free, cheerful, and gracious disposition, we might shew we are the people of God's free grace, set at liberty from the spirit of bondage, to serve him without fear, Luke i. 74, with a voluntary, child-like service, all the days of our lives.

CHAPTER XXIX.—*Of God's manifold salvation for his people, and why open, or expressed in the countenance.*

I proceed.
He is the salvation of my countenance.

As David strengthens his trust in God, by reason fetched from the future goodness of God, apprehended by faith, so he strengthens that reason with another reason fetched from God, whom he apprehends here as the salvation of his countenance. We need reason against reason, and reason upon reason, to steel and strengthen the soul against the onset of contrary reasons.

He is the salvation of my countenance; that is, he will so save as I shall see, and my enemies shall see it; and upon seeing, my countenance shall be cheered and lifted up; God's saving kindness shall be read in my countenance, so that all who look on me shall say, God hath spoken peace to my soul, as well as brought peace to my condition.

He saith not salvation, but salvations (*j*); because as our life is subject to many miseries, in soul, body, and state, public and private, &c., so God hath many salvations. If we have a thousand troubles, he hath a thousand ways of help, *Mille mali species, mille salutis erunt.* As he hath more blessings than one, so he hath more salvations than one. He saves our souls from sin, our bodies from danger, and our estates from trouble. He is the Redeemer of his people; and not only so, but 'with him is plenteous redemption,' Ps. cxxx. 7, of all persons, of all parts both of body and soul, from all ill, both of sin and misery, for all times, both now and hereafter. He is an everlasting salvation.

David doth not say, God will save me; but God is salvation itself, and nothing but salvation. Our sins only stop the current of his mercy, but it being above all our sins, will soon scatter that cloud, remove that stop, and then we shall see and feel nothing but salvation from the Lord. 'All his ways are mercy and peace,' Ps. xxv. 10, to a repentant soul that casts itself upon him.

Christ himself is nothing else but salvation clothed in our flesh. So old Simeon conceived of him, when he had him in his arms, Luke ii. 29, and was willing thereupon to yield up his spirit to God, having seen Christ, the salvation of God. When we embrace Christ in the arms of our faith, we embrace nothing but salvation. He makes up that sweet name given him by his Father, and brought from heaven by an angel to the full, Luke ii. 14; a name in the faith of which it is impossible for any believing soul to sink.

The devil, in trouble, presents God to us as a revenging destroyer, and unbelief presents him under a false vizard; but the skill of faith is, to present him as a Saviour clothed with salvation. We should not so much look what destruction the devil and his threaten, as what salvation God promiseth. To God belong 'the issues of death,' Ps. lxviii. 20; and of all other troubles, which are lesser deaths. Cannot he that hath vouchsafed an issue in Christ from eternal death, vouchsafe an issue from all temporal evils? If he will raise our bodies, cannot he raise our conditions? He that brought us into trouble can easily make a way out of it when he pleaseth. This should be a ground of resolute and absolute obedience, even in our greatest extremities, considering God will either deliver us from death, or by death, and at length out of death.

So then, when we are in any danger, we see whither to go for salvation, even to him that is nothing else but salvation; but then we must trust in him, as David doth, and conceive of him as salvation, that we may trust in him. If we will not trust in salvation, what will we trust in? and if salvation itself cannot save us, what can? Out of salvation there is nothing but destruction, which those that seek it anywhere out of God, are sure to meet with.

How pitiful then is their case, who go to a destroyer for salvation! that seek for help from hell!

Here also we see to whom to return praise in all our deliverances, even to the God of our salvation. The Virgin Mary was stirred up to magnify the Lord; but why? 'Her spirit rejoiced in God her Saviour,' Luke i. 47. Whosoever is the instrument of any good, yet salvation is of the Lord; whatsoever brings it, he sends it. Hence in their holy feasts for any deliverance, the cup they drank was called the cup of salvation; and therefore David when he summons his thoughts, what to render unto God, he resolves upon this, to take 'the cup of salvation,' Ps. cxvi. 13. But always remember this, that when we think of God as salvation, we must think of him as he is in Christ to his. For so everything in God is saving, even his most terrible attributes of justice and power. Out of Christ, the sweetest things in God are terrible. Salvation itself will not save out of Christ, who is the only way of salvation, called the way, the truth, and the life, John xiv. 6.

David addeth, 'He is the salvation of my countenance,' that is, he will first speak salvation to my soul, and say, I am thy salvation; and when the heart is cheered, which is as it were the sun of this little world, the beams of that joy will shine in the countenance. True joy begins at the centre, and so passeth to the circumference, the outward man. The countenance is as the glass of the soul, wherein you may see the naked face of the soul, according as the several affections thereof stand. In the countenance of an understanding creature, you may see more than a bare countenance. The spirit of one man may see the countenance of another's inner man in his outward countenance; which hath a speech of its own, and declares what the heart saith, and how it is affected.

Quest. But how comes God to be the salvation of our countenance?

Ans. I answer, *God only graciously shines in the face of Jesus Christ, which we with the eye of faith beholding, receive those beams of his grace, and reflect them back again.* God shineth upon us first, and we shine in that light of his countenance upon us. 'The joy of salvation,' Ps. li. 12, especially of spiritual and eternal salvation, is the only true joy: all other salvations end at last in destruction, and are no further comfortable than they issue from God's saving love.

God will have the body partake with the soul. As in matter of grief, so in matter of joy, the lantern shines in the light of the candle within.

2. Again, *God brings forth the joy of the heart into the countenance, for the further spreading and multiplying of joy to others.*

Next unto the sight of the sweet countenance of God, is the beholding of the cheerful countenance of a Christian friend, rejoicing from true grounds. Whence it is that the joy of one becomes the joy of many, and the joys of many meet in one; by which means, as many lights together make the greater light, so many lightsome spirits make the greater light of spirit: and God receiveth the more praise, which makes him so much to delight in the prosperity of his children. Hence it is, that in any deliverance of God's people, 'the righteous do compass them about,' Ps. cxlii. 7, to know 'what God hath done for their souls;' and keep a spiritual feast with them in partaking of their joy. And the godly have cause to joy in the deliverance of other Christians, because they suffered in their afflictions, and it may be in their sins the cause of them, which made them somewhat ashamed. Whence it is, that David's great desire was, that 'those who feared God might not be ashamed because of him,' Ps. lxix. 6 : insinuating that those who fear God's name are ashamed of the falls of God's people. Now when God delivers them, this reproach is removed, and those that had part in their sorrow have part in their joy.

3. Again, God will have salvation so open, that it shall appear in the countenance of his people, *the more to daunt and vex the enemies.* Cainish hypocrites hang down their heads, when God lifts up the countenance of their brethren. When the countenance of God's children clears up, then their enemies' hearts and looks are cloudy. Jerusalem's joy is Babylon's sorrow. It is with the church and her enemies as it is with a balance, the scales whereof, when one is up, the other is down. Whilst God's people are under a cloud, carnal people insult over them, as if they were men deserted of God. Whereupon they hang down their heads, and the rather, because they think that by reason of their sin, Christ and his religion will suffer with them. Hence David's care was, that the miseries of God's people 'should not be told in Gath,' 2 Sam. i. 20. The chief reason why the enemies of the church gnash their teeth at the sight of God's gracious dealing, is, that they take the rising of the church to be a presage of their ruin: a lesson which Haman's wife had learned, Esther vi. 13.

This is a comfort to us in these times of Jacob's trouble and Zion's sorrow. The captivity of the church shall return, ' as rivers in the south,' Ps. cxxvi. 1. Therefore the church may say, ' Rejoice not over me, O my enemy; though I am fallen, I shall rise again,' Mic. vii. 8. Though Christ's spouse be now as black as the pots, yet she shall be as white as the dove, Ps. lxviii. 13. If there were not great dangers, where were the glory of God's great deliverance ? The church at length will be as ' a cup of trembling,' and as ' a burdensome stone,' Zech. xii. 2. The blood of the saints cry, their enemies' violence cries, the prayers of the church cry, for deliverance and vengeance upon the enemies of the church ; and as that ' importunate widow,' Luke xi. 5, will at length prevail. Shall the importunity of one poor woman prevail with an unrighteous judge, and shall not the prayers of many that cry unto the righteous God take effect ? If there were armies of prayers, as there are armies of men, we should see the stream of things turned another way. A few Moseses in the mount would do more good than many soldiers in the valley. If we would lift up our hearts and hands to God, he would lift up our countenance. But alas! we either pray not, or cross our own prayers, for want of love to the truth of God and his people.

It is we that keep antichrist and his faction alive, to plague the unthankful world. The strength he hath is not from his own cause, but from our want of zeal. We hinder those hallelujahs by private brabbles,* coldness and indifferency in religion. The church begins at this time a little to lift up her head again. Now is the time to follow God with prayers, that he would perfect his work, and plead his own cause ; that he would be revenged not only of ours, but his enemies; that he would wholly free his church from that miserable bondage. These beginnings give our faith some hold to be encouraged to go to God, for the fulfilling of his gracious promise, that the church may rejoice in the salvation of the Lord. God doth but look for some to seek unto him ; Christ doth but stay until he is awaked by our prayers. But it is to be feared that God hath not yet perfected his work in Zion. The church is not yet fully prepared for a full and glorious deliverance. If God had once his ends in the humiliation of the church for sins past, with resolution of reformation for the time to come, then this age, perhaps, might ' see the salvation of the Lord,' which the

* That is, 'squabbles.'—G.

generations to come shall be witness of, 'we should see Zion in her perfect beauty,' Ps. l. 2. The generations of those that came out of Egypt saw and enjoyed the pleasant land which their progenitors were shut out of; who by reason of their murmuring and looking back to Egypt, and forgetfulness of the wonders which God had done for and before them, perished in the wilderness.

Use. There is little cause, therefore, of envying the present flourishing of the enemies of the church, and of joining and colluding * with them; for it will prove the wisest resolution to resolve to fall and rise with the church of Christ, considering the enemies themselves shall say, God hath done great things for them; kings shall lay their crowns at 'Christ's feet,' and 'bring all their glory to the church,' Rev. xxi. 24.

And for every Christian this may be a comfort, that though their light for a time may be eclipsed, yet it shall break forth. David at this time was accounted an enemy of the state, and had a world of false imputations laid upon him, which he was very sensible of; yet we see here, he knew at length God would be 'the salvation of his countenance.'

Obj. But some, as Gideon, may object, 'If God intend to be so gracious, why is it thus with us?' Judges vi. 13.

Ans. The answer is, salvation is God's own work, humbling and casting down is his strange work, whereby he comes to his own work. For, when he intends to save, he will seem to destroy first; and when he will justify, he will condemn first; whom he will revive, he will kill first. Grace and goodness countenanced by God, have a native inbred majesty in them, which maketh the face to shine, and borroweth not its lustre from without, which God at length will have to appear in its own likeness, howsoever malice may cast a veil thereon, and disguise it for a time. And though wickedness, as it is base born, and a child of darkness, may shelter itself under authority a while, yet it shall hide itself and run into corners. The comfort of comforts is, that at that great day, the day of all days, that day 'of the revelation of the righteous judgment of God,' the righteous shall then shine as the sun in the firmament, Dan. xii. 3; then Christ will come to be glorious in his saints, and will be the salvation of the countenance of all his. Then all the works of darkness shall be driven out of countenance, and adjudged to the place from whence they came. In the mean time, let us, with David, support ourselves with the hopes of these times.

CHAPTER XXX.—*Of God, our God, and of particular application.*

My God.

These words imply a special interest that the holy man had in God, as his God, being the ground of all which was said before; both of the duty of trusting, and of praising, and of the salvation that he expected from God. He is my God, therefore be not disquieted, but trust him. He is my God, therefore he will give me matter to praise him, and will be the salvation of my countenance. God hath some special ones in the world, to whom he doth as it were pass over himself, and whose God he is by virtue of a more special covenant; whence we have these excellent expressions, 'I will be your God, and you shall be my people,' Jer. xxxi. 33; 'I will be your Father, and you shall be my sons and daughters,' 2 Cor.

* That is, 'falling in with.'—G.

vi. 18. Since the fall, we having lost our communion with God the chief good, our happiness stands in recovering again fellowship with him. For this end we were created, and for this redeemed, and for effecting of this the word and sacraments are sanctified to us; yea, and for this end God himself, out of the bowels of his compassion, vouchsafed to enter into a gracious covenant with us, founded upon Jesus Christ, and his satisfaction to divine justice; so that by faith we become one with him, and receive him as offered of his Father to 'be all in all to us,' Col. iii. 11.

Hence it is that Christ hath his name Immanuel, God with us. Not only because he is God and man too, both natures meeting in one person, but because being God in our nature, he hath undertook this office to bring God and us together. The main end of Christ's coming and suffering was to reconcile, and to gather together in one; and, as Peter expresseth it, 'to bring man again to God,' 1 Pet. iii. 18. Immanuel is the bond of this happy agreement, and appears for ever in heaven to make it good. As the comfort hereof is great, so the foundation of it is sure and everlasting. God will be our God so long as he is Christ's God, and because he is Christ's God, John xx. 10. Thus the father of the faithful, and all other holy men before Christ, apprehended God to be their God in the Messiah to come. Christ was the ground of their interest. He was yesterday to them as well as to-day to us, Heb. xiii. Hence it is that God is called the portion, Psalm lxxiii. 26, of his people, and they his jewels, Mal. iii. 25; he is their only rock and strong tower, Psalm lxxi. 3, and they his peculiar ones.

Use. Well may we wonder that the great God should stoop so low, to enter into such a covenant of grace and peace, founded upon such a mediator, with such utter enemies, base creatures, sinful dust and ashes as we are. This is the wonderment of angels, a torment of devils, and glory of our nature and persons; and will be matter of admiration and praising God unto us for all eternity.

As God offereth himself to be ours in Christ, else durst we lay no claim to him, so there must be in us an appropriating grace of faith, to lay hold of this offer. David saith here, *My God.* But by what spirit? By a spirit of faith which, looking to God's offer, maketh it his own whatsoever it lays hold of. God offereth himself in covenant, and faith catcheth hold thereon presently. With a gracious offer of God there goeth a gracious touch of his Spirit to the soul, giving it sight and strength, whereby, being aided by the same Spirit, it layeth hold on God shewing himself in love. God saith to the soul, I am thy salvation; and the soul saith again, Thou art my God. Faith is nothing else but a spiritual echo, returning that voice back again, which God first speaks to the soul. For what acquaintance could the soul claim with so glorious a Majesty, if he should not first condescend so low as to speak peace and whisper secretly to the soul, that he is our loving God and Father, and we his peculiar ones in Christ; that our sins are all pardoned, his justice fully satisfied, and our persons freely accepted in his dear Son?

But to come more particularly to the words, *My God.* The words are pregnant. In the womb of them, all that is graciously and comfortably good is contained. They are the spring-head of all particular blessings. All particular relations and titles that it pleaseth God to take upon him, have their strength from hence, that God is our God. More cannot be said, and less will not serve the turn. Whatsoever else we have, if we have not God, it will prove but an empty cistern at last. He is our proper element. Everything desires to live in its own element: fishes in the sea, birds in the air; in this they are best preserved.

There is a greater strength in this 'My God,' than in any other title. It is more than if he had said, My King, or My Lord. These are words of sovereignty and wisdom; but this implies not only infinite power, sovereignty, and wisdom, but likewise infinite bounty and provident care; so that when we are said to be God's people, the meaning is, that we are not only such over whom God hath a power and command, but such as toward whom he shews a loving and peculiar respect.

In the words is implied: 1. A propriety and interest in God. 2. An improvement of the same for the quieting of the soul.

David here lays a particular claim, by a particular faith, unto God. The reason is: 1. The virtue of faith is, as to lay hold, so to appropriate to itself, and make its own, whatever it lays hold on; and it doth no more in this than God gives it leave by his gracious promises to do.

2. As God offers, so faith receives; but God offers himself in particular to the believing soul by his Spirit, therefore our faith must be particular. That which the sacraments seal, is a peculiar interest in Christ. This is that which hath always upheld the saints of God, and that which is ever joined with the life of Christ in us. 'The life that I live,' saith Paul, 'is by the faith of the Son of God, who loved me, and gave himself for me,' Gal. ii. 20. The spirit of faith is a spirit of application.

This is implied in all the articles of our faith. We believe God to be our Father, and Christ to be born for us; that he died for us, and rose again for our good, and now sits at the right hand of God, making requests for us in particular.

3. This is that which distinguisheth the faith of a true Christian from all hypocrites and castaways whatsoever. Were it not for this word of possession, *mine*, the devil might say the Creed to as good purpose as we. He believes there is a God and a Christ; but that which torments him is this, he can say *my* to never an article of faith.

4. A general apprehension of God's goodness and mercy may stand with desperation. Take away *my* from *God*, and take away God himself in regard of comfort. *Tolle meum, tolle Deum.* What comfort was it for Adam, when he was shut out of Paradise, to look upon it after he had lost it? The more excellencies are in God, the more our grief if we have not our part in them. The very life-blood of the gospel lies in a special application of particular mercy to ourselves. All relations that God and Christ have taken upon them imply a necessity of application. What if God be a rock of salvation, if we do not rest upon him? What if he be a foundation, and we do not build on him? What if he offers himself as a husband, if we will not accept of him, what avails it us? How can we rejoice in the salvation of our souls, unless we can in particular say, '*I* rejoice in God *my* Saviour.'

5. Without particular application, we can neither entertain the love of God, nor return love again, by which means we lose all the comfort God intends us in his word, which of purpose was written for our solace and refreshment. Take away particular faith, and we let out all the spirits of cheerful and thankful obedience.

This possessive particle, *my*, hath place in all the golden chain of our salvation. The first spring of all God's claim to us as his, is in his election of us. We were by grace his, before we were. Those that are his from that eternal love, he gives to Christ. This is hid in the breast of God, till he calls us out of the rest of the world into communion with Christ.

In answering of which call, by faith, we become one with Christ, and so one with him. Afterwards, *in justification*, we feel God experimentally to be reconciled unto us, whence arises joy and inward peace. And then, upon further *sanctification*, God delights in us as his, bearing his own image, and we from a likeness to God delight in him as ours in his Christ, and so this mutual interest betwixt God and us continues, until at last God becomes all in all unto us.

Obj. But how can a man that is not yet in the state of grace say with any comfort, My God ?

Ans. Whilst a man ' regards iniquity in his heart,' Ps. lxvi. 18, without any remorse or dislike of the same, if he saith, My God, his heart will give his tongue the lie, however in an outward profession and opinion of others he may bear himself as if God were his, upon false grounds. For there can be no more in a conclusion, than it hath from the principle and premises out of which it is drawn. The principle here is, that God is the God of all that trust in him. Now if we can make it good, that we truly trust in God, we may safely conclude of comfort from him; for the more certain clearing of which, try yourselves by the signs of trust delivered.*

It is no easy matter to say in truth of heart, *My God;* the flesh will still labour for supremacy. God should be all in all unto us; but this will not be till these bodies of flesh, together with the body of sin, be laid aside. He that says, God is my God, and doth not yield up himself unto God, raiseth a building without a foundation, layeth a claim without a title, and claimeth a title without an evidence, reckoning upon a bargain, without consent of the party with whom he would contract.

But if a man shall, out of the sight and sense of sin, thirst after mercy in Christ, and call unto God for pardon, then God, who is a God ' hearing prayer,' Ps. lxv. 2, and delighteth to be known by the name of merciful, will be ready to close and meet with the desire of such a soul, so far as to give it leave to rely upon him for mercy, and that without presumption, until he further discovers himself graciously unto it; upon sense of which grace the soul may be encouraged to lay a further claim unto God, having further acquaintance with him. Hence are those exhortations so oft in the prophets, to ' turn unto the Lord our God,' Zech. i. 3, because upon our first resolution to turn unto God, we shall find him always ready to answer those desires that he stirs up by his own Spirit in us.

We are not therefore to stay our turning unto God, till we feel him saying to our hearts, ' *I am thy God,*' Isa. xli. 10; but when he prevents us by his grace, enabling us to desire grace, let us follow the work begun in the strength of what grace we have, and then God will further manifest himself in mercy to us.

Yet God, before we can make anything towards him, lets into our hearts some few beams of mercy, thereby drawing us unto him, and reaching us out a hint to lay hold upon.

And as sin causeth a distance betwixt God and us, so the guilt of sin in the conscience, causeth further strangeness, insomuch that we dare not look up to heaven, till God open a little crevice to let in a little light of comfort at least into our souls, whereby we are by little and little drawn nearer to him. But this light at the first is so little, that in regard of the greater sense of sin, and a larger desire of grace, the soul reckons the same as no light at all, in comparison of what it desires and seeks after. Yet the comfort is, that this dawning light will at length clear up to a perfect day.

* See chap. xviii. pp. 212–218.

Thus we see how this claim of God to be our God, is still in growth until full assurance, and that there is a great distance betwixt the first act of faith in cleaving to God, offering himself in Christ to be ours, and between the last fruit, of faith the clear and comfortable feeling, that God is our God indeed. We first by faith apply ourselves to God, and then apply God to us, to be ours; the first is the conflicting exercise of faith, the last is the triumph of faith; therefore faith properly is not assurance. And to comfort us the more, the promises are specially made to the act of faith; fuller assurance is the reward of faith.

Obj. If God hath not chosen me in Christ to be his, what ground have I to trust in him? I may cast away myself upon a vain confidence.

Ans. We have no ground at first to trouble ourselves about God's election. Secret things belong to God, Deut. xxix. 29. God's revealed will is, 'that all that believe in Christ shall not perish,' John iii. 15. It is my duty therefore, knowing this, to believe, by doing whereof, I put that question, whether God be mine or no? out of all question; for all that believe in Christ are Christ's, and all that are Christ's are God's. It is not my duty to look to God's secret counsel, but to his open offer, invitation, and command, and thereupon to adventure my soul. And this adventure of faith will bring at length a rich return unto us. In war men will adventure their lives, because they think some will escape, and why not they? In traffic beyond the seas many adventure great estates, because some grow rich by a good return, though many miscarry. The husbandman adventures his seed, though sometime the year proves so bad, that he never sees it more.* And shall not we make a spiritual adventure in casting ourselves upon God, when we have so good a warrant as his command, and so good an encouragement as his promise, that he will not fail those that rely on him? God bids us ' draw near to him, and he will draw near to us,' Deut. xxix. 29. Whilst we in God's own ways draw near to him, and labour to entertain good thoughts of him, he will delight to shew himself favourable unto us. Whilst we are striving against an unbelieving heart, he will come in and help us, and so fresh light will come in.

Pretend not thy unworthiness and inability, to keep thee off from God, for this is the way to keep thee so still. If anything help us, it must be God, and if ever he help us, it must be by casting ourselves upon him; for then he will reach out himself unto us in the promise of mercy to pardon our sin, and in the promise of grace to sanctify our natures. It was a good resolution of the lepers, ' If we enter into the city, the famine is there, and we shall die, say they; if we sit still, we shall die also: let us therefore fall into the host of Assyrians, if they save us, we shall live ; if they kill us, we shall but die,' 2 Kings vii. 4. *Omnia in rebus humanis spes futurorum agunt.* So we should reason: if we sit still under the load of our sin, we shall die ; if we put ourselves into the hands of Christ, if he save us, we shall live ; if he save us not, we shall but die. Nay, surely he will not suffer us to die. Did ever Christ thrust any back from him, that put themselves upon him? unless it were by that means to draw them the nearer unto him, as we see in the ' woman of Canaan,' Mat. xv. 27. His denial was but to increase her importunity. We should therefore do as she did, gather all arguments to help our faith. Suppose I am a dog, saith she, yet I am one of the family, and therefore have right to the crumbs that fall. So, Lord,

---

* Quis pollicetur serenti, proventum; naviganti portum; militanti victoriam? Ideo navigantes vitam ventis credunt, etc. Ideo terris frumenta credimus ut cum usuris credita recipiamus.—*Salvian[us]*.

I have been a sinner, yet I am thy creature; and not only so, but such a creature as thou has set over the rest of the works of thy hands; and not only so, but one whom thou hast admitted into thy church by baptism, whereby thou wouldst bind me to give myself unto thee beforehand; and more than this, thou hast brought me under the means, and therein hast shewed thy will concerning my turning towards thee. Thou hast not only offered me conditions of peace, but wooed me by thy ministers to give up myself unto thee, as thine in thy Christ. Therefore I dare not suspect thy good meaning towards me, or question thy intendment,* but resolve to take thy counsel, and put myself upon thy mercy. I cannot think, if thou hadst meant to cast me away, and not to own me for thine, thou wouldst ever have kindled these desires in me. But it is not this state I rest in, my purpose is to wait upon thee, until thou dost manifest thyself farther unto me. It is not common favours that will content me, though I be unworthy of these; because I hear of choice blessings towards thy chosen people, that thou enterest into a peculiar covenant withal, sure mercies, Isa. lv. 3; and such as accompany salvation. These be the favours I wait for at thy hand. 'O visit me with the salvation of thy chosen,' Ps. cvi. 4, 5. O remember me with the favour of thy people, that I may see 'the good of thy chosen.' Whilst the soul is thus exercised, more sweetness falls upon the will and affections, whereby they are drawn still nearer unto God; the soul is in a getting and thriving condition. For God delights to shew himself gracious to those that strive to be well persuaded of him, concerning his readiness to shew mercy to all that look towards him in Christ. In worldly things, how do we cherish hopes upon little grounds! if there shineth never so little hope of gain or preferment, we make after it: why then should we forsake our own mercy, which God offers to be our own, if we will embrace it, having such certain grounds for our hope to rest on?

It was the policy of the servants of Benhadad to watch if any word of comfort fell from the king of Israel, and when he named Benhadad his *brother*, they catched presently at that, and cheered themselves, 1 Kings xx. 33. Faith hath a catching quality at whatsoever is near to lay hold on. Like the branches of the vine, it windeth about that which is next, and stays itself upon it, spreading further and further still. If nature taught Benhadad's servants to lay hold upon any word of comfort that fell from the mouth of a cruel king, shall not grace teach God's children to lie in wait for a token that he will shew for good to them? How should we stretch forth the arms of our faith to him, that 'stretcheth out his arms all the day long to a rebellious people!' Isa. lxv. 2. God will never shut his bosom against those, that in an humble obedience fly unto him. We cannot conceive too graciously of God. Can we have a fairer offer, than for God in Christ to make over himself unto us? which is more than if he should make over a thousand worlds. Therefore our chief care should be first by faith to make this good, and then to make it useful unto us, by living upon it as our chiefest portion, which we shall do: 1, By proving God to be our God in particular; 2, By improving of it in all the passages of our lives.

CHAPTER XXXI.—*Means of proving and evidencing to our souls that God is our God.*

1. Now we prove it to our souls, that God is ours, when we take him at his offer, when we bring nothing but a sense of our own emptiness with us,

* That is, 'design, intention.'—G.

and a good conceit of his faithfulness and ability to do us good, when we answer God in the particular passages of salvation, which we cannot do, till he begins unto us. Therefore if we be God's, it is a certain sign that God is ours. If we choose him, we may conclude he hath chosen us first: 'if we love him, we may know that he hath loved us first,' 1 John iv. 19. If we apprehend him, it is because he hath apprehended us first. Whatsoever affection we shew to God, it is a reflection of his first to us. If cold and dark bodies have light and heat in them, it is because the sun hath shined upon them first. Mary answers not *Rabboni* till Christ said *Mary* to her, John xx. 16. If we say to God, I am thine, it is because he hath first said unto us, Thou art mine; after which, the voice of the faithful soul is, 'I am my beloved's, and my beloved is mine,' Cant. vi. 3.* We may know God's mind to us in heaven, by the return of our hearts upwards again to him; only as the reflected beams are weaker than the direct, so our affections, in their return to God, are far weaker than his love falling upon us. God will be to us whatsoever we make him by our faith to be. When by grace we answer his condition of trusting, then he becomes ours to use for our good.

2. We may know God to be *our God* when we pitch and plant all our happiness in him, when the desires of our souls are towards him, and we place all our contentment in him. As this word *my* is a term of appropriation springing from a special faith, so it is a word of love and peculiar affection, shewing that the soul doth repose and rest itself quietly and securely upon God. Thus David proves God to be his God, by early seeking of him, by thirsting, and longing after his presence, and that upon good reason, 'because God's lovingkindness was better to him than life,' Ps. lxiii. 1, 2, 3, &c. This he knew would 'satisfy his soul as with marrow and fatness.' So St Paul proved Christ to be his Lord, by 'accounting all else as dung and dross in comparison of him,' Phil. iii. 8.

Then we make God our God, and set a crown of majesty upon his head, when we set up a throne for him in our hearts, where self-love before had set up the creature above him; when the heart is so unloosed from the world, that it is ready to part with anything for God's sake, giving him now the supremacy in our hearts, and bringing down every high thought, in captivity to him; making him our trust, our love, our joy, our delight, our fear, our all; and whatsoever we esteem or affect else, to esteem and affect it under him, in him, and for him; when we cleave to him above all, depending upon him as our chief good, and contenting ourselves in him, as all-sufficient to give our souls fit and full satisfaction; when we resign up ourselves to his gracious government, to do and suffer what he will, offering ourselves and all our spiritual services as sacrifices to him; when faith brings God into the soul as ours, we not only love him, but love him dearly, making it appear that we are at good terms with God, we are at a point for other things. How many are there that will adventure the loss of the love of God for a thing of nothing, and redeem the favour of men with the loss of God's! Certain it is, whatsoever we esteem, or affect most, that, whatsoever it be in itself, yet we make it our god—*Amor tuus, Deus tuus*. The best of us all may take shame to ourselves herein in that we do not give God his due place in us, but set up some idol or other in our hearts above him.

When the soul can without hypocrisy say, *My God*, it engageth us to universal and unlimited obedience. We shall be ambitious of doing that

* Dicat anima, secura dicat, Deus meus es tu, qui dicit animæ nostræ: Salus tua ego sum.—*Aug*[*ustine*] in Ps. cxxxii.

which may be acceptable and well pleasing to him; and, therefore, this is prefixed as a ground before the commandments, enforcing obedience. 'I am the Lord thy God,' therefore 'thou shalt have no other gods before me,' Exod. xx. 3, whomsoever else we obey, it must be in the Lord, because we see a beam of God's authority in them; and it is no prejudice to any inferior authority, to prefer God's authority before it, in case of difference one from the other. *Nemini fit injuria cui præponitur Deus.*

When we know we are a *peculiar people,* we cannot but be '*zealous of good works,*' Tit. ii. 14. 'If I be a Father, where is mine honour?' Mal. i. 6. Special relations are special enforcements to duty.

4. The Spirit of God, which knows the deep things of God and the depths of our hearts, doth reveal this mutual interest betwixt God and those that are his, it being a principal work of the Spirit to seal this unto the soul, by discovering such a clear and particular light in the use of means, as swayeth the soul to yield up itself wholly to God. When we truly trust, we may say with St Paul, 'I know whom I have trusted,' 2 Tim. i. 12; he knew both that he trusted, and whom he trusted. The Spirit of God, that reveals God to be ours, and stirs up faith in him, both reveals this trust to our souls, and the interest we have in God thereby. 'The Lord is my portion, saith my soul,' Lam. iii. 24; but God said so to it first. If instinct of nature teacheth dams to know their young ones, and their young ones them, in the midst of those that are alike, shall not the Spirit of God much more teach the soul to know its own father? As none knows what is in man, but the spirit of man, so none knows what love God bears to those that are his, but the Spirit of God in his. All the light in the world cannot discover the sun unto us, only it discovers itself by its own beams. So all the angels and saints in heaven cannot discover to our souls the love that is in the breast of God towards us, but only the Spirit of God, which 'sheds it into our hearts,' Rom. v. 5. The Spirit only teaches this language, My God. It is infused only into sanctified hearts; and, therefore, ofttimes mean men enjoy it, when great, wise, and learned persons are strangers to it, Mat. xi. 25.

5. The Spirit when it witnesseth this to us is called 'the Spirit of adoption,' Rom. viii. 15, and hath always accompanying of it a spirit of supplication, whereby with a familiar, yet reverend* boldness, we lay open our hearts to God as a dear father. All others are strangers to this heavenly intercourse. In straits they run to their friends and carnal shifts, whereas an heir of heaven runs to his Father, and tells him of all.

6. Those that are God's, are known to be his by special love-tokens that he bestows upon them, as,

(1.) The special graces of his Spirit. Princes' children are known by their costly jewels, and rich ornaments. It is not common gifts, and glorious parts that set a character upon us to be God's, but grace to use those gifts, in humility and love, to the glory of the giver.

(2.) There is in them a suitableness and connaturalness of heart to all that is spiritual, to whatsover hath God's stamp upon it, as his truth and his children, and that because they are his. By this likeness of disposition, we are fashioned to a communion with him. Can two walk together and not be agreed? It is a certain evidence that we are God's in Christ, if the Spirit of God hath wrought in us any impression like unto Christ, who is the image of his Father. Both Christ looking upon us, and our looking upon Christ by faith, as ours, hath a transforming and conforming power.

(3.) Spiritual comforts in distress, such as the world can neither give,

* That is, 'reverent.'—Ed.

nor take away, shew that God looks upon the souls of his with another eye, than he beholdeth others. He sends a secret messenger that reports his peculiar love to their hearts. He knows their souls, and feeds them with his '*hidden manna*,' Rev. ii. 17. The inward peace they feel is not in freedom from trouble, but in freeness with God in the midst of trouble.

(4.) Seasonable and sanctified corrections, whereby we are kept from being led away by the error of the wicked, shew God's fatherly care over us as his. Who will trouble himself in correcting another man's child? yet we oftener complain of the smart we feel, than think of the tender heart and hand that smites us, until our spirits be subdued; and then we reap the quiet fruit of righteousness. Where crosses work together for the best, we may know that we love God, Rom. viii. 28, and are loved of him. Thriving in a sinful course is a black mark of one that is not God's.

7. Then we make it appear that God is our God, when we side with him, and are for him and his cause in ill times. When God seems to cry out unto us, 'Who is on my side, who?' 2 Kings ix. 32; then if we can say as those in Isaiah, whereof one says, 'I am the Lord's, and another calls himself by the name of Jacob, and another subscribes with his hand unto the Lord,' Isa. xliv. 6, it is a blessed sign. Thus the patriarchs and prophets, apostles and martyrs, were not ashamed of God, and God was not ashamed to own them. Provided that this boldness from God proceed not only from a conviction of the judgment, but from spiritual experience of the goodness of the cause, whereby we can justify in heart what we justify in words. Otherwise men may contend for that with others, which they have no interest in themselves. The life must witness for God as well as the tongue. It is oft easier for corrupt nature to part with life rather than with lust.

This siding with God, is with a separation from whatsoever is contrary. God useth this as an argument to come out of Babylon, because we are his people: 'Come out of her, my people,' Rev. xviii. 4. Religion is nothing else but a gathering and a binding of the soul close to God. That fire which gathers together the gold, separates the dross. Nature draws out that which is wholesome in meats, and severs the contrary. The good that is to be had by God, is by cleaving to him, and him only. God loves an ingenuous and full protestation, if called to it. It shews the coldness of the times when there is not heat enough of zeal to separate from a contrary faith. God is a jealous God, and so we shall find him at last. When the day of severing comes, then they that have stood for him, shall not only be his, but his treasure, and his jewels, Mal. iii. 17.

There is none of us all but may some time or other fall into such a great extremity, that when we look about us, we shall find none to help us: at which time we shall throughly know, what it is to have comfort from heaven, and a God to go unto. If there be anything in the world worth labouring for, it is the getting sound evidence to our souls that God is ours. What madness is it to spend all our labour to possess ourselves of the cistern, when the fountain is offered to us? O beloved, the whole world cannot weigh against this one comfort, that God is ours. All things laid in the other balance, would be too light. A moth may corrupt, a thief may take away that we have here, but who can take our God away? Though God doth convey some comfort to us by these things, yet when they are gone, he reserves the comfort in himself still, and can convey that, and more, in a purer and sweeter way, where he plants the grace of faith to fetch it from him. Why then should we weaken our interest in God, for any thing this earth affords? What unworthy wretches are those, that to please a sinful man, or to feed a base lust, or to yield to a wicked custom will, as much as in them lieth, lose their interest in God? Such, little consider what an excellent privilege it is to have a sure refuge to fly unto in time of trouble. God wants not ways to maintain his, without being beholden to the devil. He hath all help hid in himself, and will then most shew it, when it shall make most for his own glory. If God be ours, it is a shame to be beholden to the devil, that ever it should be said, Satan by base courses hath made us rich. God thinks any outward thing too mean for his children, severed from himself, therefore he gives his Son, the express image of himself, 2 Cor. iv. 4, unto them. For which cause David, when he had even studied to reckon up the number of God's choice blessings, concludes with advancing of this above all, 'yea rather happy are they whose God is the Lord,' Ps. xliv. 15. If this will not satisfy the soul, what can? Labour therefore to bring thy soul to this point with God, 'Lord, if thou seest it fit, take away all from me, so thou leavest me thyself: whom have I in heaven but thee, and there is none on earth that I desire in comparison of thee?' Ps. lxxiii. 25.

CHAPTER XXXII.—*Of improving our evidences for comfort in several passages of our lives.*

That we lose not any measure of comfort in this so sweet a privilege, we must labour for skill to improve and implead the same in the several passages and occasions of our lives, and let it appear in the retail, that whatsoever is in God is mine. If I am in a perplexed condition, his wisdom is mine; if in great danger, his power is mine; if I lie sighing under the burden of sin, his grace is mine; if in any want, his all-sufficiency is mine. 'My God,' saith St Paul, 'will supply all your wants,' Philip. iv. 19. If in any danger, I am thine. Lord, save me, I am thine, the price of thy Son's blood; let me not be lost, thou hast given me the earnest of thy Spirit, and set thy seal upon me for thy own, let me neither lose my bargain nor thou thine. What is religion itself but a spiritual bond? whereby the soul is tied to God as its own, and then singles out of God whatsoever is needful for any occasion: and so binds God with his own covenant and promise. Lord, thou hast made thyself to be mine, therefore now shew thyself so, and be exalted in thy wisdom, goodness, and power, for my defence. To walk comfortably in my Christian course, I need much grace, supply me out of thy rich store. I need wisdom to go in and out inoffensively before others, furnish me with thy Spirit. I need patience and comfort, thou that art the God of all consolation, bestow it on me.

In time of desertion put Christ betwixt God and thy soul, and learn to appeal, from God out of Christ, to God in Christ. Lord, look upon my Saviour, that is near unto thee as thy son, near to me as my brother, and now intercedes at thy right hand for me. Though I have sinned, yet he hath suffered, and shed his precious blood to make my peace. When we are in any trouble, let us still wait on him, and lie at his feet, and never let him go till he casts a gracious look upon us.

So if we be to deal with God, for the church abroad, we may allege unto him that whatsoever provocations are therein, and deformity in regard of abuses and scandals; yet it is his church, his people, his inheritance, his name is called upon, in it, and the enemies of it are his enemies. God hath engaged himself to the friends of the church, that 'they shall prosper that love it,' Ps. cxxii. 6; and therefore we may with a holy boldness press him for a blessing upon the same.

So for our children and posterity, we may incline God to respect them, because they are under his covenant, who hath promised to be our God, and the God of our seed. 'Thine they were, thou gavest them me: all that I have is thine; these are those children which thou of thy rich grace hast given me. They are thine more than mine; I am but a means under thee to bring them into the world, and to be a nurse unto thy children; take care therefore of thine own children, I beseech thee, especially, when I can take no care of them myself; thou slumberest not, thou diest not, I must,' John xvii.

Flesh and blood think nothing is cared for, but what it seeth cared for by itself. It hath no eyes to see a guard of providence, a guard of angels. It takes no knowledge that that is best cared for, that God cares for. Those that have God for their God, have enlarged hearts as they have enlarged comforts. They have an everlasting spring that supplies them in all wants, refreshes them in all troubles, and then runs most clearly and freshly, when all other streams in the world are dried and stopped up. Were we skilful in the art of faith, to improve so great an interest, what in the world could much dismay us? Faith will set God against all.

It should fill our hearts with an holy indignation against ourselves, if either we rest in a condition wherein we cannot truly say, God is our God, or if, when we can in some sincerity of heart say this, that we make no better advantage thereby, and maintain not ourselves answerable to such a condition. What a shame is it for a nobleman's son to live like a beggar! for a great rich man to live like a poor peasant; to famish at a banquet; to fall when we have so many stays to lay hold on! Whereas if we could make this clear to our souls, that God is ours, and then take up our thoughts with the great riches we have in him, laid open in Christ, and in the promises, we need trouble ourselves about nothing, but only get a large vessel of faith, to receive what is offered, nay, enforced upon us.

When we can say, God is our God, it is more than if we could say, heaven is mine; or whatever good the creature affords is mine. Alas! what is all this, to be able to say, God is mine, who hath in him the sweetness of all these things, and infinitely more? If God be ours, goodness itself is ours. If he be not ours, though we had all things else, yet ere long nothing would be ours. What a wondrous comfort is this, that God hath put himself over to be ours! that a believing soul may say with as great confidence, and greater too, that God is his, than he can say his house is his, his treasure is his, his friends are his! Nothing is so much ours as God is ours, because by his being ours in covenant, all other things become ours; and if God be once ours, well may we trust in him. God and ours joined together make up the full comfort of a Christian. God! there is all to be had; but what is that to me unless he be *my* God? All-sufficiency with propriety * fully stayeth the soul.

David was now banished from the sanctuary, from his friends, habitation, and former comforts; but was he banished from his God? No; God was his God still. When riches, and friends, and life itself cease to be ours, yet God never looseth his right in us, nor we our interest in him. This comfort that God is ours, reacheth unto the resurrection of our bodies and to life everlasting. God is the God of Abraham, and so of every true believer, even when his body is turned into dust. Hence it is that 'the lovingkindness of the Lord is better than life,' Ps. lxiii. 3, because when life departs,

* That is, 'property, possession.'—G.

yet we live for ever in him. When Moses saw the people drop away so fast in the wilderness, and wither like grass, 'Thou art our foundation,' saith he, 'from one generation to another; thou art God from everlasting to everlasting,' Ps. xc. 2. When we leave the world, and are no more seen here, yet we have a dwelling-place in God for ever. God is ours from everlasting in election, and to everlasting in glory, protecting us here and glorifying us hereafter. David, that claimed God to be his God, is gone, but David's God is alive. And David himself, 'though his flesh see corruption,' Acts ii. 27, yet is alive in his God still.

That which is said of wily persons that are full of fetches * and windings, and turnings in the world, that such will never break, may much more truly be said of a right godly man, that hath but one grand policy to secure him in all dangers, which is to run to his God as to his tower of offence and defence; such a one will never be at a desperate loss so long as God hath any credit, because he never faileth those that fly unto him; and that because his mercy and truth never fails. The very lame and the blind, the most shiftless † creatures, when they had gotten the strong hold of Zion, thought then they might securely 'scorn David and his host,' 2 Sam. v. 6, 7, because though they were weak in themselves, yet their hold was strong; but we see their hold failed them at length, which a Christian's will never do.

Obj. But God seems to have small care of those that are his in the world; those who believe themselves to be his jewels, are counted the offscouring of the world, and most despised.

Ans. We must know that such have a glorious life in God, but it is 'hidden with Christ in God,' Col. iii. 3, from the eyes of the world, and sometimes from their own. Here they are hidden under infirmities, afflictions, and disgraces, but yet never so hidden but that God sometimes lets down a beam of comfort and strength, which they would not lose, to be freed from their present condition, though never so grievous. God comes more immediately to them now than formerly he was used; nay, even when God seems to forsake them and to be their enemy, yet they are supported with such inward strength that they are able to make good their claim with Christ their head, and cry 'My God' still. God never so departs but he always leaves somewhat behind him which draws and keeps the heart to him. We are like poor Hagar, who, when the bottle of water was spent, fell a crying, Gen. xxi. 17, when there was a fountain close by, but her tears hindered her from seeing it. When things go ill with us in our trades and callings, and all is spent, then our spirits droop, and we are at our wits' end, as if God were not where he was. Oh, consider, if we had all and had not God, we had nothing. If we have nothing, and have God, we have enough, for we have him that hath all, and more than all, at his command. If we had all other comforts that our hearts can desire, yet if God withdraw himself, what remains but a curse and emptiness? What makes heaven but the presence of God? and what makes hell but the absence of God? Let God be in any condition, though never so ill, yet it is comfortable; and usually we find more of God in trouble than when we are out of trouble. The comforts of religion never come till others fail. Cordials are kept for faintings. When a curtain and a veil is drawn betwixt us and the creature, then our eyes are only upward to God, and he is more clearly seen of us.

In the division of things, God bequeaths himself to those that are his for their portion as the best portion he can give them. There are many goodly

* That is, 'artifices.'—G. † That is, 'without expedients.'—G.

things in the world, but none of these are a Christian's portion. There is in him to supply all good and remove all ill, until the time come that we stand in need of no other good. It is our chief wisdom to know him, our holiness to love him, our happiness to enjoy him. There is in him to be had whatsoever can truly make us happy. We go to our treasure and our portion in all our wants; we live by it and value ourselves by it. God is such a portion, that the more we spend on him the more we may. 'Our strength may fail, and our heart may fail, but God is our portion for ever,' Ps. lxxiii. 26. Everything else teaches us, by the vanity and vexation we find in them, that our happiness is not in them. They send us to God; they may make us worse, but better they cannot. Our nature is above them, and ordained for a greater good; they can go but along with us for a while, and their end swallows up all the comfort of their beginning, as Pharaoh's lean kine swallowed up the fat, Gen. xli. 20. If we have no better portion here than these things, we are like to have hell for our portion hereafter. What a shame will it be hereafter, when we are stript of all, that it should be said, Lo, this is the man that took not God for his portion. If God be once ours, he goes for ever along with us, and when earth will hold us no longer, heaven shall. Who that hath his senses about him would perish for want of water when there is a fountain by him? or for hunger, that is at a feast? God alone is a rich portion. O, then, let us labour for a large faith, as we have a large object. If we had a thousand times more faith, we should have a thousand times more increase of God's blessings. When the prophet came to the widow's house, as many vessels as she had were filled with oil, 1 Kings xvii. 14. We are straitened in our own faith, but not straitened in our God. It falls out oft in this world that God's people are like Israel at the Red Sea, environed with dangers on all sides. What course have we, then, to take, but only to look up and wait for the salvation of our God? This is a breast full of consolation; let us teach our hearts to suck and draw comfort from hence.

Is God *our* God, and will he suffer anything to befall us for our hurt? Will he lay any more upon us than he gives us strength to bear? Will he suffer any wind to blow upon us but for good? Doth he not set us before his face? Will a father or mother suffer a child to be wronged in their presence if they can help it? Will a friend suffer his friend to be injured if he may redress him? And will God, that hath put these affections into parents and friends, neglect the care of those he hath taken so near unto himself? No, surely. His eyes are open to look upon their condition; his ears are open to their prayers; a 'book of remembrance,' Mal. iii. 16, is written of all their good desires, speeches, and actions; he hath bottles for all their tears, Ps. lvi. 8; their very sighs are not hid from him, Ps. lxxix. 11; he hath written them upon the 'palms of his hands,' Isa. xlvi. 16, and cannot but continually look upon them. Oh, let us prize the favour of so good a God, who, though he dwells on high, yet will regard things so low, and not neglect the mean estate of any; nay, especially delights to be called the 'comforter of his elect,' John xiv. 16, and the God of those that are in misery, and have none to fly unto but himself.

But we must know that God only thus graciously visits his own children; he visits with his choicest favours those only that *fear his name*, Ps. xxv. 14. As for those that either secretly undermine or openly oppose the cause and church of God and join with his enemies, such as savour not the things of God, but commit spiritual idolatry and adultery with God's enemies, the world and the devil, God will answer these as once he did the

Israelites, when in their necessity they would have forced acquaintance upon him, ' Go to the gods whom ye have served,' Judges x. 14, to the great men whose persons you have obeyed for advantage, to your riches, to your pleasures, which you have loved more than God or goodness. You would not lose a base custom, an oath, a superfluity, a thing of nothing, for me; therefore, I will not own you now. Such men are more impudent than the devil himself, that will claim acquaintance with God at last when they have carried themselves as his enemies all their days. Satan could tell Paul and Silas they were ' the servants of the living God,' Acts xvi. 17, but he would not make that plea for himself, knowing that he was a cursed creature.

Miserable, then, is their condition who live in the world, nay, in the church, without God, Eph. ii. 12. Such are in a worse estate than pagans and Jews; for, living in the house of God, they are strangers from God and from the covenant of grace; usurping the name of Christians, having, indeed, nothing to do with Christ.

Some of these, like spiritual vagabonds, as Cain, excommunicate themselves from God's presence in the use of the means, or rather like devils, that will have nothing to do with God, because they are loath to be tormented before their time. They think every good sermon an arraigning of them, and therefore keep out of reach.

Others will present themselves under the means, and carry some savour away with them of what they hear, but it is only till they meet with the next temptation, unto which they yield themselves presently slaves. These shewed themselves under a general profession, as they did, who called themselves Jews and were nothing less. But, alas! an empty title will bring an empty comfort at last. It was cold comfort to the rich man in flames, Luke xvi. 25, that Abraham called him son; or to Judas, that Christ called him friend, Mat. xxvi. 50; or to the rebellious Jews, that God styles them his people, Isa. l. 2. Such as our profession is, such will our comfort be. True profession of religion is another thing than most men take it to be. It is made up of the outward duty, and the inward man too, which is, indeed, the life and soul of all. What the heart doth not in religion is not done. *Quod cor non facit non fit.*

God cares for no retainers that will only wear his livery, but serve themselves. ' What hast thou to do to take his name into thy mouth, and hatest to be reformed? Ps. l. 16. Saul lived in the bosom of the church, yet, being a cruel tyrant, when he was in a desperate plunge, his outward profession did him no good; and, therefore, when he was environed with his enemies he uttered this doleful complaint, ' God hath forsaken me, and the Philistines are upon me,' 1 Sam. xxviii. 15. A pitiful case! Yet so will it be with all those that rest in an outward profession, thinking it enough to compliment * with God when their hearts are not right within them. Such will at length be forced to cry, sickness is upon me, death is upon me, hell is before me, and God hath forsaken me. I would have none of God heretofore, now God will have none of me. When David himself had offended God by numbering the people, then God counted him but plain David, ' Go and say to David,' &c., 2 Sam. xxiv. 12; whereas before, when he purposed to build a temple, then, ' Go, tell my servant David,' 2 Sam. vii. 5. When the Israelites had set up an idol, then God fathers them on Moses, ' *Thy* people which *thou* hast brought out of Egypt.' He would not own them as at other times then. They are my people still whilst they keep covenant. No care, no present comfort, in this near relation.

* That is, 'to pretend compliance.'—G.

The price of the pearl is not known till all else be sold, and we see the necessary use of it. So the worth of God in Christ is never discerned till we see our lost and undone condition without him, till conscience flies in our faces, and drags us to the brink of hell; then, if ever we taste how good the Lord is, we will say, 'Blessed is the people whose God is the Lord.' Heretofore I have heard of his lovingkindness, but that is not a thousandth part of what I see and feel. The joy I now apprehend is unutterable, unconceivable.

Oh then, when we have gotten our souls possessed of God, let our study be to preserve ourselves in his love, to walk close with him, that he may delight to abide with us and never forsake us! How basely doth the Scripture speak of whatsoever stands in our way! It makes nothing of them. What is man but vanity, and less than vanity! All nations but as 'a drop of the bucket,' as the 'dust of the balance,' Isa. xl. 15, things not at all considerable. Flesh looks upon them as through a multiplying glass, making them greater than they are; but faith, as God doth, sees them as nothing.

This is such a blessed condition, as may well challenge all our diligence in labouring to be assured of it; neither is it to be attained or maintained without the strength and prime of our care. I speak especially of, and in regard of, the sense and comfort of it. For the sense of God's favour will not be kept without keeping him in our best affections above all things in the world, without keeping of our hearts always close and near to him, which cannot be, without keeping a most narrow watch over our loose and unsettled hearts, that are ready to stray from God and fall to the creature. It cannot be kept without exact and circumspect walking, without constant self-denial, without a continual preparation of spirit, to want and forsake anything that God seeth fit to take from us.

But what of all this? Can we cross ourselves, or spend our labours to better purpose? One sweet beam of God's countenance will requite all this. We beat not the air, we plough not in the sand, neither sow in a barren soil; God is no barren wilderness. Nay, he never shews so much of himself as in suffering, and parting with anything for him, and denying ourselves of that which we think stands not with his will. Great persons require great observance. We can deny ourselves, and have men's persons in great admiration, for hope of some advantage; and is any more willing and more able to advance us than the great all-sufficient God? A Christian, indeed, undergoes more troubles, takes more pains, especially with his own heart, than others do. But what are these to his gains? What return so rich as trading with God? What comfort so great as these that are fetched from the fountain? One day spent in enjoying the light of God's countenance is sweeter than a thousand without it. We see here, when David was not only shut out from all comforts, but lay under many grievances, what a fruitful use he makes of this, that God was his God. It upholdeth his dejected, it stilleth his unquiet, soul; it leadeth him to the rock that was higher than he, and there stayeth him. It filleth him with comfortable hopes of better times to come. It sets him above himself, and all troubles and fears whatsoever.

Therefore wait still in the use of means till God shine upon thee; yea, though we know our sins in Christ are pardoned, yet there is something more that a gracious heart waits for us;* that is, a good look from God, a further enlargement of heart, and an establishing in grace. It was not

* Qu. 'waits for?'—ED.

enough for David to have his sins pardoned, but to 'recover the joy of salvation,' and 'freedom of spirit,' Ps. li. 12. Therefore the soul should always be in a waiting condition, even until it be filled with the fulness of God, as much as it is capable of. Neither is it quiet alone, or comfort alone, that the soul longs after, no, nor the favour of God alone, but a gracious heart to walk worthy of God. It rests not whilst anything remains that may breed the least strangeness betwixt God and us.

CHAPTER XXXIII.—*Of experience and faith, and how to wait on God comfortably. Helps thereto.*

My God. These words further imply a special experience, that David's soul had felt of the goodness of God. He had found God distilling the comfort of his goodness and truth through the promises, and he knew he should find God again the same as he was, if he put him in mind of his former gracious dealing. His soul knew right well, how good God was, and he could seal to those truths he had found comfort by, therefore he thus speaks to his soul: *My soul*, what, *my soul*, that hast found God so good, so oft, so many ways, thou *my* soul to be discouraged, having God, and my God, with whom I have taken so much sweet counsel, and felt so much comfort from, and found always heretofore to stick so close unto me! Why shouldst thou now be in such a case, as if God and thou had been strangers one to another? If we could treasure up experiments,* the former part of our life would come in to help the latter; and the longer we live the richer in faith we should be; even as in victories, every former overthrow of an enemy helps to obtain a succeeding victory. The use of a sanctified memory is to lose nothing that may help in time of need. He had need be a well-tried and a known friend upon whom we lay all our salvation and comfort.

We ought to trust God upon other grounds, though we had never tried him; but when he helps our faith by former experience, this should strengthen our confidence, and shore up † our spirits, and put us on to go more cheerfully to God, as to a tried friend. If we were well read in the story of our own lives, we might have a divinity of our own, drawn out of the observation of God's particular dealing towards us; we might say, this and this truth I dare venture upon, I have found it true, I dare build all my happiness upon it. As Paul, 'I know whom I have trusted,' 2 Tim. i. 12, I have tried him, he never yet failed me, I am not now to learn how faithful he is to those that are his. Every new experience is a new knowledge of God, and should fit us for new encounters. If we have been good in former times, God remembers the 'kindness of our youth,' Jer. ii. 2; we should therefore remember the kindness of God even from our youth. Evidence of what we have felt, helps our faith in that which for the present we feel not.

Though it be one thing to live by faith, and another thing to live by sight, yet the more we see, and feel, and taste of God, the more we shall be led to rely on him, for that which as yet we neither see nor feel. 'Because thou hast been my helper,' saith David, 'therefore in the shadow of thy wings will I rejoice,' Ps. lxiii. 7. The time was, Lord, when thou shewedst thyself a gracious Father to me, and thou art unchangeable in thy nature, in thy love, and in thy gifts.

Yea, when there is no present evidence, but God shews himself as con-

* That is, 'experiences.'—G. † That is, 'support.'—G.

trary to us, yet a former taste of God's goodness will enable to lay claim unto him still. God's concealing of himself is but a wise discipline for a time, until we be enabled to bear the full revealing of himself unto us for ever. In the mean time, though we have some sight and feeling in God, yet our constant living is not by it; the evidence of that we see not, is that which more constantly upholds the soul, than the evidence of anything we see or feel.

Yea, though our experience, by reason of our not minding of it in trouble, seems many times to stand us in no stead, but we fare as if God had never looked in mercy upon us; yet even here, some virtue remains of former sense, which with the present spirit of faith, helps us to look upon God as ours, as we have a present strength from food received and digested before. Vessels are something the better for that liquor they keep not, but runs through them.

But if experience should wholly fail, there is such a divine power in faith, as a very little beam of it, having no other help than a naked promise, will uphold the soul. Howsoever, we must neglect no help, for God oft suspends his comfort till we have searched all our helps. Though we see no light, yet we ought to search all crevices for light, and rejoice in the least beam of light, that we may see day by. It is the nature of true faith to search and pry into every corner, and if after all nothing appears, then it casts itself upon God as in the first conversion, when it had nothing to look upon but the offer of free mercy.* If at that time without former experience we did trust God, why not now, when we have forgotten our experience? The chief grounds of trusting God are always the same, whether we feel or feel not; nay, though for the present we feel the contrary, faith will never leave wrestling till it hath gotten a blessing. When faith is driven to work alone, having nothing but God, and his bare promise to rely upon, then God thinks it lies upon his credit to shew himself as a God unto us. God's power in creating light out of darkness is never more exalted, than when a guilty soul is lifted up by God to look for mercy, even when he seems armed with justice, to execute vengeance upon him; then the soul is brought to a near conformity unto Christ, who, 1, when he had the guilt of the sins of the whole world upon him; 2, when he was forsaken, and that after he had enjoyed the sweetest communion with his Father that ever creature could do; and not only so, but, 3, felt the weight of God's just displeasure against sin; and, 4, was abased lower than ever any creature was; yet still he held fast God as *his God.*

In earthly matters, if we have a title to anything by gift, contract, inheritance, or howsoever, we will not be wrangled out of our right. And shall we not maintain our right in God, against all the tricks and cavils of Satan and our own hearts? We must labour to have something, that we may shew that we are within the covenant. If we be never so little entered into the covenant, we are safe. And herein lies the special comfort of sincerity, that though our grace be little, yet it is of the right stamp, and shews us, that we are servants, and sons, though unworthy to be so. Here a little truth will go far. Hence it is that the saints in all their extremities still allege something, that shews that they are within the covenant; we are thy children, thy people, and thy servants, &c. God is mindful of his covenant, but is well pleased, that we should mind him of it too; and mind it ourselves to make use of it, as David doth here. He knew if he could bring his soul to his God, all would be quiet.

* Cum omnium incertus sit eventus, ad ea accedimus de quibus bene sperandum esse credimus.—*Sen[eca].*

God is so ready to mercy, that he delighteth in it, and delighteth in Christ, through whom he may shew mercy, notwithstanding his justice, as being fully satisfied in Christ. Mercy is his name that he will be known by. It is his glory which we behold in the face of Christ, who is nothing but grace and mercy itself. Nay, he pleads reasons for mercy, even from the sinfulness and misery of his creature, and maintains his own mercy against all the wrangling cavils of flesh and blood, that would put mercy from them; and hearken more willingly to Satan's objections, than God's arguments, till at length God subdues their spirits so far, as they become ashamed for standing out so long against him. How ready will God be to shew mercy to us when we seek it, that thus presseth upon us, when we seem to refuse it! If God should take advantage of our waywardness, what would become of us? Satan's course is to discourage those that God would have encouraged, and to encourage those whom God never speaks peace unto; and he thinks to gain both ways. Our care therefore should be, when we resolve upon God's ways, to labour that no discouragement fasten upon us, seeing God and his word speak all comfort to us.

And because the best of a Christian is to come, we should raise up our spirits to wait upon God, for that mercy which is yet to come. All inferior waitings for good things here, do but train us up in the comfortable expectation of the main.

This waiting on God requires a great strength of grace, by reason not only, 1, of the excellency of the things waited for, which are far beyond anything we can hope for in the world; but, 2, in regard of the long day which God takes before he performeth his promise; and, 3, from thence the tediousness of delay; 4, the many troubles of life in our way; 5, the great opposition we meet with in the world; 6, and scandals * ofttimes even from them that are in great esteem for religion; 7, together with the untowardness of our nature in being ready to be put off by the least discouragement. In these respects there must be more than a human spirit to hold up the soul, and carry it along to the end of that which we wait for.

But if God be our God, that love which engaged him to bind himself to us in precious promises, will furnish us likewise with grace needful, till we be possessed of them. He will give us leave to depend upon him both for happiness, and all sanctifying and quieting graces, which may support the soul, till it come to its perfect rest in God. For God so quiets the hearts of his children, as withal he makes them better and fitter for that which he provides for them. Grace and peace together. Our God is the God of grace and peace, of such graces as breed peace.

1. As he is a God of *love*, nay, love itself to us, so a taste of his love, raising up our love, is better than wine, full of nothing but encouragement. It will fetch up a soul from the deepest discouragement. This grace quickeneth all other graces. It hath so much spirits in it as will sweeten all conditions. Love enables to wait, as Jacob for Leah, seven years, Gen. xxxix. Nothing is hard to love; it carries all the powers of the soul with it.

2. As he is a God of *hope*, so by this grace, as an anchor fastened in heaven within the vail, he stayeth the soul; that though as a ship at anchor it may be tossed and moved, yet not removed from its station. This hope, as cork, will keep the soul, though in some heaviness, from sinking, and, as a helmet, bear off the blows, that they endanger not our life, Eph. vi. 17.

3. As God is a God of hope, so by hope, of *patience*, which is a grace whereby the soul resigneth up itself to God in humble submission to his

* That is, 'stumbling-blocks.'—G.

will, because he is our God, as David in extremity comforted himself 'in the Lord his God,' Ps. lxxxvi. 17. Patience breeds comfort, because it brings experience with it of God's owning of us to be his, Rom. v. 4. The soul, shod and fenced with this, is prepared against all rubs and thorns in our way, so as we are kept from taking offence. All troubles we suffer, do but help patience to its perfect work, Rom. v. 3; by subduing the unbroken sturdiness of our spirits, when we feel by experience, we get but more blows, by standing out against God.

4. The Spirit of God, likewise, is a spirit of *meekness*, whereby, though the soul be sensible of evil, yet it moderates such distempers, as would otherwise rob a man of himself; and together with patience, keepeth the soul in possession of itself. It stays murmurings and frettings against God or man. It sets and keeps the soul in tune. It is that which God, as he works, so he much delights in, and sets a price upon it, as the chief ornament of the soul. The 'meek of the earth seek God, and are hid in the day of his wrath,' Zeph. ii. 3; whereas, high spirits that compass themselves with pride as with a chain, Ps. lxxiii. 6, thinking to set out themselves by that which is their shame, are looked upon by God afar off. Meek persons will bow when others break; they are raised when others are plucked down, and stand when others that mount upon the wings of vanity, fall, Mat. v. 5; these prevail by yielding, and are lords of themselves, and other things else, more than other unquiet-spirited men: the blessings of heaven and earth attend on these.

5. So, likewise, *contentedness with our estate* is needful for a waiting condition, and this we have in our God, being able to give the soul full satisfaction. For outward things God knows how to diet us. If our condition be not to our mind, he will bring our mind to our condition. If the spirit be too big for the condition, it is never quieted, therefore God will level both. Those wants be well supplied, that are made up with contentedness, and with riches of a higher kind. If the Lord be our Shepherd, we can want nothing, Ps. xxiii. 1. This lifteth the 'weary hands and feeble knees,' even under 'chastisement,' Heb. xii. 12, wherein though the soul mourneth in the sense of God's displeasure, yet it rejoiceth in his fatherly care.

6. But patience and contentment are too low a condition for the soul to rest in, therefore the Spirit of God raiseth it up to a spiritual enlargement of *joy*. So much joy, so much light; and so much light, so much scattering of darkness of spirit. We see in nature how a little light will prevail over the thickest clouds of darkness; a little fire wastes a great deal of dross. The knowledge of God to be our God, brings such a light of joy into the soul, as driveth out dark uncomfortable conceits; this light makes lightsome. If the light of knowledge alone makes bold, much more the light of joy arising from our communion and interest in God. How can we enjoy God, and not joy in him? a soul truly cheerful rejoiceth that God whom it loveth, should think it worthy to endure anything for him. This joy often ariseth to a spirit of glory, even in matter of outward abasement. If the trouble accompanied with disgrace continue, the Spirit of glory rests upon us, and it will rest so long until it make us more than conquerors, even then when we seem conquered; for not only the cause, but the spirit riseth higher, the more the enemies labour to keep it under, as we see in Stephen, Acts vii.

With this joy goeth a spirit of courage and confidence. What can daunt that soul, which in the greatest troubles hath made the great God to be its own? Such a spirit dares bid defiance to all opposite power, setting the soul above the world, having a spirit larger and higher than the world, and seeing all but God beneath it, as being in heaven already in its head. After Moses and Micah had seen God in his favour to them, how little did they regard the angry countenances of those mighty princes, that were in their times the terrors of the world ! The courage of a Christian is not only against sensible danger, and of flesh and blood, but against principalities and powers of darkness, against the whole kingdom of Satan, the god of the world, whom he knows shortly shall be trodden under his feet, Rom. xvi. 20. Satan and his may for a time exercise us, but they cannot hurt us. True believers are so many kings and queens, so many conquerors over that which others are slaves to. They can overcome themselves in revenge, they can despise those things that the world admires, and see an excellency in that which the world sets light by ; they can set upon spiritual duties, which the world cannot tell how to go about, and endure that which others tremble to think of, and that upon wise reasons, and a sound foundation ; they can put off themselves, and be content to be nothing, so their God may appear the greater, and dare undertake and undergo anything for the glory of their God. This courage of Christians among the heathens was counted obstinacy, but they knew not the power of the Spirit of Christ in his, which is ever strongest when they are weakest in themselves ; they knew not the privy armour of proof that Christians had about their hearts, and thereupon counted their courage to be obstinacy.*

Some think the martyrs were too prodigal of their blood, and that they might have been better advised ; but such are unacquainted with the force of the love of God kindled in the heart of his child, which makes him set such a price upon Christ and his truth, that he counts not ' his life dear unto him,' Acts xx. 24 ; he knows he is not his own, but hath given up himself to Christ, and therefore all that is his, yea, if he had more lives to give for Christ, he should have them. He knows he shall be no loser by it. He knows it is not a loss of his life, but an exchange for a better.

We see the creatures that are under us will be courageous in the eye of their masters, that are of a superior nature above them ; and shall not a Christian be courageous in the presence of his great Lord and Master, who is present with him, about him, and in him ? Undoubtedly, he that hath seen God once in the face of Christ, dares look the grimmest creature in the face, yea, death itself under any shape. The fear of all things flies before such a soul. Only a Christian is not ashamed of his confidence. Why should not a Christian be as bold for his God, as others are for the base gods they make to themselves ?

7. Besides a spirit of *courage,* for establishing the soul, is required a spirit of *constancy,* whereby the soul is steeled and preserved immoveable in all conditions, whether present or to come, and is not changed in changes. And why? but because the spirit knows that God, on whom it rests, is unchangeable. We ourselves are as quicksilver, unsettled and moveable, till the spirit of constancy fix us. We see David sets out God in glorious terms, borrowed from all that is strong in the creature, to shew that he had great reason to be constant, and cleaving to him. ' He is my rock, my buckler, the horn of my salvation, my strong tower,' &c., Ps. xviii. God is a rock so deep, that no floods can undermine ; so high, that no waves can reach, though they rise never so high, and rage never so much. When we stand upon this rock that is higher than we, we may overlook

* Tertul[lian] in Apol.—Also Pliny in his famous letter to the Emperor **Trajan.** His ' inflexibilis obstinatio ' has passed into a world's proverb.—G.

all waves, swelling, and foaming, and breaking themselves, but not hurting us. And thereupon may triumphantly conclude with the apostle, that 'neither height, nor depth, shall ever separate us from the love of God,' Rom. viii. 39. Whatsoever is in the creature he found in his God, and more abundant. The soul cannot with an eye of faith look upon God in Christ, but it will be in its degree, as God is, quiet and constant. The spirit aimeth at such a condition as it beholdeth in God towards itself.

This constancy is upheld by endeavouring to keep a constant sight of God, for want of which it oft fares with us, like men, that having a city or tower in their eye, passing through uneven grounds, hills, and dales, sometimes get the sight thereof, sometimes lose it, and sometimes recover it again, though the tower be still where it was, and they nearer to it than they were at first. So it is oft with our uneven spirits: when once we have a sight of God, upon any present discouragement, we let fall our spirits, and lose the sight of him, until by an eye of faith we recover it again, and see him still to be where he was at first. The cherishing of passions take away the sight of God, as clouds take away the sight of the sun; though the sun be still where it was, and shineth as much as ever it did. We use to say, when the body of the moon is betwixt the sun and us, that the sun is eclipsed, when indeed not the sun but the earth is darkened: the sun loseth not one of its glorious beams. God is oft near us, as he was unto Jacob, and we are 'not aware of it,' Gen. xxviii. 17. God was near the holy man Asaph, when he thought him afar off. 'I am continually with thee,' saith he; 'thou holdest me by my right hand,' Ps. lxxiii. 27. Mary in her weeping passion could not see Christ before her; he seemed a stranger unto her. So long as we can keep our eye upon God, we are above the reach of sin or any spiritual danger.

CHAPTER XXXIV.—*Of confirming this trust in God: seek it of God himself. Sins hinder not: nor Satan. Conclusion and Soliloquy.*

§ I. But to return to the drawing out of our trust by *waiting*. Our estate in this world is still to wait, and happy it is that we have so great things to wait for; but our comfort is, that we have not only a 'furniture of graces,' 2 Pet. i. 5, one strengthening another as stones in an arch, but likewise God vouchsafeth some drops of the sweetness of the things we wait for, both to increase our desire of those good things, as likewise to enable us more comfortably to wait for them. And though we should die waiting, only cleaving to the promise, with little or no taste of the good promised; yet this might comfort us, that there is a life to come, that is, a life of sight and sense, and not only of taste but of fulness, and that for 'evermore,' Ps. xvi. 11. Our condition here is to live by faith and not by sight; only to make our living by faith more lively, it pleaseth God when he sees fit, to increase our earnest of that we look for. Even here God waits 'to be gracious to those that wait for him,' Isa. xxx. 18. And in heaven Christ waits for us, we are part of his 'fulness,' Eph. i. 23; it is part of his joy that 'we shall be where he is,' John xvii. 24; he will not therefore be long without us. The blessed angels and saints in heaven wait for us. Therefore let us be content as strangers to wait a while till we come home, and then we 'shall be for ever with the Lord,' Rev. xxii. 5; there is our eternal rest, where we shall enjoy both our God and ourselves in perfect happiness, being, as without need, so without desire, of the least change. When the time of our departure thither comes, then we may say as David, 'Enter now, my soul, into thy rest,' Ps. cxvi. 7. This is the 'rest which remaineth for God's people,' Heb. iv. 9, that is worth the waiting for, when we shall rest from all labour of sin and sorrow, and lay our heads in the bosom of Christ for ever.

It stands us therefore upon to get this great charter more and more confirmed to us, that God is *our God*, for it is of everlasting use unto us. It first begins at our entering into covenant with God, and continues not only unto death, but entereth into heaven with us. As it is our heaven upon earth to enjoy God as ours, so it is the very heaven of heaven, that there we shall for ever behold him, and have communion with him.

The degrees of manifesting this propriety* in God are divers, rising one upon another, as 'the light clears up by little and little till it comes to a perfect day,' Prov. iv. 18. 1. As the ground of all the rest, we apprehend God to be a God of some peculiar persons, as favourites above others. 2. From hence is stirred up in the soul a restless desire, that God would discover himself so to it, as he doth to those that are his, that he would 'visit our souls with the salvation of his chosen,' Ps. cvi. 4. 3. Hence follows a putting of the soul upon God, an adventuring itself on his mercy. 4. Upon this, God, when he seeth fit, discovers by his Spirit that he is ours. 5. Whence followeth a dependence on him as ours, for all things that may carry us on in the way to heaven. 6. Courage and boldness in setting ourselves against whatsoever may oppose us in the way, as the three young men in Daniel, 'Our God can deliver us if he will,' Dan. iii. 17. 'Our God is in heaven,' &c., Ps. cxv. 3. 7. After which springs a sweet spiritual security, whereby the soul is freed from slavish fears, and glorieth in God as ours in all conditions. And this is termed by the apostle, not only assurance, but the 'riches of assurance,' Col. ii. 2. Yet this is not so clear and full as it shall be in heaven, because some clouds may after arise out of the remainder of corruption, which may something overcast this assurance, until the light of God's countenance in heaven for ever scatters all.

There being so great happiness in this nearness betwixt God and us, no wonder if Satan labour to hinder the same, by interposing the guilt and heinousness of our sins, which he knows of themselves will work a separation; but these, upon our first serious thought of returning, will be removed. As they could not hinder our meeting with God, so they may cause a strangeness for a time, but not a parting, a hiding of God's countenance, but not a banishing of us from it. Peter had denied Christ, and the rest of the apostles had left him all alone; yet our Saviour, after his resurrection, forgets all former unkindnesses; he did not so much as object it to them, but sends Mary, who herself had been a great sinner, as an apostle to the apostles, and that presently, to tell them that he was risen, Mat. xxviii. 7; his care would have no delay. He knew they were in great heaviness for their unkindness. Though he was now entered into the first degree of his glory, yet we see his glory made him not forget his poor disciples. Above all, he was most careful of Peter, as deeper in sin than the rest, and therefore deeper in sorrow. 'Go tell Peter,' he needs most comfort. But what is the message? that 'I ascend not to my Father alone, but to your Father; not to my God only, but to your God,' John xx. 17.

And shall not we be bold to say so after Christ hath taught us, and put this claim into our mouths? If once we let this hold go, then Satan hath us where he would; every little cross then dejects us. Satan may darken

* That is, 'property, interest in.'—G.

the joy of our salvation, but not take away the God of our salvation. David, after his crying sin of murder, prays, 'Restore unto me the joy of thy salvation,' Ps. li. 12; this he had lost; but yet in the same psalm he prays, 'Deliver me from blood, O God, thou God of my salvation,' Ps. li. 14; therefore, whatsoever sense, reason, temptation, the law, or guilt upon conscience shall say, nay, however God himself, by his strange carriage to us may seem to be, yet let us cast ourselves upon him, and not suffer this plea to be wrung from us, but shut our eyes to all, and look upon God 'all-gracious and all-sufficient, who is the Father, the begetter of comfort,' 2 Cor. i. 3; the God, the creator of consolation, not only of things that may comfort, but of the comfort itself conveyed through these unto us. 'Who is a God like unto our God, that passeth by the sins of the remnant of his people?' Micah vii. 18. This should not be thought on without admiration; and indeed there is nothing so much deserves our wonderment as such mercy, of such a God, to such as we.

Since God hath 'avouched us to be his peculiar people,' Deut. xxvi. 18, let us avouch him, and since he hath passed his word for us, let us pass our words for him that we will be his, and stand for him, and to our power advance his cause. Thus David out of an enlarged spirit saith, 'Thou art my God, and I will praise thee; thou art my God, and I will exalt thee,' Ps. cxix. 28. Whatsoever we engage for God, we are sure to be gainers by. The true Christian is the wisest merchant, and makes the best adventure. He may stay long, but is sure of a safe and a rich return. A godly man is most wise for himself. We enter on religion, upon these terms, to part with ourselves, and all, when God shall call for it.

§ II. God much rejoiceth in sinners converted, as monuments of his mercy, and because the remembrance of their former sins whets them on to be more earnest in his service, especially after they have felt the sense of God's love. They even burn with a holy desire of honouring him, whom before they dishonoured, and stand not upon doing or suffering anything for him, but cheerfully embrace all occasions of expressing obedience.* God hath more work from them than from others; why then should any be discouraged?

Neither is it sins after our conversion, that nullify this claim of God to be *ours*. For this is the grand difference betwixt the two covenants, that now God will be merciful to our sins, 'if our hearts by faith be sprinkled with the blood of Christ,' Heb. x. 22. Though one sin was enough to bring condemnation, yet the free gift of grace in Christ is of many offences unto justification. And we have a sure ground for this, for the righteousness of Christ is God's righteousness, and God will thus glorify it, that it shall stand good to those that by faith apply it against their daily sins, even till at once we cease both to live and sin. For this very end was the Son of God willingly 'made sin,' Gal. iii. 13, that we might be freed from the same. And if all our sins laid upon Christ could not take away God's love from him, shall they take away God's love from us, when by Christ's blood our souls are purged from them?

O mercy of all mercies, that when we were once his, and gave away ourselves for nothing, and so became neither his nor our own, that then he would vouchsafe to become ours, and make us his by such a way, as all the angels in heaven stand wondering at; even his Son, not only taking our nature and miserable condition, but our sin upon him, that that being done

* Ex ipso dolore suo compuncti, inardescunt amore Dei. Damna præcedentia lucris sequentibus compensant.—*Greg*[*ory*].

away, we might through Christ have boldness with God as ours, who is now in heaven appearing there for us, until he bring us home to himself, and presents us to his Father for his for ever!

Think not then only that we are God's and he ours, but from what love and by what glorious means this was brought to pass. What can possibly disable this claim, when God for this end hath founded a covenant of peace so strongly in Christ, that sin itself cannot disannul it? Christ was therefore manifest, 'that he might destroy this greatest work of the devil,' 1 John iii. 5, 8. Forgiveness of sins now is one chief part of our portion in God. It is good therefore not to pore and plod so much upon sin and vileness by it, as to forget that mercy that rejoiceth over judgment. If we once be God's, though we 'drink this deadly poison, it shall not hurt us,' Mark xvi. 18. God will make a medicine, an antidote of it; and for all other evils, the fruit of them is by God's sanctifying the same, the taking away sin out of our natures; so that lesser evils are sent to take away the greater. If God could not over-rule evils to his own ends, he would never suffer them.

§ III. I have stood the longer upon this, because it is the *one thing needful*, Luke x. 42; the one thing we should desire, that this one God, in whom and from whom is all good, should be ours. All promises of all good in the new covenant, spring first from this, that God 'will be ours, and we shall be his,' Jer. xxxii. 38. What can we have more? and what is in the world less that will content us long, or stand us in any stead, especially at that time when all must be taken from us? Let us put up all our desires for all things we stand in need of, in this right we have to God in Christ, who hath brought God and us together. He can deny us nothing, that hath not denied us himself. If he be moved from hence to do us good, that we are his, let us be moved to fetch all good from him, on the same right that he is ours.

The persuasion of this will free us from all pusillanimity, lowliness, and narrowness of spirit, when we shall think that nothing can hurt us, but it must break through God first. If God give quietness, who shall 'make trouble?' Job xxxiv. 29. If God be with us, who can be against us? This is that which puts comfort into all other comforts, that maketh any burden light; this is always ready for all purposes. Our God is a present and a seasonable help. All evils are at his command to be gone, and all comforts at his command to come. It is but, go comfort, go peace, to such a man's heart: cheer him, raise him; go salvation, rescue such and such a soul in distress. So said and so done presently. Nay, with reverence be it spoken, so far doth God pass over himself unto us, that he is content himself to be commanded by us. 'Concerning the work of my hands command you me,' Isa. xlv. 11; lay the care and charge of that upon me. He is content to be out-wrestled and overpowered by a spirit of faith, as in Jacob, and the woman of Canaan, to be as it were at our service. He would not have us want anything wherein he is able to help us. And what is there wherein God cannot help us? If Christians knew the power they have in heaven and earth, what were able to stand against them? What wonder is it if faith overcome the world, if it overcomes him that made the world? that faith should be almighty, that hath the Almighty himself ready to use all his power for the good of them to whom he hath given the power of himself unto? Having therefore such a living fountain to draw from, such a centre to rest in, having all in one, and that one ours, why should we knock at any other door? We may go boldly to God now, as made 'ours, being bone of our bone, and flesh of our flesh.' We may go more comfortably to God, than to any angel or saint. God in the second person hath vouchsafed to take our nature upon him, but not that of angels. Our God and our man, our God-man is ascended unto the high court of heaven, to his and our God, clothed with our nature. Is there any more able and willing to plead our cause, or to whom we may trust business with, than he, who is in 'heaven for all things for us, appertaining to God?' Heb. v. 1.*

It should therefore be the chief care of a Christian, upon knowledge of what he stands in need of, to know where to supply all. It should raise up a holy shame and indignation in us, that there should be so much in God, who is so near unto us in Christ, and we make so little use of him. What good can any thing do us if we use it not? God is ours to use, and yet men will rather use shifts and unhallowed policies, than be beholden to God, who thinks himself never more honoured by us than when we make use of him. If we believe anything will do us good, we naturally make out for the obtaining of it. If we believe anything will hurt us, we study to decline it. And certain it is, if we believed that so much good were in God, we would then apply ourselves to him, and him to ourselves. Whatsoever virtue is in anything, it is conveyed by application and touching of it; that whereby we touch God, is our faith, which never toucheth him, but it draws virtue from him. Upon the first touch of faith, spiritual life is begun. It is a bastard in nature, to believe anything can work upon another without spiritual or bodily touch. And it is a monster in religion to believe that any saving good will issue from God, if we turn from him, and shut him out, and our hearts be unwilling. Where unbelief is, it binds up his power. Where faith is, there it is between the soul and God, as betwixt the iron and the loadstone, a present closing and drawing of one to the other. This is the beginning of eternal life, so to 'know God the Father and his Son Christ,' John xvii. 4, as thereby to embrace him with the arms of faith and love as ours, by the best title he can make us, who is truth itself.

Since then our happiness lies, out of ourselves, in God, we should go out of ourselves for it, and first get into Christ, and so unto God in him; and then labour, by the Spirit of the Father and the Son, to maintain acquaintance with both, that so God may be ours, not only in covenant, but in communion, hearkening what he will say to us, and opening our spirits, disclosing our wants, consulting and advising in all our distresses with him. By keeping this acquaintance with God, 'peace and all good is conveyed to us,' Job xxii. 21.

Thereafter as we maintain this communion further with him, we out of love study to please him, by exact walking according to his commands; then we shall feel increase of peace as our care increaseth; then he will 'come and sup with us,' Rev. iii. 20, and be free in his refreshing of us; then he will shew himself more and more to us, and manifest still a further degree of presence in joy and strength, until communion in grace ends in communion in glory.

But we must remember, as David doth here, to desire and delight in God himself more than in anything that is God's. It was a sign of St Paul's pure love to the Corinthians when he said, 'I seek not yours, but

---

* Tutius et jucundius loquor ad meum Jesum quam ad aliquem sanctorum Dei &c. Quod ego sum, fieri dignatus est Deus, non factus est quod angeli. Ad curiam Dei sui, Dei tui, præcessit Deus tuus, homo tuus; tunica tua indutus illic assidue pro nobis interpellat.—*Aug*[*ustine*].

you,' 2 Cor. xii. 14. We should seek for no blessing of God so much as for himself.

What is there in the world of equal goodness to draw us away from our God? If to preserve the dearest thing we have in the world, we break with God, God will take away the comfort we look to have by it, and it will prove but a dead contentment, if not a torment to us. Whereas, if we care to preserve communion with God, we shall be sure to find in him whatsoever we deny for him, honour, riches, pleasures, friends, all; so much the sweeter, by how much we have the more immediately from the spring-head. We shall never find God to be our God more than when, for making of him to be so, we suffer anything for his sake. We enjoy never more of him than then.

At the first we may seek to him, as rich to supply our wants, as a physician to cure our souls and bodies; but here we must not rest till we come to rejoice in him as our friend, and from thence rise to an admiration of him for his own excellencies, that being so high in himself, out of his goodness would stoop low to us. And we should delight in the meditation of him, not only as good to us, but as good in himself; because goodness of bounty springs from goodness of disposition. He doth good, because he is good.

A natural man delights more in God's gifts than in his grace. If he desires grace, it is to grace himself, not as grace, making him like unto God, and issuing from the first grace, the free favour of God; by which means men come to have the gifts of God without God himself; *dona Dei, sine Deo.* But, alas! what are all other goods, without the chief good? They are but as flowers, which are long in planting, in cherishing, and growing, but short in enjoying the sweetness of them. David here joys in God himself; he cares for nothing in the world but what he may have with his favour; and whatever else he desires, he desires only that he may have the better ground from thence to praise his God.

§ IV. The sum of all is this, *the state of God's dear children in this world is to be cast into variety of conditions*, wherein, they, consisting of nature, flesh, and spirit, every principle hath its own and proper working. They are sensible as flesh and blood; they are sensible to discouragements as sinful flesh and blood; but they recover themselves, as having a higher principle, God's Spirit, above flesh and blood in them.

In this conflicting state, every principle labouring to maintain itself, at length by help of the Spirit, backing and strengthening his own work, grace gets the better, keeping nature within bounds, and suppressing corruption. And this the soul, so far as it is spiritual, doth by gathering itself to itself, and by reasoning the case so far, till it concludes, and joins upon this issue, that the only way to attain sound peace is, when all other means fail, to trust in God. And thereupon he lays a charge upon his soul so to do, as being a course grounded upon the highest reason, even the unchangeable goodness of God; who, out of the riches of his mercy, having chosen a people in this world, which should be to the glory of his mercy, will give them matter of setting forth his praise, in shewing some token of good upon them, as being those on whom he hath fixed his love, and to whom he will appear not only a Saviour, but salvation itself; nothing but salvation. As the sun is nothing but light, so whatsoever proceeds from him to them tends to further salvation. All his ways towards them lead to that; which ways of his, though for a time they are secret, and not easily found out, yet at length God will be wonderful in them, to the admiration of his enemies themselves, who shall be forced to say, God hath done great things for them; and all from this ground, that God is our God in covenant; which words are a stern * that rule and guide the whole text.

For why should we not be disquieted when we are disquieted? Why should we not be cast down when we are cast down? Why should we trust in God as a Saviour, but that he is *our God*, making himself so to us in his choicest favours? doing that for us which none else can do, and which he doth to none else that are not his in a gracious manner. This blessed interest and intercourse betwixt God's Spirit and our spirits, is the hinge upon which all turns; without this no comfort is comfortable; with this, no trouble can be very troublesome.

Without this assurance there is little comfort in soliloquies; unless, when we speak to ourselves, we can speak to God as ours. For in desperate cases our soul can say nothing to itself to still itself, unless it be suggested by God. Discouragements will appear greater to the soul than any comfort, unless God comes in as ours.

See therefore David's art; he demands of himself why he was so cast down? The cause was apparent, because there were troubles without and terrors within, and none to comfort. Well, grant this, saith the Spirit of God in him, as the worst must be granted; yet, saith the Spirit, Trust in God. *So I have.*

Why, then, wait in trusting; 'light is sown for the righteous,' Ps. xcvii. 11; it comes not up on the sudden. We must not think to sow and reap both at once. If trouble be lengthened, lengthen thy patience.

What good will come of this?

God will wait to do thee that good, for which thou shalt praise him; he will deal so graciously with thee, as he will deserve thy praise; he will shew thee his salvation. And new favours will stir thee up to sing new songs. Every new recovery of ourselves or friends is as it were a new life, and ministers new matter of praise. And upon offering this sacrifice of praise, the heart is further enlarged to pray for fresh blessings. We are never fitter to pray than after praise.

But in the mean time I hang down my head, whilst mine enemies carry themselves highly, and my friends stand aloof.

God in his own time, which is best for thee, will be the salvation of thy countenance; he will compass thee about with songs of deliverance, and make it appear at last that he hath care of thee.

But why then doth God appear as a stranger to me?

That thou shouldst follow after him with the stronger faith and prayer; he withdraws himself, that thou shouldst be the more earnest in seeking after him. God speaks the sweetest comfort to the heart in *the wilderness*. Happily thou art not yet low enough, nor purged enough. Thy affections are not thoroughly crucified to the world, and therefore it will not yet appear that it is God's good will to deliver thee. Wert thou a fit subject of mercy, God would bestow it on thee.

But what ground hast thou to build thyself so strongly upon God?

He hath offered and made himself to be *my God*, and so hath shewed himself in former times; and I have made him *my God*, by yielding him his sovereignty in my heart; besides the present evidence of his blessed Spirit, clearing the same, and many peculiar tokens of his love which I daily do enjoy; though sometimes the beams of his favour are eclipsed.

* That is, 'rudder' or 'helm,' using the place for the thing.—G.

Those that are God's, besides their interest and right in him, have oft a sense of the same, even in this life, as a foretaste of that which is to come. To the seal of grace stamped upon their hearts, God superadds a fresh seal of joy and comfort, by the presence and witness of his Spirit; and shews likewise some outward token for good upon them, whereby he makes it appear that 'he hath set apart him that is godly for himself, as his own,' Ps. iv. 3.

Thus we see that discussing of objections in the consistory of the soul settles the soul at last, faith at length silencing all risings to the contrary. All motion tends to rest, and ends in it. God is the centre and resting-place of the soul, and here David takes up his rest, and so let us. Then whatsoever times come, we are sure of a hiding-place and sanctuary.

FINIS.

'Although the fig-tree shall not blossom, neither shall fruit be in the vines, the labour of the olive shall fail, and the fields shall yield no meat, &c., yet I will rejoice in the Lord, I will joy in the God of my salvation,' Hab. iii. 17.

'He that dwelleth in the secret place of the Most High, shall lodge under the shadow of the Almighty. I will say of the Lord, He is my refuge, and my fortress; My God, in him will I trust,' Ps. xci. 1, 2.

'My strength and my heart faileth, but God is the strength of my heart, and my portion for ever,' Ps. lxxiii. 26.

NOTES.

(a) P. 153.—Nero. Consult Long's excellent memoir of this worst of all the Cæsars, in Dr Smith's Dictionary of Greek and Roman Biography and Mythology.

(b) P. 158.—'File.' 'In good sadness, I do not know; either it is there, or it is upon a *file*, with the duke's other letters, in my tent.'—*All's Well that Ends Well*, iv. 3.

(c) P. 171.—'Restrained.' The touching saying told of many, from John Bradford to John Newton, and certainly used by the latter, on seeing a criminal ascending the gallows, 'There goes John Newton, but for the grace of God,' illustrates this.

(d) Caracciolus. The following are the title-pages of the translations referred to in foot-note, page 184:—
1. 'Newes from Italy of a second Moses, or the Life of Galeacius Caracciolus the noble Marquesse of Vico.' 4to. London. 1608.
2. 'A President to the Nobilitie of Court and Countrey, in the Life of Galeacius Caraeciolus, the noble Marquesse of Vico in the Kingdome of Naples.' 4to. 1612.

The incident noted by Sibbes is thus narrated:—

'At that time *Peter Martyr Vermilius*, a *Florentine*, was a publik preacher and reader at *Naples*. This man was a canon regular (as they call them), a man since then of great name for his singular knowledge in Christian religion, his godly manners and behaviours, and for his sweet and copious teaching; for he afterwards, casting away his monkes coule, and renouncing the superstitions of Poperie, he shone so brightly in God's church, that he dispersed and strangely drove away the darknesse and mists of popery. *Galeacius* was once content at *Cæserta* his motion to be drawn to heare *Peter Martyr's* sermon, yet not so much for any desire he had to learne, as moved and tickled with a curious humour to heare so famous a man as then *Martyr* was accounted at that time. *Peter Martyr* was in hand with *Paul's* first

Epistle to the *Corinthians*; and as he was shewing the weaknesse and deceitfulnes of the iudgement of man's reason in spirituall things, as likewise the power and efficasy of the word of God in those men in whom the Lord worketh by his Spirit, amongst other things, he vsed this similie or comparison—If a man walking in a large place see a farre off men and women dancing together, and heare no sound of instrument, he will iudge them mad, or at least foolish ; but if he come neerer them, and perseive their order, and heare their musicke, and marke their measures and their courses, he will then be of another minde, and not onely take delight in seeing them, but feele a desire in himself to beare them company, and dance with them. Even the same (said *Martyr*) betides many men, who, when they behold in others a suddain and great change of their looks, apparell, behaviour, and whole course of life, at the first sight they impute it to melancholy, or some other foolish humour ; but if they looke more narrowly into the matter, and begin to heare and perceive the harmony and sweet concent of God's Spirit and his word in them (by the ioint power of which two this change was made and wrought, which afore they counted folly), then they change their opinion of them, and, first of all, begin to like them, and that change in them, and afterwards feele in themselves a motion and desire to imitate them, and to be of the number of such men, who, forsaking the world and his vanities, doe thinke that they ought to reforme their lives by the rule of the gospell, that so they may come to true and sound holinesse. This comparison, by the grace of God's Spirit, wrought so wonderfully with *Galeacius* (as himselfe hath often tolde his friends), that from that houre he resolved with himselfe more carefully to restraine his affections from following the world and his pleasures, as before they did, and to set his mind about seeking out the truth of religion, and the way to true happinesse. To this purpose he began to reade the Scriptures every day, being perswaded that truth of religion and soundnesse of wisdom was to be drawn out of that fountaine, and that the highway to heaven was thence to be sought. And further, all his acquaintance and familiarity did he turne into such company as out of whose life and conferences he was perswaded he might reape the fruit of godlinesse and pure religion ; and thus farre in this short time had the Lord wrought with him by that sermon, as, first, to consider with himselfe seriously whether he was right or no ; secondly, to take up an exercise continuall of reading Scripture ; thirdly, to change his former company, and make choice of better. And this was done in the year one thousand five hundred fortie and one, and in the foure and twentieth yeare of his age.'

There is a marginal note, having relation to the chapter, and not to any particular sentence in it—' See how the first step of a man's conversion from popery is true and sound mortification of carnal lusts, and a change of life. See, also, how the first means to bring a man out of error to the truth is study of holy Scriptures.'

(e) P. 186.—' Idiot.' The original word here (1 Cor. xiv. 24), 'ἰδιώτης, which Sibbes renders literally, and which Wickliffe had so done long before, meant, at the period, simply a private person, as opposed to officials, and not at all, as now, a fatuous person.

(f) P. 192.—' Pity a beast over-loaden, and yet take no pity of a brother.' Sterne, weeping and moralising over a ' dead ass,' and at the very time neglecting his nearest relatives, has long ' pointed this moral.'

(g) P. 209.—Bishop Patrick and the ' Soul's Conflict.' The paragraph commencing ' The laws under which we live,' as stated in the foot-note (page 209), forms the basis of an extraordinary charge against the Puritans by Bishop Patrick, only less extraordinary than his mode of putting it. It occurs in his, it must be allowed us to say, miscalled *' Friendly* Debate betwixt two Neighbours, the one a Conformist, the other a Nonconformist,' described below.*

Perhaps the better way to deal with the charge will be to give it in full, and then see what can be said about it. Be it observed, that *C.* stands for Conformist, and *N. C.* for Nonconformist. The passage is as follows (part ii., 1669, pp. 219–222 ; in Taylor's scholarly edition of Patrick's Works, vol. v., pp. 655–57) :—

C. I must add, that you are all guilty of too much confidence, and talk as if you were infallible in your conclusions. When you see, therefore, the folly of it in another, mend it in yourselves; and do not talk hereafter as if all godly men had

* The 'Friendly Debate.' Part 1st, 1668 ; part 2d, 1669 ; part 3d, 1669-70 ; appendix to part 3d, 1669-70, with a postscript. Curiously enough, the 6th edition, ' enlarged and corrected,' does not include part 3d, or any of the additions, though published long subsequently, viz., in 1683-4.

ever been of your mind; no man of a tender conscience but held it unlawful to prescribe anything in God's worship. Everybody knows Cartwright, Reynolds, Greenham were of this opinion, as the prefacer boldly told you; and it is a wonder he did not add Dr Sibbes. For so some of your party took care the world should believe, and *chose rather to corrupt his writings, than have it thought he was of another persuasion*

N. C. I shall never believe it.

C. You may choose; but I shall prove that this good man's writings were *abused presently after his death* in this very point. For in his book called the Soul's Conflict he gave this direction, among others, to guide a soul in doubtful cases—'The laws under which we live are particular determinations of the law of God, and therefore ought to be a rule to us, *so far as they reach*. Though it be too narrow a rule to be good only so far as man's law guides unto, yet law, being the joint reason and consent of many men for public good, *hath an use* for the guiding of our actions *that are under the same. Where it dashes not against God's law*, what is agreeable to law is agreeable to conscience.' Thus the rule stood when the book first came out.* But in a very short time after, when he was newly laid in his grave, the first words were changed into these—'The laws under which we live are particular determinations of the law of God in some duties *of the second table.*'† *In which they made two restrictions of that which he had said in general words; first, they restrained the rule to the second table, and not to all things neither, but only some duties; and then they add a whole sentence, by way of example, which* was not in the first edition, *which I make no doubt was done on purpose, lest any man who read the book should think it was the Doctor's opinion, that we should conform to the orders of our governors about the worship of God, where the law of God hath determined nothing in particular, and their laws do not cross his.* But what is there done by the Jesuits worse than this? What greater injury to the dead than thus to play tricks with their books, and change their words at your pleasure.

N. C. It is very strange.

C. I have something more to tell you. As they have added here, so they have taken away in another place just before it. He is answering, I told you, this question, What course must we take for guidance of our lives in particular actions wherein doubts may arise, what is most agreeable to God's will? And one advice is this—'We must look to our place wherein God hath set us. If we be in subjection to others, their authority in doubtful things ought to sway with us.' A dangerous rule, some men thought; and therefore in the next edition *they left out those words,* 'in doubtful things;' and also blotted out this whole sentence which follows—'It is certain we ought to obey *(viz., in doubtful things of which he is speaking)*, and if the things wherein we are to obey be certain to us, we ought to leave that which is uncertain, and stick to that which is certain. In this case, we must obey those that are under God.'

N. C. Are you sure of this?

C. As sure as that I see you; though I must tell you there was a neat device to hide this fraud: for they *reprinted the book speedily with the very same title-page that was before, without giving notice that it was a second edition; and by leaving out those lines, and adding an example, as I told you, to illustrate the rule as they had restrained it, they made the pages exactly even as they were at the first.*‡ *Afterward the book was divided into chapters; and in all editions since, you will find these rules* (chap. 17) *with these alterations.*

N. C. By his own appointment, it is like.

C. Why did they not tell us so?

N. C. I know not.

C. I will tell you then. They were loth to tell a plain lie; for the Doctor died within three days after he had writ his preface to the first impression, *and therefore, it is most likely, made no alterations.* That preface was dated July the first 1635,§ and he died July the fourth. So I gather from those who put out his two last sermons, preached June 21st and 28th; and he died, say they, the Lord's day following.

* First Edition, 1635, page 364.
† From page 364 of B. I note this, as Taylor in his edition of the 'Friendly Debate' mistakenly gives a reference to C.—G.
‡ There are two editions of 1635, one of his own, another of somebody's else, but so ordered, that they seem the same. At least, they reprinted that sheet (wherein these things are contained) with these alterations, which I add lest I should not be rightly understood by all.
§ Mr Taylor adds a foot-note here—'The day of the month is not appended in the first unaltered edition, a copy of which is in the Bodleian Library.' This is an overlook. The 'unaltered edition' A is now before me, and it bears the date 'July 1. 1635.' Mr Taylor apparently turned to the 'Epistle Dedicatory,' which is undated, instead of to the address 'To the Reader.'—G.

Immediately after which came out a new impression of the same year 1635, *but not called a second edition, which they would have us believe was not till* 1636 ; a mere cheat, as I confidently affirm, *having seen and compared all.*

Not satisfied with the preceding, the charge is renewed, and, if possible, intensified in a 'general preface' to the '6th edition' [1684, ⅔ ix.; in Taylor's edition *supra*, vol. v., pp. 262–3]. That the whole may be before our readers, this fresh assault may also be given :—

'And let me beseech all those who shall cast their eyes on this preface, by no means to hearken to one sort of people among them, but to look upon them as men of an evil mind, that are perniciously bent to their own and all our destruction ; such, I mean, as persuade men to read nothing that is said for their information, and take as great care to continue their scruples as we do to remove them. An instance of which we had long ago in the corrupting of Dr Sibbes's book, called the Soul's Conflict, which hath been in many hands since, and might have done much to the settling men's minds in dutiful obedience to authority, if they of the then discontented party had not falsified his words, and quite altered the sense of his discourse. For it was intended to satisfy weak and doubtful people in those very things, as well as others, which still trouble this church ; but lest they should receive such satisfaction as to conform to public orders, when they were in any uncertainty of mind about them (as Dr Sibbes honestly advised them to do, nay, told them they ought to do, notwithstanding their doubts and scruples), there was care taken to have that passage quite blotted out of his book immediately upon his death, which happened as soon as the book had seen the light. Read the second part of this treatise, pp. 225, 226, &c., and then consider what kind of conscience this is, and how impudently it pretends to tenderness, which is so strait-laced about a ceremony, and takes such a liberty as this to *deprave* other men's writings, and make them speak contrary to their meaning. If they could be persuaded to reflect whose practice this is, and how odious it hath made those who have been guilty of it, it is possible they might be ashamed to find this foul and (as they would call it in others) anti-Christian dealing among themselves.'

Such is the charge and case of the bishop against the Puritans in all its length and breadth, and I would now make a few remarks upon it. It only requires, I apprehend, a statement of matters-of-fact to set the whole aside. But it were to dishonour the memory of the Puritans to emulate the spirit of the bishop in vindicating them.

[*a*] The text of the *sentences* (let the word be marked) in question *is* found in 'Soul's Conflict' A, the original edition, as given in the 'Friendly Debate ;' and the changes alleged are accurately represented from 'Soul's Conflict' B. But—

[*b*] The following specific notice, which the bishop, as will be shewn, knew of, but apparently found it convenient to ignore, warrants us in affirming that the omissions and additions of B, were made, if not from the dictation, at least with the sanction of Sibbes himself. It is taken from the close of the address 'To the Christian Reader :'—'By reason,' he says, 'of my absence while the work was in printing, SOME SENTENCES were MISTAKEN.'* Now, that the '*sentences*' in debate were those herein referred to, is self-evident, from this fact, that they are THE ONLY SENTENCES IN THE WHOLE BOOK changed in B. Nor is this all. For—

[*c*] As if to guard against the abuse of the 'general rule' laid down in the mistaken sentences, in absence of the after-limitations inserted in B, he adds—' Some men will be ready to *deprave* the labours of other men's, but, so good may be done, let all such ill-disposed persons be what they are, and what they will be, unless God turn their hearts.'† I remark by the way—

[*d*] That it is the more necessary to attend to the intimation by Sibbes of 'mistaken *sentences*,' inasmuch as Pickering's beautiful, but, unfortunately, inaccurate, reprint of the 'Soul's Conflict,' by a strange oversight, omits it.‡

[*e*] It may be very safely left with every unprejudiced reader to decide whether it be not plain, from the above words of Sibbes, that some of his friends, Goodwin, or Nye, or Ash (to whom he confided his MSS), had called his attention to the '*sentences*,' and received from him the modifications and corrections inserted in B, and from B to H. and in all subsequent editions. The specific noting of certain 'mistaken sentences' has no meaning otherwise. It must be kept in mind also,

---

* See page 127, line 11 from bottom, of our reprint in this volume.
† Ibid., line 10 from bottom.
‡ 'The Bruised Reed' and other pieces in the companion volume to the 'Soul's Conflict,' by Pickering, has the same beauty of typography, but even more inaccuracies.

that the 'Soul's Conflict' was posthumously published, having only been printed off while the author was on his death-bed. Again, I remark—

[*f*] That the mistake would be the more readily made, from the circumstance, that, in common with all the writings of Sibbes, he seems to have taken as the groundwork of the 'Soul's Conflict,' the brachy-graphic notes of others written down from his lips on delivery. These he simply revised.* Having in my library a volume of such 'notes,' I speak with the less hesitation.

[*g*] In the matter of editions, and the related 'charge' of 'trick,' and 'falsification,' and 'corruption,' it is UNTRUE that they [*i.e.*, the Puritans] reprinted the book speedily, with the very same title-page that was before, WITHOUT giving notice that it was a SECOND EDITION. B, was NOT a 'reprint,' was not a 'new edition,' but simply A, with leaf 364-5 inserted, and 'victory' in title-page, instead of 'victorie,' and C, *the* 'second edition,' DOES bear on its title-page these words, 'The Second Edition,' and the date, not of 1636, as the bishop would have us believe, but of 1635. I have a copy in my library, and another will be found in, respectively, University Library, Cambridge, and the Library of Trinity College, Dublin. I place below the *verbatim et literatim et punctatim* title-page.†

[*h*] It would be very idle to enter into a controversy as to the relative teaching of the sentences, as in A and B. Every dispassionate reader of both must admit that there is no change in the sentiment, but simply an expansion by way of explanation. In the original form, it was said, 'The laws under which we live . . . . . . ought to be a rule unto us, *so far as they reach*;' and it was only illustrating the extent of the obligation of the rule to add in B, 'in some duties of the second table,' &c. Would Bishop Patrick really have us regard Sibbes as teaching that the 'rule' did extend beyond the 'second table,' while we read so unmistakably, in A and B alike, the qualification, '*Where it dashes not against God's law?*' Every one who knows the works of Sibbes, knows that in a venal and time-serving semi-popish period he held with all his might, that in matters of *conscience*, the law of God contained in the word of God was the supreme and only arbiter. It is worse than slander to maintain that he would have had men 'conform to the orders of our governors about the worship of God' apart therefrom. The utmost he says, and he says even that with the preliminary caution, 'though it be TOO NARROW A RULE to be good ONLY [carefully italicised in A and B], so far as man's law guides unto,' is this . . . 'yet law . hath AN USE for the guiding of our actions THAT ARE UNDER THE SAME.'

This is sufficiently explicit, and conclusively meets that unquestioning submission to 'the powers that be,' which offered its inodorous incense at the shrine of James I., and his son Charles I.—that worshipping of 'the right divine of kings to *govern wrong*,' by which, in the indignant couplet of old Benjamin Bennet—

'The SOV'REIGN'S WILL becomes our—LAW,
The CHURCH'S WILL our—CREED.'

[*i*] As to the 'blotting out' of the second sentence (first in order), animadverted upon by the bishop, it may be sufficient to observe, that the omission of the words, 'in doubtful cases,' is explained and accounted for by the fuller statement, with example, thereafter given; and equally is the deletion of the remainder accounted for, partly by its being a mere tautology in view of the after fuller statement, and partly that there was necessarily abridgment here to admit of corresponding enlargement there, within the compass of the one leaf in B, as in A.

* 'Revised.' See address to 'Christian Reader' prefixed to 'Bruised Reed' and 'Soul's Conflict,' and the various prefaces to the posthumously published volumes. The B. R. and S. C. seem to have been more fully written out by Sibbes himself; but as Mr Ryle observes of Ward, even they, and much more the others, have all the characteristics of compositions intended for ears rather than for eyes, for hearers rather than for readers. In the haste of revision, it is easily to be understood how Sibbes passed by the 'mistaken sentences.'

† 'The SOVLES CONFLICT with it selfe, AND VICTORY over it self by *Faith*: A Treatise of the inward disquietments of distressed spirits, with comfortable remedies to establish them. Returne unto thy rest O my soule, for the Lord hath dealt bountifully with thee. By *R. Sibbs* D.D. Master of *Katherine Hall* in Cambridge, and Preacher of *Grayes Inne* London. The Second Edition. LONDON Printed by M. F. for *R. Dawlman* at the Brazen Serpent in Pauls Churchyard. 1635. 12°.' By the way, it may be noticed as an incidental confirmation of above, as to B being identical with A, that Benlowes' and Quarles's 'Verses' did *not* appear in it, but first in C. There was a '*second* edition' also of 1636, which perhaps explains, but does not in the slightest extenuate, the bishop's rash and reckless assertion, seeing he boasts of having seen and compared ALL. But indeed D, as in the case of A and B, is palpably from the same types, a mere further issue of C. Hence, probably, the designating C and D 'the second edition,' the only change being in the date 1635 into 1636. It will be noticed from our prefatory note to 'Soul's Conflict,' that there were two 'fourth' editions likewise. Nichols, in his Introduction to Pearson on the Creed, has shewn how publishers were wont to continue issuing edition upon edition, with the same date. I believe this to have been done with Sibbes's 'Soul's Conflict,' and that the long apparent interval between edition of 1651 and that of 1658 is thus explained.

That this is the true explanation, will be readily granted.

[*j*] When it is remembered who were the literary executors and editors of all Sibbes's writings. If the honoured and venerable names of Thomas Goodwin, Philip Nye, Jeremiah Burroughs, Simeon Ashe, James Nalton, be not sufficient to put to flight all charges of *unauthorised* changes or omissions, much more of 'trick,' 'falsification,' 'corruption,' then none may hope to do so. But apart altogether from Sibbes's own explicit declaration, that 'some sentences' had been 'mistaken,' and his deprecation of any 'depraving' of his writings on the strength (or rather weakness) of such mistake, the *character* of the men is more than sufficient to meet the accusations and insinuations of the 'Friendly Debate.' Finally,

[*k*] The use of the peculiar word 'deprave,'* in the second statement of his case, reveals the bishop's knowledge of Sibbes's special intimation concerning the mistaken sentences, a circumstance which aggravates his disingenuousness.

I would only add, that a similar examination of the numerous other kindred charges of the 'Friendly Debate' will satisfy any one that scarcely a page is without its over or under statement, that its citations are wrested from their context, that dogma is substituted for proof, and loud assertion for argument, while the entire spirit and temper evidence a contest for victory rather than truth.

(h) P. 214.—' The soul is made for God, and never finds rest till it returns to him again.' This seems to be a reminiscence of the well-known saying of Augustine, 'Thou madest us for thyself, and our heart is restless, until it rests in thee,' (Confess. Book i. 1).

(i) P. 243.—' No calling so mean .... enough to give account for.' I have marked this searching observation, in order to confirm it with the great and worthy John Brown of Haddington's 'Hint to Ministers,' than which few things are more striking. It was originally addressed to Dr Waugh, when a young man, and subsequently published in the 'Evangelical Magazine.' The Rev. John Brown of Haddington, *clarum et venerabile nomen*, in a letter of paternal counsels and cautions to one of his pupils newly ordained over a *small* congregation, wrote thus—' I know the vanity of your heart, and that you will feel mortified that your congregation is very small, in comparison with those of your brethren around you ; but assure yourself on the word of an old man, that when you *come to give an account of them to the Lord Christ, at his judgment-seat, you will think you have had enough.*'—Memoir of Dr Waugh, by Drs Hay and Belfrage. 1839. 8vo. Pages 64–5.

(j) P. 259.—' Salvations.' Sibbes here notes the bold and unusual expression which would seem to indicate such abundant help as meets abounding need. It is interesting to find one thus early turning from time to time to the original Hebrew as well as Greek. G.

* 'Deprave.' See *ante* page 127, line 10 from bottom.

THE SAINT'S SAFETY IN EVIL TIMES.

THE SAINT'S SAFETY IN EVIL TIMES.

NOTE.

* The 'Saint's Safety' forms a moiety of the only remaining volume published by Sibbes himself. The full title-page is given below.* These two masterly discourses form Nos. 8 and 9 of the folio, entitled 'The Saint's Cordials.' (2d edition, 1637; 3d edition, 1658). Our text follows the edition of 1633. That of 1634 is the same book with a new title.—G

* Title-page—

THE
SAINTS
SAFETIE IN
EVILL TIMES.
Delivered at St Maries in *Cambridge* the fift of *November* upon occasion of the POWDER-PLOT.
Whereunto is annexed a *Passion-Sermon*, Preached at MERCER'S CHAPPEL *London* upon Good-Friday.
As also the Happinesse of enjoying Christ laid open at the Funerall of Mr *Sherland* late Recorder of *Northampton*.
Together with the most vertuous life and Heavenly end of that Religious
GENTLEMAN.

BY

R. Sibbes, D.D., Master of *Katherine-Hall* in *Cambridge*, and Preacher at *Grayes-Inne* LONDON.
John 3. 30.
Let him increase, let me decrease.
LONDON,
Printed by M. Flesher for *R. Dawlman* at the Brazen Serpent in Pauls Church-yard. 1633.

THE SAINT'S SAFETY IN EVIL TIMES.

Behold, he travaileth with iniquity, and hath conceived mischief, and brought forth a lie.—Ps. VII. 14.

THESE be the words of David. The title shews the occasion, which was the malicious slander and cruel practices of Ahithophel or Shimei, in the time of Absalom's rebellion. The words express the *conception, birth, carriage,* and *miscarriage,* of a *plot* against David. In which you may consider, 1. What his *enemies* did. 2. What *God* did. 3. What *we all* should do: his enemies' *intention,* God's *prevention,* and our *duty;* his enemies' intention, *he travaileth with iniquity, and conceiveth mischief;* God's prevention, *he brought forth a lie;* our duty, *Behold.*

His enemy's *intention* or *action* is set out by proportion to a bodily conception. The Holy Ghost delights to present unto us the plots of wicked men under the resemblance of a bodily conception and birth, by reason of the analogy between both. The mind hath its conceptions as well as the body. The seed of this conception was some wicked thought either raised up by the heart itself, or cast in by Satan, that envious man. Not only wicked men, but their devices, are the seed of the serpent. The understanding was the womb to conceive, the will to consent. The conception was the hatching of a mischievous plot; the quickening of it was the resolution and taking it in hand; the impregnation, growing big, and travailing of it, was the carriage of it the due time; the birth itself was the execution expected, but yet miscarried and stillborn. They intended the destruction of David, but brought forth their own ruin.

1. *Quo minor necessitas peccandi, eo majus peccatum.* For the conception, observe the aggravation of the sin, he conceiveth. (1.) He was not put upon it, or forced unto it; it was voluntary. The more liberty we have not to sin, makes our sin the greater. He did not this in passion, but in cold blood. The less will, less sin. *Involuntarium minuit de ratione peccati.* Here could be no plea, because nothing is more voluntary than plotting. Where the will sets the wit a work to devise, and the body to execute mischief, it shews the spreading and largeness of sin in any man; for the will being the desire of the whole man, carries the whole man with it.

Voluntas appetitus totius suppositi. Besides, when a man sins voluntarily, there is less hope of amendment, because his will is not counselable; if the defect were in the understanding of a man, then sound direction might set it right; but where the will is set upon a thing, and is the only reason of itself (as when a man will, because he wills) there counsel will not be heard; for, tell a roving person that he is out of the way, he knows it well enough already, and means not to take your direction; but tell an honest traveller that ignorantly mistakes his way, and he will thank you. So tell a popish atheist that he is in an error, he heeds it not, because he is a papist for bye-ends, not in judgment, and resolves to be so, bring what reasons you can, his hope being to rise that way. Though the will follow some kind of understanding, yet it is in the power of the will what the understanding shall consult and determine of; and, therefore, unless the malice of the will be first taken away by grace, it will always bias our judgments the wrong way.

2. Neither was this plot only voluntary, but with delight, because it was a conception; births are with more pain. Delight carries the whole strength and marrow of the soul with it; much of the soul is where delight is.

3. Again, it was a spiritual sin. The spirit of a man is the chief seat of God's good Spirit, wherein he frames all holy devices and good desires. The spirit is either the best or the worst part in a man. Here Satan builds his nest and forges all his designs, his masterpieces, his powder-plots. The chief curse or blessing of God is upon the spirits of men. If men be raised never so high in the world, yet if they are given to a malicious and devilish spirit, they are under a most heavy judgment, carrying Satan's stamp upon them. Diseases that seize upon the spirits of men, as pestilential diseases, &c., are more deadly than those that seize upon the humours. Spiritual wickednesses are the most desperate wickednesses. Sins are more judged by the mind than by the fact.

4. And as it was a spiritual sin, so it was artificial. There was a great deal of art and cunning in it; and in evil things, the more art, the worse. Art commends other things, but it makes sin the more *sinful*. *Doli non sunt doli, ni astu colas*. When men are witty to work mischief, and wise to do evil, then they are evil in grain. It is best to be a bungler at this occupation. Ingenuous men carry their hatred open; but this plot was spun with so fine a thread as could not easily be discerned.

5. Again, they were very diligent in it, for it was a curious web. And as in weaving, head and hand, eye and foot, all go together, so here they mustered up all their wits. Judas is awake when Peter sleeps.

6. And which is worst of all, they were so well pleased with the brat of their own brain that they travailed of it. It increases guilt when men upon view and sight of their plot grow so far in love with it that they long to be delivered of it. The more the soul dwells upon any sinful plot, the more estrangement there is from God; because the happiness of the soul consists in cleaving to God the fountain of all good. The more deliberation any man takes in sinning, the more his soul is pleased with wickedness. A heart long exercised in sin will admit of no impression of grace; for the spirits are so absorbed with other designs that they are dry and dead to better things. Many thousands are in hell at this day for suffering their spirits to shove them too far into sin. Many suck out the delight of sin before they act it, as Esau pleased himself by thinking 'the day of mourning for his father would come, wherein he might be revenged of his brother,' Gen. xxvii. 41.

7. Yet this sin was not only spiritual and imminent, but transient likewise. It reached against the second table, and, therefore, against the principles of nature, and against society, out of which God gathers a church. There was false witness and murder in this sin. In this respect it is that

the sins of the second table are greater than the sins of the first, because they are against more clear light. A natural conscience hath a clearer eye in these things. Here is light upon light; for both grace and nature condemn these sins. Yet for order in sinning, the rise of all sin against man, is our sinning against God first, for none sin against men, but they sin against God in the first place, whereupon the breach of the first commandment is the ground of the breach of all the rest; for if God were set up in the heart in the first place, there parents would be honoured, and all kind of injury suppressed for conscience sake. The Scripture gives this as a cause of the notorious courses of wicked men, 'that God is not in all their thoughts,' Ps. x. 4. They forget there is a God of vengeance and a day of reckoning. The fool would needs enforce upon his heart, 'that there is no God,' Ps. xiv. 1, and what follows: 'Corrupt they are, there is none doth good, they eat up my people as bread,' &c. They make no more bones of devouring men and their estates, than they make conscience of eating a piece of bread. What a wretched condition hath sin brought man unto, that the great God who 'filleth heaven and earth,' Jer. xxiii. 24, should yet have no place in the heart which he hath especially made for himself! The sun is not so clear as this truth, that God is, for all things in the world are because God is. If he were not, nothing could be. It is from him that wicked men have that strength they have to commit sin, therefore sin proceeds from atheism, especially these plotting sins; for if God were more thought on, he would take off the soul from sinful contrivings, and fix it upon himself.

But by whom and against whom was this plotting? by children of the church, not uncircumcised Philistines. Opposition is bitterest betwixt those that are nearest, as betwixt the flesh and the spirit in the same soul, between hypocrites and true-hearted Christians in the same womb of the church. Brethren they were, but false brethren; children, but strange children. Children by the mother's side, all bred in the same church, but had not the same father. Children by the mother's side only, are commonly persecutors. Popish spirits count it presumption to know who is their father, which shews them to be bastard children. The greatest sins of all are committed within the church, because they are committed against the greatest light; whereupon that great sin against the Holy Ghost (which, like Jonah his whale, devours all at once) is not committed out of the church at all. Oh! beloved, how should we reverence the blessed truth of God and gracious motions of his Spirit! If it be sin to kill infants in the womb, what is it to kill the breed of the blessed Spirit in our hearts!

But against whom was this plot directed? Even against David, a prophet and a king, a kingly prophet, a man after God's own heart, 1 Sam. xiii. 14; Acts xiii. 22, though not according to theirs; a sacred person, and therefore inviolable. 'Touch not mine anointed, and do my prophets no harm,' Ps. cv. 15, was a prohibition from heaven. David was a man eminent in goodness, and goodness invested in greatness is a fair mark for envy to shoot at. What men for sloth care not to do, for weakness cannot, or for pride will not, imitate, that they malign, sitting cursing and fretting at the bottom of the hill, at those which they see go above them, whose life giveth witness against them. When goodness shines forth, it presently meets with envy, until it come to the height to be above envy, as the sun at the highest hath no shadow. Envy hath an ill eye. It cannot look on goodness without grief. The spirit that is in us lusteth after envy. Pursuing of goodness in men, and men for goodness, is a sin of a deep dye, because whosoever hates a man for goodness, hates goodness itself; and he that hates goodness itself hates it most in the fountain, and so becomes a hater of God himself; and if Christ were in such a man's power he should escape no better than his members do. For Christ is joined either in love or hatred with his cause and children. He and his have common friends and common enemies. Men think they have to deal with silly men, but they shall one day find that they have to deal with the great Lord of heaven and earth.

But what was the manner of carrying their design? This cruel plot was cunningly carried, for they kill him in his good name first, and accuse him as an enemy to the state, that so their slanders may make way for violence. Satan is a liar first, and then a murderer, yea therefore a liar that he may be a murderer the better. He is first a serpent, then a liar; and first a lion couchant, then a lion rampant. He teaches his scholars the same method. Cruelty marcheth furiously, and under warrant with privilege, when it hath slander to countenance it. Taint men once in the opinion of the world, and then they lie open to any usage. It is not only safe but glorious to oppose such, and thus virtue comes to have the reward due to wickedness, and passes under public hatred. The open cause and pretence is one, and the inward moving cause another, which perhaps lies hid till the day of 'revelation of the secrets of all flesh,' Rom. ii. 5, as in a clock the wheels and the hand appear openly, but the weights that move all are out of sight.

But what course took David herein? Innocency was his best apology, and when that would not do, then patience. He saw God in the wrongs he suffered, 'God bade Shimei,' &c., 2 Sam. xvi. 10. But this invites more injuries, therefore by prayer he lays open his soul to God. David's prayer prevailed more in heaven than Ahithophel's policy could do on earth. Carnal men are pregnant and full of wiles and fetches* to secure themselves, but godly men have one only refuge and hiding-place, yet that is a great one, namely, to run to God by prayer, as to their rock and tower of defence in their distresses. From all this that hath been said there ariseth these conclusions :—

First, that *even the best of God's saints are liable to be the subjects of the plots of wicked men.* (1.) From an antipathy between the two contrary seeds in them. (2.) Because God will not have his children love the world, therefore he suffers the world to hate them. (3.) They are strangers here, and therefore no wonder if they find strange entertainment from them that think themselves at home. There hath ever been from the beginning of the world a continual conspiracy of Satan and his instruments against God and goodness. Emperors and kings became Christians, but Satan never yet became a Christian, but hath always bestirred himself to maintain the first division, and never yet wanted a strong faction in the world.

Secondly, observe that *it is the character of a man wicked in an high degree, to contrive wickedness.* The reason is: (1.) Because it is a disposition of such as are given up by God to a reprobate sense, and it is reckoned among other vile sins, that they are full of maliciousness, and inventors of ill, &c. A son of Belial carries a froward heart and devises mischief, Prov. vi. 14. (2.) It shews that malice is so connatural to such, that they cannot sleep unless they cause some to fall; 'wickedness comes from the wicked' (as *naturally* and *speedily*), Prov. iv. 16, as poison from a spider. (3.) It argues such kind of men work out of a vicious habit, which is a stamping of a second ill nature upon the former, whenas their hearts are exercised

* That is, 'artifices.'—G.

to do mischief. (4.) It shews they are of the devil's trade, whose only work is to hurt and mischief all he can, those that are broken loose from him. Certainly such people as these are the children of the devil in an higher degree than ordinary. It is said, when Judas began to betray Christ, 'the devil entered into him,' Luke xxii. 3. He was the child of the devil in some degree before, but now the devil took stronger possession of him; his unnatural treason did in some sort change him into the very form of the devil. When Simon Magus sought to turn away the deputy from the faith, St Paul had no fitter terms for him than to style him, 'Thou full of all subtlety and mischief, and child of the devil,' Acts xiii. 10. And indeed there is no disposition so contrary to the sweet Spirit of God, which is a Spirit of love and goodness, as this is.

Use 1. Learn hence therefore, as you love God, to abhor this hateful disposition. The serpent indeed was 'wiser than all the beasts of the field,' Gen. iii. 1, yet when he became an instrument of mischief, he was cursed above all the rest, Gen. iii. 14. Satan labours to serve his turn of the best wits; but what greater curse can befal a man than to serve the basest creature in the basest service, and that with our best abilities? Men of a devilish spirit carry God's curse under zeal,* yea, they carry the devil in their brain, in all their works of darkness; for, alas, what should the subtilty of foxes, and fierceness of lions, and malice of devils do, in an heart dedicated to Christ? Such men work from a double principle, the illness of their own disposition within, and Satan going with the tide of that, whose chief labour is to make a prey of men of the best parts, that by them he may either snare others, or else vex them that have so much wit or grace as not to be catched by his baits. This is a course contrary to humanity as we are men, contrary to ingenuity† as we are civil men, and contrary to religion as we are Christian men, and plainly argueth that such persons are led with another spirit than their own, even by the prince that ruleth in the air.

Our care and duty, therefore, should be to submit our spirits to the sweet guidance and government of God's good Spirit, to be contented that every device and imagination of our hearts should be captivated to higher and better reasons than our own.

We are not wise enough of ourselves that our own wills and wit should be our first movers. Everything is perfected by subjection to a superior; where there should be a subordination to higher wisdom, there to withdraw our understanding and wills, is mere rebellion. That which the prophet speaks is too true of many in these days, 'Thy wisdom hath made thee to rebel,' Is. xlvii. 10. Such are too wise to be saved.

Use 2. We need not be ashamed to learn some things of our very enemies. If they be so pragmatical for evil, why should not we be as active for good? I am sure we serve a better Master. True love is full of inventions; it will be devising of good things. So soon as ever our nature is changed, the stream of the soul is turned another way, the bent of it is for God. Alas, it is a small commendation to be only passively good, and it is a poor excuse to be only passively ill. A good Christian thinks it not enough to see good done by others, but labours to have a hand in it himself; and he that suffers evil to be done, which he might have opposed and hindered, brings the guilt thereof upon his own head. 'Curse you Meroz,' saith God, 'for not helping the Lord against the mighty,' &c., Jud. v. 23. What shall we think then of those that help the mighty against the Lord, that cast oil to kindle where they should cast water to quench, that inflame the rage of

---

* Qu. 'seal?'—ED.   † That is, 'ingenuousness.'—ED.

great persons, when they should labour to reduce all to a moderation? Of this spirit was that apostate which stirred up the emperor to kill man, woman, and child of the Protestants, with all their kindred and alliance, fearing lest any living should revenge the other's quarrel.*

We see God hath stooped so low as to commend his cause unto us, as if he stood in need of our help, and usually what good he doth to us is conveyed by men like ourselves; therefore, we should labour to appear on his side, and own his cause and children. In the house of God there be vessels of all kinds. Some are of more honourable use than others. Some make the very times and places good where they live, by an influence of good. Others, as malignant planets, threaten misery and desolation wherever they come. These are the calamities of the times. Men may know whether they be vessels of mercy or no, by the use they are put to; the basest of people are fit enough to be executioners; the worst of men are good enough to be rods of God's wrath. How much better is it to be full of goodness, as the Scripture speaks of Josiah and Hezekiah, &c.! Indeed, what is a man, but his goodness? Such men live desired, and die lamented. Yea, their very 'name is as the ointment of the apothecary poured out,' Cant. i. 3. They leave a sweet savour in the church behind them.

Now I come to their miscarriage. They brought forth a lie; a lie in regard of their expectation, their hopes deceiving them, but a just defeating in regard of God. It was contrary to their desire, but agreeable to God's justice. Neither were they disappointed only so as to miss of what they intended, but they met with that misery they intended not; yea, even with that very misery which they thought to bring upon David.

This defeating ariseth by five steps: 1, they were *disappointed;* 2, they fell into *danger;* 3, they were *contrivers* of this danger *themselves;* 4, there was a penal *proportion*, they *fell* into the *same* danger which they plotted for *another;* 5, they were a means of doing *good* to him whom they devised *evil* against; and *raised* him, whom they thought to pull *down.* David sped the better for Shimei's malice, and Ahithophel's policy. See all these five likewise in the example of Haman and Mordecai. 1, Haman missed of his plot; 2, he fell into danger; 3, he fell into the same danger which he contrived himself; 4, he fell into the same danger which he contrived for Mordecai; and 5, was the means of Mordecai's advancement. It had been enough to have woven a spider's web, which is done with a great deal of art, and yet comes to nothing; but to hatch a cockatrice's egg, that brings forth a viper which stings to death, this is a double vexation. Yet thus God delighteth to catch the 'wise in the imagination of their own hearts,' Luke i. 51, and to pay them in their own coin. The wicked carry a lie in their right hand; for they trust in man, which is but a *lie;* and, being liars themselves too, no marvel if their hopes prove deceitful, so that, while they sow the wind, they reap the whirlwind, Hosea viii. 7.

Reason. (1.) The reason of God's dealing in this kind is, *first,* in regard of *himself.* God will not lose the glory of any of his attributes; he will be known to be God only wise, and this he will let appear, then especially, when wicked men think to overreach him.

(2.) Secondly, in regard of his tender care over his children, they are as the apple of his eye; and as they are very near, so they are very dear to him. They cost him dear; they are his jewels, and he gave a *Jewel* of infinite price for them. He is interested in their quarrels, and they in his.

* Qu. 'Massacre of St Bartholomew, 1572?'—G.

If they be in any misery, God's bowels yearn for them. He is always awake, and never slumbereth, as we see in the parable, the master of the house waked while the servants slept, Mat. xxv. 1, *et seq.* God's eye is upon them for good. He hath them written in the 'palms of his hands,' Isa. xlix. 16. Christ carries them always in his breast. Christ, who is the husband of his church, is Lord of heaven and earth, and hath all power committed to him, Mat. xxviii. 18, John xvii. 2, and will rule in the midst of his enemies. He is the only Monarch of the world, and makes both all things and persons serviceable to his own end and his church's good. He is higher than the highest. Satan, the god of the world, 2 Cor. iv. 4, is but his and his church's slave. All things are the church's, to further its best good.

(3.) Another reason is, *the insolence of the enemies*, whose *fierceness turns at length to God's praise*, Ps. ix. 16; for as he is a just Lord, so he will be known to be so by executing of judgment. It shall appear that there is 'a God that judgeth the earth,' Ps. lviii. 11.

(4.) Again, God's children will give him *no rest*. When he seems to sleep, they will awake him with their prayers. 'They will not let him go without a blessing from him,' Gen. xxxii. 26. They will prevail by importunity, as the widow in the gospel, Luke xviii. 5. Having to deal with a just God, in a just cause, against common enemies, his as well as theirs, they bind him with his own promises; and he is content to be bound, because he hath bound himself first. He will not lose that part of his title whereby he is known to be a 'God hearing prayers,' Ps. lxv. 2.

Obj. But it will be objected that wicked men do not only set themselves against the people of God, but prevail over them, even to the scorn of the beholders. Tully could say '*The gods shew how much they esteem of the Jewish nation, by suffering them so often to be conquered.*'* Hath not antichrist a long time prevailed, and was it not foretold that the beast should prevail? Rev. xiii. Where is, then, the *bringing forth of a lie*?

Ans. I answer, (1.) the enemies have power, but no more than is given them of God, as Christ answered Pilate, John xix. 11. They prevail indeed, but it is for a time, a limited time, and that a short one too, ten days, &c., Rev. ii. 10: and what is this to that vast time of their torment? The time will come, when there shall be no more time for them to persecute in.

(2.) Besides, even when they do prevail, it is but over part only, not over the whole. They prevail over persons, it may be, not over the cause: that stands impregnable. They prevail over men's lives, perhaps, but not over their spirits, which is that they chiefly aim at. A true Christian conquers when he is conquered. Stephen prevailed over his enemies when they seemed to prevail over him. God put glory upon him, and a spirit of glory into him, Acts vii.

(3.) The church's enemies may prevail in some place, but then, as the sea, they lose in another. The more they cut down God's people, as Pharaoh did the Israelites, the more they multiply; and the more they are kept straight,† the more they spread and are enlarged. God suffers the enemies of his truth to prevail, in some passages, to harden their hearts the more for destruction, as Pharaoh prevailed in oppressing the Israelites,

---

* This is one of only two notices of the Jews, that are found in the voluminous works of Cicero. It occurs in Orat. Pro L. Flacco, c. 28. As Sibbes rather paraphrases than translates, the true and vivid original may be given:—'.... Nunc vero hoc magis, quod illa gens, quid de imperio, nostro sentiret ostendit armis; quam cara Diis immortalibus esset, docuit, quod est victa, quod elocata, quod servata.'—G.

† Qu. 'strait?'—ED.

and Herod in killing John, &c. But yet, lay the beginning and the end together, and then we shall see they prevailed not, and so far as they did prevail, it tended only to hasten their own ruin, because the present success lifts up the heart. We see antichrist prevailed, but spiritually, only over those 'whose names were not written in the Lamb's book of life,' Rev. xiii. 7, and outwardly over the saints; for so it was prefixed, Rev. xviii. 24, that he should *make war* with the saints, *and overcome them:* and this was objected as a fiery dart against the Christians in those times, that therefore they might think their cause naught, because they were so prevailed over;* but they, by help of the Spirit of God, understood so much of the Revelation as concerned themselves, and used this as a weapon, confessing that they were the conquered people of God, but yet the people of God still. But the chief stay and satisfaction of the soul herein, is to look to the day of the righteous judgment of God, when we shall see all promises performed, all threatenings executed, and all enemies trodden for ever under Christ and his church's feet.

Use 1. This is a point of marvellous comfort, when Israel can say, 'They have afflicted me from my youth, but yet they have not prevailed over me,' Ps. cxxix. 1. The gates of hell may set themselves against the church, but shall not prevail. The church is not ruled by man's counsel. We neither live nor die at man's appointment. Our lives are not in our own hands, or Satan's, or our enemies', but in God's. They can do no more, they shall do no less, than God will, who is our life, and the length of our days. God may give way a while, that the 'thoughts of many may be revealed,' Luke ii. 35, and that his glory may shine the more in raising his children, and confounding his enemies; but he will put a period in his due time, and that is the best time. There is a day of Jacob's trouble, when his enemies say, 'This is Sion, whom none regards,' Jer. xxx. 7; but God sets bounds both to the time of his children's trouble, and to the malice of the wicked. 'Their rod shall not rest over-long upon the back of the righteous,' Ps. cxxv. 3. God will put a *hook into the nostrils* of these leviathans, and draw them which way he pleaseth.

Use 2. Again, we see here that mischievous attempts are successless in the end; for did ever any harden themselves against God and prosper long? Let Cain speak, let Pharaoh, Haman, Ahithophel, Herod; let the persecutors of the church for the first two hundred years; let all that ever bore ill-will towards Sion, speak, and they will confess they did but kick against the pricks, and dash against the rocks. The greatest torment of the damned spirit is, that God turns all his plots for the good of those he hates most. He tempted man to desire *to become like God*, Gen iii. 5, that so he might ruin him; but God *became man*, and so restored him. God serveth himself of this archpolitician and all his instruments; they are but executioners of God's will while they rush against it. Joseph's brethren sold him that they might not worship him, and that was the very means whereby they came at length to worship him. God delights to take the oppressed party's part. Wicked men cannot do God's children a greater pleasure than to oppose them, for by this means they help to advance them.

Why wicked plots miscarry. The ground of the miscarriage of wicked plots is, that Satan and his, maintain a damned cause, and their plots are under a curse. Every one that prays, 'Thy kingdom come,' prays by consequence against them as opposers of it; and how can the men and plots of so many curses but miscarry, and prove but as the untimely fruit of a

* Cicero, *ante*.—G.

woman? They are like the grass on the house-top, which perks above the corn in the field, but yet no man prays for a blessing upon it. When men come by a goodly corn-field, every one is ready to say, God bless this field, &c. Beloved, it is a heavier thing than atheistical spirits think of, to be under the curse of the church; for as God blesseth out of Sion, so usually the heaviest curses come out of Sion. Woe be to the Herods and Julians of the world, when the church, either directly or indirectly, prays against them.

Use 3. This is a ground of staying the souls of God's people in seeming confusion of things. There is an harmony in all this discord. God is fitting his people for a better condition even when they are at the worst, and is hardening and preparing the wicked for confusion, even when they are at the best. 'The wicked practise against the righteous, but God laugheth them to scorn,' Ps. ii. 4; for he seeth all their plottings, and his day is a-coming. Whilst they are digging pits for others, there is a pit a-digging and a grave a-making for themselves. They have a measure to make up, and a treasure to fill, which at length will be broken open, which, methinks, should take off them which are set upon mischief from pleasing themselves in their plots. Alas! they are but plotting their own ruin, and building a Babel which will fall upon their own heads. If there were any commendation in plotting, then that great plotter of plotters, that great engineer, Satan, would go beyond us all, and take all the credit from us. But let us not envy Satan and his in their glory. They had need of something to comfort them. Let them please themselves with their trade. The day is coming wherein the daughter of Sion shall laugh them to scorn. There will be a time wherein it shall be said, 'Arise, Sion, and thrash,' Micah iv. 13. And usually the delivery of God's children is joined with the destruction of his enemies; Saul's death, and David's deliverance; the Israelites' deliverance, and Egyptians' drowning. The church and her opposites are like the scales of a balance; when one goes up, the other goes down.

Haman's wife had learned this, that if her husband began once to fall before the Jews, he should surely fall. Wicked men have an hour, and they will be sure to take it; and God hath his hour too, and will be as sure to take that. The judgments of the wicked are mercies to the church. So saith David, 'He slew mighty kings, Og king of Bashan, for his mercy endureth for ever,' &c., Ps. cxxxvi. 20.

God hath but two things in the world that he much regardeth; his truth, and his church, begotten by his truth;* and shall we think that he will suffer long, wretched men who turn that wit and power which they have from him against his truth and church? No, assuredly; but he will give them up by that very wit of theirs, to work their own destruction; they shall serve their turn most whom they hate most. God sits in heaven, and laughs them to scorn. Shall God laugh, and we cry? They take counsel together on earth, but God hath a counsel in heaven that will overthrow all their counsels here. Mark the bitter expressions in Scripture, 'Why do the heathen rage,' Ps. ii. 1, without fear or wit? 'Go to now, saith God, gather a council,' &c., Isa. viii. 9. Beloved, it goes to the heart of proud persons to be scorned, especially in the miscarriage of that which they count their masterpiece; they had rather be counted devils than fools. Let us *work wisely*, saith Pharaoh, when he was never more fool, Exod. ii. 10. They usurp upon God, and promise themselves great

* 'God hath but two things,' &c. This sentiment, which is repeated in the 'Fountain Sealed,' is quoted by Bishop Patrick in his 'Friendly Debate,' against Bridge. See Taylor's edition of Patrick, vol. v. pp. 509–10.—G.

matters for the time to come, whereas that is only God's prerogative, and they neither know what the womb of their counsels, nor what the womb of to-morrow, may bring forth. That which they are big of may prove an abortive, or a viper to consume the womb that bred it. 'Go to now,' saith the prophet, 'all ye that kindle a fire: walk in the light of your fire, but take this of me, you shall lie down in sorrow,' &c., Isa. li. 11. The Scripture is full of such expostulations and upbraidings. 'Man is become like one of us, saith God,' Gen. iii. 22. When men will have a way of their own, and think themselves wiser than God, then it stands upon God's honour to outwit them. 'Yet God is wise,' saith the prophet, Isa. xxxi. 2. You think to go beyond God. Deceive not yourselves. *God is wise*, and you shall find him to be so. He hath a way to go beyond you. Do not many men spin a fine thread, and weave a fair web, when by their turnings and devices they turn themselves into hell? 'Woe be to them that dig deep,' saith the prophet, 'and think to hide their counsels from the Lord,' Hosea ix. 2, 3. God hath an eye to see into the most secret and dark conveyances of business. God hath a key to open the closet of their hearts, let them be never so close locked up. Oh, that men would more fear this all-seeing eye of God, and be wise for themselves, and not against themselves. It is a miserable wisdom when men are wise to work their own ruin. Beloved, when men have had all their plots, God hath a plot still beyond them. He takes them failing in something or other. Their devices are like a curious clock; if the least thing be out of frame, all is marred. God suffers them to spin a fine thread a great while, and at length cuts the web, and there is an end. And they may thank themselves for all this, for they carry a justification of God in their own breasts. They perish because they will perish; and this will be the torment of all torments to graceless persons, that they pulled destruction upon themselves. Malice blinds the understanding in Satan and his instruments; for, if their malice were not above their wit, would they, to gratify their ill affections, knowingly rush into the displeasure of God, and into such courses as will unavoidably bring their ruin? Malice drinks up the greatest part of its own poison. 'His own iniquity shall take the wicked himself,' saith Solomon, 'and he shall be holden with the cords of his own sin,' Prov. v. 22.

This may be enlarged to all sinful courses. Every sinner worketh a deceitful work, and *bringeth forth a lie*. Augustine saith well, *every sin is a lie* (*a*). Men would be happy, yet they will not live so as they may be happy; what more deceitful than this? It will be the complaint of every sinner at length, that was Eve's, the 'serpent hath deceived me,' Gen. iii. 13. It was St Paul's complaint, Rom. viii. 8, and it will be the complaint of all sinful wretches at the last day. What hath pride profited us? what can the favour of men, upon whom we bear ourselves, do us good now? Sin promiseth us contentment, continuance, secresy, full satisfaction, &c., but doth it make good this? Were ever any, when the beginning and ending was laid together, established by wickedness? Take it from God himself (we have a commission to speak it),' Say, it shall not go well with the wicked, though they escape an hundred times,' Eccl. viii. 12, 13, yet it is but a reprieval for some further service which God hath to do by them. 'Be not deceived, God is not mocked,' Gal. vi. 7. When we can be more subtle than the devil, or more strong than God, we may think to thrive by sin. Can we think God will alter the course of divine justice for us? had we not better believe this than find it so hereafter? Beloved, hell is for those to feel that will not believe. Certain it is, that those who will sin, notwithstanding God's justice, shall be severely punished, notwithstanding his mercy. God is not more peremptory in any one thing than in this, ' If any man bless himself in an ill way, my wrath shall smoke against him,' Deut. xxix. 19, 20 ; therefore it is a good prayer, Lord, *give me not over to lying*, that is, not to trust in that which will lie and deceive me.

This is the unhappiness of us ministers, all other professions are believed when they discover danger, but ' who believeth our report?' Isa. liii. 1. We are men's ' enemies, because we tell them the truth,' Gal. iv. 16 ; we labour to take away the sweet morsels from men, their Herodiases (*b*), and to divide betwixt men and their sins, which they love better than their souls. No creature but man, loves that which will be its own bane. Only wretched man seeks happiness in the way to misery, and heaven in the way to hell. I beseech you therefore, as you would not be deceived, (as indeed who would?) take heed of the deceitful works of darkness. Satan that tempts us is but a lying spirit (which he is not ashamed to confess), 1 Kings xxii. 22, and sin is like unto him. What got Ahab by his vineyard ? Judas by his thirty pieces of silver ? what got Haman, and so of the rest, by their sins at the last ? Men are usually ashamed of an ill bargain, because the very thought thereof upbraids them with weakness and folly. Whatever we get by sin for the present, it will prove the worst bargain that ever we made. Oh, therefore, let us use our wits and parts to better purpose ; if we will needs be plotting, let us plot for eternity ; that is worth the plotting for. Let us plot how to avoid Satan's plot. Our time is short, opportunity, the flower of time, shorter. Our talents are many, our accounts strict, our judge unpartial. Let us be ' sowing to the Spirit,' Gal. vi. 8 ; let us labour to be like our Judge, who went about doing his Father's work, John xvii. 4, and came to destroy the works of the devil, 1 John iii. 8. Oh, beloved, shall we build up that which Christ came to destroy ? All his miracles tended to good ; he wrought the salvation of those that wrought his destruction ; he shed his blood for those that shed his blood. Satan is all for mischief, and rather than he will not do hurt, he is content to be set about drowning of swine, Mark v. 14. And such are all those that are led with his spirit, men witty to destroy and acute to malice others, who take a great deal of pains to go to hell and carry others with them. Those that are skilful in the story of nature, write of the scorpion, that he whets his tail often upon stones, that so it may be sharp and ready for a mischief. Some crooked wits there are which make it their exercise to vex the quiet of the land ; it is as natural to them as poison to a scorpion.

But our happiness is, how to be like the idea, the pattern of all grace, and the glory of our nature, by whom we hope to be saved. Our happiness is to bring forth fruit, and our own fruit ' in due season,' Ps. i. 3 ; to have opportunity, ability, and a heart to do good. How comfortable is death when it takes men so doing ? The time will be ere long, when it will comfort us above all things in the world besides, that we have been honoured to be instruments of doing good, and stood in the gap to hinder evil. Beloved, we serve a good master. We shall not lose a good word for a good cause. There is a ' book of remembrance, Mal, iii. 16, for every good word and work we do. When wicked men have beaten their brains, spent their spirits, and wasted their strength, what becomes of them at length ? A conscience often wounded will receive no comfort, but take God's part against itself. When the other powers are wearied, then conscience comes and doth its office ; then the eyes of the soul are open to see what it would not see before, then sin that ' lay at the door,' Gen. iv. 7 (*c*), at the going out of this life, flieth in our faces. Pleasure and profit, for which wicked men project and contrive so much, comes all to nothing ; but sin itself, and the punishment of it, abides for ever. Men, like popes, will dispense with themselves, and conceit a latitude and breadth in their courses, that they may do so and so, and yet do well at last, but who tells them this ? Is it not a spirit of illusion ? Indeed, punishment is often deferred ; it comes not like thunder and lightning all at once, yet as sure as God is true, sin will be bitterness in the end. When the honey is gone, the sting will remain.

To conclude this point ; when we are tempted to any hurtful design, let us look upon Christ, and that great project for our redemption undertaken by him, and reason thus with ourselves : hath he plotted and wrought my salvation, and shall I plot against him in his members ?

I beseech you, stir up your hearts to conceive and bring forth good purposes. Satan is an enemy to all strong resolutions and masculine conceptions, endeavouring to kill them in the very birth. Alas, how many good thoughts are conceived whilst the word is hearing, which yet prove abortive and stick in the birth ! How few actions come to their due ripeness and perfection ! I am sure our encouragements to good are far more than our encouragements to evil. We serve a better master, and for better wages. They may prosper for a time, but nothing is more wretched than the happiness of wicked men ; it first hardens them, and then destroys them, Prov. i. 32.

Our only way is, 1, to get into Christ ' the true vine,' John xv. 1, then we shall take and bear fruit presently, and draw and suck out of him the same disposition.

2. And then lay up good principles, and look with a single eye to the main end of our life, and see that all the particular passages of our life tend to that. It is an argument of a narrow heart to be wise in some particular business, for some particular end, and yet to be careless in the main. Other creatures are carried by a particular instinct to some particular thing. A spider is witty to catch flies, a bird to build nests, &c. As man hath larger parts, so he should have larger aims.

That which we should especially labour for is, 1, to be good in ourselves ; and 2, to do all the good we can to others, even as God our Father is good, and doth good ; and the further our good extends, the more we resemble our Father. Such as we are, such are our thoughts, such are our devices. A good man will devise of liberal things, &c. Every vermin can do mischief. We see some are never in their element but when they are plotting or working mischief, as if they were born for no other end but to exercise the graces of men better than themselves. It is a poor commendation to be counted a cunning person for self ends. Alas ! the heart of man, which is ' deceitful above measure,' Jer. xvii. 9, hath abundance of turnings and windings in it, and can suggest tricks enough to circumvent the best of us.

I come, in the third place, to our duty, which is to ' behold,'—the ordinary beacon kindled to discover some extraordinary thing.

Quest. But what is here to be beheld ?

Ans. Behold the subtlety, malice, and restless endeavour of the enemies of goodness. Is it not a matter with grief to be beheld, that one member should tear another ? that one, professing the same religion, should study to supplant and devour another ? Behold, likewise, their bootless enterprise, *they bring forth a lie.*

But especially behold the mercy of God to his children ; his wisdom in discovering, his justice in confounding, the mischievous practices of their enemies, making them the workers of their own ruin.

The things which especially deserve our beholding are either, 1, things excellent, and so are all God's works in their season, yea, justice itself; or, 2, things rare, as comets and eclipses; or else, 3, great things, as stars of the first magnitude, &c.

Even such, and much more, is God's mercy to his children, and justice against his enemies. Behold what great things he hath done for them, Ps. cxxvi. 2. Shall the heathen say so, and shall not Israel much more? Beloved, we ought to seek out God's works, and shall we not take notice of them when they are offered to our view? This is especially the duty of the saints of God. 'All thy works praise thee, and thy saints bless thee,' saith David, Ps. cxlv. 10. The works of God praise him by our mouths and by our tongues. Were it not for some few that by a more divine light and spiritual eye see more of God than others do, what glory should God have in the world? God hath not brought us on the stage of this world to be mere gazers, but to extract something out for our own use, and to give him the glory of his excellencies. But we are too wise to admire anything. It is a matter too mean for our parts to take notice of God and his works. You have some that can see nothing in the works of God worth the admiring; and yet they will have men's persons in admiration, in hope of some advantage by them. We are apt to admire any outward excellency, like the disciples, before the Holy Ghost came upon them, who stood admiring of the goodly stones of the temple. When our minds are thus taken up, it were good if we heard Christ speaking to us as he did to them, 'Are these the things you wonder at?' Mark xiii. 1.

Beloved, it is our duty to observe special occurrences, not out of any Athenian curiosity, but to begin our employment in heaven now, whilst we are upon earth; to take occasion from thence to bless God. We should compare the rule and the event together, and observe what truth or attribute God makes good by that which is so fallen out; see how God commenteth upon himself by his own actions; and from observation of particulars it is good to rise to generals, as Deborah from the destruction of one enemy to the destruction of all. 'So let all thy enemies perish, O Lord,' Judges v. 31. This was Moses's song, and Hannah's, and the Virgin Mary's, &c. They mounted from a consideration of their own particular, and had their thoughts enlarged with the mercy and justice of God, to others in succeeding generations.

And among all God's works we should more take notice of his mercy to the church than of his justice towards his enemies, because his justice is, as it were, a foil to give lustre to his mercy. God delighteth more in mercy, as being his proper work, issuing from his own bowels, than in works of justice that are occasioned by the malice of men. God is wonderful in his saints, and more in saving them than in destroying his enemies. Considering, therefore, that mercy bears the chief office in the great works of God, we ought to dwell most in consideration thereof, and feed our thoughts more with the meditation of his saving works to his church than of the ruin of his enemies.

We pray *hallowed be thy name.* Unless we practise what we pray for, we mock God, and deceive our own souls. Let not God lose any glory by us; let not us lose such a pledge of future happiness as glorifying God is. 'Oh that men would praise the Lord,' saith David, who, fearing lest God should lose any glory from his creatures, stirs up angels and all creatures to 'bless the Lord,' Ps. cxlviii. 2, 3. God takes it very unkindly when we do not observe especially, the excellent pieces of his workmanship. 'A fool considereth not this,' &c., Ps. xcii. 6.

The Lord hath done marvellous things for his church of late, whereof we should rejoice. We should do as Moses did when he came out of the sea, and as the church, in resemblance of that deliverance from Egypt, did, who sang the song of Moses, being delivered from their spiritual Pharaoh, Rev. xv. 3.

We see now the vial poured upon the sun, we see the prophecies against antichrist's kingdom in fulfilling. God hath vouchsafed to strengthen our faith by experience. We have something to lay hold on, which may encourage us to expect more from God, and to look for those hallelujahs to be sung from all creatures in heaven and earth, upon the utter confusion of antichrist; which, whosoever labours to hinder any kind of way, hinders the glory of God, and the joy of his people.

It is good to observe how the Scripture sets out the enemies of God's church, in a double representation, 1, as terrible, terming them lions, bulls, &c.; 2, as base, comparing them to chaff and dust before the wind, dung, &c., Ps. x. 4, that when we see them in their present ruff and jollity, we should stay ourselves with consideration of their future baseness. Faith looks on things as present, because it looks upon them in the word of Jehovah, who will give a being to all his promises and threatenings; and therefore faith is called the subsistence of 'things not seen,' Heb. xi. 1, (*d*) because it gives a kind of being of things to the mind and affections of man, as if they were present. Therefore the believing of the final deliverance of God's people, and the ruin of his enemies, cannot but raise up the souls of good men to a marvellous degree of joy and thankfulness to God. Who would not fear to cleave to antichrist, if they did but present to themselves by faith, the certain ruin of that state, which the Scripture sets down, in a prophetical manner, as a thing already present? 'Babylon is fallen,' &c., Rev. xviii. 2.

But to come to a more particular application, suitable to the present time. The occasion and the text are as parallel as may be. Our gunpowder-plotters (*e*) were as pregnant in mischief as ever these. For conception, it could not but come from beneath the vault. There was the very quintessence of devilishness in it. Satan emptied all his bowels, as it were, in this project. If all the devils in hell were set awork to devise the like, they could hardly do it. There was scarce from the beginning of the world, a design more prodigious and unmerciful, of greater depth and extent of villany. Were [it] not [for] this anniversary commemoration of it, posterity would hardly believe that a plot so hellish could be hatched in the hearts of men, of English men, of Catholic men, as they would be termed, of men so borne withal, notwithstanding their dangerous correspondency with foreign enemies, and but half subjects, their better parts, their spirits, being subject to another visible head, who can untie the bond of allegiance at his pleasure.

Neither did they only conceive this hellish wickedness, but were big of it, and kept it close many months, and pleased themselves in the same, as monstrous and misshapen as it was. There wanted neither wit, nor counsel, nor combination, nor secret encouragement to effect it.

Nay, it was an holy villany, sealed with oaths, sacrament, and all the bonds of secrecy that could be invented. Oh horrible profanation, to set God's seal to Satan's plot. But God, who delighteth to confound all presumptuous attempts, discovered it when it should have come to the birth, and so it proved but the untimely fruit of a woman.

They *brought forth a lie,* for whereas they intended to have blown up king and kingdom, churchmen and church, statesmen, yea, the whole state itself, all at once, without any warning to prepare themselves for another world, they not only missed of this, but brought that ruin upon themselves which they intended to others; whereas they thought for ever to have established their (religion, shall I call it, or idolatry, or) superstition, they have by this means made it more odious than ever before; as the northern gentleman could say, that though he was not able to dispute, yet he had two arguments against popery, equivocation and the gunpowder-treason. But they turn it off easily, as they think. Alas! it was but the plot of a company of unfortunate gentlemen. It was our happiness that they were unfortunate; whereas if it had succeeded well, they would have had other terms for it. Successful villany goeth for virtue.

Well, the net is broken, and we are delivered. God thought of us when we thought not of him, and awaked for us when we were asleep (here is a place for *behold*), for what a miserable face of things would there have been if their plot had succeeded!

Now what return shall we make for all this? They conceived mischief, let us conceive praise, and travail of holy resolutions to give up ourselves to God, who hath given us our king, our state, yea, ourselves to ourselves. He hath given us our lives more than once, every one of us in particular, especially in the last heavy visitation.* But had it not been better for many in regard of their own particular, to have been swept away in that deluge, than to live longer to treasure up further wrath to themselves? Many are not content to go to hell alone, but they will draw as many others as they can into their fellowship here, and torment hereafter. Oh beloved, the preservation of such, is but a reservation to further judgment! What good got the king of Sodom by being delivered once, and then after to be consumed with 'fire and brimstone from heaven? Gen. xix. What got Pharaoh by being delivered from ten plagues, and then to perish in the sea? Exod. xiv. What are all our temporal deliverances, if we live still in sin, go on in sin, die in our sins, and so perish eternally? Blessings, without return of due thanks, increase the guilt of sin, and the increase of guilt causeth the increase of judgments.

The most proper homogeneal way of thanks, is to stir up ourselves to a greater hatred of that religion. They would fain free it, as if it were the fault of some persons only; but alas! what can be else distilled from those dangerous points they hold (as that, *the pope hath temporal jurisdiction over princes, that he may excommunicate them; that he may, out of fulness of power, dispense with the oath of allegiance: that he cannot err; that subjection to him is a point of absolute necessity to salvation, &c.*) What, I say, can be distilled from these opinions, but treason in a people that live under a prince of a contrary religion? The dispositions of many of them are better than their positions.

However perhaps the present pope† may be more moderate and neutral, yet this is the infusion of their religion wherever it prevails, and these tenets shall be acted and in full force when they please, and it will please them when it shall be for the advantage of the Catholic cause. This was Bellarmine's tenet, *If the pope should err in commanding vice or forbidding virtue, the church is bound to believe vice to be good, and virtue to be ill, or*

---

* The plague.—G.   † Urban VIII *(f).*—G.

else it should sin against conscience; for it is bound to believe what he commands.* Thus they make the judgment of man the rule of truth and falsehood, good and evil; whereas truth is truth, and that which is false is false, whether men think so or no. There is an intrinsical evil in evil, which the judgment of any man cannot take away; and the truth and goodness of things stands upon eternal grounds, not flexible or alterable by the will of any creature; otherwise it were all one as to think the course of the sun should be guided by a dial. Is there any hope of their coming to us when they had rather have the rules of nature and religion, which are as unmoveable as a mountain of brass, to vary, than be thought to confess that the pope may err! which indeed is the grand and leading error of all. But how should we expect our words should prevail, whenas the great works of God prevail not at all with them? The efficacy of error is so strong in many, that though they should see the vial poured out 'upon the throne of the beast,' Rev. xvi. 10, yet will they not repent.

For ourselves, we cannot better shew our thankfulness for this deliverance, by means whereof we enjoy our lives and our religion, than to preserve that truth, that is grounded upon the foundation of truth, which hath been derived unto us from those that went before, who held out the same truth; that hath been sealed by the blood of so many martyrs; that hath been established by the authority of gracious princes; that God hath given witness to by so many deliverances; that concurs with the confessions of all reformed churches; that God hath blessed with a constant tenor of peace, even to the rejoicing of all neighbour churches, to the envy of our enemies, and to the admiration of all.

We see all countries round about us in a confusion, and we, as it were the 'three young men in the fiery furnace,' safe, Dan. iii., without so much as smoke or smell of fire; as if we were the only people of God's delight. Now, what is that which God careth most for amongst us, but his truth? which, if we suffer, as much as in us lieth, to take any detriment, God may justly make us the spectacles of his wrath to others, as others have been to us. Beloved, God hath a cause and a people in the world, which he esteemeth more than all the world besides. Let us therefore own God's cause and people; his side one day will prove the better side.

I beseech you consider, what hurt have we ever had by the Reformation of religion? hath it come naked unto us? hath it not been attended with peace and prosperity? hath God 'been a barren wilderness to us?' Jer. ii. 31. Hath not God been a wall of fire about us? which, if he had not been, it is not the water that compasseth our island could have kept us. So long as we keep Christ's truth, Christ will keep us. Otherwise, trust to it, Christ and his truth will leave us. No nation under heaven hath so much cause to say 'Behold' as we have. Men are ready upon all occasions to be sensible of civil grievances (as in Solomon's time gold was as stones in the street, 2 Chron. i. 15, ix. 27), but we should be sensible of the spiritual favours we enjoy. If we look upon other kingdoms abroad, what nation under heaven hath the like cause to bless God for religion, for prince, for peace, &c., as we have? Beloved, we cannot better deserve of our king, church, and state, than to give up our lives to God who hath thus blessed us. The greatest enemies of a church and state, are those that provoke the highest Majesty of heaven, by obstinate courses against the light that shineth in their own hearts. It is seriously to be considered what Samuel saith to the people; and therefore, if not for love of our-

---

* See original in note *g*.—G.

selves, yet for the love of our king, religion, and state, let us take heed of provoking courses, and take heed of tiring the patience of God over-long. To conclude all, it is prayer that gets, but thankfulness witnessed by obedience that keeps, blessings. And what can our thoughts devise, our tongues utter, or our lives express, better, than the praise of our good God, that ever loadeth us with his benefits? that so God may delight still to shew himself unto us in the ways of his mercy, and think thoughts of love towards us, and dwell amongst us to the world's end.

NOTES.

(a) P. 306.—Augustine saith well, every sin is a lie. From De Civitate Dei, xlv. iv. 1, ' Unde non frustra dici potest, omne peccatum esse mendacium.'

(b) P. 307.—' Sweet morsels . . . . their Herodians.' This is probably a misprint for Herodiases, and the reference to Mat. xiv. 3, 6, Mark vi. 17, 22.

(c) P. 307.—' Sin . . . lay at the door,' Gen. iv. 7. For very interesting remarks on this passage, in the sense of Sibbes's quotation, consult Kalisch *in loc*, specially page 139 (Hist. and Critical Commentary on Old Testament . . . Genesis. 1858).

(d) P. 310.—' The *subsistence* of things not seen,' Heb. xi. 1. $ὑπόστασις$ is rendered ' substance ' in our authorised version. Professor Sampson of America *in loc* accepts Sibbes's translation, and observes, ' It is not only true of faith, that it is a " firm persuasion " of the existence of such things, but that it gives them, so to speak, "*present subsistence.*" It gives them the force of present realities. This sense, therefore, includes the other, and is for this reason preferable, that, while it expresses all that is expressed by the other, it gives more fulness and strength to the apostle's words ' (Critical Commentary on Hebrews. New York, 1856).

(e) P. 310.—' Our gunpowder plotters.' Sibbes preached numerous sermons on the anniversary of the memorable conspiracy known by the name of ' the gunpowder plot.' It was so designated from its design having been, by springing a mine under the Houses of Parliament, to destroy the three estates of the realm. It was discovered on Nov. 5th. 1605. An excellent summary of the facts will be found in a small volume dedicated to ' the plot,' by the Rev. Thomas Lathbury of Bristol, and a full ' history ' in the standard work of David Jardine, Esq.

(f) P. 311.—' The present pope . . . . Urban VIII.' Consult Ranké (History of the Popes, ii. 104, *seq.*) for the extraordinary career of this very remarkable pope. His bearing toward England at the time of Sibbes's sermon explains the halffavourable opinion expressed. He was raised to the tiara in 1623, and died in 1644.

(g) P. 311.—This extraordinary quotation will be found in Bellarmine, De Pontifice, book iv. c. 5—' Si autem Papa erraret præcipiendo vitia vel prohibendo virtutes, teneretur Ecclesia credere vitia esse bona et virtutes malas, nisi vellet contra conscientiam peccare.' G.

THE SAINT'S SAFETY IN EVIL TIMES:*

MANIFESTED BY ST PAUL, FROM HIS EXPERIENCE OF GOD'S GOODNESS IN GREATEST DISTRESSES.

Notwithstanding the Lord stood with me, and strengthened me, that by me the preaching might be fully known, and that all the Gentiles might hear: and I was delivered out of the mouth of the lion. And the Lord shall deliver me from every evil work, and will preserve me unto his heavenly kingdom; to whom be glory for ever and ever. Amen.—2 TIM. IV. 17, 18.

BLESSED St Paul, being now an old man, and ready to sacrifice his dearest blood for the sealing of that truth which he had carefully taught, sets down in this chapter what diverse entertainment he found, both from God and man, in the preaching of it. As for men, he found they dealt most unfaithfully with him, when he stood most in need of comfort from them. Demas, a man of great note, in the end forsook him; Alexander the coppersmith (thus it pleases God to try his dearest ones with base oppositions of worthless persons) did him most mischief; weaker Christians forsook him, &c. But mark the wisdom of God's Spirit in the blessed apostle, in regard of his different carriage towards these persons. Demas, because his fault was greater, by reason of the eminency of his profession, him he brands to all posterity, for looking back to Sodom and to the world, after he had put his hand to the plough. Alexander's opposing, because it sprung from extremity of malice towards the profession of godliness, him he curseth. 'The Lord reward him,' &c. Weaker Christians, who failed him from want of some measure of spirit and courage, retaining still a hidden love to the cause of Christ, their names he conceals, with prayer that God would not lay their sin to their charge. But whilst Paul lived in this cold comfort on earth, see what large encouragement had he from heaven! 'Though all forsook me, yet,' says he, 'God did not forsake me, but stood by me, and I was delivered out of the mouth of the lion. And the Lord will deliver me,' &c.

In the words, we have, in Paul's example, an expressing of that general truth set down by himself: 'And not only so, but we glory in tribulations

---

* In the 'Saint's Cordial's' editions of this sermon, it is said to have been 'preached at Paul's Crosse, upon a speciall solemne occasion, Aug. 5.'—G.

also, knowing that tribulation worketh patience; and patience, experience; and experience, hope,' &c., Rom. v. 3. So here affliction breeds experience of God's mercy in our deliverance, and experience breeds hope of deliverance for the time to come; and both his experience and hope stirs him up to glorify God, who was his deliverer; so that here offer unto us to be unfolded—

1. Paul's *experience of God's loving care of him in his deliverance past.*
2. *His assured hope, built upon his experience, for the time to come;* set down in two branches:
   (1.) *The Lord will deliver me from every evil work.*
   (2.) *He will preserve me to his heavenly kingdom.*
3. *The issue he maketh of both; as they flow from God's grace, so he ascribes him the glory of both.* 'To whom be glory for ever and ever. Amen.'

For the first, I find that most, both ancient and modern writers, by *lion* understand Nero, that cruel tyrant, thirsty of blood, especially of Christians (*h*). Some also understand it to be a proverbial speech, to express extremity of danger, both which are true. But if we take the words in the just breadth of the apostle's intent, we may by lion understand *the whole united company of his cruel enemies*, as David in many places hath the like; and, by the mouth of the *lion*, the present danger he was in by reason of their cruel malice. Whence observe:

1. *That enemies of the truth are (oft for power, always for malice) lions.*
2. *That God suffers his dearest children to fall into the mouths of these lions.*
3. *That in this extremity of danger God delivers them.*

For the second, his hope built upon his experience; both* branches thereof hath its limitation and extent. The Lord shall deliver me, not from evil suffering, but from evil works. This he could boldly build on. He could not conjecture what he should suffer, because that was in the power of others; but he could build upon this, what God would give him grace to do. And so he limits his confidence, 'He will deliver me from evil works, and he will preserve me.' From what? From danger? from death? No; here is the limitation: 'He will preserve me to his heavenly kingdom.' He will not preserve me from death (and yet he will do that whilst I can do his service by my life), but sure I am he will preserve me beyond death to a state of security and happiness. 'He will preserve me to his heavenly kingdom.'

And then for the third. After his experience, confidence, and hope well built, as his fashion is, when his heart was once warmed, he breaks out into *thanksgiving*, in the consideration of God's favours past, and to come. His tongue is large thereupon, and God hath the fruit of it. 'To whom be glory for ever;' and lastly, he seals up all with the word, 'Amen.'

'I was delivered out of the mouth of the lion,' &c. Beloved, by nature we are all lions, and nothing will alter us, save the effectual knowledge of Christ. Education may civilise, but not subdue. A sound knowledge of God's truth hath a changing power; for when the spirit becomes tender, and when the heart, which lies in a cursed estate, under and in danger of, the wrath of a just God, whose eye cannot spare iniquity unrepented of, is cited and affrighted effectually by the spirit of bondage, it will cast down, and pull sorrow from the strongest spirit, making it melting and tender. Again, in this estate, when the soul hath felt favour shining upon it; when

* That is, 'each of the' branches.—G.

the eye is opened to see the high prerogatives and exceeding riches of Christ; when we find ourselves that we are delivered from the lion's mouth, we cannot but shew that pity to others, which we felt from God ourselves. Paul thirsts as eagerly after the conversion of others now, as ever he did for their blood before, Acts ix. 22. The jailor also, a man by nature, custom, and calling, hardened in the practice of cruelty, Acts xvi. 83; yet after he had felt the power of God's blessed truth, shewed forth those bowels of pity he felt from Christ, which were shut before (*i*).

Let us then be thankful, that God hath changed us from being lions, and with meekness submit ourselves unto God's ordinances, desiring him to write his law, not only in our understandings, but in our very hearts and bowels, that we may not only know that we should walk harmless and full of good, Jer. xxxi. 83, but be so indeed, resembling him by whom we hope to be saved, in a right serviceable pliableness to all duties of love.

And because our imperfect measure of mortification in this life, hinders us from a full content in one another's communion, let this make us the more willing to be translated to God's holy mount, where, being purged from all such lusts as hinder our peace and love, we shall fully enjoy one another, without the least falseness or distrust. Then shall we see total accomplishment of these promises, which are but in part fulfilled in this life.

Obs. 1. That God suffereth his children to fall into the *mouth of lions*, or into some danger proportionable, wherein they shall see no help from him, is a truth clear as the sun. The history of the church in all ages shews as much. Was not Christ in the mouth of the lion, so soon as born, when Herod sought to kill him? Mat. ii. 18. Did not Satan and all the spiritual powers of hell daily come about him, like ramping and roaring lions? And hath it not been thus with God's church from Abel to this present, as appears by the children of Israel in Egypt, at the Red Sea, and in their journey to Canaan, being environed round about with cruel enemies, and dangers on every side, like Daniel in the midst of lions? So far God gave them up to the power of their enemies, that the wisest of the heathen judged them a forlorn people, hateful to God and men.* For particular instances, see Job and David, so near as there was but a step between them and death.

Besides, God often awakens the consciences of his children, and exerciseth them with spiritual conflicts; their sins, as so many lions, stand up against them, ready to tear their souls. Nay, rather than those that belong to God shall want that, which will drive them unto him, God himself will be a lion unto them, as unto Ephraim, Hos. v. 14,† which made David pray, 'Oh Lord, rebuke me not in thine anger, neither chasten me in thy hot displeasure,' Ps. vi. 1. Of all the troubles which a child of God undergoeth in his way to heaven, these bring him lowest. When the body is vexed and spirit troubled, it is much; but when God frowns, when neither heaven nor earth yields comfort to a distressed soul, no evil in the world is like to this. Imagine the horror and straits of such a soul, when all things seem against it, and itself against itself, as near to the pains of the very damned in hell.

The reasons of this dispensation of God are: 1, because we are so desperately addicted to present things, and so prone to put confidence in the

---

* Cicero. See *ante*, p. 303.—G.

† 'For I will be unto Ephraim as a lion, and as a young lion to the house of Judah: I, even I, will tear and go away; I will take away, and none shall rescue him.'

arm of flesh, that unless God driveth us from these holds, by casting us into a perplexed estate, we shall never know what it is to live by faith in God alone, when all other props are pulled away, and when the stream of things seems cross unto us. That God therefore may train us up to live the spiritual life of the just, which is by faith in him, when all else fail, he suffereth us to fall into the lion's mouth, that so our prayers, which are the flame of faith, may be more ardent and piercing, rather cries than words. 'Why criest thou unto me,' saith God to Moses, Exod. xiv. 15. When was this? Even when he knew not what way to turn him. It was out of the depths that David cried most earnestly unto God, Ps. cxxx. 1; and Christ, in the days of his flesh, cried unto God with strong cries and tears, in a deep distress, and was also heard in that which he feared, Heb. v. 7. Strong troubles force from the afflicted strong cries. Even experience shews, in prosperity, and a full estate, how faint and cold the prayers and desires of men are.

2. Besides, it is meet that the secrets of men's hearts should be discovered; for when all is quiet, we know not the falsehood of our own hearts. Some over-value their strength, as Peter, Mat. xxvi. 33; others underprize themselves, and the gifts and graces of God's Spirit in them, thinking that they want faith, patience, love, &c., who yet, when God calleth them out to the cross, shine forth in the eyes of others, in the example of a meek and faithful subjection. The wisdom of God therefore judgeth it meet, that there should be times of sifting, that both the church and ourselves may know what good or ill is in us, what soundness or looseness remains in our hearts. When, therefore, we are wanting in fanning ourselves, God in love takes the fan into his hand.

It is likewise behoveful that false brethren may be discovered. Afflictions are well called trials, because then it is known what metal men are made of, whether pure or reprobate silver. Think it not strange then, when our estate seems desperate. It is but with us after the manner of God's dearest ones; why should we have a severed condition from them? Remember this, that God, as he suffers his children to fall into the lion's mouth, so he delivers them out; and that he never leaves his, especially in extremity, but in fit case of soul to receive the greatest comfort, and to render him the greatest glory. For then it is known to be God's work: our extremity is his opportunity. God will especially shew himself at such a time, and make it appear that the church stands not by man's strength. When Christians are at a loss, and know not which way to turn themselves, then is God nearest hand and careth most for them.

And this the Lord doth, both for the greater shame of those that contrive mischief (when they make themselves surest to bring their wicked plots and purposes to pass, then their designs are most frustrated); as also to draw on others not yet called; that they, seeing God's immediate care over his church and children, may come in and obtain like protection and deliverance.

The manner how God delivereth his children out of the lion's mouth is diverse.

Divers ways how God delivers from the lion's mouth:—1. *By suspending their malice for the time.* As in Noah's ark the fierceness of the wild creatures was stopped by divine power from preying upon the tamer, so the lions' mouths were stopped from preying upon Daniel in the lions' den, Dan. vi. 22.

2. *By stirring up one lion against another;* as the Persians against the

Babylonians, Grecians against Persians, Romans against the Grecians, and the other barbarous nations, as the Goths and Vandals, against them; so whilst lions spit their fury one upon another, the sheep are quiet. Thus the Turks and other enemies have kept popish princes from raging and tyrannising over the church to the height of their malice.

3. *By casting something unto these lions, to divert them another way from their intended prey;* as when a man is in danger, a dog is cast unto the lion (*j*). Thus, when Saul was ready to devour David, the Philistines made a breach upon him, invaded the land, and turned his fury another way, 2 Sam. xxiii. 27.

4. *By altering and changing lions to be lambs;* as when Paul was set upon havoc and mischief, God, by changing his heart, gave the churches cause to glorify God for him, of whom before they were most afraid.

5. *God shews himself a lion to these lions;* by breaking their teeth and jaw-bones, striking them with sudden and fearful judgment; as Herod, Acts xii. 23, and the persecuting emperors; and as in '88, when God with his four winds fought for us against the enemies of his truth.*

6. *By making them lions to themselves:* witness Ahithophel, Saul, and other such-like enemies of God's children.

7. Again, *God maketh them friends without changing their disposition,* by putting into their hearts some conceit for the time, which inclineth them to favour: as in Nehemiah, God put it into the king's heart to favour his people, Neh. ii. 8. Esau, Gen. xxxiii. 4, was not changed, only God for the time changed his affections to favour Jacob. So God puts it into the hearts of many, groundedly-naught, to favour the best persons.

8. Lastly, *God maketh his own children sometimes lions to their adversaries;* for the image of God shining in his children, hath a secret majesty in it, and striketh an awe upon wicked men. So Pharaoh at length could not endure to see Moses and Aaron any more, Exod. x. 28; and Felix trembled whilst Paul disputed of temperance and judgment, Acts xxiv. 25.

Use; of instruction and consolation. Thus we see the Lord knows how to deliver his, and can if he will; and will do it in their extremities, when is most for his glory, his people's comfort, and confusion of his own and their enemies. Never despair therefore of thyself or the church of God: it shall, rather than fail, breed in the lion's den. Paul salutes the Philippians, from the church in Cæsar's house, Phil. iv. 22, a place in appearance little fitter for a church than hell itself. What though things seem past recovery abroad? When they are at the worst, then are they nearest mending. When the task of brick was doubled by Pharaoh upon Israel, Exod. v. 11, then came Moses to work out their deliverance. When the Jews heard news of their liberty to return from captivity, they were as those that dreamed, Ps. cxxvi. 1; they could not suddenly believe it, it seemed so strange a thing, in that their hopeless estate. Learn we then, from this dealing of God with his people, in the midst of all extremities, to allege unto God the extremity we are in: 'Help, Lord, for vain is the help of man,' Ps. lx. 11, is a prevailing argument. Allege the pride of enemies, the presumption of those that fear not God, &c., and that he only, can give issue from death, when he will. And as God brings us to heaven by contraries, so let us in one contrary believe another: hope against hope, in misery look for mercy, in death for life, in guiltiness for forgiveness.

---

* The reference is to the Armada, proudly called 'the Invincible.' It arrived in the Channel July 19th 1588. A fortnight later all Spanish vessels that had not been sunk were in full flight.—G.

Learn to wrestle with God when he seemeth thy enemy; oppose unto God his former dealings, his nature, his promise, &c. Job had learned this, 'Though he kill me, yet will I trust in him,' Job xiii. 15. Be of Jacob's resolution, 'I will not leave hold of thee, until I get a blessing,' Gen. xxxii. 26. Whatsoever we are stript of, let us never forsake our own mercy, Jonah ii. 8. This one word, 'I despair,' takes away God and Christ all at once. We must remember our sins are the sins of men, but mercy is the mercy of God. God will never leave us, but be with us, whilst we are with him. The world and all comforts in it, leave a man when they can have no more use of him nor he of them. Satan leaves his sworn vassals at their wits' end when he hath brought them into danger. But blessed be for ever our gracious God, then of all other times he is nearest to help us, when we stand most in need of him. He was never nearer Moses than when Moses seemed furthest from comfort, Exod. iii. 2; never nearer Jacob than when heaven was his canopy and a stone his pillow, Gen. xxviii. 12; never nearer Joseph than when in prison; Jonah, than in the belly of the whale, for God went down with him; never nearer Paul than when in the dungeon, Acts xvi. 25. A Christian is not alone when left alone, not forsaken when forsaken, 2 Cor. iv. 9. God and his angels supply them the want of other comforts. Is it not a greater comfort that a prince should come in person to a subject and cheer him up, than send a meaner man? 'And whence is this to me,' said Elizabeth, 'that the mother of my Lord should come unto me? Luke i. 43. Is it not the greatest comfort to a Christian soul when God, in want of means, comes immediately himself unto us, and comforts us by his Spirit? For in defect of second causes, comforts are ever sweetest. Therefore, in all extremities let us wait and hope still for mercy. 'If the vision stay,' saith Habakkuk, 'wait, for it will come,' Hab. ii. 3.

Differences of godly and wicked. This is a main difference betwixt the child of God and a person destitute of sound grace; for the child of God in extremity, recovers himself, as David, after a great conflict, gets still the upper hand, 'Yet, my soul, keep thou silence unto God, for God is yet good to Israel,' Ps. lxxiii. 1, as if he should say, Though, when I look upon my present outward condition, I stagger, yet, when I consider more deeply of his dealing, I am resolved God is good to Israel. Thus, after much tossing, they get up upon that rock which is higher than they. But those who are not upright-hearted, in any great extremity, sink down with despair, as heavy bodies, to the centre of the earth, without stop. The reason is, in their best estate they never were acquainted with relying upon God, but bore themselves up with fleshly helps, which, being taken away, they must needs fall downright. But a sincere Christian, in midst of his flourishing estate, acquainteth himself with God, and sets not his heart upon present things. Job says, that which he feared in his best case, that befel unto him, Job iii. 25. Therefore they can rest upon God's mercy when other props are taken away.

Of our support in spiritual losses. Yet there be divers degrees of upholding us when we are at a spiritual loss. For usually, in what measure we, in the times of our peace and liberty, inordinately let loose our affections, in that measure are we cast down, or more deeply in discomfort. When our adulterous hearts cleave to outward things more than becomes chaste hearts, it makes the cross more sharp and extreme. For that which is not enjoyed with over much pleasure, is parted withal without over much grief. But for spiritual extremities, oftentimes the strongest, feel them with quickest sense; for God herein respects not always sins past, or more or less measure of grace, as in Job's case, who could, without much distemper of soul, endure extremities of body and estate, but when God wrote bitter things against him, presently he begins to sink, and but begins only; for when he was at worst, he stays himself upon his Redeemer, to the glory of God's grace, and shame of the devil. Thus sometimes God makes his children triumph, whom he sets as champions in defiance of Satan. They, in weakness, think they shall utterly fail and perish, but their standing out in greatest conflicts shews the contrary.

But to come to that which I intend chiefly to insist on, 'the Lord shall deliver me from every evil work,' &c., wherein we may see—

1. *The author of his safety.*
2. *The deliverance itself.*

The author is the Lord. No less than an almighty power is necessary to deliver from any evil work. For such is our inclinableness to join with temptation, such the malice and strength of our enemy, so many be the snares, and so cunningly spread in everything we deal withal, that whatsoever delivereth us must be above Satan and our own evil hearts; more wise, more powerful, more gracious to preserve us than any adverse power can be to draw us unto evil works. In which case, well said Moses when God, in his wonted glorious presence, refused to go along with them. O, saith Moses, if thou go not with us, carry us not hence, Exod. xxxiii. 15.

'Deliver' supposeth danger, possible or present. Beloved, our lives are such as stand in need of perpetual deliverance. Our estate here is wavering. The church lives always in tents, and hath never any hope of rest until the day of triumph. Therefore, after forgiveness of sins, follows 'lead us not into temptation;' because, though sins past be forgiven, yet we are in danger to be led into temptation. Let none promise a truce to himself, which God promiseth not. If Satan and our corruptions join, we cannot be quiet. After sins of youth we are in danger of sins of riper age; for though by grace, in some sort, sin be subdued, yet, until it be wholly mortified, there will be some stirring up, until that which is imperfect in us be abolished.

But I hasten to that which follows. 'The Lord will deliver me from every evil work.'

Whence, from the form of the argument, observe that we ought to reason with God from former experience to future, 1 Sam. xvii. 37; 2 Cor. i. 10. Yea, it is a binding argument with God. He loves to be sued and pressed from former mercies, and suffers them to be bonds unto him. Men will not do so, because their fountain is soon drawn dry; but God is a spring that can never be emptied. As he was able to help in former time, so he is also for the time to come. He is always, I AM JEHOVAH; always where he was; his arm is not shortened. What he hath done heretofore he can do now.

Use. We should therefore register God's favours, which is the best use we can put our memories to, and make them so many arguments to build upon him for time to come, as David, 'The Lord that delivered me,' saith he, 'out of the paw of the lion, and out of the paw of the bear, will deliver me out of the hand of this Philistine,' 1 Sam. xvii. 37. Oh, were we but acquainted with this kind of reasoning with God, how undaunted would we be in all troubles! We should be as secure for the time to come as for the time past, for all is one with God. We do exceedingly wrong our own souls, and weaken our faith, by not minding of God's favours. How strong in faith might old men be, that have had many experiences of God's love, if they would take this course! Every former mercy should strengthen our faith for a new, as conquerors, whom every former victory encourageth to a new conquest. So old favours should help us to set upon God afresh.

But what is the limitation here? 'From every evil work.' Which words we will first touch a little severally, and then consider more particularly of them.

Sometimes God speaks of duties as they issue from man, because, indeed, the will is man's, from whence the duty comes, and therefore the Scripture speaks, as though the duty came from us, because the powers are ours from whence they spring. Sometimes the Scripture speaks of holy duties as they issue from a higher power, from God. So here, the Lord will deliver me from every evil work, he means that God would stir up his heart to a care to avoid evil works. We are agents and patients in all we do. We are agents, because the powers are ours; we are patients, because the Lord doth all. Now it is the language of the Holy Ghost for the most part, when he speaks of good duties, to go to the fountain, especially when faith is to be strengthened.

Quest. But how doth God deliver?

Ans. By keeping us from occasions, or by ministering strength if occasions be offered. By giving occasions of good, and by giving a heart to entertain those occasions. He preserves us from evil works, (1) *by planting the graces of faith and of fear in us*, whereby we are preserved; and by peace, which guards our souls from despair and tumultuous thoughts. Yea, he preserves us from evil works, through faith, unto his heavenly kingdom, Phil. iv. 7.

In a word, (2) *God preserves his children by making them better*, by weakening corruptions, by his Spirit stirring up a clear sight and hatred of the same in them, and by withdrawing occasions which might prevail over us, and by keeping us from betraying ourselves unto them; by chaining up Satan until our strength be such as may encounter him. A great mercy it is, though little thought on, that God letteth not loose Satan upon us every moment. How should this stir us up, with David, to thankfulness and dependence upon God.

He delivers also wicked men from dangers, not out of any love to their persons, but because he hath some base service for them to undertake, to exercise the patience of his children, and vex others better than themselves, which is not fit for godly men to do. They are only God's rod, and their deliverance is no preservation, but a reservation to worse mischief. It is not a bettering deliverance.

But God delivers his, graciously, not only from danger, but from those evil works they are subject to fall into in their danger. It is not ill to suffer ill, but to do ill. For doing ill makes God our enemy; suffering ill doth not. Doing ill, stains and defiles the soul, and blemisheth the image of God in us; suffering ill doth none of this. Doing ill, hinders communion and acquaintance with God; suffering ill doth not. God is more immediately acquainted with the soul in suffering ill. Doing ill is the cause of all ills; suffering ill comes from doing ill. The ill of sin, is the ill of ills, because it is evil itself, and the cause of all other whatsoever. We may thank our ill in doing, for our ill in suffering; and therefore the apostle is well assured what he says, 'The Lord will deliver me from every evil work,' not from every inward infirmity and weakness, but from every evil work that is scandalous and offensive to him.

It is an aggravation of ill when it is manifested; for then it either taints or grieves others. Indeed so soon as the resolution of the soul hath passed it, when the will resolves on such a thing, it is done, both in good and evil, before God. But in regard of the world, and of the church we live in; the bringing of the work upon the stage, as it were, is an aggravation of evil; because, besides the hurt which is done to evil men, good men are either hurt or vexed at it. Therefore the apostle saith, 'the Lord will deliver me from every evil work.' This, a Christian should especially labour for, that God in all things would keep him free from sin. Yea, this differenceth a Christian from another man. Take a carnal man when he is like to fall into danger, he studies how to get out of suffering evil, not how to prevent doing evil; he plots, devises, and entangles himself in his own wit, and makes the matter worse by equivocation, and such like sinful courses, as we might learn from the papists, if we had not enough from our own breast. But Paul's care was to be delivered from *evil works*. For a man indeed is never overcome, let him be never so vexed in the world by any, till his conscience be cracked. If his conscience and his cause stand upright, he prevails still; 'in all these things we are more than conquerors,' Rom. viii. 37, saith the apostle. The meaning is, sufferings cannot quell our courage, they cannot stain our conscience, they do not hurt the cause, but it gets victory in despite of them; so that our courage is undaunted and our conscience abides unstained. Let it be our care therefore to take heed of evil works. Look into the world and see what is the care of most men we converse with, Oh, if they can get such a place, if they can get such an estate! Aye, but it cannot be had without sinful abasement, without cracking of conscience, and unlawful engagement. Oh, say they, it is no matter, God will pardon all, I care not so I may have my wish. This is the heart of many graceless persons that are not led with heavenly respects. But take a Christian, and he had rather beg, do anything in the world, than do a thing unworthy his profession, unbeseeming the gospel, or that high calling whereunto he is called. 'Shall such a man as I do this?' Neh. vi. 11; he will not, and therefore his care is to take heed of ill works; for then he is sure to have God his friend, who hath riches and honour enough for him, because 'the earth is the Lord's and the fulness thereof,' Ps. xxiv. 1. This is the care of a judicious well-instructed Christian.

But mark the *extent* from *every* evil work. St Paul' scare is not for one or two, but that God would keep him from *every* evil work. Why so?

Why St Paul says from every evil work. Because he that truly hates one sin, will hate all the kinds of it. Both come from the same love of God. He that loves God as he should, will hate whatsoever God hates; 'and have respect to all God's commandments,' as the psalmist speaks, Ps. cxix. 128. Partial obedience is indeed no obedience at all; for he that obeys one, and not another, obeys not simply because of the commander, to yield obedience unto him; but only to satisfy his own corrupt nature, picking and choosing what pleases himself, which belongs not to an inferior, but to a superior to do. And therefore, such make themselves gods, in that they single out easy things that do not oppose their lusts, which are not against their reputation, &c., and therein perhaps they will supererogate, and do more than they need, only because they will have a compensation with God, that he should quit with them for other things. I have done that, and therefore he must bear with me in this. Oh! but there is no compensation here. A man is never so straitened but he may escape without sin. There is no pretence will serve; but we must abstain from *every* evil work. Satan keeps many men in his snare by this, and so he hath them safe in one sin, he cares not; therefore he will suffer them to hear, read, and pray, &c., holding them fast in one reigning sin, wherein he will let them alone till the time of some great affliction, or death; and then he will roar upon them. Oh beloved! we cannot provide worse for our own souls, than to cherish a purpose of living in any one sin, for that is enough for the devil to hold his possession in us by, and at the hour of death to claim us for his own. 'If we regard any iniquity in our heart, the Lord will not hear our prayers,' Ps. lxvi. 18. I beseech you therefore, let us labour to have clear consciences, freeing ourselves from a purpose to live in any sin; that in all our slips and failings we may say with an honest heart, my purpose was not to do this, but to refrain from wickedness.

Again, he speaks of this for the time to come; the Lord *will* deliver me from evil. A true Christian is as careful to avoid sin for the time to come, as to be freed from the guilt of sins past. Judas may desire to have his conscience freed from former sins, but Judas cannot desire to be a good man for the time to come. Nothing argues a good conscience more than this. The most wicked wretch that breathes, may desire to have his conscience stilled, and yet never have any purpose or power to abstain from sin; but like a dog, after he hath disgorged himself, return to his vomit again. True repentance is a turning from former evils to a contrary good. Our grief no further yields comfort of sound repentance, than it hath care attending, for prevention of sin; according to that which Christ said to the woman taken in adultery, 'Go, and sin no more,' John v. 14, and as David prays, 'Purge me, O Lord, and cleanse me, but withal, establish me with thy free Spirit for the time to come,' Ps. li. 2, 12. As if he should say, Lord, I know it is not in man to order his own ways, I desire not the forgiveness of my sins that thereby I might with more liberty offend thy majesty, but with pardoning grace, I beg preventing grace. No false heart can move such a desire as this to God. A gracious heart that prays aright, prays as well that God would preserve him from future sin, as forgive him his former sins. It is a ridiculous thing of the papists to make confession of a sin which they mean to commit: as some late traitors confessed such and such things which they were to act, and were straight absolved for it. So your cursed duellists, that will pray and repent, when they mean presently to fall one upon another. Is this repentance, when a man is inveigled with the sin he means to commit; and cannot overcome himself in the case of revenge? Do these men think they repent? No, certainly; repentance is of sins past, and the carriage of every true Christian is to avoid evil for the time to come.

Again, it is here a perpetuated act: The Lord will deliver me still from every evil work. Whence you see that in every evil work we are tempted to, we need delivering grace; as to every good work, assisting grace. Indeed, our whole life, if we look upwards, is nothing but a deliverance, but if we look to ourselves, it is nothing but danger and a warfare, and therefore we have need of a deliverance. How little a temptation turns over a great man! as sometimes a little wind turns over your mighty galleys. We see this in David and Solomon; and, if God leave us to ourselves, even the strongest man in the world, how soon is he overturned! In the midst of sinful occasions, how ready are we to join with them, and betray our own souls!

But from the whole, take it as it comes from God altogether, the truth is thus much, *that a Christian, who is privy to his own soul of good intentions to abstain from all ill for the present, may presume that God will assist him against all ill works for the time to come.* I say a Christian, that hath his conscience telling him that he means to be better, and is not in league with any sin, may believe this for the time to come, that God will keep him from evil works. I speak this, because many who are yet sinners think it in vain to strive, for they shall never be better. What dost thou talk, man? Hast thou a mind to be better? God will meet thee one time or other. Is thy will at liberty? He that gives thee the will, will also give thee the deed. Is not this the promise, that God will deliver thee from every evil work? And, therefore, away with all discouragements.

Obj. O but there are sons of Anak, mighty giants, that molest me; my sins are as so many giants to stop my proceeding; I shall never be better!

Solution. Say not so; nay, rather thou *wilt* not be better. Thou art in league with some secret sin, thy heart riseth against those that reprove thee of it, thine own conscience tells thee that thy heart is naught; for if thou wouldst set thyself to obey God in truth, assuredly he would deliver thy soul. And therefore the apostle, to prevent such doubts, speaks of deliverance from evil works as coming from God.

Obj. But some may object, We sin every day; and 'if we say we have no sin, we deceive ourselves, and the truth is not in us,' 1 John i. 8.

Ans. You must not understand this phrase legally, in the rigour of it, as that God will deliver us from every ill thought, or rising in the heart, or from every outward slip and failing, &c.; but by every evil work, the apostle means every reproachful sin that breaks the peace of our conscience, that swallows up a man's salvation. From such kind of sins that bring a stain and discredit unto a man's profession, that wound his soul, and may discourage others, the Lord will deliver his; he will keep them from greater sins altogether, and from being in league with lesser. You know in falls there are several degrees; there is a slip, a falling, and a falling on all four; as we say, a flat falling. Now God will deliver his children from falling so foully.

2. *How God delivers from ill works by not delivering.* Nay, sometimes he will deliver them from evil works, by not delivering them from evil works. He will deliver from great ill works, by letting them alone in lesser ill works. God delivers from evil divers ways; he delivers from falling into ill, and he delivers out of ill when we are fallen; he delivers from ill likewise by supporting us; nay, which is more, he delivers from ill works by ill works.

Quest. How is that?

Solution. How do physicians deliver from an apoplexy? from a lethargy? Is it not by casting the sick person into an ague, to awaken that dull sickness? So God, to cure the conscience of a man, when he sees him in danger of security by those soul-killing sins, pride, covetousness, looseness, hypocrisy, and the like, suffers him sometimes to fall into less offences, to awake his conscience, that being roused up he may fly to God's mercy in Christ. So infinite is God's care this way, that he will deliver either from ill works, or from the evil of ill works; or, if he deliver not from ill works, yet he will deliver us from worse works by those ill works. Austin saith, I dare presume to say, it is profitable for some men to fall.* If a man be of a proud, peremptory disposition, or of a blockish, dull, and

* 'It is profitable for some men to fall.' Consult 'Confessions Book I., xi. 18; and Book VII. xx. 26.—G.

secure nature, it is good he should be acquainted what sin he carries in his breast, where his corruptions are, &c., that so he may know himself and his danger the better.

Use. I beseech you make use of this, to help your faith and thankfulness. When we are delivered from evil works, it is God that doth it. The consideration whereof, methinks, should strengthen our faith against Satan and all his fiery darts, and encourage us to set confidently upon any corruption that we are moved to by others, or our own natural inclination. It is God's enemy, and it is my enemy; it is opposite to God's will, and it is an enemy to my comfort. God will take my part against that which is opposite to him. He hath promised me to assist me against every evil work by his Holy Spirit. A Christian is a king, Rev. i. 6; and he hath the triumphing Spirit of Christ in him, which will prevail over all sin in time.

Obj. But some poor soul may object, Alas! I have been assaulted by such a corruption, a long time, in a grievous manner, and am not yet delivered from it.

Ans. God doth by little and little purge out corruption. As every stroke helps the fall of the oak, the first stroke helps forward; so every opposing of corruption, never so little, helps to root it out, and it is weakened by little and little, till death accomplish more mortification.

But to proceed. God doth not only deliver from evil works, but preserves us to his heavenly kingdom. We must take *preserve* here in its full breadth. He preserves us whilst he hath any work for us to do in this life; and when he will have us live no longer, he will preserve us to heaven; howsoever, by death he takes us away, yet even then the Lord still preserves us.

Under-preservers of the saints. He will preserve us in our outward estate, by himself, and by under-preservers, for there be many such under God; as angels that are his ministering spirits, and magistrates, who are the shields of the earth; they may preserve under God; and likewise ministers, that are the chariots and horsemen of Israel, and good laws, &c. But God is the first turner of the wheel; we must see him in all other preservers whatsoever. And therefore the apostle, in the language of the Holy Ghost, and of Canaan, saith here, 'The Lord will preserve me,' Ps. xlvii. 9; 2 Kings ii. 12. And rather than a man shall miscarry when God hath anything for him to do, God will work a miracle.

The three men could not be burned in the fire, Dan. iii. 25 and vi. 12; God so suspended the force thereof. Daniel could not be devoured of the greedy lions, &c. Rather than God's purpose shall fail, that a man should perish before the time that God hath allotted him, the lions shall not devour, and the fire shall not burn. God hath measured our glass and time, even to a moment; and as our Saviour Christ, out of knowledge of this heavenly truth, saith, 'My time is not yet come,' John vii. 6, so let us know that, till our hour comes, all the devils in hell cannot hurt one hair of our head. And this is a wondrous ground of confidence, that we should carry ourselves above all threatenings, and above all fears whatsoever. 'Thou canst do nothing except it were given thee,' John xix. 10, saith Christ to bragging Pilate, who boasted of his power. Alas! what can all the enemies of God's people do except God permit them?

If a king or a great man should say to an inferior, Go on; I will stand by thee, and preserve thee; thou shalt take no harm: what an encouragement were this! Oh, but when God shall say to a Christian, Walk humbly before me, keep close to my word, be stedfast in the ways of holiness, **fear not man, you are under my protection and safeguard**: what an encouragement is this to a believing soul!

But put case we cannot be preserved from death; for so it was here with the apostle, he died a bloody death. Why, let us observe his blessed carriage in all this, and do likewise. I regard not that, saith he; do your worst, God will preserve me still. So it should be the bent of a Christian's soul to come to God with this limitation, in his faith and in his prayer: Lord, if thou wilt not deliver me from suffering ill, preserve me from doing ill; if thou wilt not preserve me from death, preserve me from sinful works. This we may build on, that either God will preserve us in life, or if we die, he will preserve us in death to his heavenly kingdom. And *sometimes God preserves by not preserving from death;* for indeed death keeps a man from all danger whatsoever. He is out of all gun-shot, when he is once dead. Death is a deliverance and a preservation of itself: it sends a man to heaven straight; and therefore the apostle knew what he said, 'The Lord will preserve me to his heavenly kingdom.'

That is, he will preserve me till I be possessed of heaven; he will go along with me in all the passages of my life; he will carry me through all, and bring me thither at last. As the angel that struck off Peter's bolts, 'shined in the prison,' Acts xii. 7, and carried him out into the city, so God by his Spirit shines into our souls, and carries us through all the passages of this life, never leaving us, till he have brought us to his heavenly kingdom.

And not to open unto you things that are beyond my conceit, much more my expression, what a state this heavenly kingdom is, unto which St Paul hoped to be preserved! Observe, briefly, thus much :—1, It is a kingdom of all conditions the freest ; 2, the most glorious ; 3, the most abundant in all supplies ; 4, it is a heavenly kingdom ; 5, it is an everlasting kingdom.

The excellency of the heavenly kingdom. Things, the nearer the heavens they are, the purer they are. 1, heaven is a most holy kingdom : no uncleanness can enter there ; 2, it is a large kingdom ; and 3, an everlasting kingdom. Other men's kingdoms determine with their persons ; perhaps they may live to out-live their glory in the world, as Nero did (the king that Paul was under now, when he wrote this epistle), who came to a base end. But this kingdom can never be shaken. God's preservation shall end in eternal glory.

Use 1. *Here is a special ground to God's children of perseverance in well-doing.* What! doth God undertake even from himself, to deliver us from evil works, which might endanger our salvation, and to preserve us until he have put us into heaven! Where is the popish doctrine of falling away, then? *Obj.* Oh, but I may sin, and so fall away. *Sol.* Aye, but God will deliver us from evil works; he takes away that objection. He that keeps heaven for us, keeps us for heaven, till he have put us into possession of it. 'We are kept (we are guarded (*k*), as the word is) by the power of God to salvation,' 1 Pet. i. 5. Salvation is kept for us, and we for that. If we endanger heaven any way, it is by ill works, and God keeps us from them. What a most comfortable doctrine is this!

Use 2. But, to add a second against that foolish, vain, and proud point of *popish merit.* We see what a strain they are in. 1. Before conversion they will have merit of congruity, that it befits the goodness of God, when we do what we can, that we should have grace. 2. When we are in the state of grace, they will have merit of condignity; but how can that be, whenas free grace runs along in all? God preserves us from evil works, and preserves us to his heavenly kingdom, of his mere love and mercy. Where then is the merit of man? Indeed, we do good when we do good, but God enables us; we speak to the praise of God, but he opens our mouth; we believe, but God draws our heart to it: as Austin says, we move, but God moves us.*

Use 3. I beseech you, observe further here: *How complete God's favours are to his.* He deals like a God, that is, *fully and eternally*, with his children. If he deliver, it is from the greatest evil; if he preserve, it is to the greatest good. Who would not serve such a master? Oh, the baseness of the vile heart of man, that is a slave to inferior things, and afraid to displease men, never considering what a blessed condition it is, to be under the government of a gracious God, that will keep us from ill, if it be for our good, for ever, outwardly from evil works, inwardly from the terrors of an ill conscience, that will preserve us here in this world, and give us heaven when we have done. I beseech you, let this complete and full dealing of God quicken us to a holy courage and constancy in his service.

Use 4. And see here a *point of heavenly wisdom; to look, when we are in any danger, with the apostle, to the heavenly kingdom.* When we are sick, look not at death. Paul cared not for that, but says he, 'The Lord will preserve me to his kingdom.' He looked to the bank of the shore. As a man that goes through a river hath his eye still on the shore, so the apostle had his eye fixed upon heaven still. I beseech you therefore, in all dangers and distresses whatsoever, if you would keep your souls without discouragements, as you should, be much in heaven in your thoughts, minding the things above, and conversing with God in your spirits. Look to the crown that is held out to us; let our minds be in heaven before our souls. It is a wondrous help to our weakness in the time of trouble, not to think, I am full of pain, I must be turned into the grave, and rot, and what shall become of me then? &c. Away with this carnal reasoning. It much weakens faith, and damps the hearts of Christians.

Use 5. Again, *How doth this arm the soul with invincible courage in any trouble.* God may call me to trouble, but he will preserve me in it that I shall not stain my conscience. What a ground of patience is this! Patience is too mean a word; what a ground of joy and triumphing is it! 'We rejoice under the hope of glory,' Rom. v. 2. A Christian should triumph in soul over all evils whatsoever, and be, as the apostle saith, 'more than a conqueror,' Rom. viii. 37; considering that God will be present with him all his life long, and after that, bring him to an everlasting kingdom. What an encouragement is this! Heaven is holy, and shall we not fit ourselves for that blessed estate? There is much holiness required for heaven; the sinful, wicked, malicious, poisonful world, lays reproaches upon holiness; but 'without it no man shall see God,' Heb. xii. 24. Doth that man believe he shall obtain a heavenly kingdom, who never fits himself with holiness for it? Oh no; 'Faith and hope have this efficacy in the breast, wheresoever they are, to frame the heart to the thing believed.' If I believe a kingdom to be where righteousness and holiness dwelleth, this belief forceth me to carry myself answerable to the state there, 2 Pet. iii. 13. And therefore, saith the apostle, ' our conversation (*l*) is in heaven, from whence we look for the Saviour,' &c., Philip. iii. 20. Because he was assured of heaven, therefore he conversed as a citizen of heaven before he came there. He praised God,

* 'We move, but God moves us.' A frequent saying in his 'Confessions.' Consult Book VII., iii. 4.—G.

kept himself undefiled of the world, and conversed with the best people; every way he carried himself, as much as earth would suffer him, as they do in heaven. Certainly, 'he that hath the hope of a heavenly kingdom, is pure as Christ is pure,' 1 John iii. 3. He endeavours and aims to be holy as God is holy, who hath called him. Faith is of efficacy to conform a Christian's carriage to the likeness of him whom he believes to be so excellent. And therefore they are infidels, and have no saving faith; profane persons, who live in sins that stain their consciences, and blemish their conversation, not believing that there is a heaven. 'Deceive not yourselves; neither whoremongers, nor adulterers, nor extortioners,' &c., 1 Cor. vi. 9, shall inherit the kingdom of God. Do men who live in these sins, without remorse, think to come to heaven? as though they should come out of the puddle to heaven? No, no; 'away, you workers of iniquity, I know you not,' Mat. xxv. 41, saith Christ. Let no man cherish presumptions of a heavenly kingdom, except he abstain from all sins against conscience. The apostle, when he would urge to holiness of life, uses this argument: 'If you be risen with Christ, seek those things that are above, where Christ is, at the right hand of the Father,' Col. iii. 1.

Well, let us oft, I beseech you, present unto our souls the blessed condition to come, which will be effectual to quicken and stir us up to every good duty, and comfort us in all conditions whatsoever. What will a man care for crosses and losses and disgraces in the world, that thinks of a heavenly kingdom? What will a man care for ill usage in his pilgrimage, when he knows he is a king at home? We are all strangers upon earth, now in the time of our absence from God; what if we suffer indignities, considering that we have a better estate to come, when we shall be somebody! What if we pass unknown in the world! It is safe that we should do so; God will preserve us to his heavenly kingdom, and all that we suffer and endure here, it is but a fitting for that place. David was a king anointed many years ere he was actually possessed of his kingdom; but all that time between his anointing and his investing into the kingdom, it was a preparation of him by humility, that he might know himself, and learn fitness to govern aright. So we are anointed kings as soon as we believe; for when we believe in Christ, who is a king, priest, and prophet, we communicate with his offices; we have the same blessed anointing poured on our head, and runs down about us, Ps. cxxxiii. 2. But we must be humbled by crosses, and fitted for it; we must be drawn more out of the world, and be heavenly-minded first.

Rules to discern what our interest in heaven is. Would you know some rules of discerning whether heaven belongs to you or not? In brief, do but remember the *qualification of them that must reign;* those that labour daily to purge themselves of all pride and self-confidence; that see no excellency in the creature, in comparison of heaven; that see a vanity in all outward things which makes them humble in the midst of all their bravery; those that see themselves empty of all, without God's favour, 'the poor in spirit, &c., theirs,' saith Christ, ' is the kingdom of heaven,' Mat. v. 3.

2. *Faith makes us kings,* because thereby we marry the King of heaven; the church is the queen of heaven, and Christ is the king of heaven. Where this grace is in truth, happiness belongs to that soul.

3. *Those that are kings have a royal spirit.* The hopes of a young prince puts into him a great deal of spirit, otherwise, perhaps, above his disposition. So all that are kings have a royal spirit in some measure, which raiseth them above all earthly things, and maketh them see all other things to be nothing

in comparison of Christ, to be but 'dross and dung,' as holy St Paul saith, Philip. iii. 8. Those therefore that are slaves to their base lusts, to riches, honour, pleasure, &c., know not what belongs to this heavenly kingdom. What, do men think to reign in heaven, when they cannot reign over their own base corruptions! We see David prays to God for an 'enlarged spirit,' Ps. li. 12, that he might be capable of the best things; and certainly those that have this knowledge are of a spirit above the world, '*more excellent than their neighbours*,' as the wise man saith, Prov. xii. 26. You cannot shake them with offers of preferment, or with fears; they will not venture their hope of eternity for this or that base earthly thing; they are of a more royal spirit than so.

I beseech you therefore, let us discern of our spirits what they are; whether God hath established us with a free spirit or not. The kingdom of heaven is begun upon earth; the door whereby we must enter in is here. Those graces must be begun here which must fit us for happiness hereafter. As the 'stones of the temple,' 1 Kings vi. 7, were first hewn and then laid upon the temple, so we must be hewn and fashioned here, ere we can come thither. Those that are not fitted and squared now, must never think to be used of God as living stones of his temple then. A word now of Paul's use of all, and so I conclude:

'*To whom be glory for ever and ever.*'

When he had mentioned the heavenly kingdom, and set himself by faith, as it were, in possession of it, he presently begins the employment of heaven, 'to praise and glorify God,' even whilst he was on earth. For faith stirs us up to do that which we shall do, when we obtain the thing believed. It is called 'the evidence of things not seen,' Heb. xi. 1; and makes them, as it were, present to the soul. Because when we are in heaven indeed, we shall do nothing else but praise God. Faith apprehends it, as if he were now there, for all is sure to faith, God having said it, who will do it; and sets the soul upon that employment here, which it shall have eternally with God hereafter.

It is therefore Christian wisdom, to fix our souls on good meditations, to have them wedded to good thoughts, to have those *præclaras cogitationes*, befitting Christians, that may lead us comfortably in our way to heaven. Let a man think of God's deliverances past, and that will strengthen his faith for the future deliverances. Let him think of future deliverances, and that will lead him to a kingdom, to praise God; and this praising of God will stretch his soul, for ever and for ever; as if there were no time sufficient to glorify God, that is so excellent and glorious. What a blessed condition is this, to have God's Spirit warming our souls and perfuming our spirits with holy ejaculations, continually putting us upon the employment of heaven, till at length it hath safely brought us thither.

Here then is the use of all uses. What is the former use which Paul makes of the experience of God's deliverance? The Lord hath delivered me, and therefore he will deliver me. But what use doth he make of this, that God will deliver him? To glorify God. Here is the end of all ends, to praise God. Happy we when God's end and our end meet together. He hath made all for his own glory; and when we, with a single eye, can aim at that too, what a sweet harmony is there!

1. To direct us in this duty in praising God, let us with Paul, for I go no further than the text leads me, *seriously meditate on God's mercies, both past and to come*. Nothing moves thankfulness more than this. A Christian when he looks backward hath comfort, and when he looks forward he sees

comfort still: for preservation, and kingdoms, and crowns abide for him. If a man would praise God, therefore, let him consider how graciously God hath dealt with him. He hath delivered me already by Jesus Christ, from sin and eternal wrath; and he will deliver me from every evil work to come, that may endanger my salvation. Think of these things, and see whether your hearts can be cold and dead or no; see if your spirits can be straitened. Certainly both heart and mouth will be full. Thou canst not but say, in the apprehension of God's mercies, 'To him be glory for ever.'

2. *Consider the kinds of favours thou receivest.* They are either positive or privative, spiritual or temporal. Positive—the Lord will preserve me; privative—the Lord will deliver me from every evil work. Temporal—the Lord in this life will keep me; spiritual—he will deliver me from the power of sin. Eternal—he will preserve me to his heavenly kingdom. Think forward or backward, outward or inward, spiritual or temporal: wherever you look, tell me if you can do otherwise than break out with the holy apostle in the praises of so good a God.

And 3. *Think of the greatness of all these:* the greatness of the deliverance from sin and damnation. The apostle, to make himself the more thankful, saith he was delivered out of the mouth of the lion. He had large apprehensions of God's goodness. So should we, beloved, consider the greatness of the misery we are in by nature, being slaves of Satan, in danger to slip into hell every moment; and when God hath secured us from this, think of the greatness of the benefit, a 'heavenly kingdom.' When we think, not only of the benefits, but of the greatness of them, it is a wondrous encouragement to be thankful. Labour then to have a due and high esteem of every mercy. God hath brought us out of *darkness into marvellous light*, saith the apostle, 1 Pet. ii. 9; *great is the mystery of godliness*, 1 Tim. iii. 16; and *the unsearchable riches of his grace*, Eph. iii. 8. He had not words big enough to express God's goodness. 'Oh, the height, and breadth, and depth, and length of his love,' Eph. ii. 18. When we consider these dimensions, our thankfulness must be answerable.

4. Again, if you would be thankful, *labour to have humble spirits, to see God in all things;* and then you will sacrifice to him alone; not to thy parts and graces, friends, abilities, &c. The meek are fit to pray to God. 'Seek the Lord, ye meek of the earth,' Zeph. ii. 3; and an humbled, meek, soul, is the fittest to praise God of any other. He that knows he is worthy of nothing, will bless God for anything. He that knows he hath nothing in himself, will be thankful for the least measure of grace. An humble soul is a thankful soul. We see it was Paul's disposition here. He gives all to God, which makes him so break out in praising his name.

5. Again, if we would be thankful, as Paul here, and begin heaven upon earth, *labour to be assured of salvation,* and perseverance in thy Christian course. The papists, that speak against assurance and perseverance, kill prayer and praising of God. Shall a man praise God for that which he doubts of? I cannot tell whether God will damn me or not; perhaps I am but fitted as a sheep to the slaughter, &c. How shall a man praise God for any blessing he enjoys, when these thoughts are still with him? How shall a man praise God for salvation, when perhaps he shall not come to it? How shall a man praise God for that which perhaps he may fall from before he die? when perhaps he is God's to-day, and may be the devil's to-morrow? How can there be a hearty thanks, but when a man can say, 'The Lord will deliver me from every evil work,' that by mine own weakness, and Satan's malice, I may occasionally fall into, betwixt this and

heaven? Therefore, if we would praise God as we should, let us work our hearts to labour after assurance of God's favour; let us redeem our precious time, and every day set some time apart to strengthen our evidences for heaven, which will set us in a continual frame to every good work.

Thus we see, out of Paul's example, how we should be disposed here, to be in heaven before our time. For *undoubtedly he who praiseth God is so much in heaven, as he is given to thankfulness;* for he is in that employment now, which shall be there altogether. But how long doth he desire that God should have glory? For ever and ever.

Obs. A Christian should have the extent of his desires of God's glory carried to eternity. Upon what ground? Because God intends him glory for ever and ever. A Christian that is assured of his salvation, is assured that God will eternally glorify him. He knows that Christ is king for ever; he knows that Christ is a priest for ever; he knows that the state and condition that he is kept for, is everlasting: ' it is an inheritance immortal and undefiled, that fadeth not away,' 1 Pet. i. 4; and therefore he saith, Hath God eternal thoughts of my good? and is Christ an eternal head, an eternal king to rule me, both in life and in death? Surely I will extend my desires of his glory as far as he extends his purpose to do me good. Now, his purpose to do me good is for eternity, and my desire that he may have glory shall be for eternity, *world without end,* Eph. iii. 21. This is the disposition of a gracious soul, not that God may be honoured by him alone, but of all. To whom be praise, not by me, but by all. I am not sufficient enough to praise him. To him be praises in the churches, throughout all ages, for ever. David had not largeness enough in himself to bless God; and therefore he stirs up his spirits and all within him to praise his holy name, Ps. ciii. 1, as if all were too little to set out the glory of God's infinite goodness, mercy, wisdom, and power: those gracious attributes that shew themselves glorious in bringing man to salvation, and in governing the church.

Use. Learn this duty therefore: *if we will make good to our own souls, that we are in the state of grace, we must plot for eternity, and endeavour to lay a ground and foundation, that the church may flourish for eternity.* No man can warrant himself to be a good Christian, but he that labours to have the church and commonwealth flourish; to have a happy kingdom, happy government, and happy laws. Not only to have the church in his own family, but that the church may flourish in those that stand up when we are gone the way of all flesh; and therefore to declare the mind of God, and his favours to us, and our children, that they may strengthen their experience, with their fathers' experience, and say to God, Thou art the God of my fathers, therefore be my God. Those that are called to places of dignity, should consider that it is required at their hands to labour that there should be means to continue religion, even to the world's end, if it may be, and to stop all the breaches in this kind. And if it were possible, it were to be wished that there were set up some lights in all the dark corners of this kingdom, that might shine to those people that sit in darkness, and in the shadow of death.

2. One way is, *to have a care that there be no breaches made upon the sound doctrine that is left unto us, and hath been sealed up by the blood of so many martyrs.* We had it dearly. It hath been taught by our forefathers, and sealed with their blood; and shall we betray it? No; let us labour to deliver it to our posterity, from hand to hand, to the coming of Christ; and then we shall in effect, and not in word only, do that which Paul saith

here—labour to glorify God for ever and ever, both in the church and in heaven. Surely those that will glorify God in heaven, he will have them so disposed to glorify him on earth.

It is a dangerous thing when persons are naught. We see what comes of it, especially if they be great. It is said of Manasseh, when God had forgiven him his sin, yet afterwards God plagued the kingdom for the sins that Manasseh committed, 2 Kings xxiv. 3. How can this be? Because he by his sin, though he repented himself, yet set the kingdom in an evil frame. And no question but he had naughty principles; and among people that are given to licentiousness, if there be anything in great men, it will go to posterity after them. So that when governors are naught, they are not only a poison to the church and state while they live, but the mischief of it is after and after still. And so it is in the best things. If the governor be good, he lays a foundation of good for the kingdom in time to come, as well as for his own time.

How will it shame a man when he shall think, I do these things now, but what will posterity think of me? what will be the remembrance of it when I am gone? Then my name will stink. The wicked emperor Nero was of this resolution when he should die: 'Let heaven and earth mingle together,' saith he, 'when I am gone.'* He knew himself to be so naught, and that he should be so evil spoken of, that he wished there were no posterity, but that the world might end with him. So it is the wishes of those that are wretches themselves, and that lay a foundation of wretched times after. They wish that heaven and earth may mingle, that no man might censure them when they are gone. What a shameful condition is it for men to gratify a number of unruly lusts, and give such sway to them as to do ill while they live, and to lay a foundation of misery for after times.

On the contrary, what a good thing is it, like Josiah and Nehemiah, to be full of goodness while we live, and to lay a foundation of happiness and prosperity to the church and state when we are gone! What a happy thing is it, when a man is gone, to say such a man did such a thing! He stood stoutly for the church, for religion; he was a public man; he forgot his own private good for the public; he deserved well of the times wherein he lived. What a blessed commendation is this, next to heaven, to have a blessed report on earth, and to carry such a conscience as will comfort a man that he hath carried himself well, and abounded in well-doing.

I beseech you let us think of this 'for ever and ever.' It is not enough that we be good in our times that are circumscribed to us. But as God hath given us immortal souls, and preserves us to immortal glory, and a crown of immortality, so let our thoughts and desires be immortal, that God may be glorified in the church, world without end. Oh, what a sweet comfort will it be when we are on our deathbed, to think what we have done in our lifetimes! Then all our good actions will come and meet together, to comfort and refresh our souls.

Encouragements to glorify God. The better to encourage us to glorify God while we are here, and to lay a foundation to eternise his glory for the time to come, consider, 1. *God's gracious promise:* 'Those that honour me I will honour,' 1 Sam. ii. 30. If we had enlarged hearts to honour God, God would honour us. He hath passed his word for it. If a king should say so, O how would we be set on fire! how much more when the King of kings saith it!

* The dying saying of Nero has been recorded, 'Dedecorosè vixi, turpiùs peream.' —See Tacitus, lib. xv.—G.

2. Consider that *we honour ourselves when we honour God*. Nay, the more we honour God, the more we are bound to God; for it is from him that we honour him. The sacrifice comes from him, as well as the matter for which we sacrifice. He found a ram for Abraham to sacrifice, Gen. xxii. 13. He gives the heart to be thankful. The more we are thankful, the more we shall be thankful, and the more we ought to be thankful for our thankfulness.

3. *The more we praise God, the more we should praise him*, for it is the gift of God. When God sees we honour him, and frame ourselves that we may be such as may honour him, by emptying and disabling ourselves to be sufficient to do him any service, he will bestow more upon us. As men cast seed upon seed where there is fruitful ground, but they will sow nothing upon a barren heath. So the more we set ourselves to do good in our places, the more we shall have advantage thereunto; and the more we do good, the more we shall do good. When God sees we improve our talents so well that he trusts us withal, he will trust us with more.

4. Again, consider *our glorifying and praising God causeth others to do so*, which is the main end wherefore we live in this world. It is the employment of heaven, and we are so much in heaven as we are about this work. And when God gives us hearts to glorify him here, it is a good pledge that he will afterward glorify us in heaven. Who would lose the comfort of all this, to be barren, and yield to his base, unbelieving, dead heart? to save a little here? to sleep in a whole skin? and adventure upon no good action? Who would not rather take a course that hath such large encouragements attending it both in life and death? I beseech you think of these things. Christ, ere long, will come to be glorified in all those that believe, 2 Thes. i. 10. He will come to be glorified in his saints. Our glory tends to his glory. Shall we not glorify him all we can here, by setting forth his truth, by countenancing his children and servants, by doing good, and deserving well of ungrateful times we live in? Let men be as unthankful as they will, we look not to them, but to the honour of God, the credit of religion, the maintenance of the truth, &c. Let men be as they will be, base and wicked, enemies to grace and goodness, we do it not to them, but to God. Consider this. Will Christ come from heaven ere long to be glorified in us, and shall not we labour to glorify him while we are here? He will never come to be glorified in any hereafter, but those that glorify him now. As we look, therefore, that he should be glorified in us, and by us, let us glorify him now; for so he condescends to vouchsafe to be glorified in us and by us, that he may also glorify us.

Quest. St Paul saith, the wife is the glory of the husband, 1 Cor. xi. 7. What means he by this? *Solution.* That is, she reflects the graces of a good husband. If he be good, she is good; she reflects his excellencies. So let every Christian soul that is married to Christ, be the glory of Christ, reflect his excellencies, be holy as he is holy, 1 Pet. i. 15, fruitful as he was in doing good, meek and humble as he was; every way be his glory; and then, undoubtedly, when he comes to judge us, he will come to be glorified in us, having been before glorified by us.

Beloved, these and such considerations should set us on work how to do Christ all the honour we can. As David saith, 'Is there any of Jonathan's posterity alive, that I may do good unto them for his sake?' 2 Sam. ix. 1, so, considering we shall be so glorified by Christ, and that he will do so much for us in another world, we should inquire, Is there any of Christ's posterity here, any of his children in this world, that I may do good unto them? Is there any way wherein I may shew my thankfulness, and I will do it? Let us consider that we shall be for ever and ever glorified. The expression of it is beyond conceit. We shall never know it till we have it. Let this, I beseech you, stir us up to study how we may be thankful to God, set forth his glory, and deserve well of the church and times wherein we live. God hath children and a cause in the world which he dearly loves, let us own the same, and stand for it to the uttermost of our power, maugre all the spite and opposition of Satan and his wicked instruments.

The Lord in mercy settle these truths upon our hearts, and encourage us in his most holy way.

NOTES.

(*h*) P. 315.—' I find that most ancient and modern writers by 'lion' understand Nero. . . . . This is the common view of ' the Fathers;' and, of contemporaries of Sibbes, of Thomas Hall of King's Norton. All wishing to obtain much learning and quaint application will not be disappointed if they consult the latter's ' Exposition' of 2 Timothy, c. iii.-iv. (folio, 1658). See pp. 449–50. ' When we consider the position of the apostle,' observe Webster and Wilkinson, ' the good confession he maintained in spite of desertion and discouragement, we may reasonably conceive he refers to ὁ ἀντίδικος ἡμῶν διάβολος ὡς λεων ὠρυόμενος, 1 Peter v. 8.' (Greek Testament, with Notes Grammatical and Exegetical, vol. ii. 1861.) It will be noticed that Sibbes adopts the impersonal reference. Psalm xxii. 21, Proverbs xxvi. 13, illustrate his interpretation.

(*i*) P. 316.—' Jailor . . . . . bowels of pity.' See this subject treated with no common power and pathos from the text, Acts xvi. 33, ' He washed their stripes,' by Bishop Brownrig, who succeeded Sibbes as Master of Katherine Hall. ('Sermons,' folio, vol. i. pp. 273–291.)

(*j*) P. 318.—' Casting something unto these lions, to divert them another way.' A singularly beautiful expansion of this thought may here be given from a volume of ' Sermons,' by the late Rev. Dr Henderson of Galashiels, with whom Sibbes was an especial favourite:—

' Death is the last enemy,—the last with whom the believer shall be called to contend during his period of conflict and trial. When the struggle is over, which issues in the dissolution of his earthly tabernacle, it may be said that his " warfare is accomplished." He may appear to the eye of sense to sink and perish in the mortal strife; but to the eye of faith, in the view of the angel bands who look on, and in his sight to whom belong the issues from death, he escapes and triumphs. He has passed from the land of the enemy—from the field of war and danger. He has left his body, indeed, behind, a prey to corruption. Death may wreak on *it* his fury. *But it is as one who has thrown down his garment to be torn and trampled by the wild beasts in its rage; while he himself hastens away to the refuge which opens before him.* So does the soul enter into rest. . . . ' (Sermons on Doctrinal and Practical Subjects. 1 vol. 8vo, 1843, pp. 244–5.)

(*k*) P. 326.—' We are kept (we are *guarded*, as the word is).' Sibbes very frequently quotes this text; and invariably returns upon his rendering of 'guarded' instead of 'kept.' Demarest, who adopts it, may profitably be consulted. (Translation and Exp. of 1 Peter. New York, 1851.)

(*l*) P. 327.—' Our *conversation* is in heaven. . . . . . He conversed as a *citizen* of heaven before he came there, Philip iii. 20. The original is τὸ πολίτευμα = commonwealth, or perhaps citizenship. Cf. Ellicott *in loc*, who gives the literature of the text and word.
G.

CHRIST IS BEST; OR, ST PAUL'S STRAIT.

CHRIST IS BEST; or, ST PAUL'S STRAIT.

NOTE.

'Christ is Best' follows the 'Saint's Safety in Evil Times' in the volume described, (See note at page 296). Its separate title-page is given below.* It forms No. 11 of 'Saints' Cordials,' (2d ed. 1637, and 3d ed. 1658); and is therein entitled, 'Christ is Best; or, A Sweet Passage to Glory.'—G.

* Title-page—

CHRIST IS BEST:
OR,
ST PAUL'S STRAIT,
A
SERMON PREAched at the Funerall of
Mr Sherland, late Recorder of Northampton.
By R. SIBBS, D.D. [as before].
Psal. 42. 2.
London, Printed by M. F. for R. Dawlman, at the Brazen Serpent in Paul's Churchyard. 1634. 8°.

CHRIST IS BEST;

OR,

ST PAUL'S STRAIT.

For I am in a strait between two, having a desire to depart, and to be with Christ, which is best of all; nevertheless, to abide in the flesh is most needful for you.—PHIL. I. 23, 24.

THE apostle Paul here, had a double desire, one in regard of himself, to be with Christ; another, out of his love of God's church and people, to abide still in the flesh; and between these two he is in a great strait, not knowing which to choose. But the love of the church of Christ triumphed in him, above the love of his own salvation, so as he was content, out of self-denial, to want the joys of heaven for a time, that he might yet further comfort the people of God.

In the words you have, 1, *St Paul's straits;* 2, his *desires* that caused them, as in regard of himself, which was *to be with Christ;* so, in respect of the church of God, which was *to abide still here;* 3, the reasons of both, (1) *to be with Christ* is far better for me, (2) *to abide in the flesh* more needful for you; and 4, his resolution upon all, being willing for the church's good *still to abide here,* rather than go to heaven and enjoy his own happiness.

St Paul's soul was as a ship, between two winds, tossed up and down, and as iron between two loadstones, drawn first one way, then another; the one loadstone was his own good, to be in heaven; the other was the good of God's people, to abide still in the flesh.

Obs. Observe hence *that the servants of God are oftentimes in great straits.* Some things are so exceeding bad that, without any deliberation or delay at all, we ought presently to abominate them, as Satan's temptations to sin, to distrust, despair, &c. Some things also are so good that we should immediately cleave unto them, as matters of religion and piety. There should be no delay in these holy businesses. Deliberation here, argues weakness. Some things, again, are of an ambiguous and doubtful nature, requiring our best consideration. Such was Paul's strait in this place. He had reasons swaying him on both sides; and such is the happy estate of a Christian, that whatsoever he had chosen had been well for him; only, God who rules our judgments, will have us to make choice. God might have determined whether Paul should live or die, but he would not without Paul's choice. That which is good, is not good to us, but upon choice and advice. When God hath given us abilities to discourse and examine things, he will have us make use of them, and therefore the apostle useth reasons on both sides, it is better to die for me, it is better to live for you, &c.

Wicked men have their deliberations, and their straits too; but it is with the rich man in the gospel, what they shall do, how they may pull down their barns, and build bigger, &c., Luke xii. 18. Their main strait is at the hour of death; live they cannot, die they dare not. There is so much guilt of sin upon their consciences, they know not which way to turn themselves. Oh, what fearful straits will sin bring men into! But the apostle was straitened in an higher nature than this, whether it were better for the glory of God (which he aimed at above all) for him to go to heaven and enjoy happiness in his own person, or to abide still, for the comfort of God's saints, on earth.

The ground of this difficulty and strait was his present desire.

I have a desire. Desires are the immediate issue of the soul, the motion and stirring of the same to something that likes it. When there is anything set before the soul having a magnetical force, as the loadstone, to draw out the motions thereof, we call that desire, though for the present it enjoys it not.

1. St Paul's desire was, *spiritual;* not after happiness, so much as holiness. 'O miserable man that I am,' saith he, 'who shall deliver me from this body of death?' Rom. vii. 24. His desire of death was to be freed from the *body of sin*, more than to be taken out of the flesh; and his desire of holiness, to have Christ's image stamped on his soul, was more than of eternal happiness. Nature cannot do this. It is a work above the flesh, for that will not hear of departing, but rather bids God and Christ depart from it.

2. This desire came from a *taste of sweetness in communion with Christ;* and those desires that most ravish the soul in apprehension of heavenly things are ever the most holy. St Paul knew what a sweet communion Christ was.

3. It was a *constant* desire. He doth not say I desire, but I have a desire, I carry the same about me, and that carries me to a love of Christ and his members.

4. It was *efficacious*, not a naked velleity, not a wish of the sluggard, I would, and I would, but a strong desire, carrying him even through death itself to Christ. Desires thus qualified are blessed desires. As where we see vapours arise, there are springs usually below them, so where these desires are, there is always a spring of grace in that soul. Nothing characteriseth a Christian so much as holy and blessed desires, for there is no hypocrisy in them.

I desire to depart. There must be a *parting* and a departing; there must be a parting in this world with all outward excellencies, from the sweet enjoyment of the creatures; there must be a parting between soul and body, between friend and friend, and whatever is near and dear unto us. All shall determine in death.

And there must be a *departing* also. Here we cannot stay long; away we must; we are for another place. Oh that we could make use of these common truths! How far are we from making a right use of the mysteries of salvation, when we cannot make use of common truths which we have daily experience of! Holy Moses, considering the suddenness of his departure hence, begged of God to teach him to number his days, that he might apply his heart unto wisdom, Ps. xc. 12.

Death is but a departing (*a*), which word is taken from loosing from the shore, or removing of a ship to another coast. We must all be unloosened from our houses of clay, and be carried to another place, to heaven. Paul labours to sweeten so harsh a thing as death, by comfortable expressions of it. It is but a sleep, a going home, a laying aside our earthly tabernacle, to teach us this point of heavenly wisdom, that we should look on death as it is now in the gospel, not as it was in the law and by nature; for so it is a passage to hell, and lets us in to all miseries whatsoever.

Some things are desirable for themselves, as happiness and holiness; some things are desirable not for themselves, but as they make way to better things, being sour, and bitter to nature themselves; as physic is desired not for itself, but for health. We desire health for itself, and physic for health, so *to be with Christ* is a thing desirable of itself; but because we cannot come to Christ but by the dark passage of death, saith Paul, *I desire to depart*, that so my death may be a passage to Christ; so that death was the object of St Paul's desire so far as it made way for better things.

I desire to depart, and to be with Christ.

To be with Christ that came from heaven to be here on earth with us, and descended that we should ascend; to be with him, that hath done and suffered so much for us; to be with Christ that delighted to be with us; to be with Christ that emptied himself, and became of no reputation, that became poor to make us rich; to be with Christ our husband, now contracted here, that all may be made up in heaven, this was the thing Paul desired.

Quest. Why doth he not say, I desire to be in heaven?

Ans. Because heaven is not heaven without Christ. It is better to be in any place with Christ than to be in heaven itself without him. All delicacies without Christ are but as a funeral banquet. Where the master of the feast is away, there is nothing but solemnness. What is all without Christ? I say the joys of heaven are not the joys of heaven without Christ; he is the very heaven of heaven.

True love is carried to the person. It is adulterous love, to love the thing, or the gift, more than the person. St Paul loved the person of Christ, because he felt sweet experience that Christ loved him; his love was but a reflection of Christ's love first. He loved to see Christ, to embrace him, and enjoy him that had done so much and suffered so much for his soul, that had forgiven him so many sins, &c.

The reason is, because it is best of all. To be with Christ is to be at the spring-head of all happiness. It is to be in our proper element. Every creature thinks itself best in its own element, that is the place it thrives in, and enjoys its happiness in; now Christ is the element of a Christian. Again, it is far better, because to be with Christ is to have the marriage consummate. Is not marriage better than the contract? is not home better than absence? To be with Christ is to be at home. Is not triumph better than to be in conflict? but to be with Christ is to triumph over all enemies, to be out of Satan's reach. Is not perfection better than imperfection? Here all is but imperfect, in heaven there is perfection; therefore that is much better than any good below, for all are but shadows here, there is reality. What is riches? what are the worm-eaten pleasures of the world? What are the honours of the earth, but mere shadows of good? 'At the right hand of Christ are pleasures indeed,' Ps. xvi. 11, honours indeed, riches indeed; there is reality.

If we speak of grace, and good things, it is better to be with Christ than enjoy the graces and comforts of the Holy Ghost here. Why? because they are all stained and mixed. Here our peace is interrupted with desertion and trouble. Here the joys of the Holy Ghost are mingled with sorrow. Here the grace in a man is with combat of flesh and spirit, but in heaven there is pure peace, pure joy, pure grace: for what is glory but the perfection of grace. Grace indeed is glory here, but it is glory with conflict. The Scripture calls grace glory sometimes, but it is glory with imperfection. Beloved, perfection is better than imperfection, therefore to be with Christ is far better.

And is it much 'far better' to die, that we may be with Christ, than to live here a conflicting life? Why should we then fear death, that is but a passage to Christ? It is but a grim sergeant that lets us into a glorious palace, that strikes off our bolts, that takes off our rags, that we may be clothed with better robes, that ends all our misery, and is the beginning of all our happiness. Why should we therefore be afraid of death? it is but a departure to a better condition? It is but as Jordan to the children of Israel, by which they passed to Canaan. It is but as the Red Sea by which they were going that way. Therefore we have no reason to fear death. Of itself it is an enemy indeed, but now it is harmless, nay, now it is become a friend, amicable to us, a sweet friend. It is one part of the church's jointure, death. 'All things are yours,' saith the apostle, Paul and Apollos, 'life and death,' 1 Cor. iii. 22. Death is ours and for our good. It doth us more good than all the friends we have in the world. It determines and ends all our misery and sin; and it is the suburbs of heaven. It lets us into those joys above. It is a shame for Christians therefore, to be afraid of that that Paul here makes the object of his desire.

But may not a good Christian fear death?

I answer, Not, so far as a Christian is led with the Spirit of God, and is truly spiritual; for the Spirit carries us upward. But as far as we are earthly and carnal, and biassed downward to things below, we are loath to depart hence. In some cases God's children are afraid to die, because their accounts are not ready. Though they love Christ, and are in a good way, yet notwithstanding, because they have not prepared themselves by care, as a woman that hath her husband abroad and desires his coming, but all is not prepared in the house, therefore she desires that he may stay awhile; so the soul that is not exact, that is not in that frame that it should be in, saith, 'Oh stay a while that I may recover my strength, before I go hence and be no more seen,' Ps. xxxix. 13; but as far as we are guided by the Spirit of God sanctifying us, and are in such a condition as we should be in, so far the thoughts of death ought not to be terrible to us; nor indeed are they.

Beloved, there is none but a Christian that can desire death; because it is the end of all comfort here, it is the end of all callings and employments, of all sweetness whatsoever in this world. If another man that is not a Christian, desire heaven, he desires it not as heaven, or to be with Christ as Christ; he desires it under some notion suitable to his corruption; for our desires are as ourselves are, as our aims are. No carnal worldly man, but hath carnal worldly aims. A worldly man cannot go beyond the world. It is his sphere. A carnal man cannot go beyond the flesh. Therefore a carnal man cannot desire heaven. A man that is under the power of any lust, can desire nothing but the satisfying of that lust. Heaven is no place for such. None but a child of God can desire that; for if we consider heaven, and *to be with Christ*, to be *perfect holiness*, can he desire it that hates holiness here? can he desire the image of God upon him that hates it in others and in himself too? can he desire the communion of saints, that of all societies hates it the most? can he desire to be free from sin, that engulfs himself continually in sin? He cannot, and therefore as long as he is under the thraldom and dominion of any lust he may desire heaven indeed, but it is only so far as he may have his lusts there, his pleasures, honours, and riches there too. If he may have heaven with that, he is contented; but alas! brethren, heaven must not be so desired. St Paul did otherwise; he desired *to be dissolved, to be with Christ*. He desired it as the perfection of the image of God, under the notion of holiness and freedom from sin, as I said before.

Which is far better.

Obs. Again, we see that *God reserves the best for the last* (*b*). God's last works are his best works. The new heaven and the new earth are the best; the second wine that Christ created himself was the best; spiritual things are better than natural. A Christian's last is his best.

God will have it so, for the comfort of Christians, that every day they live, they may think, my best is behind, my best is to come, that every day they rise, they may think, I am nearer heaven one day than I was before, I am nearer death, and therefore nearer to Christ. What a solace is this to a gracious heart! A Christian is a happy man in his life, but happier in his death, because then he goes to Christ; but happiest of all in heaven, for then he is *with Christ*. How contrary to a carnal man, that lives according to the sway of his own base lusts! He is miserable in his life, more miserable in his death, but most miserable of all after death. I beseech you, lay this to heart. Methinks, considering that death is but a way for us to be with Christ, *which is far better*, this should sweeten the thinking of death to us, and we should comfort ourselves daily that we are nearer happiness.

Quest. But how shall we attain this sanctified sweet desire that Paul had, to die, and be with Christ?

Ans. 1. *Let us carry ourselves as Paul did*, and then we shall have the same desires. St Paul, before death, in his lifetime, 'had his conversation in heaven,' Phil. iii. 1. His mind was there, and his soul followed after. There is no man's soul comes into heaven, but his mind is there first. It was an easy matter for him to desire to be with Christ, having his conversation in heaven already. Paul in meditation was, where he was not, and he was not where he was. He was in heaven when his body was on earth.

2. Again, *St Paul had loosed his affections from all earthly things*; therefore it was an easy matter for him to desire to be with Christ. 'I am crucified to the world, and the world is crucified to me,' &c., Gal. vi. 14. If once a Christian comes to this pass, death will be welcome to him. Those whose hearts are fastened to the world, cannot easily desire Christ.

3. Again, holy St Paul *laboured to keep a good conscience in all things*. 'Herein I exercise myself, to have a good conscience towards God and men,' &c., Acts xxiv. 16. It is easy for him to desire to be dissolved, that hath his conscience *sprinkled with the blood of Christ*, Heb. x. 22, free from a purpose of living in any sin. But where there is a stained, defiled, polluted conscience, there cannot be this desire; for the heart of man, naturally, as the prophet saith, 'casts up mire and dirt,' Isa. lvii. 20. It casts up fears, and objections, and murmurings, and repinings. Oh, beloved, we think not what mischief sin will do us, when we suffer it to seize upon our consciences; when it is once written there *with the claw of a diamond*,

and *with a pen of iron*, Jer. xvii. 1, who shall get it out? Nothing but great repentance and faith, applying the blood of Christ. It is no easy matter to get it off there, and to get the conscience at peace again; and when conscience is not appeased, there will be all clamours within. It will fear to appear before the judgment-seat. A guilty conscience trembles at the mention of death. Therefore I wonder how men that live in swearing, in looseness, in filthiness, in deboisedness* of life, that labour to satisfy their lusts and corruptions, I wonder how they can think of death without trembling, considering that they are under the guilt of so many sins. Oh, beloved, the exercising of the heart to keep a clear conscience, can only breed this desire in us to depart, and to be with Christ. You have a company of wretched persons, proud enough in their own conceits, and censorious. Nothing can please them, whose whole life is acted by Satan joining with the lusts of their flesh, and they do nothing but put stings into death every day, and arm death against themselves, which when once it appears, their conscience, which is a hell within them, is wakened, and where are they? They can stay here no longer; they must appear before the dreadful Judge; and then where are all their pleasures and contentments, for which they neglected heaven and happiness, peace of conscience, and all? Oh, therefore let us walk holily with our God, and maintain inward peace all we can, if we desire to depart hence with comfort.

4. Again, Paul had got *assurance that he was in Christ, by his union with him.* 'I live not,' saith he, 'but Christ lives in me,' Gal. ii. 19. Therefore labour for assurance of salvation, that you may feel the Spirit of Christ in you, sanctifying and altering your carnal dispositions to be like his. 'I know whom I have trusted,' 2 Tim. i. 12, saith he. He was as sure of his salvation, as if he had had it already. How few live as if they intended any such matter as this, assurance of salvation, without which how can we ever desire to be dissolved, and to be with Christ? Will a man leave his house, though it be never so mean, when he knows not whither to go? Will a man leave the prison, when he knows he shall be carried to execution? Oh, no; he had rather be in the dungeon still. So when there is guilt on the soul, that it is not assured of salvation, but rather hath cause to fear the contrary, can it say, 'I desire to depart, and be with Christ,' &c.? No; they had rather abide in the flesh still, if they could, for ever, for all eternity. Therefore, if we would come to Paul's desire, labour to come to the frame of the holy apostle's spirit. He knew whom he had believed; he was assured that nothing could separate him from the love of God, neither life, nor death, nor anything whatsoever that could befall him, Rom. viii. 38, 39.

5. *Paul had an art of sweetening the thoughts of death.* He considered it only as a departure from earth to heaven. When death was presented unto him as a passage to Christ, it was an easy matter to desire the same; therefore it should be the art of Christians to present death as a passage to a better life, to labour to bring our souls into such a condition, as to think death not to be a death to us, but the death of itself. Death dies when I die, and I begin to live when I die. It is a sweet passage to life. We never live till we die. This was Paul's art. He had a care to look beyond death, to heaven; and when he looked upon death, he looked on it but as a passage to Christ: so let it be our art and skill. Would we cherish a desire to die, let us look on death as a passage to Christ, and look beyond it to heaven. All of us must go through this dark passage to Christ (*c*), which when we consider as Paul did, it will be an easy matter to die.

* That is, 'debauchery.'—G.

I come now to the next words—*Nevertheless, to abide in the flesh is more needful for you.*

This is the other desire of Paul, that brought him into this strait. He was troubled whether he should die, which was far better for himself, or live, which was more needful for them; but the love of God's people did prevail in holy St Paul, above the desire of heaven, and the present enjoying his own happiness. Oh, the power of grace in the hearts of God's children, that makes them content to be without the joys of heaven for a time, that they may do God's service, in serving his church here upon earth.

Obs. 1. Observe hence, *that the lives of worthy men, especially magistrates and ministers, are very needful for the church of God.*

The reason is, because God's manner of dispensation is, to convey all good to men, by the means of men like ourselves for the most part; and this he doth to knit us into a holy communion one with another. Therefore it is needful that holy men should abide. In regard of the church of God, their lives are very useful.

If we consider good, the great benefit that comes by them, we shall easily yield to this; for what a deal of sin doth a good magistrate stop and hinder! When there were good judges and good kings in Israel, see what a reformation there was. Antichrist could not come in when the Roman empire flourished, 2 Thes. ii. 7, though now the Roman empire hinder the fall of antichrist, because antichrist hath given her the cup of fornication, and they are drunk with the whore's cup; but at the first it was not so. Beloved, whilst good magistrates and good ministers continue in a place, there is a hindrance of heresies and sin, &c. If they be once removed, there is a floodgate opened for all manner of sin and corruption to break in at. Yea, there is abundance of good comes in by gracious persons.

1. By their *counsel and direction:* 'The lips of the righteous feed many,' Prov. vii. 21.

2. By their *reformation of abuses, by planting God's ordinances and good orders,* whereby God's wrath is appeased. They stand in the gap, and stop evil. They reform it, and labour to establish that which is pleasing to God.

3. Gracious persons, in what condition soever they are, *carry the blessing of God with them.* Wheresoever they are, God and his blessing goes along with them.

4. They do a great deal of good *by their pattern and example.* 'They are the lights of the world,' Philip. ii. 15, that give aim to others in the darkness of this life.

5. They can by their *prayers bind God,* as it were, *that he shall not inflict his judgments.* They do a world of good by this way. A praying force and army is as good as a fighting army. Moses did as much good by prayer, as the soldiers in the valley when they fought with Amalek. They are favourites with God in heaven, therefore St Paul saith, *It is needful for you that I abide in the flesh.* Gracious men are public treasures, and storehouses, wherein every man hath a share, a portion; they are public springs in the wilderness of this world, to refresh the souls of people; they are trees of righteousness, that stretch out their boughs for others to shelter under, and to gather fruit from. You have an excellent picture of this in Daniel, in the dream of Nebuchadnezzar, Dan. iv. 21. The magistrates there, are compared to a great tree, wherein the birds build their nests, and the beasts shelter themselves; so a good magistrate, especially

if he be in great place, is as a great tree for comfort and shelter. Oh, beloved, the lives of good men are very useful. A good man, saith the philosopher, is a common good; because as soon as ever a man becomes gracious, he hath a public mind, as he hath a public place, nay, whether he hath a public place or no, he hath a public mind. It is needful, therefore, that there be such men alive.

If this be so, then we may lament the death of worthy men, because we lose part of our strength in the loss of such, God's custom being to convey much good by them; and when there is scarcity of good men, we should say with Micah, Woe is me; the good is perished from the earth, Micah vii. 2. They keep judgments from a place, and derive a blessing upon it. Howsoever the world judgeth them, and accounts them not worthy to live, yet God accounts the world unworthy of them. They are God's jewels, they are his treasure and his portion, therefore we ought to lament their death, and to desire their lives; and we ought to desire our own lives, as long as we may be useful to the church; and be content to want heaven for a time. Beloved, it is not for the good of God's children that they live; as soon as ever they are in the state of grace they have a title to heaven, but it is for others. When once we are in Christ, we live for others, not for ourselves. That a father is kept alive, it is for his children's sake; that good magistrates are kept alive, it is for their subjects' sake; that a good minister is kept alive, out of the present enjoying of heaven, it is for the people's sake that God hath committed to him to instruct; for, as Paul saith here, in regard of my own particular, *it is better for me to be with Christ*.

Use. If God convey so much good by worthy men to us, then what wretches are they that malign them, persecute them, &c., speak ill of those that speak to God for them? Doth the world continue for a company of wretches, a company of profane, blasphemous, loose, disorderly livers? Oh no; for if God had not a church in the world, a company of good people, heaven and earth would fall in pieces. There would be an end presently. It is for good people only that the world continues. They are the pillars of the tottering world, they are the stakes in the fence, they are the foundation of the building, and if they were once taken out, all would come down; there would be a confusion of all. Therefore those that oppose and disquiet gracious and good men are enemies to their own good; they cut the bough which they stand on; they labour to pull down the house that covers themselves, being blinded with malice and a diabolical spirit. Take heed of such a disposition. It comes near to the sin against the Holy Ghost to hate any man for goodness; because, perhaps, his good life reproacheth us. Such a one would hate Christ himself if he were here. How can a man desire to be with Christ when he hates his image in another? Therefore if God convey so much good by other men that are good, let us make much of them, as public persons, as instruments of our good. Take away malice, and pride, and a poisonful spirit, and all their good is ours. What hinders that we have no good by them? Pride and an envious spirit, &c.

Obs. A second thing that I observe hence is this, *holy and gracious men, that are led by the Spirit of God, can deny themselves and their own best good for the church's benefit*. They know that God hath appointed them as instruments to convey good to others; and knowing this, they labour to come to Paul's spirit here, to desire to live, to have life in patience, and death in desire in regard of themselves; for it were much better for a good man to be in heaven, out of misery, out of this conflicting condition with the devil and devilish-minded men.

Reason 1. The reason is, because a good man, as soon as he is a good man, *hath the spirit of love in him*, and 'love seeketh not its own,' 1 Cor. xiii. 5, but the good of another; and as the love of Christ and the love of God possesseth and seizeth upon the soul, so self-love decays. What is gracious love but a decay of self-love? The more self-love decays, the more we deny ourselves.

2. Again, God's people have the *Spirit of Christ in them*, who minded not his own things, 1 Cor. x. 24. If Christ had minded his own things, where had our salvation been? Christ was content to leave heaven, and to take our nature upon him, to be Emmanuel, God with us, that we might be with God for ever in heaven. He was content, not only to leave heaven, but to be born in the womb of a virgin. He was content to stoop to the grave. He stooped as low as hell in love to us. Now, where Christ's Spirit is, it will bring men from their altitudes and excellencies, and make them to stoop to serve the church, and account it an honour to be an instrument to do good. Christ was content to be accounted, not only a servant of God, but of the church. 'My righteous servant,' &c., Isa. liii. 11. Those that have the Spirit of Christ have a spirit of self-denial of their own. We see the blessed angels are content to be ministering spirits for us, and it is thought to be the sin of the devil, pride, when he scorned to stoop to the keeping of man, an inferior creature to himself. The blessed angels do not scorn to attend upon a poor child, 'little ones.' A christian is a consecrated person, and he is none of his own. He is a sacrifice as soon as he is a Christian. He is Christ's. He gives himself to Christ; and as he gives himself, so he gives his life and all to Christ, as Paul saith of the Corinthians, they gave themselves and their goods to him, 2 Cor. viii. 5. When a Christian gives himself to Christ, he gives all to Christ; all his labour and pains, and whatsoever he knows that Christ can serve himself of him for his church's good and his glory. He knows that Christ is wiser than he; therefore he resigns himself to his disposal, resolving, if he live, *he lives to the Lord;* and if he die, *he dies to the Lord,* Rom. xiv. 8; that so, whether he live or die, *he may be the Lord's.*

Use 1. Oh, beloved, that we had the spirit of St Paul, and the Spirit of Christ, *to set us a work to do good while we are here,* 'to deny ourselves,' Titus ii. 12. Oh, it would be meat and drink, as it was to our blessed Saviour Christ, to do good all kinds of ways. Consider all the capacities and abilities we have to do good, this way and that way, in this relation and that relation, that we may be trees of righteousness, that the more we bear the more we may bear. God will mend his own trees. He will purge them and prune them to 'bring forth more fruit,' John xv. 2. God cherisheth fruitful trees. In the law of Moses, when they besieged any place, he commanded them to spare fruitful trees. God spares a fruitful person till he have done his work. We know not how much good one man may do, though he be a mean person. Sometimes one poor wise man delivereth the city, Eccles. ix. 15; and the righteous delivereth the land. We see for one servant, Joseph, Potiphar's house was blessed, Gen. xxxix. 3. Naaman had a poor maidservant that was the occasion of his conversion, 2 Kings v. Grace will set anybody a-work. It puts a dexterity into any, though never so mean. They carry God's blessing wheresoever they go, and they bethink themselves when they are in any condition to do good, as he saith in Esther iv. 14, 'God hath called me to this place, perhaps for this end.' We should often put this *quære* to ourselves, Why hath God called me to this place? for such and such a purpose?

Now, that we may be fruitful as Paul was, let us labour to have humble spirits. God delights in an humble spirit, and not in a proud spirit, for that takes all the glory to itself. God delights to use humble spirits, that are content to stoop to any service for others, that think no office too mean.

2. Get *loving* hearts. Love is full of invention, how shall I glorify God? how shall I do good to others? how shall I bring to heaven as many as I can? Love is a sweet and boundless affection, full of holy devices.

3. Labour to have *sufficiency in our places*, that you may have ability to do good. Oh, when these meet together, ability and sufficiency; and a willing, a large, and gracious heart and a fit object to do good to, what a deal of good is done then!

4. And when we find *opportunity of doing any good, let us resolve upon it*, resolve to honour God, and serve him in spite of flesh and blood; for we must get every good work that we do out of the fire, as it were; we must get it out with travail, and pains. We carry that about us that will hinder us. Let us therefore labour to have sincere aims in that we do to please God, and then resolve to do all the good we can.

To stir us up to be more and more fruitful in our places, let us consider we live for others, and not for ourselves, when we are good Christians once. It was a good speech of that godly Palsgrave, great grandfather to him that is (Frederick the godly they called him), when he was to die, *Satis vobis*, saith he, *I have lived hitherto for you, now let me live for myself*. We live here all our life for others, therefore let us think while we live, how we may do most good in the church of God.

For encouragement hereunto consider, God will undertake to recompense all the good we do, to a 'cup of cold water,' Mark ix. 41. We shall not lose a sigh, a groan, for the church. God would account himself dishonoured if it should not be rewarded. He hath pawned his faithfulness upon it; 'he is not unfaithful to be unmindful of your good works,' Heb. vi. 10.

Nay, we have a present reward and contentment of conscience: as light accompanies fire, so peace and joy accompany every good action. All is not reserved for heaven. A Christian hath some beginnings of happiness here. When he doth that that is contrary to flesh and blood, how full of sweet joy is a fruitful soul! Those that are fruitful in their places never want arguments of good assurance of salvation. It is your lazy, lukewarm Christian that wants assurance. Therefore I beseech you be stirred up, to live desired in the world, and die lamented; labour to be useful in your places all you can; to be as the olive and fig-tree, delighting God and man, and not to cumber the ground of the church with barrenness. Sins of omission,—because men were not fruitful in their places,—was a ground of damnation; 'cast the unprofitable servant into outer darkness,' Mat. xxv. 30; put case he did no harm; aye, but he was *unprofitable*. Such was the cursed disposition of Ephraim; he brought forth fruit to himself. Oh this looking to ourselves. When we make ourselves the beginning and the end of all the good we do, it is an argument of a barren person. None ever came to heaven but those that denied themselves.

I see I cannot proceed in this point. You may by the Spirit of God enlarge it in your thoughts and bring home what hath been said, to your own souls. Labour that you may be such as others may make use of you, and not be the burdens and calamities of the time, as many are, that live for nothing but to do good men good by vexing of them. That is all the good they do; by vexing their patience they exercise their grace a contrary way.

Let us not be briars and unfruitful plants, labouring to be great by the public miseries. As they say, great fishes grow big by devouring many little ones; as a dragon comes to be great by devouring many little serpents, so many grow great by the ruin of others. Oh beloved, it had been better for such that they had never been born. Therefore as we desire to have comfort when we die, let us labour to be fruitful while we live. St Paul, when the time came that he should die, when he had done his work, you see he that was thus full of self-denial, how gloriously he ended his days. The second Epistle to Timothy was the last epistle that ever he wrote, and when he had done his work, saith he, 'I have fought a good fight, I have kept the faith, I have finished my course: from henceforth there is a crown of righteousness reserved for me,' 2 Tim. iv. 7. What a glorious end is here! and indeed those that are thus careful, and fruitful in their lives and conversations, end their days full of comfort, and resign their souls to God with full assurance of a blessed change, and only those. For you have many, when they come to die, what hinders them? Oh I have been unfruitful, I have not done that good that I might, I have not 'wrought out my salvation with fear and trembling,' Philip. ii. 12. In such a thing I have done ill, such a thing I have omitted. So they are enemies to their own comfort. Enlarge this in your own meditations, and consider what will comfort you hereafter, when you shall need most comfort. So I leave the text, and come to the occasion.

This holy and blessed man whose funeral now we solemnize, was of St Paul's spirit. He did *desire to die, and be with Christ;* he had a desire while he lived to take all opportunities to do good. I speak of that time when he lived, that is, when he was good, for we live no longer than we are good. Let us not reckon that life, wherein we do no good. After God had wrought upon his heart, he had a public heart to do good. If I wanted matter to speak of, I could tell you of his alliance and birth, having two worthy judges of reverend esteem, the one his grandfather, the other his uncle. The one bred him, the other cherished and promoted his study and endeavours; but what should I speak of these things when he hath personal worth enough? I need not go abroad to commend this man, for there were those graces and gifts in him that made him so esteemed, that verily, I think, no man of his place and years lived more desired, and died more lamented.

1. For his parts of nature, they were pregnant and solid; but as one said to Melancthon, his disposition and loving mind did gain as much love from men as his parts, though they were great.

2. His learning was good; for beside his own profession, he was a general scholar, and had good skill in that we call elegant learning, and controverted points of divinity. He was a good divine. Indeed, in the turning of his life, when he should have adventured upon a profession, he had some thoughts of being a divine, had not his friends, especially his uncle, Judge Yelverton, (d) disposed him otherwise, by promoting his study in the law; and when he took upon him that profession, he grew so in it, that he was a credit to the profession for integrity, sincerity, and ability.

3. For his disposition he was every way a man of an excellent sweet temper; mild, and yet resolute; meek, and yet bold where cause was; discreet, yet not over-discreet, so as not to stand out in a good cause in the defence of it; he was humble, yet thought himself too good to be instrumental to any services other than stood with the peace of his conscience; he was tractable and gentle, yet immovably fixed to his principles of piety

and honesty; he was exact in his life, yet not censorious; very conscionable and religious, but without any vain curiosity; indeed, he was every-way of a sweet temper. If he stood out in dislike of any, in any matter, he carried it usually with evidence of such sincerity, and denial of self-seeking, that he usually prevailed where he put in.

4. To come to his private personal carriage, it was very pious. He was wont to sequester himself from his employment and labour, to bring his heart under to God, to the guidance of God's Spirit: his study was to study to die; for he gathered choice things out of the sermons he heard about death, many years before he died, to lay up store of provision against that time; and two or three terms before he died he had a special care to inquire of nearer communion with God. He inquired of those he conversed with of the way to attain the same, and was willing to hear any discourses that tended that way.

5. For his care of the Sabbath, it was his delight. His custom was, after sermon, to retire and ruminate upon what he had heard, to turn it into his spirit. Alas, for want of this, how many sermons are lost in this great city! how much seed is spilt in vain! What nourishment can there be without digestion? it is the second digestion that breeds nourishment; when we chew things, and call them to mind again, and make them our own. This was his custom every Sabbath.

6. For his carriage to others, he was a constant friend, and his study was, to labour to make those good he conversed withal. He conversed with few, but they were the better for him, he was so fruitful; and he would have intimate society with none, but he would do good or take good from them. You have many in the society where he lived, that may bless God all the days of their life that ever they knew him.

7. For his carriage in his government of the place where he lived, I think there are none that are able to judge, but will give him the testimony of a faithful, prudent governor. He was so careful of the town where he was recorder, that he provided for them after his death, and gave them a large legacy, two hundred merks, to set the poor on work.

8. For the honourable society wherein he was a governor, he carried himself with that resolution, for good order and good exercises, and was such a strict opposer of any abuse, which he judged to be so, that the house will have a special want of him.* I fear, rather, I desire from my soul, that that honourable society may so flourish as they may have no want of good Master Sherland.

9. For his more public carriage, by virtue of his place at Northampton, where he was recorder, he was called to be a member of the body-representative in Parliament, wherein both his ability and spirit appeared to all that knew him. You may see by this what manner of man we have lost.

He died before he was come to the middle of his years, a young man to speak of; and he did a great deal of work in a little time. God had ripened him for his business extraordinarily, and gave him a spirit to bestir himself to do all the good he could. These be wondrous ill times, beloved, to lose such men as he was; therefore we have cause to lay it to heart the more. The commonwealth wants him, the town and country where he lived will want him, the society where he was a governor will want him, the family where he was a governor will find a miss in him. He went wisely in and out; he was able for family duties; he had more than ordinary sufficiency;

* Qu. 'want of him, I fear: rather, I desire?' &c.—ED.

he was of Joshua's mind, ' Choose who you will serve, but I and my house will serve the Lord,' Josh. xxiv. 15; and to help him the more, he had the happiness to marry into a religious family; he had a good helper.

Now for the church. Though his profession was the law, yet that will have a great want of him. He was a hearty and true promoter of the cause of religion, and shewed his love to the church, by his care of it now he is departed. He gave four hundred pounds to buy in impropriations; he gave an hundred pounds for the breeding up of poor scholars, and there is never a good minister round about where he lived, but had encouragement from him. Indeed, he was a man of special use and service; and as he honoured God in his life, so God hath honoured him in his death, as you may see by this honourable assembly of worthy people, met in love to him.

His death was, as the death of strong men useth to be, with conflicts between nature and his disease, but with a great deal of patience; and in his sickness time he would utter Paul's disposition, Oh, saith he, you keep me from heaven, you keep me from glory, being displeased with those that kept him alive, with conference out of love.

He had a large heart to do good, for though he were fruitful, and studied to be fruitful, yet oft in his sickness in a complaining manner he would say, Oh, I have not been so wise for my own soul as I ought to be; I have not been provident enough in taking opportunities of doing and receiving good.

Beloved, shall such a man as he was, so careful, so fruitful, so good, shall he complain thus? what shall a company of us do? Beloved, those that have warmed their hearts at the fire of God's love, they think zeal itself to be coldness, and fruitfulness to be barrenness. Love is a boundless affection. He spake not this from want of care; but love knows no bounds. Therefore he took the more opportunities of doing good.

Well, I beseech you, beloved, let not this example pass without making good use of it. God will call us to a reckoning, not only for what we hear, but for what we see: he will call us to a reckoning for the examples of his people. Therefore, as we see here what a holy disposition was in St Paul, and in this blessed man now with God, so let us labour to find the same disposition in ourselves. Paul hath now his desire; he is dissolved, and he is with Christ, that is best of all. This holy man hath his desire; he desired not to be kept from his glory and happiness, on which his mind was set before. Let us therefore labour with God in the use of good means, to have the same disposition; and in this moment let us provide for eternity; out of eternity before, and eternity after, issueth this little spot of time to do good in. Let us sow to the Spirit, account all time lost that either we do not or take not, good in. Opportunity is God's angel. Time is short, but opportunity is shorter. Let us catch at all opportunities. This is the time of worship. Oh, let us sow now. Shall we go to sowing then, when the time comes that we should reap? Some begin to sow when they die, that is the reaping time. While we have time let us do all good, especially where God loves most, to those that are good.

Consider the standings and places that God hath set us in; consider the advantages in our hands, the price that we have; consider that opportunity will not stay long. Let us therefore do all the good we can, and so if we do, beloved, we shall come at length to reap that, that this blessed saint of God, St Paul here in the text, and this blessed man, for whose cause we are now met, do enjoy. Therefore, if we desire to end our days in joy and comfort, let us lay the foundation of a comfortable death now betimes. To die well is not a thing of that light moment as some imagine: it is no easy matter. But to die well is a matter of every day. Let us daily do some good that may help us at the time of our death. Every day by repentance pull out the sting of some sin, that so when death comes, we may have nothing to do but to die. To die well is the action of the whole life. He never dies well for the most part that dies not daily, as Paul saith of himself, 'I die daily,' 1 Cor. xv. 31; he laboured to loose his heart from the world, and worldly things. If we loose our hearts from the world and die daily, how easy will it be to die at last! He that thinks of the vanity of the world, and of death, and of being with Christ for ever, and is dying daily, it will be easy for him to end his days with comfort. But the time being past, I will here make an end. Let us desire God to make that which hath been spoken effectual, both concerning Paul, and likewise concerning this blessed man, for whose cause we are met together.*

* Sherland. In addition to the splendid eulogy of Sibbes, it may be noted here, that Sherland was one of the lay 'feofees' to buy in livings. (Fuller's Church History, ed. Brewer, vi. 67; and see Prynne's Canterburie's Doom, p. 385.) He impeached Buckingham. (Heylin's Laud, p. 143.)—G.

NOTES.

(a) P. 339.—'Death is but a *departing* . . . which word is taken from loosing from the shore, or removing of a ship to another coast.' See Luke viii. 38, and 2 Tim. iv. 6, and Phil. 1. 23 (all in the Greek).

(b) P. 341.—'God reserves the best for the last.' This more than once repeated saying of Sibbes, probably suggested to Thomas Brooks the titles of two of his minor writings, *(a)* 'A String of Pearls; or the Best Things Reserved till Last,' (1657); *(b)* 'A Believer's Last Day is his Best Day,' (1651).

(c) P. 342.—' All of us must go *through this dark passage to Christ.*' Sir William Davenant has finely used this saying—

'O harmless Death! whom still the valiant brave,
    The wise expect, the sorrowful invite,
And all the good embrace, *who know the grave*
    A short dark passage to eternal light.'

Longfellow has the same thought:

'The grave is but a cover'd bridge, leading from light
    To light, *through a brief darkness.*'

(d) P. 347.—'Judge Yelverton.' Consult Foss's 'Judges of England.'

G.

CHRIST'S SUFFERINGS FOR MAN'S SIN.

CHRIST'S SUFFERINGS FOR MAN'S SIN.

NOTE.

'Christ's Sufferings' follows 'Christ is Best,' and closes the 'first part' of the volume. It was reprinted in the 'Saint's Cordial's' (2d edition, 1637; 3d edition, 1658), forming No. 7. The separate title-page is subjoined.*—G.

* Title-page—

CHRISTS
SUFFERINGS,
FOR
MANS SINNE.

Laid open in a Passion Sermon at *Mercers Chappell* London, vpon Good Friday.

By R. SIBBS, D.D.

ISAY. 53. 5.

He was wounded for our *transgressions, and bruised for* our *iniquities; the chastisement of our peace was upon* him, *and with* his *stripes are* wee *healed.*

LONDON,
Printed by *M. F.* for *R. Dawlman*, at the Brazen Serpent in *Pauls* Churchyard. 1634.

CHRIST'S SUFFERINGS FOR MAN'S SIN.

About the ninth hour Jesus cried with a loud voice, Eli, Eli, lama sabachthani? that is to say, My God, my God, why hast thou forsaken me?—MAT. XXVII. 46.

THE dying speeches of men of worth, are most remarkable. At that time they stir up all their spirits and abilities which remain, that they may speak with greatest advantage to the hearts of others, and leave the deeper impression behind them.

These be some of the last words of our blessed Saviour's, uttered from the greatest affection, with the greatest faith, and to the greatest purpose, that ever any words were spoken, and therefore deserve your best attention.

In this portion of Scripture you have Christ's compellation, *My God;* and his complaint, *Why hast thou forsaken me?* 1. A compellation with an ingemination or reduplication of the words, *My God, my God,* to shew the strength of his affection and desire of help at this time.

2. A complaint by way of expostulation, *Why hast thou forsaken me?* I will draw all that I have to say into these four propositions:

1. That Christ was *forsaken.*
2. That he was very *sensible of it,* even unto complaint, *Why hast thou forsaken me?*
3. His *disposition and carriage in this extremity.* His faith failed not; *My God, my God.* His present grief tied him the closer and faster to his God.
4. Neither was it only faith, but a faith *flaming in prayer,* whereby he expressed that God was his God. He not only prayed but cried to him, 'My God, my God,' &c. This is the sum of what I intend.

1. Christ being in extremity was *forsaken.*
2. Being forsaken, he was very *sensible of it;* and from sensibleness complains, pouring out his soul into the bosom of his Father.
3. And not only complains, but *believes certainly that his Father will help him.*
4. And to strengthen his *faith* the more, he puts it forth in *prayer.* The fire of faith in his heart kindled into a flame of prayer (and that not in an ordinary manner, but in strong supplications), he cried out, 'My God, my God, why hast thou forsaken me?' To come to the particulars.

Obs. 1. *Christ was forsaken.*

I will briefly touch upon some circumstances, and then fall upon the point itself, as,

1. The *time* wherein he was *forsaken*—a time of darkness (*the sixth hour*), in which there was a darkness over the whole earth, and in the land of Judea especially. Neither had he darkness without only, but within likewise. His soul was troubled from a sense of his Father's displeasure, Mat. xxvi. 38. Two eclipses seized upon him together,—the one of the glorious light of the sun, the other of the light of his Father's countenance. He must needs be in a disconsolate estate, and doubly miserable, that is encompassed with such darkness. Whatsoever was done to Christ our surety, shall be done to all that are out of him. Blackness of darkness is reserved for them. As Christ wanted the comfort of light from heaven, so those that are out of Christ shall have no comfort from any creature at the last: the sun shall not shine upon them, the earth shall not bear them, they shall not have a drop of water to cool their tongues. They were formerly rebels against God, and now every creature is ready to serve the Lord against them. When the king is displeased with a man, which of his servants dare to countenance him?

This darkness being in Judea, did likewise portend the miserable condition of the Jews here, and that eternal darkness in the world to come, which should be their portion if they repented not.

2. Another circumstance may be this, *God was a great while ere he removed his heavy displeasure from Christ.* He was three hours in torment; and though God delayed him long, yet he said nothing till now by way of complaint. We should beware of darkness of spirit in trouble. God may delay help to his dearest children, as here he did to his only Son, to perfect the work of sanctification in them. Therefore, submit to his will, rest contented with whatever he sends, look to thy Head and Saviour, &c. But of this more anon.

3. *His greatest grief and conflicts were towards his latter end*, towards the shutting up and close of his life. Though a little after he saith, 'All is finished,' yet now he cries out, 'My God, my God, why hast thou forsaken me?' Afflictions are sharpest toward our ends. I speak this for prevention of discomfort in those that find extremities upon them. When miseries are extreme, help is nearest. They will either mend or end then. The darkness is thickest a little before the morning appears; and Satan raged most a little before his casting down.

As also to prevent security from seizing upon people. Take heed of deferring repentance till thy last hours; there may be a confluence of many extremities then upon thee, pains of body, terrors of conscience, Satan's temptations, God's wrath, &c. When all these meet together, and the poor soul, in its best strength, finds enough to do to conflict with any one of them, what an unhappy condition will that be! Oh, put not off your repentance to this time. But I pass these circumstances, and come to the point of forsaking itself.

In the unfolding whereof I will shew,

1. In what *sense* Christ was *forsaken*.
2. In what *parts* he was forsaken.
3. Upon what *ground*. And,
4. To what *end* all this forsaking of Christ was.

For the first, forsaking is nothing else but when God leaves the creature to itself, either in regard of comfort or of grace and assistance. I will shew you how Christ was left of his Father, and how he was not left.

(1.) *How Christ was not forsaken.* He was not forsaken in regard of *God's love*, for 'My Father loveth me,' saith he, John iii. 35, 'because I give my life for my sheep,' John x. 11. God never loved Christ more than now, because he was never more obedient than at this present.

(2.) Nor in regard of *union*, for there was no separation of his divine nature from the human. There was a suspension of vision, indeed; he saw no comfort for the present from God, but there was no dissolution of union; for the divine nature did many things in this seeming forsaking. That was it which supported his human nature to sustain the burden of our sin and the wrath of God, as also that gave merit and worth of satisfaction to his sufferings.

(3.) Neither was this forsaking in regard of *grace*, as if faith, or love, or any other grace, were taken from Christ. Oh, no; for he believed, before he said, '*My God, my God.*' Would he have committed his dearest jewel into the hands of God if he had not believed in him?

Quest. How, then, was Christ forsaken?

Ans. 1. *In regard of his present comfort and joy.* He could not else have been a sacrifice; for as we cannot suffer by way of conformity to Christ, unless there be some desertion, that we may know the bitterness of sin, no more could Christ have suffered for our iniquities had there not been a suspension of light and comfort from his gracious soul.

2. He was not only privatively deprived of all joy and happiness, but *positively he felt the wrath and fury of the Almighty,* whose just displeasure seized upon his soul for sin, as *our surety.* All outward comforts likewise forsook him. The sun withdrew his light from above, and everything below was irksome to him. He suffered in all the good things he had, body, soul, good name, in his eyes, ears, hands, &c. He was reproached, and forsaken of all comforts about him. He had not the common comfort of a man in misery, pity; none took compassion upon him; he was the very object of scorn.

Quest. But in what part was Christ forsaken?

Ans. In all, both in body and soul too, as may plainly appear.

(1.) First, because he was our surety, and we had stained our souls, and bodies too, offending God in both (but in soul especially, because that is the contriver of all sin, the body being but the instrument). Some sins we call spiritual sins, as pride, malice, infidelity, and the like; these touch not the body, yet are the greatest sins of all other.

(2.) Secondly, if he had not suffered in his soul the sense of God's displeasure why should he thus cry out, whenas the poor thieves that suffered by him made no such exclamation? If he had suffered in body only, the sufferings of Paul and Moses had been more, for they wished to be separated from the joys of heaven out of a desire to promote God's glory on earth. Therefore it was, he saith in the garden, 'My soul is heavy unto death,' Mat. xxvi. 38.

Obj. Some will grant that Christ suffered in soul, but, say they, it was by way of sympathy, for there are sufferings of soul immediately from God, and sufferings by way of sympathy and agreement with the body, whenas the soul hath a fellow-feeling of the torments thereof; and so Christ suffered in soul indeed.

Ans. That is not all, beloved, but there were immediate sufferings, even of his soul also, which he groaned under. God the Father laid a heavy stroke upon that. He was smitten of the Lord, Isa. liii. 4; and when God deals immediately with the soul himself, and fills it with his wrath, no creature in the world is able to undergo the same. None can inflict punishment upon the soul but God only. Satan may urge and press arguments of discouragement, and affright us with God's displeasure; but the inflicting of anger upon the soul issues immediately from the hand of the Almighty. We must here, therefore, consider God as a righteous Judge, sitting in heaven in his judgment-seat, taking the punishment of the sins of all his people upon Christ. There was a meeting together of all the sins of the faithful, from Adam to the last man that shall be in the world, as it were, in one point upon him, and the punishment of all these was laid on his blessed shoulders, who suffered for them in both body and soul.

3. *Conclusion.* But how could Christ be forsaken of God, especially so forsaken as to suffer the anger of his father, being an innocent person?

Ans. 1. I answer, first, the Paschal lamb was an innocent creature, yet if the Paschal lamb be once made a sacrifice, it must be killed. Though Christ were never so unblameable, yet, if he will stoop to the office of a surety, he must pay our debt, and do that which we should have done. If a prince's son become a surety, though his father love him and pity him never so much, yet he will say, Now you have taken this upon you, you must discharge it.

2. Secondly, as in natural things the head is punished for the fault of the body, so Christ, by communicating his blessed nature with ours, made up one mystical body, and suffered for us.

Quest. But upon what ground should Christ become our surety?

Ans. 1. Because he was able to discharge our debt to the uttermost. He was more eminent than all mankind, having two natures in one, the manhood knit to the Godhead.

2. Christ most willingly gave himself a sacrifice for us.

3. He was designed and predestinated to this office, yea, he was anointed, set out, and sealed for this business by God himself; and is not this sufficient ground why he should become our surety? especially if we consider,

4. That Christ took the communion of our nature upon him for this very end, that he might be a full surety, that his righteousness being derived to us, and our guilt to him, God's wrath might be satisfied in the self-same nature that offended. You see in societies and cities, if some people offend, the whole city is oftentimes punished. Though perhaps many are guiltless in it, yet by reason of the communion, all are punished. So likewise a traitor's son, that never had any hand in his father's sin, but behaved himself as an honest subject should do, yet, having communion with the person of his father, being indeed a piece of him, is thereupon justly disinherited by all law.

Obj. But how could Christ take our sins upon him and not be defiled therewith?

Quest. He took not the *stain* of our sins, but the *guilt* of them. Now in guilt there is two things.

1. A worthiness and desert of punishment.
2. An obligation and binding over thereunto.

Christ took not the desert of punishment upon him, from any fault in himself; he took whatsoever was penal upon him, but not culpable. As he was our surety, so he everyway discharged our debt, being bound over to all judgments and punishments for us.

Now we owe unto God a double debt.

1. A debt of obedience; and if that fail,
2. A debt of punishment.

And both these hath Christ freed us from: first, by obeying the will of his Father in everything; and, secondly, by suffering whatsoever was due to us for our transgressions.

Some heretics that would shake the foundation of our faith, will grant Christ to be a *Mediator* to intercede for us, and a *Redeemer* to set us at liberty from slavery, &c., but *not* to be a *surety* to pay our debt, by way of satisfaction to God for us.

Let such remember, that God's pleasure to redeem lost mankind, is not so much by way of power and strength, as by way of justice, and therefore it is said, Heb. vii. 22, ' Christ is become our surety;' and Paul, when he became a mediator to Philemon for Onesimus, a fugitive servant, did it by way of surety, ' If he owe thee anything I will discharge it,' Philem. 18; and Christ Jesus our Mediator blessed for ever, so intercedeth unto God for us, as that he fully satisfies his justice for our offences.

Quest. But why was Christ thus forsaken of his Father?

Ans. 1. To satisfy God for *our forsaking of him.* Christ's forsaking was satisfactory for all our forsakings of God. Beloved, we all forsook God in Adam, and indeed what do we else in every sin we commit, but forsake the Lord, and turn to the creature? what are all our sins of pleasure, profit, ambition, and the like, but a leaving of *the fountain of living waters,* to fetch contentment from ' broken cisterns,' Jer. ii. 13.

2. But Christ was chiefly forsaken, *that he might bring us home again to God*, that there might be no more a separation betwixt his blessed Majesty and us.

Some shallow heretics there are, that would have Christ to be an *example* of *patience* and *holiness* in his life and death, and do us good that way only. Oh no, beloved, the main comfort we receive from Christ is by way of satisfaction. There must be first grace, and then peace in our agreement with God. Sweetly, saith Bernard, I desire indeed to follow Christ as an example of humility, patience, self-denial, &c., and to love him with the same affection that he hath loved me; but I must eat of the Passover-Lamb, that is, I must chiefly feed on Christ dying for my sins. So every true Christian soul desires to follow Christ's obedience, humility, patience, &c., and to be transformed into the likeness of his blessed Saviour. Whom should I desire to be like more than him, that hath done so much for me? But yet the main comfort I receive from Christ, is by eating his body and drinking his blood; my soul feeds and feasts itself most of all upon the death of Christ, as satisfying for my sins. And what a comfort is it that Christ being our surety, hath made full satisfaction for all our sins. Surely * we shall never be finally and wholly forsaken, because Christ was forsaken for us. Now we may think of God without discomfort, and of sin without despair. Now we may think of the law of death, the curse and all, and never be terrified—why? Christ our surety hath given full content of divine justice for wrath and law, sin and curse, &c. They are all links of one chain, and Christ hath dissolved them all. Now sin ceaseth, wrath ceaseth, the law hath nothing to lay to our charge; death's sting is pulled out. How comfortably, therefore, may we appear before God's tribunal! Oh, beloved, when the soul is brought as low as hell almost, then this consideration will be sweet, that Christ was forsaken as a surety for me; Christ overcame sin, death, God's wrath, and all for me; in him I triumph over all these. What welcome news is this to a distressed sinner! Whenever thy soul is truly humbled in the sense of sin, look not

* That is, ' assuredly.'—G.

at sin in thy conscience (thy conscience is a bed for another to lodge in), but at Christ. If thou be a broken-hearted sinner, see thy sins in Christ thy Saviour taken away; see what he hath endured and suffered for them; see not the law in thy conscience, but see it discharged by Christ; see death disarmed through him, and made an entrance into a better life for thee. Whatsoever is ill, see it in Christ before thou seest it in thyself; and when thou beholdest it there, see not only the hurt thereof taken away, but all good made over to thee; for 'all things work together for the best to them that love God,' Rom. viii. 28. The devil himself, death, sin, and wrath, all help the main; the poison and mischief of all is taken away by Christ, and all good conveyed to us in him. We have grace answerable to his grace. He is the first seat of God's love, and it sweetens whatever mercy we enjoy, that it comes from the fountain, *God the father*, through Christ unto us. I beseech you embrace the comfort that the Holy Ghost affords us from these sweet considerations.

Again, in that Christ was forsaken; and not only so, but endured the displeasure and immediate wrath of God, seizing upon his soul, and filling his heart with anguish at this time, we may learn hence.

How to discern the ugliness of sin. 1. *In what glass to look upon the ugly thing, sin, to make it more ugly unto us.* Beloved, if we would conceive aright of sin, let us see it in the angels tumbled out of heaven, and reserved in chains of darkness for offending God, Jude 6; see it in the casting of Adam out of paradise, Gen. iii. 23, 24, and all us in him; see it in the destruction of the old world, and the Jews carried to captivity, in the general destruction of Jerusalem, &c. But if you would indeed see the most ugly colours of sin, then see it in Christ upon the cross, see how many sighs and groans it cost him, how bitter a thing it was to his righteous soul, forcing him to weep tears of blood, and send forth strong cries to his Father, 'My God, my God, why hast thou forsaken me?' If sin but imputed to Christ our surety, so affected him that was God-man, and lay so heavy upon his soul, what will it do to those that are not in Christ? Certainly, the wrath of God must needs burn to hell; he will be a 'consuming fire,' Heb. xii. 29, to all such. See sin therefore chiefly in the death of Christ. How odious it is to God, that it could be no otherwise purged away than by the death of his beloved Son. All the angels in heaven, and all the creatures in the world could not satisfy divine justice for the least sin. If all the agonies of all creatures were put into one, it were nothing to Christ's agony; if all their sufferings were put into one, they could not make satisfaction to divine justice for the least sin. Sin is another manner of matter than we take it to be. See the attributes of God, his anger against it, his justice and holiness, &c. Beloved, men forget this. They think God is angry against sin indeed, but yet his justice is soon satisfied in Christ. Oh, we must think of the Almighty as a holy God, separated from all stain and pollution of sin whatsoever, and so holy that he enforced a separation of his favour from Christ, for becoming our surety, and Christ underwent a separation from his Father, because he undertook for us. So odious is sin to the holy nature of God, that he left his Son while he struggled with his wrath for it; and so odious was sin to the holy nature of Christ, that he became thus a sacrifice for the same. And so odious are the remainders of sin in the hearts of the saints, that all that belong to God have the Spirit of Christ, which is as fire to consume and waste the old Adam by little and little out of them. 'No unclean thing must enter into heaven,' Rev. xxi. 27. Those that are not in Christ by faith, that have not a shelter in him, must suffer for their transgressions eternally, 'Depart, ye cursed, into everlasting fire,' Mat. xxv. 41; so holy is God that he can have no society and fellowship with sinners.

Do you wonder why God so much hates sin, that men so little regard, not only the lewd sort of the world, but common dead-hearted persons, that set so little by it, that they regard not spiritual sins at all, especially hatred, malice, pride, &c., clothing themselves with these things as a comely garment? Certainly you would not wonder that God hates sin, if you did but consider how sin hates God? What is sin but a setting of itself in God's room, a setting the devil in God's place? for when we sin we leave God, and set up the creature, and by consequence Satan, that brings the temptation to us; setting him in our hearts before God. Beloved, God is very jealous, and cannot endure that filthy thing sin, to be in his room. Sin is such a thing as desires to take away God himself. Ask a sinner when he is about to sin, Could you not wish that there were no God at all, that there were no eye of heaven to take vengeance on you? Oh aye, with all my heart. And can you then wonder that God hates sin so, when it hates him so, as to wish the not being of God? Oh marvel not at it, but have such conceits of sin as God had when he gave his Son to die for it, and such as Christ had, when in the sense of his Father's anger he cried thus, 'My God, my God,' &c.

The deeper our thoughts are of the odiousness of sin, the deeper our comfort and joy in Christ will be after; therefore I beseech you work your hearts to a serious consideration what that sin is that we cherish so much, and will not be reproved for, and which we leave God and heaven, and all to embrace; conceive of it as God doth, that must be a Judge, and will one day call us to a strict account for the same.

If Christ cried out thus, 'My God, my God, why hast thou forsaken me?' as being our surety for our sins, we may see what to conceive of sin, and of God the better.

But above all things I desire you to see often in this glass, in this book of Christ crucified (it is an excellent book to study), the mercy of God and the love of Christ, the height, and depth, and breadth of God's love in Jesus Christ, which hath no dimensions. What set God on work to plot this excellent work of our salvation and redemption by such a surety,—was it not mercy? Did not that awaken wisdom to reconcile justice and mercy to* Christ? But what stirred up this wisdom of God? Oh, bowels of compassion to man! He would not have man perish, when the angels did, without remedy.

Therefore let us desire to be inflamed with the love of God, that hath loved us so much. All the favours of God in Christ tend, next after satisfaction to justice, to inflame our hearts to love him again. Wherefore else are the favours of creation and providence? How sweet is God in providing for our bodies, giving us not only for necessity, but abundance, withholding no comfort that is good for us, &c.

But chiefly in his masterpiece, God would have us apprehend the greatest love of all other, because there he hath set himself to glorify his mercy more than anything else! Therefore we may well cry with the apostle, 'Oh the height of his love,' &c., Ephes. iii. 18. I beseech you fix your thoughts on this, think not now and then slightly of it, but dwell on the meditation of the infinite love of God in Christ, till your hearts be enlarged and warmed and inflamed with the consideration thereof; and then love will set you forward

* Qu. 'by?'—ED.

to all good works. What need we bid you be liberal to the poor, to be good subjects, just in your dealings, &c. ? All this may be spared when there is a loving heart. And when shall we have loving hearts ? When they are kindled and fired at God's fire; when they are persuaded of God's love, then the apprehension of his love will breed love in our hearts again; and that is the reason why the apostles are not so punctual as heathen authors in particularities of duties. They force upon men especially the love of God, and the ground-points of religion, as knowing when the heart is seasoned with that once, it is ready prepared to every good duty. Think seriously of this, 'The love of Christ constraineth me,' 2 Cor. v. 14. There is a holy violence in love; there is a spiritual kind of tyranny and prevailing in this grace.

One thing further we may learn from this forsaking of Christ, viz., that, *It is no strange thing for God's dear children to be forsaken.*

To have the apprehension of their sins, and the wrath of God, to be forsaken, in regard of sense of all comfort, do we not see it done in the natural Son? and shall we wonder that it is done in the adopted sons? We see this forsaking was in the natural branch, and shall we wonder that it is done in the grafted branches? It was done to the green tree, and shall we wonder if it be done in the dry? No, certainly.

The whole church complains, Ps. lxix. 21; of drinking gall and wormwood, Ezek. xxxvi. 3; that God was hid in a cloud, Lam. iii. 15, &c. Both the head complains, and the body too, as we see in David, Job, and other saints; so that there is a kind of desertion and forsaking that the child of God must undergo.

Quest. What is the ground and end of it?

Ans. 1. First, God's prerogative is such, that sometimes when there is no great sin to provoke him to withdraw comfort, yet will he leave holy men to themselves, to shew that he will do as pleaseth him.

2. Another ground is, our own estate and condition. We are here absent from the Lord, strangers on earth. Now we would take our pilgrimage for our country, if we had always comfort and new supplies of joy.

3. Again, our disposition is to live by sense more than by faith. We are as children in this. We would have God ever smile upon us, that we might walk in abundance of comfort; and I cannot blame Christians for desiring it, if they desire the work of grace in the first place; if they desire the work of God in them, rather than the shining of comfort by the Spirit, for that is the best work. Now because Christians desire rather to live by sight than by faith, wherein they might honour God more, he leaves them ofttimes. Sight is reserved for another world, for the church triumphant. There we shall have sight enough; we shall see God face to face.

4. Sometimes God's children are negligent, and keep not a holy watch over their souls; they cleave to the creature too much, and then no wonder though God forsake them, since they will have stolen waters of their own, and fetch comfort elsewhere.

5. But one main ground is, conformity to Christ. He suffered for our sins, and God will conform the members in some measure to their head. Though Christ drank the cup of God's wrath to the bottom, yet we must sip and taste a little, that we may know how much we are beholden to Christ; and there are few that come to heaven, few that truly belong to God, but they know what sin is, and what the wrath of God is, first or last. The wrath of God is the best corrosive in the world to eat out sin. A little anger of God felt in the conscience will make a man hate pride and malice, and all sin whatsoever.

Quest. But for what end doth God leave his children, as he did here our blessed Saviour?

Ans. 1. In regard of himself.

2. In regard of his children.

1. In regard of himself, he leaves them that he may comfort them more afterwards; that he may bring more love with him; and that they may love him more than before. There will, after a little forsaking, be a mutual reflection of love between God and a Christian. God delights to shew himself more abundantly after a little forsaking, and the soul enlargeth itself after it hath wanted the love of God; for want enlargeth the capacity of the soul, and want makes it stretch itself to receive more comfort when it comes. God doth this for the increase of his love to us, and of our love to him again. He both draws nigh to us, and goes away, in regard of feeling for our good.

2. That we may be more watchful over our hearts for the time to come; that there may be a more perfect divorce and separation wrought in us to the creatures. Our adulterous hearts have 'stolen delights' that God likes not; and, therefore, when we have smarted for it in the anger and displeasure of God, a divorce will be wrought. It is hard to work a separation from sin, sin and the soul being so nearly invested together; yet God therefore uses this way of spiritual desertion to effect the same.

3. Likewise to make a Christian soul ransack and search the ground of all the comforts that are left him by God. It will make him rifle and search all the Scriptures. Is there any comfort for me, poor wretch, that am troubled with sin? It will make him search the experience of other Christians. Have you any word of comfort for me? It will make him regard a gracious man as 'one of a thousand.' It will make him stretch his heart in all the degrees of grace. Have I any evidence that I am the child of God, and not a cast-away? It will make him search his heart in regard of corruption. Is there any sin that I am not willing to part with? &c. Beloved, God many times leaves us; and not only leaves us, but makes our naked conscience smart for sin. Oh! this is a quickening thing! A child of God that is of the right stamp will not endure to be under God's wrath long. Oh, it is bitter! He knows what it is to enjoy communion with God. He will not endure it. Therefore, it stirs him up to all manner of diligence whatsoever.

Quest. But is there no difference between Christ's sufferings and smart, for sin and ours?

Ans. Yes (1), the sufferings of Christ came from the vindictive * and revenging † hand of God, as a just Judge; but ours proceed from him as a loving Father; for God, when we are in Christ, is changed. He layeth aside the person of a Judge. Having received full satisfaction in Christ, he is now in the relation of a sweet Father to us.

(2.) Again, there is difference in the measure. We take but a taste of the cup, sweetened with some comfort and moderated; but Christ drank deep of the same.

(3.) In the end and use. The sufferings and forsaking of Christ were satisfactory to divine justice; but ours are not so, but only medicinal. The nature of them is quite changed. They are not for satisfaction; for then we should die eternally; disable the satisfaction of Christ. They are crosses indeed, but not curses. Whatsoever we suffer in soul or body is a cross, but not a curse unto us; because the sting is pulled out. They are all medicinal cures to fit us for heaven. Whatsoever we suffer in our in-

* That is, 'vindicative, vindicatory.'—G.   † That is, 'avenging.'—G.

ward or outward man, prepares us for glory, by mortifying the remainders of corruptions, and fitting us for that blessed estate.

(4.) All other men's deaths are for themselves. As Leo saith, *Singula in singulis (a)*; they are single deaths for single men. But it is otherwise here; for all the children of God were forsaken in their head, crucified in their head, and died in Christ their head. Christ's death was a public satisfaction. No man dieth for another, let the papists say what they will; only Christ died for all, and suffered for his whole body. And thus much of the first general, that *Christ was forsaken.*

2. The second is this, *Christ was very sensible of it*, even to complaint and expostulation, *My God, My God*, &c. Why should it be thus between the Father and the Son? between such a Father and such a Son, a kind, loving Father to his natural, obedient, and only Son? The word is strong, beloved, he was not only forsaken, but exposed to danger, and left in it, being very sensible of the same. Every word here expresseth some bowels. He doth not say, the Jews have forsaken me; or my beloved disciples and apostles that I made much of have forsaken me, or Pilate would not do the duty of a true judge; my feet are pierced, my head is wounded, my body is racked, hanging on the cross, &c.; he complains of none of these, though they were things to be complained of, and would have sunk any creature to have felt that in his body that he did, but that which went nearest to him, was this, 'Oh, my God, why hast *thou* forsaken me?' I stand not upon others forsaking, but why hast *thou* forsaken me? I stand more upon *thy* forsaking than the forsaking of all others. Christ was very sensible of this; it went to his very heart.

But what special reason was there that Christ should take this so deeply?

1. First of all, because *the lovingkindness of the Lord is better than life itself*, as David the type of Christ well said, Ps. xiii. 8; the forsaking of God being indeed worse than death. The lovingkindness of the Lord is that that sweeteneth all discomforts in the world; the want of that embitters all comforts to us. If we be condemned traitors, what will all comforts do to a condemned man? The want of God's love embitters all good, and the presence thereof sweeteneth all ill; death, imprisonment, and all crosses whatsoever. Therefore Christ having a sanctified judgment, in the highest degree, judgeth the loss of this to be the worst thing.

2. *The sweeter the communion is with God the fountain of good, the more intolerable and unsufferable is the separation from him;* but none had ever so near and sweet a communion with God as Christ our Mediator had, for he was both God and man in one person, the beloved Son of his Father. Now the communion before being so near and so sweet unto him, a little want of the same must needs be unsufferable. Things the nearer they are, the more difficult the separation will be; as when the skin is severed from the flesh, and the flesh from the bones, oh, it is irksome to nature; much more was Christ's separation from the sense of his Father's love. Those that love, live more in the party loved, than in themselves. Christ was in love with the person of his Father, and lived in him. Now to want the sense of his love, considering that love desires nothing but the return of love again, it must needs be death unto him.

3. Another ground that Christ was thus sensible, was, *because he was best able to apprehend the worth of communion with God, and best able to apprehend what the anger of God was.* He had a large judgment, and a more capacious soul than any other; therefore being filled with the wrath of God,

he was able to hold more wrath than any man else. He could deepest apprehend wrath, that had so deep a taste of love before.

4. Again, in regard of his body: the grief of Christ, both in *body* and *soul*, was the greatest that ever was, for he was in the strength of his years; he had not dulled his spirits with intemperancy; he was quick and able to apprehend pain, being of an excellent temperature.

Use. Was Christ so exceeding sensible of the want of his Father's love, though it were but a while? I beseech you then, let us have merciful considerations of those that suffer in conscience, and are troubled in mind. Oh, it is another manner of matter than the world takes it for! It is no easy thing to conflict with God's anger, though but a little. It was the fault of Job's friends; they should have judged charitably of him, but they did not. Take heed, therefore, of making desperate conclusions against ourselves or other, when the arrows of the Almighty stick in us, when we smart and shew our distemper in the apprehension of the terrors of the Lord seizing upon our souls. God is about a gracious work all this while; the more sensible men are of the anger of God, the more sensible they will be of the return of his favour again.

There are some insensible, stupid creatures, that are neither sensible of the afflictions they suffer in body, nor of the manifestation of God's anger on their soul. Notwithstanding, he follows them with his corrections, yet they are as dead flesh, unmoveable; therefore, 'Why should I smite them any longer,' &c., Isa. i. 5, saith God.

This comes from three grounds:

(1.) From *pride*, when men think it a shame for such Roman spirits as they are to stoop.

(2.) Or from *hypocrisy*, when they will not discover their grief, though their conscience be out of tune.

(3.) Or else out of *stupid blockishness*, which is worst of all, when they are not affected with the signs of God's wrath. It is a good thing to be affected with the least token of God's displeasure, when we can gather by good evidence that God hath a quarrel against us. You see how sensible Christ was, and so will it be with us if we get not into him betimes; we shall be sensible of sin one day whether we will or no; conscience is not put in us for nought. You may stupify and stifle the mouth of conscience with this or that trick now, but it will not be so for ever; it will discharge its office, and lay bitter things to our charge, and stare in our faces, and drive us to despair one day. Sin is another matter when it is revealed to conscience than we take it, howsoever we go blockishly and stupidly on now. It is sweet in the temptation and allurement, but it hath an ill farewell and sting. If we could judge of sin as we shall do when it is past, especially when we come to our reckoning at the hour of death, and at the day of judgment, then we would be of another mind; then we would say that all sinners, as the Scripture terms them, 'are fools,' Ps. xciv. 8. But to go on.

Christ we see expresseth his *sensibleness by complaint;* 'My God, my God, why hast thou forsaken me?'

Caution. Here some cautions must be rendered that we do not mistake. Christ complains not *of* God but *to* God.

Obj. Was Christ ignorant of the cause of God's forsaking him?

Ans. No, he knew the cause, for his sufferings were intolerable; but taking our nature upon him, he takes our speech also, and expresseth himself like to a miserable man; having the greatest affliction that ever was upon a creature. The divine nature of Christ stopped the excess of any passion; he was turbated but not perturbated; he was moved with the sins of men, but not removed; he was as water in a clear glass. There is nothing but water though you stir it never so much: if there were mud in it, it would soon be unclean. We cannot stir our affections and complain but with a tincture of sin. It was not so with Christ. He knew when to raise and when to allay his affections; and though there were much nature in these affections, a natural shunning of grief, and a natural desire of God's presence; yet here was grace to direct and sanctify the same; for nature sometimes carries grace with a stronger wind, more fully when they go both in one current, as here. It was grace to have the love of God, yea, it was death to be without it, and it was sinless nature to desire ease; for without sin nature may desire ease, so it be with submission of itself to God. For the soul may have divers desires as there are divers objects presented to it. When the soul apprehends release and ease, it rejoices and is glad; but when upon higher considerations and better ends there is pain presented to the soul to do it good, the soul may desire that, and upon deliberation choose that it refused before. A man may have his hand cut off, and cast his wares into the sea, that he would not willingly do, yet when upon deliberation he considers, I shall save my life by it, he will do it. So Christ by a natural desire, without sin, might desire release of pain, but when it was presented to him, what shall become of the salvation of men and obedience to God then? Upon these considerations, that respected higher ends, there might be another choice; so in things subordinate one to another, one thing may cross another, and yet all be good too.

But you must know this likewise, that forsaking and to be sensible of forsaking, is no sin, especially when it is not contracted by any sin of ours. It is a suffering, but not a sin; and to be sensible of it is no sin. It is rather a sin to be otherwise affected. God allows those affections that he hath planted in us: he hath planted fear and sorrow in presenting dolorous objects. If a man do not sorrow in objects of sorrow, he is not a man after God's making. God allows grief and fear in afflictions and trouble, always remembering it be with submission to him, 'Not as I will, but as thou wilt,' Matt. xxvi. 30.

Again, consider Christ was now in a conflicting condition between doubting and despair, the powers of hell being round about him. Satan as he was busy about him at the entrance into his office, Mat. iv. 1–11, so he was now vexing his righteous soul with temptations, 'God hath forsaken thee,' and this and that. We know not the malice of Satan at such a time; but certainly the powers of hell were all let loose then upon him. The truth is, God had a purpose to finish his sufferings presently upon his complaint, and because he will have us all receive what we receive, even Christ himself, by prayer and opening our desires to him, God suffers Christ to complain, and pour out his supplication into his bosom, that presently after, he might be released of all, seeing he had now fully satisfied for the sins of man.

Use. The use of it in a word is this, *That God having stooped so low to poor creatures, to be a father and a friend to them,* will suffer them familiarly (as there is a great deal of familiarity in the spirit of adoption), yet reverently, to lay open their griefs into his bosom, and reason the case with his Majesty, without sin, Why, Lord, am I thus forsaken? what is the matter? where are the sounding of thy bowels? where are thy former mercies? &c. There is another kind of familiarity between God and his children than the world takes notice of; yet withal remember, they are not murmuring complaints, but seasoned with faith and love, as here, *my* God, *my* God still. Whence you see that,

Christ in his greatest extremities had a spirit of faith.

3. There is a question between the papists and us about Christ's faith; they will have him to be a comprehender and a traveller, &c. Indeed, he needed no justifying faith to apply anything from without him, because he had righteousness enough of his own; but yet to depend upon God as his Father, so he had faith; neither was he alway in the state of happiness, for that distinction is a confusion of the abasement of Christ and his exaltation. Howsoever, there was the happiness of union (the human nature being alway united to the Godhead), yet there was not alway the happiness of vision; he did not see the face of God, for then why did he cry out, 'My God, my God,' &c. ? Sight was due to him from his incarnation in himself considered, not as our surety. Now that which made a stop of the influence of comfort to his soul was, that he might fully suffer for our sins, that he might be humbled and tempted, and suffer even death itself. Therefore, in regard of the state of humiliation, there was faith in him, faith of dependence; there was hope in him, and he made great use thereof to support himself.

Quest. But what supported the faith of Christ in this woeful, rueful estate he was in, being forsaken of God as our surety?

Ans. Christ presented to his faith these things.

1. The unchangeable nature of God, *my God*, &c. 'Whom he once loves, he loves to the end,' John xiii. 1; therefore he lays claim to him; thou hast been my God heretofore, and so thou art still.

2. Again, faith presented to the soul of Christ, God's manner of dealing. He knew well enough that God by contraries brings contraries to pass. He brings to heaven by the gates of hell, he brings to glory by shame, to life by death, and therefore resolves, notwithstanding this desertion, I will depend upon *my* God.

3. Again, Christ knew well enough that God is nearest in support when he is furthest off in feeling. So it is oft, where he is nearest the inward man, to strengthen it with his love, he is furthest off in comfort to outward sense. To whom was God nearer than Christ in support and sanctifying grace? and yet to whom was he further off in present feeling? Christ knew that there was a secret sense of God's love, and a sensible sense of God's love; he had a secret sense of God that he was his Father, because he knew himself to be his Son, but he had it not sensibly. Faith must be suitable to the thing believed. Now Christ, in saying My God, suits his faith to the truth that was offered to him; he knew God in the greatest extremity to be nearest at hand. 'Be not far off, for trouble is near,' &c., Ps. xxii. 11.

This should teach us in any extremity or trouble, to set faith on work, and feed faith with the consideration of God's unchangeable nature, and the unchangeableness of his promises, which endure for ever. We change, but the promise changeth not, and God changeth not; *my God* still: 'The word of the Lord endureth for ever,' 1 Pet. i. 25. God deals with his people in a hidden manner; he supports with secret, though not with sensible comfort, and will be nearest when he seems to be furthest off his children. I beseech you, acquaint yourselves with these things, and think it not strange that God comes near you in desertions, considering that it was so with Christ. Present to thy soul the nature of God, his custom and manner of dealing, so shalt thou apprehend favour in the midst of wrath, and glory in the midst of shame. We shall see life in death; we shall see through the thickest clouds that are between God and us. For as God shines in the heart in his love secretly through all temptations and troubles, so there is a spirit of faith goes back to him again: my God, my God. For faith hath a quick eye, and seeth through contraries. There is no cloud of grief but faith will pierce through it, and see a father's heart under the carriage of an enemy. Christ had a great burden upon him, the sins of the whole world; yet he breaks through all. I am now sin, I bear the guilt of the whole world, yet under this person that I sustain, I am a son, and God is my God still, notwithstanding all this weight of sin upon me. And shall not we, beloved, say, My God, in any affliction or trouble that befalls us? Oh yes. In the sense of sin, which is the bitterest of all, and in the sense of God's anger, in losses and crosses, in our families &c., let us break through those clouds, and say, My God, still.

Obj. But you will say, I may apprehend a lie; perhaps God is not my God, and then it is presumption to say so.

Ans. Whosoever casts himself upon God, out of the sense of sin, to be ruled by God for the time to come, shall obtain mercy. Now, dost thou so? doth thy conscience tell thee, I cast myself upon God for better direction; I would be ruled as God and the ministry of the Word would have me hereafter. If so, thou hast put this question out of question: thou doubtest whether God be thy God; I tell thee God is the God of all that seek him, and obey him in truth. But thy conscience tells thee thou dost this, certainly then, whatsoever thou wert before, God is now beforehand with thee. He offers himself to be thy God, if thou trust in him, and wilt be ruled by him; and not only so, but he entreats us (we should beseech him, but he entreats us, such is his love), nay, he commands us to believe in his Son Jesus Christ. Now, when I join with God's entreaty, Oh Lord, thou offerest thyself, thou invitest me, thou commandest me, I yield obedience and submit to thy good word; then the match is stricken and made up in doing so. God is thy God, and Christ is thy Christ, and thou must improve this claim and interest here, in all the passages of thy life long. Lord, thou art my God, therefore teach me; thou art my God, I have given myself to thee, I have set up thee in my heart above all things, thou art in my soul above all sin, above all profits and pleasures whatsoever, therefore save me, and deliver me, have pity upon me, &c. The claim is good when we have truly given ourselves up to him, else God may say, 'Go to the gods you have served,' Jud. x. 14; men were your gods, for whom you cracked your consciences, riches and pleasure were your gods, go to them for succour.

Oh, beloved, it is a harder matter to say, *My God*, in the midst of trouble, than the world takes it. There was a great conflict in Christ when he said, My God, when he brake through all molestations and temptations of Satan, together with the sense of wrath, and could say notwithstanding, My God. There was a mighty strong spirit in him. But no wonder; faith is an almighty grace, wrought by the power of God, and laying hold upon that power, it lays hold upon omnipotency, and therefore it can do wonders, it overcomes the invincible God. He hath made a promise, and cannot deny his promise; he cannot deny himself and his truth. Put case his dealing be as an enemy. His promise is to be as a friend to those that trust in him: he is merciful, forgiving sins; his nature now is such. Satisfaction to his justice makes him shew mercy.

I speak this that you might beg of God the gift of faith, which will carry you through all temptations and afflictions, yea, even through the shadow of death; as David saith, 'Though I walk in the valley of the shadow of death, yet will I fear no ill,' Ps. xxiii. 4. Why? Because thou art with me, my God and my shepherd. Though we be in the valley of the shadow of death, yet notwithstanding, if God be with us, if we be in covenant with him, and can lay just claim to his promise, by giving up ourselves to him, we shall not fear. One beam of God's countenance, when we are in covenant with him, will scatter all clouds whatsoever. I beseech you, therefore, labour more and more for this precious grace of faith, and increase it by all sanctified means, hearing the word, reading the Scriptures, and treasuring up promises, considering what special use we have of this above all other graces. But to proceed.

Christ here doth not only believe, but

4. *He vents his faith by prayer.*

Good works are but faith incarnate, faith working. They differ not much from it. So prayer is but faith flaming, the breath of faith, as it were. For when troubles possess the soul, it sends out its ambassador presently, it speeds prayer forth, and prayer stays not till it come to heaven, and there takes hold upon God, and gets a message and answer from him back, to comfort the soul. Faith and prayer are all one in a manner. When the soul hath any great desire of grace, or is in grief, apprehending the displeasure of God, faith would, if it could, work to heaven; but we are on earth, and cannot till we die. Therefore when it cannot go to heaven, it sends prayer, and that mounts the soul aloft, and wrestles with God, and will give him no rest till the petition be granted, and it can say, My God.

Therefore, if you have any faith at all, exercise it, and make it bright by often prayer: 'The prayer of faith prevails much,' James v. 15. How shall they call on him in whom they have not believed? Indeed it is no prayer at all without faith; great faith, great prayer; weak faith, weak prayer; no faith, no prayer: they both go on in an even strength. Christ here prays to God under this complaint, *Why hast thou forsaken me?* There is a hidden prayer in it, Oh do not forsake me, deliver me out, &c.

I beseech you, even as you would have comfort from the fountain of comfort, that usually conveys all grace and comfort to us by a spirit of prayer, labour to be much in communion with God in this blessed exercise, especially in troubles: 'Call upon me in the day of trouble,' Ps. l. **15.** The evil day is a day of prayer; of all days, in the day of trouble especially, 'make your request known to God,' Phil. iv. 6.

Obj. But perhaps God will not hear me.

Ans. Yes, this fruit follows: 'The peace of God which passeth all understanding shall keep your hearts and minds,' Philip. iv. 7. When you have eased your souls into the bosom of God by prayer, you may go securely, and know that he will let you reap the fruit of your prayers in the best time.

Obj. Yea, but I have prayed long, and have had no answer.

Ans. Wait in prayer; God's time is the best time. The physician keeps his own time; he turns the glass,* and though the patient cry out that he torments him, it is no matter, he knows his time. The goldsmith will not take the metal out of the fire till it be refined. So God knows what to do; wait his good leisure. In the mean time, because we must have all from God by prayer, I beseech you, derive all from him this way; pray for evreything, and then we shall have it as a blessing indeed.

* The allusion is to the 'hour-glass,' the then common measure of time, as the watch is now.—G.

Obj. But put the case I cannot pray, as sometimes we are in such a case that we cannot make a large prayer to God.

Ans. Then do as Christ did, cry; if thou canst not pray, groan and sigh, for they are the groans and the sighs of God's Spirit in thee. There is a great deal of oratory in these words. What is the use of eloquence but to persuade? and what could persuade God more than when Christ shewed how he esteemed his love, and how he was now, in the absence of it, environed with grief before him? Here was rhetoric. If Christ had not spoken, his wounds had said enough, and his pitiful case spake sufficiently. Everything hath a voice to cry for mercy. But he adds his voice to all, and cries vocally aloud, 'My God, my God, why hast thou forsaken me?'

Beloved, if you acquaint yourselves with God in prayer, then you may go readily to him in any extremity. Therefore, in time of health and prosperity, cherish communion with his blessed Majesty, make him your friend; and upon every good occasion improve this plea, O my God. If we have riches, if we have a friend in the court, we will improve them; if we have anything, we will make use of it. Have we a God, and will we not improve him? Have we a God that is our God, and do we want grace? Do we want comfort, and strength, and assistance, and have we a God, the fountain of all, to go to? Shall we have such a prerogative as this, to have Jesus Christ to be our great peacemaker, that we may go boldly to the throne of grace through him, and shall we not improve the same? We may go boldly to God, and welcome, because God is infinite, and the more we go and beg, the more he gives. We cannot exhaust that fountain. O let us improve this blessed prerogative; then we shall live the life of heaven upon earth. Especially when the conscience is troubled with sin, as Christ was now with the displeasure of his Father, then let us go to God, and plead with his Majesty, and we may plead lawfully with him—Lord, thy justice is better satisfied in Christ, than if thou shouldst send me to hell; if thou wilt, thou mayest destroy me (for conscience must come to a great resignation; it cannot desire mercy, but it must see its own misery); Lord, thou mayest justly call me to hell, but it would not be so much for thy glory; thou art more glorious in satisfying thy justice in Christ, than if thou shouldst damn me to hell. Why? Because God's justice is better satisfied in Christ. Man sinned, but God-man satisfied for sin; man would be like God in pride, God becomes man in humility. The expiation of God is greater than the sin of man. He prayed for his persecutors, and gave his life for them. Doth not this proportion more the justice of God than the sin of man? The law doth but require a nocent person, a guilty person to suffer. Christ was innocent. The law requires that man should suffer. Christ was God. Therefore Christ hath done more than satisfied the law. The satisfaction of Christ is more than if we had suffered. We are poor men,—creatures. That was the satisfaction of God-man. Our sins are the sins of finite persons, but he is infinite. Therefore, the soul may plead, Lord, I am a wretched sinner, but I should take away thee, and take away Christ, if I should despair; I should make thee no God, and make Christ no Christ, if I should not accept of mercy; for Christ is given to me, and I labour to make him mine own, by laying hold of him. Faith hath a power to make everything its own that it toucheth; particular faith (which is the only true comfortable faith) makes general things mine. When the soul can lay a particular claim to God as his God, by giving himself to him only, then we may plead in Christ better satisfaction to God's justice, than if he should cast us into hell. What a stay is this for a distressed soul to make use of!

Beloved, the church of God, the mystical body of Christ, is thus forsaken in other countries, besides many particular humble, broken-hearted Christians at home, who find no beams of God's love and mercy. What shall we do? Let the body imitate the head, even go to God in their behalf, and pour out your complaints before him: Lord, where are thy mercies of old? where are thy ancient bowels to thy church? why should the enemy triumph, &c. God delights when we lay open the miseries of his people, and our own particular grievances before him. If there be a spirit of faith in it, oh! it works upon his bowels. If a child can but say, O father, O mother! though he can say not a word more, the bowels are touched, there is eloquence enough; so when we can lay open the pitiful state of God's poor church, what a blessing may we obtain for them? It is thy church, Lord, thine own people, thy name is called upon them, and they call upon thy name; though they have sinned, yet thou deservest to be like thyself, and Christ hath deserved mercy for them. Thus, if we contend with God, and keep not silence, and give God no rest, faith would work wonders. The state of the church would not be long as it is, if we would all improve our interest in heaven in their behalf. Beloved, Christ struggled with the powers of darkness and the wrath of his Father a while, but presently after, all was finished; so let us contend boldly, 'Fight the good fight of faith,' 2 Tim. iv. 7, and not yield to desperate suggestions. Let faith stir up prayer, and prayer go to God; and ere long it shall be said of the church, and of all particular troubles, All is finished. Then we shall enjoy the sweet presence of God, 'where is fulness of joy,' Ps. xvi. 11, and that *for evermore.* The presence of God is that the child of God desires above all things in the world; it quickens and strengthens him; it puts zeal and fire into him; it doth all. What will not the presence of God do when a man enjoys his face? Therefore, let us be content to conflict here, to be exercised a while in faith and prayer. We shall surely say ere long, 'I have finished my course, I have kept the faith; henceforth is laid up for me a crown of righteousness,' 2 Tim. iv. 8.

I beseech you learn these lessons and instructions from our blessed Saviour. We cannot have a better pattern than to be like him, by whom we all hope to be saved another day. So much for this time.

NOTE.

Page 362, line 3d from top, 'As Leo saith,' &c. The reference (rather than quotation) is to Leo, Serm. 64, De Passione Domini, 13, wherein occurs the following: —'Singulares quippe in singulis mortes fuerunt, nec alterius quisquam debitum suo fine persolvit, cum inter filios hominum unus solus Dominus Noster Jesus extiterit in quo omnes crucifixi, omnes mortui, omnes sepulti, omnes etiam sint suscitati.' G.

THE CHURCH'S VISITATION.

THE CHURCH'S VISITATION.

NOTE.

'The Church's Visitation' forms a treatise expository of 1 Pet. iv. 17–19, in four separate but related discourses. The original title-page is given below.* It makes the 'second part' of the volume described at page 296. These four sermons were reprinted in the 'Saints Cordials' (2d ed. 1637, 3d ed. 1658), where they are numbered as 12th to 15th.—G.

* Title-page—

THE
CHVRCHES
VISITATION :
DISCOVERING
The many difficulties and tryalls of
Gods Saints on earth :
Shewing wherein the fountaine of
their happinesse consists :
Arming Christians how to doe, and
suffer for CHRIST ;
And directing them how to commit
themselves, and all their wayes to
God in holinesse here, and
happinesse hereafter.

Preached in sundry Sermons at Grayes-
Inne, LONDON,

By R. S. D.D.

LONDON,
Printed by *M. F.* for *R. Dawlman*, at the
Brazen Serpent in *Pauls* Church-
yard. 1634.

THE CHURCH'S VISITATION.

SERMON I.

For the time is come that judgment must begin at the house of God, and if it begin at us, what shall the end be of them that obey not the gospel? &c.—1 PET. IV. 17, 18, 19.

OUR nature, as it is very backward to do good, so likewise to suffer evil; therefore the blessed apostle exhorts us at the latter end of this chapter, 'not to think it strange concerning the fiery trial, but to rejoice, inasmuch as we are made partakers of Christ's sufferings; wherein are many grounds of patience and comfort to the children of God.

(1.) That the thought of troubles should not be *strange* but *familiar* to them. Acquainting our thoughts with them, taketh away offence at them; though it be a *fiery trial*, yet it shall consume nothing but dross.

(2.) Then Christ joineth with us *in suffering*. Better to be in trouble with Christ, than in peace *without* him.

(3.) *The issue will be glorious;* for the Spirit of glory will not only support us with his presence, but rest still upon us.

To other grounds of comfort, he addeth some in the words of my text, as,

1. First, *that the church is God's house*, and therefore he will have a care of it.

2. That he will do it in the fittest *season*. Such is the exigence of the church and people of God, that they require a sharp visitation; and, therefore, such is God's love, that he appoints out a certain time for them.

3. From the different conditions of the *godly* and *ungodly* in *suffering;* both suffer, but differ much; (1) in order, *God begins with his own house;* (2) in measure, *where shall the ungodly appear?* Their judgment shall be most terrible and certain. It is set down by way of interrogation and admiration; what shall their end be? And as Pharaoh's dreams were doubled for more certainty, so here is a double question to make the matter more out of question, [1] what shall their end be that obey not the gospel? [2] where shall the ungodly and sinners appear?

Here is no unnecessary waste of words and arguments, for the Spirit of God knows that all is little enough to fortify the soul against the evil day. Unless the soul be well balanced, it will soon be overturned when storms arise. Therefore, the apostle in these three verses sets down, 1, some *foundations* of comfort; and, 2, an *encouragement* to build upon them, 'wherefore let them that suffer,' &c.

The points considerable in the 17th verse are these:—

1. *That God's church is his house.*
2. *That this house of his will need purging; it will gather soil.*
3. *When God sees the exigent of it, that it must be so, he will be sure to visit and judge his own house.*
4. *That there is a certain time when he will do it, which those that are wise may easily gather.* For God comes not upon his church on the sudden, as a storm, or tempest, &c., but he gives them fair warning. There is a season when God begins judgment with his own house.
5. Lastly, *Why God begins with his own church and people.*

Of these in order.

Obs. 1. *That the Church of God is his own house.* First, *The Church of God is God's house.* God hath two houses, the *heavens*, which are called his house, because he manifests his glory there, and the *church* here below, wherein he manifests his *grace*. Yea, the whole world, in a sort, is his house, because he manifests his power and wisdom in it; but heaven and his church, in a more peculiar manner; and that in these respects:

(1.) Because God by his grace hath *residence* in his church.

(2.) Because by the means of salvation,—the *word*, and *sacraments* there administered,—he doth *feed* his church, as in a house.

(3.) A man *rests* and takes *contentment* in his *house;* so God takes his best contentment in his church and *people;* they are the most beloved of all mankind.

(4.) As in a house we use to lay up our jewels and precious things; so God lays up in his church whatsoever is precious,—his praises, his graces, yea, whatsoever is good and of high esteem, that he bestows upon his church and people.

For the further clearing of this, we must know that the church and children of God are said to be his house, either,

[1.] As a *family* is said to be a house; or,

[2.] As the *fabric* or *building* is said to be the house.

God provides for his church as his own house. First, a man provides for his family, and he that neglects it, is worse than an infidel, 1 Tim. v. 8; so doth God provide for his church. The very dragons and ostriches, the worst of the creatures, all have some respect to their young ones; much more will God provide for his own. And as a man protects his house from all enemies, so will God protect his church and people, and be *a wall of fire*, and a defence round about them.

Now there is a mixture in the church, as in a house, of good and bad vessels; but the godly are especially God's house. As for hypocrites and false professors, they are no more in the house, than the excrements are in the body; they are in the body, but not of the body; and therefore, as Ishmael, Gen. xxi. 10, they must be cast out at length.

The heart of true Christians is God's private closet. And as in every house or building, there are some open places, and some private closets, &c., so is it here. God hath his private chamber, and his retiring-place, which is the heart of every true Christian. He counts it not sufficient to dwell in his house at large, but he will dwell in the best part of it, the heart and the affections. Therefore 'he knocks at the doors of our hearts for entrance,' Rev. iii. 20, and his best children are glad he will reside in them. They set him up in the highest place of their souls, and set a crown upon him;

their desire is, that God may govern and rule their whole conversation; they have no idol above God in their hearts.

Use 1. What a wonderful mercy is this, that we are God's house; that he will vouchsafe to dwell and take up his lodging in such defiled houses as our souls are. It is no mean favour, that God should single out us poor wretches, to have his residence and abiding place in our souls, considering there is so much wickedness in the hearts of the best of us.

Oh what comfort ariseth to a Christian soul from the due meditation of this point. If we are God's house, then God will be our house; 'Thou art our habitation,' saith Moses, 'from generation to generation,' Ps. xc. 1. Howsoever we shuffle in the world, now here and now there, having no certain place of abode, but are here to day, and gone to-morrow, yet in God we have an house, 'Thou art our habitation;' he is ours, and we are his. And what a comfort is this that we are God's house. Certainly God will provide for his own house. He that lays this charge upon others, and hath put that affection and care of provision into others for their families, will he neglect his own? he that makes us love, and puts that natural affection into us of those that belong unto us, hath he not infinitely more in himself? whenas that which we have, is but a beam or ray from his infinite brightness.

Use 2. This should then, instruct us to labour that God may dwell largely and comfortably in us, to deliver up all to this keeper of our house, and suffer him to rule and reign in us. The Romish Church is become the habitation of devils; that which was Bethel, is now become Bethaven (*a*). Why? because they would not suffer God to rule in his own house, but would have coadjutors with Christ, as if he were not a sufficient head of the church to govern it, but he must have a vicar, the pope; who, as if Christ were took* weak, will not suffer him to exercise his kingly office, unless he may support and help him. Thus they set up the abomination of desolation in the temple of God.

O beloved, it much concerns us to cleanse and purify our hearts, that so we may entertain Christ, and he may delight to abide and dwell with us. You know how heinously he took it, when his house was made a den of thieves, Luke xix. 46, and will he not take it much worse that our hearts should be made the very sinks and cages of all manner of uncleanness?

How should we beg and cry to God that he would whip out these noisome lusts and corruptions out of the temple of our hearts by any sharp correction or terror of conscience whatsoever, rather than suffer them to reside there, still to grieve his good Spirit. We should take a holy state upon us, as being *temples of the Holy Ghost*, and therefore too good to be defiled with sin. Our hearts should be as the holy of holies; and therefore the apostle exhorts us 'to abstain from all filthiness both of flesh and spirit,' for this cause, 'that God may dwell amongst us,' 2 Cor. vii. 1; for, 'what communion hath light with darkness?' 2 Cor. vi. 14.

Use 3. Are God's people his house? Then let the enemies of the church take heed how they deal with them, for God will have a special care of his own house. Howsoever he may seem for a time to neglect his children, yet remember this, they are his house still; and no ordinary house, but a temple, wherein sacrifice is offered to him continually; and 'he that destroyeth the temple of God, him will God destroy,' 1 Cor. iii. 17.

Quest. Here a question would be answered, which some uncharitable spirits make, and that is this, Whether England be the house of God, or no?

* Qu. 'too?'—ED.

Ans. That the Church of England is God's house. I answer: the whole catholic militant church is but one house of God, though there be divers branches of the same. As there is but one main ocean of the sea, yet as it washeth upon the British coast it is called the British sea; and as it washeth on the Germans, the German sea, &c. It hath divers names of the divers countries which it passeth through, nevertheless there is still but one main sea; so it is with the house of God. God hath but one true church in the whole world, which spreads itself into divers nations and countries upon the face of the earth; one branch whereof is among us at this day.

Quest. How prove you that?

Ans. Doth not Christ dwell amongst us by his ordinances, and by his Spirit working effectually in the same? If a house be not in perfect repair, is it not still a house? I beseech you, let us rather give God cause to delight to dwell within us, than call in question whether he dwelleth amongst us or no.

Obs. 2. *That the house of God needs visiting and purging, and the reasons of it.* But to proceed. Hence further we see that the house of God after some time will need visiting and purging, seeing it will soon gather soil. There will abuses and disorders creep into it, so that it will need reformation. And this the apostle seems to insinuate when he saith, 'The time is come that judgment must begin at the house of God.' The Lord saw cause for what he did. For,

1. First,—Such is the weakness of man's nature, that evil things soon discourage us; and good things, except we wrestle with our spirits, prove a snare to the best. Even the church of God, after a long time of peace, is apt to gather corruption, as water doth by standing, and as the air itself will do if it have not the wind to purge it. And as it is in the bodies of men, if they be not curiously looked unto; after a certain time, they will gather such a burden of humours as will rise to a distemper, so that they must be let blood or purged, &c., so it is with the church of God. Such is the infirmity of man's nature and the malice of Satan, that enemy to mankind, that the best of God's people will quickly gather some distemper or other, and stand in need of purging. You know a house will gather dust of itself, though clean at the first.

2. Most certain it is that the church of God cannot be long without some affliction, considering that it is now in a state of pilgrimage, absent from God, in another world as it were. We live in a gross, corrupt air, and draw in the corruption of the times, one defiling another. 'I am a man of polluted lips,' saith Isaiah, 'and dwell with men of polluted lips,' Isaiah vi. 5; ill neighbours made him the worse.

Use. This should stir us up to lament the miserable estate of man's nature, that even the best of men, the church and people of God, whilst they remain in this world, stand in need of continual purging and winnowing. Crosses are as necessary to us as our daily bread, because we carry that about us which wants them. We are as much beholden to God's corrections as to his comforts, in this world. The church needs keeping under, for the most part. God will not have us settle upon our dregs, Ps. lv. 19; Jer. xlviii. 11. This should teach us to bewail our condition, and to desire to be at home, where we shall need no purging, where we shall be as free from sorrow as from sin, the cause of it.

Obs. 3. *That God will come to visit and purge his house when need is.* Observe we further, *that as the church will stand in need of chastisements, so*

God will come and visit his temple when need is, and but when need requires neither;* for God is no tyrant, yet he will shew that he hates sin wheresoever he finds it, even in his own dear children and servants, Amos iii. 2.

If God should bear with the abuses and sins of his own church and people, it would seem that sin was not so contrary to his holy disposition as it is. Therefore, in whomsoever he finds sin, he will punish it. Our blessed Saviour found this true, when he took upon him the imputation of our sins, and became but only a surety for us. You see how it made him cry out, 'My God, my God, why hast thou forsaken me?' Mat. xxvii. 46. Those glorious creatures, the very angels themselves, when they kept not their own standing, God would endure them no longer, but thrust them out of heaven.

Obj. But why doth God chiefly afflict his own people more than others?

Ans. 1. *Why God afflicts his own people before others. Because they are of his own family, and are called by his name*, Num. vi. 27. Now the disorders of the family tend to the disgrace of the governor of it. The sins of the church touch God more nearly than others, and therefore 'judgments must begin at the sanctuary first,' Ezek. iv. 6. 'I will be sanctified in all that come near me,' saith God when he smote Aaron's sons, Lev. x. 3. The nearer we come to God, if we maintain not the dignity of our profession, undoubtedly the more near will God come to us in judgment. We see the angels, who came nearest to God of all others, when once they sinned against him, they were tumbled out of heaven, and cast into the bottomless pit. Heaven could then brook them no longer.

2. Beloved, *the gospel suffers much through the sides of professors.* What saith the wicked worldling? These be your professors! See what manner of lives they lead! what little conscience they make of their ways! &c. Little do men know how much religion is vilified, and the ways of God evil spoken of, through the loose carriage of professors of the gospel, as if there were no force in the grace and favour of God to make us love and obey him in all things; as if religion consisted in word only, and not in power. What a scandal is this to the cause of Christ! It is no marvel God begins with them first. 'You have I known above all the families of the earth, and therefore will I punish you,' Amos iii. 2. A man may see and pass by dirt in his grounds, but he will not suffer it in his dining chamber; he will not endure dust to be in his parlour.

3. *The sins of the godly more heinous than others.* The sins of God's house admit of a greater aggravation than the sins of others; for, (1) they are committed against more *light;* (2) against more *benefits and favours;* (3) their sins in a manner are *sacrilege.* What! to make 'the temple of God a den of thieves,' to defile their *bodies* and *souls*, that are bought with the precious blood of Jesus Christ, is this a small matter? Again, (4) their sins are *idolatry;* for they are not only the *house* of God, but the *spouse* of God.

Now, for a spouse to be false and adulterous, this is greater than fornication, because the bond is nearer; so the nearer any come to God in profession, the higher is the aggravation of their sin, and as their sin grows, so must their punishment grow answerable and proportionable. They, therefore that know God's will most of all others, must look for most stripes if they do it not, Luke xii. 47, 48.

Use 1. *No privilege can exempt us from God's judgment.* Hence, therefore, learn that no privilege can exempt us from God's judgments, nay, rather the contrary. Where God doth magnify his rich goodness and mercy to a people, and is, notwithstanding, dishonoured by them, he will at last,

* That is, 'He will neither visit nor purge it, except when need requires.'—ED.

magnify his righteous justice in correcting such disobedient wretches. Some of the fathers (Augustine, Salvianus) were forced to justify God in visiting his church more sharply than other people, because Christians are so much worse than others, by how much they should be better. Their sins open the mouths of others to blaspheme. We should not bear out ourselves on this, that we are God's house, but fear so much the more to offend him, else all our privileges will but increase our guilt, not our comfort.

Use 2. Secondly, if God begins with his own house, let the church be severe in punishing sin there most of all; because God's wrath will break out first there. What a shame is it that the heathen should make such sharp laws against adultery and other sins, and we let them pass with a slight or no punishment at all! No doubt but God blesseth a State most, when sin is discountenanced and condemned most; for then it is the State's sin no longer, but lieth upon particular offenders. But I hasten.

Obs. 4. *God appoints a particular time for his visitation.* As God will visit his church, *so there is a certain time for it.* God, as he hath appointed a general day to *judge the world in,* so he appoints particular times of judgment in this life; he is the wise dispenser of times. God doth not always whip his church, but his ordinary course is to give them some respite, as, Acts ix. 31, after Paul's conversion, the church had joy, and grew in the comforts of the Holy Ghost. God hath rejoicing days for his people as well as mourning days; fair weather as well as foul; and all to help them forward in the way to heaven. Beloved, God gives many happy and blessed times to encourage weak ones at their first coming on, that they may the better grow up in goodness, and not be nipped in the bud; but after a certain time, when through peace and encouragement they grow secure and careless, and scandalous in their lives, then he takes them in hand and corrects them. God hath scouring days for his vessels.

Quest. What be those times wherein God will visit his church?

Ans. 1. *What be the times of God's visitation?* I answer, in general, the time of visiting the church of God is from Abel to the last man that shall be in the earth. The church began with blood, continues with blood, and shall end with blood. The whole days of the church are a time of persecution. 'From my youth upward,' saith the psalmist, 'I have suffered,' Ps. lxxxviii. 15. So may the church of God say, 'Even from my cradle, from my infancy,' I have been afflicted; yea, 'for thy sake we are killed all the day long, and counted as sheep for the slaughter,' Ps. xliv. 22. But this is not here meant.

.2. *The church is afflicted when the light of the gospel hath most clearly shined.* The time for the church of God to suffer is when the glorious manifestation of the gospel is more than in former times. We see the ten first persecutions were after that general promulgation of the gospel, whereby the world was more enlightened than formerly (*b*). We read in the Revelation of a *white horse* that Christ rides on, and a *pale horse* of famine, and a *red horse* of persecution that followed after him, Rev. vi. 2, 4, 8. So presently after the preaching of the gospel, comes the fan and the axe, or though not very presently, yet after a certain time, when our need requires it; for God will wait a while to see how we entertain his glorious gospel, and whether we walk worthy of it or not.

3. *That now is the time of the church's affliction.* More particularly, even now is the time of Jacob's trouble; even now God hath put a cup into the church's hand, and it must go round. The sword hath a commission to devour, which is not yet called in.

Quest. But what be the more especial times wherein a man may know some judgment is like to fall upon the church of God?

Ans. 1. *How we may know when some judgment approacheth.* The Scripture is wondrous full in the point. God usually, before any heavy judgment, visits a people with lesser judgments. His footsteps first appear in some small token of his displeasure; but if that prevails not, then *he brings a greater.*

Sign 1. 'This, and this have I done,' saith the Lord, 'and yet ye have not returned unto me,' Amos iv. 6, 7. There be droppings before the ruin of a house. Lesser judgments make way for greater, as a little wedge makes way for a greater; and, therefore, where less afflictions prevail not, there cannot but be an expectation of greater. 'Why should I smite you any more?' saith God; 'you fall away more and more,' Isa. i. 5; that is, I must have a sweeping judgment to carry you clean away.

Sign 2. Again, usually before some great calamity *God takes away worthy men*, 'the councillor, and the captain, and the man of war,' Isa. iii. 2, 3. This is a fearful presage that God threateneth some destruction, for they are the pillars of the church and the strength of the world; they are those that make the times and places good wherein they live; for they keep away evil and do good by their example and by their prayers many ways. A good man is a common good. The city thrives the better, as Solomon saith, for a righteous man, Prov. xi. 10, 11, Eccles. ix. 15. Therefore, we have cause to rejoice in them, and it is an evil sign when such are removed.*

Sign 3. God usually visits a people when some *horrible crying sins reign amongst them*, as (1) atheism. Beloved, God stands upon his prerogative then, when he is scarce known in the world; when they say, Where is God? God sees us not, &c. So, likewise (2), when idolatry prevails. This is spiritual adultery and a breach of covenant with God. Again (3), when divisions grow amongst a people. Union is a preserver. Where there is dissension of judgment, there will soon be dissension of affections; and dissipation will be the end if we take not heed. For the most part, ecclesiastical dissensions end in civil; and therefore we see, before the destruction of Jerusalem, what a world of schisms and divisions were amongst the Jews. There were Pharisees and Sadducees, &c. It was the ruin of the ten tribes at length, the rent that Jeroboam caused in religion. It is a fearful sign of some great judgment to fall upon a church, when there is not a stopping of dissensions. They may be easily stopped at first, as waters in the beginning; but when they are once gotten into the very vital parts of the church and commonwealth, we may see the mischief, but it is hardly † remedied.

Sign 4. Again, *when sin goes with some evil circumstances and odious qualities, which aggravate the same in the sight of God*, as when sin grows ripe, and abounds in a land or nation. At such a time as this a man may know there is some fearful judgment approaching.

Quest. But when is sin ripe?

Ans. 1. When it is impudent; when men grow bold in sin, making it their whole course and trade of life. When men's wicked courses are their 'conversation,'‡ they cannot tell how to do otherwise.

2. When sin grows common and spreads far. It is an ill plea to say, Others do so as well as I. Alas! the more sin, the more danger.

3. When there is a security in sinning, without fear or dread of the Almighty, as if men would dare the God of heaven to do his worst. Oh,

---

* Compare reflections on Sibbes's own death, by Catlin. Appendix to Memoir, pp. cxxxiii-v.—G.   † That is, 'with difficulty.'—G.

‡ That is, 'habitual.' Compare 2 Peter ii. 7; 1 Peter i. 15, *et alibi*.—G.

beloved, such persons as go on still in their sins to provoke the Lord, do put a sword, as it were, into God's hands to destroy themselves.

The old world, you know, was very secure. No doubt, they mocked at holy Noah when he made the ark, as if he had been a doting old man. Notwithstanding, he foretold them of the wrath to come. And our Saviour, Christ, saith, 'Before the end of the world it shall be as in the days of Noah,' Mat. xxiv. 38. Beloved, God hath his 'old worlds' still. If we have the same course and security of sinning, we must look for the same judgments. And, therefore, compare times with times. If the times now answer former times, when God judged them, we may well expect the same fearful judgments to fall upon us.

Sign 5. *Unfruitfulness threateneth a judgment upon a people.* When God hath bestowed a great deal of cost and time, he looks we should answer his expectation in some measure. The fig-tree in the gospel had some respite given it, by reason of the prayers of the vine-dresser; but afterward, when it brought forth no fruit, it was cut down and cast into the fire. Beloved, who amongst us would endure a barren tree in his garden? That which is not fit for fruit is most fit for fire. We can endure a barren tree in the wilderness, but not in our orchards. When God, the great husbandman in his church, sees that upon so great and continual cost bestowed upon us, we remain yet unfruitful, he will not suffer us long to cumber the ground of his church.

Sign 6. Again, *decay in our first love* is a sign of judgment approaching. God threatened the church of Ephesus to remove his candlestick from among them, for their 'decay in their first love,' Rev. ii. 4; that having surfeited of plenty and peace, he might recover her taste by dieting of her. Decay in love proceeds from disesteem in judgment; and God cannot endure his glorious gospel should be slighted, as not deserving the richest strain of our love. The Lord takes it better where there is but little strength and a striving to be better, than when there is great means of grace and knowledge, and no growth answerable, but rather a declining in goodness. I beseech you lay these things to heart. The Lord is much displeased when Christians are not so zealous as they should be; when there is not that sweet communion of saints among them, to strengthen and encourage one another in the ways of holiness as there might be; when there is not a beauty in their profession to allure and draw on others to a love and liking of the best things; when there is not a care to avoid all scandals that may weaken respect to good things, and bring an evil report on the ways of God; when they labour not with their whole hearts to serve the Lord in a cheerful manner, &c. The very not serving God answerable to encouragements, is a certain sign of ensuing danger, Deut. xxviii. 47.

Use. Therefore, I beseech you, let us look about us whether these be not the times wherein we live, that judgment must begin at the house of God. The Lord complains in Jeremiah, Jer. viii. 7, that the turtle and other silly creatures knew the time of their standing and removing, but his people did not know his judgments. Do the creatures know their times and seasons, and shall Christ complain that we know not the day of our visitation? What a shame is this! I beseech you, let us know and consider our times. If we have a time of sinning, God will have a time of punishing.

And have we not just cause to fear that judgment is not far from us, when we see a great part of God's house on fire already in our neighbouring countries? We have had lesser judgments, and they have not wrought kindly with us; we need a stronger purge. If we look to the carriage of men, what sin is less committed now than formerly? How few renew their covenant with God, in sincerity of resolution, to walk closely with him!

And what the judgment will be, we may probably foresee, for usually the last judgment is the worst. We have had all but war, the worst of all; for in other judgments we have to deal with God, but in this we are to deal with men, whose very mercies are cruelties, Prov. xii. 10. The sword hath a long time been shaken over our heads, a cloud of war hath hung over us to affright us, but we rest still secure in our sinful courses, and think 'to-morrow shall be as to-day,' Isa. lvi. 12, and that 'no evil shall come nigh us,' &c., Micah iii. 11. O the frozen hearts of Christians, that thrust the evil day far from them! do we not see the whole world in a manner in a combustion round about us, and we, as 'the three young men in the fiery furnace,' Dan. iii., untouched? Beloved, we have outstripped them in abominable wickedness; and however the Lord is pleased that we should only hear a noise and rumour of war, yet we in this land have deserved to drink as deep of the cup of the Lord's wrath as any people under heaven.

Quest. What course should we take to prevent the judgment of God, and keep it from us?

Ans. Of the means to prevent and escape God's judgments. 1. *Labour to meet God by speedy repentance, before any decree be peremptorily come forth against us.* As yet there is hope to prevail; for, blessed be God, as we have many things to fear, so we have many things to encourage us to go unto God with comfort. We have enjoyed a succession of gracious princes that have maintained the truth of God amongst us; we have many godly magistrates and ministers, together with the ordinances, and many other experiences of God's love vouchsafed unto us. We have yet time to seek the Lord. Let us not defer till the very time of judgment come upon us; for that is but self-love.

Note. Assure thyself thus much, thou canst have no more comfort in troubles and afflictions when they do come, than thou hast care to prevent them before they come; answerable to our care in preventing now, will be our comfort then.

Therefore if we would be hid in the day of God's wrath; if we would have God to set his mark upon us, and write us in his book of remembrance, and to gather us when he 'makes up his jewels,' Mal. iii. 16; if we would have him to own us then, look to it now, get now into Christ, be provided now of a sound profession of religion, and that will be as an ark to shelter us in the evil day. What we know let us do, and then we shall be built on a rock, that if waves or anything come, we shall not be stirred.

Usually God in dangerous times leaveth some ground of hope, which worketh differently with men. Such as are carnal, grow presumptuous hereupon; but the godly are drawn nearer to God upon any appearance of encouragement; the good things they enjoy from God, work in them a more earnest desire to please him.

It is the custom of the Spirit of God to make doubtful, imperfect, and as it were half promises, to keep his people still under some hope; whence we read of these and such like phrases in Scripture, 'It may be God will shew mercy,' Amos v. 15; and 'who knoweth whether he will hear us?' &c., Joel ii. 14.

2. Again, *examine and try, upon what ground thou professest religion,* whether it will hold water or no, and stand thee in stead when evil times shall come. Beloved, it nearly concerns us all, seriously to consider and narrowly to search,

upon what grounds we venture our lives and souls; try our graces, our knowledge, repentance, faith, love, &c., of what metal they are. Those that have coin, bring it to the touchstone, and if it prove counterfeit they presently reject it and will have none of it. O that we had this wisdom for matters of eternity! If men would search and plough up their own hearts, they would not need the ploughing of God's enemies. We should not need God's judgments, if we would judge ourselves. The church complained that the enemies had made long furrows on her back, but if she had ploughed herself, she had saved the enemies that labour, Ps. cxxix. 3.

3. Before any judgment comes, *let us store up the fruits of a holy life;* every day be doing something; do that now, which may comfort thee then; store up comforts against the evil day. When the 'night is come, we cannot work,' John ix. 4. Let us therefore 'walk while we have the light,' John xii. 35; let us look about us and do what good we can 'whilst we have time,' as the apostle saith, 1 Cor. vii. 29. The time will come ere long that thou wilt wish, O that I had that opportunity and advantage of doing good as I have had! O that I had such means of doing good as I have had! but then it will be too late; then that whereby thou shouldst do good, will be in thy enemies' hands; and therefore, while we have time, let us be doing and receiving all the good we can.

4. Again, if we would have God to shield us, and be an hiding-place in the worst times, *let us mourn for our own sins and the sins of the times wherein we live.* Let us keep ourselves unspotted of the sins of the world; let us not bring sticks to the common fire; let us not make the times worse for us, but better, that the times and places we live in may bless God for us.

And let us not only mourn for the sins of the times, but labour also to repress them all we can, and stand in the gap, endeavouring by our prayers and tears to stop God's judgments.

5. *And we should set a high price upon that religion and the blessings of God which we do enjoy,* lest we force God to take them from us; and so we come to know that, by the want of it, which we did not value when we possessed it. Oh, let us esteem the treasure of the gospel at a higher rate than ever we have done. We see how it is slighted by most of the world; how they shake the blessed truths of God, and call them into question, being indifferent for any religion. Is this our proficiency, beloved? It behoves us to store up all the sanctified knowledge we can, and to take heed we yield not to any, that would either weaken our judgment in religion, or our affections to the best things. We should, every one in his place, labour to stop dissensions in this kind, and knit our hearts together as one man in unity and concord. Factions have always fractions going with them. Unity makes strong, but division weakeneth any people. Even Satan's kingdom, Mat. xii. 25, 26, divided against itself, cannot stand.

What is the glory of England? Take away the gospel, and what have we that other nations have not better than ourselves? Alas, if we labour not to maintain truth, we may say with Eli's daughter, 'The glory of God is departed from us,' 1 Sam. iv. 21.

Sarah had her handmaid; and so hath religion been attended with prosperity and peace, preservation and protection amongst us, even to the admiration* of other countries. Shall we not, therefore, make much of that religion, which, if we had it alone, joined with many crosses and sufferings, yet were an inestimable and unvaluable blessing? And shall we not now much more, considering it hath been attended by so many mer-

* That is, 'wonder.'—G.

cies, cherish and maintain the same all we can? Do we think it will go alone when it goes, whensoever God removes it from us? No, no. Therefore, I beseech you, let us highly esteem of the gospel, whilst we do enjoy it. If we suffer that to be shaken any way, our peace and prosperity will then leave us, and judgment upon judgment will come upon us. If we will not regard the truth of God, which he esteemeth most, he will take away outward prosperity, which we esteem most.

But I come to the fifth point, *that judgment must begin at the house of God.*
Quest. Why doth God begin with his own church and people?
Ans. Reason 1. Usually because he useth *wicked* men and the *enemies* of his church for that base service, *to correct and punish them.*
Reason 2. *To take away all excuse from wicked men.* That they, seeing how severely God deals with his own dear children, might be stirred up to look about them, and consider what will become of themselves at the last, if they go on in their sinful courses. So many crosses as befall God's children, so many evidences against secure carnal persons; for if God deal thus with the green tree, what will he do with the dry? If he scourge his children thus with rods, certainly the slaves shall be whipped with scorpions.
Reason 3. God begins with his own servants, *that his children might be best at last.* If he should not begin with them, they would grow deeper in rebellion against him, and attract more soil and filth to themselves, and be more and more engaged to error and corruption. God's love to his people is such, that he regards their correction before the confusion of his enemies.
Reason 4. Again, God doth this, *that when he sends them good days afterwards, they might have the more taste and relish of his goodness.* After an afflicted life, we are more sensible of happy times. God deals favourably, therefore, with a man when he crosseth him in the beginning of his days, and gives him peace in his latter end.

This is a point of marvellous comfort and encouragement to the faithful servants of God; for,

Use 1. *Though God correct them sharply, yet he shews thereby they are of his household.* When a man corrects another, we may know it is his child or servant, &c. God shews that we are of his house and family by the care he takes to correct us. The vine is not hated because it is pruned, but that it may bring forth more fruit; the ground is not hated because it is ploughed, nor the house because it is cleansed.

Quest. But what is meant by judgment here?
Ans. Judgment is correction moderated to God's children. Judgment is twofold in Scripture. The statutes of God are called judgments, and the corrections of God are called judgments. The statutes are called judgments, because they judge what we should do, and what we should not do. Now, when we do not that we should, he is forced to judge us actually with real judgments.

The real judgments of God are either (1), upon the *wicked,* and so they are judgments *in fury,* for there is not the least taste of his love in them to wicked men. They can make no sanctified use of them, because they are not directed to them for their good; or (2), to *God's children,* and so they are *moderate corrections;* and therefore the prophet so often urgeth, ' Correct us, Lord, in judgment,' &c., Jer. x. 24. God always moderates afflictions to his own children, but as for the wicked, he sweeps them away as dung, as dross, and as chaff, &c.

Use 2. Again, *it is a comfort to God's children that he begins with them first.* Rather than God will suffer them to perish and be condemned with the world, he begins with them here. They have their worst first, and the better is to come.

Use 3. This likewise is some comfort, that the *time* when God corrects his children is most *seasonable* and fit for them. God pruneth his trees in the fittest time. A plant cut unseasonably, dieth, but being cut in due time it flourishes the better. All the works of God are beautiful in their season. Every Christian may truly say, God loves me better than I do myself. He knows the best time of purging and visiting his people. 'This is the time of Jacob's trouble,' &c., Micah ii. 3. Therefore we should lay our hands upon our mouths, kiss the rod, and stoop under judgments, as considering God's time to be the best time, and that he knows better what is good for us than we do ourselves.

Thus you see, though we have cause of fearing God's judgments, yet there is something to comfort us in the midst of all. God mingles our comforts and crosses together whilst we are here, both to keep us in awe of offending his Majesty, and to encourage us in well-doing. *Securitatis custos timor.* Therefore let us always look what matter of fear and what matter of hope we have, for both these are operative affections. *Spes exercitat ad opus.* Oh that I could stir up this blessed fear in you. It is that which preserves the soul; and God hath promised that 'he will put his fear into our hearts, that we shall not depart from him,' Jer. xxxii. 40. I beseech you, ply the throne of grace, and desire the Lord that it may be to every one of your souls according to his good word.

Labour likewise for encouragement in the ways of holiness. Blessed be God, yet we have a time of respite. God forbears us with much patience and goodness. Answerable to our good courses that we take now, will be our comfort in the evil day. If we carelessly go on in sin, and think it time enough to renew our covenant with God then, when his judgments are abroad and ready to cease* upon us, we do but delude our own souls, and expose ourselves to inevitable dangers. Mark what the Lord saith, Because I called, and you would not hear, &c., therefore will I laugh at your destruction, Prov. i. 24, 26. Is it not strange that the merciful God should laugh at the calamity of his poor creatures? Yet thus it is with every wilful sinner that dallies with God, and puts off his repentance from time to time. God will take pleasure in the ruin of such a man, and laugh when his fear cometh, because those that seek him then, do it not out of any love or liking of God and the ways of goodness, but merely out of self-love and respect to their own welfare.

* Qu. 'rest?' or 'fall?'—ED.

NOTES.

(a) Page 375.—'That which was Bethel, is now become Bethaven.' That is, what was 'Bethel,' which means 'house of God,' was become 'Bethaven,' which means 'house of idols;' a sort of *jeu de mot* applied to Bethel, after it became the seat of the worship of the golden calves.

(b) Page 378.—'First ten persecutions.' The first was under Nero, A.D. 64; the second under Domitian, 95; the third under Trajan, 100; the fourth under Adrian, 118; the fifth under Severus, 197; the sixth under Maximinus, 235; the seventh under Decius, more bloody than any preceding; the eighth under Valerian, 257; the ninth under Aurelian, 272; and the tenth under Diocletian, which lasted ten years, 302. G.

THE UNGODLY'S MISERY.

SERMON II.

And if it first begin at us, what shall the end of those be that obey not the gospel!—1 PET. IV. 17.

THESE words are propounded by way of admiration,* as if the apostle had been at his wits' end, and could not certainly set down how great the judgment should be, of those that obey not the gospel, it was so terrible and unavoidable. The points considerable are these :—

Three points considerable. 1. *That the seeming prosperity of the wicked shall have an end.*

2. *That it is wisdom to consider the end of graceless persons.*

3. *The description of them;* in these words, *they are such as obey not the gospel.*

Obs. 1. *The seeming prosperity of the wicked shall have an end.* It is naturally in the hearts of carnal persons, to think it shall be always well with them, whereas the prophet saith, the happiness of a wicked man is but 'as a candle, that ends in a snuff,' Prov. xxiv. 20, or like a rose, the beauty whereof suddenly fades, and nothing remains but the prickles. The favours of men, for which they so much offend God, shall have an end; their strength shall end, their pleasure shall end, (alas, they are but pleasures of sin for a season!) their life itself, the foundation of all their comforts, that shall have an end; but their sins, by which they have offended God, shall never have an end. See what a fearful judgment follows every wicked wretch; that which he sins for, his honour, riches, delights, all shall vanish and come to nothing; they shall not be able to afford him one drop or dram of comfort at his dying day; but the sin itself, the guilt of that, and the punishment due to the same, shall endure for ever, to torment his soul, without serious repentance and turning to God in time.

Obs. 2. *The happiness of the wicked is momentary; their misery endless.* But secondly, if the happiness of wicked men shall have an end, and their misery shall have no end, *let us not be dazzled with their present happiness, so as to imitate their evil ways;* let us tremble at their courses, whose end we tremble at. If we walk in the same path, shall we not come to the

* That is, 'amazement.'—G.

same end? All wicked men that delight in the company one of another here, are brethren in evil, and shall be like a company of tares, all cast into hell-fire together hereafter. It is pity they should be severed then that will not be severed now. Those men's courses, therefore, which we follow here, of their judgment we shall participate eternally afterwards.

Use. Let this admonish us to have nothing to do with sinful persons, nor to be troubled with their seeming prosperity. 'They stand in slippery places,' Ps. lxxiii. 18. God lets them alone for a while, but their pleasure will end in bitterness at last; all their riches shall end in poverty and beggary. 'They shall not have a drop of water to cool their tongues,' Luke xvi. 24, 25. All their honour and greatness shall end in confusion and shame, and lie in the dust ere long. Indeed, we should rather pity them, if we consider their latter ends. Alas, what shall become of them ere long! The fall of these wretches shall be so terrible, that Peter could not set it down, but leaves it to the admiration of the reader, What shall the end of such be! &c.

One difference betwixt a wise man and a fool is, that a wise man considers his end, and frames his life suitable thereunto. Therefore if we would be truly wise, let us consider the end of those things in this world, which wicked men offend God for, and set so light by heaven and everlasting happiness for the procurement of. Alas, whatsoever is here, shall have an end! A Christian should frame his course answerable to eternity, that when his happiness shall end in this world, it may begin in the world to come, else we may outlive our happiness.

Present happiness aggravates future and eternal misery. This is the misery of wicked men, that their souls are eternal, but their happiness is determined in this life. Here that ends; but their misery is infinite, and hath no end at all. Look what degree of excellency any creature hath, if it be good; the same degree of misery it hath if it be evil. What made the angels worse than other creatures when they sinned, but only this? they were most excellent creatures, and therefore when they became evil, their excellency did but help them to subsist and be more capable of punishment. A wise man understandeth his misery. *Sapiens miser plus miser.* Now the angels when they fell became more miserable, because they were more capacious, and sensible of it, being spirits.

So man being sinful and evil, his end will be more miserable than any inferior creature, because he was more happy. His happiness helps him to more misery. How should this stir up every one to look about him, and not to prize himself by any outward excellency whatsoever! The more excellent thou art, the more miserable if thou sin against God. It is of all unhappiness the most unhappy thing, for a man to live happily here a while, and be eternally miserable afterwards; for our former happiness tends to nothing else but to make us more sensible of future miseries. What is all the felicity of great persons, when they die and leave this world? Alas, it soon comes to nothing, and serves but to make them apprehensive of more misery than meaner persons are capable of: what shall the end of such be? &c.

Obs. 8. *The endless miseries of the wicked should warn us from the love of their present pleasures and profits.* From this, that the apostle leaves the punishment of all sinful wretches to admiration and wonderment, rather than to expression, for indeed it is above expression, we may learn—*when we are tempted to any sin or unlawful course, to consider thus with ourselves* · Shall I, for a pleasure that will end, have a judgment that shall never end?

for the favour of men that will fail, shall I lose the perpetual favour of God, whose wrath is a consuming fire, and burns to hell? shall I for a little profit, lose my soul eternally? Beloved, as the good things of a Christian, even in this life, are admirable beyond expression, ' peace that passeth all understanding,' Philip. iv. 7, and ' joy unspeakable and glorious,' 1 Pet. i. 8, &c., so when God awakens our consciences, those gripes and pangs and terrors of soul, which follow after sin committed, are unutterable and inconceivable. I beseech you therefore, whenever you are solicited to sin, for profit or pleasure, &c., set before your eyes the fading and perishing condition of these things, and the everlastingness of that judgment which attends upon them. Oh that we were wise this way!

Obs. 3. I come now to the third particular; *Those that obey not the gospel,* wherein we have—

1. A description of the *thing.*
2. And then of the *persons.*

The thing is the *gospel of God;* the persons are *wicked men.* God is the author of the gospel. It comes out of his breast, sealed with authority. Whence learn this, by the way, *that in refusing the blessed gospel, we have to deal with God himself.* It is God's word and gospel. Therefore when you reject it, you reject God; in receiving it, you receive God. You deal with God himself, when you deal with the ministers of his word. Therefore whenever you partake of the ordinances, say, with good Cornelius, ' We are now in the presence of God, to hear what he will say,' Acts x. 33.

Quest. But, what is it to obey the gospel?

Ans. To obey the gospel is to *entertain the offers of it;* for indeed though the gospel command us to believe in the Son of God, yet withal it offers the very command unto us; to believe in Christ, being in effect a command to receive him, which supposeth an act of giving and tendering something to us. Now when we do not receive and entertain with our whole heart Christ and his benefits, freely offered, we disobey the gospel, and so procure danger to ourselves.

But more particularly, he obeys the gospel *that is sensible of his own miserable and sinful condition, and from a sense thereof hungereth after the grace and favour offered in Jesus Christ to pardon sin,* which when he hath once obtained, [he] walks answerable to that great mercy received. He that receives whole Christ to justify him, and sanctify him too; that receives Christ as a king to rule him as well as a priest to save him, such a one receives the gospel. But those that are not sensible of their misery, or if they be, will not go to Christ, but, as desperate persons, fling away the potion that should cure them, these are far from obeying the gospel of God. Such likewise as pretend, Oh, Christ is welcome with the pardon of sin, but yet live in gross wickedness, against knowledge and conscience, and suffer him not to bear sway in their hearts, as if Christ came by blood alone, and not by water; whereas indeed he came as well by water to sanctify us, as by blood to die for us.

Many there are that think they obey the gospel, who are indeed very rebels and enemies unto it. They welcome the gospel, and they hate popery, &c., but notwithstanding they will be their own rulers, and live as they list; they will not deny themselves in their beloved sins; they are full of revenge, notwithstanding the gospel saith, ' This is my commandment, that you love one another,' John xv. 12. That ' bids them deny ungodliness and worldly lusts, and live soberly,' Titus ii. 12 ; yet they will riot, and follow their base courses still. The gospel teacheth a man to acknowledge God in all his ways, to deal with God in all things he goes about. Now, when a man lives without God in the world, saying, *God is merciful*, and *Christ is a Saviour*, and yet persists in those ways which seem good in his own eyes, never looking to God to guide him, or his law to rule him, how can such a one be said to obey the gospel?

That works have no place in the act of justification. But some others there are amongst us, that regard not Christ and his satisfaction alone, but join faith and works together in justification; they will have other priests, and other intercessors than Christ. Alas! beloved, how are these men fallen from Christ to another gospel, as if Christ were not an all-sufficient Saviour, and able to deliver to the uttermost! What is the gospel but salvation and redemption by Christ alone? Gal. ii. 16.

Therefore Rome's church is an apostate church, and may well be styled an adulteress and a whore, because she is fallen from her husband Christ Jesus.

And what may we think of those that would bring light and darkness, Christ and antichrist, the ark and Dagon together; that would reconcile us, as if it were no such great matter! Beloved, they that join works with Christ in matter of justification, err in the foundation. The very life and soul of religion consists in this. What was the reason the Jews stumbled at this stumblingblock, and were never benefited by Christ? Why? They set up a righteousness of their own, which could not stand, but soon failed them. So when a man sets up a righteousness of his own, neglecting the righteousness of Christ, it is impossible he should ever be saved, living and dying in that error, Philip. iii. 10.

Why disobedience against the gospel is so great a sin. Therefore, I beseech you, take heed of disobeying the gospel of Jesus Christ in any kind whatsoever, for of all sins this is the greatest, as shall appear by these reasons.

Reason 1. First, *because sins against the gospel are sins against those attributes, wherein God will glorify himself most*, as his grace, mercy, lovingkindness, &c. Therefore the gospel is called grace, because it publisheth, offers, and applies grace. Now sins against mercy are greater than sins against justice; for God hath made all things for the glory of his mercy. Even among men, are not sins against favours the greatest sins? To wrong a man whether he deserves well or ill is an offence. But what man will have his courtesies rejected, though never so mean? Love deserves love; favour deserves respect again. But now when we obey not the gospel, we neglect and despise the goodness and mercy of God. Oh what excellent blessings doth the gospel reveal, if we had hearts to value them! Doth not the gospel bring salvation! Is it not the word of *grace*, the word of *life*, the word of the *kingdom?* Beloved, I beseech you, lay these things to heart, for whensoever you refuse the gospel of Christ, you refuse with it the word of grace, of the kingdom of heaven, and eternal life, and all. Therefore the sins of the gospel must needs be the greatest sins.

Reason 2. Again, *sins against the greatest light are most sinful.* What makes sin out of measure sinful, but this, when it is committed against a great measure of light? What makes a man fall foul? It is not when he falls in a mist, or in a dark night, every one will pity him then; alas, he wanted light; but when he falls at noon-day. Beloved, had we lived in former times, when the light was not poured forth so abundantly as now it is, our sin had been the less; but now in this clear sunshine of the gospel, for us to live in sins condemned by so great a light, either in our judgment or practice, it must needs make our sin the greater. 'If I had not come and spoken to them,' saith our Saviour, 'they had had some pretence for their sins,' John xv. 22; but when Christ had once poken, all excuse was taken away; they could not then say they knew not the will of God; and this is the reason of that speech of the apostle, 'Now you are in the light, walk as children of light,' Eph. v. 8. 'And this is the condemnation, that men hate light (not that men for want of light stumble, but), that men love darkness more than light,' John iii. 19. It is not the sin itself, but the love and liking of sin which aggravates men's wickedness, whenas the malice and poison of their hearts rebel against the discovery of God's good pleasure in Christ.

Negative infidelity is a lesser sin than disobedience to the gospel. No people out of the church are capable of this sin; for how can they sin by infidelity and unthankfulness for the gospel that never had it? And therefore negative infidelity is, as it were, no sin in comparison, 'If I had not come among them, they had had no sin,' saith Christ, John xv. 22. Negative I call that, whenas men believe not, having no means, as infidels and heathens, &c. And therefore as they sin without the gospel, so they shall be damned without the gospel. The rule of their damnation shall be the law of nature written in their hearts; for this is an undoubted truth, *no man ever lived answerable to his rule;* and therefore God hath just ground of damnation to any man, even from this, that he hath not lived answerable to the rule of his own conscience. So that we need not fly to reprobation, &c.

Reason 8. Again, another aggravation of sins against the gospel is, *that they sin against the better covenant.* The first covenant was, *Do this and live,* against which we all sinned, and *were under the curse.* But now we are under a more gracious covenant, *a covenant of mercy,* 'Believe in the Lord Jesus Christ and we shall be saved.' Therefore sin now must needs be more heinous; for if we sin against the gospel, either by presumption or despair, or else by profaneness, professing the gospel but denying the power of it, &c., 2 Tim. iii. 5, there is no remedy left for us. If a man sin against the law, against moral honesty and civil righteousness, there is a remedy in the gospel for him; but when a man sins against the sweet love and goodness of God, in rejecting the gospel of his dear Son, mercy itself shall not save such an one. That must needs be a strange sin that makes a man worse than a Sodomite, yet we read it 'shall be easier for Sodom and Gomorrah in that day,' Mat. x. 15, than for those that hear the gospel, the blessed allurements and invitations to believe, and to lead an holy life answerable to our faith and calling, and yet live in sins against conscience, despising the precious blood of Christ.

Herod was a wretched man, yet notwithstanding it was said, he added this to all, 'he put John in prison, a preacher of the gospel,' Luke ii. 20. Sins against the gospel in a loose malignant professor, are many times worse than all the rest. Oh therefore take heed of sinning against the favour and goodness of God; for this will confound us at the day of judgment, when we shall think, What! was so great mercy offered me, and did I slight it in this manner? Have I lost the favour of God, eternal life, and the glorious company of the saints in heaven, for a base pleasure of sin for a season? to gratify a brutish lust? Have I lost Christ and all the good by him for ever, only to satisfy my sinful disposition? to please a carnal friend? &c. Oh, how will this lie heavy upon the soul another day! We shall not need accusers. Our own hearts shall justify the sentence of God against us, be it never so sharp, that we have refused mercy, so often tendered to us in the blood of Christ. Mark what St Paul saith, 'The Lord Jesus shall be revealed from heaven in flaming fire, taking vengeance upon those that know not God, and obey not his glorious gospel,' 2 Thess. i. 7, 8. He saith not only on those that are swearers and profane persons, but ignorant sots that care not to know God, though they be not open sinners. He saith not, those that persecute the gospel or oppose it, shall be punished with eternal destruction from the presence of God, which is true; but those that sin in a less degree, 'such as obey not the gospel, 2 Thess. i. 8; that value not this inestimable jewel ; that sell not all to buy this pearl, Mat. xiii. 46 ; unto whom all the world is not dross and dung, Philip. iii. 8, in respect of the glorious gospel of Christ Jesus. How shall they escape 'which neglect so great salvation ?' Heb. ii. 3.

Oh, say some, this concerns not me, I thank God there is mercy in Christ, and I hope for pardon, &c. Beloved, here is the bane of men's souls, they will be their own carvers, and take of the gospel what they list. Oh, so much of Christ as concerns their own good they will have ; so much as concerns their pleasure and profit ; so much as they may have, and be proud too, and be devilish and evil in their life and conversation too. This they allow of. And it is pity he should live *that regards not Christ* in justification. But so much as concerns mortification and self-denial, as crosses them in their sinful courses, this they are strangers to. But, we must know, the gospel doth not only bring salvation, but it teacheth a man ' to deny ungodliness and worldly lusts,' Titus ii. 12 ; to put off himself, his whole self, that he might have no judgment, nor no affection contrary to God.

To make this more plainly appear, take these few instances.

Instance 1. The very first lesson which the gospel enjoineth, is to ' cut off our right hand, and pull out our right eye,' that is, to deny ourselves in those sins which are most useful and gainful to us. Now when this is pressed in particular, to some that live in their secret beloved sins, presently they begin to hate this blessed truth, and the ministry thereof. They know so much as will damn them, but so much, as without the which they cannot be saved, that they oppose. Contenting themselves with a bare form and outside of religion, they come to church, and take their books, and read, and hear, and receive the sacrament, &c., and in these outward performances they rest. Alas, beloved, what are these ? I tell you, all the privileges of the gospel do but aggravate thy damnation, if thou are not better by them; for as they are in themselves invaluable privileges, and even ravish the heart of a true child of God ; so when they are not entertained to purpose, they make our sin the more heinous. Every man is willing to accept of Christ, but it must be upon their own terms ; and what are those ? So they may enjoy their worldly delights ; so they may increase their estates by such unlawful means, and not be crossed. So long they are content that Christ and the gospel shall be theirs ; but otherwise, if they cannot enjoy Christ upon their own terms, that is, if they cannot go to heaven and to hell too, they will rather regard their own profits and pleasures, than regard Christ. Oh, how do these poor wretches delude their own souls ! Beloved, the embracing and obeying the gospel is a spiritual marriage betwixt Christ and the believer. Now, you know in marriage the will is given up to the husband; the wife is no more her own, but at his disposing. So when once we are truly united unto Christ, we take him for better for worse. We must suffer with him, yea, live and die with him, and esteem him above all ; we must take Christ upon his own terms, or else he will not be had. If we love not ' him above father and mother (yea and life itself), we are not worthy of him,' Mat. x. 37 ; and therefore all that do not thus obey the gospel are rebels, and shall have the reward of rebels if they repent not in time. Were it not a comely thing, think you, for a company of traitors that had this condition propounded to them, if you will come in and live as good subjects you shall have a pardon, for them to go on presumptuously in their rebellion still, and think to have favour when they please? Would not a sharp execution be the just desert of such persons?

Instance 2. Again, Christ propounds pardon and forgiveness of sins upon this condition, that we will come in and live as wives* and as obedient subjects to his blessed Spirit, and not in swearing, filthiness, and other abominable courses, of which the Scripture saith, 'such shall never inherit the kingdom of heaven,' 1 Cor. vi. 9; and yet notwithstanding, Satan hath so bewitched many poor wretches, that they think their case is good, and it shall go well with them, be their lives never so loose and opposite to the ways of God. They bless themselves when God doth not bless them, but rather curse them to their faces. The devil himself is likely to be saved as soon as such graceless persons as these, without repentance. No, no; if ever they expect a pardon, they must live as subjects; if they frame not themselves to be guided by Christ, and come under his government, to be ruled according to his will, they have nothing to do with mercy and salvation: 'those mine enemies, that will not have me rule over them, bring them hither, and slay them before me,' &c., Luke xix. 27. We mock Christ if we will not suffer him to rule us.

Obj. But I cannot obey the gospel of myself.

Ans. It is true we cannot, no more than we can obey the law; nay, it is harder to obey the gospel than to obey the law in a man's own strength; for there are the seeds of the law in our nature, but there are none of the gospel. That is merely† supernatural. The promises are above nature to apprehend them; therefore a supernatural strength is required to plant the excellent grace of faith in our hearts. But though we be as unable to believe and obey the gospel as the law, yet here is the difference; together with the unfolding of our miseries by the gospel, the Spirit of God goes along to sustain us. The law finds us dead, and gives us no strength, but leaves a man cursed still; the gospel likewise finds us dead, but it leaves us not so, and therefore it is called 'the ministry of the Spirit,' Gal. iii. 5. 'Received you the Spirit by the law, or by the gospel?' Gal. iii. 2. God's blessed Spirit goes together with the sweet message of salvation and eternal life, and this Spirit doth not only open our understandings, but incline and bend our wills and affections to embrace the truth that is offered. Seeing, therefore, the Spirit which accompanieth the gospel is mighty and powerful in operation, let none pretend impossibility. For though they find not the sweet blaze of the Spirit at the first or second hearing, yet let them still attend upon grace, 'waiting at wisdom's gate,' Prov. viii. 34, and the angel will come at length and stir the waters. God will make the means effectual first or last, to those that in truth of heart seek unto him; for the gospel is the chariot of the Spirit, and the golden conduit through which the Spirit runs, and is conveyed to us. Therefore if thou wouldst not disobey the gospel, withstand not the Spirit of God working by the same.

How the Spirit works with the gospel. Now the Spirit works with the gospel by degrees. 1. It bringeth some to be willing to hear the gospel, who yet presently neglect and disregard the same. 2. Others are more obedient for a time, 'as the stony ground,' Mat. xiii. 5, but because they

---

* That is, as 'submissive.' See page 390, line 7 from bottom.—G.

† That is, 'wholly.'—G.

opened not their hearts to the working of the Spirit only, but will be ruled partly by carnal wisdom, and partly by the Spirit, it leaves them at last altogether. 3. But some there are who give up themselves wholly to the government of Christ, to be ruled in all things by his blessed Spirit, highly esteeming the treasures of heaven, and comforts of a better life, above all the fading outward felicities which this world can afford; who would not gain any earthly thing, hurt their consciences, or once defile themselves with unfruitful works of darkness; fearing lest they should in anything dishonour Christ, or grieve his good Spirit; and to such only hath the gospel come in power.

Therefore, I beseech you, seriously consider of this truth. *If you would not disobey the gospel, disobey not the Spirit accompanying the same;* deal faithfully with your own souls. Which of you all hath not some time or other had his heart warmed with the sweet motions of God's Spirit? Oh, do not resist these holy stirrings within you; give way to the motions of the blessed Spirit of God; second them with holy resolutions to practise the same; let them sink deep into your hearts, root them there, and never give over the holy meditation of them, till you make them your own, till you come to see grace and the state of Christianity, to be the most amiable and excellent thing in the world, and sin and carnal courses to be the most accursed thing in the world, worse than any misery, than any beggary, torment, or disgrace whatsoever. Beloved, till we have our spirits wrought upon to this high esteem of good things, and to a base undervaluing of all things else, we shall rebel against Christ first or last; for until such time as the heart of man is overpowered with grace, he cannot but disobey the gospel, either by shutting it out altogether, or by making an evil use of what he knoweth, thereby turning the 'grace of God into wantonness,' Jude 4, or else by revolting from the truth received altogether. When times of temptation come, unsound Christians will do one of these three, either despise, refuse, or revolt from the truth. Therefore I beseech you, let your hearts be cast into the mould and fashion of the gospel of Christ, let it be soundly bottomed and engrafted in you, that so you may grow more and more obedient to the truth revealed, and so your end shall not be theirs here, *which obey not the gospel of Jesus Christ.*

Quest. But how may I come to obey the gospel?

Ans. Beg *earnestly of God, in the use of the means* (else prayer is but a tempting of God), *that thy soul may be convinced what evil is in thee, and what evil is towards thee, unless thou repent.* Labour for sound conviction; for you shall not need to stir up a man that is condemned to seek out for a pardon, or a man that feels the smart of his wound to get balm to cure it. Oh, no; when our hearts are once truly humbled and pierced with a sight of our sins, then Christ will be Christ indeed unto us. Now mercy is sweet at such a time; anything for a Saviour then, and not before. Therefore labour every day to see more and more into the venomous and filthy nature of sin; make it as odious to thy soul as possibly thou canst; hearken to the voice of conscience; give it full scope to speak what it can, that so thou mayest fly to Christ. Consider how God plagueth us in this world for sin; how it fills us with fears and horrors, causing our consciences to torment us, and fly in our faces; consider what threatenings are denounced against sin and sinners, for the time to come; consider the fearful judgments of God upon others for sin, how it cast Adam out of paradise, the angels out of heaven, being so offensive to God, that it could no otherwise be expiated than by the death and bloodshedding of the Lord Jesus. I beseech you, let your hearts dwell upon these things, and consider with yourselves how bitter you have found it to offend God, though now it be a time of mercy.

2. Secondly, consider how the gospel lays open Christ unto us; 'This is his commandment, that we believe in the Lord Jesus,' 1 John iii. 23. He that commands us to do no murder, not to steal, &c., commands us likewise to believe in Christ. He commands us to love our own souls so much, as to take the remedy which may cure them; so that now it is our duty to be good to our poor souls; and we offend God if we be not merciful to our own souls. Oh! what a favour is this, that God should lay a charge upon me not to reject my own mercy, as it is in Jonah, 'They who follow lying vanities forsake their own mercies,' Jonah ii. 8. If I do not love my own soul, and accept of mercy offered, 'I make God a liar,' 1 John v. 10, and offend his majesty.

3. Again, consider how God allures those that might except against mercy. Alas, I am laden with sin, will some poor soul say! Why! 'Come unto me, all you that are heavy laden, and I will ease you,' Mat. xi. 28. But I have offended God, I have broken my peace, &c., yet 'I beseech you, be reconciled to God,' 2 Cor. v. 20; though you have offended, yet there is hope. Do but consider how ready God is to help you, how continual his mercies are, and how he stretcheth out his hands to receive us.

4. Consider further, what a sweet regiment* it is to be under Christ, as a king, and as an husband. Will he not provide for his own family, for his own subjects? Beloved, it is not mere dominion that Christ stands upon; he aims at a fatherly and husband-like sovereignty, for the good of his children and spouse. It is their welfare he looks after. Therefore, I beseech you, be in love with the government of Jesus Christ, his blessed Spirit. Oh! it is a sweet regiment!* For the Spirit of God leads us quietly, enlightening our understandings upon judicious grounds what to do, by strength of reason; altering our natures, and bettering us every way, both in our inward and outward man. It never leaves teaching and guiding of us till it hath brought us to heaven and happiness.

To conclude, mark what the apostle saith here, 'What shall be the end of those that obey not the gospel?' He cares not what they know. Many say, we have heard the word, and we have received the sacrament, &c. It is no matter for that, how stands the bent of your souls? what hath your obedience been? This is that God looks after. Every man can talk of religion, but where is the practice? A little obedience is worth all the discourse and contemplation in the world; for that serves but to justify God's damning of us, if we live not answerably. Value not yourselves, therefore, by your outward profession, neither judge of your estate in grace, by the knowledge of good things. Nothing but the power of godliness, expressed in our lives, will yield real comfort in the day of trial.

Our obedience must be free. And we should labour that our obedience be 'free and cheerful,' Ps. cx. 3; always upon the wing, as we say, for that is evangelical obedience. God's people under the gospel are a voluntary, ready people, 'zealous of good works,' Tit. ii. 14. Oh! beloved, did we but consider what God hath done for us here, and what he means to do for us in another world, how would our hearts be enlarged in duty to his majesty! Did we but consider of his inestimable love in the Lord Christ, pardoning such wretches as we are, and not only so, but accepting our service and us to life everlasting; taking us from the lowest misery to the highest happiness; from the lowest hell to the highest heaven; of traitors

* That is, 'government.'—C.

to be sons; of slaves to be heirs of the kingdom, &c. Oh! did we but seriously consider and believe these things, how would they warm our hearts, and make us pliable and constant to every good work and way!

The apostle having tasted the sweet favour of God in Christ, might well use it as a motive to quicken others. 'I beseech you by the tender mercies of Christ,' &c., Rom. xii. 1. He knew this was a powerful argument, and if that wrought not upon men's hearts, nothing would.

Let our obedience, therefore, be cheerful; for now we are not in the oldness of the letter. We have not a legal covenant since Christ's coming, but we serve God 'in the newness of the Spirit,' Rom. vii. 6; that is, considering that the Spirit is given in more plenty since his ascension, we should be more spiritual and heavenly in our service of God. Considering that our Head is already entered into that high and holy place, and we, ere long, shall be present with him, having but a spot of time to pass here below, how ready and zealous should we be in obedience to God's will! and not suffer a heavy lumpishness and deadness of spirit to seize upon us in holy performances. But I hasten to the second amplification.

THE DIFFICULTY OF SALVATION.

SERMON III.

If the righteous scarcely be saved, where shall the wicked and ungodly appear?
—1 PET. IV. 18.

What is meant here by righteousness, to wit, a man endued with evangelical righteousness. By 'righteous' here, is meant that evangelical righteousness which we have in the state of the gospel, namely, the righteousness of Christ imputed to us; for Christ himself being ours, his obedience and all that he hath becomes ours also; and whosoever partaketh of this righteousness which is by faith, hath also a righteousness of sanctification accompanying the same, wrought in his soul by the Spirit of God, whereby his sinful nature is changed and made holy; for 'if any man be in Christ, he is a new creature,' 2 Cor. v. 17. The same Spirit that assures us of our interest in Christ, purifies and cleanseth our hearts, and worketh a new life in us, opposite to our life in the first Adam; from whence flows new works of holiness and obedience throughout our whole conversation. There must be an inward inherent righteousness, before there can be any works of righteousness. An instrument must be set in tune before it will make music; so the Spirit of God must first work a holy frame and disposition of heart in us, before we can bring forth any fruits of holiness in our lives. For we commend not the works of grace as we do the works of art, but refer them to the worker. All that flows from the Spirit of righteousness are works of righteousness. When the soul submits itself to the spirit, and the body to the soul, then things come off kindly. Take a man that is righteous by the Spirit of God: he is righteous in all relations; he gives every one his due; he gives God his due; spiritual worship is set up in his heart above all; he gives Christ his due by affiance in him; he gives the holy angels their due, by considering he is always in their presence, that their eye is upon him in every action he doth, and every duty he performs; the poor have their due from him; those that are in authority have their due. If he be under any, he gives them reverence and obedience, &c.; 'he will owe nothing to any man but love,' Rom. xiii. 8; he is righteous in all his conversation; he is a vessel prepared for every good work. I deny not but he may err in some particular; that is nothing to the purpose. I speak of a man as he is in the disposition and bent of his heart to God and goodness, and so there is a thread of a righteous course, that runs along through his whole conversation. The constant tenure of his life is righteous. He hungers and thirsts after righteousness, and labours to be more and more righteous still, every way, both in justification, that he may have a clearer evidence of that, as also in sanctification, that he may have more of the 'new creature' formed in him, that so he may serve God better and better all his days. Now, if this man shall *scarcely be saved*, where shall the sinner and ungodly appear? Where you have two branches.

1. *The righteous shall scarcely be saved.*
2. *The terrible end of sinners and ungodly*, where shall they appear? &c.

Now in that the righteous man thus described by me *shall scarcely be saved*, consider two things.

1. *That the righteous shall be saved.*
2. *That they shall scarcely be saved.*

The righteous are saved. What do I say? the righteous *shall be saved?* He is saved already. 'This day is salvation come to thine house,' saith Christ to Zaccheus, Luke xix. 9. ' We are saved by faith, and are now set in heavenly places together with him,' Eph. ii. 6. We have a title and interest to happiness already. There remains only a passage to the crown by good works. We do not, as the papists do, work to merit that we have not, but we do that we do in thankfulness for what we have. Because we know we are in the state of salvation ; therefore we will shew our thankfulness to God in the course of our lives.

How can we miss of salvation when we are saved already? Christ our head being in heaven, will draw his body after him. What should hinder us? The world? Alas!* we have that *faith* in us, 'which overcometh the world,' 1 John v. 4. As for the flesh, you know what the apostle saith, ' We are not under the law, but under grace,' Rom. vi. 14. The spirit in us always lusteth against the flesh, and subdues it by little and little ; neither can Satan nor the gates of hell prevail against us ; for the grace we have is stronger than all enemies against us.

God the Father is our Father in Christ, and his love and gifts are without repentance, Rom. xi. 29. When once we are in the state of salvation, ' he will preserve us by faith to salvation,' 1 Pet. i. 5 ; and we are knit to God the Son, who will lose none of his members. The marriage with Christ is an everlasting union ; whom he loves, ' he loves to the end,' John xiii. 1. As for God the Holy Ghost, saith Christ, ' I will send the Comforter, and he shall be with you to the end,' John vi. 14, 16. The blessed Spirit of God never departs where he once takes up his lodging. There is no question, therefore, of the salvation of the righteous ; they are, as it were, saved already.

Use. Let this teach us thus much, that in all the changes and alterations which the faith of man is subject unto, he is sure of one thing: all the troubles, and all the enemies of the world shall not hinder his salvation. ' If it be possible the elect should be deceived,' Mat. xxiv. 24 ; but it is not possible. O what a comfort is this, that in the midst of all the oppositions and plottings of men and devils, yet notwithstanding, somewhat we have, that is not in the power of any enemy to take from us, nor in our own power to lose, namely, *our salvation.* Set this against any evil whatsoever, and it swallows up all. Put case a man were subject to an hundred deaths, one after another, what are all these to salvation ? Put case a man were in such grief, that he wept tears of blood ; alas ! in the day of salvation all tears shall

---

* This is one of many instances, in Sibbes, of a peculiar use of the interjection 'Alas!' See also last line of this page.—G.

be wiped from his eyes. Set this, *I shall be saved,* against any misery you can imagine, and it will unspeakably comfort and revive the soul beyond all.

Obj. But it is here said, he *shall scarcely be saved.*

Ans. This is not a word of doubt, but of difficulty. It is not a word of doubt of the event, whether he shall be saved or no—there is no doubt at all of that—but it is a word of difficulty in regard of the way and passage thither. So it is here taken, which leads me to a second point, that *the way to come to salvation is full of difficulties.*

1. Because there is much ado to get Lot out of Sodom, to get Israel out of Egypt. It is no easy matter to get a man out of the state of corruption. O the sweetness of sin to an unregenerate man! O how it cuts his very heart to think what pleasures and what profits, and what friends, and what esteem amongst men he must part withal! What ado is there to pull him out of the kingdom of Satan, wherein the *strong man,* Luke xi. 21, held him before!

2. Again, it is hard in regard of the sin that continually cleaves to them in this world, which doth, as it were, shackle them, and compass them about in all their performances. 'They would do well, but sin is at hand,' Rom. vii. 21, ready to hinder and stop them in good courses; so that they cannot serve God with such cheerfulness and readiness as they desire to do. Every good work they do, it is, as it were, pulled out of the fire; they cannot pray, but the flesh resists; they cannot suffer, but the flesh draws back. In all their doing and suffering they carry an enemy in their own bosoms that hinders them. Beloved, this [is] no small affliction to God's people. How did this humble Paul, when no other affliction lay upon him! 'O wretched man that I am, who shall deliver me from this body of death?' Rom. vii. 24. It was more troublesome to him than all his irons and pressures whatsoever.

3. Besides, it is a hard matter in regard of Satan; for he is a great enemy to the peace of God's children. When they are once pulled out of his kingdom, he sends floods of reproaches and persecutions after them, and presently sends hue and cry, as Pharaoh after the Israelites. Oh, how it spites him! What! shall a piece of dust and clay be so near God, when I am tumbled out of heaven myself! Though I cannot hinder him from salvation, I will hinder his peace and joy; he shall not have heaven upon earth.* I will make him walk as uncomfortably as I can. Thus the devil, as he is a malignant creature, full of envy against God's poor saints, so he is a bitter enemy of the peace and comfort which they enjoy; and therefore troubles them with many temptations from himself and his instruments, to interrupt their peace, and make the hearts of God's people sad all he can.

4. Then, by reason of great discouragements and ill-usage which they find in the world from wicked men, who are the devil's pipes, led with his spirit to vex and trouble the meek of the earth; for, though they think not of it, Satan is in their devilish natures; he joins and goes along with their spirits in hating and opposing the saints of God; for, indeed, what hurt could they do but by his instigation? How are good men despised in the world! How are they made the only butt† to shoot at! Alas! beloved, we should rather encourage men in the ways of holiness. We see the number of such as truly fear God is but small, soon reckoned up. They are but as grapes after the vintage, or a few berries after the shaking; one of a city, two of a tribe, Micah vii. 1, Jer. iii. 14. They have little encouragements from any, but discouragements on all sides.

---

* 'Heaven upon earth' is the title of one of Thomas Brooks's most Sibbes-like works.—G.   † That is, 'a mark.'—G.

5. Besides this, scandal makes it a hard matter to be saved; to see evil courses and evil persons flourish and countenanced in the world. Oh, it goes to the heart of God's people, and makes them stagger at God's providence. It is a bitter temptation, and shakes the faith of holy men, as we see, Ps. lxxiii., Jer. xii. 1, 2. Again, it makes the heart of a good Christian bleed within him, to see scandals arise from professors of the gospel, when they are not so watchful as they should be, but bring a reproach upon religion by their licentious lives.

Yea, God's children suffer much for their friends, whose wicked courses are laid to their charge, and sometimes even by their friends; for whilst they live here, the best of all are subject to some weakness or other, which causeth even those that are our encouragers, through jealousy or corruption, one way or another, to dishearten and trouble us in the way to heaven.

6. This, likewise, makes the way difficult; we are too apt to offend God daily, giving him just cause to withdraw his Spirit of comfort from us, which makes us go mourning all the day long; wanting those sweet refreshments of spiritual joy and peace we had before. The more comfort God's child hath in communion with God, the more he is grieved when he wants it. When Christ wanted the sweet solace of his Father upon the cross, how did it trouble him! 'My God, my God, why hast thou forsaken me?' Mat. xxvii. 46. How did he sweat water and blood in the garden, Luke xxii. 44, when he felt but a little while his Father's displeasure for sin! Thus is it with all God's children; they are of Christ's mind in their spiritual desertions.

And when they have gotten a little grace, how difficult is it to keep it! to keep ourselves in the sense of God's love! to manage our Christian state aright! to walk worthy of the gospel, that God may still do us good, and delight to be present with us! What a great difficulty is it to be always striving against the stream, and when we are cast back to get forward still, and not be discouraged till we come to the haven! None comes to heaven but they know how they come there.

Why God will have the righteous with such difficulty saved. Now, God will have it thus to sweeten heaven unto us. After a conflicting life peace is welcome; heaven is heaven indeed after trouble. We can relish it then. Because God will discard hypocrites in this life, who take up so much of religion as stands with their ease and credit in the world, avoiding every difficulty which accompanies godliness, but, so they may swim two ways at once, go on in their lusts still and be religious withal. This they approve of. Therefore, God will have it a hard matter to be saved, to frustrate the vain hopes of such wretches. Alas! it is an easy matter to be an hypocrite, but not to live godly.

Use. If the righteous be saved with much ado, then never enter upon the profession of religion with vain hopes of ease and pleasure, that it shall be thus and thus with thee, &c. Herein thou dost but delude thy own soul, for it will prove otherwise. Forecast, therefore, what will fall, and get provision of grace beforehand to sustain thee. As, if a man were to go a dangerous journey, he provides himself of weapons and cordials, and all the encouragements he can, lest he should faint in the way; whereas he that walks for his pleasure provides nothing. He cares not for his weapon or his cloak, because if a storm comes he can run under shelter or into a house, &c. He that makes religion a recreation can walk a turn or two for his pleasure, and when any difficulty arises can retire and draw in his horns again. An hypocrite hath his reservations and politic ends, and therefore what needs he any great provision to support him, when he knows how to wind out of trouble well enough, rather than to stand courageously to anything. But a true Christian, that makes it the main work of his life to please God, arms himself for the worst that can befall him, and will be saved through thick or thin, smooth or rough, whatsoever comes on it. So God will save his soul, he cares not, but rejoiceth, with Paul, if by any means he can attain the resurrection of the dead, Phil. iii. 11, by any means, it is no matter what. Let fire and fagot meet with him, yet he is resolved not to retire for any trouble or persecution whatsoever that stands between him and happiness. He is purposely armed to break through every opposition to the best things, and whatever may separate his soul from the favour of God. I beseech you, beloved, think of these things, and let it be your wisdom to make the way to heaven as easy as you can. To this end,

1. *Beg the Spirit of Christ.* You know the Holy Spirit is full of life and strength; it is a Spirit of light and comfort and whatsover is good. The Spirit of God is like the wind; as it is subtle in operation and invisible, so it is strong and mighty, it bears all before it. Oh! therefore, get this blessed Spirit to enlighten thee, to quicken thee, to support thee, &c., and it will carry thy soul courageously along, above all oppositions and discouragements whatsoever in the way to happiness.

2. *Get likewise the particular graces of the Spirit*, which will much cheer thee in thy Christian course. Above all, labour for a spirit of humility. An humble man is fit to do or suffer anything. A proud man is like a gouty hand, or a swelled arm, unfit for any Christian performance; he is not in a state to do good; but an humble man is thankful that God will honour him so far as to let him suffer for the cause of Christ. He is wondrous empty and vile in his own eyes, and admires* why God should reserve such infinite matters for so base a worm as he is.

When Christ would have us take his yoke upon us, he advises us 'to learn of him to be meek and lowly,' &c., Mat. xi. 29. Some might say, This yoke is heavy, it will pinch me and gall me. No, saith our Saviour, it shall be very light and easy. But how shall I get it to be so? Why! get but an humble and meek spirit, and that will bring rest to your souls.

3. Again, *labour for a spirit of love.* 'Love is strong as death,' Cant. viii. 6; it will carry us through all. The love of Christ in the martyrs, when the fire was kindled about them, made them despise all torments whatsoever. This will warm our hearts and make us go cheerfully to work. Let but a spirit of love be kindled in God's child, and it is no matter what he suffers; cast him into the fire, cast him into the dungeon, into prison, whatsoever it be, he hath that kindled in his heart, which will make him digest anything. We see the disciples, when they had the Spirit of Christ within them to warm their hearts, what cared they for whipping, or stocks, &c.? You see even base, carnal love will make a man endure poverty, disgrace, what not! and shall not this fire that comes from heaven, when it is once kindled in our hearts, prevail much more? What will make our passage to heaven sweet if this will not? Nothing is grievous to a person that loves.

4. *Exercise your hope likewise..* Set before your eyes the crown and kingdom of heaven; those admirable things contained in the word of God, which no tongue can express. Let hope feed upon these delicates; cast anchor in heaven, and see if it will not make thee go on cheerfully in a Christian course.

Faith will *overcome the world;* all the snares of prosperity that would hinder us on the right hand. Faith, it presents things of a higher nature to the soul; better than they. Faith likewise overcomes temptations on the

* That is, ' wonders.'—G.

left hand; all terrors and discomforts whatsoever. It considers these are nothing to 'the terror of the Lord,' 2 Cor. v. 11. Therefore 'faith is called the evidence of things not seen,' Heb. xi. 1, because it presents things that are absent as present to the soul. If life and happiness be once truly presented to our hearts, what can all the world do to hinder our passage thither?

5. Lastly, we should much endeavour *the mortification of our lusts;* for what is it that makes the way to heaven irksome unto us? Is it not this corrupt and proud flesh of ours, which will endure nothing, no, not the weight of a straw, but is all for ease and quiet, &c.? It is not duty which makes our way difficult, 'for it was meat and drink to Christ, to do the will of his Father,' John iv. 34.

Quest. Why is it not so with us?

Ans. Because he was born without sin. When Satan came he found nothing of his own in him; but when he solicits us, he finds a correspondency betwixt our corrupt hearts and himself, whereby having intelligence what we haunt, and what we love, he will be sure to molest us. The less we have of the works of Satan in us, the less will be our trouble; and the more we do the will of God, and strive against our corruptions, the more will be our comfort. This will make holy duties delightful to us; but if we favour and cherish corruption, it will make religion harsh. For the ways of wisdom are ways of pleasure in themselves, and to the regenerate, &c. I come now to the second clause.

'*Where shall the sinner and ungodly appear?*'

What he means by sinner. By sinner he means him that makes a trade of sin. As we say, a man is of such a trade, because he is daily at work of it, and lives by it, so a man is a trader in sin, that lives in corrupt courses. For it is not one act that denominates a sinner, but the constant practice of his life.

Now this question, Where shall the ungodly appear? implies a strong denial, He shall be able to appear nowhere; especially in these three times.

1. *In the day of public calamity,* when God's judgments are abroad in the world. The wicked are as chaff before the wind, as wax before the sun, as stubble before the fire. When God comes to deal with a company of graceless wretches, how will he consume and scatter them, and sweep them away as dung from the face of the earth! he will universally make a riddance of them at once. Where shall a Nabal stand when judgment comes upon him? 1 Sam. xxv. 37. Alas! his heart is become a stone. Where shall Belshazzar appear when he sees the handwriting upon the wall? Dan. v. Oh how the wicked tremble and quake when God comes to judge them in this world, though they were a terror to others before!

2. But where shall they stand *in the hour of death?* when the world can hold them no longer; when friends shall forsake them; when God will not receive them; when hell is ready to devour them, &c.

3. And lastly, where shall the sinner appear *at the day of judgment,* that great and terrible day of account, when they shall see all the world in a combustion round about them, and the Lord Jesus coming in flaming fire, 'with his mighty angels, to take vengeance on such as obey not the gospel?' 2 Thess. i. 8. How will they then call for 'the mountains to cover them, and the hills to fall upon them, to hide them from the face of him that sitteth on the throne, and from the wrath of the Lamb,' &c., Rev. vi. 16. Beloved, I beseech you, let the meditation of these things sink deep into your hearts, dwell upon them, remember that they are matters which nearly concern your soul, and no vain words, touching you and your welfare.

THE SAINT'S HIDING-PLACE IN THE EVIL DAY.*

SERMON IV.

Wherefore let them that suffer according to the will of God commit their souls to him in well-doing, as to a faithful Creator.—1 Pet. IV. 19.

Though divinity be clear in other differences from carnal or natural reasons, yet it hath homogeneal reasons and grounds of its own, whence come inferences as natural as for the tree to bear fruit, or the sun to shine; so upon the former divine grounds (for it is a matter of suffering wherein we must have pure divinity to support our souls), the apostle comes to bring a spiritual inference suitable to the same in the words read unto you. *Wherefore*, concluding all to be true that was said before, *let them that suffer*, &c. Wherein consider, 1. That the state and condition of God's children is to *suffer*. 2. The dispensation of that *suffering*, they suffer not at all adventures, but *according to the will of God*. 3. Their duty in this estate, namely, *to commit the keeping of their souls to God*.

In the *duty* we have these particulars comprehended:—1. An action, *to commit*. 2. An object, what we must commit, *the soul*. 3. The person to whom, *to God*. 4. The manner, *in well-doing*. Lastly. The reason which should move us hereunto, implied in these words, *as unto a faithful Creator*. Whatsoever may support the doubting of a godly man in any trouble, and enforce upon him this duty of committing his soul to God, is briefly comprised in this, that God stands in that near relation of a Creator, yea, of a faithful Creator, to us. This is the scope of the words.

Obs. 1. *That the state of God's children is to suffer*, yea, to suffer *of God;* for sometimes he seems to be an enemy to his dearest servants, as unto Job. But chiefly they are in a militant estate and condition here.

1. *Why God's children must suffer here.* Because they live among those that they cannot but suffer from, wheresoever they live. Suppose they live among Christians, yet there are many Christians in name that are not so in deed. There hath been secret underminers in all ages; and what else may they look for but suffering from these? All that ever truly feared God and

* This title of the present sermon, which is taken from the reprint in the 'Saint's Cordials,' is preferred, to that placed over it in the original volume, viz., 'The Saints Safety in Evil Times,' inasmuch as at page 297, *seq.*, other two bear this heading.—G.

made conscience of their ways have found afflictions among false brethren. It was never heard of that a sheep should pursue a wolf.

2. They must suffer also in regard of themselves; for the truth is, the best of us all have many lusts to be subdued, and a great deal of corruption to be purged out, before we can come to heaven, that pure and holy place into which no unclean thing can enter, Rev. xxi. 27. Though a garden be never so fruitful, yet after a shower it will need weeding. So, after long peace, the church of God gathers soil, and needs cleansing.

Obj. But some carnal wretch will say, I thank God I never suffered in my life, but have enjoyed peace and prosperity, and my heart's content in everything.

Ans. In the best estate there will be suffering one way or other. Then, suspect thyself to be in a bad estate, for every true Christian suffers in one kind or other, either from without or within. Sometimes God's children are troubled more with corruption than with affliction; at other times their peace is troubled both with corruption within and with affliction without; at the best, they have sufferings of sympathy. Shall the members of Christ suffer in other countries, and we profess ourselves to be living members, and yet not sympathise with them? We must be conformable to our Head before we can come to heaven. But the dispensation of our suffering is according to the will of God, where note two things.

1. *That it is God's will we should suffer.*
2. *When we suffer we suffer according to his will.*

To pass briefly over these, as not being the thing I aim at,

God's will concerning our suffering is permissive in respect of those that do us harm; but in regard of our patient enduring injuries, it is his approving and commanding will. We are enjoined to suffer, and they are permitted to wrong us.

Obj. It seems, then, there is some excuse for those that persecute the saints. They do but *according to God's will;* and if it be so, who dares speak against them?

Ans. It is not God's commanding will, but his suffering will. He useth their malice for his own ends. God lets the rein loose upon their necks. As a man is said to set a dog upon another when he unlooseth his chain, so God is said to command them when he lets them loose to do mischief. They are full of malice themselves, which God useth as physicians do their poison to cure poison. God and they go two contrary ways, as a man in a ship walks one way, but is carried another. In the death of Christ the will of Judas and the rest went one way, and God's will another. So, in all our sufferings, when God useth wicked men, their will is destructive and hostile, but God's will is clean otherwise, aiming at the good of his people in all this. Nebuchadnezzar did the will of God in *carrying the people captive.* However, he thought not so, Isa. x. 7. Every sinful wretch that offers violence to the poor saints, imagine they do God good service in it, whenas, indeed, they do but execute the malice and venom of their own hearts. In the highest heavens, as they say in philosophy, the first thing moved is by a violent motion. The sun is carried about the heavens violently against its own proper motion, which inclines to a clean contrary course. So God dealeth with wicked men; he carries them they know not whither. They are set to do mischief, and God useth their sinful dispositions for his own ends, which plainly shews that God is without all fault, and they without all excuse.

Obs. But observe further, *that we never suffer but when God will.* And, beloved, his will is not that we should always suffer, though generally our estate be so in one kind or other. God is *not always chiding*, Ps. ciii. 9, but hath times of breathing and intermission, which he vouchsafes his children for their good. He knows if we had not some respite, some refreshment, we should soon be consumed and brought to nothing. 'The Lord knows whereof we are made, and considers we are but dust,' Ps. ciii. 14. Therefore he saith, 'Though for a season you are in heaviness, yet rejoice,' &c., 1 Pet. i. 6.

And this the Lord doth out of mercy to his poor creatures, that they might not sink before him, but gather strength of grace, and be the better fitted to bear further crosses afterwards. You know, Acts ix. 31, after Saul's conversion, when he was become a Paul, then the church had rest, and increased in the comforts of the Holy Ghost. God gives his people pausing times, some *lucida intervalla* (*a*). Our time of going into trouble is in God's hands; our time of abiding trouble is in God's hands; our time of coming out is in God's hands. As in our callings he preserves our going out and our coming in, so in every trouble that befalls us we come in and tarry there, and go out of the same when he pleaseth. He brings us to the fire as the goldsmith puts his metals and holds them there, till he hath refined them and purged out the dross, and then brings them out again. 'Our times,' as David saith excellently, 'are in thy hands, O Lord,' Ps. xxxi. 15. Beloved, if our times were in our enemies' hands we should never come out. If they were in our own hands we should never stay in trouble, but come out as soon as we come in; nay, we would not come into trouble at all if we could choose. Beloved, everything of a Christian is dear unto God; his health is precious, his blood is precious; especially precious to the Lord is the death of his saints, Ps. cxvi. 15. Do you think, therefore, he will let them suffer without his will? No; he will have a valuable consideration of all those that are malignant persecutors of his people at last. And it is for matters better than life that God lets his children suffer here; for, alas! this life is but a shadow, as it were, nothing. God regards us not as we are in this present world, but as strangers; therefore, he suffers us to sacrifice this life upon better terms than life, or else he would never let us suffer for his truth, and seal it with our dearest blood, as many of the saints have done.

Use. I beseech you, therefore, considering all our sufferings are by the appointment and will of God, let us bring our souls to an holy resignation unto his Majesty, not looking so much to the grievance we are under as to the hand that sent it. We should with one eye consider the thing, with another eye the will of God in the same. When a man considers, I suffer now, but it is by the will of God'; he puts me upon it, how cheerfully will such an one commit his soul to the Lord! It is as hard a matter to suffer God's will as to do his will. Passive obedience is as hard as active. In the active we labour that what we do may please God; in the passive we must endeavour that what he doth may please us. Our hearts are as untoward to the one as to the other. Therefore, let us beg of God to bring our wills to the obedience of his blessed will in everything. Would you have a pattern of this? Look upon our blessed Saviour, to whom we must be conformable in obedience if ever we will be conformable in glory. 'Lo, I come,' saith he; 'I am ready to do thy will, O Lord,' Heb. x. 9. What was the whole life of Christ but a doing and a suffering of God's will? 'Behold, it is written in the volume of thy book that I should do thy will,' ver. 7, and here I am ready pressed for it. It should be, therefore, the disposition of all those that are led by the Spirit of Christ, as all must be that hope to reign with him, to be willing to suffer with Christ here, and say with him, Lord, I am here ready to do and suffer whatsoever thou requirest! When once we are brought to this, all the quarrel is ended between God and us.

I come now to that which I chiefly intend, which is the Christian's duty. *Let him commit his soul to God in well-doing.* Wherein observe,

1. The manner *how* he must commit, *in well-doing.*
2. What, *his soul.*
3. To whom, *to God.*
4. The reasons moving, implied in these words, *as unto a faithful Creator.*

Now this *well-doing* must be distinguished into two times.

1. *Before our suffering.* When a son of Belial shall offer violence to a poor saint of God, what a comfort is this, that he suffers in well-doing! Oh, beloved, we should so carry ourselves that none might speak evil justly against us, that none, unless it were wrongfully, might do us hurt. We should be in an estate of well-doing continually in our general and particular callings. We must not go out of our sphere, but serve God in our standings, that if trouble comes it may find us in a way of well-pleasing, either doing works of charity or else the works of our particular calling wherein God hath set us. In all that befalls thee look to this, that thou suffer not as an evil doer, 1 Pet. iv. 15.

2. So likewise *in suffering*, we must commit our souls to God in well-doing in a double regard.

1. *We must carry ourselves* generally *well in all our sufferings.*
2. In particular, *we must do well to them that do us wrong.*

First, I say, *in* affliction our carriage must be generally good in respect of God, by a meek behaviour under his hand, without murmuring against him.

2. In regard of the cause of God, that we betray it not through fear or cowardice, through base aims and intentions, &c., but endeavour to carry it with a good conscience in all things. When we make it clear by managing anything, that we are led with the cause and conscience of our duty, it works mightily upon them that wrong us. (1.) It wins those that are indifferent; and (2.) confounds the obstinate, and stops their mouths. Therefore, let us carry ourselves well, not only before, but in suffering. We may not fight against them with their own weapons, that is, be malicious as they are malicious, and rail as they rail. Beloved, this is as if a man should see another drink poison, and he will drink, too, for company; he is poisoned with malice, and thou, to revenge thyself, wilt be poisoned too. What a preposterous course is this! Ought we not rather to behave ourselves as befits the cause of Christ, as becomes our Christian profession, and as befits him whose children we are?

We should have an eye to God, and an eye to ourselves, and an eye to others, and an eye to the cause in hand; so we shall do well. We must not commit our souls to God in idleness, doing nothing at all, nor yet in evil doing, but in well doing. We must have a care, if we would suffer with comfort, not to study how to avoid suffering by tricks, so to hurt the cause of Christ. This is to avoid suffering, by sin, to leap out of one danger into another. Is not the least evil of sin worse than the greatest evil of punishment? What doth a man get by pleasing men, to displease God? Perhaps a little ease for the present. Alas! what is this to that inexpressible horror and despair which will one day seize upon thy soul eternally for betraying the blessed cause and truth of Christ? How can we expect God should own us another day, when we will not own him in his cause, and his members, to stand for them now? Think on that speech of our Saviour, 'Whosoever shall be ashamed of me, or of my words in this adulterous and sinful generation, of him shall the Son of man be ashamed when he cometh in the glory of his Father,' Mark viii. 38.

Therefore, avoid not any suffering *by sin*. See how blessed St Paul carried himself in this case. 'The Lord,' saith he, 'hath delivered me, and will deliver me,' 2 Tim. iv. 18. From what? from death? No; *from every evil work*. What! will God keep him from evil sufferings? No; for immediately after he was put to death. What then? Why! he will preserve me from every evil work, that is, from every sinful act, which may hurt the cause of Christ, or blemish my profession. This was it Paul chiefly regarded; not whether he will preserve me from death or trouble, I leave that to him; but this I hope and trust to, that he will preserve me from every evil work to his heavenly kingdom. Thus should it be with every Christian in the cause of religion, or in a cause of justice, &c.; for there is not any good cause but it is worth our lives to stand in, if we be called to it. It is necessary we should be just; it is not so necessary we should live (*b*). A Christian's main care is how to do well; and if he can go on in that course, he is a happy man.

Obj. But I cannot do well, but I shall suffer ill.

Ans. Labour, therefore, to carry thyself well in suffering evil, not only in the general, but even in particular, towards those persons that do thee wrong; endeavour to requite their evil with good. There is a great measure of self-denial required to be a Christian, especially in matter of revenge, 'to pray for them that curse us, to do good to them that persecute us,' &c., and so 'heap coals of fire upon our enemies' heads,' Prov. xxv. 22, Rom. xii. 20. How is that? There are—

1. Coals of conversion.
2. Coals of confusion.

How in suffering we heap coals of fire. You know coals do either melt or consume. If they belong to God, we shall heap coals of fire to convert them, and make them better by our holy carriage in suffering. If they be wicked, graceless wretches, we shall heap coals of fire to consume them; for it will aggravate their just damnation when they do ill to those that deserve well of them.

Obj. Some will say, Christianity is a strange condition, that enforceth such things upon men, that are so contrary to nature.

Ans. It is so, indeed, for we must be new-moulded before ever we can come to heaven. We must put off our whole self; and he is gone a great way in religion, that hath brought his heart to this pass. None ever overcame himself in these matters out of religious respects, but he found a good issue at last. It is a sweet evidence of the state of grace, none better, when a man can love his very enemies, and those that have done him most wrong; it is an argument that such a man hath something above nature in him. What is above nature, if this be not, for a man to overcome himself in this sweet appetite of revenge? Revenge is most natural to a man; it is as sugar, as the heathen saith; and for a man to overcome himself in that, it argues the power of grace and godliness in such a one.

As Christianity is an excellent estate, an admirable advancing of a man to a higher condition, so it must not seem strange for those that are Christians to be raised to a higher pitch of soul than other men. See how our

Saviour dealt in this particular, 'Father, forgive them, they know not what they do,' Luke xxiii. 34; and so likewise Stephen, being led by the same Spirit of Christ, desired God 'not to lay this sin to their charge,' Acts vii. 60; and so all the martyrs in the first state of the church, when the blood of Christ was warm, and the remembrance of Christ was fresh, were wont to pray for their enemies, committing their souls to God in well doing.

The excellent victory of suffering. I beseech you let us labour by all means possible to bring our hearts hereunto. If anything overcome, this will do it, *to suffer well.* The church of God is a company of men that gain and overcome by suffering in doing good. Thus the dove overcomes the eagle, the sheep overcomes the wolf, the lamb overcomes the lion, &c. It hath been so from the beginning of the world. Meek Christians, by suffering quietly, have at length overcome those that are malicious, and have gained even their very enemies to the love of the truth. What shall we think, then, of the greatest part of the world, who never think of suffering, which is the first lesson in Christianity, but study their ease and contentment, accounting the blessed martyrs too prodigal of their blood, &c.?

Others there are, who, if once they come to suffer, presently fall to shifting and plotting, how to get forth again by unlawful means; oftentimes making shipwreck of a good conscience, and dishonouring the gospel of God. I beseech you consider these things. Every man would have Christ, and be religious, so long as they may enjoy peace and quietness; but if once trouble or persecution arises, then farewell religion; they cast off their profession then. I wish this were not the case of many seeming Christians in these our days.

But suppose a man carry himself *ill* in *suffering?*

There is not the least promise of comfort in Scripture to such a man, unless he *return,* and seek the Lord by timely repentance; for all encouragement is to *well-doing.* Oh, what a pitiful thing is it for the soul to be in such a state, as that it dares not commit itself to God! A man in evil doing cannot go home to his own conscience for comfort, nor have any inward peace in the least action he performs, so long as he doth it with false aims, and carnal affections, &c. Who would deprive himself of the comfort of suffering in a good cause for want of integrity? I beseech you, therefore, carry yourselves well in anything you either do or suffer, otherwise no blessing can be expected; for we tempt the Lord, and make him accessory to us, when we commit our souls to him in ill-doing: even as your pirates and other miscreants in the world, that will rob and steal, and do wickedly, and yet pray to God to bless them in their base courses (*c*); what is this but to make God like themselves, as if he approved their theft and horrible blasphemy?

But *what* must we commit to God *in well-doing?* The keeping of our *souls.* The soul is the more excellent part, witness he that purchased the same with his dearest blood. 'What will it profit a man,' saith our Saviour, 'to gain the whole world and lose his own soul?' Mark viii. 36. Who could know the price of a soul better than he that gave his life for redemption of it? Yea, if the whole world were laid in one balance and the soul in another, the soul were better than all. Therefore, whatsoever estate thou art in, let thy first care be for thy soul, that it may go well with that. You know in any danger or combustion, suppose the firing of an house, that which a man chiefly looks after is his jewels and precious things, 'I have some wealth in such a place, if I could but have that I care for no more, let the rest go;' so it is with a Christian, whatsoever becomes of him in this world, he looks to his precious soul, that that may be laid up safely in the hands of God. Suppose a man were robbed by the highway, and had some special jewel about him, though every thing else were taken away from him, yet so long as that is left he thinks himself a happy man, and saith, they have taken away some luggage, but they have left me that which I prize more than all: so it is with a Christian, let him be stripped of all he hath, so his soul be not hurt, but all safe and well there, he cares not much.

Quest. But what should we desire our souls to be *kept from* in this world?

Ans. From sin and the evil consequences thereof. Beloved, we have great need our souls should be kept by God; for alas! what sin is there but we shall fall into it, unless God preserve us in peace and comfort, and assurance of a better estate. What would become of our poor souls if we had them in our own keeping? Ahithophel had the keeping of his own soul, and what became of him? First, he did run into the sins of treason, and afterwards, being a wicked politician, and an atheist, having no delight in God, was the executioner of himself (*d*). We shall be ready, as Job saith, to tear our own souls if God hath not the keeping of them; we shall tear them with desperate thoughts, as Judas, who never committed his soul to God, but kept it himself, and we see what became of him. The apostle bids us go to God in prayer, and committing our souls to him, to keep from sin, despair, distrust, and all spiritual evil whatsoever, ' and then the peace of God which passeth all understanding,' as the word in the original is, ' shall guard* our souls in Christ,' Phil. iv. 7. Our souls have need of guarding, and we of ourselves are not sufficient to do it; therefore we should commit them unto God, for except he preserve us we shall soon perish.

Wicked men think that they have no souls. I am ashamed to speak of it, and yet notwithstanding the courses of men are such, that they enforce a man to speak that which he is ashamed of. What do I speak of committing your souls to God, when many thousands in the world live as if they had no souls at all? I am persuaded that your common swearers, and profane wretches, who wrong their souls to pleasure their bodies, and prostitute both body and soul, and all to their base lusts, think for the time that they have no souls; they think not that there is such an excellent immortal substance breathed into them by God, which must live for ever in eternal happiness or endless misery. Did they believe this they would not wound and stain their precious souls as they do; they would not obey every base lust out of the abundance of profaneness in their hearts, even for nothing, as many notorious loose persons do. Oh could we but get this principle into people, that they have immortal souls, which must live for ever, they would soon be better than they are; but the devil hath most men in such bondage that their lives speak that they believe they have no souls, by their ill usage of them.

Obj. But must we not commit our *bodies* and our *estates* to God, as well as our souls?

Ans. Yes, all we have; for that is only well kept which God keeps; but yet in time of suffering we must be at a point† with these things. If God will have our liberty, if he will have our life and all, we must hate all for Christ's sake; but we must not be at such a point with our souls, we must keep them close to God, and desire him to keep them *in well-doing.*

Obj. Suppose it come to an exigent, that we must either sin and hurt our souls, or else lose all our outward good things?

See note *k*, page 334.—G. † That is, ' make light of.'—ED.

Ans. Our chief care must be over our souls. We must desire God to preserve our souls, whatsoever becomes of these; our principal care must be that that be not blemished in the least kind; for, alas! other things must be parted with first or last. This body of ours, or whatsoever is dear in the world, must be stripped from us, and laid in the dust ere long. But here is our comfort, though our body be dead, yet our souls are themselves still; dead St Paul is Paul still. Our body is but the case or tabernacle wherein our soul dwells; especially a man's self is his soul; keep that and keep all. I beseech you, therefore, as things are in worth and excellency in God's account, let our esteem be answerable. You have many compliments in the world, how doth your body, &c., mere compliments indeed, but how few will inquire how our souls do? alas! that is in poor case. The body perhaps is well looked unto, that is clothed, and care taken that nothing be wanting to it, but the poor soul is ragged and wounded, and naked. Oh that men were sensible of that miserable condition their poor souls are in.

Beloved, the soul is the better part of a man, and if that miscarries, all miscarries. If the soul be not well, the body will not continue long in a good estate. Bernard saith sweetly, 'Oh, body, thou hast a noble guest dwelling in thee, a soul of such inestimable worth that it makes thee truly noble.' Whatsoever goodness and excellency is in the body, is communicated from the soul; when that once departs, the body is an unlovely thing, without life or sense. The very sight of it cannot be endured of the dearest friends. What an incredible baseness is it therefore, that so precious a thing as the soul is, should serve these vile bodies of ours! Let the body stay its leisure; the time of the resurrection is the time of the body. In this life it should be serviceable to our souls in suffering and doing whatsoever God calls us unto. Let our bodies serve our souls now, and then body and soul shall for ever after be happy; whereas, if we, to gratify our bodies, do betray our souls, both are undone.

Beloved, the devil and devilish-minded men, acted with his spirit, have a special spite to the soul. Alas! what do they aim at in all their wrongs and injuries to God's children? Do they care to hurt the body? indeed, they will do this rather than nothing at all; they will rather play at small game than sit out. The devil will enter into the swine rather than stand out altogether. Some mischief he will do, however; but his main spite is at the soul, to vex and disquiet that, and taint it with sin all he can. Considering therefore that it is Satan's aim to unloose our hold from God, by defiling our souls with sin, so to put a divorce betwixt his blessed majesty and us, oh! let it be our chief care to see to that which Satan strikes at most! He did not so much care, in Job's trouble, for his goods, or for his house, or children, &c. Alas! he aimed at a further mischief than this! his plot was how to make him blaspheme and wound his soul, that so there might be a difference betwixt God and him. He first tempts us to commit sin, and afterwards to despair for sin.

Quest. But to whom must the soul be *committed?*

Ans. Our souls must be committed to God. Commit the keeping of your souls to God. Indeed, he only can keep our souls. We cannot keep them ourselves; neither can anything else in the world do it. Some when they are sick will commit themselves to the physician, and put all their trust in him. When they are in trouble they will commit themselves to some great friend; when they have any bad, naughty cause to manage, they will commit themselves to their purse, and think that shall bear them out in anything. One thinks his wit and policy shall secure him, another that his shifts may shelter him, &c.; and indeed the heart of man is so full of atheism, that it can never light upon the right object, *to trust God alone*, until it sees everything else fail, as being insufficient to support the soul, or to yield any solid comfort in times of extremity and distress.

Quest. But why must we commit our souls to God ?

Ans. Because he is a *faithful Creator*. Whence observe,

Obs. That the soul of man being an understanding essence, will not be satisfied and settled without sound reasons. Comfort is nothing else but reasons stronger than the evil which doth afflict us; when the reasons are more forcible to ease the mind than the grievance is to trouble it. It is no difficult matter to commit our souls to God when we are once persuaded that he is a *faithful Creator*. A man commits himself to another man, and hath no other reason for it, but only he is persuaded of his ability and credit in the world; that he is a man of estate and power to do him good. So it is in this business of religion. Our souls are carried to anything strongly when they are carried by strong reasons, as in this particular of trusting God with our souls. When we see sufficient reasons inducing thereto, we easily resign them into his hands. This shews that popery is an uncomfortable religion, which brings men to despair. They have no reason for what they maintain. What reason can they give for their doctrine of doubting, transubstantiation, perfect obedience to the law, &c.? These are unreasonable things. The soul cannot yield to such absurdities. It must have strong reasons to stablish it, as here, to consider God as a *faithful Creator*, &c. There is something in God to answer all the doubts and fears of the soul, and to satisfy it in any condition whatsoever. This is the very foundation of religion; not that any worth can accrue to the Creator from the creature, but that there is an all-sufficiency in the Creator to relieve the poor creature. If a man consider in what order God created him, it will make him trust God. Paradise and all in it were ready for him, so soon as he came into the world. God created us after his own image, that as he was Lord of all things, so we should be lord of the creatures. They were all at his service, that he might serve God. Therefore after everything else was created, he was made, that so God might bring him as it were to a table ready furnished.

And not only in nature, but in holiness, having an immortal and invisible soul resembling God. We must take God here as a Creator of our whole man, body and soul, and of *the new creature* in us. God made man at the first, but that was not so much as for God to be made man, to make us new creatures. God created our bodies out of the dust, but our souls come immediately from himself. He breathes them into us, and in this respect he is a higher Creator than in the other; for when we had marred our first making, and became more like beasts than men, for indeed every one that is not like God sympathiseth with beasts or devils one way or other, God in Christ made us new again. Yea, God became man to enrich us with all grace and goodness, to free us from the hands of Satan, and bring us to an eternal state of communion with himself in heaven. For all the old heaven and the old earth shall pass away, and the old condition of creatures, and a new life shall be given them. God that made the new heaven and the new earth, hath made us for them. Considering therefore that God gave us our first being, and when we were worse than naught, gave us a second being in regard to our new creation, how should it stir us up to commit our souls unto him! especially if we consider that in him we 'live and move and have our being,' Acts xvii. 28; that there is not the least thought and affection to goodness in us but it comes from God; we are what we are by his grace.

Quest. What is the reason that love descends so much?

Ans. Because a man looks upon that which is his own and loves it. Now God looks upon us as upon those into whom he hath infused mercy and goodness, and he loves his own work upon us; and therefore having begun a good work, will perfect the same. Do not men delight to polish their own work? As in the first creation God never took off his hand till he had finished his work, so in the second creation of our souls he will never remove his hand from the blessed work of grace till he hath perfected the same; therefore we may well commit our souls to him.

Obj. But suppose a man be in a desperate estate, and hath no way of escaping?

Ans. Remember that God is the same still; he hath not forgot his old art of creating, but is as able to help now as ever, and can create comforts for thee in thy greatest troubles. As in the first creation he made light out of darkness, order out of confusion, so still he is able out of thy confused and perplexed estate to create peace and comfort. Thou knowest not what to do perhaps, thy mind is so troubled and disquieted; why, commit thy soul to God; he can raise an excellent frame out of the chaos of thy thoughts. Therefore be not dismayed; consider thou hast God in covenant with thee, and hast to deal with an almighty Creator, who can send present help in time of need. Dost thou want any grace? dost thou want spiritual life? Go to this Creator, he will put a new life into thee; he that made all things of nothing can raise light out of thy dark mind, and can make fleshy thy stony heart, though it be as hard as a rock. Therefore never despair, but frequent the means of grace, and still think of God under this relation of a Creator; and when he hath begun any good work of grace in thee, go confidently to His Majesty, and desire him to promote and increase the same in thy heart and life. Lord, I am thy poor creature, thou hast in mercy begun a blessed work in me, and where thou hast begun thou hast said thou wilt make an end. When thou createdst the world, thou didst not leave it till all was done; and when thou createdst man thou madest an end. Now, I beseech thee, perfect the *new creature* in my soul. As thou hast begun to enlighten mine understanding and to direct my affections to the best things, so I commit my soul unto thee for further guidance and direction to full happiness.

NOTES.

(a) P. 403.—' Lucida Intervalla.' This is the title of a very singular volume by Carkesse. 4to. 1679.

(b) P. 405.—' It is necessary we should be just; *it is not so necessary we should live.*' The memorable reprimand of the man who, engaged in a disreputable business, and defending himself against the sarcasms of Dr Samuel Johnson, pleaded he 'must live.' 'Not at all, Sir; there is no necessity for *your* living,' enforces the apophthegm of Sibbes. It is one of the gems preserved by Boswell.

(c) P. 406.—' Miscreants .... that will rob and steal and do wickedly, and yet pray to God to bless them in their base courses.' The 'Thugs' and the appalling system of 'Thuggism' furnish apt examples of this. Consult Arnold's 'Marquis Dalhousie's Administration of the Punjaub,' just issued, for narrative of their suppression in India. It contains many startling illustrations of Sibbes's words.

(d) P. 407.—' Ahithophel . . . *a wicked politician.*' 'Ahithophel,' or the 'Wicked Politician,' is the title of one of Nathaniel Carpenter's curious tractates. 4to. 1629.

G.

THE SAINT'S HIDING-PLACE IN THE EVIL DAY.*

SERMON V.

Wherefore let them that suffer according to the will of God, commit their souls to him in well-doing, as to a faithful Creator.—1 Pet. IV. 19.

I am now to treat of that other attribute of God, which should move us to trust in him, namely, as he is a *faithful* Creator. Now God is faithful, 1. In his *nature*. He is I am, always like himself, immutable and unchangeable. 2. In his *word*. He expresseth himself as he is. The word that comes from God is an expression of the faithfulness of his nature. 3. In his *works*. 'Thou art good, and dost good,' as the psalmist saith, Ps. cxix. 68. God being faithful in himself, all must needs be so that proceeds from him. Whatsoever relation God takes upon him, he is faithful therein. As he is a Creator, so he preserves and maintains his own work. As he is a Father, he is faithful in discharging that duty to the full, for his children's good. As he is our Friend, he likewise performs all the duties of that relation, &c. And why doth God stoop so low to take these relations upon him, but only to shew that he will certainly accomplish the same to the utmost? Whence is it that men are faithful in their relations one towards another, that the father is faithful to his child? Is it not from God, the chief Father? That a friend should be faithful to his friend, is it not from God, the great Friend?

All his ways are mercy and truth, Ps. xxxv. 10. They are not only merciful and good and gracious, but mercy and truth itself. If he shew himself to be a Father, he is a true father, a true friend, a true creator and protector. As one saith, 'Shall I cause others to fear, and be a tyrant myself?'† All other faithfulness is but a beam of that which is in God. Shall not he be most faithful that makes other things faithful?

Now, this faithfulness of God is here a ground of this duty of committing ourselves to him; and we may well trust him whose word hath been seven times tried in the fire, Ps. xii. 6. There is no dross in it. Every word of God is a sure word; his truth is a shield and buckler; we may well trust in it. Therefore, when you read of any singular promise in the New

---

* Title.—See Note p. 401.
† Qu.—'Be a tyrant to myself?'—G. Rather, 'Shall I cause others to fear tyrants, and be a tyrant myself?'—Ed.

Testament, it is said, 'This is a faithful saying,' &c., 1 Tim. i. 15; that is, this is such a speech as we may trust to; it is the speech of a *faithful* Creator.

Considering, therefore, that God is so faithful every way in his promises and in his deeds, let us make especial use of it. Treasure up all the promises we can of the forgiveness of sins, of protection and preservation; that he will never leave us, but be *our God to death*, &c., and then consider withal that he is faithful in performing the same. When we are affrighted by his majesty and his justice, and other attributes, then think of his mercy and truth. He hath clothed himself with faithfulness, as the psalmist saith. In all the unfaithfulness of men whom thou trustest, depend upon this, that God is still the same, and will not deceive thee.

When we have man's word, we have his sufficiency in mind, for men's words are as themselves are. What will not the word of a king do? If a man be mighty and great, his word is answerable. This is the reason why we should make so much of the word of God, because it is the word of Jehovah, a mighty Creator, who gives a being to all things, and can only be Lord and Master of his word. We know God's meaning no otherwise than by his word. Till we come to the knowledge of vision in heaven, we must be content with the knowledge of revelation in the word.

And in every promise, single out that which best suiteth with thy present condition. If thou art in any great distress, think upon the almighty power of God. Lord, thou hast made me of nothing, and canst deliver me out of this estate. Behold, I fly unto thee for succour, &c. If thou art in perplexity for want of direction, and knowest not what to do, single out the attribute of God's wisdom, and desire him to teach thee the way that thou shouldst go. If thou art wronged, fly to his justice, and say, O God, to whom vengeance belongeth, hear and help thy servant. If thou be surprised with distrust and staggering, then go to his truth and faithfulness. Thou shalt always find in God something to support thy soul in the greatest extremity that can befall thee; for if there were not in God a fulness to supply every exigent* that we are in, he were not to be worshipped, he were not to be trusted.

Man is lighter than vanity in the balance. Every man is a liar, that is, he is false. We may be so, and yet be men too, but God is essentially true. He cannot deceive and be God too. Therefore ever, when thou art disappointed with men, retire to God and to his promises, and build upon this, that the Lord will not be wanting in anything may do thee good. With men there is breach of covenant, nation with nation, and man with man. There is little trust to be had in any; but in all confusions here is comfort. A religious person may cast himself boldly into the arms of the Almighty, and go to him in any distress, as to a faithful Creator that will not forsake him.

Use. Oh, let us be ashamed that we should dishonour him who is ready to pawn his faithfulness and truth for us. If we confess our sins, 'God is faithful to forgive them,' 1 John i. 9. He will not suffer us to be tempted 'above that which we are able,' 1 Cor. x. 13. When we perplex ourselves with doubts and fears whether he will make good his promise or not, we disable His Majesty. Do we not think God stands upon his truth and faithfulness? Undoubtedly he doth, and we cannot dishonour him more

---

* That is, exigency. Brooks uses 'exigents' in the title of one of his raciest books, viz., 'The Mute Christian under the Smarting Rod, with Sovereign Antidotes against the most miserable *Exigents*.' 12mo, 1669.—G.

than to distrust him, especially in his evangelical promises. We make him a liar, and rob him of that which he most glories in, his mercy and faithfulness, if we rest not securely upon him.

See the baseness of man's nature. God hath made all other things faithful that are so, and we can trust them; but are ever and anon questioning the truth of his promise. We may justly take up Salvian's complaint in his time, 'Who hath made the earth faithful to bring forth fruit,' saith he, 'but God? Yet we can trust the ground with sowing our seed. Who makes man faithful, who is by nature the most slippery and unconstant creature of all other, but God only? Yet we can trust a vain man, whose breath is in his nostrils, and look for great matters at his hands, before an all-sufficient God, that changeth not. Who makes the seas and the winds faithful, that they do not hurt us, but God? And yet we are apt to trust the wind and weather sooner than God, as we see many seamen that will thrust forth their goods into the wide ocean in a small bark, to shift any way, rather than trust God with them.'

Yea, let Satan, by his wicked instruments, draw a man to some cursed politic reasons, for the devil doth not immediately converse with the world, but in his instruments, and he will sooner trust him than God himself. So prone are our hearts to distrust the Almighty, to call his truth in question, and to trust the lies of our own hearts and other men's, before him. Let us, therefore, lament our infidelity, that having such an omnipotent and faithful creator to rely upon, yet we cannot bring our hearts to trust in him. There are two main pillars of a Christian's faith :—

1. The power of God.
2. The goodness of God.

These two, like Aaron and Hur, hold up the arms of our prayers. Let our estate be never so desperate, yet God is a Creator still. Let our sins and infirmities be never so great, yet he hath power to heal them. Oh, how should this cheer up our souls, and support our drooping spirits in all our strivings and conflicts with sin and Satan, that we yield not to the least temptation, having such an almighty God to fly unto for succour.

We must not trust the creature. 'Cursed is that man which makes flesh his arm,' Jer. xvii. 5. He that we trust in, must be no less than a Creator. 'Cease from man, whose breath is in his nostrils,' saith God, he is a poor creature as thyself is; raised of nothing, and shall come to dust again. If we would be trusting, as we needs must, for we are dependent persons, and want many things whilst we are here, let us go to the fountain, and not to broken cisterns for comfort.

It is no small privilege for a Christian to have this free access to God in times of extremity. Be we what we can be, take us at our worst in regard of sin or misery, yet we are his creatures still. I am the clay, thou art the potter; I am a sinful wretch, yet I am the workmanship of thy hands. O Lord, thou hast framed me and fashioned me, &c. No wicked person in the world can, upon good ground, plead in this manner, though they may say to God, *I am thy creature*, yet they have not the grace in their troubles to plead this unto him. Why, Lord, though I be a rebellious son, and am not worthy to be called thy servant, yet I am thy creature, though a sinful one. Surely, had we faith, we would take hold by a little. The soul of man is like the vine, it winds about and fastens upon every little help. Faith will see day at a little hole; and where it sees anything it will catch at it, as the woman of Canaan. Christ calls her dog. Why, be it so, Lord, *I am a dog*, yet I am one of the family though I be a dog; therefore *have mercy on me.*

Oh, it is a sweet reasoning thus to cling about God, and gather upon him; it is a special art of faith. Though a carnal man may reason thus, as having a ground from the truth of the thing, yet he hath not grace to reason out of an affection thereunto. Though he should say, Lord, I am thy creature; yet his heart tells him thus, if he would hearken to it, I am thy creature, Lord, but I have made all my members that I have received from thee, instruments to sin against thee, and I purpose not to reform; my tongue is an instrument of swearing, lying, and profane speeches; my hands are instruments of bribery and violence, continually working mischief in thy sight; my feet carry me to such and such filthy places, and abominable courses; mine own heart tells me that I fight against thee, my Creator, with those very limbs and weapons which thou hast given me. Beloved, the conscience of this so stifles the voice of a wilful sinner, that notwithstanding he acknowledgeth himself to be God's creature, yet he cannot with any comfort plead for mercy at his hand in times of distress.

But to a right godly man this is an argument of special use and consequence; in the midst of troubles he may allege this, and it binds God to help him. We see great ones when they raise any, though perhaps there is little merit in them, yet they call them their creatures; and this is a moving argument with such to polish their own work still, and not to desert them. Will it not be a prevailing argument with God then, for a Christian to plead with him? Lord, thou hast raised me out of nothing, yea, out of a state worse than nothing; I am thy poor creature, forsake not the work of thine own hands. We may see what a fearful thing sin is in God's eye, that the works of *our* hands should make God depart from the work of *his* hands, as he will certainly do at the day of judgment: 'Depart, you cursed,' &c., Mat. xxv. 41. Though we be his creatures, yet because we have not used those gifts and abilities which he hath given us to serve His Majesty, he will not endure the sight of us in that day.

But that you may the better practise this duty of committing your souls to God, take these directions.

1. *Directions how to commit our souls to God.* First, *see that thou be thy own man.* It is an act of persons free to covenant. Our souls must be ours before we can commit them to God. Naturally we are all slaves to Satan; the *strong man* hath possession of us, and therefore our first care must be to get out of his bondage, to which purpose we should much eye the sweet promises and invitations of the gospel, alluring us to accept of mercy and deliverance from sin and death, as—' Come unto me, all you that are weary and heavy laden,' &c., Mat. xi. 28, and so cast the guilt of our souls upon God to pardon first, and then to sanctify and cleanse, that we may no more return to folly, but lead an unspotted life before him for the time to come.

It is therefore a silly course and dangerous, which poor worldly wretches take, who think *Lord, have mercy upon them,* will serve their turn, and that God will certainly save their souls; whenas they were never yet in the state of grace or reconciliation with him, nor never had any divorce made between them and their sins, and consequently never any league between God and their souls to this day.

Beloved, when once a man hath alienated his soul from God by sin, he hath then no more command of it; for the present it is quite out of his power. Now, when we would commit our souls to God aright, we must first commit them to him to pardon the guilt of sin in them. When this is done, God will give us our souls again, and then they may truly be said to be our own, and not before. It is the happiness of a Christian that he is not his own, but that whether he live or die, he is the Lord's.

Direction 2. In the second place, *we must labour to find ourselves in covenant with God;* that is, *to find him making good his promises to us, and ourselves making good our promises to him.* For a man cannot commit himself to God, unless he find a disposition in his heart to be faithful to him.

There is a passive fidelity, and an active. 1. Passive faithfulness is in the things that we give trust unto, as, such a one is a sure, trusty man, therefore I will rely upon him. 2. Active faithfulness in the soul is, when we cast ourselves upon a man that is trusty, and depend upon him. The more a man knows another to be faithful, the more faithful he will be in trusting of him; and thus we must trust God, if ever we expect any good at his hands; and our dependence on him binds him to be the more faithful to us. He is counted a wicked man indeed, that will deceive the trust committed to him. Trust begets fidelity; it makes a good man the more faithful, when he knows he is trusted.

Learn therefore to know thyself to be in covenant with God, and to trust him with all thou hast; train up thyself in a continual dependence upon him. He that trusts God with his soul, will trust him every day in everything he hath or doth. He knows well, that whatsoever he enjoys is not his own, but God's; and this stirs him to commit all his ways and doings to his protection, esteeming nothing safe but what the Lord keeps. He sees 'it is not in sinful man to direct his own steps,' Jer. x. 23; and therefore resigns up his estate, his calling, his family, whatsoever is near and dear unto him, to the blessed guidance and direction of the Almighty. Oh, thinks he, that I were in covenant with God, that he would own me for his, and take the care of me, how happy should my condition then be!

He will likewise commit the church and state wherein he lives to God; and strengthens his faith daily by observing God's faithful dealing with his people in every kind.

How behoveful it is for Christians thus to inure themselves to be acquainted with God by little and little, first trusting him with smaller matters, and then with greater. How can a man trust God with his soul, that distrusts him for the petty things of this life? 'They that give to the poor are said to lend unto the Lord,' Prov. xix. 17; and 'if we cast our bread upon the waters, we shall find it again,' Eccles. xi. 1. Beloved, he that parts with anything to relieve a poor saint, and will not trust God with his promise to recompense it again, but thinks all is gone, and he shall never see it more, &c., exceedingly derogates from the truth and goodness of the Almighty, who hath promised to return with advantage whatsoever we give that way. He hath secret ways of his own to do us good, that we know not of. A man is never the poorer for that which he discreetly gives. It is hard to believe this; but it is much harder for a man to commit his soul to God when he dies, with assurance that he shall partake of mercy, and be saved at the last day.

Direction 3. Again, *take heed of these evil and cursed dispositions that hinder us from the performance of this duty;* as namely, carnal wit and policy, and carnal will and affection, &c. There is a great deal of self-denial to be learned, before we can go out of ourselves and commit all to God; ere we can cast ourselves into his arms, and lay ourselves at his feet. Therefore take heed that we be not ruled, either by our own carnal policy or others', to knit ourselves to that; for I beseech you, do but think, what is true in all stories, not only in the Scripture, but elsewhere, the most unfortunate men that ever were, otherwise wise enough, were always too confident of themselves. The greatest swimmers, you know, are often drowned, because relying overmuch on their own skill, they cast themselves into danger, and are swallowed up of the deep. Even confidence in wit is usually unfortunate, though it be great. Let Solomon be an example. You see how he strengthened himself by carnal supports; but what became of all? Alas, it soon vanished and came to nothing. The Jews would run to the reed of Egypt, and that ran into their hands; instead of helping, it hurt them. God takes delight to overthrow the ripeness of all the carnal policy of man, that advanceth itself against his word and gospel. Take heed of confidence in prosperity, in wit, in strength; take heed of whatsoever hinders the committing of our souls to God; and alway remember, that honesty is the best policy; and that God reconciled in Christ is the best sanctuary to flee unto. 'The name of God is a strong tower,' saith Solomon; 'the righteous flee thereto, and are safe,' Prov. xviii. 10.

That carnal policy hinders our safety. Let Christians therefore have nothing to do with carnal shifts, and politic ends; for they have a strong rock, and a sure hold to go to; the Almighty is their shield. Beloved, God will be honoured by our trusting of him, and those that will be wiser than God, and have other courses distinct and contrary to him, must look for confusion in all their plots. A Christian should thus think with himself, let God be wise for me; his wisdom shall be my direction; his will shall be the rule of my life; he shall guide me and support me; I will adventure upon no course that I dare not commit my soul with comfort to God in.

Oh beloved, if we tender our own welfare, let us shun all unwarrantable courses, and adventure upon no action whatsoever, wherein we cannot upon good grounds desire the Lord's protection. It is a fearful estate for a man to undertake such courses, as that he cannot if he were surprised by judgment, suddenly commit himself to God in. The throne of iniquity shall not abide with God; he will not take a wicked man by the hand, nor own him in a distressful time.

Study therefore, I beseech you, to be always in such a blessed condition, as that you may, without tempting of God, in a holy boldness of faith, resign up your souls to him. A guilty conscience cannot seek the Lord; naturally it runs away from him. Peace is not easily gotten, nor the gap soon made up; therefore preserve conscience clear and unspotted, if thou wouldst have God thy refuge in time of need. Adam when he had sinned ran from God; Peter, when our Saviour discovered more than an ordinary majesty in his miracles, said, 'Lord, depart from me, I am a sinful man,' Luke v. 8. It is the work of flesh and blood to depart from God, but when a man goes to God, it is a sign he hath more than flesh and blood in him; for this cannot be done without a supernatural work of faith; which alone will make a sinful conscience fly to God, and look to him as a father in Christ, and desire him by his almighty power, whereby he created heaven and earth, to create faith in the soul. And when thou hast cast thy soul into the arms of the Almighty, labour to settle it there, and to quiet thyself in the discharge of thy duty; say thus, now I have done that which belongs to me, let God do that which belongs to him; I will not trouble myself about God's work, but in well-doing commit my soul to him, and let him alone with the rest.

Christians should not outrun God's providence, and say, what shall become of me? this trouble will overwhelm me! &c. but serve his providence in the use of the means, and then leave all to his disposal. Especially this duty is needful in the hour of death, or when some imminent danger approacheth; but then it will be an hard work, except it be practised aforehand.

Direction 4. Labour therefore for *assurance of God's love betimes*, get infallible evidences of thy estate in grace, that thou art a renewed person, and that there is a thorough change wrought in thy heart; that God hath set a stamp upon thee for his own, and that thou hast something above nature in thee; then mayest thou cheerfully say, 'Father, into thy hands I commend my spirit; I am thine, Lord, save me, &c.,' Luke xxiii. 46, otherwise having no interest in God, how canst thou expect any favour from him? Oh the sweet tranquillity and heaven upon earth which those enjoy who have God to be their friend!

This lays a heavy prejudice upon antichristian religion, which maintains a doctrine of doubting, affirming that we ought not to labour for assurance of God's favour. Oh beloved, what deprives a poor Christian soul of comfort more than this? Alas! how can a man at the hour of death commit his soul into the hands of Almighty God, that staggers whether he be his child or no? and knows not whether he shall go to heaven or hell? Therefore it should be our daily endeavour, as we would have comfort in the time of resigning and giving up our souls to God, to gather evidences of a good estate; that we are in covenant with him; that he is our Father; and that we are his children in Christ Jesus.

For will a man trust his jewels with an enemy, or with a doubtful friend? How can the swearer commit his soul to God? How can loose livers and your filthy, unclean wretches, that live in continual enmity against the Lord, commit themselves with any comfort unto him? They pray, 'Lead us not into temptation,' Mat. vi. 13, and yet run daily into temptations, into vile houses and places of wickedness, wherein they feed their corruptions, and nothing else. They say, 'Give us this day our daily bread,' and yet use unwarrantable courses, seeking to thrive by unlawful means.

Beloved, a man can commit his soul with no more comfort to God than he hath care to please him. If a man knows such a one hath his evidences and leases, and may hurt him when he list, how careful will he be of provoking or giving offence to such a man? Suppose we knew a man that had the keeping of a lion, or some cruel beast, and could let it loose upon us at his pleasure, would we not speak such a one fair, and give him as little cause of discontent as may be? Beloved, God hath devils and wicked men in a chain, and can, if we offend him, set loose all the powers of darkness upon us; he can make conscience fly in our faces, and cause us to despair and sink. All our evidences and assurances of salvation are in God's hands; he can bring us into a state full of discomfort and misery, and make us in a manner to feel the very flashes and scorchings of hell itself. Oh who would offend this God, much less live in the practice of any sin, and yet think of committing their souls to him!

Direction 5. To encourage you the more to trust in God, *observe the constant course of his dealing towards you*. 'Lord, thou hast been my God from my youth,' saith David; 'upon thee have I hung ever since I was took out of my mother's womb; forsake me not in my gray hairs, when my strength faileth me,' &c., Ps. lxxi. 6, 9, xvii. 18. We should gather upon God, as it were, from former experience of his goodness, and trust him for the time to come, having formerly found him true. Beloved, it is good to lay up all the experiments of God's love we can, that we may trust him at the hour of death; for all our strength then will be little enough to uphold our faith. When many troubles shall meet in one, as it were in a centre, then a world of fears and distractions will seize upon our souls, the guilt of sin past, thoughts of judgment to come, forsaking of our former lusts and delights, trouble of mind, pain of body, &c. We have need of much acquaintance with God, and assurance of his love at such a time. Therefore let us learn daily to observe the experience of his goodness towards us, how when we have committed ourselves to him in youth, he hath been a God from time to time in such and such dangers to us. Ancient Christians should be the best Christians, because they are enriched with most experiences. It is a shame for ancient Christians to stagger, when they yield up their souls to God, as if they had not been acquainted with him heretofore. You see how David pleads to God, 'Thou hast redeemed me,' Ps. xxxi. 5; he goes to former experience of his mercy; therefore now into thy hands I commend my spirit in this extremity. This psalm is a practice of this precept; here is the precept, ' Commit your souls to God, as a faithful Creator;' here is the practice of David, 'Into thy hands I commend my spirit, for thou hast redeemed me, O Lord God of truth,' &c. Therefore, I beseech you, let us treasure up experience of God's goodness, that so when extremities shall come, we may go boldly to him, upon former acquaintance with his majesty; and being strengthened with former experience. I beseech you, let us labour to practise these and the like rules prescribed, to encourage us in the performance of so necessary a duty.

Obj. But will not God keep us without we commit ourselves unto him?

Ans. We must commit our souls to God if we would be preserved. I answer, God having endued us with understanding and grace, will do us good in the exercise of those powers and graces that he hath given us; he will preserve us, but we must pray for it. Christ himself must ask before he can have: ' Ask of me, and I will give thee the heathen for thine inheritance,' Ps. ii. 8, &c. We should therefore make it a continued act, every day of our lives, to commit all we have to the Lord's disposal; and to that end observe how he dischargeth the trust committed to him upon all occasions; how faithful he is in delivering his poor church in greatest extremities, and ourselves also even in our worst times. ' Thou never failest those that trust in thee,' saith David, and ' How excellent is thy lovingkindness, O God, therefore the children of men shall trust under the shadow of thy wings,' Ps. xxxvi. 7. Daily experience of God's lovingkindness will make us daily to trust under the shadow of his wings. It should therefore be our continual course to observe the goodness, kindness, faithfulness, and other attributes of God, and often to support our souls with them.

Think, I beseech you, how he numbers the very bones of men; they are all written in his book of providence; he knows every joint, every part which he hath made; he knows his own workmanship; therefore we may well commit our souls to him. Doth God number our superfluities, and not our natural and essential parts? Even our very hairs are numbered; our tears are taken notice of, and put into his bottle; our steps are told; our desires are known; our groans are not hid. We shall not lose a sigh for sin, so particular is God's providence. He watcheth continually over us. There is not any of our members but they are all written in his book, so that he will not suffer ' a bone to be broken,' Ps. xxxiv. 20. We should therefore daily resign up our souls to his merciful tuition,* and bind ourselves to lead unblameable lives before him, resolving against every sinful course, wherein we would be afraid to look his Majesty in the face. What a comfortable life were the life of Christians, if they would exercise them-

* That is, 'protection.'—ED.

selves to walk as in the presence of the Almighty! This is that which the Scripture speaks of Enoch, Gen. v. 24, and the rest, who are said to have walked with God; that is, to have committed themselves and their souls to him, as *to a faithful Creator.*

Obj. Of wicked men's preserving, who do not commit their souls to God. It may be objected, here is a great deal of labour and striving against corruptions indeed; may not a man walk with God without all this ado? We see wicked men, that never commit their souls to God, grow fat and lusty, and have as good success in the world as the strictest men that are.

Ans. 1. I answer, God many times preserves such wretches; but, alas! that preservation is rather a reservation for a worse evil to come upon them. 'There is a pit a-digging for the wicked,' Ps. xxxvii. 13, 38. He flourisheth and bears out all impudently, under hope of success; but his grave is a-making, and his present prosperity will but aggravate his future misery.

2. Sometimes God preserves wicked men for other ends. It may be he hath some to come of their loins, who of wicked shall be made good.

3. Again, God will be in no man's debt. Those that are civilly good shall have civil prosperity, as the Romans had. They had a commonwealth well governed, and they prospered many years together. As Chaucer observes, God preserves wicked men from many calamities; he gives them civil wisdom, good carriage, &c.; and answerable to those common gifts, he gives them preservation and protection, &c.; but then there is vengeance on their souls the while. Those that commit not themselves carefully and watchfully to God, have dead, secure souls, without any life of grace or power of godliness in them. I speak this to waking Christians, that would know in what case they should live; walking in the sense and assurance of God's love; they, I say, ought to practise this duty of committing the keeping of their souls to God in well-doing, as to a faithful Creator.

What it is to commit our souls to God. Neither is it so easy a matter to commit our souls to God as many fondly imagine. It is not the mumbling over a few prayers, saying, Lord, receive my soul, &c., will serve the turn. These are good words indeed, and soon learned; but, alas! who cannot do this? Our study, therefore, should be to know the depth and meaning of the same; how that we are not only to commit the essence of our souls to God, that he would take them into heaven when we die; but also to commit the affections of our souls to him, that he might own us and govern us whilst we live; for how are our souls known, but by those active expressions in our affections, which immediately issue from them, when we commit all our thoughts, desires, and affections to him, setting him highest in our souls, and making him our hope, our trust, our joy, our fear, &c.?

Thus I have spoken of the duty, and of the *thing* to be committed, *our souls;* and *to whom, to God;* and the *manner, in well-doing;* and *why? because he is a faithful Creator.*

Now, I beseech you, consider how nearly it concerns us all to be thoroughly acquainted with the practice of this duty. God knows what extremities we may fall into. Certainly in what condition soever we be, either public or private, whether in contagion and infection, or war and desolation, happy are we if we have a God to go to. If we have him to retire to in heaven, and a good conscience to retire to in ourselves, we may rest secure. 'Though the earth be removed, and the mountains be carried into the midst of the sea,' Ps. xlvi. 2, 4, yet we shall be safe; that is, though the order of nature were confounded, yet there is a river shall refresh the house of God. There are chambers of divine protection, that the

Christian enters into, as the prophet saith, 'Enter into thy chambers,' Isa. xxvi. 20; and God is his habitation still. If a Christian had no shelter in the world, yet he hath an abiding place in God continually; as God dwells in him, so he dwells in God. Satan and all other the enemies of man must break through God before they can come to us, when once we commit ourselves to him, as to a tower and habitation, and enter into him as into an hiding place. The enemies must wrong him before they can hurt us, so blessed an estate it is to be in God, having commended our souls to him, as unto a *faithful Creator*.

Obj. But we see many of God's dear children, that commit themselves to his care and protection, miscarry, and go by the worst in the world.

Ans. 1. Beloved, it is not so, for when they commit themselves to God, they are under safety; and if he keep them not *out* of trouble, yet he will preserve them *in* trouble. 'I will be with thee in the fire, and in the water,' saith God, Isa. xl. He saith not, I will keep you out of the fire, and out of the water, for he brought many holy martyrs into it; some were drowned, some burned, &c. Though God will not keep us out of trouble, yet he will preserve our spirits in trouble; nay, God many times by a small trouble preserves us from a greater. Even the sufferings of the godly are oft preservations to them. Was not Jonah preserved by the whale? What had become of him if that had not swallowed him up? A whale that one would have thought should be a means to destroy him, was a means to carry him to the coast, and bring him safely to land.

Again, God seems for a time indeed to neglect his children when they commit themselves unto him, but mark the issue; 'all the works of God are beautiful in their season,' Eccl. iii. 11. He suffers them it may be, a long time to be in danger and trouble, till he hath perfected the work of mortification in their hearts, and crucified their confidence in earthly things, till he hath made them more sensible of the evil of sin, and watchful against it; but wait a while, and you shall see 'that the end of the righteous man is peace,' Ps. xxxvii. 37.

God's presence and assistance to support his children in trouble is invincible; they have gladness and comfort that we wot not of; they commit the safety of their souls to God, and he seems to neglect them, if we look to their outward man, but they have a paradise in their conscience. God preserves their souls from sin, and their consciences from despair. They have an invisible protection. There was a fence about Job that the devils saw, and a guard of angels that Elias saw, and that his servant saw afterwards, 2 Kings vi. 14, 15. Wicked men see not the guard of spirits that is about the children of God; as Christ saith, 'they have meat the world knows not of,' John iv. 32; they feed on hidden comforts.

As for carnal men, they do not commit themselves to God; they have no preservation, but rather a reservation to further evil. Pharaoh was kept from the ten plagues, but was drowned in the sea at last; and Sodom was kept by Abraham; he fought for them, but yet it was destroyed with fire and brimstone afterwards.

Let us then try our trust in God. Those that intend to embark themselves and their estates in a ship, will be sure to try it first. This committing of our souls to God, must be our ship to carry us through the waves of this troublesome world to the heavenly Canaan of rest and peace. We should therefore search and prove the same, whether it be indeed safe and sound, able to support our souls in the evil day, and not leak and prove insufficient for us.

How to know when we trust God aright. Trial 1. Those that commit themselves to God aright, *are far from tempting his majesty.* God will be trusted, but not tempted. What though things fall not out according to thy expectation; yet wait thou, and think God hath further ends than thou knowest of. God will do things in the order of his providence, therefore if we neglect that, it is our own fault if he do not help us. If Christ had committed his health to God, and had cast himself down from the pinnacle, what an act had this been! but he would not so tempt the Almighty. Neither should we unadvisedly run into dangers, but serve his providence upon all occasions. God useth our endeavour to this very end. He saves us not always immediately, but by putting wisdom into our hearts to use lawful means, and using those means he will save us in them. A Christian therefore should be in a continual dependence upon God, and say, I will use these means, God may bless them; if not, I will trust him; he is not tied to the use of means, though I be.

Trial 2. Again, those that commit their souls, or anything to God, *find themselves quieted therein.* Is it not so amongst men? If a man commit a jewel to a trusty friend, is he not secure presently? Have we not God's word and faithfulness engaged, that he will not leave us nor forsake us, but continue our all-sufficient God and portion to our lives' end? Why then are we disquieted? Those that are full of cares and fears may talk their pleasure, but they never yet had any true confidence in God: for faith is a quieting grace, it stills the soul; 'being justified by faith, we have peace with God,' Rom. v. 1. Those that are hurried in their life with false doubts and perplexities, 'What shall become of me? What shall I eat, and what shall I drink?' &c., though they use lawful means, yet commit not themselves to God as they should; for where there is a dependence upon God in the use of means, there is an holy silence in the party. All stubborn and tumultuous thoughts are hushed in him. ' My soul, keep silence to the Lord,' saith David, ' and trust in God; why art thou so vexed within me?' Ps xlii. 11. Still there is a quieting of the soul where there is trust. Can that man put confidence in God that prowls for himself, and thinks he hath no Father in heaven to provide for him? Doth that child trust his father, that, besides going to school, thinks what he shall put on? how he shall be provided for, and what inheritance he shall have hereafter? Alas: this is the father's care, and belongs not to him. Wheresoever these distractions are, there can be no yielding up of the soul to God in truth.

There be two affections which mightily disturb the peace of Christians. 1. Sinful cares; and 2. sinful fears. To both which we have remedies prescribed in the Scripture. 1. 'Fear not, little flock,' saith Christ, 'for it is your Father's will to give you a kingdom,' Luke xii. 32; as if he had said, Will not he that gives you heaven, give you other things? In nothing be careful, saith the apostle, that is, in a distracting manner, but do your duty, and then ' let your requests be made known to God, and the peace of God shall keep you,' Phil. iv. 7; and therefore were we redeemed from the hands of our enemies, that we might ' serve him without fear all our days,' Luke i. 74.

A Christian should keep an inward sabbath in his soul, and go quietly on in doing all the good he can. What a fearful thing is it to see men lie grovelling in the earth, and live without God in the world, troubling and turmoiling themselves how to compass this thing and that thing, as if they had no God to seek unto, nor no promise to rely upon.

Trial 3. Again, where this committing of a man's self and his soul to God is, *there will be a looking to God only, in all a man doth,* not fearing any danger or opposition that may befall him from without. As the three young men said to Nebuchadnezzar, 'Our God can keep us if he will,' Dan. iii. But what if he will not? 'Yet know, O king, that we will not worship nor fall down before thy image.' So it is with a Christian; foreseeing some danger, disgrace, or displeasure of this or that man which may befall him, he resolveth notwithstanding, in despite of all, to commit himself to God in doing his duty, come what will. Whether God will save him or no, he will not break the peace of his conscience, or do the least evil. He is no fool, but foresees what may befall him for well-doing. This inconvenience may come, and that trouble, yet he sets light by these. He hath an eye to heaven, and sees more good to himself in the Creator that gave him his being of nothing, and more good for the time to come, that will make him a blessed saint in heaven, than there can be ill in the creature. Therefore, come what can come, his heart is fixed to trust the Lord, and rather than he will displease him, desert his honour and his cause, or do any unworthy action, he will commit himself to God in the greatest dangers.

Reason of trusting in God. The ground hereof is this: a Christian is the wisest man in the world, and he understands well enough that God is all-sufficient. He sees there is a greater good in God than he can have in the creature, and counts it madness to offend God to please the creature; because there is a greater evil to be expected from God than from the creature, though it were the greatest monarch in the world. Considering, therefore, that he hath his best good in his union with God, and in keeping his peace with him, he will not break with him for any creature. And thus he doth wisely, for he knows if he lose his life he shall have a better life of God than he hath in his body; for God is his life, God is his soul and his comfort, and he hath his being from God. He is his Creator, and he hath a better being in God when he dies than he had when he lived; for our being in God makes us happy, and therefore Christ saith, *He that loves his life,* before God and a good cause, *hates it,* and *he that hates his life* when Christ calls for it, *loves it,* John xii. 25, for he hath a better life in him. We give nothing to God, but he returns it a thousand times better than we gave it. Let us yield our lives to him. We shall have them in heaven if they be taken away on earth. He will give us our goods a thousandfold. We shall have more favour in God than in any creature, and therefore a Christian, out of this ground, commits himself to God, though he foresee never so much danger like to fall upon him.

Trial 4. Again, if we do *in deed and not in pretence* commit ourselves to God, as to a faithful Creator, *we will not limit his majesty,* as many carnal hearts do. Oh, if God will do so and so for them, then they would trust him. If they had but so much to live on a year, and such comings in, &c., then they would depend upon God. But they must have a pawn and so much in hand first. What a shame is it that we should trust the vilest man in the world as far as we see him, and yet, unless we have somewhat to lean on, we will not trust God! Beloved, when a man limits God in anything, such a one may talk, but he trusts him not at all. Indeed, we should indent with God, and tie him to look to the salvation of our souls; but for other things leave them to his own wisdom, both for the time, for the manner and measure, do what he will with us. Suppose it come to the cross, hath he not done greater matters for us? Why then should we distrust him in lesser? If times come that religion flourish or goes downward, yet rely on him still. Hath he not given his Son to us, and will he not give heaven also ? Why do we limit the Holy One of Israel, and not cast ourselves upon him, except he will covenant to deal thus and thus with us ?

A true Christian hath his eye always heavenward, and thinks nothing too good for God. O Lord, saith he, of thee I have received this life, this estate, this credit and reputation in the world. I have what I have, and am what I am of thee, and therefore I yield all to thee back again. If thou wilt serve thyself of my wealth, of myself, of my strength, thou shalt have it. If thou wilt serve thyself of my credit and reputation, I will adventure it for thee. If thou wilt have my life, of thee I had it, to thee I will restore it, I will not limit thy majesty; come of it what will, I leave it to thy wisdom; use me and mine as thou wilt; only be gracious to my soul, that it may go well with that, and I care not. Thus we should wholly resign ourselves to the Lord's disposal, and thereby we shall exceedingly honour his majesty, and cause him to honour us, and to shew his presence to us for our good, which he will assuredly do if we absolutely yield up ourselves to him. But if a man will have two strings to his bow, and trust him so far but not so far, so he may be kept from this danger or that trouble, &c., this is not to deal with God as an omnipotent Creator; for he that doth a thing truly in obedience to God, will do it generally to all his commands. So far as the reason of his obedience reaches, his trust extends. He that commits anything to God will commit all to him. He chooseth not his objects. But upon the same ground that he commits his soul to God when he dies, he commits his estate, liberty, and all he hath while he lives. He can never rely on God for greater matters, that distrusts him in lesser.

Trial 5. Again, a man that truly trusts God *will commit all his ways unto him;* he will take no course but what he is guided in by the Lord. He looks for wisdom from above, and saith, Lord, though it is not in me to guide my own way; as thy word shall lead me, and the good counsel of thy Spirit in others direct me, so I will follow thee. He that commits not his ways to God, will not commit his comforts to him. God must be our counsellor as well as our comforter. Therefore the wise man bids us ' acknowledge God in all our ways, and lean not to our own wisdom,' Prov. iii. 5. Most men look how safe their counsels are, not how holy and agreeable to God. Is this to trust in him? Will God save us at last, and yet suffer us to live as we list now? Deceive not yourselves; he that will have his soul saved must commit it to God beforehand to be sanctified.

Trial 6. Again, those that commit themselves aright to God *will commit their posterity to him,* their wives and children, &c.

Obj. Why! do not men make their wills and commit their goods to them?

Solution. Oh! but how do they resign them? How covetous and full of distrust are they! I must leave such a child so much and so much; and why, I pray you? Because God cannot bless him else? O fearful! is God tied to means? cannot he bless with a little as well as with a great deal? Is not ' the earth the Lord's, and the fulness thereof?' Ps. xxiv. 1. Why must God have so much in hand, or else he cannot enrich and raise up thy children? Oh! consider, he hath declared himself to be the father of the fatherless, and looks to the widow in a special manner; he doubles his providence there; he provides for all, but takes special notice of them; therefore quiet thyself, they are in covenant with God, and God is thy God, and the God of thy seed also; therefore if thou wilt commit thy soul, why not thy wife, children, goods? &c.

Look into the course of God's people in all times. Those that have left but little with honest dealing, God hath blessed the same exceedingly; whereas those that have left great matters ill gotten, instead of a blessing have often left a curse and a snare behind them. Why then should men take indirect courses, and wound their consciences for worldly pelf?

Consid. 1. Consider, 1, thy children are God's and not thine; he gave them to thee at first, and he can provide hereafter when thou art gone. Thou art the father of their body, but he is the father of their soul.

2. He provided for them before they were born. Doth not he provide care and affection in the mother's heart? Doth he not provide suck in the mother's breasts? and will he not care for them now they are born as well as he did before they came into the world? It is atheism to think such a thought. Those that commit themselves to God in one thing will do so in all things, otherwise they deceive their own souls; for it is a universal act that runs through their whole life. Committing is an action of trust, and there is a kind of intercourse of trust between God and a Christian continually.

Trial 7. Lastly, those that commit themselves to God *will be faithful stewards in whatsoever he hath trusted them withal.* Thou committest thyself and thy health and estate to God, and at length thou wilt commit thy soul when thou diest unto him. 'Very well; but what doth God trust thee withal? Hath he not trusted thee with a body and a soul, with a portion of goods, with place, time, strength, and abilities to do good? Hast thou not all thou hast from God as a steward, to improve for thy Master's advantage? If ever thou expectest the performance of what thou hast put in him, be faithful in that trust which he hath committed to thee. Those that have misused their bodies and wounded their souls in their lives, how can they commit them to God at their deaths? How dares the soul look up to him, when the life hath been nothing else but a perpetual offending of his majesty?

I beseech you, let us learn this wholesome lesson! Great is our benefit thereby. 'He that trusts in the Lord shall be as Mount Sion, that cannot be moved.' We may be shaken, but shall never be removed. The earth is shaken with earthquakes, but the earth keeps its own centre still. Our best peace is in God, and our chiefest safety in his protection. 'I laid me down to rest, because thou, Lord, watchest over me,' Ps. iii. 5, saith the prophet; and, 'Return, O my soul, to thy rest, for the Lord hath been very beneficial to thee,' Ps. cxvi. 7. Is it not a good thing to have a sweet security of soul that whether I sleep or wake, whether I be at home or abroad, live or die, I have a providence watching over me better than mine own? When I yield myself up to God, his wisdom is mine, his strength is mine; whatsoever he hath it is for me, because I am his. What a heaven upon earth is this, that a Christian, out of a holy familiarity with God, can resign up his soul to him upon all occasions! Set heaven and salvation aside, what greater happiness can be desired? How sweet is a man's rest at night after he hath yielded himself to God by faithful prayer?

Use. Exhortation. I beseech you, let us be acquainted with the practice of this duty, and labour to be in such a state as God may own us, and receive our poor souls to himself. Let us keep them pure and undefiled, and labour to improve our talents, that when we give anything to God, we may say, Lord, according to the grace I have received I have kept it, and therefore now return it to thee again.

Beloved, when trouble of conscience comes, when sickness and death comes, what will become of a man that hath not this sweet acquaintance with

God? He was a stranger to God in the time of prosperity, and God is now a stranger to him in adversity. Saul was a profane-spirited man; he did not acquaint himself with God in the time of his happiness, and therefore in time of distress he goes first to the witch, and then to the sword-point. So fareth it with all wicked wretches in their great extremities. No sooner doth any evil betide them, or the least danger approach them, let conscience never so little fly in their faces, &c., but presently they go to cursed means, and run upon desperate conclusions.

Therefore, as we desire to die even in God's arms, and yield up ourselves into the very hands of the Almighty with comfort, let us daily inure ourselves to this blessed course of committing ourselves and all our ways to him in doing good.

'Come and see,' saith the Scripture, John i. 46. Beloved, if you will not believe me, make trial of this course a while. Did you once taste the sweetness of it, how would your drooping spirits be cheered up!

Let a man continually keep a good conscience, and he shall be satisfied with peace at last. Suppose he meets with danger and opposition in the world, this may seem harsh at the first. Oh, but he shall know afterwards what it is to part with anything for Christ's sake, to commit his cause, or whatsoever he hath, unto God, as to a faithful Creator! Then we taste of God to the purpose when we put him to it, for God will not be indebted to us. We never find such sweet immediate comfort from him as when we deny ourselves comfort of the creature for his sake.

Little do we know what times may befall us. There is much danger abroad, and we have cause to fear, not far from us. It may be the clouds even now hang over our heads. Oh, if we would be hid in the day of the Lord's wrath, and have no evil come nigh our dwellings, let us, above all things in the world, make sure our interest in Christ, and title to the promise. We should seek to know God more, and then we would trust him more. 'They that know thy name will trust in thee,' saith David, Ps. ix. 10. Oh, the blessed estate of a Christian, that now he may be acquainted with God; that through Christ there is a throne of grace to fly unto! I beseech you, improve this happy privilege; and then, come what will, come famine, come danger of war or pestilence, &c., God will be a sanctuary and an abiding place to you. A Christian carries his rock and sure defence about him. 'I will be unto them a little sanctuary in all places,' saith God. What a comfort is it to have a 'wall of fire' still compassing us about, a shield that our enemies must break through before they can come at us! He that trusts in God shall be recompensed with mercy on every side. It is no matter what dangers compass him. Though he be in the midst of death and hell, or any trouble whatsoever, if he commits himself to God in obedience, out of good grounds of faith in his word, hes hall be safe in the evil day.*

* As explained in prefatory note, 'The Church's Visitation' forms the 'second part' of a volume. I annex the quaint notice for the guidance of readers, as wishing to preserve everything traceable to the pen of Sibbes:—

To THE READER.—Reader, in this Booke there are two parts. The one begins at the *Church's Visitation,* and goes on orderly to page 240, and there it ends. This I call the *second part.* All the rest, from the beginning and so forward, I count the first part. Therefore, when thou art directed to the fourth or fifth page, because thou shouldest not looke in both nor mistake, I have set it thus : 1, 4, which is, 1 part, 4 page ; or 2, 5, the second part and fifth page.'

INDEX

NOTE. The principle acted upon in the construction of this General Index was to select *thoughts* rather than mere *words*. An effort has been made to include all the former. The 'Tables' given in the original and early editions are *substantially* incorporated, but frequently under more definite and concise headings. Where, as in '*Christ*,' the references would have been so numerous as to confuse, as many as possible have been distributed under other topics. G.

Abasement, of Christ, 6; whence, 7; fruit of, 7.
Absence, of God's Spirit discourageth, 398.
Accepted, in Christ, 12.
Action and *Actions*, how to know whether from a good ground, 82; what are to be imputed to weak Christians, 75, 76; what, are the principles of them, 191.
Activity, grace is active and vigorous, 60, 61.
Adam, advance from Adam's state in Christ, 19, 31.
Admiration, admire God's love, 263.
Adventure, of faith, makes a rich return, 266.
Affection and *affections*, their conflict one with another, 152; how to be ordered, 159; in case of God's dishonour no affection is excessive, 159; why they do not always follow the judgment, 254; God most to be affected, 268.
Affliction and *Afflictions*, must take heed of impatiency in, 67; why we are oft foiled with small and courageously pass through great, 94.
America, progress of, 101.
Anger, 118.
Appearance, of salvation in the countenance, whence and why, 260.
Applause, seek not, 30, 31.
Application, of mercy in particular, necessary, reasons, 264; in the wicked it is a lie, 265; no easy matter to say '*my* God,' 265; when it is right, 267; a shame not to improve it, 272.
Approach, comfort in to God, 13.
Arguments, with God, 21; for faith to come to God, 246.
Art, in bearing of troubles, 148; in misery to think of matter of joy, 240; aggravates sin, 298.
Ascension, the Spirit given more abundantly since Christ's, 23.
Assurance, by the Spirit, 19, 22; faith and yet no full assurance, 62; what to do in the want of, 252; to be sought betimes, 417.
Atheism, brings judgment, 302.
Attributes, of God are to be applied to ourselves, 412.

Austerity, in ministers to be used wisely, 53, 98.

Back, faith with strong reasons and arguments, 245.
Beauty, of a well-ordered soul, 167; of Christian's works performed in season, 248, 249.
Behold, 4, 5.
'*Beloved*,' Christ, 11, 12.
Bilney, his offence at a preacher, 230.
Blasphemous, thoughts, how known and expelled, 63; temptations to blaspheming, and how checked, 227.
Boldness, to come before the throne of grace, how bred in us, 47; of conscience, 95.
Books, all written to amend the book of conscience, 149.
Breach, of inward peace: still look at thyself therein, 171.
Brethren, false, discovered by affliction, 317.
'*Bruised Reed*,' 33–101; what, 43; they must be as, with whom Christ deals, 43; Christ will not break the, 43, 44; signs of one truly bruised, 46; why it is necessary, 44; means of, 47; measure of, 47, 48.

Calamity, in the common, the wicked dare not appear, 400.
Calling, mean, 294.
'*Cast down*,' casting down disquiets, why, 142; remedies against, 143.
Caution, in forecasting changes, 163.
Censure, of others, must not be rash, 44; although it be the censure of the church, 55; or of the civil magistrate, 55; or private Christians, 56; cencensure not distempered Christians, dangerous to do so, 141.
Change, of nature, changeth all, 181; changes must be forethought of, 165; caution in, 163; directions for forethinking in troubles, 163, 164.
Character, of a good soul, 234, 235.
Children, of God are known by God's correcting them, 383; the devil their enemy, 397; must be committed to God, 424.
Choice, should rest in God's, 10.
Chosen, Christ of God, how, 10.
CHRIST, Description of, 1–31; withdraws himself, 4, 30; prophecy fulfilled thereby, 4; nearness to God, 4–11; calling and qualification, 4, 15, 16; execution of that calling, 4, 15; manner thereof, 4, 15, 29; a servant, 5–11; abasement, 6, 7; head of elect, 9; chosen and choice, 10; the Beloved, how, 11, 12; comfort, 12, 13, 14; God and man, 17; a priest, 17; full supply in, 20; fullness of, 23; to be offered to God, 21; ascended, 23; riches of, 24; strives not, 29; an especial servant of God in the work of our redemption, 42; he will not break the bruised reed, 43; his office calls him to this work, 43; he was clothed

with our nature, that he might succour the tempted, 45; though oft he seem an enemy, yet he is a true friend indeed, 71; is an all-sufficient comforter, 72; we should not harbour hard conceits of, 72; he doth rule as Lord over his own, 82; the government of his church is well ordered, 82; we should all submit to his government, 91; he alone maketh us victorious, 91, 92, 93; is salvation, clothed in man's flesh, 259; is Best, or St Paul's Strait, 335–350; his sufferings for man's sin, 351–369.

Christian, combat, we must fight before the victory, 95, 96, 97; calling: what is the true ability to it? grace, not gifts only, 242; particular calling, directions for it, 243.

Church, compared to weak things, 43; it should be merciful in censures, 55; as Christ, so should we commiserate the distressed church, 76; the Church of Rome is tyrannical over wounded consciences, 77; the church shall have victory, 97; visitation, 371–384; of God, is his house, 374; why, 374; he provides for it, 374; whether the English Church be God's house, 376; proved, 376; the church needs purging, 376; God cleanseth it when need is, 376, 377; it should severely punish sin, 378; it is God's spouse, 390; impregnable, 303.

Combat, spiritual, how discerned from that of common grace and light, 153.

Comfort, Christ is a complete and all-sufficient comforter, 70, 72; consolation to weak Christians, 86; that our victory lies with Christ, not ourselves, 97; who fit for comfort, 48; in the church's troubles, 244, 261; amiss, sought in sanctification, 138; have and hold comfort, grow up in holiness, 139; a sin not to comfort the afflicted, 195; how comfort tendered doth no good: miscarriages, 196.

Comforters, in way of humanity, many: few in way of Christianity, 192; graces necessary in a good, 193; method of comforting, 193, 194.

Commonness, of sin is a sign it is ripe, 379.

Communicative, grace is, 61, 62.

Communion, with God, 75; with saints, 75; with God, to be sought, how Christians have continual ground of it, 249; of friends, in watching over one another, 189; in comforting one another, 190.

Complain, of thyself, not of God nor others, 151.

Conception, of mind is like the body, 297.

Concupiscence, not severely censured by papists, 172.

Condition, of life, none wherein we may not exercise some

Condition—contd
grace, 170; a man can be in no condition wherein God is at a loss and cannot help him, 203.

Confidence, in a man's self the way to fall, 94; in ourselves, how chased away, 197; for mercies, warranted to us as well as to David or others, 250.

Conflict, of grace and corruption much casts us down, 237; should make us trust in God the more, 237, 238; in man's soul, kinds and degrees of them, 152; Conflict, Soul's, 119–294.

Conjunctions, four wonderful, 6.

Conscience, is a judge within us, 87; how it becomes bold, 95; how tortured, 70; how stilled, 70; how it is tender, 57; not clear brings disquietness, 139; good, fears not death, 339.

Consideration, the best objects of it, 181.

Constancy, in sin to be shunned, 298.

Contentment, contented meekness becomes a Christian in that estate which he is in, 65, 66; contentment to be framed to ourselves, and how, 164; a special means of quieting the soul, 161.

Continuance, of sin, or sins of continuance dangerous, 229; how to be dealt withal, 229, 230.

Conversion, before and after, need of bruising, 44.

Correction, shews we are God's children, 383.

Corruption, how far curbed or repressed by God, 177; remaining in an holy heart natural, uncontrollable, 171; what follows, 173.

Court, of conscience, why backward to keep, 146.

Cowardice, in God's ways to be avoided, 116, 117.

Creator, comfort from God as, 409, 413, 414.

Dark, times, why, 24.

Deal, with thyself in all afflictions to get quietness, 162.

Death, comfort in, 241, 242; in the state after, 242; compared to a wild beast, 334; a short dark passage, 334; a departing, 339; how Paul desired it, 339; not to be feared by a Christian, 340; may be desired by a wicked man, 340, 341; our ends must be considered, 386; of the godly to be lamented, and why, 344; their death a sign of judgment, 379.

Defects, three main, in man, 16; in life, rise from defects in trust, 222; a supply for all, 238.

Delay, not the praising of God, 254.

Deliberation, in what things to be used, 337.

Delight, is brought into the soul by grace, 58.

Denial, Self,—of ourselves necessary, wherein, 168; notes of it, 169.

Deliverance, we have daily from God, should cause us to glorify him, 329.

Description, of Christ, 3–31.

Desertion, then Christ should be put between God and us, 271.

Desires, how ordered, 60; what, 338.

Despair, of mercy, no cause of it, 287; may be where there is only a general apprehension of mercy, 264; to be avoided, 318.

Devil, enemy to God's children, 397.

Difference, between a carnal Christian and another, 251.

Diligent, to sin, 298.

Direction, in our ways afforded by grace, 60.

Discouragement, in affliction, incident to God's people, 133; causes, in ourselves, privative, positive, 136, 137; we are apt to cast down ourselves, 142; reasons against, the hurt that comes by it, 143; crosseth our own principles, 145; in times of, should not think too much of our corruptions, 156; a godly man knows how to bear himself in, 157.

Disobedience, against the gospel, the greatest sin, why, 388; how known, 391.

Disputations, their censure, 54; when jangling, see how they disquiet the peace of the church, 77.

Disquiet, we may be disquieted for that which it is not sinful to be disquieted for, 155; disquietness, three notes of that which is not befitting, 156; for sin, when it exceeds measure, 156; disquietment, proper for the soul, beside those of the body, 160; cause of all, 199.

Distempers, fall, if arrainged before reason, 145.

Distrust, the cause of all disquiet, 199.

Division, in a land forerunner of judgment, 379, 380.

Doctrine, should keep sound what has been left us pure, 331.

Doubts, and needless scruples, how hushed, 68; arise from popish doctrine of works, 133; Romish, disallowed, 417.

Duty, not to be hindered by consideration of our infirmities, 65; indisposition to duty, how known and prevented, rules, 66; discouragements, in whom they arise, 67; more to be thought of than comfort, 247; to be done with united forces or spirits, 139

Election, not known, no hindrance to our trust in God, 266; Christ head of, 9.

Eloquence, of Ambrose converted Augustine, 184.

End, our, must be considered, 386.

Enemy, Christ, though he seems so awhile, yet in the end he proves a true friend, 71; enemies of the church, comfort against them, 244; to be

Enemy—contd
prayed for, 405, 406; represented two ways, 311.

Envy, not prosperity of the wicked, 262; snarls at great goodness, 299.

Estate (= state), of a Christian, how to be judged, 137.

Eternity, our desire of God's glory should be carried into, 331.

Event, of things not to be too much forecasted, 141.

Evidence, of faith more constantly upholds the soul than sight, 278.

Evil, in an holy Christian not to be too much looked upon, 141; nor evils of the time 141; evils of sin, 154; we must not plot to do it, 307; difference between, done and suffered, 321; manifestation, aggravates it, 322.

Example, of others, of what force, 56; of governors prevail, 332.

Excellency, of God to be branched out for our several uses, 271.

Exercise, of grace, a means to keep it alive, 74; cautions, 75; preserves the soul, 199.

Experience, of God treasured up in the heart would much help faith, 277; to be called to mind, 216; communicated to others, 217; of God's care and love expressed, we may collect the future, 320, 417.

Extremities, whereunto the godly are suffered to fall, and why, 216.

Failure, failings pardoned where is no malicious intention, 248; how to make use of Christ in, 21.

Faith, upheld by promises, 5; may have, and no assurance, 62; strong and weak, how each stands, 85; weak, how it prevails, 86; how shaken, 110; to be strengthened, 110; must own God especially, 262, 263; why, 264; relies on a double principle, 213; why so requisite in Christians, 213; shaken by the devil and wicked ones, 134; must be prized, and how this may be, 217, 218; in us no seeds of, as of obedience, 222; its efficacy, 399; takes hold by little, 414; active and passive, 415; is strengthened by deliverance, 325; sign of our interest in heaven, 328.

Faithfulness, of God to be trusted in, 412; he is faithful, 411; we must be faithful in what he trusts to us, 424.

Falling, the way to fall is to be confident, 94.

Fame, commit to God, 30, 31.

Fancy, to be limited and restrained, 188; proper use of, 183.

Fathers, ancient, not always to be relied on, 42, 43.

Favours, how to preserve some of God's favour, 276; former make the soul more sensible of contrary, 131.

Fear, disturbs peace, 421.

GENERAL INDEX 433

Fight, must be before victory, 95, 96, 97.

Flax, smoking, Christ will not quench, 51; rules to know whether we are, 58; general rules of trial, 59; particular signs, 61.

Friends, living, spiritual privileges by them, 191; departure, comfort in, 246.

Fruitfulness required, 345; means to attain it, 346.

Fulness, of Christ, 21.

Future, care and love in God collected by things past, 417, 418.

Gain, for the Church of Rome proves tyrannical over conscience, 77.

Glory, Glorify, God for his deliverances, 329; our desire of God's glory should be infinite, 331; makes others do so, 333 (see *Honour*); a way to glorify God, 330.

God, love of, 7; God and man in Christ, 17; arguments with, 21; makes every man a governor over himself, 149; still left to a good heart when all others fail, 198; only is the object of trust, 203; cannot out of Christ, be thought on comfortably, 204; is some men's specially, 262; hence is the spring of all good, 264; when we prove this to our souls, 267; tokens of it, 269; comfort by it in extremities, 270; presence sweeteneth all places and states, 130; his glory more to be regarded than our own good, 247; is many salvations to his people, 259, 294; a rock not to be undermined, 259; the church is his house, 374; and he ours, 375; our bodies and all to him, 407; he is faithful, 411; we must be our own ere we can give ourselves to him, 414; must commit ourselves to him if we would be kept, 418; must eye him in all we do, 422, 423; rely on him, 423; he will be known in his attributes, 302, 303; his love to his, 302; he is overcome by prayer, 303; author of our deliverance, 320; our glorifying him makes others do it, 333; we must be faithful in what he trusts us, 424; God's attributes to be applied to ourselves, 412; must be in covenant with God, 414; comfort from God as a creator, 410, 413, 414; must be glorified for his deliverances, 329; trust his faithfulness, 412.

Godly men, when best disposed, 162; can restrain themselves in distempers, 148; can make good use of privacy, 148; afflicted more than others, why, 377; their sins greater than others, 377; seem neglected, but end is peace, 420; shall not be subdued, 304; their prosperity makes way for the subversion of the wicked, 304; they suffer, 316; yet differing from the wicked,

Godly men—*contd*
319; in straits, 337; death, how to be lamented, 344; bring good where they are, 344; deny best good for the church, 344; good men dying, sign of coming judgment, 379; must be actively as well as passively good, 301, 302.

Gospel, and law, how they differ, 29, 59; ministry of the Spirit, 23; in rejecting it we reject God, 387, 388; sin against worse than against the law, 389; it lays open Christ, 393; disobedience thereunto a great sin, 388; how known, 392.

Government, of Christ over his people, 79; victorious, 84, 91; we should all submit to it, 91; is opposed, 96; reasons, 96; well-ordered, 80; mean gifts not neglected but cherished by Christ, 49; good to be under Christ's, 393.

Governors, examples avail, 331.

Grace, in a small measure at first, 49; much in worth, 49; doth not waste corruption all at once but by degrees, 50; Christ cherishes weak beginners, 51; should be imitated therein, 52, 53; God looks at the truth of grace, not the measure, 58; often scarcely discernible, 50; yet discerned, as fire by light, 59, 60; direction, 60; delight, 60; is active, 61; pliable, communicative, 61, 62; working upward, 62; spreading, growing, 62; as grace increaseth, so doth the sense of sin, 62, 63; means how Christ preserveth, 74; exercise thereof, means to keep it alive, 75; why growth is insensible, 90; shall in the end be a glorious and visible conqueror, 84; of the Spirit make way to heaven easy, 399; delivering, needed against temptation, 323.

Great, in most danger, and why, 147, 192; greatness of sin may encourage us to go to God, 228; joined with goodness envied, 299.

Grief, more for sin than punishment, 48; gathered to a head will not be quieted at the first, 131; casteth down as joy lifteth up, 141; how to be mitigated, 189; faulty, when, 156; even godly, is to be bounded, 157; how to be ordered aright, 158; for sin, why we want it so much, 233; what to do in want of, 236; it is not all at first, 236; of contrition and of compassion, 158.

Growth, in laying claim to God, 266.

Guard, over the soul to be kept, 177.

Gunpowder, treason, 310, 311.

Happiness, present, aggravates eternal misery, 386.

Hatred, of sin, a good sign of grace, notes of it, 235.

Hear, Hearken, why God hears weak prayers, 71.

Heart, of man, not easily

brought to God, 200; to be most watched and kept in temper, 142; though vile shall be fitted for God, comfort, and glory, 238; enlarged to praise God is the chief deliverance, 252; of Christians first cheered by God, then their countenance, 260; of a Christian is God's closet, 374; discovered in affliction, 317.

Heaven, how to make the way thither easy, 399; faith a sign of our interest in, 328; pride purged also a sign, 328.

Help, helps against our infirmities, 58; by others in discerning our state, 209; where none is, yet trust in God, 209.

Hiding-place, saint's, in the evil day, 401–425; God sometimes hides himself, 111, 112.

Holiness, of God no discouragement to true Christians in their many infirmities, 238; 239; Holy Ghost, work of, distinguished, 18.

Honour, honouring God we honour ourselves, 333; a sign of a good state, 331, (see *Glorify*).

Hope, the main support of a Christian, 202; difference from faith, 203; most in a hopeless ground, 266; hour of mercy not yet past, 232; must be exercised, 399.

Humility, taught, 8, 9, 30; why to be laboured for, 30; humble persons comforted, 232; to humble us God does not need to go beyond ourselves, 160; nor we, 171.

Idle, life is ever a burden to itself, 139; idleness is the hour of temptation, 182.

Idolatry, ground of it, 21; brings judgment, 379.

Ignorance, of Christ's merciful disposition a block to comfort, 69.

Imagination, and opinion, cause of much disquiet, 178; how it hurteth us, 180; how sinful imaginations work in the soul, 179; remedy and cure of, 180; opportunities of helping it to be sought and taken, 183; how it may be made serviceable in spiritual things, 184; not impossible to rule, 188; misconceptions, 188.

Immanuel, a name of nature, and office, 263.

Impatience, under the cross, hurtful, 67.

Impediments, should not discourage, 238.

Impudence, in wicked men more than in devils, 275; sign of the ripeness of sin, 379, 380.

Inclinations, of soul to the creature should be at first subdued, 221.

Indifferent, things not too hastily to be censured in others, 56.

Indisposition, to duty, rules then to be observed, 66.

Infidelity, negative is less than disobedience against the gospel, 389.

Infirmities, should not discour-

Infirmities—contd
 age us from duty, 71, 72; what are sins of, 68, 69; in whom, 69; helps against them, 58.
Instinct, supernatural leads the godly to God, 246.
Interest, in God, the ground of trusting in him, 246.

Johnson, Dr. saying of, 410.
Judging, of others, must avoid rashness, 44; when proceed such different, by the saints of themselves, 50; take heed how we judge others, 55; rules to help us in, 88; inferiors should think well of superiors, 56; conscience a judge, 87.
Judgment, 26, 27; word of God is, 27; sanctification, 27; what it is to bring unto victory, 77, 78; a good man's judgment is refined, 78; Satan principally strives to corrupt, 71; how to know when it is victorious, 66; directions how to make our judgments victorious, 88; well employed will raise up a dejected spirit, 144, 145; how to know when near, 379; how to prevent, 381; will begin at God's house, why, 383; what it is, and its divisions, 383; wicked shall not appear in day of, 400; consideration and examination, means to escape, 381; mourning for our own and others' sins, why, 382; no privilege can exempt from, 377.

Kindness, churlishly refused is a high provocation, 76; should be required, 77.
Kinds, of judgment. (See *Sickness*, *Weak*).
Knowledge, its necessity, 81.

Latimer, three prayers, all granted, 250.
Law and gospel, how they differ, 59; extent of law of God to be considered, and its spirituality, 176; less to sin against than against the gospel, 389.
Least mercy of God to be prized, 255.
Liberty, Christian's may not be unknown nor abused, 140, 161.
Life of a Christian, a life of trouble, 160; a mixture of good and evil, 249; hid, 273; lose most by yielding to ourselves, 147; communion with Christ, 87.
Lions, all naturally such, 315.
Lord, Christ is, over his own, 82, 83.
Love, of God, 7; Christ loved by God, how, 11; requires love, 79; labours to keep alive, 89; such as can return, 143, 144; of God to be looked at in every mercy, 254; tokens from God, arguing he is ours, 269; not to be questioned, grounds, 212, 213; decay of, a sign of judgment, 380; requisite for a Christian, 399; it descends, why, 410; assurance of God's love to be sought betimes, 417; present too much, 317.

Luther, assured of a particular mercy in prayer, 250.

Magistrates, how far they may be mild and when rough, 55; needful to the church, 343.
Man, union to Christ, 6; and God united, 6.
Massacre, of Huguenots in France terrible afterward to the king, 149.
Mean, no calling, 294.
Means, must be used, not neglected, 89; whether relied on or no, 225.
Mediator, there is none so pitiful as Christ, 75, 76.
Meekness, contented becomes a Christian, 66.
Mercy, abused, 22, 23; of Christ, will not break the bruised reed, 43, 44; not less in heaven than on earth, 45; how we may know ourselves rightly qualified for mercy, 46; signs of one fitly qualified for, 47; means to qualify us, 47; who do offend against Christ's mercy, 73; who may lay claim to, 75; abused, turns to fury, 73; of God must not be limited by man's sins, 229; it is God's name, he pleads for it, 279; of Christ must not be presumed on, 390; exceptions against Christ's mercy, 393; God's must be specially noted, 309; consideration of is the way to glorify him, 330.
Meritorious. (See *Grace*).
Ministers, how they should carry themselves to the weak, 53; not to preach too austerely, 54; not too darkly, 54; nor doubtfully in disputes, 54; hardly believed, 307.
Mischief, to contrive is the sign of a man notoriously wicked, 300; therefore to be abhorred, 301.
Moderators, catholic, 388.
Moon, in the change, nearest the sun, so we to God in greatest dejection, 135.
Mortification, necessary, 400.
Motions, of sin to be at first crushed, 166.
Mourning, for our own sins and of others is the way to avert judgment, 382.
Murder, of the tongue, 135.

Nature, of Christ is tender to weak Christians, therefore should not despair, 71; our nature ill, 63; unclean naturally, 63; of man since sin came in, subject to misery, 132; proved and applied, 132, 133; favourers, enemies of grace, 175; divine the only counter-poison of sin, 177; natural righteousness in Adam, 173; natural sin in us, voluntary, 174; nature and Christianity different, 405.
Necessity, of bruising, 44.

Obedience, 24, 25; Spirit given to the obedient, 24, 25; must not be hindered by consideration of our infirmity, 66, 71, 72; rules to observe when indisposed to, 66; discourage-

Obedience—contd
ments, whence, 66, 67; Christ though gentle, looks for, 79; to the gospel, what, 387; who have it not, 387; not of ourselves, but wrought, 391, 392; free and cheerful, 393, 394; active and passive, 403.

Objects, of religion or conversation not to be substituted, 218.

Obscure, and dark preaching censured, 54.

Offenders, offence against God takes not away trust in, 199.

Office, of ministry only in the Spirit, 19; of Christ, in what order performed, 16.

Omission, of duties breeds trouble, 140; not to be slighted, 66.

'One', good man may do much good, 345.

Opinions, of others not to be too much heeded, 141, 163, 164.

Opposition, to Christ's government, why, 95, 96, 97; to sin in the godly is universal, 155; is bitterest among those that are nearest, 299.

Original, sin, how it defiles and spreads, 63, 64.

Others, matters, how to be minded, 345.

Out, Outward, outward things no fit stays, 219, 220.

Overjoying, in outward comforts breeds troubles, 140.

Particulars, rise from the generals, 309.

Passions, conflict one with another, 132; not to be put to our troubles, 164; hid till drawn out, and how this is, 165.

Patience, in suffering, 67.

Patrick, Bishop, charge of falsification by, refuted, 290–294.

Paul, St, his strait, or Christ is best, 335–350.

Peace, of conscience, when lost, 70; how recovered, 70; epitome of all good, 168; a sign we have committed ourselves to God, 421; disturbed by cares, 421; end of the godly man, 420.

Perseverance, in grace warranted and how, 237.

Pity, Christ is a most pitiful mediator, 75, 76.

Policy, carnal, 415; hinders our safety, 416; to be avoided.

Portion, of the godly in God alone, 273.

Posterity, commit to God, 423; motive, 424.

Power, Christ brings us through all difficulties, 93, 94; what power this is, 97, 98; we have over ourselves, is of God, 197.

Praise, in trouble, more minded by the godly than their delivery, 247; special times to praise God, 246, 247; no easy matter to praise God aright, 252; conditions, 254, 255; motives, 257; means of performing it, 257, 258.

Prayer, means to obtain the spirit of, 26; though weak yet acceptable, 65; why God accepts, 65, 66; needful to keep ourselves in temper, 147; heard, signs of, 256; and praise depend each on other, 247, 257; must pray before we get, 418; for our enemies, 405, 406; God overcome, by 303.

Preaching, 27, 28.

Pre-eminence, of Christ, 18.

Preparation, prepare for an alteration of thy state and spirit, 141.

Presence of God in the worst times, 248.

Present, too much addicted to, 316, 317.

Preservation, is from God, 325. (See *Providence*).

Pride, of the Romish church, who stumble at Christ's lowliness, 77; if purged a sign of interest in heaven, 328; to be avoided, 345; must be taken down though the spirit be dejected, 147; and passion, mischievous, 146.

Priestly office of Christ, 16, 17.

Privilege, none exempt from judgment, 382.

Professors, loose life wounds the gospel, 377.

Promises. Christ promised in the Old Testament, 3; of God, what they are in different respects, 212; not all reserved for heaven, 250, 251.

Property in God chiefly to be laboured for, 264.

Prophetical office of Christ, 16.

Prosperity, seeming, of the wicked shall have an end, 385, 419; must not grieve at, 385, 386; continual of a bad estate, a sign, 402.

Providence of God, makes all good to us, 204; a special stay of our faith, 205; what God is he makes good by, 205; graces to be exercised in by observing, 207; God will keep us if we commit ourselves to him, 418; eye him in all, 422, 423; rely on him, 423; commit posterity to, 424 (see *Preservation*).

Quenching the Spirit, how, 74; helps to cherish, 74, 75.

Questions, about needless disputes, their censure, 54.

Quiet, mistrust thyself when all is, 97.

Real, praises of God necessary, 255; things put out troublesome thoughts, 181.

Reason, true religion not contrary to, 80; for sin, none at all, 245; of a godly man, divine, 245.

Redemption, wonder of, 7; Christ a special instrument of, 42.

Reed, Bruised, 33–101.

Relapse, relapses pardonable and curable, 231.

Relations, wherein we stand to God must be all answered, and how, 215.

Religion, not to be entered on with hopes of pleasure and ease, 398; reformation of, hath brought blessings, 312.

Repentance, begins in the love

Repentance—contd
of God, 184; a way to turn away wrath, 381.
Reproach, expression of malice, 109; not to be cast down, for 109; David sensible of, 113, 114.
Reprobates, 25.
Resolution, needful in a Christian 100, 253; want of it breeds disquiet, 140; firm and peremptory, to be affirmed, 201; renew it, 201; quickly, 202.
Resurrection, its end, 85.
Riches, of Christ, 24; carry ourselves answerable to, 21.
Righteousness, righteous, what meant thereby, 395; they are saved, yet hardly, why, 396, 397, 398.
Rome, tyrannical over afflicted conscience, 77.

Sacraments, of the Lord's Supper its nature, 67.
Saints, Safety in Evil Times, 295–334; hatred of wicked men, 300; Hiding-place in the Evil Day, 406–425.
Salvation, chosen to, 9; of God plentiful and manifold, 259; to be thought upon in trouble, 259; the golden chain of it, 264; difficulty of, 394–400; certainty of, 396; certain.
Sanctification, 27; Christ is our, as well as justification, 79.
Satan, his objections answered, 98; when overcome by weak means is most outrageous, 98; why he prevails sooner over us than Christ, 63; and his instruments still casting down the godly, 134; cunning in divers humours of Christians, 137; discourages when God encourages, 279; studies to unloose the heart from God, 223; to divide between God and us, 223.
Scandal, makes it hard to be saved, 398.
Scruples, needless, how remedied, 62.
Security, mark of ripeness of sin, 379.
Self-, denial requisite to praise God, 252; self, what in the godly and what in others, 160; self-denial required, 345.
Servants, how, 5; comfort that he was, 9; offer Christ in our service, 10.
Serve, servant, Christ a servant, 5–11; humility taught thereby, 8, 9.
SIBBES, RICHARD, never before edited, xiii; plan and spirit of this edition, xiv, xv; '*Heavenly*' his usual designation, xix; neglect of contemporaries to write his Life, xix; Isaac Walton, Dr William Gouge, Richard Baxter, John Davenport, Goodwin, &c., &c., xx-xxii; his own indifference to posthumous fame, xxiii, xxiv; spellings of the name, xxiv, xxv; Bishop Montagu's allusion, xxv; his birth-place Tostock not Sudbury, xxvi; Zachery Catlin MS, xxvii; born 1577, parent-

age, xxvii; Tostock and vicinity described, xxvii, xxvii; removed to Thurston, xxix; 'wheel-wright' shop. xxix; school, 'leather-suited,' xxx; 'Free-School,' Bury St Edmunds, xxxi; contemporary boys, xxxi; father withdraws Master Richard, xxxiii; friends interfere and send him to St John's College, Cambridge, xxxiii-xxxiv; B.A. 1598–9 and other degrees to B.D. in 1610, xxxiv; his conversion under Paul Bayne, modest reticence approved, xxxiv, xxv; 'Memorial' as to 'Trinity Lectureship,' xxxv, xxxvi; subscribers, 'common people,' xxxvi; success, conversion of John Cotton, xxxvii-viii; Thomas Goodwin. xxxviii; character of prevalent 'preaching,' xxxviii-ix; deprived of Lectureship and 'outed' from Fellowship, xxxix; Preachership of Gray's Inn, London, secured by Sir Henry Yelverton, xxxix-xl; date corrected, xi; illustrious auditory, xl, xli: Lord Bacon '*a bruised reed*', xli, xlii; Shakespeare, xlii; Archbishop Ussher seeks to have him transferred to Trinity College, Dublin, xlii; correspondence. xlii-xlviii; accepts 'Mastership' of Catherine Hall, Cambridge, xlviii; history of this College and Sibbes' success, xlix, *seq.*; Preston and Sibbes, contemporaries and hearers, l-liv; Trinity Lectureship again, liv; testimonies, lv-lvi; students, lvii; Puritans watched, lvii; the Elector Palatine and Sibbes' interest and efforts, lvii-viii; Laud persecutes, Star-chamber, lix; preacher of Gray's Inn under surveillance, lx; Sibbes uncontroversial, lx; faithful outspeaking, lxi; sad and strange yet not strange hatred of Laud, lxii, *seq.*; popish services, lxiv, *seq.*; all good and true men harrassed by the Protestant primate, lxvi *seq.*; Puritan literature the very life-blood of the literature of the age. lxvii; worthlessness of the 'writings' of the Laudian divines, lxviii; noble words of Sibbes, lxviii, *seq.*; 'Feoffees' another handle for persecuting Sibbes, lxx; contemporary events, lxx, *seq.*; extracts from Laud's 'Journal' and 'Defence', lxxxiii, *seq.*; character of Laud delineated, lxxix-lxxxi; Sibbes' 'Introductions' to works of contemporaries, Whitaker, Paul Bayne, Henry Scudder, Ezekiel Culverwell, Dr John Preston, John Smith, John Ball, Richard Capel, lxxxi-cx; presentation to Vicarage of Trinity by the king, cxi; another relaxation of 'order' of Gray's Inn, cxii; Bishop Williams and Sibbes, cxii-xiii; letter to Goodwin, cxiv-xvi; emigrants to 'New England,'

SIBBES—contd
cxvii; visits to country mansions of nobility by Sibbes, cxviii, seq.; church of Thurston, cxxi-xxiii; 'The Beginning of the End,' retrospect, cxxiii-iv; character, testimonies, the English Leighton, cxxiv. seq.; 'The Valley of the Shadow of Death, last sermons, will, illness, death, burial, cxxvii, seq.; conclusion, cxxxi; appendix, Zachary Catlin's 'Memoir' of Sibbes, annotated, cxxxiii-xli, Sibbes' family and name, cxli-ii; successors of Sibbes in his offices, cxliii.

Sickness, comfort in, 240.

Siding, with God in evil times, 270.

Sight, of God not always alike, reasons, 278.

Signs, of a good estate, 137.

Sin, is laid open to the sense by the light of grace, 59, 60; of infirmity, what, 68, 69; in whom, 67; more grieve for sin than punishment, 48; original, spreads, 63, 64; ever unreasonable, 146; the greatest trouble, 241; avoid not trouble by sin, 241; sweet in doing, bitter in reckoning, 228; God punishes it wherever he sees it, 377; when ripe, 379; against the gospel is against God's attributes, 388; greatest against greatest light, 388; nearest must be parted with, 390; effects, 392; sweet, 397; sticks to all, 397; sins of the second table grounded on the first, 298, 299; full of deceit, 306, 307, 311; God delivers from great, 324; abstinence from present, the way to be delivered from future, 323, 324; art and diligence aggravate, 298; church must punish, 378; sinners, what, 400.

Slandering, and depraving others' actions, the devil's office, 56; a cloak for cruelty, 300.

Soliloquies, of special use, 191.

Solitariness, ill for afflicted ones, 195; intolerable to the wicked, why, 149.

Sorrow, weakens the heart, 142; not required for itself, 232; cannot make satisfaction, 233; dangerous overmuch, 233; popery in it, 234; comfortable degree of, for sin, when, 235.

Soul, union with the body, 6; most constant state in respect of sin, 28; to be cited and pressed to give account, 147; excellency in reflecting on itself and judging all its issues, 149; debased by wicked men, 150; should be first set in order, 131; needs more than itself to uphold it, 160; temper, when right, 157; over-borne gets free, 202; gracious, most sensible of the want of spiritual means, 131; knows when it is well and ill, 132; committed to God, 406, 407, 408, 418; why, 409; must be done sincerely, 422; reasons, 422; directions, 414; what it is, 419; how we may know when we commit it to God, 421; even in the most desperate state, 414, 415; desire to be kept from sin, 407; wicked think they have none, 407; must be respected above other things, 407, 408; not satisfied but by strong reasons, 409; carried away with delight, 409.

Spirit, an evidence, 14; put on Christ, 15; work of, 18; assurance by, 19, 22; striving, 22; gospel by, 23; reprobates have, 25; by prayer, 26; how to know we have, 14; degrees of receiving, 15; given and received by Christ, how, 17; three things received, 18, 19; how Christ gives, 23, 24; of Christ gives, 23, 24; of God, how far it dwells in the earthly-minded, 96; how our spirit is helped against our infirmities, 57, 58; the word is the breath of, 74, 75; how it works with the gospel, 391; its power, 399; chiefest part of man, 298; supports us in spiritual losses, 319; a royal, sign of our interest in, 328.

Spouse, of Christ is the church, 390.

Stones, of the temple, 5.

Strait, St Paul's, or Christ is Best, 335–350.

Suffering, with patience, 67; of the godly and ungodly differ, 373; it is best for God's children, 401, 402; comes when God will, 402, 403; must look from whence it comes, 403; well-doing before well-suffering, 404; not to be avoided by sin, 405; in well-suffering heaps coals of fire on our enemies, 405, 406; we overcome by, 406; no by-respects in, 406.

Supply, our, whence, 20.

Symmetry, of the soul most lovely, 167.

Sword, of the Wicked, 103–118.

Temptation, Christ was clothed with our flesh to favour the tempted, 45; reason why Satan prevails sooner over us than over Christ, 63; divine, what it is, 133; considerations against, 386; God will not be tempted, 421; grace requisite against those times, 323.

Tenderness, must be shewn to weak Christians, 53; conscience is tender, 45, 53.

Thanks, best when it tends to praise, 254; should be large, 254; never without some taste of mercy, 256; special help in our afflicted condition, 256; excellent use of it, 258.

Things, 410, the 'one thing'.

Thomas, mistake about, 101.

Thoughts, blasphemous, when they come from the devil, and how to repel them, 63; evil, their original, and how remedied, 63, 64; to be set in order every morning, 186; are not free, 186, 187; danger of that

Thoughts—contd
opinion, 187; of praise should be precious to us, 249.

Time, an appointed, for God visiting his church, 378, 384; when that is, 378; we must use time present in doing good against the day of judgment, 382; the wicked shall not appear in these special times, 400; must avoid sin for the time to come, 323.

Titles, empty, of goodness bring empty comfort at last, 275; ours in God to be maintained, 277, 278.

Trade, of conversing with God, the richest in the world, 253.

Treasury, in Christ, 20.

Trial, of trust, whether it be right, 226; comfort against the fiery, 373.

Trinity, the whole agree in the work of our redemption, 43.

Troubles, outward, appointed to help the soul inwardly, 149; onward, threefold miscarriage of it, 156.

Trust, is the means to bring God and the soul together, 203; to settle, know the mind as well as the nature of God, 212; trust must answer the truth of God, 213; directions about, 214; whether we may friends, riches, or helps, 318; a sin so to do, 219; in self not to be trusted, 220; should follow God's order of promising, 221; trial of ourselves exceedingly necessary, 165; must not trust to flesh, 413; God's children are prone to trust in themselves.

Unfruitfulness, a sign of coming judgment, 380.

Ungodly, misery of, 385–394.

Uniformity, necessary in the lives of Christians, 168.

Unthankfulness, to God most sinful, 253, 254; detestable to God and man, 256.

Unworthiness, may not keep from God, 266.

Us, all good in Christ before, 18; how the Spirit takes from Christ and gives to, 18; how put on Christ for, 21, 22.

Use, sanctified, of all troubles to God's children, 198.

Vainglorious, be not, 30; why to be avoided, 30.

Values, ground whence to, Christians, 14.

Victory, of truth will appear at last, 88; the government of Christ a victorious, why for a while the enemy seems to prevail, 90; how to know when we shall be victorious, 87; three degrees of, 88; directions how to make our judgments victorious, 88; by Christ alone obtained, and how he brings judgment to victory, 93, 94; a fight before, 95, 96, 97; lies in Christ, not in ourselves, 97; church shall have, 99; over ourselves, signs of, 169; how it may be obtained, 170.

Visitation, Church's 371–384.

Wait, waiting on God a necessary duty, 251; what it is, 251; be ever in a waiting condition, 277; difficult helps, 279.

Watchfulness, our remissness herein, what evil it brings, 74.

Weak, Christians, how they must be heartened with tenderness, 45, 53; a caution for them, 52; may sometimes be dealt with more roughly, 55; men should not pry into their weaknesses, 56; means to work us to receive them, 61, 62; weakness, what, 65; doth not debar from mercy, 65; what actions to be imputed to weak Christians, 69; in whom sins of infirmity, 69, 70; weak faith, how it prevails, 90; Christ helps, 90; the church compared to weak things, 43; prayers accepted, 65; why, 65; faith, how strengthened, 325.

Wicked, Sword of, 103-118; their end, 385; confidence of their torment should wean us from the world, 386; they are reserved to further plagues, 419, 420; shall not prevail over the godly, 302; though for a time over their persons, yet not over their cause, 303; get nothing by persecuting the church, 304; in their enterprises they are but to work God's will, 304; their plots against the church miscarry, 305; as fools, 305.

Will, of man hath a sovereignty, 174; of the godly conformable to God's will, 247; of itself cannot be rectified but by the understanding, 373; God's, that men suffer, how, 402; wilfulness aggravates sin, 297.

Wisdom, the ways of God as ways of, 80; spiritual, great help unto us in our Christian course, 83; carnal, is folly, 301, 302, 305.

Woman (see *Affections*).

Wonders, 4-8; shallow things wondered at, 8;

Word, Spirit given in, 23, 24; of God, judgment, 27; the breath of the Spirit, 74, 75; like himself, 412.

Works, justify not, 388;

World, Worldly, worldly good hath some evil, and worldly evil some good, 166; worldlings, excuses to keep them from Christ, 94, 95.

Yet, not in hell nor at worst, a mercy, and undeserved, 248.

Youth, to be curbed quickly, 147.

Also from Benediction Books ...
Wandering Between Two Worlds: Essays on Faith and Art
Anita Mathias
Benediction Books, 2007
152 pages
ISBN: 0955373700

Available from www.amazon.com, www.amazon.co.uk

In these wide-ranging lyrical essays, Anita Mathias writes, in lush, lovely prose, of her naughty Catholic childhood in Jamshedpur, India; her large, eccentric family in Mangalore, a sea-coast town converted by the Portuguese in the sixteenth century; her rebellion and atheism as a teenager in her Himalayan boarding school, run by German missionary nuns, St. Mary's Convent, Nainital; and her abrupt religious conversion after which she entered Mother Teresa's convent in Calcutta as a novice. Later rich, elegant essays explore the dualities of her life as a writer, mother, and Christian in the United States-- Domesticity and Art, Writing and Prayer, and the experience of being "an alien and stranger" as an immigrant in America, sensing the need for roots.

About the Author

Anita Mathias is the author of *Wandering Between Two Worlds: Essays on Faith and Art.* She has a B.A. and M.A. in English from Somerville College, Oxford University, and an M.A. in Creative Writing from the Ohio State University, USA. Anita won a National Endowment of the Arts fellowship in Creative Nonfiction in 1997. She lives in Oxford, England with her husband, Roy, and her daughters, Zoe and Irene.

Visit Anita at http://www.anitamathias.com.

The Church That Had Too Much
Anita Mathias
Benediction Books, 2010
52 pages
ISBN: 9781849026567

The Church That Had Too Much was very well-intentioned. She wanted to love God, she wanted to love people, but she was both hampered by her muchness and the abundance of her possessions, and beset by ambition, power struggles and snobbery. Read about the surprising way The Church That Had Too Much began to resolve her problems in this deceptively simple and enchanting fable.

The Meek Shall Inherit the Earth
Anita Mathias
Benediction Books, 2013
38 pages
ISBN: 9781781393956

"Blessed are the meek, for they shall inherit the earth," Jesus says in his most puzzling Beatitude. Puzzling, because, if we are honest, it does not feel true to our experience. So do the meek inherit the earth? Is this true? Or isn't it? In The Meek Shall Inherit the Earth, an extended meditation on the power of gentleness, Anita Mathias grapples with this mystifying Beatitude.

About the Author

Anita Mathias is the author of *Wandering Between Two Worlds: Essays on Faith and Art.* She has a B.A. and M.A. in English from Somerville College, Oxford University, and an M.A. in Creative Writing from the Ohio State University, USA. Anita won a National Endowment of the Arts fellowship in Creative Nonfiction in 1997. She lives in Oxford, England with her husband, Roy, and her daughters, Zoe and Irene.

Visit Anita at http://www.anitamathias.com

Francesco, Artist of Florence: The Man Who Gave Too Much
Anita Mathias
Benediction Books, 2014
52 pages (full colour)
ISBN: 978-1781394175

In this lavishly illustrated book by Anita Mathias, Francesco, artist of Florence, creates magic in pietre dure, inlaying precious stones in marble in life-like "paintings." While he works, placing lapis lazuli birds on clocks, and jade dragonflies on vases, he is purely happy. However, he must sell his art to support his family. Francesco, who is incorrigibly soft-hearted, cannot stand up to his haggling customers. He ends up almost giving away an exquisite jewellery box to Signora Farnese's bambina, who stands, captivated, gazing at a jade parrot nibbling a cherry. Signora Stallardi uses her daughter's wedding to cajole him into discounting his rainbowed marriage chest. His old friend Girolamo bullies him into letting him have the opulent table he hoped to sell to the Medici almost at cost. Carrara is raising the price of marble; the price of gems keeps rising. His wife is in despair. Francesco fears ruin.

* * *

Sitting in the church of Santa Maria Novella at Mass, very worried, Francesco hears the words of Christ. The lilies of the field and the birds of the air do not worry, yet their Heavenly Father looks after them. As He will look after us. He resolves not to worry. And as he repeats the prayer the Saviour taught us, Francesco resolves to forgive the friends and neighbours who repeatedly put their own interests above his. But can he forgive himself for his own weakness, as he waits for the eternal city of gold whose walls are made of jasper, whose gates are made of pearls, and whose foundations are sapphire, emerald, ruby and amethyst? There time and money shall be no more, the lion shall live with the lamb, and we shall dwell trustfully together. Francesco leaves Santa Maria Novella, resolving to trust the One who told him to live like the lilies and the birds, deciding to forgive those who haggled him into bad bargains--while making a little resolution for the future

www.ingramcontent.com/pod-product-compliance
Lightning Source LLC
Chambersburg PA
CBHW030100170426
43198CB00009B/435